"*Meet the Puritans* is a wonderful gift to the church of Jesus Christ, and a valuable resource for students and lovers of the Puritans. We owe a debt of gratitude to Joel Beeke and Randall Pederson for this labor of love."

—DR. TOM ASCOL, Pastor, Grace Baptist Church in Cape Coral, Florida, and Executive Director, Founders Ministries

"Joel Beeke and Randall Pederson's *Meet the Puritans* will assist us greatly to provide a valid biblical and crystal-clear Reformed antidote for the cancer of the Prosperity Gospel that is spreading like wild-fire through Africa. The God-honoring, well-balanced, holistic spirituality of head, heart, and hands of the Puritans is now made accessible in a comprehensive yet simple, understandable way. This should become standard compulsory reading for the African pastors who are preparing themselves for ministry of the Word in God's kingdom. We firmly believe that this kind of theology and spirituality, through God's grace, will make a significant difference in the midst of desperate poverty, thousands of terminally ill HIV patients, and millions of orphans. What Africa needs is transformation through the renewing of mindsets (Rom. 12:1-2) that hold people in chains of poverty because of a lack of biblical work ethics, Christian stewardship, and, above all, Christ-centered lives. *Meet the Puritans* will assist us greatly in making all the counsel of God known and equipping church leaders to be instruments of heartfelt change and transformation through acquiring a simple yet profound Reformed worldlife view."

— DR. P.J. (FLIP) BUYS, Principal, Mukhanyo Theological College, KwaMhlanga, South Africa, and Chairperson, African Region of World Reformed Fellowship

"What a marvelous idea, and what a wonderful resource! In one volume we are introduced to some of the greatest minds in the history of the church as we are invited to 'meet the Puritans' and become acquainted with their writings. Although appreciation for Puritan theology and writings has grown over the last half century, the literature was missing a comprehensive introduction to the main authors; now that has been corrected in a volume that will at once stimulate further reading, refresh our acquaintance with the past, and renew our appreciation for the theological legacy carried to us on a stream of Puritan literature. The authors are to be congratulated on completion of the project; the church will be enriched as a consequence."

—DR. IAIN D. CAMPBELL, Pastor, Back Free Church of Scotland, Isle of Lewis, Scotland

"Those Puritans, the masters of connecting Reformed theology and practical Christian living, can and do speak for themselves. But still —Joel Beeke and Randall Pederson's pointed and helpful summaries of 150 biographies and 700 books make an enormous difference. Now we can easily and reliably learn the personal stories underneath the passionate theology, and see more deeply into the issues which these godly men were called to address. For many years now Beeke has reminded us of the role of the Dutch Further Reformation people in the history of Reformed piety, and it's fitting that he would be the one to add them, and the Scots too, to the grand procession of the British and New Englanders whom we think of more readily. 'Global Puritanism' and how to understand and value it, is really what this remarkable book gives us. It opens so many doors into biblical wisdom and deep gospel, and it will work well for the beginner and mature student of biblical piety."
—DR. D. CLAIR DAVIS, Professor of Church History Emeritus,
Westminster Seminary, Philadelphia

"*Meet the Puritans* maps the terrain of Puritan literature available in English with extraordinary comprehensive, keen insight, and respectful appreciation. Anyone wishing to travel into this remarkable world will benefit enormously from this unique and important new study. Both useful and inspiring, it is an astonishing accomplishment."
—DR. JAMES A. DEJONG, President, Dutch Reformed Translation Society

"*Meet the Puritans* is another welcome incentive to be thankful to God for what He has given in the Puritans—in their lives, their sermons, their ministry, and their example."
—REV. PAUL DEN BUTTER, Emeritus Pastor,
Christelijke Gereformeerde Kerk, the Netherlands

"Finally, a reliable guide book to a vast, fertile, and little-traveled continent. From encyclopedic knowledge, disciplined by scrupulous research, Joel Beeke and Randall Pederson have compiled a Puritan *Baedeker* for our time. In these pages we can learn what the Puritans have to offer and where to find it. A marvelous encouragement to more extensive exploration!"
—PASTOR EDWARD DONNELLY, Principal,
Reformed Theological College, Belfast, Northern Ireland

"Beeke and Pederson have made an extraordinary contribution to the literature that promotes the rich heritage of our Puritan forebears. Not only does this work give us a comprehensive overview of the entire Puritan movement, but its concise and eloquent descriptions of each reprinted Puritan allow us to meet them in a new and unique way. Most importantly, this work will whet one's appetite for the theology of the Puritans—a theology that aims to produce a Christ-centered, intelligent piety. May God use this work greatly to further expand the remarkable resurgence of Puritan literature in the English-speaking world."

— REV. BARTEL ELSHOUT, Pastor, Heritage Reformed Congregation, Chilliwack, British Columbia, and translator of Wilhelmus à Brakel's *The Christian's Reasonable Service*

"Here is a most useful book of information and inspiration calling us to a fuller appreciation of English, Scottish, and Dutch experimental Calvinists of the seventeenth century. This careful study is a place to begin and to progress in meeting the Puritans."

—DR. W. ROBERT GODFREY, President, Westminster Seminary California

"Since the late 1950s, an increasing number of evangelicals have been re-discovering the wealth of the piety and theology of their Puritan forebears. Those new to this material can feel overwhelmed by the wide choice of authors and works being offered. *Meet the Puritans* is an invaluable guide to the most significant portion of our devotional and theological inheritance."

—DR. CRAWFORD GRIBBEN, author of *The Irish Puritans*

"Anything that furthers the reading and study of the Puritans I wish to recommend. I am grateful for *Meet the Puritans*, because I think it is immensely important to make their writings more known."

—REV. COR HARINCK, Emeritus Pastor, Gereformeerde Gemeenten, the Netherlands

"This valuable volume fills a major lacuna and is sure to become the standard reference work for the study of the Puritans and their literary remains. For all who are interested in the Puritans, an indispensable work."

—DR. MICHAEL HAYKIN, President, Toronto Baptist Seminary

"*Meet the Puritans* is a book we have been waiting for! It makes history with respect to the Puritans come alive and will surely awaken further interest in the writings of these divines who were the greatest preachers after the apostles."

—DR. MARTIN HOLDT, Pastor, Constantia Park Baptist Church, Pretoria, South Africa

"The Puritans exceed all others, both in quality of exposition and in balancing doctrine, experience, and practice. I am thrilled with this timely work, which will surely encourage many to read the Puritans for themselves. The biographies are gripping; it is especially helpful to include the Scottish and Dutch divines. A superlative resource."

—PASTOR ERROLL HULSE, author of *Who are the Puritans?*

"Over fifty years since interest in the Puritans and their work was reborn in Britain and America, enthusiasm for their writings has spread around the globe. There is now a third generation delving into their works. This biographical volume will provide an invaluable resource to all who have discovered the writings of these great men, but who want to see the 'face' of their authors. May it serve to carry a love for the Puritans to a fourth generation and beyond!"

—REV. MARK G. JOHNSTON, Pastor, Grove Chapel, Camberwell, England

"*Meet the Puritans* is a picture gallery of the Puritan brotherhood in England, Scotland, and Holland and a reference facility for their writings, rolled into one. A labor of love on the part of its compilers, may it produce the same in many readers."

—DR. HYWEL R. JONES, Professor of Practical Theology,
Westminster Seminary California

"Part of reformation is recovery, and that includes especially recovery of the past. *Meet the Puritans* is an important tool for recovering the pulse of piety that lived among God's people as a result of their return to the Bible and to the church's historic affection for spiritual matters. This volume ought to find an enduring place in that genre of religious writing called 'spiritual biography,' as a guidebook for further exploration and enjoyment."

—DR. NELSON KLOOSTERMAN, Professor, Mid-America Reformed Seminary

"If space on your library shelves is limited, here is one volume that will do the work of ten or twenty, giving you access to the lives of the men behind the Puritan books you value so highly. Having a guide to all that has been printed since the 1950s will help you explore the field of Puritan literature more widely, and choose more wisely as you build your own collection. Knowing more of the lives, trials, and real achievements of these great Christians will add greatly to your understanding and appreciation of their writings."

—REV. RAY B. LANNING, Pastor, Associate Reformed
Presbyterian Church, Grand Rapids, Michigan

"The stories of the lives of prominent Puritans and their illustrations in *Meet the Puritans* promote a personal touch that will arouse considerable interest for all kinds of readers and motivate them to read the Puritans more regularly for themselves. The authors have met their aim to be sufficiently simple for the educated layman who is just beginning to read Puritan writings and sufficiently instructive so that the more mature Puritan reader can learn and glean from it. *Meet the Puritans* will surely be the standard work to which God's people will turn as they seek to know and benefit from the godly men who lived and ministered during this period of church history. What a treasure this book will be for many reasons, one being that it makes the lives and some of the materials of a wide variety of Puritans available in one volume."

—Dr. Wayne Mack, Director of Strengthening Ministries International

"Comprehensive in character and encyclopedic in scope, this work will serve as a sterling reference volume for all those who study Puritanism for decades to come. This labor of learning is an unsurpassed source for easy accessibility to all the important Puritan figures, their biographies, and their major writings. We can be extremely grateful to the authors and to God's providential provisions in making this unparalleled resource available to a wide audience."

—Dr. Donald K. McKim, author of *Ramism in William Perkins' Theology*

"*Meet the Puritans* is a very useful and comprehensive compilation of Puritan biography and bibliography which focuses specifically upon the Puritan reprints of the last 50 years. It is particularly outstanding for its compact thoroughness of each biography and its incisive summaries of each reprint. May every faithful minister of the gospel and serious student of God's Word secure and utilize this precious treasure!"

—Pastor Jerry Marcellino, Laurel, Mississippi;
Moderator, Fellowship of Independent Reformed Evangelicals

"The writings of the Puritans are the richest deposit of practical Christian instruction produced since the days of the Apostles and those who mine Puritan gold are lavishly rewarded for their effort. *Meet the Puritans* is a monumental accomplishment and a long-needed addition to the tools available for those serious about unearthing the treasure. Joel Beeke and Randall Pederson have done us a great service."

—Dr. Robert P. Martin, Pastor,
Emmanuel Reformed Baptist Church, Seattle, Washington

"The resurgent appetite for Puritan literature has produced long booklists and heavy bookshelves. Intimidated students and busy pastors ask, 'Where do I start?' Regular readers of the Puritans ask, 'Where do I go from here?' The obvious answer to both questions now is, *Meet the Puritans*. I am confident that God will mightily use this mind-enriching, heart-warming, and soul-satisfying publication to arouse new interest in the Puritans, to stimulate demand for their books, and so to multiply among us the Christ-centered lives they so passionately promoted."

—Dr. DAVID MURRAY, Pastor, Free Church of Scotland (Continuing), Stornoway, Scotland

"*Meet the Puritans* is a work to read and treasure. The sheer bulk of Puritan writings can be overwhelming unless some guide is handy. This is just what we need. Those who know and love the Puritans will find new vistas opening up, while those who want to begin will find helpful direction."

—Dr. ROBERT OLIVER, Lecturer, London Theological Seminary, and author of *History of English Calvinistic Baptists*

"*Meet the Puritans* provides well researched biographies of the Puritans and Puritan-minded Scotsmen and Dutch divines, as well as useful and appealing information on the contents of their books published during the last fifty years. This fascinating book supplies a long-felt want."

—Dr. WILLEM J. OP 'T HOF, Professor in the History of Reformed Pietism, Vrije Universiteit, Amsterdam

"One of my many blessings over the last thirty-five years of ministry has been the rediscovery of the Puritans. No men have influenced me more. One thing lacking, however, has been thorough and readable details of their lives. We know them as shadows more or less through their books, but they have often lacked the lineaments of personality. *Meet the Puritans*, with its biographical sketches, fills the gap. How great it is to know better the men that have been such a blessing to me!"

—Dr. JOSEPH A. PIPA, JR., President, Greenville Presbyterian Theological Seminary, South Carolina

"*Meet the Puritans* is a monumental work that represents a milestone in the revival of interest in the Puritans. I am greatly indebted to the Puritans for the biblical and spiritual guidance I first received as a young man through the literature of the Banner of Truth Trust, and later, during the thirty-eight years I have been a minister. If it wasn't for the reprints of the Puritans, my ministry would have been greatly impoverished."

—Rev. Cornelis (Neil) Pronk, Emeritus Pastor,
Free Reformed Church, Ontario

"The Puritans are the best friends that Christians could have in a day of doctrinal confusion. For that reason we welcome this new volume which Dr. Beeke and Mr. Pederson have provided for our generation by setting the Puritan divines so accessibly before us. These spiritual forefathers, who deserve to be more than honored names in history, are introduced to us here in a way that should influence for good our own personal lives and the life of our churches."

—Rev. Maurice Roberts, Pastor,
Free Church of Scotland (Continuing), Inverness, Scotland

"There is no other resource quite like *Meet the Puritans*; it will prove indispensable for anyone who likes to read the Puritan divines and their spiritual children. What's more: The brief biographies of these teachers of yesteryear are of immense assistance in getting to know something of the men behind all the familiar Puritan names, and even some men who are not so familiar. I thank God for the labor of love that Dr. Beeke and Randall Pederson have undertaken: *Meet the Puritans* would have not been completed had not these men persevered through many years of reading and research in order to bless us with this great work. May the Lord reward all of us (and them), for taking up and reading this most worthy volume!"

—Dr. Lance Quinn, Pastor,
The Bible Church of Little Rock, Arkansas

"*Meet the Puritans* is a breathtaking achievement. The book is noteworthy for its comprehensiveness. Also outstanding is the easy access that it provides to factual information about the Puritan movement and the lives and writings of individual Puritans. For anyone wishing to acquire or maintain an acquaintance with the Puritans, this is an indispensable book."

—Dr. Leland Ryken, author of *Worldly Saints*

"*Meet the Puritans* is an invaluable resource for any reader of these spiritual and theological giants. Like the subject of this book, this work will stretch your mind and enrich your heart both in appreciation of the Puritans and encourage your growth in experimental piety. All who value this period of church history owe a great debt to Beeke and Pederson."

—DR. TOM SCHWANDA, Associate Professor of Christian Formation and Ministry, Wheaton College

"*Meet the Puritans* helps us as Koreans to grasp more fully the Puritans as well as the Scottish and Dutch Further Reformation divines. By reading this book, I trust that God will stir up the hearts of many readers to stand for the truth at this present time when so many reject sound teaching and wander off into man-centered traditions."

—REV. CHANGWON SEO, Pastor, Seoul, Korea, and Chairman of the KIRP (Korean Institute for Reformed Preaching)

"John Udall, in his preface to the 1637 edition of his commentary on Lamentations, wrote, 'The Lord make us able and willing to travel with all carefulness in that heavenly labor of searching out the unspeakable treasures of knowledge and wisdom that lie hidden in his blessed Word.' Our labors in this will be greatly assisted by this excellent volume, *Meet the Puritans*, as it opens to us these men and their writings, which in turn seek to cause us to drink deeply of the inexhaustible fountain of Holy Scripture."

—REV. DENIS SHELTON, Retired Minister, Presbyterian Reformed Church, Sydney, Australia

"*Meet the Puritans* should be the first volume anyone with any interest in the Puritans picks up. The bite-size biographies are inspirational and set the heart ablaze to read the writings of these great men. A masterly piece of research that is the result of a twenty-year labor of love."

—TIM SHENTON, author of *Christmas Evans*

"Beeke and Pederson have done the Christian community and historical theology a wonderful service by providing a very handy introduction and orientation to the recently published writings of Puritanism and to the Puritans writers themselves. A special strength of the collection is the inclusion not only of English and American Puritans, but also of the 'old writers' of the Dutch Further Reformation."

—DR. DON SINNEMA, Professor of Theology, Trinity Christian College, Palos Heights, Illinois

"*Meet the Puritans* explores the lives, world, and works of the Puritans with a thoroughness they deserve. The biographies challenge and inspire, the tastes of their writings richly edify, and the guide to modern reprints discovers new horizons of reading. This book will have the beginner fall in love with the Puritans for the first time, and will greatly help those who already cherish these men and their books."

—REV. JOHN THACKWAY, Pastor, Holywell,
Flintshire, Wales, and Editor of *Bible League Quarterly*

"I was blessed in the first Puritan books I studied. They were readable, helpful, intensely practical, and fascinating. The first, of course, was *Pilgrim's Progress*, studied in school and read with increasing pleasure and growing discernment ever since. The second was at University in 1959, at the time of the first explosion of Banner of Truth books. It was Thomas Watson's *Body of Divinity*. I found more distilled emotion and enlightenment in a single page than in many contemporary books. The next book had to be Owen. Everyone was mentioning him in the college coffee break and so I sat and read *Spiritual Mindedness* in the reference library in the Hayes, Cardiff. It confirmed I had entered a new world. The next practical help was *Precious Remedies against Satan's Devices* by Thomas Brooks, a large, green hardback published by Sovereign Grace Publishers in 1960. Years later it became a series of sermons. I was also to derive much profit from Thomas Watson's *Divine Cordial*, or as it was later called, *All Things for Good*. Very recently, I have been delighted with Thomas Brooks's book on personal devotion, *The Secret Key to Heaven*. Another discovery over recent years has been the writings of the Cardiff-born Puritan, Christopher Love. Who were these mighty men? At last there is a splendid book which fills in some of the gaps in our knowledge, a friendly companion on the shelves of Puritan volumes to be consulted."

—PASTOR GEOFF THOMAS, Alfred Place Baptist Church, Aberystwyth, Wales

"Since the 1950s, there has been a growing thirst for accessible Puritan literature in Christian circles, a thirst which has resulted in a most encouraging growth in the number of reprinted Puritan works now available. In this book, Joel Beeke and Randall Pederson have provided not only a clear and thorough guide to those works which have been republished, but also biographies of the Puritan authors themselves which allow the reader to understand more fully the context in which each work was written. This book will be invaluable both to those coming to the Puritans for the first time and to those who are familiar with their works but are looking for a sure-footed guide to help them in their reading."

—DR. CARL TRUEMAN, Professor of Church History
and Historical Theology, Westminster Seminary, Philadelphia

"As the world has its own canon of saints and heroes, Christianity has its cloud of witnesses, among whom the Puritans—as *Meet the Puritans* reaffirms—are most prominent in the areas of experimental theology and exemplary piety."

—PROFESSOR FRED VAN LIEBURG, Vrije Universiteit, Amsterdam

"In the past, collections of biographies have proved to be of immense value; and Christian believers are still being spiritually enriched by volumes written by Edmund Calamy, Walter Wilson, James Reid, Benjamin Brook, Erasmus Middleton, Thomas Smith, and others. But this book, while making use of information contained in earlier works, promises and delivers something more: a history of English Puritanism, followed by nearly one hundred and fifty informative sketches of those Puritans, Scottish Presbyterians, and divines of the Dutch Further Reformation, whose works have been republished in the last fifty years— all this along with perceptive assessment of many of their excellent works. The idea for such a book, brilliantly conceived, has now been made a reality with evident piety and meticulous scholarship. Beautifully produced, this book will surely become a classic and standard work. May the Lord be pleased to bless it, and to revive, in our needy day, the theology, experience, and practice of authentic Puritanism!"

—PASTOR MALCOLM H. WATTS, Emmanuel Church, Salisbury, England

"At last! Beeke and Pederson have produced the volume that readers of Puritan literature have been wanting for years. Whether you've just discovered the treasures penned by the Puritans, or have known these timeless works well and want to mine their riches more deeply, this book is for you."

—DR. DONALD S. WHITNEY, Associate Professor of Biblical Spirituality, Southern Baptist Theological Seminary, Louisville, Kentucky

"The Puritans were men of precise minds and burning hearts, devoted to following Scripture fully and to adorning the doctrine of their God and Savior in all things. Their lives are to be studied by all who love biblical holiness, and their writings are to be pondered deeply by all who have Christ's interests at heart. This invaluable work, so carefully, lovingly, and judiciously produced, will introduce a new generation of Christians to these spiritual giants of the seventeenth century in a way that can only stimulate desire to become better acquainted with them. That can only be good for the church of the twenty-first century."

—DR. ANDREW WOOLSEY, Pastor, Evangelical Presbyterian Church, Crumlin, Northern Ireland

Meet the Puritans

With a Guide to Modern Reprints

Meet the Puritans

With a Guide to Modern Reprints

Joel R. Beeke
and
Randall J. Pederson

Reformation Heritage Books
Grand Rapids, Michigan

REFORMATION HERITAGE BOOKS
2965 Leonard St., NE
Grand Rapids, MI 49525
616-977-0599 / Fax 616-285-3246
e-mail: orders@heritagebooks.org
website: www.heritagebooks.org

10 digit ISBN # 1-60178-000-1
13 digit ISBN # 978-1-60178-000-3

First printing, November 2006
Second printing, February 2007

For additional Reformed literature, both new and used, request a
free book list from Reformation Heritage Books at the above address.

With heartfelt appreciation to my faithful United Kingdom friends for your spiritual fellowship, your open pulpits and open homes, and your invitations to speak at conferences in the homeland of the Puritans:

Gareth and Ceri Edwards
David and Elisabeth George
Erroll and Lyn Hulse
Mark and Fiona Johnston
Peter and Jill Masters
David and Shona Murray
Iain and Jean Murray
Robert and Rachel Oliver
Maurice and Sandra Roberts
Ken and Rosemary Stockley
John and Margaret Thackway
Geoff and Iola Thomas
Malcolm and Jill Watts
Andrew and Joan Woolsey

—JRB

❧

To my dear **Sarah**, for all her love and support;
to my parents, **Gary and Rosamary Pederson**,
for their encouragement through the years;
and to **Tyler James**—may you grow up
reading and loving the Puritans.

—RJP

Contents

Puritan Biographies and Book Reviews

Preface

The Puritans [were] burning and shining lights. When cast out by the black Bartholomew Act, and driven from their respective charges to preach in barns and fields, in the highways and hedges, they in a special manner wrote and preached as men having authority. Though dead, by their writings they yet speak: a peculiar unction attends them to this very hour; and for these thirty years past I have remarked, that the more true and vital religion hath revived either at home or abroad, the more the good old puritanical writings, or the authors of a like stamp who lived and died in communion of the Church of England, have been called for.... Their works still praise them in the gates; and without pretending to a spirit of prophecy, we may venture to affirm that they will live and flourish, when more modern performances of a contrary cast, notwithstanding their gaudy and tinseled trappings, will languish and die in the esteem of those whose understandings are opened to discern what comes nearest to the scripture standard.

— George Whitefield, *Works*, 4:306-307

Why produce a guide to the literature left to us by the English Puritans and their counterparts in Scotland and the Netherlands? To answer that question we must begin by recalling how little interest there was in the Puritans for much of the twentieth century.

As Whitefield predicted, demand for "the good old puritanical writings" continued strong in the generations that followed him, until well into the nineteenth century. This interest in the Puritans culminated in the efforts of Alexander Grosart and others to produce standard editions of the Puritans' works.

In the last years of the nineteenth century, however, a very different mindset came to prevail among Christians on both sides of the Atlantic. The Calvinism of the Puritans was discarded as an outmoded system of Christian thought, and the high view of Scripture that was the very heartbeat of Puritanism was displaced by a much different view, proclaimed to be more scholarly or more scientific to disguise its real character as sheer unbelief and apostasy.

The call for "the good old puritanical writings" was silenced, and the works of the Puritans ceased to issue from the presses of Great Britain and North America. If not thrown into the trash or sold for scrap, the works of the Puritans languished unread on library shelves or went unsold, even at bargain rates, in used bookshops and stalls.

Under God it was the ministry of Dr. Martyn Lloyd-Jones in London that helped to create a demand for Puritan books. He so often referred to Puritan works in his preaching that people asked him where they could be found. He directed them to the Evangelical Library. Then he also chaired the Puritan Conference from its beginning in 1950 several years before the Puritan reprints began to appear. Thus, many people were longing for them by the time that they were available.

The situation changed dramatically beginning in the latter half of the 1950s, spearheaded by the Banner of Truth Trust's new Puritan reprints. A new generation of Christians, already beginning to look more deeply into the truths of Scripture and the teaching of the Reformed Confessions, now began to relish the written legacy of the Puritans in their quest for guidance and understanding. Demand began to grow for new editions of "the good old puritanical writings."

Since that time Puritan literature has so multiplied that few book-lovers can afford to purchase all that is being republished. What books should one buy? Where can one find a brief summary of each Puritan work and a brief description of the author?

This guide answers these questions by providing a brief biography of each Puritan author whose works have been reprinted since 1956 and a short review of those books. We hope this will help purchasers of Puritan books, interest other readers in the Puritans, and guide those already immersed in Puritan literature to further depths of study.

Definition of Puritanism

Just what is meant by the term *Puritan*? Many people today use the term to describe a morose and legalistic brand of Christianity that borders on fanaticism. Much of this stereotype was the product of nineteenth-century anti-Puritan sentiments. While subsequent cultures have expressed various opinions of the Puritans, it is helpful to chronicle a brief history of the term and to assess the movement as objectively as possible.

The term *Puritan* was first used in the 1560s of those English Protestants who considered the reforms under Queen Elizabeth incomplete and called for further "purification" (from the Greek word *katharos*, "pure"). Its negative connotation derived from its being a translation of the Latin term *catharus* (Puritan) or *cathari* (Puritans; from *katharos*), a title given to medieval heretics (Gordon S. Wakefield, "The Puritans," in *The Study of Spirituality*, ed. Cheslyn Jones, Geoffrey Wainwright, and Edward Yarnold, p. 438). For William Perkins (1558-1602), often called "the father of Puritanism," *Puritan* was a "vile term" that described people with perfectionist tendencies (*The Works of Mr. William Perkins*, 1:342, 3:15). Leonard J. Trinterud concludes, "Throughout the sixteenth century it was used more often as a scornful adjective than as a substantive noun, and was rejected as slanderous in whatever quarter it was applied" (*Elizabethan Puritanism*, pp. 3ff.).

The terms *Puritan* and *Puritanism* stuck, though what they mean has changed over the years. Twentieth-century scholars offer various opinions on what the terms actually intend to describe. William Haller sees the "central dogma of Puritanism [as] an all-embracing determinism, theologically formulated doctrine of predestination" (*The Rise of Puritanism*, p. 83). Perry Miller finds the "marrow of Puritan divinity" in the idea of the covenant (*Errand into the Wilderness*, pp. 48–49); and Alan Simpson, in the concept of conversion (*Puritanism in Old and New England*, p. 2). Christopher Hill emphasized the social and political ideas in Puritanism (*Society and Puritanism*). John Coolidge linked the Puritan emphasis to a rejection of the Anglican doctrine of *adiaphora*, or things indifferent (*The Pauline Renaissance in England: Puritanism and the Bible*).

Richard M. Hawkes offers this summary: "Was [English Puritanism] essentially a theological movement, emphasizing covenant theology, predestination, and a reformed church service? Or was the heart of the matter political, asserting the inalienable rights of conscience before God, the rule of natural law over arbitrary prerogative courts, the dependency of the king in parliament, the foundation of state authority in the people? Some modern research has pointed to a third possibility, that the essence of Puritanism was its piety, a stress on conversion, on existential, heartfelt religion" ("The Logic of Assurance in English Puritan Theology," *Westminster Theological Journal* 52 [1990]:247).

All of these concerns and more are involved in Puritanism. More simply put, we would assert that the Puritans embraced five major concerns and addressed each of them substantially in their writings:

- The Puritans sought to search the Scriptures, collate their findings, and apply them to all areas of life. In so doing, the Puritans also aimed to be confessional and theological, and drew heavily on the labors of dedicated Christian scholarship.

- The Puritans were passionately committed to focusing on the Trinitarian character of theology. They never tired of proclaiming the electing grace of God, the dying love of Jesus Christ, and the applicatory work of the Holy Spirit in the lives of sinners. Their fascination with Christian experience was not so much motivated by an interest in their experience per se as it was in their desire to trace out the divine work within them so that they could render all glory to their Triune Lord.

- In common with the Reformers, the Puritans believed in the significance of the church in the purposes of Christ. They believed therefore that the worship of the church should be the careful outworking and faithful embodiment of her biblical faith, and so Puritanism was a movement that focused on plain and earnest preaching, liturgical reform, and spiritual brotherhood. Likewise, the Puritans believed that there was an order or polity for the government of the church revealed in Scripture, and the well-being of the church depended on bringing her into conformity to that order.

- In the great questions of national life presented by the crises of their day, the Puritans looked to Scripture for light on the duties, power, and rights of king, Parliament, and citizen-subjects.

- In regard to the individual, the Puritans focused on personal, comprehensive conversion. They believed with Christ that "except a man be born again, he cannot see the kingdom of heaven" (John 3:3). So they excelled at preaching the gospel, probing the conscience, awakening the sinner, calling him to repentance and faith, leading him to Christ, and schooling him in the way of Christ. Likewise, the Puritans believed with James that "faith, if it hath not works, is dead being alone" (James 2:17). So they developed from Scripture a careful description of what a Christian ought to be in his inward life before God, and in all his actions and relationships in this life, at home, in the church, at work, and in society.

In this book, the term *Puritan* is used as a combination of all the concerns presented above. Thus, we have included not only those Puritans who were ejected from the Church of England by the Act of Uniformity in 1662, but also those in England and North America who, from the reign of Elizabeth I until 1689 (and in a few cases, on into the eighteenth century), worked to reform and purify the church and to lead people toward godly living consistent with the Reformed doctrines of grace. J.I. Packer summarizes this understanding of Puritanism well: "Puritanism was an evangelical holiness movement seeking to implement its vision of spiritual renewal, national and personal, in the church, the state, and the home; in education, evangelism, and economics; in individual discipleship and devotion, and in pastoral care and competence" (*An Anglican to Remember—William Perkins: Puritan Popularizer* [St. Antholin's Lectureship Charity Lecture, 1996], pp. 1-2).

Peter Lewis rightly says that Puritanism grew out of three needs: (1) the need for biblical preaching and the teaching of sound Reformed doctrine; (2) the need for biblical, personal piety that stresses the work of the Holy Spirit in the faith and life of the believer; and (3) the need to restore biblical simplicity in liturgy, vestments, and church government, so that a well-ordered church life would promote the worship of the Triune God as prescribed in His Word (*The Genius of Puritanism*, pp. 11ff.). Doctrinally, Puritanism was a kind of vigorous Calvinism; experientially, it was warm and contagious; evangelistically, it was aggressive, yet tender; ecclesiastically, it was theocentric and worshipful; politically, it aimed to be scriptural, balanced, and bound by conscience before God in the relations of king, Parliament, and subjects.

The Puritans were by no means a monolithic movement any more than were the Reformers, or, for that matter, any major group of theologians in church history. They too had their differences, not only ecclesiastically and politically, but also theologically. There were men among them who imbibed error, such as Richard Baxter on justification and John Preston on the atonement. Yet, for the most part, there was a remarkable unity of thought, conviction, and experience among the Puritans.

How to Profit from Reading the Puritans

With the Spirit's blessing, Puritan writings can enrich your life as a Christian in many ways as they open the Scriptures and apply them practically, probing your conscience, indicting your sins, leading you to repentance, shaping your faith, guiding your conduct, comforting you in Christ and conforming you to Him, and bringing you into full assurance of salvation and a lifestyle of gratitude to the triune God for His great salvation. Here are six characteristics that permeate Puritan literature and account for its continuing relevance and power:

1. *They shape life by Scripture.* The Puritans loved, lived, and breathed Scripture, relishing the power of the Spirit that accompanied the Word. They regarded the sixty-six books of Scripture as the library of the Holy Spirit graciously bequeathed to Christians. They viewed Scripture as God speaking to them as their Father, giving them the truth they could trust for all eternity. They saw it as Spirit-empowered to renew their minds and transform their lives.

The Puritans searched, heard, and sang the Word with delight and encouraged others to do the same. Puritan Richard Greenham suggested eight ways to read Scripture:

with diligence, wisdom, preparation, meditation, conference, faith, practice, and prayer. Thomas Watson provided numerous guidelines on how to listen to the Word: come to the Word with a holy appetite and a teachable heart. Sit under the Word attentively, receive it with meekness, and mingle it with faith. Then retain the Word, pray over it, practice it, and speak to others about it.

The Puritans called believers to be Word-centered in faith and practice. Richard Baxter's *Christian Directory* showed how the Puritans regarded the Bible as a trustworthy guide for all of life. Every case of conscience was subjected to Scripture's directives. Henry Smith said, "We should set the Word of God always before us like a rule, and believe nothing but that which it teacheth, love nothing but that which it prescribeth, hate nothing but that which it forbiddeth, do nothing but that which it commandeth."

If you read the Puritans regularly, their focus on the Scriptures becomes contagious. Though their commentaries on Scripture are not the last word in exegesis, the Puritans show how to yield wholehearted allegiance to the Bible's message. Like them, you will become a believer of the living Book, concurring with John Flavel, who said, "The Scriptures teach us the best way of living, the noblest way of suffering, and the most comfortable way of dying."

2. *They marry doctrine and practice.* The Puritans did this by addressing the mind, confronting the conscience, and wooing the heart.

• *Addressing the mind.* The Puritans refused to set mind and heart against each other but taught that knowledge was the soil in which the Spirit planted the seed of regeneration. They viewed the mind as the palace of faith. "In conversion, reason is elevated," John Preston wrote. Cotton Mather said, "Ignorance is the mother not of devotion but of heresy."

The Puritans understood that a mindless Christianity fosters a spineless Christianity. An anti-intellectual gospel quickly becomes an empty, formless gospel that doesn't get beyond "felt needs." That's what is happening in many churches today. Tragically, few understand that if there is little difference between what Christians and unbelievers believe with their minds, there will soon be little difference in how they live. Puritan literature is a great solution to this problem.

• *Confronting the conscience.* The Puritans were masters at naming specific sins, then asking questions to press home conviction of those sins. As one Puritan wrote, "We must go with the stick of divine truth and beat every bush behind which a sinner hides, until like Adam who hid, he stands before God in his nakedness."

Devotional reading should be confrontational as well as comforting. We experience little growth if our consciences are not pricked daily and directed to Christ. Since we are prone to run for the bushes, we need daily help to be brought before the living God "naked and opened unto the eyes of him with whom we have to do" (Heb. 4:13). In this, no writers can help us as much as the Puritans.

• *Engaging the heart.* It is unusual today to find books that feed the mind with solid biblical substance and move the heart with affectionate warmth, but the Puritans do both. They reason with the mind, confront the conscience, and appeal to the heart. They write out of love for God's Word, love for the glory of God, and love for the souls of readers. They set forth Christ in His loveliness, moving us to yearn to know Him better and live wholly for Him.

3. *They focus on Christ.* According to Thomas Adams, "Christ is the sum of the whole Bible, prophesied, typified, prefigured, exhibited, demonstrated, to be found in every leaf, almost in every line, the Scriptures being but as it were the swaddling

bands of the child Jesus." Likewise, Isaac Ambrose wrote, "Think of Christ as the very substance, marrow, soul, and scope of the whole Scriptures."

The Puritans loved Christ and wrote much about His beauty. Samuel Rutherford wrote: "Put the beauty of ten thousand thousand worlds of paradises, like the Garden of Eden in one; put all trees, all flowers, all smells, all colors, all tastes, all joys, all loveliness, all sweetness in one. O what a fair and excellent thing would that be? And yet it would be less to that fair and dearest well-beloved Christ than one drop of rain to the whole seas, rivers, lakes, and fountains of ten thousand earths." Thomas Goodwin echoed this thought, saying, "Heaven would be hell to me without Christ."

Would you know Christ better and love Him more fully? Immerse yourself in Puritan literature, asking the Spirit to sanctify it to you in a Christ-centered way.

4. *They show how to handle trials.* We learn from the Puritans that we need affliction to humble us (Deut. 8:2), to teach us what sin is (Zeph. 1:12), and to bring us to God (Hos. 5:15). As Robert Leighton wrote, "Affliction is the diamond dust that heaven polishes its jewels with." The Puritans show us how God's rod of affliction is His means to write Christ's image more fully upon us, so that we may be partakers of His righteousness and holiness (Heb. 12:10–11).

If you are presently undergoing trials, read William Bridge's *A Lifting Up for the Downcast,* Thomas Brooks's *A Mute Christian Under the Rod,* and Richard Sibbes's *A Bruised Reed.* They will show you how every trial can bring you to Christ, to walk by faith and to be weaned from this world. As Thomas Watson wrote, "God would have the world hang as a loose tooth which, being easily twitched away, doth not much trouble us." Also, read *The Rare Jewel of Christian Contentment* by Jeremiah Burroughs. It will teach you how to learn contentment through trial. Then, the next time you are buffeted by others, Satan, or your own conscience, you will carry those trials to Christ and ask Him, by His Spirit, to sanctify them so that you may model spiritual contentment for others.

5. *They show how to live in two worlds.* Richard Baxter's *The Saint's Everlasting Rest* shows the power that the hope of heaven has to direct, control, and energize our life here on earth. Despite its length (800-plus pages), this classic became household reading in Puritan homes. It was surpassed only by John Bunyan's *Pilgrim's Progress,* which is an allegorical outworking of this same truth. Bunyan's pilgrim is heading for the Celestial City, which he never has out of his mind except when he is betrayed by some form of spiritual malaise.

The Puritans believed that we should have heaven "in our eye" throughout our earthly pilgrimage. They took seriously the two-worldly, now/not-yet dynamic of the New Testament, stressing that keeping the "hope of glory" before our minds should guide and shape our lives here on earth. Living in the light of eternity necessitated radical self-denial. The Puritans taught us to live, knowing that the joy of heaven makes amends for any losses and crosses that we must endure on earth if we follow Christ. They taught us that preparing to die is the first step in learning to live.

6. *They show us true spirituality.* The Puritans promoted the authority of Scripture, biblical evangelism, church reform, the spirituality of the law, spiritual warfare against indwelling sin, the filial fear of God, the art of meditation, the dreadfulness of hell and the glories of heaven. So read the Puritans devotionally, and then pray to emulate their spirituality. Ask questions like these: Are we, like the Puritans, thirsting to glorify the triune God? Are we motivated by biblical truth and biblical fire? Do we share the Puritan view of the vital neces-

sity of conversion and of being clothed with the righteousness of Christ? Do we follow them, as they followed Christ?

Where to Begin

If you are just starting to read the Puritans, begin with Thomas Watson's *Heaven Taken by Storm*, John Bunyan's *The Fear of God*, John Flavel's *Keeping the Heart*, Thomas Brooks's *Precious Remedies Against Satan's Devices*, and Richard Sibbes's *Glorious Freedom*, then move on to the works of John Owen, Thomas Goodwin, and Jonathan Edwards.

For sources that introduce you to the Puritan lifestyle and theology, begin with Leland Ryken's *Worldly Saints: The Puritans As They Really Were* (Grand Rapids: Zondervan, 1990), Peter Lewis's *The Genius of Puritanism* (Morgan, Penn.: Soli Deo Gloria, 1997), and Erroll Hulse's *Who are the Puritans? and what do they teach?* (Darlington, England: Evangelical Press, 2000). Then move on to James I. Packer's *A Quest for Godliness: The Puritan Vision of the Christian Life* (Wheaton, Ill.: Crossway Books, 1990).

We have striven to make our guide useful both for those who are just beginning to read the Puritans and for those who are more advanced in Puritan theology and studies. Consequently, there will be some material that the beginner will find a bit difficult to grasp and other material that the more advanced will find rather elementary. In the main, however, we trust that this book will be an informative and stimulating guide to all who are seeking to know more about the Puritan divines and the recently reprinted books that they wrote.

Criteria and Sources Used

This book began in the 1980s with a series of articles written for the *Banner of Truth* (U.S.) entitled, "Meet the Puritans . . . in Print!" Those articles covered Puritans reprinted from the 1950s through 1985. Ten years later, "Reading the Best in Puritan Literature: A Modern Bibliography," *Reformation and*

Revival 5, 2 (1996):117-158, covered reprinted Puritan titles from 1986 to 1996. *Meet the Puritans* expands this material and covers books reprinted for half a century, from 1956 through 2005. In all, it contains comments on close to 700 volumes from more than 75 publishers, and nearly 150 brief biographies. Some biographies are substantially longer than others because of the importance of the individual in Christian history and literature, or because of the amount of biographical material available. Also, some of these longer biographies are adapted from articles or book introductions that we have written, and are printed here with permission.

We have not usually attempted to include all the paperback editions of a particular author when his complete works have been reprinted. Nor have we included more than one edition of a book that has been reissued two or more times. In most cases, we noted the reprint of highest quality. In a few instances, when the quality was nearly equal, we gave preference to the edition that is still in print. In every case, we supplied the publisher, number of pages, and date of publication behind the title. Each author's titles are listed alphabetically, except in cases when the author's "works" have been reprinted. In those cases, the entry of the author's works is placed first. In subsequent entries by that author an asterisk (*) is placed before each title that is *not* included in the author's works. We regret that we are not able to indicate whether or not a title is currently in print as many books in this guide come into print or go out of print every single year. Since we would like to update this book periodically, we welcome suggestions from readers on Puritan titles that were reprinted in the last half century (1956-2005) that we may have missed. Please forward them to Joel R. Beeke, 2965 Leonard Street, NE, Grand Rapids, Michigan 49525, USA. Our updated information on new reprinted Puritan publications will be regularly updated and posted on the Puritan Resource Center's page of www.puritanseminary.org.

Several appendices are included. The first covers multi-authored Puritan titles; the second, Scottish writers who fit our definition of Puritan; the third, Dutch Further Reformation writers, sometimes called "Dutch Puritans," translated into English; and fourth, an annotated bibliography of a sampling of secondary sources on the Puritans printed in the last twenty years. This last appendix could easily be augmented to become a full monograph by itself. Instead, in addition to the short annotated bibliography of the fourth appendix, we include a non-annotated bibliography of several hundred secondary sources at the end of this book. The concluding appendix serves as a final word on Puritanism from J.I. Packer.

For time parameters, men and women are included whose writings reflect Puritan convictions in the period from William Perkins (1558-1602) to Jonathan Edwards (1703-1758), sometimes called "the last Puritan." Forerunners of the Puritans, such as John Bradford and John Hooper, have not been included. In some cases, it was difficult to determine whether or not to include a particular writer, particularly those who opposed Puritan ecclesiology, such as Thomas Adams, Richard Baker, Joseph Hall, Nathaniel Hardy, and Ezekiel Hopkins. In these cases, since their writings bear the Puritan stamp of spirituality that Whitefield refers to in the opening quotation of this preface, we have included them.

Regarding sources used, we freely consulted the major encyclopedias and standard reference works on the Puritans. The most useful have been H.C.G. Matthew and Brian Harrison's *Oxford Dictionary of National Biography* (60 vols.; *Oxford DNB*), Leslie Stephen and Sidney Lee's *Dictionary of National Biography* (22 vols.; *DNB*), *The New Schaff-Herzog Encyclopedia of Religious Knowledge* (15 vols.), M'Clintock and Strong's *Cyclopedia of Biblical, Theological, and Ecclesiastical Literature* (12 vols.),

Allen Johnson and Dumas Malone's *Dictionary of American Biography* (10 vols.), John Strype's *Ecclesiastical Memorials* (7 vols.), *Appletons' Cyclopaedia of American Biography* (6 vols.), Erasmus Middleton's *Evangelical Biography* (4 vols.), Edmund Calamy's *The Nonconformist's Memorial* (4 vols.; also, Samuel Palmer's 3 vol. edition), A.G. Matthews's *Calamy Revised,* Jay Green's *Encyclopedia of Christianity* (4 vols.), Anthony à Wood's *Athenae Oxonienses* (4 vols.), S. Allibone's *A Critical Dictionary of English Literature and British and American Authors* (4 vols.), James Darling's *Cyclopaedia Bibliographica* (3 vols.), Benjamin Brooks's *Lives of the Puritans* (3 vols.), and Thomas Fuller's *Abel Redevivus; or, The Dead Yet Speaking: The Lives and Deaths of Modern Divines* (2 vols.) as well as his *Worthies of England* (2 vols.). Due to the paucity of material on certain Puritans, we have relied heavily at times on these sources. For information on the Puritans who served at the Westminster Assembly, James Reid's *Memoirs of the Westminster Divines* and William Barker's *Puritan Profiles* have been most helpful. We have also consulted studies on individual Puritans. In cases where sources have contradicted each other, we have used the *Oxford DNB* as our final source of authority.

For appendix 2, we have used the *Dictionary of Scottish Church History & Theology*, edited by Nigel Cameron; for appendix 3, we have consulted F.W. Grosheide and G.P. Van Itterzon's *Christelijke Encyclopedie* (6 vols.), J.P. DeBie and J. Loosjes's *Biographisch Woordenboek van Protestantsche Godgeleerden in Nederland* (5 vols.), D. Nauta's *Biografisch Lexicon voor de Geschiedenis van het Nederlandse Protestantisme* (4 vols.), and B. Glasius's *Biografisch Woordenboek van Nederlandsche Godgeleerden* (3 vols.).

As for book descriptions, we have summarized each volume, frequently offering a savory quotation from the book under review to whet the potential reader's appetite. When material from the publisher has factually described a book's content, we have on occasion woven some of that material into our summary.

For a topical and textual index to the writings of the Puritans, see Robert P. Martin's *A Guide to the Puritans*, which includes most of the books reviewed in this volume. Martin's book is a necessary complement to this volume for those who are serious about knowing and studying the themes and texts handled in the Puritan tradition.

To keep this book a reasonable length, we have not used footnotes. In most cases, quotations of some length include the author and title reference in the text. For complete bibliographical data of secondary sources, check the bibliography at the end of this book. Spelling has been modernized in the titles of, and quotations from, antiquarian books. Capitalization has followed the Chicago Manual of Style: hence, "King Charles," but "the king"; "Bachelor of Arts degree" or "Doctor of Divinity degree" as titles, but "bachelor's degree" or "doctorate in divinity" as general terms.

Finally, it should be noted that thousands of books written by Puritans are *not* included in this book because they have not been reprinted since the 1950s. In some cases, titles not reprinted have been referred to in the biographical portions of this book. Scores of Puritans, however, have not had any of their titles reprinted; hence you will look in vain for their names on the contents pages. We contemplated compiling a list of all such authors and titles, but this would take up too many pages to retain our one-volume format. For good reference guides to Puritans and primary sources not mentioned in this book, see especially Benjamin Brook's *Lives of the Puritans*, James Reid's *Memoirs of the Westminster Divines*, and the *Oxford DNB*. For those interested in information on antiquarian Puritan titles that have not yet been reprinted, contact the Puritan Resource Center (2965 Leonard Street N.E., Grand

Rapids, Michigan 49525, USA), which houses a collection of more than 3,000 titles by and about the Puritans.

Acknowledgements

We thank Rev. Ray B. Lanning for editorial assistance and especially for supplying a glossary of seventeenth-century words and events from Presbyterian Scotland, Puritan England, and New England that may be unfamiliar to modern readers. We trust that you will find this glossary helpful, particularly when reading the biographical material. Thanks, too, to Phyllis TenElshof for editing; to Gary den Hollander, Kate DeVries, Sharla Kattenberg, Dr. Robert Oliver, Rev. John Thackway, Dr. Fred van Lieburg, and Kelly Ziegler for proofreading; to Alastair Roberts for assistance during an internship; to Linda den Hollander for her typesetting; and to Jay T. Collier for help in wrapping up details down the final stretch. A heartfelt thanks to Dr. Jan VanVliet for contributing to the entry on William Ames, to Rev. Cornelius Pronk for coauthoring the entry on Theodorus Frelinghuysen, and to Dr. Tom Schwanda for assisting with the entry on Isaac Ambrose.

We thank Iain Murray for his detailed suggestions in response to our first two drafts, and for instilling a love for Puritan literature in us through the Puritan reprints of Banner of Truth Trust books, his own books, and his valued friendship. We are also grateful to Kelly Kapic and Randall Gleason for allowing us to reprint their "A Brief History of English Puritanism." Our heartfelt thanks is extended to Don Kistler for providing most of the illustrations of the English Puritans contained in this book and for sharing our vision and love for Puritan reprints. Thanks, too, to DenHertog Publications for allowing us to borrow illustrations of the Dutch Further Reformation divines, to Caffy Whitney for her artwork in providing illustrations for William Perkins and William

Ames used both on the cover and in the book, and to Amy Zevenbergen for designing the dust jacket.

The theological students at Puritan Reformed Theological Seminary were a major impetus for persevering with this book. We are grateful to several students who provided material that assisted us with an entry. We pray that these students may be as godly and able ministers of the gospel for our generation as the Puritans were for theirs.

We wholeheartedly thank our dear wives, Mary Beeke and Sarah Pederson, for their patience, support, and enthusiasm throughout this project. We are humbled to be blessed with wives whose lives manifest, by God's grace, the kind of biblical piety that Puritan literature powerfully promotes.

Finally, we acknowledge our God and Savior, who, by His grace, has fed us so richly through our Puritan-minded English, Scottish, and Dutch forebears. We trust that, as you read of their lives and peruse their books, you will concur with James I. Packer's assessment: "In a time of failing vision and decaying values, [the Puritans are] a beacon of hope calling us to radical commitment and action when both are desperately needed."

— JRB/RJP

Illustrations

English and American Puritans

Scottish Divines

Dutch Further Reformation Divines

Abbreviations and Addresses of Publishers

AAS: American Antiquarian Society, 185 Salisbury Street, Worcester, Massachusetts 01609

AMS: AMS Press, Inc., Brooklyn Navy Yard, Building 292, Suite 417, 63 Flushing Avenue, Brooklyn, New York 11205

AP: Aldine Press

Arno: Arno Press—now an imprint of Ayer Company Publishers, 400 Bedford St., Suite 322, Manchester, New Hampshire 03101

Ashgate: Ashgate Publishing Co., Old Post Road, Brookfield, Vermont 05036

Baker: Baker Book House, 6030 E. Fulton, Ada, Michigan 49301

BB: Blue Banner Publications, Livingstone House, 16 Edward St., Kilsyth G65 9DL, Scotland

Bedford: Bedford Publishers, 33 Irving Place, New York, New York 10003

Berith: Berith Publications (a division of Tentmaker Publications, see address below)

B&H: Broadman & Holman, 127 Ninth Avenue North, MSN 114, Nashville, Tennessee 37234

BP: The Bunyan Press, 23 Haslingden Close, Harpenden, Herts AL5 3EW, England

BTT: Banner of Truth Trust, The Grey House, 3 Murrayfield Road, Edinburgh EH12 6EL, Scotland; American office: P.O. Box 621, 63 E. Louther St., Carlisle, Pennsylvania 17013

CFP: Christian Focus Publications, Geanies House, Fearn, Tain, Ross-shire IV20 1TW, Scotland

CMP: Cornmarket Press, 42/43 Conduit Street, London W1R 0NL, England

Crossway: Crossway Books, 1300 Crescent St., Wheaton, Illinois 60187

CVHM: Connecticut Valley Historical Museum, 220 State Street, Corner of State and Chestnut Streets, Springfield, Massachusetts 01103

DA: Dust and Ashes, 170 Washington Ave., Muskegon, Michigan 49441

Da Capo: Da Capo Press Inc.

Degraaf: DeGraaf, Zuideinde 40, Postbus 6, 2420 AA, Nieuwkoop, Netherlands

Dover: Dover Publications, Inc., 31 East 2nd Street, Mineola, New York 11501

Ebenezer: Ebenezer Publications

Eerdmans: Wm. B. Eerdmans Publishing, 255 Jefferson S.E., Grand Rapids, Michigan 49503

EP: Evangelical Press, 12 Wooler St., Darlington, County Durham DL1 1RX, England

FCM: Focus Christian Ministries Trust, 6 Orchard Road, Lewes, East Sussex BN7 2HB, England

FPP: Free Presbyterian Publications, 133 Woodlands Rd., Glasgow G3 6LE, Scotland

FUP: Frederick Ungar Publishing Co., 250 Park Avenue South, New York, New York 10003

GM: Gospel Mission, P.O. Box 318, Choteau, Montana 59422

Harvard: Harvard University Press, 79 Garden St., Cambridge, Massachusetts 02138

HP: Hendrickson Publishers, P.O. Box 3473, Peabody, Massachusetts 01961

IO: International Outreach, P.O. Box 1286, Ames, Iowa 50010

IVP: InterVarsity Press, P.O. Box 1400, Downers Grove, Illinois 60515

JB: James Begg Society, 20 Abbotswell Crescent, Kincorth, Aberdeen AB12 5AR, Scotland

JC: James Clarke Press, P.O. Box 60, Cambridge CB1 2NT, England

JFCP: James Family Christian Publishers

Johnson: Johnson Reprint Corporation

K&K: Klock & Klock

Kregel: Kregel Publishers, P.O. Box 2607, Grand Rapids, Michigan 49501

LSUP: Louisiana State University Press, P.O. Box 25053, Baton Rouge, Louisiana 70894

LUP: Lehigh University Press, 2002 Lehigh University, 27 Memorial Drive West, Bethlehem, Pennsylvania 18015

MP: Maranatha Publishers

MQ: McGill-Queen's University Press, 3430 McTavish Street, Montreal, Quebec H3A 1X9 Canada

NP: Naphtali Press, P.O. Box 141084, Dallas, Texas 75214

NR: Netherlands Reformed Book and Publishing, 123 Leffingwell N.E., Grand Rapids, Michigan 49525

NUP: Nebraska University Press, 233 North 8th Street, Lincoln, Nebraska 68588

OP: Old Paths Publications, 1 Bittersweet Path, Willowstreet, Pennsylvania 17584

PA: Presbyterian's Armoury Publications, P.O. Box 662, Burnie TAS 7320, Australia

Pilgrim: Pilgrim Press

PL: Peter Lang, 275 Seventh Avenue, 28th floor, New York, New York 10001

PP: Pietan Publication, 26 Green Farm Road, New Ipswich, New Hampshire 03071

P&R: Presbyterian and Reformed Publishing, P.O. Box 817, Philipsburg, New Jersey 08865

PUP: Princeton University Press, 41 William St., Princeton, New Jersey 08540

RAP: Reformed Academic Press, P.O. Box 8599, Greenville, South Carolina 29604

RE: Maranatha Publications, P.O. Box 66212, Mobile, Alabama 36606

Reiner: Reiner Publications

RHB: Reformation Heritage Books, 2965 Leonard St. N.E., Grand Rapids, Michigan 49525

Rhwym: Rhwym Books, P.O. Box 1706, Cambridge, Massachusetts 02238

ROR: Richard Owen Roberts, P.O. Box 21, Wheaton, Illinois 60189

RP: Reformation Press, 11 Churchhill Dr., Stornoway, Isle of Lewis PA87 2NP, Scotland

SDG: Soli Deo Gloria, a division of Ligonier Ministries, P.O. Box 547500, Orlando, Florida 32854

SF: Scholars' Facsimiles and Reprints

SG: Solid Ground Christian Books, P.O. Box 660132, Vestavia Hills, Alabama 35266

SGP: Sovereign Grace Publishers, P.O. Box 4998, Lafayette, Indiana 47903

SGT: Sovereign Grace Trust Fund

Smith: Peter Smith Publishers, 5 Lexington Ave., Gloucester,
   Massachusetts 01930
SPR: Sprinkle Publications, P.O. Box 1094, Harrisonburg,
   Virginia 22801
SWRB: Still Waters Revival Books, 4710-37A Ave., Edmonton,
   Alberta T6L 3T5, Canada
TENT: Tentmaker Publications, 121 Hartshill Rd., Stoke-on-Trent,
   Staffs ST4 7LU, England
TP: Tanski Publications
UC: University of Chicago Press, 1427 East 60th Street, Chicago,
   Illinois 60637
UGP: University of Georgia Press, 330 Research Drive, Athens,
   Georgia 30602
UIP: University of Illinois Press, 1325 South Oak Street, Champaign,
   Illinois 61820
UMP: University of Massachusetts Press, P.O. Box 429, Amherst,
   Massachusetts 01004
UNC: University of North Carolina Press, 116 South Boundary Street,
   Chapel Hill, North Carolina 27514
UPA: United Press of America, Boston Way, Lanham, Maryland 20706
UPP: University of Pennsylvania Press, 4200 Pine Street,
   Philadelphia, Pennsylvania 19104
VH: Vision Harvest, P.O. Box 680, Haymarket, Virginia 20168
WJ: Walter J. Johnson, Inc.
Yale: Yale University Press, P.O. Box 209040, New Haven,
   Connecticut 06520
Zoar: Zoar Publications, Christian Bookshop, 21 Queen St.,
   Ossett, West Yorkshire WF5 8AS, England
Zondervan: Zondervan Publications, 5300 Patterson S.E.,
   Grand Rapids, Michigan 49512

*Publishers without addresses are no longer in existence. Many of the books reviewed
in this book can be found in your local Christian bookstore or can be obtained directly from the publisher. If you cannot locate certain titles, contact Reformation
Heritage Books, 2965 Leonard St. NE, Grand Rapids, Michigan 49525 (phone: 616-
977-0599; e-mail: orders@heritagebooks.org; website: www.heritagebooks.org).*

Puritan Biographies
and
Book Reviews

The Puritans were not unlearned and ignorant men. The great majority of them were Oxford and Cambridge graduates—many of them fellows of colleges, and some of them heads or principals of the best colleges in the two Universities. In knowledge of Hebrew, Greek, and Latin, in power as preachers, expositors, writers, and critics, the Puritans in their day were second to none. Their works still speak for them on the shelves of every well-furnished theological library. Their commentaries, their expositions, their treatises on practical, casuistical, and experimental divinity, are immeasurably superior to those of their adversaries in the seventeenth century. In short, those who hold up the Puritans to scorn as shallow, illiterate men are only exposing their own lamentable shallowness, their own ignorance of historical facts, and the extremely superficial character of their own reading.

The Puritans, as a body, have done more to elevate the national character than any class of Englishmen that ever lived. Ardent lovers of civil liberty, and ready to die in its defence—mighty at the council board, and no less mighty in the battlefield—feared abroad throughout Europe, and invincible at home while united—great with their pens, and no less great with their swords—fearing God very much, and fearing men very little,—they were a generation of men who have never received from their country the honor that they deserve.

—J.C. Ryle (introduction to
Thomas Manton's *Works*, 2:xi)

A Brief History of
English Puritanism
━━◆◆◆━━

Protestant ideas from Wittenberg spread rapidly throughout
Europe, reaching England during the reign of Henry VIII
(1509-1547). The English monarch used the pretense of religious reform as an opportunity to break with the Catholic
Church so he could legally divorce, remarry, and hopefully
produce a male heir. During the short reign of his sickly son
Edward VI (1547-1553), the theology of Luther and Calvin
was introduced into the English Church by Archbishop
Thomas Cranmer (1489-1556) through his book of *Homilies*
(1547), his *Book of Common Prayer* (1552), and his *Forty-Two
Articles of Religion* (1553). However, these reforms were quickly
reversed during the "bloody" reign of Mary Tudor (1553-1558).
She reinstated the Latin mass and enforced English allegiance
to the Roman pope at the cost of 270 Protestant martyrs,
including Thomas Cranmer.

When Queen Elizabeth (1533-1603) came to the throne in
1558, many who had fled to Europe in order to escape persecution under Mary returned to England with hopes of
continuing the reforms begun under Edward VI. Though the
Queen appointed some of the "Marian exiles" to positions of
influence (including six bishops), many felt that her Acts of
Uniformity (1559-1562) left the church only "half reformed,"
since she failed to rid England of the clerical vestments and
ceremonies remaining from Catholicism. Her demand for
strict observance of Cranmer's *Book of Common Prayer* and *Articles of Religion* did little to satisfy their longing for the sort of
biblical preaching they had experienced in the great

Reformed churches on the continent. Horrified by the immoral and incompetent clergy tolerated by English episcopacy, Thomas Cartwright (1535-1603) convinced many through his Cambridge lectures in 1570 that the road to reform required the more disciplined Presbyterian model practiced in Geneva. By 1586, a *Book of Discipline* began to circulate quietly among concerned ministers; it outlined new patterns for public worship that insured the preaching of the Word and proper administration of the sacraments.

Once the Queen overcame the international threat of Catholicism by defeating the Spanish Armada in 1588, she turned her attention again to reinforce conformity within the English church. Her new Court of High Commission under Archbishop John Whitgift (1530-1604) suspended hundreds of clergy, accusing them of sedition and disloyalty in her Act Against Puritans issued in 1593. Some of the ejected ministers continued preaching in lectureships sponsored by sympathetic Puritan gentry while a few began to gather congregations in private homes. Although Elizabeth successfully ended any organized efforts to reform the church, a "spiritual brotherhood" of reform-minded moderates continued to flourish. Patrick Collinson explains that this was especially true in Cambridge where students flocked to hear the sermons of William Perkins (1558-1602), the "prince of the Puritan theologians." During his ministry at Great St. Andrews Church, Perkins kept the university press busy printing his books on Reformed theology and practical divinity that were eagerly read throughout England. Equally influential was Laurence Chaderton (1538-1640), the "pope of Cambridge Puritanism," who for nearly forty years as master of Emmanuel College trained many of the most talented Puritan preachers of the next generation.

Since James I (1566-1625) was a Calvinist, his accession to the throne in 1603 revived Puritan hopes for further reforms.

Denying accusations that they were "schismatics aiming at the dissolution" of the English church, the Puritan brotherhood presented their requests to the new king in *The Millenary Petition* (1603), which was signed by a thousand ministers. They appealed for changes in the administration of baptism and use of vestments, the need for self-examination before Communion, the replacement of absent bishops with clergy able to preach, and greater restraint by the ecclesiastical courts in excommunicating laypersons and suspending ministers.

In 1604, James I held a conference at Hampton Court to consider their requests. However, recognizing that his royal supremacy was tied to the English episcopacy, James openly declared his fears: "No bishop, no king." Although he agreed to produce a fresh translation of the Bible to assist English preachers (the King James Version), he demanded that all clergy conform to the liturgy and government of the Church of England. To insure this, the king began a new campaign to impose ceremonial conformity through his bishops. From 1604 to 1609, nearly ninety ministers were suspended from office, including John Robinson (1575-1625), who migrated to the Netherlands with fellow separatist William Bradford (1589-1657), the future governor of Plymouth colony. In 1609, William Ames (1576-1633) was also ejected from Cambridge University and fled to the Netherlands where he became one of the greatest Puritan theologians.

After these initial suspensions, James I grew more tolerant toward Puritan pastors due to pressure from sympathetic members of Parliament. Tensions were further eased by the king's support of Calvinism at the Synod of Dort (1618-1619) and by a growing number of moderate Puritans who found ways to compromise in order to continue their service within the English church. They were led by Laurence Chaderton, who continued as master of Emmanuel College until 1622, and Richard Sibbes (1577-1635), who served as preacher at Holy

Trinity Church in Cambridge and later at Gray's Inn in London. Sibbes's moderate stance on ecclesiastical matters allowed his popularity as a preacher to grow even during the contentious reign of King Charles I (1625-1640).

Charles's marriage in 1625 to Henrietta Maria, a devout Catholic, sparked immediate fears among Puritan ministers and Parliament that the new king intended to lead England back to Rome. Suspicions grew when Charles appointed his trusted adviser, William Laud (1573-1645), as the bishop of London in 1628. Although Laud opposed the authority of the pope, his reintroduction of many Catholic forms of worship and support of Arminian theology distressed the Puritan clergy. After Charles dissolved Parliament and assumed personal rule in 1629, Bishop Laud unleashed a bitter persecution of Puritans. He prohibited the preaching of predestination, required all clergy to use the prayer book and clerical dress, and made the laity kneel while receiving Communion. After his appointment as archbishop of Canterbury in 1633, Laud opposed the Puritan observance of the Sabbath by demanding that the *Book of Sports* be read from every pulpit upon threat of suspension.

Hounded by Laud's agents, many Puritans chose to emigrate either to the Netherlands or to New England. In 1630, John Winthrop (1588-1649) led the first great Puritan exodus to Massachusetts aboard the *Arbella* (with Simon and Anne Bradstreet) as part of a seven-ship flotilla. During the next decade, some of the most esteemed preachers in England, including John Cotton, Thomas Hooker, and Thomas Shepard joined 13,000 emigrants who sailed to New England.

The escalation of Laud's repressive tactics in 1637 proved disastrous for King Charles. His barbaric treatment of Puritan nonconformists like William Prynne (1600-1669), whose ears were cut off and face branded with hot irons, brought back memories of the brutal persecutions against Protestants under Queen Mary. Laud's attempt to enforce Anglican liturgy on the

Scottish Presbyterians galvanized their national resistance leading to their adoption in 1638 of the National Covenant that affirmed the Reformed faith and freedom of the church in Scotland. The king's failed war against the Scottish "Covenanters" and his refusal to work with Parliament incited more opposition, ultimately forcing Charles to flee London in May 1642. In league with the Scottish Presbyterians and with the support of the Puritan clergy, the Long Parliament rejected Charles's claim of the divine right of kings, plunging the country into civil war. Charles and his cavalier army proved no match for the brilliant leadership of Oliver Cromwell (1599-1658) and his New Model Army of Puritan soldiers. Parliament arrested Archbishop Laud and executed him for treason in 1645. After the defeat of the Royalists, Charles negotiated from prison a secret treaty with the Scots that led to further hostilities. For his role in prolonging the civil war, the king was tried and executed on January 30, 1649.

Throughout the English Civil War (1642-1648), under the direction of Parliament, over one hundred Puritan leaders assembled at Westminster Abbey to draft a new confession of faith for the national church. Although they generally agreed on Calvinistic theology, differences arose between the majority who advocated a national Presbyterian church, and a small but vocal minority of Independents, led by Thomas Goodwin, who argued for the right of congregations to govern themselves. They finally reached a compromise that advocated the voluntary formation of congregational presbyteries throughout the country. The Church of Scotland immediately approved the Westminster Confession upon its completion in 1647, followed by Congregationalists in New England in 1648. A decade later, English Congregationalists meeting in London adopted the Westminster Confession in their Savoy Declaration (1658) with only minor modifications on church government. Thus, the Westminster Confession became the doctrinal standard for Puritan theology.

In spite of the great achievement at Westminster, any semblance of solidarity among nonconformists quickly disappeared with the end of the monarchy. After the creation of a new Commonwealth, the political tensions between Presbyterians and Independents in Parliament continued to escalate. To avoid political gridlock, Cromwell dissolved Parliament in 1653 and ruled the country as Lord Protector until his death in 1658. Cromwell's guarantee of religious freedoms allowed unprecedented growth among nearly all religious sects. Independents were promoted to positions of great power within the Puritan Commonwealth. John Owen, for example, was appointed vice-chancellor of Oxford, a former royalist stronghold. Unfortunately, the new religious freedoms were short lived. Richard Cromwell's failed attempt to succeed his father created a complex political crisis that precipitously led to the restoration of the monarchy in 1660. In spite of promises by Charles II to preserve liberty of conscience, Anglican loyalists driven by revenge pressured the king to restore religious conformity through a series of acts known as the Clarendon Code (named after Lord Chancellor Edward Hyde, earl of Clarendon).

Thus began the period of dissent that resulted in the persecution and imprisonment of many famous Puritan pastors, including John Bunyan and Richard Baxter. In 1662, the Act of Uniformity required Puritan ministers to repudiate their denominational ordinations, renounce their oath to the Solemn League and Covenant, and be reordained under the bishops. Nearly two thousand ministers (a fifth of all the clergy) refused to conform and were ejected from their parishes on St. Bartholomew's day, August 24, 1662. The Conventicle Act in 1664 banning nonconformists from preaching in the fields or conducting services in homes was followed in

1665 by the Five Mile Act, which prohibited ejected ministers from coming within five miles of their former parishes or any city or town.

Although Puritans were barred from the pulpits and universities, the repressive measures could not silence their pens. After 1662, under the shadow of persecution, they produced some of their most cherished devotional and theological works (e.g., *Pilgrim's Progress*). Although the hopes of a Puritan commonwealth continued to flicker in New England, the strength of Puritanism was quickly fading in old England. Sadly, most of the leading Puritans died before the lifting of persecution in 1689 by the Toleration Act under William and Mary. Banned from English churchyards even after their death, many Puritans, including John Bunyan, Thomas Goodwin, and John Owen, were buried in a special nonconformist cemetery in Bunhill Fields, London. By the end of the century, much of the Puritan passion to reform the Church of England was redirected into the forming of various dissenting denominations then lawfully permitted by the English government.

> — taken from *The Devoted Life*, edited by Kelly M. Kapic and Randall C. Gleason. Copyright (c) 2004 by Kelly M. Kapic and Randall C. Gleason. Used with permission of InterVarsity Press, P.O. Box 1400, Downers Grove, IL 60515. www.ivpress.com

Thomas Adams

(1583-1652)

Thomas Adams graduated from Trinity College, Cambridge, with a Bachelor of Arts degree in 1602, and four years later, with a Master of Arts degree from Clare College. Ordained deacon and priest in the Lincoln diocese in 1604, he served as curate of Northill, Bedfordshire from 1605 to 1611. When his new patron dismissed him, Adams's parishioners signed a petition stating that he had "behaved himself soberly in his conversation, painfully in his calling, lovingly amongst his neighbors, conformable to the orders of the Church, and in all respects befittingly to his vocation" (J. Maltby, *Prayer Book and People in Elizabethan and Early Stuart England*, p. 78). This testimony may have assisted Adams in securing an appointment the following year as vicar of Willington, Bedfordshire.

In 1614, he became vicar of Wingrave, Buckinghamshire, and then moved to London in 1619, where he was given the rectories of St. Benet Paul's Wharf and the small church of St. Benet Sherehog. For his first five years in London, he also held the lectureship of St. Gregory's, a parish of 3,000. Later on, he preached occasionally at St. Paul's Cross and Whitehall, and served as chaplain to Henry Montagu, First Earl of Manchester and Chief Justice of the king's bench.

Adams was a powerful preacher, a much-quoted writer, and an influential divine. Prominent leaders in church and state, such as John Donne and the earl of Pembroke, were among his friends.

Adams was more of a Calvinist Episcopalian than a Puritan. He was not opposed to kneeling to receive communion and feared that the abolition of episcopacy advocated by some Puritans would lead to Anabaptism. Nonetheless, Adams is included here because he embraced Puritan theology, polemics, and lifestyle. J. Sears McGee writes, "Like Puritans he craved careful observation of the Sabbath and was deeply hostile to Rome, the Jesuits, and the papacy, as well as to idleness, over-indulgence in worldly pleasures, and conspicuous consumption in all its forms" (*Oxford DNB*, 1:261). These things, combined with his eloquent style of writing, led Robert Southey to describe him as "the prose Shakespeare of the Puritan theologians."

Adams shared the Puritan concern to purge the Church of England of remaining vestiges of Roman Catholicism or "popery," as it was then called. His open expression of this concern and his identification with the Puritans in many areas offended William Laud, archbishop of Canterbury; doubtless, this hindered his preferment in the church. At the same time, Adams was staunchly loyal to the king, and so found himself in disfavor with Cromwell and probably suffered being sequestered under the Commonwealth, left to live out his days dependent on charity in what he called, in the dedication of his posthumously published *Anger and Man's Comfort* (1653), his "necessitous and decrepit old age."

Little is known of the latter part of Adams's career. He appears to have written nothing for print during the last twenty years of his life. He died in 1652. Alexander B. Grosart wrote of him: "Thomas Adams stands in the forefront of our great English preachers. He is not as sustained as Jeremy Taylor, nor so continuously sparkling as Thomas Fuller, but he is surpassingly eloquent and brilliant, and much more thought-laden than either."

The Complete Works of Thomas Adams (TP; 3 vols., 1,148 pages; 1998). In 1629, Adams organized his sermons into a massive folio, subsequently printed in three volumes in the Nichol's series reprint of 1861-1866. Adams's sermons have been admired since their first printing; they "placed him beyond all comparison in the van of the preachers of England, and had something to do with shaping John Bunyan.... His numerous works display great learning, classical and patristic, and are unique in their abundance of stories, anecdotes, aphorisms, and puns" (*Encyclopedia Britannica*, 11th ed., 1:181).

Volume 1 of Adams's works contains his sermons on Old Testament texts, such as "God's Bounty" on Proverbs 3:16, and "Mystical Bedlam" on Ecclesiastes 9:3. Volume 2 contains his sermons on New Testament texts, and volume 3 contains the remaining corpus of New Testament sermons as well as meditations on the Apostles' Creed and a fifty-page memoir of Adams by Joseph Angus.

Adams's sermons are evangelically eloquent and biblically faithful. James I. Packer writes:

> His fondness for evangelical allegorizing and verbal pyrotechnics, however, makes his sermons lively rather than weighty. His doctrine is unambiguously Calvinistic, but with a pastoral rather than a speculative or controversial orientation. He does not go deeply into the subject of Christian experience, but is warmly evangelical in extolling the power of Christ, and grace, and faith. The themes on which he is most constant and full, however, are the varieties of sin, the anatomy of hypocrisy, and the stratagems of Satan. Like all the Puritans, he is a thoroughly theocentric thinker, and says much that is illuminating on the ways of God in dealing with sinners in both mercy and judgment. He shows no sympathy with the Puritan program of church reform, but dismisses it as he does all forms of sectarianism and

separatism. He is vigorously outspoken against Rome (*The Encyclopedia of Christianity*, ed. Edwin H. Palmer, 1:63).

*A *Commentary on the Second Epistle General of St. Peter*
(SDG; 899 pages; 1990). In 1633, Adams published an extensive commentary on the Second Epistle of Peter. It was never included in any edition of his works. However, the 900 pages of double-columned print was edited by James Sherman and printed in London in 1839. The work is exegetically reliable and stylistically adept. Much useful theological knowledge is conveyed in striking phrases. Spurgeon commented that this book was the best Puritan commentary printed under James Sherman's editorship. It is "full of quaintness, holy wit, bright thought, and deep instruction; we know of no richer and racier reading," Spurgeon said.

For example, on 2 Peter 3:9 ("The Lord is not slack concerning his promise"), Adams writes, "Another cause of the Lord's seeming slackness to deliver us for the present, is our slackness to praise him for deliverances past. Unthankfulness; this is the witch, the sorceress, whose drowsy enchantments have made us even forget God himself. If we forget him, can he be blamed for slackness to remember us?" (p. 688).

Henry Ainsworth

(1569-1622)

Born of yeoman stock in Swanton Morley, Norfolk, Henry Ainsworth completed his formal education as a scholar first at St. John's, and later at Gonville and Caius College, Cambridge, from 1586 to 1591. He associated himself with the Puritan party in the church, but eventually joined the Separatists, those Congregationalists who would not wait for reform to work from within. These early Congregationalists were derided on all sides as "Brownists," after the name of their earliest public representative, Robert Browne (c. 1550-1633), who made himself a byword for extremism and instability.

Persecution in England soon compelled Separatists to take refuge in the Netherlands. Ainsworth arrived in Amsterdam around 1593, where he lived in poverty and obscurity, laboring as a porter for a bookseller. Soon his brilliant gifts as a Hebraist and his studies in rabbinics opened the way to better things. The exiled part of the London Separatist congregation regrouped in Amsterdam under Ainsworth's leadership as "doctor" or teacher of the church. Ainsworth was the author "wholly or in part" of the church's confession of faith issued in 1596, one of the earliest creeds or platforms of Congregationalism. The text of the Confession of 1596 has been reprinted with introduction and notes as "The Second Confession of the London-Amsterdam Church" in Williston Walker, *The Creeds and Platforms of Congregationalism* (New York: The Pilgrim Press, 1991).

In 1597, Ainsworth was joined by Francis Johnson (1562-1618), who became pastor of the church. The two came to a parting of the ways over a much-mooted point of Congregationalist polity, viz., whether decisions of the church's officers should be subject to review by the congregation. After many efforts at reconciliation, Ainsworth and his supporters withdrew in 1610 to go their own way as the "Ainsworthians."

For the next twelve years Ainsworth filled his hands with preaching and teaching and found himself engaged in controversies great and small, all the while pursuing his studies and producing a host of written works, among them some true monuments of scholarship, including his *Annotations*. Ainsworth has been called "the most steadfast and cultured champion of the principles represented by the early Congregationalists." As such he was greatly despised, but his abilities and accomplishments as a scholar could not be denied. His contrasting reputations had the result that "many, like the encyclopaedists L. Moréri and J.H. Zedler, have made two Henry Ainsworths—one Dr. Henry Ainsworth, a learned biblical commentator; the other H. Ainsworth, an arch-heretic and 'the ringleader of the Separatists at Amsterdam'" (*Encyclopaedia Britannica*, 11th ed., 1:440-41).

Ainsworth justly had a reputation for true godliness and graciousness. One of his many contributions to Christian literature was "Ainsworth's Psalter," his metrical version of the Psalms, used by Separatists in the Netherlands and carried across the sea to Plymouth Plantation by the Pilgrim Fathers in 1620, two years before Henry Ainsworth died.

⇒◆◆◆⇐

Annotations on the Pentateuch, or the Five Books of Moses; the Psalms of David, and the Song of Solomon (SDG; 2 vols., 1524 pages; 1991). Ainsworth did his best work on the Psalms, which he translated into English in both prose and meter. His work has often been consulted by English translators of the Old

Testament. Ainsworth interprets the Song of Solomon alle-gorically, viewing it as "treating of man's reconciliation unto God, and peace by Jesus Christ, with joy in the Holy Ghost."

American and British divines praised Ainsworth's *Annotations*. Philip Doddridge wrote, "Ainsworth on the Pentateuch, Psalms, and Solomon's Song, is a good book, full of very valuable Jewish learning; and his translation is, in many places, to be pre-ferred to our own, especially on the Psalms."

Ainsworth's *Annotations* has long been a necessity in a pastor's library. His comments are precise, and his expertise in antiquity enables him to offer unique insights on various passages.

Henry Airay

(1560-1616)

Henry Airay was born near Lake Windermere, in Westmorland. His father, William Airay, was either the brother-in-law or the favorite servant of a wealthy clergyman, Bernard Gilpin, remembered as "the apostle of the North" for his many labors and charitable activities there. Through Gilpin's kindness, Henry was educated in the local grammar school Gilpin had built and endowed, and later sent up to Oxford at Gilpin's expense. Although Gilpin died while Airay was still an undergraduate, Gilpin made provision in his will for Airay's continued education.

Airay began his studies in St. Edmund's Hall in 1580, but soon transferred to Queen's College, where he was awarded the degrees of Bachelor of Arts (1583), Master of Arts (1586), Bachelor of Theology (1594), and Doctor of Divinity (1600). Airay became a fellow in 1586 and held several college offices in the next few decades. In 1599, he was elected provost of Queen's, and in 1606, became vice-chancellor of Oxford. During his vice-chancellorship, Airay took William Laud to task for preaching what Airay regarded as "popery in St. Mary's."

Around 1586, Airay was ordained to the ministry and became a frequent and zealous preacher in the university. His *Lectures on Philippians* (published posthumously in 1618) is reckoned a specimen of his preaching, his faithful exposition of the Reformed faith, and his opposition to all that savored of "popery" in the national church.

Airay accepted the rectorship of Charlton-on-Otmoor, near Oxford, in 1606. In 1615, he became rector of Bletchingdon, Oxfordshire. He died on October 6, 1616. A year later, Christopher Potter, a cousin whom Airay made his executor, eulogized Airay as "noted and esteemed for his holiness, his integrity, his learning and gravity, his indefatigable pains in the discharge of his ministerial function, [and] his singular wisdom and dexterity in the government of our [Queen's] college, which, by God's blessing upon his care, hath sent forth many learned ministers into the church."

Lectures upon the Whole Epistle of St. Paul to the Philippians (TENT; 410 pages; 2001). The substance of ninety-five sermons, Airay's *Philippians* (reprinted from the Nichol's series, 1864) conveys a thorough grasp of Paul's thought and clear instruction with poignant applications on each passage. In these sermons, Airay insists on putting Pauline teaching into action. Prolific without being repetitive, this volume is punctuated with Christ-centered thoughts such as the following on Philippians 3:10: "I note two reasons why the apostle reckoned afflictions a vantage unto him: first, because in afflictions he had fellowship with Christ. Second, because by afflictions he was made like unto Christ" (p. 259).

Airay's *Philippians* is, as Alexander Grosart says, his "one abiding monument." Also bound with this volume is Thomas Cartwright's commentary on Colossians (see Cartwright).

Joseph Alleine

(1634-1668)

Born at Devizes, Wiltshire, early in 1634, Joseph Alleine loved and served the Lord from childhood. A contemporary witness identified 1645 as the year of Alleine's "setting forth in the Christian race." From eleven years of age onward, "the whole course of his youth was an even-spun thread of godly conversation." When his elder brother Edward, a clergyman, died, Joseph begged that he might be educated to take Edward's place in the ministry of the church. He entered Oxford at age sixteen and sat at the feet of such great divines as John Owen and Thomas Goodwin.

Alleine began his studies at Lincoln College in 1649. Two years later, he became a scholar of Corpus Christi College, where the faculty was, in general, more thoroughly Puritan than at Lincoln. Alleine studied long hours, often depriving himself of sleep and food. He graduated from Oxford in 1653 with a Bachelor of Arts degree and became a tutor and chaplain of Corpus Christi. He also devoted much time to preaching to prisoners in the county jail, visiting the sick, and ministering to the poor.

In 1655, Alleine accepted the invitation of George Newton, vicar of St. Mary Magdalene Church, Taunton, Somerset, to become Newton's assistant. Taunton, a wool-manufacturing city of some 20,000, was a Puritan stronghold. Shortly after moving to Taunton, Alleine married his cousin, Theodosia Alleine, whose father, Richard Alleine, was minister of

Batcombe, Somerset (see below). She was an active woman who feared God deeply. Early in their marriage, she ran a home school of about fifty scholars, half of them boarders. She would later serve as her husband's biographer after his death.

Alleine rose early, devoting the time between four and eight o'clock in the morning to the exercises of private worship. His wife recalled that he "would be much troubled if he heard smiths or other craftsmen at work at their trades, before he was at communion with God: saying to me often, 'How this noise shames me! Doth not my Master deserve more than theirs?'"

His ministry in Taunton as preacher and pastor was very fruitful. Richard Baxter recalled Alleine's "great ministerial skillfulness in the public explication and application of the Scriptures—so melting, so convincing, so powerful." Alleine was also an excellent teacher, devoting much time to instructing his people, using the Shorter Catechism. He was a passionate evangelist. One contemporary wrote, "He was infinitely and insatiably greedy of the conversion of souls, wherein he had no small success."

Ejected for nonconformity in 1662, Alleine took the opportunity to increase his public labors, believing that his remaining time was short. He preached on average one or two sermons every day for nine months until he was arrested and cast into the Ilchester prison. The night before, Alleine had preached and prayed with his people for three hours and had declared, "Glory be to God that hath accounted me worthy to suffer for His gospel!"

Alleine's prison cell became his pulpit as he continued to preach to his people through the prison bars. He also wrote numerous pastoral letters and theological articles. Released on May 20, 1664, after about a year in prison, he resumed his forbidden ministry until arrested again on July 10, 1665 for holding a conventicle. Once more released from prison, his remaining time was "full of troubles and persecutions nobly borne." He returned to Taunton in February, 1668, where he became very ill. Nine months later, at age thirty-four, weary from hard work and suffering, Alleine died in full assurance of faith, praising God and saying, "Christ is mine, and I am His— His by covenant."

———◦◆◦———

The Act of Conformity (RE; 47 pages; n.d.). This small, polemical tract is bound with RE Publications' edition of Alleine's *Alarm to the Unconverted*. It is not included in the list of Alleine's works compiled by Charles Stanford in 1861. No one is certain that it was written by Alleine, though its style is similar to that of his other works. The work is an in-depth examination of the Oath of Allegiance passed on August 24, 1662, and whether or not a nonconformist minister could conscientiously subscribe to it. *The Act of Conformity* offers an emphatic "No," saying, "Taking this oath will encourage Parliament (when they shall see how glibly and smoothly we swallow every pill) to think themselves either infallible in imposing, or us as ductile, flexible and sequatious souls" (p. 45).

An Alarm to the Unconverted (BTT; 148 pages; 1995). This evangelical classic was first printed in 1671 (subtitle: *A Serious Treatise on Conversion*), when 20,000 copies were sold, and subsequently reprinted in 1675 as *A Sure Guide to Heaven*, which was the title given to the latest BTT editions. It is a powerful manual on conversion and the call of the gospel, as the chapter titles reveal: Mistakes about Conversion; The Nature of Conversion; The Necessity of Conversion; The Marks of the Unconverted; The Miseries of the Unconverted; Directions to the Unconverted; The Motives to Conversion.

Alleine's model of Puritan evangelism is well suited to correct today's distortions of the gospel. For example, he shows us that dividing the offices and benefits of Christ is not a new idea. The true convert is willing to receive Christ, both as Savior from sin and as Lord of one's life. He asserts:

> All of Christ is accepted by the sincere convert. He loves not only the wages but the work of Christ, not only the benefits but the burden of Christ. He is willing not only to tread out the corn, but to draw under the yoke. He takes up the commands of Christ, yea, the cross of Christ. The unsound convert takes Christ by halves. He is all for the salvation of Christ, but he is not for sanctification. He is for the privileges, but does not appropriate the person of Christ. He divides the offices and benefits of Christ. This is an error in the foundation. Whoever loves life, let him beware here. It is an undoing mistake, of which you have often been warned, and yet none is more common (p. 45).

This book, reprinted some five hundred times and the most famous of Alleine's nineteen treatises, has been used for the conversion of many souls. It greatly influenced the evangelistic approach of famous preachers such as George Whitefield and Charles Spurgeon. Despite a smattering of statements that may be misconstrued as promoting human ability in salvation, Alleine's classic remains a golden example of evangelistic preaching and a spur to personal evangelism.

The Life and Letters of Joseph Alleine (RHB, 332 pages, 2003). A definitive biography of Alleine has yet to be written. The longest sustained seventeenth-century narrative was written by his wife, Theodosia, following his ejection and imprisonment after the passing of the Act of Uniformity in 1662. In 1672, four years after his death and a year after the first printing of *Alarm to the Unconverted,* Alleine's *Christian Letters, Full of Spiritual Instructions* was printed in London. The following year, fragments of biographical information and personal reminiscences were brought together by his widow and Richard Baxter and were printed with his letters. That volume was reprinted with corrections in 1677 as *The Life and Death of that Excellent Minister of Christ Mr. Joseph Alleine* (London: Nevil Simmons).

Additional printings of the 1677 volume with minor additions or deletions took place in 1806, published by J. Gemmill; in 1829, by the American Sunday School Union; and in 1840, by Robert Carter in New York. The RHB reprint of 2003 includes the Carter edition, plus two letters from the Gemmill edition and three letters from Alleine's *Remains*. Thus, for the first time, all forty-nine of Alleine's extant letters are printed in one volume. An appendix contains George Newton's *Sermon Preached at the Funeral of Mr. Joseph Alleine* (London: Nevil Simmons, 1677).

Charles Stanford's biography, *Joseph Alleine: His Companions and Times*, appeared in 1861. Though Charles Spurgeon called it an "admirable biography," it, too, is incomplete, no doubt partly due to the paucity of details of Alleine's life. Although Alleine's *Life and Letters* suffers somewhat from not being a sustained narrative, it has the advantage of having been written by Alleine's contemporaries. Allowing for some repetition and hagiographical tendencies, these pages display the portrait of a minister who had a large heart for God and for the precious souls of those who sat under his ministry.

In this book, Richard Baxter wrote chapter 1 of Alleine's biography. Richard Alleine, his father-in-law, wrote chapter 3. Other chapters were written by his senior colleague, George Newton (chap. 4), his widow (chap. 6), and his close friend and ministerial colleague, Richard Fairclough (chap. 9). The remaining chapters were written by several close friends who preferred to remain anonymous.

Valuable as the account of Alleine's life by his contemporaries is, his letters which form the second half of the book are of greater worth. While the narrative of his life gives us an account of his outward circumstances, his letters reveal the secret springs of his heart, exhibiting the fervor of an evangelist, the heart of a pastor, and the patience of a sufferer for Jesus Christ. Many of these letters were written from prison to parishioners in Taunton when he was no longer able to minister the Word of God to them in person. With their emphasis on Christ and true godliness, these letters breathe the atmosphere of heaven itself. Here is a passage expressing his love for his people in Taunton:

> You are a people much upon my heart, whose welfare is the matter of my continual prayers, care, and study. And oh that I knew how to do you good! How it pities me to think how so many of you should remain in your sins, after so many and so long endeavors to convert you and bring you in! Once more, oh beloved, once more hear the call of the Most High God unto you. The prison preaches to you the same doctrine that the pulpit did. Hear, O people, hear; the Lord of life and glory offers you all mercy, and peace, and blessedness. Oh, why should you die? Whosoever will, let him take of the waters of life freely. My soul yearns for you. Ah, that I did but know what arguments to use with you; who shall choose my words for me that I may prevail with sinners not to reject their own mercy? How shall I get within them? How shall I reach them? Oh, that I did but know the words that would pierce them! That I could but get between their sins and them (pp. 150-51).

Truly, as Iain Murray writes, "Never did the evangel of Jesus Christ burn more fervently in any English heart!"

When the Scottish missionary Alexander Duff (1806-78) read this book, he was deeply impressed by Alleine's rich variety of gifts and graces, mature judgment, fervent devotion, and pervasive seriousness. Duff wrote: "What inextinguishable zeal! What unquenchable thirstings after the conversion of lost sinners! What unslumbering watchfulness in warning and edifying saints! What profound humility and self-abasement in the sight of God! What patience and forbearance,

what meekness and generosity, what affability and moderation! What triumphant faith—what tranquil, yet rapturous
joy!" No wonder John Wesley called Alleine "the English
Rutherford."

In a day when the desire for personal happiness and
self-esteem have replaced the biblical mandate for holiness of
life, a reading of Alleine's life and letters can be a real tonic to
the soul.

The Precious Promises of the Gospel (SDG; 40 pages; 2000).
This booklet is extracted from Richard Alleine's *Heaven Opened.*
It is one of the two chapters written by Joseph Alleine. Imper-
sonating God in addressing His people, Alleine provides us
with a moving declaration of the loving, merciful heart of the
Triune God, revealed in the promises of Scripture, which are
woven into nearly every sentence.

Richard Alleine
(1611-1681)

The uncle and father-in-law of Joseph Alleine, Richard Alleine was born in Ditcheat, Somersetshire, where his father was rector of the parish church for more than fifty years. His father served as his tutor, preparing Richard to go to Oxford at age nineteen, where he matriculated at St. Alban's Hall, completing a Bachelor of Arts degree in 1631. He then continued his studies at New Inn College until he was awarded a master's degree with high honors in 1634.

Alleine was ordained priest in the diocese of Salisbury on March 2, 1634. The following year, he was appointed chaplain to Sir Ralph Hopton. Already before the civil war, Alleine began assisting his aged father at Ditcheat. In 1642, Richard Alleine moved to Batcombe, Somerset, where he ministered effectively for more than twenty years. He soon declared himself a Puritan by subscribing both to the Solemn League and Covenant of 1643, and then to a local confession, "The Testimony of the Ministers in Somersetshire to the Truths of Jesus Christ," five years later. Alleine was much loved in Batcombe for his preaching and his tender care of souls. *Godly Fear* (1664), a collection of his sermons, reveals his tenderness in pastoral ministry.

Alleine was ejected from his parish in 1662 for nonconformity. The passing of the Five Mile Act compelled him to take refuge in the neighboring village of Frome Selwood, where he continued to preach in private homes until his death in 1681.

He was fined on several occasions for holding conventicles in other villages also, but due to his popularity, the magistrates dared not imprison him.

Alleine was known for his piety and soul-searching ministry as well as his writings, all of which are spiritual and practical in nature. One writer relates the story of what happened to his four-volume work, *Vindication of Godliness* (*Vindiciae Pietatis*):

> His *Vindiciae Pietatis* (which first appeared in 1660) was refused license by Archbishop Sheldon, and was published in common with other nonconformist books, without it. It was rapidly bought up and "did much good to mend this bad world." Roger Norton, the king's printer, caused a large part of the first impression to be seized on the ground of its not being licensed and to be sent to the royal kitchen. Glancing over its pages, however, it seemed to him a sin that a book so holy—and so saleable—should be destroyed. He therefore bought back the sheets, says Calamy, for an old song, bound them and sold them in his own shop. This in turn was complained of, and he had to beg pardon on his knees before the council-table; and the remaining copies were sentenced to be "bisked," or rubbed over with an inky brush, and sent back to the kitchen for lighting fires. Such "bisked" copies occasionally still occur. The book was not killed (*Encyclopedia Britannica*, 11th ed., 1:690).

***

Heaven Opened: The Riches of God's Covenant (SDG; 343 pages; 2000). In this book, Alleine discusses the nature and blessings of God's covenant with His people. Alleine outlines in great detail the roles of God, Christ, the Spirit, the earth, the angels of light, the powers of darkness, death, and the kingdom in the covenant. Then he speaks of the fruits of the covenant in the believer's life.

The book begins: "Good news from heaven! The day-spring from on high hath visited this undone world! After a deluge of sin and misery, behold the bow in the cloud! The Lord God hath made and established a new covenant, and this is it that hath cast the first beam on the dark state of lost and fallen man, and hath brought life and immortality to light. This covenant is the hope of sinners, and the riches of saints, the Magna Charta of the city of God. The forfeited lease of eternity renewed; God's deed of gift, wherein he hath, on fair conditions, granted sinners their lives, and settled upon his saints an everlasting inheritance."

It ends with an equally moving exhortation to sinners and saints. Addressing backslidden saints, Alleine writes, "Christians, bewail lost conscience, and let it be recovered."

Instructions About Heart-work (SDG; 411 pages, 2003). First published in 1681, this little-known treatise by Alleine (his last published work) is an extensive exposition of Proverbs 4:23: "Keep thy heart with all diligence; for out of it are the issues of life." The author aims to teach readers the proper way to keep their hearts, stressing what is to be done on God's part and on the believer's part. The goal throughout is that believers may grow in exercising grace and in embracing full assurance of salvation.

Alleine closes his treatise with these searching words: "Will you be persuaded, will you be prevailed upon, thus to prepare and bring over your hearts to the Lord? Thus to preserve and keep them pure and faithful to him? And so trust to his faithfulness? Might I prevail with you in this, I had done my work, and having put you thus into safe custody, should there be bold to leave you in this confidence, that you should be thenceforth 'all kept by the mighty power of God, through faith unto salvation.'"

Like Flavel's *Keeping the Heart*, which is also on Proverbs 4:23, Alleine's work is packed with practical, spiritual in-

struction. No sin is left unexposed; no hypocrite is left excused. It is a most searching treatment of practical godliness,
bearing the mark of one personally sifted by God.

The World Conquered by the Faithful Christian (SDG; 172
pages; 1995). In this book, Alleine uses the Pauline military
motif of Christian warfare, viewing the believer's existence in
this world as a continual battle against spiritual evil. He explains the believer's armor, the believer's enemies, and the
believer's victory. Most of the book focuses on how to obtain
victory in spiritual warfare—victory in contentment, in a
steady mind despite outward changes, in a willingness to die,
in living by faith, in being crucified with Christ, in being sealed
by the Spirit, in looking to the reward, and in heavenly joys. In
all this, Alleine stresses that nothing less than victory will do.

This book encourages battle-weary saints to stay the
course, looking to Jesus. Alleine concludes, "A true Christian
has his enemies under his feet even while he is in the fight. He
is a soldier as soon as he is a saint, and he is a conqueror as soon
as he is a soldier. His very taking up arms ensures his victory."

Alleine considers Sabbath observance and frequent
attendance at the Lord's Supper to be a critical part of the
Christian's strength in a fallen world. In explaining proper
self-examination for the Lord's Supper, Alleine writes, "Repentance, if it is sincere, will be universal. It will extend to
every known sin. He who does not repent of everything that
is evil truly repents of nothing" (p. 131).

Vincent Alsop

(1630-1703)

Vincent Alsop was born in South Collingham, Nottinghamshire, in 1630, the son of George and Judith Alsop. His father served as rector in South Collingham. Alsop attended Uppingham grammar school, and matriculated at St. John's College, Cambridge, in 1648. He became an assistant teacher at Oakham School, Rutland, and, in 1657, married the daughter of Benjamin King, the local minister, who influenced Alsop to embrace Puritanism vigorously. That same year Alsop obtained the curacy of Langham, a parish bordering on Oakham.

About 1660, Alsop served the congregation at Wilby, Northamptonshire, but was ejected in 1662 for nonconformity. He continued to preach privately in the area, and was confined for six months in a Northampton jail for praying with a sick person. In 1672, he was able to minister in his house at Geddington under the Declaration of Indulgence. He succeeded Thomas Cawton, Jr., as minister of Tothill Street, Westminster, in 1677 and served there until his death in 1703. After his death, Calamy became Alsop's successor.

Alsop was particularly known in his day as an avid polemist and "emancipator of Restoration dissent." He wrote several works attacking the errors of his day, such as his 1675 *Anti-Sozzo*, which criticized the perceived Socinianism of

William Sherlock. Alsop's polemical vigor somewhat subsided when his son, who had participated in the Monmouth rebellion of 1685, was imprisoned for possible charges of treason. Alsop was able to obtain pardon for his son two years later, probably due to his conciliatory efforts between James II and the nonconformists (Alsop and a handful of other prominent Presbyterians supported the king when the situation deteriorated with high-Anglican officials). Alsop's efforts for reform set the stage for eighteenth-century nonconformists, such as Calamy, who became his successor at Tothill Street.

——◆◆◆——

Practical Godliness: The Ornament of All Religion (SDG; 172 pages; 2003). First printed in 1696, this treatise, which consists of several sermons preached on Titus 2:10, commands us to "adorn the doctrine of God our Savior in all things." In addition to providing numerous directions on how to practice godliness each day by living according to the promises of the gospel and the precepts of the law, Alsop buttresses his argument for the advance of personal godliness by stressing the sanctification of the Sabbath (in which "all practical religion rises, falls, ebbs and flows") and the sanctification of family religion ("It is in vain to dream that congregations will be holy, if families be profane"). Appended is Alsop's rare 67-page treatment of the scriptural theology of clothing and fashions, which is remarkably relevant for our day.

Isaac Ambrose
(1604-1664)

Isaac Ambrose was born in 1604, the son of Richard Ambrose, vicar of Ormskirk, Lancashire. Entering Brasenose College, Oxford, in 1621, he graduated with a Bachelor of Arts degree in 1624, and was ordained to the ministry. He became vicar of the parish church in Castleton, Derbyshire, in 1627, then served at Clapham, Yorkshire, from 1629 to 1631. The following year he received a Master of Arts degree from Cambridge.

Through the influence of William Russell, Earl of Bedford, Ambrose was appointed one of the king's four itinerant preachers for Lancashire, and took up residence in Garstang, a Lancashire town between Preston and Lancaster. The king's preachers were commissioned to preach the Reformation doctrines in an area that was strongly entrenched in Roman Catholicism. Shortly thereafter, he was married.

About 1640, Lady Margaret Hoghton selected him as vicar of Preston in Amounderness. As long as Ambrose lived in Preston, he enjoyed the warm friendship of the Hoghton family. It was to their ancestral woods and tower near Blackburn, east of Preston, or Weddicre Woods near Garstang, that Ambrose retired each May to be alone, searching the Scriptures, praying, and meditating upon God. His sermon, "Redeeming the Time," preached to the large congregation assembled for Lady Hoghton's funeral, was long remembered in Lancashire. At the time of the Reformation, many in Preston, especially the local gentry, had clung to the Roman Catholic faith. When the first civil war began, Preston remained loyal to the king and became the headquarters for the Royalists in Lancashire. Nonetheless, Ambrose declared himself a Puritan and a Presbyterian when he subscribed to the Solemn League and Covenant of 1643, and he was one of the ministers who served on the committee of Parliament appointed to oversee the ejection of "scandalous and ignorant ministers and schoolmasters" during the Commonwealth.

Preston became a battleground between the opposing forces of king and Parliament. Ambrose was arrested twice (1642 and 1643) for his Presbyterian beliefs, but he was quickly released on both occasions because of his friendship with the Hoghtons and other neighboring gentlemen and his own reputation for godliness. When Bolton was taken by the Royalists in 1644, Ambrose took refuge in Leeds. Cromwell defeated the Royalist troops at the battle fought in Preston in 1648. This victory concluded the second civil war.

Presbyterianism in Lancashire was served well by Ambrose in the 1640s and early 1650s, though not without strife. On several occasions he served as moderator of the Lancashire classis, and, in 1648, was a signatory of the harmonious consent of the Lancashire Presbyterian clergy, which expressed solidarity with the Westminster Assembly and opposed calls for toleration. In 1649, the local committee for the relief of plundered ministers ordered him to be briefly imprisoned in London. When Ambrose returned to minister in Preston, he faced ongoing persecution. Finally, in 1654, he gave up his post there, perhaps due in part to illness (*Oxford DNB*, 1:921).

Ambrose moved north to become minister of Garstang, where he was ejected from his living in 1662 because of nonconformity. He lived in retirement among his friends at Preston, dying suddenly of apoplexy on January 23, 1664. It was said of him: "He was holy in life, happy in his death, honored of God, and held in high estimation by all good men."

Ambrose was a Christ-centered and warmly experiential author. He spoke of himself as a son of Boanerges and Barnabas, though his writings and ministry appear to have reflected more of the latter than the former. His writings are remarkably free of polemics. "As a religious writer Ambrose has a vividness and freshness of imagination possessed by scarcely any of the Puritan nonconformists. Many who have no love for Puritan doctrine, nor sympathy with Puritan experience, have appreciated the pathos and beauty of his writings, and his *Looking unto Jesus* long held its own in popular appreciation with the writings of John Bunyan" (*Encyclopedia Britannica*, 11th ed., 1:800). A collection of his works appeared in 1674 and was reprinted at least seven times over the next two centuries.

Several of Ambrose's significant books have not been reprinted for more than a century. These include the first works from his pen, *Prima* and *Ultima*, written in 1640. *Prima* presents the message of regeneration and *Ultima* deals with the last things, including life, death, judgment, hell, a correct understanding of purgatory, and heaven. These works were followed by *Media*, written in 1650. This lengthier treatise on sanctification examines the spiritual duties that the believer should engage in to grow in grace and deeper union with Christ. Ambrose was a strong proponent of keeping a diary to record daily experiences with God. Unfortunately, his diary has been lost, though he did include two lengthy samples in *Media*. These reveal his deep passion for seeking and experiencing the "joy unspeakable and full of glory" of Jesus Christ, our divine bridegroom.

Ambrose's *Communion with Angels* was first published with his *Works* in 1674. This work traces the ways in which God's divine messengers assist the believer at the various periods of life from birth to the judgment. According to Ambrose, angels defend and keep us safe from the temptations of the devil and act as God's servants and instruments of providence. Angels may work in our dreams and therefore we must be careful to discern the origin of our dreams to see if they are of God. While still strongly experimental in nature, this is Ambrose's most speculative work.

———◆◆◆———

The Christian Warrior: Wrestling with Sin, Satan, the World, and the Flesh (SDG; 150 pages; 1997). In this work on spiritual warfare, originally written in 1661 but apparently first published with the *Works* in 1674, Ambrose presents three key truths: (1) all God's people must be warriors, (2) we have powerful and malicious enemies to contend with, and (3) we must wrestle and strive against these enemies.

Basing his work on Ephesians 6:12, Ambrose explains how a Christian must wage spiritual battle against sin, the world, the flesh, and Satan. He shows how Satan attacks us at different times and under different conditions in life, and how we can prepare to withstand his assaults. His ten ways to cope with sinful anger are extremely helpful (pp. 110-116).

Ambrose's directives are insightful, probing, and succinct. For instance, Ambrose advises, "Be not satisfied with sudden pangs of affection, but labor to preserve those impressions which the Spirit has made on your soul" (pp. 64-65).

Looking Unto Jesus (SPR; 694 pages; 1986). After a serious illness in the early 1650s, Ambrose wrote a devotional on what the Lord had done for his soul, titled *Looking unto Jesus, or the Soul's Eyeing of Jesus as Carrying on the Great Work of Man's Salvation* (1658). The book, which stresses experiential identification with Jesus in thought and behavior, soon became a classic of Christ-centered divinity. Its readers feel they are standing on holy ground.

Ambrose describes numerous aspects of Christ's ministry. For example, he presents Jesus' ministry from eternity and during His life from a nine-point perspective: knowing Jesus, considering Jesus, desiring Jesus, hoping in Jesus, believing in Jesus, loving Jesus, rejoicing in Jesus, calling on Jesus, and conforming to Jesus in a particular aspect of His ministry. Regarding conformity to Christ in His resurrection, Ambrose writes, "Look much at Christ raised, Christ glorified. [Let us] see our own personal vivification linked inseparably unto, and bottomed immovably upon the resurrection of Christ. When we can by faith get a sight of this, how courageously and successfully the soul will grapple in the controversies of the Lord against the devil, and our own deceitful hearts.... O that I could set my faith more frequently on Christ's resurrection, so that at last I could see it by the light of God to be a destinated principle of my vivification in particular!" (pp. 490-91).

This book has been reprinted many times, influencing many Christians over the centuries to pursue a closer walk with God. It equals Samuel Rutherford's *Letters* in its Christ-centeredness.

WILLIAM AMES

William Ames

(1576-1633)

William Ames (Latinized as "Amesius") was born in 1576 at Ipswich, Suffolk, then a center of robust Puritanism. Ames's father, also named William, was a well-to-do merchant with Puritan sympathies; his mother, Joane Snelling, was related to families that would help to found Plymouth Plantation in the New World. Since both parents died when he was young, he was reared by his maternal uncle, Robert Snelling, a Puritan from nearby Boxford. From childhood, Ames was steeped in the vigorous Puritanism of his time and place.

Ames's uncle spared no expense for his education, sending him in 1594 to Christ's College at Cambridge University, known for its undiluted Puritanism and Ramist philosophy. Ames rapidly displayed his proclivity to learn. He graduated with a Bachelor of Arts degree in 1598. In 1601, he received a Master of Arts degree, was elected fellow at Christ's College and ordained to the ministry, and underwent a dramatic conversion experience under the "rousing preaching" of William Perkins.

Following this profound spiritual transformation, Ames declared that "a man may be *bonus ethicus* [a moral person in outward religion], and yet not *bonus Theologus* [a sincere-hearted Christian]" (*Fresh Suit Against Human Ceremonies*, 1633, 1:131). To be a *bonus Theologus* became Ames's life-long concern,

which revealed itself in a practical Christianity that expressed
the inner piety of an obedient, redeemed heart.

Ames quickly became the moral compass and conscience
of the College. But this role was short-lived. King James's
edict at the 1604 Hampton Court Conference strengthened
the conviction that any Puritan activity at the colleges involving criticism of the Church of England must be suppressed.
Puritan spokesmen were soon stripped of their degrees and
dismissed. The process culminated in 1609 with the appointment of Valentine Cary, who hated Puritanism, to the
mastership rather than William Ames, who was far more
qualified for the position. On December 21, 1609, when Ames
preached a stinging sermon on St. Thomas's Day—an annual
festivity at Cambridge which had become increasingly rau-
cous over the years—and denounced gambling, administering
the "salutary vinegar of reproof," the college authorities had
him taken into custody and suspended him from his academic
degrees and ecclesiastical duties.

Before he was formally expelled, Ames left his position as
a fellow. After a brief period as city lecturer in Colchester,
George Abbott, bishop of London, forbade Ames to preach. In
1610, Ames decided to seek the freer academic and ecclesiastical climate of the Netherlands. There he remained in exile for
the rest of his life.

Ames first went to Rotterdam where he met John Robinson, pastor of the English Separatist congregation at Leiden.
Some of the congregation's members were soon to establish
Plymouth Plantation in the New World and become known
as the Pilgrim fathers of New England. Ames could not persuade Robinson to abandon his Separatist sentiments,
namely, that the Puritan churches should separate "root and
branch" from the Church of England, but Ames did succeed in
tempering some of his more radical views.

Following a brief stay in Rotterdam and Leiden, Ames
was employed from 1611 to 1619 by Sir Horace Vere, com-

mander of English forces in the Netherlands, to serve as military chaplain for those forces stationed at the Hague. Here Ames presided over a small congregation, acted as spiritual counselor to the Vere family, ministered to the troops during military campaigns, and wrote four books against the Arminianism that had precipitated an ecclesiastical crisis. This crisis among the Dutch pitted the Remonstrants (Arminians), promoters of the doctrine of free will, against the Contra-Remonstrants (Calvinists), who maintained the orthodox doctrine of predestination. Ames's skill as a systematic theologian in this debate won him considerable acclaim as the "Augustine of Holland" and "the hammer of the Arminians" (*Oxford DNB*, 1:943). Eventually, the Arminian issue was addressed at an international Synod in the Dutch city of Dordrecht (1618-1619). Because of his expertise in addressing issues of the Arminian struggle, Ames, while a non-voting member of the synod, was called to be the chief theological advisor and secretary to Johannes Bogerman, the presiding officer. The synod ruled in favor of the historic Calvinist position on all five points raised by the Arminians.

An anti-Arminian purge in ecclesiastical, political, and academic circles followed the synod's rulings, leaving a professorship vacant at Leiden University. Ames was elected to fill the chair, but the long arm of the English state prevailed. Ames, recently dismissed from his post in the Hague under pressure from the English authorities, found the post at Leiden University closed to him as well due to King James's opposition.

During his first decade in the Netherlands, Ames married twice. He first married a daughter of Ursula Sotherton and John Burges, his predecessor at The Hague, but she died shortly after they married, leaving no children. In 1618, he married Joan Fletcher; together, they had three children, Ruth, William, and John.

To support his family, Ames turned to private lecturing and tutoring university students for three years after the Synod of Dort. His little private "house college" at Leiden resembled on a small scale the Staten College, an academy presided over by Festus Hommius. Theological students lived in Ames's home, and he taught them Puritanism and systematic theology. He later developed some of these lectures into his famous *Marrow of Theology*.

In 1622, officials at Franeker University, a relatively new institution in the province of Friesland, ignored the English authorities and appointed Ames as professor of theology. On May 7, 1622, Ames gave his inaugural address on the urim and thummim of the high priest's breastplate. Four days after his inauguration as professor, he received the Doctor of Theology degree upon successfully defending thirty-eight theses and four corollaries on "the nature, theory, and practical working of Conscience" before Sibrandus Lubbertus, senior professor on the faculty. In 1626, he was appointed Rector Magnificus, the highest honorary academic office in the university.

During his eleven-year tenure at Franeker, Ames became known as the "Learned Doctor" who tried to "puritanize" the entire university. Ames acknowledged the university was orthodox in doctrine, but did not feel that a majority of the faculty and student body were sufficiently Reformed in practice. The faculty, in particular, were too dependent on Aristotelian logic for Ames's comfort, and inadequately emphasized human responsibility and the exercise of the human will in Christian living. Therefore, Ames once again organized a kind of rooming house or "college" in his house within the university where tutorial sessions, lectures, and numerous theological discussions took place. As Rector, he promoted piety, enforced Sabbath observance, shortened Christmas and Easter holidays, and tightened student discipline. His efforts produced what was called "the Reformation of the 1620s."

Through lecturing and prolific writing during his Franeker years, Ames maintained a strong anti-prelatical and anti-Arminian stance, but his greatest contribution was in theology and ethics, which he saw as a unified system that helped the Christian live a life of genuine piety. Here he wrote his two greatest works, *Medulla theologiae* (*The Marrow of Theology*) and *De conscientia* ("Of the Conscience," translated in English as *Conscience with the Power and Cases Thereof*). In his system of theological and moral divinity, Ames incorporated the Ramist philosophy and method he had learned at Cambridge. Developed by Petrus Ramus (1515-1572), a sixteenth-century French Reformed philosopher, Ramism sought to correct the artificial sophistry of the Aristotelianism of the day, characterized by a breach between life and thought, between knowing and doing, and, in the case of the religious life, between theology and ethics.

Through his teaching, Ames established his own reputation as well as that of the academy where he taught. Students came from all over Europe to study under him. His most famous pupil was Johannes Cocceius, who would later carry the development of covenant theology well beyond Ames's thought. Yet Ames was not content, for all was not well at the university. Some students and faculty members did not appreciate Ames's efforts to achieve deeper or further reformation. A clique of professors, led by Johannes Maccovius, sabotaged Ames's efforts. Moreover, continuing arguments between Ames, Lubbertus, and his Aristotelian colleague Maccovius poisoned the intellectual climate at Franeker, while the damp sea air of Friesland eroded Ames's health. Those problems, combined with his wife's desire to rejoin her countrymen, convinced Ames to look for a new place in which to serve.

In 1632, Ames accepted an invitation from his friend Hugh Peter to join him in co-pastoring the church of English refugees at Rotterdam. Ames was attracted to the post because of Peter's vision of a covenant-centered congregation that strove for a purged membership of regenerate believers who truly practiced their faith. Peter also wanted Ames to help the church develop a Puritan college in Rotterdam.

In late summer, 1633, Ames finally headed south to Rotterdam. In the fall, the Maas River breached its banks, and Ames, already unwell, became even more ill after his house was flooded. He died of pneumonia on November 11 at the age of fifty-seven in the arms of Hugh Peter. To the end, he remained firm in faith and triumphant in hope.

Shortly before his death, Ames seriously considered joining his friend John Winthrop in New England, but God had another "New World" in mind for him. Four years after Ames's death, his wife and children went to live in the Puritan settlement of Salem, Massachusetts. They brought Ames's library with them, which formed the nucleus of the original library for Harvard College, though fire later destroyed most of the books.

Ames's influence was perhaps greatest in New England, where his *Marrow* became the primary text at Harvard and was often read and quoted throughout the colonies. Then, too, his writings on church issues laid the groundwork for non-separating Congregationalism in New England, a movement that maintained that the Congregational churches of Massachusetts Bay Colony ought to support the further reformation of the Church of England rather than separation from it. The Cambridge Platform of 1648 in particular reflects Ames's thought. Then, too, his Ramism was eagerly embraced and became characteristic of New England Puritanism. Cotton Mather called Ames "that profound, that sublime, that subtle, that irrefragable—yea, that angelic doctor."

Ames's influence was also great in the Netherlands, where he became known for his opposition to Arminianism. He influenced Dutch thinking in many ways, especially in his development of casuistry, that is, how to deal with specific "cases of conscience." Gisbertus Voetius, professor at Utrecht and leader of the Dutch Further Reformation, was profoundly influenced by Ames's ideas. Petrus van Mastricht, another renowned Dutch writer, also drew heavily on Ames, particularly his covenantal thinking and casuistry.

Nearly all of Ames's books were printed in the Netherlands, many in Latin for the international scholarly community. *The Marrow of Theology* and *Conscience, with the Power and Cases Thereof* were soon both translated into Dutch and reprinted at least four times in the seventeenth century.

Ironically, Ames was least influential in his homeland of England, although there, too, he was considered Perkins's most important disciple and heir. Ames's major works were widely circulated and influenced Calvinistic theology in England throughout the seventeenth century. His *Marrow* was particularly highly esteemed by the Puritans. Thomas Goodwin said that "next to the Bible, he esteemed Dr. Ames, his *Marrow of Divinity*, as the best book in the world."

———◆◆◆———

Conscience, with the Power and Cases Thereof (WJ; 293 pages; 1975). Samuel Morrison, a Harvard historian, describes this important manual of Puritan casuistry (first published in Latin, 1630; in English, 1639) as "one of the most valuable sources of Puritan morality." It passed through nearly twenty printings in less than thirty years.

Ames mentions in the preface how he listened as a youth to Master Perkins expound the Puritan way of handling cases of conscience, which profoundly impacted him and directed the course of his life and ministry. Ames's casuistry, however, is more precise and integral to his theology than Perkins's. Perkins relies more on medieval case divinity, whereas Ames develops a more Word-centered case divinity, most evident in his explication of humanity's obedience to God within the framework of the Decalogue.

Conscience naturally flows from and serves as a commentary, as it were, on Book 2 of the *Marrow*. Ames himself stated as much: "If there are some who desire to have practical matters better explained, especially those of the latter part of this *Marrow*, we shall attempt, God willing, to satisfy them in a special treatise, which I mean to write, dealing with questions usually called 'cases of conscience.'"

A collection of five books, *Conscience* moves from a theoretical treatment of the nature of conscience to very practical applications. Its core content first came to light in Ames's defense of the theses and corollaries connected with his promotion to the Doctor of Theology degree at Franeker University in 1622. Eight years after that defense, Ames published this undertaking as a work on moral theology that filled a gap in the developing system of Reformed thought. Richard Baxter, who built his own *Christian Directory* on Ames's casuistry, said that although Perkins did valuable service in promoting Reformed casuistry, Ames's work, though briefer, was superior: "Ames hath exceeded all."

The first Book in *Conscience* defines conscience as "a man's judgment of himself, according to the judgment of God of him." It offers a theoretical treatment of what constitutes conscience before going into detail about the working of conscience.

In Book 2, Ames describes what a case of conscience is: "a practical question, concerning which, the Conscience may make a doubt." This section explains sin, entry into the state of grace, the ongoing battle between flesh and spirit, and conduct in the Christian life. Book 2 could easily serve as a compendium of Reformed theology.

Book 3, titled "Of Man's Duty in General," asks about "the actions, and conversation of [man's] life." Ames says the sign of true obedience is submissively placing God's will ahead of the will of the creature, even when that will does not appear to work towards the creature's advantage. This is accomplished by exercising the disciplines of an obedient life—humility, sincerity, zeal, peace, virtue, prudence, patience, temperance—and by avoiding practices that hinder an obedient walk, such as drunkenness, sins of the heart, and sins of the tongue.

These three books take up about a third of *Conscience*. Following these preliminary matters of definitional statements and conceptual elaborations on conscience and obedience, Ames now concentrates on his real concern for ethics or moral theology by asking how cases of conscience are to be adjudicated. The simple answer is: by proper understanding and application of the moral law. This is where *Conscience* picks up the theme from Book 2 of the *Marrow*.

Books 4 and 5 elucidate the moral law regarding one's duty toward God and one's neighbor. Man's duty to God covers the entire spectrum of the obedient Christian walk, from love towards God in public and private worship to the keeping of the Sabbath. Ames discusses general topics such as the church, but he also covers specific topics such as prayer and singing. He properly prepares the reader for Book 5 on interpersonal relations by first settling any uncertainty the believer may have about his relationship to God. In Book 5, which has fifty-seven chapters and is twice as long as book 4, Ames discusses cases of conscience that might come up in interpersonal relationships. He grounds all his teaching in the last six of the Ten Commandments.

The Marrow of Theology (Baker; 353 pages; 1997). First published in Latin in 1627, Ames's *Medulla theologiae* was the standard theological textbook for New England Puritans for over a hundred years. It was generally regarded as the best succinct summary of Calvinistic theology ever written. Thomas Hooker and Increase Mather recommended the *Marrow* as the most important book beyond the Bible for making a sound theologian. Mather said it was the only book other than the Bible that was a necessary prerequisite for entering the ministry. Ames's work was eventually succeeded as a seminary theological text by Francis Turretin's *Institutes of Elenctic Theology* and Charles Hodge's *Systematic Theology*.

The theology of this book is all about practical Christianity—a Christianity of the whole man, not just of the intellect, will, or affections. It demonstrates Ames's passion that thought and life should represent a single system of practical, vital Christianity. Ames tried to show that theology does not deal primarily with statements about God, but rather with knowledge of how to live to God, i.e., "in accord with the will of God."

Ames held to the primacy of volition. Faith involves "an act of the whole man—which is by no means a mere act of the intellect," he wrote, but the act of the will in believing the gospel is that which, by the Spirit's grace, makes knowledge saving. Saving knowledge, therefore, differs from mere knowledge by involving the wholehearted commitment of the will. Ames writes, "Although faith always presupposes a knowledge of the gospel, there is nevertheless no saving knowledge in anyone...except the knowledge which follows this act of the will and depends upon it" (1.1.3-4).

By focusing on the will as the center of faith, Ames wanted to demonstrate that true piety takes place in a covenant relationship between the sinful creature and the redeeming Creator. Faith as an act of the will is a true mark of covenant obedience as the creature is asked to respond with faith and obedience to the covenant promises offered freely in Christ. Covenant theology is the heart of Ames's theological system.

The *Marrow* is organized according to the Ramist system of dichotomies, which pursues the theme that theology, the doctrine of living to God, consists of, first, "faith" (Book 1, chapters 1-41, pages 77-216), or what one believes, and second, "observance" (Book 2, chapters 1-22, pages 219-331), or how one practices faith and does good works in obedience to God. Such works flow from and add life and meaning to faith. Those two major categories—faith and observance—comprise the fountainhead from which Ames's entire theological system flows.

After defining faith as "the resting of the heart on God" and setting forth faith as an act of the whole man, especially the will, Ames discusses the object of faith, which is God. Following his teaching on the knowledge and essence of God (Book 1, chapters 4-5; hereafter, 1.4, 5), Ames sets forth God's "efficiency," which he defines as the "working power of God by which He works all things in all things (Eph. 1:11; Rom. 11:36)" (1.6). He then discusses God's decree as the first exercise of God's efficiency (1.7). He establishes that everything happens because of God's eternal good pleasure as demonstrated in His creation and providence (1.8, 9). God's preserving grace extends over the created order, while the special government that God exercises toward humanity, the "intelligent creature," is the covenant of works (1.10). By violating this conditional covenant, humanity tragically fell into sin. That fall had serious and eternal consequences, including spiritual and physical death and the propagation of original sin (1.11-17).

But there is still hope. Condemnation is overturned by restorative grace through redemption. Through the person and work of Christ, fallen humanity can have renewed fellowship with God. All of this happens solely for God's good pleasure and out of His "merciful purpose" (1.18-23).

In chapter 24, titled "The Application of Christ," Ames's covenant theology becomes more obvious. The means through which the covenant of redemption between God and Christ comes to fruition is the covenant of grace, which the Scriptures call the "new covenant." In other words, the "application of Christ" is administered covenantally. After explaining how the new covenant differs from the old, Ames asserts that the essence of the covenant of grace continues through different historical eras until, finally, in the last day, believers will be swept up into glory, and the covenant of grace inaugurated at the fall will finally be consummated.

Ames places the doctrine of predestination as part of the doctrine of assurance (1.25). For Ames, assuring grace belongs with his examination of the order of salvation, which he explains before moving through "union by calling," justification, adoption, sanctification, and glorification (1.26-30).

Ames then devotes two chapters to the *subject* of the application of redemption, the church (1.31-32), then addresses the *way* or *means* of the application of redemption, devoting chapters to Holy Scripture (1.34), the ministry (1.33, 35), the sacraments (1.36, 41), and ecclesiastical discipline (1.37). Finally, Ames explains how God administers the covenant of grace (1.38, 39, 41).

Book 2 offers the second half of Ames's system of theology: the observance or obedience that accompanies faith. Obedience is accomplished through virtue and good works, and is manifested in religion (love to God) as well as justice and charity (love to neighbor). Here Ames explains how the first table of the law and its theological virtues are the foundation of religion and worship of God, while the second table of the law and its charitable virtues constitute the paradigm for interpersonal behavior. This blueprint for the Christian life is expressed by acting toward God and each other as the Ten Commandments prescribe (2.1-22). Ames worked out Book 2 in detail in his *Conscience* (see above).

The Marrow of Theology clearly and systematically sets forth the essence of Puritan thought about God, the church, and the world. It is essential for understanding the Puritan view of covenant, sanctification, and activism, and is highly recommended for laypeople and theologians alike. It ought to be a part of every pastor's library and every church library.

Technometry (UPP; 202 pages; 1979). In this work, Ames presents the general structure of the Puritan-Ramist intellectual system. This framework, which consists of an encyclopedic outline of all knowledge, is called "technometry," or technology. The book offers a systematic treatment of the liberal arts and their integration with theology. It inspired the "technological theses" that were argued at early Harvard and Yale commencement exercises. Ames's methodology is precise and comprehensive.

Robert Asty
(1642-1681)

Robert Asty was born to Robert and Ellen Asty in 1642 at Stratford, in the borough of West Ham, Essex, when that part of the country was a stronghold of Puritanism. His father was one of the ministers ejected from their livings in the Church of England on St. Bartholomew's Day, August 24, 1662. While the father was forced out, the son chose to stay out, for conscience's sake.

The younger Robert Asty opened a grammar school in the village of Dedham, Essex, in 1663, where he taught for ten years. In 1668, he married Lydia Sammes, daughter of his pastor, John Sammes, minister at Coggeshall, Essex. The Astys had seven children, three of whom preceded their father in death. Their second son, John, studied for the ministry alongside Isaac Watts, and the two were afterwards associated as colleagues in the ministry of the Independent churches.

In 1674, Asty moved north to be the teacher of a Congregational church at Norwich, Norfolk. There he labored until 1681, when he succumbed to smallpox and died suddenly on October 14 at age thirty-nine.

A Treatise of Rejoicing in the Lord Jesus in All Cases and Conditions. (SDG; 250 pages; 2002). This is Asty's best-known work. It was first published in 1683, then again in 1901 and 1990. In explaining Habakkuk 3:17-18, Asty probes the soul to uncover causes for darkness and discouragement in the lives of God's people. He then provides wise counsel on how relief can be found in Christ. He offers a thoroughly biblical battle plan to combat the foe of spiritual discouragement. He also offers important helps against the assaults of darkness for both newborn saints and seasoned pilgrims.

Asty provides many instructions on how to wait on Christ and how to be assured of a personal, saving interest in Him. His directions to believers in chapter 4, "while in the dark concerning their [saving] interest in Christ," are particularly helpful. He advises: strengthen the direct act of faith in Christ; rejoice in the Spirit's strengthening and upholding graces; labor to increase grace and holiness; wait upon God; diligently attend all the means of grace; rejoice in the "dawnings of the day, even when you cannot see the sun in its noonday brightness"; prefer service for Christ above assurance in Christ; glean comfort from former experiences; show kindness to all spiritual mourners; and be willing to continue "walking in the dark" for as long as God will keep you there.

Asty reminds believers that they are to rejoice in Christ no matter what their circumstances. He writes, "Fear not, soul, do not weep over your empty bottle, do not weep over your lost estate, do not weep over your past comforts, but look up to the fullness of Jesus. He hath enough for your relief, He can command the fullness of the earth into your condition, and give it you by what hand He pleaseth."

At the close of the book, Asty pleads, "O, come and draw thy comforts from Christ, and do not draw them from the creature; do not draw them from secondary helps, but draw them from the Fountain; do not sit down at the streams, but away to the Fountain, to the Ocean, that is always full!"

The book also includes two sermons, "The Hope of the Saints in Heaven" (Col. 1:5) and "A Christian's Freedom from Condemnation in Christ" (Rom. 8:1).

Sir Richard Baker

(c. 1568-1645)

Richard Baker was born at Sissinghurst, Kent, to a wealthy family. His father, John Baker, had served as a member of Parliament (1554-55) and was a lawyer, and his mother, Catherine, was a daughter of Reginald Scott, of Scots Hall, Ashford, Kent. Richard entered Hart Hall, Oxford, as a 16-year-old commoner. He later left Oxford to study law in London, and traveled on the continent to acquire languages and experience cultures. He returned to Oxford to complete a master's degree in 1594.

Baker served as a Commons member for Arundel in 1593 and for East Grinstead in 1597, and was knighted by James I in 1603. He was much esteemed for his intellectual prowess, particularly in logic and philosophy. For some time, he served as a justice of the peace for Middlesex, then in 1620, he was made High Sheriff of Oxfordshire. He was also Lord of Middle Aston and of other lands in Essex, Gloucestershire, Kent, and Oxfordshire.

He married Margaret Mainwaring, daughter of Sir George Mainwaring of Ightfield, Shropshire, though that meant he would act as surety for her family's substantial debts. By 1625, Baker was reported as a debtor to the crown. The government seized his property in Oxfordshire, and from 1635 until his death ten years later he was incarcerated at Fleet Prison.

Though under close watch, he had freedom to write; while a prisoner, he produced twelve books. Many of his writings are historical in nature, the most famous being *A Chronicle of the Kings of England*. His most evangelical work is his *Meditations and Disquisitions upon Certain Psalms*. Though not a Puritan from a political standpoint, he is included here because of these meditations' Puritan theological flavor.

———◆◆◆———

Meditations and Disquisitions upon Certain Psalms (SPR; 449 pages; 1988). This book includes meditations on Psalm 1, the penitential psalms (6, 32, 38, 51, 102, 130, 143), and the seven consolatory psalms of David (23, 27, 30, 34, 84, 103, 116). Baker's expositions are eloquent and experiential. For instance, commenting on Psalm 51, Baker writes, "If it be thy pleasure, O God, to withdraw thy presence from me, to make me sensible of my weakness, yet cast me not off from thy presence in displeasure, to make me despair of thy love."

William Bates

(1625-1699)

William Bates was one of the most popular and esteemed preachers among the Nonconformists; a master of the Puritan's plain style of preaching, his stress on piety earned him the name "silver-tongued." Born in November 1625, he was the son of William Bates, gentleman of St. Mary Magdalene parish, Bermondsey, Surrey. He graduated from Queen's College with a Bachelor of Arts degree in 1645 and a Master of Arts degree in 1648. The following year he became vicar of Tottenham, Middlesex, and a few years later succeeded William Strong as vicar of St. Dunstan-in-the-West. Like other Puritans, Bates often lectured at the famous morning exercises at Cripplegate Church.

According to Richard Baxter, Bates played a major role in negotiations for the restoration of Charles II. As a reward, he was appointed royal chaplain in 1660. That same year, he was appointed as a commissioner for the approbation of ministers by the Rump Parliament and, by royal mandate, was given a doctorate in divinity from Cambridge University. The following year, he represented the Presbyterians as a commissioner at the Savoy Conference, where one purpose was to review public liturgy, including the identification of weaknesses in *The Book of Common Prayer*.

Bates's first wife died young, as did his first daughter. At age thirty-six, he married Margaret, the 21-year-old daughter of Edward Gravenor, gentleman of St. Giles Cripplegate. She outlived him by a generation.

In 1662, Bates was one of 2,000 ministers ejected by the Act of Uniformity. Yet he did not take offense. In his farewell sermon to the St. Dunstan's church, he made no mention of the coming ejections, other than to say rather mildly in his conclusion that his nonconformity was motivated only by his fear of offending God. He then added, "If it be my unhappiness to be in an error, surely men will have no reason to be angry with me in this world, and I hope God will pardon me in the next" (*Oxford DNB*, 4:327).

Bates labored for the next ten years, often with men like Thomas Manton, Edmund Calamy, and Richard Baxter, for the inclusion of nonconformists within the Anglican church and for toleration of other churches. On two occasions, he addressed William III and Mary on behalf of his fellow nonconformists. All of these efforts remained largely fruitless, however, for Charles never fulfilled his promises to work toward nonconformist inclusion.

After his ejection, Bates often preached in the vicinity of St. Dunstan's, most commonly at the house of the countess of Exeter and in a room over Temple Bar Gate, beside his old church. From 1669 onward, he apparently served as one of the lecturers at a dissenting congregation at Hackney. In 1672, he was licensed as a Presbyterian teacher and was appointed to lecture at Pinner's Hall (later called the Ancient Merchants lecture). When Daniel Williams was expelled from this lectureship in 1694, Bates surrendered his lectureship and founded the Salters Hall lecture, where he drew large crowds.

Throughout the last decades of his life, Bates had several brushes with the authorities, including at least three fines for holding conventicles, despite his irenical character, mild manner of preaching, growing reputation as a respectable scholar, and friendships with leading Anglican authorities such as Archbishop Tillotson. Bates remained a leading Puritan until the end of his life, often being invited to preach at the funerals of close Puritan friends, including Richard Baxter, Thomas Manton, Thomas Jacomb, and David Clarkson.

Bates died in Hackney on July 21, 1699, survived by his second wife, Margaret. The sermon at Bates's funeral, preached by John Howe, a close friend of more than forty years, was a rich testimony to his godly life and diligent study. His excellent library, purchased by Daniel Williams, helped establish the Dr. Williams's Library, now situated at Gordon Square, London.

<hr />

The Complete Works of William Bates (SPR; 4 vols., 2085 pages; 1990). Bates's writings were first collected in a 1700 folio edition; in 1815, they were printed in four volumes, from which this reprint is photolithographed.

All of Bates's writings convey good scholarship, wide reading, and careful writing. John Howe called Bates a "devourer of books," and one who yearned to study about God and set forth His love and mercy: "Into what transports of admiration and love of God, have I seen him break forth," Howe said (*Works of Bates*, 1:xviii). That comes to the fore in Bates's most frequently reprinted book, *The Harmony of the Attributes of God* (1674). His chapters on the mercy of God are some of the finest ever written on this precious subject. Here are four practical inferences Bates draws from reveling in the infinity of divine love: "(1) Redeeming love deserves our highest admiration and most humble acknowledgments. (2) The love of God discovered in our redemption, is the most powerful persuasive to repentance. (3) The transcendent love that God hath expressed in our redemption by Christ, should kindle in us a reciprocal affection to him. (4) What an high provocation is it to despise redeeming mercy, and to defeat that infinite goodness which hath been at such expense for our recovery?" (1:329-40).

Some consider Bates's greatest work to be *The Four Last Things* (1691), a short, poignant treatment on death, judgment, heaven, and hell. His 50-page treatise *On Divine Meditation* is typically Puritan and one of the best in its field, covering succinctly the basics of its nature, necessity, time, advantages, rules, and applications. His other major publications include *The Select Lives of Illustrious and Pious Persons, Discourses on the Existence of God, The Immortality of the Soul, The Great Duty of Resignation, The Danger of Prosperity, Sermons on the Forgiveness of Sins,* and *The Sure Trial of Uprightness. Complete Works* includes numerous sermons and several treatises on Christian living, all of which are succinctly written and packed with edifying material. If you are looking for a Puritan who always writes well, is both practical and heavenly, and is never tedious, read Bates's *Works.*

RICHARD BAXTER

Richard Baxter

(1615-1691)

Richard Baxter was born in 1615, in Rowton, near Shrewsbury, in Shropshire. He was the only son of Beatrice Adeney and Richard Baxter, Sr. Because of his father's gambling habit and inherited debts, and his mother's poor health, Richard lived with his maternal grandparents for the first ten years of his life. When his father was converted through "the bare reading of the Scriptures in private," Richard returned to his parental home, and later acknowledged that God used his father's serious talks about God and eternity as "the Instrument of my first Convictions, and Approbation of a Holy Life" (*Reliquiae Baxterianae*, 1:2-4).

Baxter's education was largely informal; he later wrote that he had four teachers in six years, all of whom were ignorant and two led immoral lives. Nevertheless, he had a fertile mind, and enjoyed reading and studying. A prolonged illness and various books—particularly William Perkins's *Works*—were the means God used to "resolve me for himself," Baxter wrote (*Reliquiae Baxterianae*, 1:3-4). When he was fifteen, he was deeply affected by Richard Sibbes's *The Bruised Reed*: "Sibbes opened more the love of God to me, and gave me a livelier apprehension of the mystery of redemption and how much I was beholden to Jesus Christ." Subsequently, Ezekiel Culverwell's *Treatise of Faith* (1623) "did me much good" (ibid., 1:4-5).

Baxter's education took a turn for the better when he transferred to the Wroxeter grammar school, where he received some tuition support from a schoolmaster named John Owen. His best teacher there was an erudite minister, Francis Garbet, who took a real interest in Baxter. At the age of sixteen, under Owen's persuasion, Baxter decided to forego university in favor of placing himself under the instruction of Owen's friend, Richard Wickstead, chaplain at Ludlow Castle, who tutored him rather half-heartedly for eighteen months.

In 1633, Baxter went to London under the patronage of Sir Henry Herbert, Master of the Revels, in the court of Charles I. Joseph Symonds and Walter Cradock, two godly Puritan ministers in London, roused his sympathy for nonconformity, but he stayed in London only four weeks. Having become dissatisfied with the worldly court life in London and desiring to care for his ailing mother, he returned home in 1634; his mother died in May of 1635. He spent the next four years privately studying theology, particularly that of the scholastics, including Aquinas, Scotus, and Ockham.

At age twenty-three, having as yet "no scruple at all against subscription," and thinking "the Conformists had the better cause" (ibid., 1:13), Baxter was ordained deacon by John Thornborough, the elderly bishop of Worcester. For nine months he served as master of the school founded at Dudley, a center of nonconformity. In 1639, he became an assistant minister at Bridgnorth, Shropshire, where he developed a deeper appreciation for nonconformity.

In 1641, Baxter became curate at Kidderminster. Though many among a rather corrupt and crude population of hand-loom workers were initially offended by his forceful preaching and stress on a controlled Lord's Supper and on church discipline, his seventeen-year ministry there (1641-42, 1647-61) bore substantial fruit. He preached as "a dying man to dying men," which, with the Spirit's blessing, resulted in numerous conversions. His praying was no less intense: "His soul took wing for heaven and rapt up the souls of others with him"

(Leonard Bacon, *Select Practical Writings of Richard Baxter* [New Haven, 1831], 1:262).

During the early days of the Civil War, Baxter supported, and on occasion accompanied, the Parliamentary Army. He preached before Cromwell, but he was uncomfortable with the Protector's toleration of separatists. Though he was only an occasional "conformer," Baxter favored being part of an established church and opposed the Solemn League and Covenant of 1643. He also believed that the antinomian tendencies of some of the soldiers and preachers, such as Tobias Crisp and John Saltmarsh, were antithetical to practical Christian living. Their teaching prompted him to write *Aphorisms of Justification* (1649), in which he argued for a combination of divine grace and human cooperation in justification.

In 1647, Baxter's prolonged illnesses compelled him to leave the army. He recuperated at the Worcestershire home of Sir Thomas and Lady Rous, where he wrote the first part of *The Saints' Everlasting Rest.* He later said he wrote it as a labor of love while "looking death full in the face and yet experiencing the sufficient grace of God."

After he recovered, Baxter returned to Kidderminster, where he concentrated on writing. "My writings were my chiefest daily labor," he wrote, whereas "preaching and preparing for it, were but my recreation" (*Reliquae*, p. 85). He also catechized church members two days each week. He went from home to home with an assistant, speaking with each family for one hour and providing each family with an edifying book or two, usually written by himself. He said of these visits, "Few families went from me without some tears, or seemingly serious promises [to strive] for a godly life." He added, "Some ignorant persons, who have been so long unprofitable hearers, have got more knowledge and remorse of conscience in half an hour's close disclosure, than they did from ten year's public preaching" (ibid., 1:83ff.).

The home visits bore fruit. The congregation kept over-flowing its meeting place so that five galleries had to be added. When Baxter came to Kidderminster, scarcely one family on each street among the 800 families honored God in family worship. By the end of his ministry in 1661, there were streets on which every family did so. On the Sabbath, he writes, "you might hear an hundred families singing Psalms and repeating sermons, as you passed through the streets." Of the approxi-mately six hundred people who became full communicants under his ministry, he adds, "There was not twelve that I had not good hopes of, as to their sincerity" (ibid., 1:84-85).

Baxter worked hard, despite chronic pain from the age of twenty-one until the end of his life. He suffered from tubercu-losis and feared consumption. In the years following the Restoration, he left Kidderminster for London, where he often preached at St. Dunstan's and lectured at Pinner's Hall and Fetters Lane. He pleaded in vain, however, at the Savoy Con-ference (1661) for the non-prelatical, synodical form of episcopacy devised by Archbishop James Ussher (1581-1656) and for a Puritan revision of the Prayer Book.

In 1662, Baxter was ejected from the Church of England by the Act of Uniformity. He continued to preach for the rest of his life where he could, but never gathered a congregation of his own. J. I. Packer writes, "Miscalled a Presbyterian, Bax-ter was a reluctant Nonconformist who favored monarchy, national churches, liturgy and episcopacy, and could accept the unsympathetically revised 1662 Prayer Book. But the 1662 Act of Uniformity required renunciation on oath of Puritan ideals of reformation as a condition of incumbency in the restored Church of England, and Baxter balked at that" (New Dictionary of Theology, p. 83).

After his ejection, when he was almost fifty, Baxter mar-ried one of his converts, Margaret Charlton, who was in her early twenties. The disparity of their ages caused some consternation for a time, but the excellence of their marriage in Christ silenced the rumors. Margaret proved to be a devout Christian and faithful wife who earnestly yearned for the salvation of souls. Baxter's tenderness toward her, and her godliness, are described in *Breviate of the Life of Mrs. Margaret Baxter* (1681). There Baxter writes that he "never knew her equal" in practical divinity, for she was "better at resolving a case of conscience than most Divines that ever I knew." Consequently, Baxter habitually shared all cases with her except for those that compelled confidentiality (*Breviate*, pp. 67-68).

The Baxters settled in London. Prelates and magistrates hounded Baxter for most of his remaining years. He was imprisoned at least three times for preaching and never again resumed a pastoral charge; even his books were taken from him. His response was, "I found I was near the end of both that work and that life which needeth books, and so I easily let go all." Once, even the bed on which he was lying sick was confiscated.

After James II took the throne in 1685, Baxter was charged with attacking episcopacy in *Paraphrase on the New Testament* and was brought before Lord Chief Justice Jeffreys. Jeffreys charged Baxter with seditious behavior, calling him "an old rogue who poisoned the world with his Kidderminster doctrine." Jeffreys went on to exclaim, "This conceited, stubborn, fanatical dog—that did not conform when he might have been preferred; hang him!" The bishop of London intervened, and Baxter was spared a public whipping, though he was still imprisoned for five more months.

Baxter eventually benefited from the Toleration Act of 1689, introduced by William and Mary to protect nonconformists. His last days were spent in the pleasant surroundings of Charterhouse Square. He occasionally preached to large crowds there, but he spent most of his time writing. When he was dying and a friend reminded him of the benefits many had received from his writings, Baxter replied, "I was but a pen in

God's hand, and what praise is due to a pen?" By the time he died on December 8, 1691, Baxter had written about 150 treatises, as well as hundreds of unpublished letters and papers.

Baxter's writings are a strange theological mix. He was one of a few Puritans whose doctrines of God's decrees, atonement, and justification were anything but Reformed. Though he generally structured his theology along Reformed lines of thought, he frequently leaned towards Arminian thinking. He developed his own notion of universal redemption, which offended Calvinists, but retained a form of personal election, which offended Arminians. He rejected reprobation. He was greatly influenced by the Amyraldians and incorporated much of their thinking, including hypothetical universalism, which teaches that Christ hypothetically died for all men, but His death only has real benefit to those who believe. For Baxter, Christ's death was more of a legal satisfaction of the law than a personal substitutionary death on behalf of elect sinners.

Baxter's approach to justification has been called neonomianism (that is, "new law"); he said that God has made a new law offering forgiveness to repentant breakers of the old law. Faith and repentance—the new laws that must be obeyed—become the believer's personal, saving righteousness that is sustained by preserving grace. Baxter's soteriology, then, is Amyraldian with the addition of Arminian "new law" teaching. Happily, these erroneous doctrines do not surface much in Baxter's devotional writings, which are geared mainly to encourage one's sanctification rather than to teach theology.

Baxter professed to resent having to write polemical treatises: "Controversies I have written of, but only to end them, not to make them." Hans Boersma has shown, however, that though irenic in some respects, Baxter could be provocative as well (see *A Hot Pepper Corn: Richard Baxter's Doctrine of Justification in its Seventeenth-Century Context of Controversy* [Zoetermeer: Boekencentrum, 1993]).

A Call to the Unconverted (Zondervan; 170 pages; 1953). This classic evangelistic "tract," based on Ezekiel 33:11, reveals Baxter's passionate concern for evangelism. It is an earnest and reasoned appeal to the unsaved to turn to God and accept His offered mercy. Here is one example:

> If thou die unconverted, there is no doubt to be made of thy damnation; and thou are not sure to live an hour, and yet art thou not ready to turn and to come in? Oh miserable wretch! Hast thou not served the flesh and the devil long enough yet? Hast thou not enough of sin? Is it so good to thee? or so profitable for thee? Dost thou know what it is, that thou wouldst yet have more of it? Hast thou had so many calls and so many mercies, and so many blows, and so many examples? Hast thou seen so many laid in the grave, and yet art thou not ready to let go thy sins and come to Christ? What? After so many convictions and gripes of conscience, after so many purposes and promises, art thou not ready yet to turn and live? Oh that thy eyes, thy heart were opened to know how fair an offer is now made to thee! and what joyful message it is that we are sent on, to bid thee come, for all things are ready (pp. 70-71).

Stressing that sinners "die because they will die; that is, because they will not turn," Baxter says, "So earnest is God for the conversion of sinners, that he doubleth his commands and exhortations with vehemency, Turn ye, turn ye; why will ye die?" Discernment is necessary in reading this book, since Baxter's unsound views do occasionally surface.

Dying Thoughts (Baker; 144 pages; 2004). Based on Philippians 1:23, "For I am in a strait betwixt two, having a desire to depart, and to be with Christ, which is far better," Baxter sets forth a proper attitude towards the present life and the life hereafter. *Dying Thoughts* was written shortly before Baxter's death in 1691. It breathes a spirit of vital faith in the promises of God.

This reprint was abridged by Benjamin Fawcett. It also contains an excellent introductory essay by Edward Donnelly, "A Corrective for Reformed Preachers," which gleans practical lessons for ministers from Baxter's preaching.

The Practical Works of Richard Baxter (SDG; 4 vols., 4,201 pages; 2000). Baxter authored about 150 books, of which several were folios of more than a million words. If his entire works were ever to be printed, they would amount to more than double the size of Owen's. Most of Baxter's books are homiletical, catechetical, biographical, historical, practical, philosophical, ethical, or polemical in nature, though he also published commentaries, poetry, and politics. Keeble writes, "Puritanism had always utilized the press, but there had never been a literary career like this, either in scale or in success: Baxter was the first author of a string of bestsellers in British literary history" (*Oxford DNB*, 4:430).

Baxter's practical writings were usually the most popular. His *Practical Works* were published in four folio volumes in London in 1707, then helpfully edited by William Orme and republished in twenty-three volumes in 1830, after which H. R. Rogers's four-volume set was published in 1868. The SDG reprint in 2000 is of the Rogers set.

The first volume, *A Christian Directory* (1673), offers keen insights into the life of the believer, expounding practical and casuistical divinity in more than a million words. No Puritan work on applied theology has approached the popularity, scope, or depth of this treatise. With widespread interest in counseling and practical, biblical living in today's church, this reprint of Baxter's work should be a welcome addition to every library and to anyone who wishes to give solid scriptural answers to man's most important questions.

Volume 2, titled *A Call to the Unconverted* (1658), contains that work unabridged, plus eleven treatises, including *The Reasons of the Christian Religion, The Unreasonableness of Infidelity, A*

Treatise of Conversion, and *The Character of a Sound, Confirmed Christian*. Volume 3 contains *The Saints' Everlasting Rest* (1649), *A Treatise of Self-Denial* (1659), *Dying Thoughts* (1683), and other miscellaneous treatises. Volume 4 contains the unabridged version of the masterful treatise *The Reformed Pastor* (1656), as well as *The Catechising of Families, The Vain Religion of the Formal Hypocrite*, various sermons, and thirteen smaller treatises, including *The Cure of Melancholy and Overmuch Sorrow, by Faith*— perhaps the most undervalued work of Baxter. In it, Baxter, as a physician of souls, probes with remarkable insight into the human psyche and offers suggestions for the cure of depression and other mental ailments. For example, Baxter says, "As much as you can, divert them from the thoughts which are their trouble; keep them on some other talks and business; break in upon them and interrupt their musings; rouse them out of it, but with loving importunity; suffer them not to be long alone; get fit company to them, or them to it; especially, suffer them not to be idle, but drive or draw them to some pleasing works which may stir the body, and employ the thoughts" (*Practical Works*, 4:933).

The Reformed Pastor (BTT; 256 pages; 1999). Abridged from the original work, this edition offers a more accessible look at Baxter's pastoral theology. Writing this book out of a deep determination to rectify the pastoral neglect he had experienced as a young man in the West Midlands, Baxter describes in zealous detail the oversight pastors are to have over themselves first and then over their flocks, out of heartfelt love for souls (Acts 20:28).

By "Reformed" in the title, Baxter does not only mean that pastors should be "Calvinistic," but they must be "revived." He excels in convincing ministers of their high calling to pursue personal revival and to take up their work seriously and prayerfully. Certain portions of this book are remarkably convicting, such as Baxter's denunciation of pastoral pride. He

also offers much practical guidance for dealing with the
perennial problems of instructing and guiding the church.
This is Baxter at his best.

Philip Doddridge writes of this work: "*The Reformed Pastor*
should be read by every young minister, before he takes a people under his stated care; and, I think, the practical part of it
reviewed every three or four years; for nothing would have a
greater tendency to awaken the spirit of a minister to that zeal
in his work, for want of which many good men are but shadows
of what they might be, if the maxims and measures laid down
in that incomparable treatise were strenuously pursued."

Reliquiae Baxterianae (RE; 312 pages; n.d.). This work contains considerably less than half of the original which first
appeared in 1696 under the editorship of Matthew Sylvester.
While the original, which has never been reprinted in its entirety, has been called "a confused and shapeless hulk," it
remains an important source for seventeenth-century history.
Edmund Calamy (1671-1732) condensed Baxter's work into a
more readable edition and published it in 1702. In 1925, J. M.
Lloyd Thomas edited an unsatisfactory abridgment, *The Autobiography of Richard Baxter* (London: Dent). The current edition,
published in the 1990s, though uneven in quality, contains fascinating insights into Baxter's life and offers valuable nuggets
of wisdom, particularly for ministers.

The Saints' Everlasting Rest (CFP; 704 pages; 1999). This is
deservedly one of the most valued of Baxter's practical works.
He wrote most of the book when he was far from home and
had no book but the Bible to consult. Being ill for many
months and expecting to die, he fixed his thoughts on the believer's eternal rest in Christ. After he recovered, Baxter
preached these thoughts in his weekly lectures at Kidderminster. Thomas Doolittle, a native of Kidderminster who later

became a well-known Puritan minister and author, dated his conversion to the time when he heard these lectures.

In 1650, Baxter published the substance of his lectures as the first of many practical writings. William Bates wrote of this book: "To allure our desires, he unveils the sanctuary above, and discovers the glories and joys of the blessed in the divine presence, by a light so strong and lively, that all the glittering vanities of this world vanish in the comparison, and a sincere believer will despise them, as one of mature age does the toys of children. To excite our fear, he removes the screen, and makes the everlasting fire of hell so visible, and represents the tormenting passions of the damned in such dreadful colors, as, if duly considered, would check and control the unbridled, licentious appetites of the most sensual wretches."

The Puritan minister John Janeway said that his conversion was greatly influenced by reading Baxter's book. Referring to the part of the book that explains heavenly contemplation, Janeway wrote to a friend, "There is a duty, which, if it were exercised, would dispel all cause of melancholy: I mean heavenly meditation and contemplation of the things to which the true Christian religion tends. If we did but walk closely with God one hour in a day in this duty, O what influence would it have upon the whole day besides, and, duly performed, upon the whole life! This duty, with its usefulness, manner, and directions, I knew in some measure before, but had it more pressed upon me by Mr. Baxter's *Saints' Everlasting Rest*, a book that can scarce be overvalued, and for which I have cause for ever to bless God."

Lewis Bayly

(c. 1575-1631)

L ewis Bayly was born around 1575 at Carmarthen, Wales, where Thomas Bayly, who probably was his father, was serving as curate at that time. Lewis and his first wife, who was probably Judith Appleton, had their first son in 1595, followed by four additional children. Bayly secured the living of Shipston-on-Stour, in Worcestershire, in 1597, and three years later was presented to the crown living of Evesham in the same county, where he served as headmaster of the grammar school.

Bayly soon became known for his preaching and was appointed a chaplain to Prince Henry within a few years of King James's accession. In 1606, he was presented to the rectory of Llanedi, Carmarthenshire, but remained largely at Evesham. Though he was a conformed Calvinist who respected the authority of the church, Bayly emphasized Puritan-like piety. Shortly after his wife passed away in 1608, he began to work on turning some of his sermons into what would become a Protestant classic, *The Practice of Piety*.

In 1611, Bayly became treasurer of St. Paul's Cathedral. In that same year, he earned a Bachelor of Divinity degree from Oxford and a doctorate in divinity in 1613. About that time, he succeeded Henry Mason at St. Matthew's Friday Street in London. He was made prebendary of Lichfield in 1614 and, two years later, chaplain to the king. In December 1616, he was consecrated as bishop of Bangor, a position he held until his death.

Bayly's Puritan convictions occasioned frequent conflict both at court and in his remote diocese of North Wales. In

1621, he was imprisoned for several months for his opposition to the Book of Sports. Fresh charges, endorsed by Archbishop William Laud, were brought against him in 1626 but resulted in nothing more than continued harassment. In 1630, Bayly was accused of ordaining clergy who had not fully accepted the doctrine and discipline of the Church of England. He successfully defended himself. He died in October 1631, survived by his wife and four sons.

———→◆◆◆←———

The Practice of Piety: Directing a Christian Walk, that He May Please God (SDG; 343 pages; 1997). In the seventeenth and eighteenth centuries, this classic Protestant work was one of the most universally read English devotional books after John Bunyan's *Pilgrim's Progress*. Bunyan himself traced the beginning of his spiritual convictions to the reading of Bayly's handbook. One Puritan pastor even complained that his flock regarded the devotional as equally authoritative as the Bible.

First published in the early 1600s (the exact date is unknown, but was probably 1611), *The Practice of Piety* was reprinted in 1612 in an amplified form. By 1643 it had reached its thirty-fourth English edition; by 1714, its fifty-first English edition; by 1792, its seventy-first English edition. In 1842, Grace Webster produced an edition with biographical notes. Throughout these centuries, *The Practice of Piety* has been translated in most European languages, including Dutch (1620), French (1625), Welsh (1629), German (1629), Polish (1647), and Romansch (1668). New England Puritans even translated it into the language used by Native Americans in Massachusetts (1665).

The Practice of Piety is filled with scriptural and practical guidelines on the pursuit of holy living. The author begins his work with "a plain description of God [in] his essence, person, and attributes." This doctrine is the basis for piety; every grace that sinners need springs from the gracious character of God.

Bayly arranges his work around the two destinies of mankind. We either are traveling the broad way to destruction or by divine grace are on the narrow way leading to life eternal. The unrepentant sinner has misery as his constant companion in infancy, in youth, and especially in adulthood and the later years of life. From the tragic scene of hell as a bottomless lake reserved for those who die unregenerate, Bayly turns to the un-speakable glories of heaven. Stressing the necessity of true faith and holy living, he concludes: "Get forthwith the oil of piety in the lamp of thy conversation, that thou mayest be in continual readiness to meet the bridegroom."

The rest of the book explains how to attain and maintain readiness for Christ's second advent. Bayly shows how to overcome seven obstacles: wrong teaching, the bad example of prominent persons, God's patience in delaying a sinner's punishment, presuming upon God's mercy, ungodly com-pany, the fear of piety (as if it made its possessors depressed), and the illusion of a long life. Bayly then stresses how piety is to be cultivated, offering wise advice on the spiritual disci-plines of prayer, Bible-reading, meditation, psalm-singing, Sabbath-keeping, stewardship, the commemoration of the Lord's Supper, and walking daily with God. He shows how to guide our thoughts, words, and actions in times of health as well as in times of sickness and affliction. He provides direc-tives to protect us from despair and the fear of death. In short, this is a book about how to live godly and die well.

Bayly's book, which has been credited as a fundamental influence in the rise of pietism (*Oxford DNB*, 4:463), is not without shortcomings. It lacks a strong evangelical emphasis and consequently says little on how one becomes a Christian. At places, it tends to foster the type of introspective medita-tion that leads to the very melancholy he sought to avoid.

Paul Baynes

(c. 1573-1617)

Born in London about 1573, Paul Baynes matriculated at Christ's College, Cambridge, in 1591, where he lived so dissolutely that his father removed him from the family inheritance until he showed signs of repentance. Shortly after his father's death, he was converted and soon became known for his godliness, "sharpness of wit, variety of reading, depth of judgment, aptness to teach, holy and pleasant language, wise carriage, and heavenly conversation." He received a Bachelor of Arts degree from Cambridge in 1594 and a master's degree in 1597. He served as a fellow in Christ's College from 1600 to 1604, and succeeded William Perkins as lecturer of St. Andrews, Cambridge, in 1602. Large crowds attended his ministry; some traveled great lengths to hear his expositions.

Baynes continued the experimental predestinarian tradition established by Perkins. Comparing Perkins and Baynes to Elijah and Elisha, William Ames wrote that the spirit of Elijah "was by experience found to be doubled" on Baynes (preface to Baynes's *The Diocesans Trial*).

Baynes refused to subscribe to the rules of the Church of England, for which he was silenced in 1608 by Samuel Harsnet, chancellor to Archbishop Bancroft. Baynes then preached as occasion would allow and distinguished himself as a spiritual counselor. Samuel Clarke calls him "an excellent casuist, and thereupon many doubting Christians repaired to him for satisfaction in cases of conscience" (*Lives*, pp. 30-31). His *Christian*

Letters contain numerous consolations to afflicted believers in all conditions. Baynes was, according to Alexander Grosart, "the honored guest of Puritan gentlemen all over England."

These gifts caused Baynes further persecution. Seeking to have him banished, Harsnet formally charged him with violating the Conventicle Act. When summoned before the Privy Council, he handled himself so well that all charges were dropped. One member of the council confessed, "He speaks more like an angel than a man, and I dare not stay here to have a hand in any sentence against him."

Baynes lived out his last years in poverty and in ill health, dying in Cambridge in 1617. He had a difficult deathbed. Doubts and fears brought him into fierce spiritual conflict; faith, however, conquered in the end. He was succeeded at St. Andrews by Richard Sibbes, who had been converted under Baynes and affectionately called him "our Paul."

Baynes published nothing during his lifetime. We are indebted to William Ames and other Puritans for seeing at least ten of Baynes's works through the press shortly after Baynes's death. Several important books by Baynes have not yet been reprinted, such as a commentary on the first two chapters of Colossians, a treatise on the Lord's Prayer, *Help to True Happiness, The Trial of a Christian's Estate, A Caveat for Cold Christians, A Counterbane against Earthly Carefulness, An Epitome of Man's Misery and Deliverance, The Mirror or Miracle of God's Love unto the World of His Elect, Two Godly and Fruitful Treatises,* and *Brief Directions Unto a Godly Life.* Baynes's books excel in magnifying the sovereignty of God's grace and in probing the depths of man's depravity.

⸺◆⸺

A Commentary on St. Paul's Epistle to the Ephesians (TENT; 424 pages; 2002). First published in 1643 and reissued in the nineteenth century, Baynes's commentary on Ephesians is a solid piece of Puritan exposition, marked by exegetical precision, doctrinal astuteness, and experiential depth. The commentary, which is his *magnum opus*, contains the substance of lectures preached at St. Andrews, Cambridge. Richard Sibbes wrote of the Ephesians commentary: "The greatest shall find matter to exercise themselves in; the meaner, matter of sweet comfort and holy instruction; and all confess that he hath brought some light to this Scripture."

In exegeting Ephesians 1:13-14, Baynes attempts to bring harmony between the Reformed and Puritan views by uniting the Spirit's roles as indweller and seal. He distinguishes being sealed by the Spirit (which all believers possess) and being made conscious of such sealing (which only those who are conscious of the graces of the Spirit experience). He relates the consciousness of the Spirit's sealing to full assurance of faith, picturing the Christian's growth in assurance as stages. "Childhood" lacks full assurance, "middle age" has some measure of assurance, and "old age" usually possesses much assurance (cf. Beeke, *Quest for Full Assurance*, pp. 202-203).

Robert Bolton

(1572-1631)

Robert Bolton was born in 1572 at Blackburn, Lancashire. He was admitted to Lincoln College, Oxford, in 1592, but soon transferred to Brasenose College, Oxford, where he graduated with a Bachelor of Arts degree in 1596. In 1602, he became a fellow of Brasenose. He soon established himself as an able university lecturer as well as a gifted logician, linguist, and philosopher.

After hearing William Perkins deliver a commencement address, Bolton called him "a barren empty fellow, and a passing mean scholar." Shortly after that, however, God convicted Bolton of his sins through his conversations with Thomas Peacock, fellow of the house where Bolton was staying. As one biographer writes, "The Lord ran upon him as a giant, taking him by the neck and shaking him to pieces, as he did Job; beating him to the very ground, as he did Paul, by laying before him the ugly visage of his sins, which lay so heavy upon him, as he roared for grief of heart, and so affrighted him, as I have heard him say, he rose out of his bed in the night for very anguish of spirit" (M. Bolton's Last and Learned Work of the Four Last Things [1635], pp. 15-16). Several months later, Bolton was set at liberty in Christ. Shortly after his conversion, he felt called to the ministry.

After earning a Bachelor of Divinity degree at Oxford in 1609, Bolton became minister of Broughton, in Northamptonshire. He remained there until his death in 1631. Bolton was a dignified, eloquent, faithful, and godly pastor, whose preaching stressed both the heinousness of sin and God's offers of grace. He was scriptural, earnest, and affectionate, and conveyed a singular passion for the good of never-dying souls. His biographer, J.F. Denham, writes, "This simplicity of intention was peculiarly approved and honoured of God, who by his ministry convinced many hundreds of their spiritual need, and of the ability and willingness of the Saviour to sanctify and to redeem" (*Afflicted Consciences*, p. xxxiii).

Bolton loved to preach on the historical material of Scripture. In the course of his ministry, he preached on nearly every historical chapter of the Old and New Testaments. On every holy day and every Friday before a sacrament, he customarily expounded on an entire chapter.

Bolton was in constant demand as a spiritual counselor, both at home and abroad. His books reflect that experience, summarizing half a century of Puritan thought on sanctification and the principles of Christian living.

Despite his busyness, Bolton's devotional habits were strong. He habitually prayed six times a day and observed days of humiliation, especially before the Lord's Supper. One biographer wrote, "He used such humility, and such fervency and faith with God, as if he had been a child talking with his parent."

Bolton died December 17, 1631, after a painful, prolonged illness. His sickbed served as a pulpit from which he spoke to his family and numerous visitors. He often expressed his ardent longing to be with Christ, saying, "Oh, when will this good hour come? When shall I be dissolved? When shall I be with Christ?" Two days before he died, he said, "I feel nothing in my soul but Christ, with whom I heartily desire to be." He said he had never taught anything in his sermons that he had not first sought to "work on my own heart." When he said farewell to his children, he reminded them of what he had often taught them, and said that he "was persuaded that none of them durst think to meet him at the great tribunal in an unregenerate state."

⟶✦⟵

The Carnal Professor (SDG; 156 pages; 1992). Bound with Thomas Goodwin's *Christ Set Forth*, this book is a solemn work on man's natural sinfulness and Christ's exceeding sufficiency. Bolton's text for this treatise is Romans 8:13, "For if ye live after the flesh ye shall die, but if through the Spirit ye mortify the deeds of the body, ye shall live." He says of this work, "Thou hast here in brief the soul of man unboweled before thine eye, and that mass of corruption lodging in a carnal heart (together with its power and plague) discovered unto thee, wherein is plainly demonstrated the miserable condition of a man guided by the flesh, and the happiness attending such as are led by God's Spirit; as also the bitter conflict of these two opposite inmates in believing souls, with the means of victory."

Discourse About the State of True Happiness (WJ; 156 pages; 1979). This reprint offers Bolton's sermons on Psalm 1:1, 2: "Blessed is the man that walketh not in the counsel of the ungodly, nor standeth in the way of sinners, nor sitteth in the seat of the scornful. But his delight is in the law of the Lord; and in his law doth he meditate day and night." In classic Puritan fashion, Bolton contends that man's chief happiness can be found only in God and in living a godly life before Him, and solemnly warns against seeking happiness anywhere else.

Bolton says of happiness, "There is no possibility of attainment, but by pureness of heart, holiness of life, constancy in a course of sanctification, which only lead unto the face and presence of God, where, and with whom alone is the highest perfection of bliss, a river of infinite pleasures, the well of life, and endless rest of all created desires."

The Four Last Things: Death, Judgment, Hell, Heaven (SDG; 144 pages; 1994). This book contains the last sermons Bolton preached before his death. Much of its instruction is on how to prepare for impending judgment and one's final destiny in heaven or hell. Half of the book is spent on how to prepare for death.

Writing of the joys of heaven, Bolton declares, "Let me tell you beforehand, that the excellency, glory, and sweetness thereof no mortal heart, finite mind, created understanding, can possibly conceive and comprehend" (p. 93). In the back of this edition is an abridgment of Bolton's scarce work, *Helps to Humiliation*, based on Acts 2:37.

General Directions for a Comfortable Walking with God (SDG; 450 pages; 1995). This treatise, first published in 1626 and reprinted in 1837, is a major work of Puritan casuistry. But Bolton first wrote it as a guide for himself. He divides this work into two sections: General Preparatives and Particular Directions. In the first section, Bolton considers ten ways to loosen sin's grip on the soul: abandon your loved sin, hate hypocrisy, exercise self-denial, live the life of faith, form right conceptions of Christianity, guard against worldliness, be warmed with the love of God, treasure reconciliation with God, keep your heart, and meditate on future bliss. In the second section, he describes Christian duties, such as tending family, governing the tongue, and managing every action of our lives.

J. I. Packer wrote of Bolton's *Comfortable Walking* and *Instructions* (see next entry): "Richard Baxter went over all this ground a generation later in much greater detail, and with a greater power of thought, but Bolton yields nothing to Baxter in experimental warmth and depth, and sometimes surpasses him."

Instructions for Comforting Afflicted Consciences (SDG; 390 pages; 1991). The Puritans addressed every aspect of the inner life of man—mind, heart, conscience, memory, and will. Bolton's *Instructions* (1626) provides one of the best early Puritan works on consoling the afflicted believer in all those aspects.

Section 1, Part 1 shows man's great need, based on Proverbs 18:14, to store up "heavenly comforts" in his heart. It admonishes the indifferent, the sensualist, and those who oppose faithful preaching, and it addresses the problem of persecution. Section 1, Part 2 describes the intolerableness of a wounded conscience. It explains why some do not always feel the sting of sin, and it provides twenty persuasives against sin.

Section 2, Part 1 shows how wrong it is to comfort those who do not sorrow over sin or who do so for wrong reasons. Bolton explains how ministers should apply comfort to such people—neither too little nor too much. Section 2, Part 2 deals with the right methods and ways to cure afflicted consciences.

Section 3, Part 1 addresses ways of comfort that arise from outside of us and from within us through the Scriptures and the marks of grace. It also tells how those marks may be identified. Section 3, Part 2, the longest section of the book, deals with maladies of the conscience and various ways to heal each one. Here Bolton especially offers help for dealing with a tormented soul. Most of that advice flows out of a lifetime of counseling many troubled believers, including some from the Continent, who sought Bolton's spiritual counsel.

This edition, reprinted from the 1831 edition, also contains a memoir of the life of Bolton.

Samuel Bolton

(1606-1654)

This scholar and member of the Westminster Assembly was not related to his namesake above. Samuel Bolton was born in London in 1606, was educated at Manchester School, matriculated as a pensioner at Christ's College, Cambridge, in 1625, and graduated with a Bachelor of Arts degree in 1629 and a Master of Arts in 1632.

Bolton became curate of Harrow, Middlesex, in 1634; minister of St. Martin Ludgate, London, in 1638; and then, in 1641, minister of St. Saviour's, Southwark. During his ministry there, he was also appointed lecturer at St. Anne and St. Agnes, Aldersgate, and was delegated as a member of the Westminster Assembly.

In 1645, Bolton became master of Christ's College, Cambridge (1645). Even then, however, he continued to preach regularly in London, especially at St. Andrew's, Holborn, because "his desire to win souls to Christ by preaching was so great" (Calamy, p. 25). Later, he served as vice-chancellor of Cambridge University (1650-52).

Bolton wrote seven books, most of which were collections of revised sermons. They reveal him as a clear, warmly experimental, orthodox interpreter of Scripture. He lived as he preached, taught, and wrote.

He died October 15, 1654, at the age of forty-eight, after a
long illness. At his funeral, he was described as a God-fearing,
other-worldly divine whose preaching "snatched our souls by
vigorous sympathy." In his will, he asked "to be interred as a
private Christian, and not with the outward pomp of a doctor,
because he hoped to rise in the Day of Judgment and appear
before God not as a doctor, but as a humble Christian."
Edmund Calamy preached at his funeral.

The Arraignment of Error (SDG; 460 pages; 1999). Notwithstanding its title, this book aims to show why unnecessary
controversy ought to be avoided as well as why errors on essential doctrines must be firmly opposed. Its title page
summarizes the questions addressed:

> A discourse serving as a curb to restrain the wantonness
> of men's spirits in the entertainment of opinions, and as
> a compass whereby we may sail in the search and finding
> of truth, distributed into six main questions.
>
> Question 1. How may it stand with God's, with Satan's,
> and with a man's own ends, that there should be erro-
> neous opinions?
>
> Question 2. What are the grounds of abounding errors?
>
> Question 3. Why are so many carried away with errors?
>
> Question 4. Who are those who are in danger?
>
> Question 5. What are the means of examining opinions,
> and the characteristics of truth?
>
> Question 6. What ways has God left in His Word to sup-
> press error and correct erroneous persons?
>
> Under which general questions, many other necessary
> and profitable queries are comprised, discussed, and re-
> solved. And, in conclusion of all, some motives and

means conducing to a happy accommodation of our present differences are subjoined.

The Arraignment of Error addresses the question: If there is one truth and one gospel, why are there so many divisions among God's people? Bolton's answer is that errors abound to try and sift God's children, thus preparing them to hold the truth dear. He addresses other questions as well, such as: Why does God allow errors in the church? What should we do when godly men disagree on doctrinal matters? What is the importance of synods and councils in settling matters? Bolton teaches that both the pastoral use of synods and the power of the civil magistrate are necessary, but both should be limited, clearly defined, and subjected to Scripture. He writes with conviction: "The Word of God and God in His Word, the Scripture and God in Scripture is the only infallible, supreme, authoritative rule and judge of matters of doctrines and worship, of things to be believed and things to be done."

The True Bounds of Christian Freedom (BTT; 224 pages; 2001). First published in 1645, this book explains the place of the law in the Christian's life. Living in an age in which licentiousness and immorality abound, we cannot recommend this book enough. Bolton's analysis is piercing. While opposing Antinomianism, he assures the believer that the law is not a death sentence, but rather an encouragement to do good works. The law is to be loved and cherished, not feared and disobeyed.

After defining the nature of true freedom, Bolton answers six related questions: Are Christians free from the moral law as a rule of obedience? Are Christians free from all punishments and chastisements for sin? If a believer is under the moral law as a rule of duty, is his liberty in Christ infringed? Can Christ's freemen sin themselves back into bondage? May Christ's freemen perform duties for the sake

of reward? Are Christians free from obedience to men?
Bolton concludes his treatise by saying, "It is my exhortation
therefore to all Christians to maintain their Christian freedom by constant watchfulness."

Christian Freedom first appeared under the endorsement of
John Downame, who described it as a "solid, judicious, pious
and very profitable" book. In this edition, S.M. Houghton provides a poignant summary of the historical background to
Bolton's book in an appendix (pp. 225-30).

John Boys

(1571-1625)

John Boys was committed to the Church of England; however, he was deeply evangelical and shared with his Puritan contemporaries a love for true, experimental religion. He was born at Elmton, in Eythorne, Kent, to Thomas Boys, a gentleman from a long-established family in east Kent, and his wife, Christian Searles, daughter and coheir of John Searles of Wye. John Boys was educated at King's School, Canterbury, and entered Corpus Christi College, Cambridge, in 1586, where he earned a Bachelor of Arts degree in 1590 and a master's degree in 1593. That year, he moved to a fellowship at Clare Hall, where he earned a Bachelor of Divinity degree in 1600.

In 1597, Boys was presented with the living of Betteshanger, Kent, which he retained all his life. He preached at St. Paul's Cross in London at the age of twenty-eight and was awarded a doctorate in divinity in 1605. In 1599, Boys received the living of Tilmanstone, which he resigned in 1618 to become rector of Great Mongeham. In 1603, he received the rectory of Hollingbourne as a third Kent living. The following year, he married Angela Bargrave, daughter of Robert Bargrave of Bridge, near Canterbury.

Boys was a favorite of Archbishop Whitgift, and King James I made him Dean of Canterbury in 1619, a position he retained until his death. In 1620, he was appointed to the Court of High Commission. Because of his influential positions, Boys was able to promote piety and spiritual reform among his fellow clergy. As a predestinarian Calvinist, he was especially noted for his staunch Protestantism. He died in his study at Elmton on September 26, 1625, and was buried in the cathedral four days later.

———◆◆◆———

The Works of John Boys (SDG; 789 pages; 1997). Boys himself compiled a one-volume edition of his works in 1622, which included his systematic sermonic exposition of the church's prescribed lectionary—a ten year project. It also included five miscellaneous sermons, and eleven books of postils first published between 1609-1617. The postils were so popular that they were reissued at least a dozen times in the first decade.

The SDG reprint is photolithographed from an 1854 edition published in New York by Stanford and Swords, which is based on a 1629 London edition. It contains Boys's exposition of Scripture passages used in the services of Morning and Evening Prayer and Holy Communion in *The Book of Common Prayer*, as well as his writings on the Psalms, expositions on the epistles and gospels, and comments on the Apostles' Creed, the Lord's Prayer, and the Ten Commandments.

Spurgeon said Boys was "one of the richest of writers," being "all essence." Indeed, Boys's writing is lively, witty, clear, and profound. He made complex doctrine plain and practical.

Anne Bradstreet

(1612-1672)

Anne Bradstreet was the first American to publish a book of poetry. Born in 1612 in Northampton, England, she was the daughter of Thomas Dudley and Dorothy Yorke. Her father had led volunteer soldiers in the English Reformation and Elizabethan Settlement, and her mother was a gentlewoman of noble descent.

When she was sixteen, Anne married Simon Bradstreet, a twenty-five year old assistant at the Massachusetts Bay Company. He was the son of Simon Bradstreet, Sr., Puritan minister of Horbling. Anne and her family had immigrated to America on the *Arbella* in 1630 (the same ship that John Winthrop traveled on). Many perished on that three-month journey, but the Bradstreets arrived safely in Salem and moved to Boston, where they united briefly with the church served by John Cotton before moving on to Newtown (now Cambridge), and eventually to Ipswich and Andover. During the first years of their settlement, Anne wrote several poems expressing her devotion to God and love for her husband as well as describing her struggles with the New World, winter, and sickness. After a bout with tuberculosis, she wrote, "Upon a Fit of Sickness" (1632).

Early in marriage, Bradstreet worried that her failure to conceive was a result of God's displeasure, but her fears were alleviated in 1632 when she became pregnant with Samuel, the first of her eight children. For the next thirty-seven years,

Anne wrote hundreds of poems, which she often called "my children." These religious, meditative poems reveal her exemplary faith and her love for her children and her husband. Most were written during long periods of loneliness while her husband was away on political errands.

Bradstreet spent much time with her children, reading to them and teaching them as her father had taught her when she was young. She also shared poetry with them. She later wrote to her children about her passion for meditative poetry: "I have not studied in this that you read to show my skill, but to declare the truth, not to set forth myself, but the glory of God."

Bradstreet was also active in politics. She was one of the founders of Newtown and helped settle North Andover, where she lived from 1645 until her death. Her husband held several public offices and eventually became governor of Massachusetts.

In 1650, Bradstreet's poems were introduced to the public when her brother-in-law, John Woodbridge, took them to London. Apparently, they were published by Stephen Bowtell without Bradstreet's consent. The collection was published as *The Tenth Muse lately sprung up in America. Or Several Poems, compiled with great variety of Wit and Learning by a Gentlewoman in those parts.* The book was soon listed as one of the most saleable books in England.

In later years, Bradstreet revised these early poems and added eighteen more for a second edition. Nathaniel Ward, famed preacher of Ipswich, wrote the preface and published the work in Boston in 1678, six years after Bradstreet's death, as *Several Poems compiled with great variety of wit and learning, full of delight.*

Bradstreet died of tuberculosis on September 16, 1672. The warm and simple style of her writing was appreciated in her own day and has since earned her a place among America's more famous poets.

The Complete Works of Anne Bradstreet (Belknap Press; 336 pages; 1981). This collection shows Bradstreet's Puritan spirit, charm, sensibility, and wit. Unlike other editions, this one incorporates the 1650, 1678, and 1867 Andover texts, providing the complete corpus of her work. Also included are prefatory comments by Nathaniel Ward, John Rogers, and others.

To My Husband and Other Poems (Dover Publications; 80 pages; 2000). This collection of poetry, selected from a number of Bradstreet's works, reveal the thoughts of a remarkably sensitive and well-educated woman. Exhibiting great range and beauty, these poems include odes to her husband and children, a formal elegy in honor of Queen Elizabeth I, and loving epitaphs honoring her deceased parents and grandchildren. Grouped according to category (love poems, home life, religious meditations, dialogues, and lamentations), the poems exhibit Bradstreet's intellectual prowess as well as her Puritan convictions.

William Bridge
(1600-1670)

William Bridge was a native of Cambridgeshire. He entered Emmanuel College, Cambridge in 1619, where he earned a bachelor's degree in 1623 and a master's degree in 1626, then served for several years as a fellow at the college. While a student at Cambridge, he was greatly influenced by John Rogers's lectures at Dedham, Essex.

Bridge was ordained a priest in the Church of England in 1627. Two years later, he was appointed a lecturer at Saffron Walden, Essex, where he began to show some nonconformist influence, refusing to wear the surplice and hood on the basis that he had not been licensed by a bishop. In 1631, he was licensed and did conform. About that time, he was appointed lecturer at Colchester, Essex, and was also asked to give the Friday lectures at St. George's Tombland, Norwich. In 1632, he became rector of St. Peter Hungate in Norwich. In 1634, he was brought before the consistory court and temporarily suspended for espousing limited atonement and condemning Arminians. Two years later, the new bishop of Norwich, Matthew Wren, who led a vicious campaign against nonconformity, deprived Bridge. Bridge's supporters petitioned the king on his behalf, claiming that Wren was undermining the economy. Bridge did not respond to charges made against him, but remained in Norwich until he was excommunicated and ordered away from English soil.

Archbishop Laud wrote to the king, "Mr. Bridge of Norwich rather than he will conform, hath left his Lecture and two Cures, and is gone into Holland." Charles I responded in the margin, "Let him go: we are well rid of him."

Bridge settled in Rotterdam by May of 1636, where he succeeded Hugh Peters and began co-pastoring a congregation with John Ward. He renounced his Church of England ordination and was ordained as an Independent by John Ward, whom he in turn ordained. Eventually Ward was deposed in 1639 for opposing Bridge and recycling too many old sermons. Jeremiah Burroughs replaced Ward as Bridge's co-pastor.

Bridge returned to England in 1641, where he became better known for his Puritan views. In 1642, he was appointed as a member of the Westminster Assembly of Divines and proved himself a noted Independent. With Burroughs, Thomas Goodwin, Philip Nye, and Sidrach Simpson, he wrote *An Apologetical Narrative* to promote Congregational polity and present objections to Presbyterianism.

In 1642, Bridge accepted a position as town preacher at Yarmouth, where he organized an Independent church, and formally became its pastor in the fall of 1643. He labored there until 1662, when he was ejected from the pulpit by the Act of Uniformity.

Bridge was an excellent preacher, able scholar, and prolific writer with a well-furnished library. He arose at 4 a.m. each day to search the Scriptures, confess his sins, and commune with God. He often studied for seventeen hours a day, yet did not become an ivory tower theologian. His parishioners viewed him as a charitable and candid pastor whose ministry helped many people.

Bridge was often called to preach before the Long Parliament and was consulted by Parliament on church-related issues. He was also a prominent member of the Savoy Conference and a well-known writer.

Bridge spent his last years at Yarmouth and Clapham, Surrey, where he preached for an Independent church, which he probably founded. Reportedly, "the people flooded in such numbers to hear him that by 7 a.m. there is no room to be got" (Barker, *Puritan Profiles*, p. 87). He died in Clapham on March 12, 1671.

⟫◆◆⟪

The Works of William Bridge (SDG; 5 volumes; 1990). First published in three volumes in 1649, in two volumes in 1657, and later expanded to include all the writings of Bridge in five volumes in 1845, *The Works of William Bridge* (reprinted from the 1845 edition) is full of practical Puritan teaching. Topics such as the gospel mystery, the great things of faith, Christ and the covenant, and evangelical repentance are covered with keen insight and pastoral warmth.

Chapters in volume 1 include: "The Great Gospel Mystery of the Saints' Comfort and Holiness," "Satan's Power to Tempt and Christ's Love to and Care of His People Under Temptation," "Grace for Grace, or the Overflowings of Christ's Fullness Received by All Saints," "The Spiritual Life, and In-being of Christ in All Believers," "Scripture Light the Most Sure Light" (sermons on 2 Peter 1:19 which elicited a response from the Quaker, George Whitehead), and "The Righteous Man's Habitation in the Time of Plague and Pestilence" (an exposition of Psalm 91 to encourage believers while the plague ravaged London). Volume 2 includes: "A Lifting up for the Downcast," "Five Sermons on Faith," and "The Freeness of the Grace and Love of God to Believers Discovered." Volume 3 contains "Christ and the Covenant" (a series of ten sermons taken down by note-takers), "Christ in Travail," and "Seasonable Truths in Evil Times" (nine sermons preached in the London area, including one that asserts the repression of nonconformists is part of God's design to test them). Volume 4 contains "Seventeen Sermons on Various Subjects and Occasions" and "Evangelical Repentance." Volume 5 contains "The Sinfulness of Sin and the Fullness of Christ," "Eight Sermons," "A Word to the Aged," "The Wounded Conscience Cured" (asserts the right of subjects to defend themselves and of parliament to declare what the law is), "The Truth of the Times Vindicated" (insists that truth must be defended even as it acknowledges that civil war is the worst form of conflict), "The Loyal Convert" (condemns "service-book men" who do not uphold the Solemn League and Covenant), and "The Doctrine of Justification by Faith Opened."

A *Lifting Up for the Downcast* (BTT; 288 pages; 1988). This book, based on Psalm 42:11, is a collection of thirteen sermons on spiritual depression. It has helped hundreds of God's people battle discouragement. Bridge addresses the following causes of depression: great sins, weak grace, miscarriage of duties, lack of assurance, temptation, desertion, affliction, and inability to serve. This book is packed with comforting advice showing why believers ought not be discouraged no matter what their condition.

The final sermon, "The Cure of Discouragements by Faith in Jesus Christ," is worth the price of the book. "Be sure that you do not go to God without Christ, but with Christ in your arms," Bridge says (p. 276).

A *Word to the Aged* (SDG; 20 pages; 2003). In this booklet, William Bridge addresses particular sins to which the elderly are most inclined, such as a complaining spirit, bitterness, and impenitence. Pointing to the Lord Jesus Christ as the remedy for the sins and infirmities of old age, he gives counsel on improving the remaining years of the elderly so that their lives might more glorify the Lord and be pleasing to Him.

Thomas Brooks
(1608-1680)

Thomas Brooks was born in 1608. He entered Emmanuel College, Cambridge, in 1625, where such New England Puritans as Thomas Hooker, John Cotton, and Thomas Shepard were also educated, but he appears to have left before graduating. Brooks was ordained as a preacher of the gospel in 1640 and became a chaplain to the parliamentary fleet, serving for some years at sea. That ministry is mentioned in some of his "sea-devotions" as well as his statement: "I have been some years at sea and through grace I can say that I would not exchange my sea experiences for England's riches."

After the Civil War, Brooks became minister at the church of St. Thomas the Apostle, Queen Street, London (1648-1651). He was often called to preach before Parliament. In 1652, he became rector of St. Margaret's, New Fish Street Hill, which was the first church that burned to the ground in the Great Fire of London (1666). Like Thomas Goodwin and John Owen, Brooks preferred the Congregational view of church government. In 1662, he fell victim to the notorious Act of Uniformity.

After being ejected from his living, Brooks continued to preach in London, where he apparently suffered little persecution. He became minister of a congregation at Moorfields, near St. Margaret's. Unlike many ministers, he stayed in

London during the Great Plague of 1665, faithfully tending his flock. In 1672, he was licensed to preach according to the terms of the Declaration of Indulgence, but that license was revoked in 1676.

Brooks lost his first wife, Martha Burgess, a godly woman whom he greatly treasured, in 1676. He wrote of her, "She was always best when she was most with God in a corner. She has many a whole day been pouring out her soul before God for the nation, for Zion, and the great concerns of her own soul." He later married a young God-fearing woman named Patience Cartwright (Alexander Grosart puts it succinctly: "she spring-young, he winter-old" [*Works of Brooks*, 1:xxxv]), who proved a most worthy companion.

Brooks died in 1680 and was buried in Bunhill Fields, London's famous nonconformist cemetery. John Reeve, who preached at the funeral, said Brooks had "a sweet nature, great gravity, large charity, wonderful patience, and strong faith."

The Works of Thomas Brooks (BTT; 6 vols., 3,000 pages; 2001). This six-volume compilation by James Nichol is a treasure. Volume 1 contains Alexander B. Grosart's memoir of Brooks as well as "Precious Remedies Against Satan's Devices," "Apples of Gold" (a popular work for young men and women printed seventeen times from 1657 to 1693), "The Mute Christian under the Smarting Rod," and "A String of Pearls."

Volume 2 contains "An Ark for All of God's Noahs," "The Privy Key of Heaven," and "Heaven on Earth." Volume 3 contains "The Unsearchable Riches of Christ" and "A Cabinet of Jewels." Volume 4 contains "The Crown and Glory of Christianity," consisting of 58 sermons on Hebrews 12:14. Volume 5 contains "The Golden Key to Open Hidden Treasures," "Paradise Opened," and "A Word in Season." The last volume contains "London's Lamentations" (a remarkable work of corporate confession), "The Glorious Day of the Saints'

Appearance," "God's Delight in the Progress of the Upright," "Hypocrites Detected," "A Believer's Last Day His Best Day," "A Heavenly Cordial," and "The Legacy of a Dying Mother."

Of all the Puritan divines reprinted by James Nichol in the 1860s, Brooks was the most popular. Both the practical subjects he undertakes and the manner of his presentation make "his sentences as memorable as melodies." Moreover, his spiritual insights are presented directly and fervently, and are replete with Scripture. As a fellow minister said of Brooks: "He had a body of divinity in his head and the power of it in his heart." Peter Lewis said, "We may add, in his books too" (*Genius of Puritanism*, p. 29).

We recommend Thomas Brooks highly. He communicates profound truths in a simple manner and is appropriate reading for young people and adults. His writings exude spiritual life and power and are particularly comforting for true believers. If limited to the purchase of a few sets of Puritan works, be sure to buy and read Brooks.

Heaven on Earth: A Treatise on Assurance (BTT; 320 pages; 1983). There is no higher privilege than to be a child of God and to know it, for assurance brings joy to worship and prayer, and strength and boldness to our witness. Failure and weakness in all these areas can often be traced back to a lack of assurance. Brooks spells out the wonders of assurance in this book.

Chapter 1 asserts that believers may attain assurance, and chapter 2 addresses why some believers lack assurance while others enjoy it in a particularly large measure. Chapter 3 grapples with impediments that hinder assurance and how those can be removed. Chapter 4 offers motives to encourage believers not to stop short of obtaining well-grounded assurance. Brooks's ten advantages to assurance ought to motivate any believer—it offers heaven on earth, sweetens life's changes, keeps the heart from desiring the world, assists communion with God, preserves from backsliding, produces holy bold-ness, prepares a man for death, makes mercies taste like mercies, gives vigor in Christian service, and leads to the soul's enjoyment of Christ.

Chapter 5, the heart of the book, sets forth "ways and means of gaining a well-grounded assurance." Brooks's sec-tion on the "things that accompany salvation"—knowledge, faith, repentance, obedience, love, prayer, perseverance, and hope—offers more than a hundred pages of savory divinity. In itself it serves as a practical handbook on the marks of grace. Chapter 6 exposes counterfeit assurance by describing the marks of well-grounded assurance and characteristics of the Holy Spirit's internal witness. The closing chapter shows how to strengthen assurance and regain lost assurance.

The Mute Christian under the Smarting Rod (GM; 118 pages; n.d.). This work was originally published in 1658 with the subtitle, "The Silent Soul with Sovereign Antidotes." A second edition appeared in 1660 and thereafter was in great demand. Brooks presents many points to prove his theme that it is "the great duty and concern of gracious souls to be mute and silent under the greatest afflictions, the saddest providences, and sharpest trials they meet with in this world." He answers every thinkable objection against exercising spiritual submis-sion in affliction. This classic is highly recommended for anyone going through trials they cannot change.

Precious Remedies Against Satan's Devices (BTT; 256 pages; 1984). This book offers sorely needed lessons on the sub-tleties of Satan's devices. "The strange opposition that I met with from Satan, in the study of the following discourse, hath put an edge upon my spirit, knowing that Satan strives mightily to keep these things from seeing the light that tend eminently to shake and break his kingdom of darkness, and to lift up the kingdom and glory of the Lord Jesus Christ, in the souls and lives of the children of men," writes Brooks in the preface of this book.

Brooks describes twelve of Satan's devices and their remedies, then focuses on eight devices Satan uses to keep believers from using the means of grace. He provides remedies for those devices that keep saints in a sad, doubting condition. Finally, he provides remedies for the abuse of riches, for pride of learning, for divisions among the godly, and for the excuse of ignorance. An appendix considers five more devices of Satan, seven characteristics of false teachers, six propositions concerning Satan, and ten helps against his devices. The ten helps provide an adequate summary of the book: walk by the rule of God's Word, don't grieve the Spirit, strive for heavenly wisdom, resist Satan's first motions, labor to be filled with the Spirit, remain humble, pursue watchfulness, retain communion with God, fight Satan by drawing strength from the Lord Jesus, and be much in prayer.

One reason for this reprint, according to George Smeaton, is that Christian authors of former times treated the seductive influence and terrible power of Satan in ways "greatly more full and suggestive than in the literature of the present day." We greatly need the guidance Brooks provides in this book. Though Satan's tools may change over the centuries, his devices remain constant; hence, this classic will never be outdated.

Smooth Stones Taken from Ancient Brooks (SDG; 269 pages; 2001). This book of quotes from the writings and sermons of Thomas Brooks was compiled by Charles Spurgeon, a great lover of the Puritans. In his preface to the book, Spurgeon wrote: "As a writer, Brooks scatters stars with both his hands. He has dust of gold: in his storehouse are all manner of precious stones. Genius is always marvelous, but when sanctified it is matchless." Here is one precious stone: "There is no such way to attain to greater measures of grace than for a man to live up to that little grace he has."

John Bunyan

(1628-1688)

John Owen said of John Bunyan, a powerful preacher and the best-known of all the Puritan writers, that he would gladly exchange all his learning for Bunyan's power of touching men's hearts. John Bunyan was born in 1628 at Elstow, near Bedford, to Thomas Bunyan and Margaret Bentley. Thomas Bunyan, a brazier or tinker, was poor but not destitute. Still, for the most part, John Bunyan was not educated well. He became rebellious, frequently indulging in cursing. He later wrote, "It was my delight to be taken captive by the devil at his will: being filled with all unrighteousness; that from a child I had but few equals, both for cursing, swearing, lying, and blaspheming the holy name of God" (*Works of Bunyan*, ed. George Offor, 1:6). Sporadic periods of convictions of sin helped restrain some of that rebellion, however.

When Bunyan was sixteen years old, his mother and sister died a month apart. His father remarried a month later. Young Bunyan joined Cromwell's New Model Army, where he continued his rebellious ways. Fighting in the Civil War sobered him considerably, however. On one occasion, his life was wonderfully spared. "When I was a soldier, I with others, was drawn out to go to such a place to besiege it. But when I was just ready to go, one of the company desired to go in my room; to which when I consented, he took my place, and

JOHN BUNYAN

coming to the siege, as he stood sentinel he was shot in the head with a musket bullet and died" (ibid.).

Bunyan was discharged from the army in 1646 or 1647. His military experience was later reflected in his book, *The Holy War*.

In 1648, Bunyan married a God-fearing woman whose name remains unknown, and whose only dowry was two books: Arthur Dent's *The Plain Man's Pathway to Heaven* and Lewis Bayly's *The Practice of Piety*. When Bunyan read those books, he was convicted of sin. He started attending the parish church, stopped swearing (when rebuked by a dissolute woman of the town), and tried to honor the Sabbath. After some months, Bunyan came into contact with some women whose joyous conversation about the new birth and Christ deeply impressed him. He mourned his joyless existence as he realized that he was lost and outside of Christ. "I cannot now express with what longings and breakings in my soul I cried to Christ to call me," he wrote. He felt that he had the worst heart in all of England. He confessed to be jealous of animals because they did not have a soul to account for before God.

In 1651, the women introduced Bunyan to John Gifford, their pastor in Bedford. God used Gifford to lead Bunyan to repentance and faith. Bunyan was particularly influenced by a sermon Gifford preached on Song of Solomon 4:1, "Behold thou art fair, my love, behold thou art fair," as well as by reading Luther's commentary of Galatians, in which he found his own experience "largely and profoundly handled, as if [Luther's] book had been written out of my own heart" (cited by Greaves, *John Bunyan*, p. 18). While walking through a field one day, Christ's righteousness was revealed to Bunyan's soul and gained the victory. Bunyan writes of that unforgettable experience:

> One day, as I was passing in the field, this sentence fell upon my soul: Thy righteousness is in heaven; and methought withal I saw with the eyes of my soul, Jesus

Christ, at God's right hand; there, I say, as my righteousness; so that wherever I was, or whatever I was a-doing,
God could not say of me, He wants my righteousness, for
that was just before Him. I also saw, moreover, that it was
not my good frame of heart that made my righteousness
better, nor yet my bad frame that made my righteousness
worse; for my righteousness was Jesus Christ Himself, the
same yesterday, today, and forever. Now did my chains
fall off my legs indeed. I was loosed from my afflictions
and irons; my temptations also fled away. Now I went
home rejoicing for the grace and love of God. I lived for
some time very sweetly at peace with God through
Christ. Oh! methought, Christ! Christ! There was nothing
but Christ that was before my eyes. I saw now not only
looking upon this and the other benefits of Christ apart,
as of His blood, burial, and resurrection, but considered
Him as a whole Christ! It was glorious to me to see His
exaltation, and the worth and prevalency of all His benefits, and that because now I could look from myself to
Him, and would reckon that all those graces of God that
now were green in me, were yet but like those cracked
groats and fourpence-halfpennies that rich men carry in
their purses, when their gold is in their trunk at home!
Oh, I saw that my gold was in my trunk at home! In Christ
my Lord and Saviour! Now Christ was all (*Grace Abounding*, paragraphs 229-32, pp. 129-31).

The year 1654 was a momentous one for Bunyan. He
moved to Bedford with his wife and four children under the
age of six; his firstborn, Mary, was blind from birth. That same
year, he became a member of Gifford's church, and was soon
appointed deacon. His testimony became the talk of the town.
Several people were led to conversion in response to it. By the
end of the year, he had lost his beloved pastor to death.

In 1655, Bunyan began preaching to various congregations
in Bedford. Hundreds came to hear him. He published his first
book the following year, *Some Gospel Truths Opened*, written to

protect believers from being misled by Quaker and Ranter teachings about Christ's person and work. Two years later, Bunyan published *A Few Sighs from Hell*, an exposition of Luke 16:19-31 about the rich man and Lazarus. The book attacks professional clergy and the wealthy who promote carnality. It was well received, and helped establish Bunyan as a reputable Puritan writer. About that same time, his wife passed away.

In 1659, Bunyan published *The Doctrine of the Law and Grace Unfolded*, which expounds his view of covenant theology, stressing the promissory nature of the covenant of grace and the dichotomy between law and grace. This helped establish him as a thoroughgoing Calvinist, though it led to false charges of antinomianism by Richard Baxter.

In 1660, while preaching in a farmhouse at Lower Samsell, Bunyan was arrested on the charge of preaching without official rights from the king. When told that he would be freed if he no longer preached, he replied, "If I am freed today, I will preach tomorrow." He was thrown into prison, where he wrote prolifically and made shoelaces to provide some income for twelve and a half years (1660-1672).

Prior to his arrest, Bunyan had remarried, this time to a godly young woman named Elizabeth. She pleaded repeatedly for his release, but judges such as Sir Matthew Hale and Thomas Twisden rejected her plea. So Bunyan remained in prison with no formal charge and no legal sentence, in defiance of the *habeas corpus* provisions of the Magna Carta, because he refused to give up preaching the gospel and denounced the Church of England as false (see Bunyan's *A Relation of My Imprisonment*, published posthumously in 1765).

In 1661 and from 1668-1672, certain jailers permitted Bunyan to leave prison at times to preach. George Offer notes, "It is said that many of the Baptist congregations in Bedfordshire owe their origins to his midnight preaching" (*Works of Bunyan*, 1:lix). His prison years were times of difficult trials, however.

Bunyan experienced what his *Pilgrim's Progress* characters Christian and Faithful would later suffer at the hands of Giant Despair, who thrust pilgrims "into a very dark dungeon, nasty and stinking." Bunyan especially felt the pain of separation from his wife and children, particularly "blind Mary," describing it as a "pulling of the flesh from my bones."

Prison years, however, were productive years for Bunyan. In the mid-1660s, Bunyan wrote extensively, with only the Bible and *Foxe's Book of Martyrs* at his side. In 1663, he wrote *Christian Behaviour*, intended as a handbook for Christian living and a response against charges of antinomianism, as well as a last testament, since Bunyan expected to die in prison. He also finished *I Will Pray with the Spirit*, which expounded 1 Corinthians 14:15, and focused on the Spirit's inner work in all true prayer. In 1664, he published *Profitable Meditations*; in 1665, *One Thing Needful*, *The Holy City* (his understanding of church history and the end times), and *The Resurrection of the Dead*. This latter work is a sequel to *The Holy City*, in which Bunyan expounds the resurrection from Acts 24:14-15 in a traditional way, and then uses his prison torments to illustrate the horrors that await the damned following the final judgment. In 1666, the middle of his prison-time, he wrote *Grace Abounding to the Chief of Sinners*, in which he declared, "The Almighty God being my help and shield, I am determined yet to suffer, if frail life might continue so long, even till the moss shall grow upon my eyebrows, rather than violate my faith and principles." During the last part of his imprisonment, he finished *A Confession of My Faith, A Reason for My Practice*, and *A Defence of the Doctrine of Justification*, an uncompromising criticism of the rising tide of Pelagianism among the Nonconformists and latitudinarianism among the Anglican establishment.

The Bedford congregation, sensing some relaxation of the law against preaching, appointed Bunyan as pastor on January 21, 1672, but Bunyan was not released until May. He had been the first to suffer under Charles II and was the last to be released. His long years in Bedford's county prison made him a martyr in the eyes of many.

Bunyan had enjoyed only a few years of freedom when he was again arrested for preaching and put in the town jail. Here he wrote *Instruction for the Ignorant* (a catechism for the saved and unsaved that emphasizes the need for self-denial), *Saved by Grace* (an exposition of Ephesians 2:5 that encourages the godly to persevere in the faith notwithstanding persecution), *The Strait Gate* (an exposition of Luke 13:24 that seeks to awaken sinners to the gospel message), *Light for Them That Sit in Darkness* (a polemical work against those who oppose atonement by Christ's satisfaction and justification by His imputed righteousness, especially the Quakers and Latitudinarians), and the first part of his famous *Pilgrim's Progress.* That book, which sold more than 100,000 copies in its first decade in print, has since been reprinted in at least 1,500 editions and translated into more than two hundred languages, with Dutch, French, and Welsh editions appearing in Bunyan's lifetime. Some scholars have asserted that, with the exception of the Bible and perhaps Thomas à Kempis's *The Imitation of Christ*, this Bunyan classic has sold more copies than any other book ever written.

John Owen, minister of an Independent congregation at Leadenhall Street, London, successfully appealed for Bunyan to Thomas Barlow, bishop of Lincoln, who used his influence at court to secure Bunyan's release from prison on June 21, 1677. Bunyan spent his last years ministering to the Nonconformists and writing. In 1678, he published *Come and Welcome to Jesus Christ*, a popular exposition of John 6:37 that movingly proclaims a strong free offer of grace to sinners to fly to Jesus Christ and be saved. This book went through six editions in the last decade of Bunyan's life. In 1680, he wrote *The Life and Death of Mr. Badman*, described as "a series of snapshots depicting the commonplace attitudes and practices against which Bunyan regularly preached" (*Oxford DNB*, 8:707). Two years later, he published *The Greatness of the Soul* and *The Holy War*. In 1685, he published the second part of *Pilgrim's Progress*, dealing with Christiana's pilgrimage, *A Caution to Stir Up to Watch Against Sin*, and *Questions About the Nature and the Perpetuity of the Seventh-day Sabbath*.

In the last three years of his life, Bunyan wrote ten more books, of which the best-known are *The Pharisee and the Publican*, *The Jerusalem Sinner Saved*, *The Work of Jesus Christ as an Advocate*, *The Water of Life*, *Solomon's Temple Spiritualized*, and *The Acceptable Sacrifice*. Most of those books were reproduced in paperback by William Frasher in the 1960s through Reiner Press, in Swengel, Pennsylvania. They are not listed separately in this book because they are included in Bunyan's *Works*.

In 1688, Bunyan died suddenly from a fever that he caught while traveling in cold weather. On his deathbed, he said to those who gathered around him, "Weep not for me, but for yourselves. I go to the Father of our Lord Jesus Christ, who will, no doubt, through the mediation of his blessed Son, receive me, though a sinner; where I hope we ere long shall meet, to sing the new song, and remain everlastingly happy, world without end" (*Works of Bunyan*, 1:lxxviii). After telling his friends that his greatest desire was to be with Christ, he raised his hands to heaven, and cried, "Take me, for I come to Thee!" and then died. He was buried in Bunhill Fields, close to Thomas Goodwin and John Owen.

⸺◆◆◆⸺

The Works of John Bunyan (BTT; 3 vols., 2,400 pages; 1999). Bunyan was unusual among the Puritans in that he had little formal education. Nevertheless, he read exhaustively, and the Holy Spirit blessed his studies. He became a prolific writer and wrote more than sixty works in sixty years. Many of those have been overshadowed by *Pilgrim's Progress* and *The*

Holy War, but they are still worthy of reading. Bunyan's works are a treasure of scriptural, experiential truth. He was a Spirit-taught theologian who had the gift of interpreting evangelical truth for the masses.

Bunyan was one of the most popular Puritans, no doubt because, while possessing the Word-centeredness and depth of doctrine and experience of other Puritans, he presented truth with warm simplicity. Several publishers have reprinted Bunyan's individual works. Most recently, SDG has reprinted *The Fear of God*, in which Bunyan addresses the objects and reasons for fearing God, the various kinds of fear, the character and effects of godly fear, and the privileges and uses of this doctrine. BTT has also reprinted five of Bunyan's works (*The Acceptable Sacrifice, All Loves Excelling, Come and Welcome to Jesus Christ, The Jerusalem Sinner Saved*, and *Prayer*) in the Puritan Paperback Series. GM has reprinted *Groans of a Lost Soul, Solomon's Temple Spiritualized*, and *Advice to Sufferers*, among others.

For those wishing to own the best of what Bunyan has written, the BTT edition of George Offor's 1854 compilation is the best option. It offers fifty-five of Bunyan's works in three volumes. The first volume contains valuable introductions and an eighty-page memoir of Bunyan's life and times. Volumes 1 and 2 contain his experimental, doctrinal, and practical works, such as *Christ a Complete Saviour* and *The Fear of God*. Volume 3 has Bunyan's allegorical, figurative, and symbolical works, such as *The Pilgrim's Progress, The Holy War*, and *The Life and Death of Mr. Badman*, as well as a compendious index.

Christiana's Journey; Or, The Pilgrim's Progress, The Second Part (BP; 150 pages; 1993). This edition contains the text of *Christiana's Journey* and seventy-three beautiful full-page oil paintings by Albert Wessels, which especially engage children.

Bunyan may have been motivated to write the second part of *Pilgrim's Progress* in which Christiana and other female characters, as well as children, play prominent roles to depict a

more subdued way in which the Holy Spirit often works conversion in typical church members. Hence Christiana and her
children do not fall into the Slough of Despond nor have such
a dramatic experience at the cross as Christian did. Christian
and Christiana traverse much of the same ground, which
shows the universality of believers' spiritual experiences, but
the section on Christian is more autobiographical while the
section on Christiana is more corporate and normative, showing a more typical morphology of conversion.

Grace Abounding to the Chief of Sinners (AP; 243 pages; n.d.).
An indispensable source for Bunyan's early life and conversion, this autobiographical classic chronicles his life from
infancy to his imprisonment in 1660. Text on the remainder of
Bunyan's life is supplied by the editor. It provides an open and
candid look into his life struggles, showing that God's grace
abounds to even the chief of sinners. Richard Greaves writes,
"Although conventional in structure, *Grace Abounding* tran-
scends contemporary examples of the genre in its depth of
psychological experience, its riveting account of Bunyan's
struggle to keep from succumbing to pervasive, numbing despair, and his agonizing wrestling with biblical texts" (*Oxford
DNB*, 8:705).

    Grace Abounding was published six times during Bunyan's
lifetime, and has been reprinted scores of times over the centuries. This reprint is taken from the eighth edition.

The Holy War (Reiner; 454 pages; 1974). This allegory, second only to *Pilgrim's Progress*, bears the full title of *The Holy
War, made by King Shaddai upon Diabolus, for the Regaining of the Me-
tropolis of the World; or, the Losing and Taking again of The Town of
Mansoul.* Reiner's edition contains the valuable "explanatory,
experimental, and practical notes" of George Burder and
sixty-eight engravings.

Macauley claims that *The Holy War*, written after Bunyan's imprisonment, "would be the best allegory ever written if *Pilgrim's Progress* did not exist." *The Holy War* is more difficult to read but is also more profound in places than *Pilgrim's Progress* partly because it involves several levels of allegory. "Mansoul is not only the soul of each believer and the allegorical person-ification of Christianity but the symbol of England itself" (*Oxford DNB*, 8:707). *The Holy War* contains valuable counsel on how to fight the good fight of faith. It will richly reward the meditative reader.

The Pilgrim's Progress (Reiner, 1974; BTT, 1983; BP, 1999). This is a moving, allegorical account of spiritual warfare expe-rienced by a wayfaring pilgrim traveling from the City of Destruction to the Celestial City, in which Bunyan allegorizes his own religious experience as a guide for others. "Christian is both pilgrim and warrior, and the message of *The Pilgrim's Progress* is not only a call to embrace and persist in the Chris-tian life, but also a summons to battle the forces of evil" (*Oxford DNB*, 8:705).

Bunyan's insights into mankind's desperate plight and God's redeeming grace make this a legendary classic. Regen-eration, faith, repentance, justification, mortification, sanctification, and perseverance are poignantly painted for us in biblical, doctrinal, experiential, and practical detail.

Among the more than two dozen reprints of Bunyan's classic since 1960, three are worthy of mention. First, an excel-lent edition of both parts of *Pilgrim's Progress* containing the invaluable explanatory notes of Thomas Scott, original mar-ginal notes, and textual support, has been reprinted by Reiner (1974), and is the most helpful edition. It includes a helpful 50-page memoir of Bunyan by Josiah Condor.

Second, Banner of Truth Trust published a deluxe edition in 1983, which includes original marginal notes and references from Scripture, both parts of *Pilgrim's Progress*, and a series of sketches by William Strang.

Third, Bunyan Press has issued a handsome, coffee-table volume containing the complete text of *Pilgrim's Progress* along with a beautiful collection of more than seventy oil paintings by Albert Wessels. This edition is excellent for helping children grasp the classic story. A number of retellings of Bunyan's famous story have been printed for children by other publishers.

Anthony Burgess

(d. 1664)

Anthony Burgess, "a pious, learned, and able scholar, a good disputant, a good tutor, an eminent preacher, a sound and orthodox divine" (Wallis, *Sermons*, p. 15), was born to the son of a schoolmaster at Watford, Hertfordshire. He entered St. John's College, Cambridge, in 1623, and graduated with a Bachelor of Arts degree in 1627. He then transferred to Emmanuel College, where he was elected to a fellowship, and earned a Master of Arts degree in 1630. In the early 1630s, Burgess tutored John Wallis, the future Savillian professor of geometry, who, like Burgess, would become a member of the Westminster Assembly, and William Jenkyn, best known as the author of a thorough exposition of Jude.

Burgess served as vicar of Sutton Coldfield, Warwickshire, from 1635 to 1662, except for some years in the 1640s. During the Civil War, the king's soldiers mercilessly persecuted Puritan ministers, ransacking their houses and evicting their families. Burgess fled to Coventry for safety from the king's army, where he became one of the chaplains to the parliamentary garrisons and associated with several godly ministers, including Richard Baxter.

From Coventry, Burgess joined the Westminster Assembly of Divines, where he became known for his theological astuteness and piety. During his years in London, he preached to Parliament on at least six occasions; these sermons show a thoroughly biblical emphasis, an emphasis on maintaining church discipline, and an abhorrence of antinomian errors. In 1645, he replaced the expelled Thomas Crane as vicar of the Guildhall church of St. Lawrence Jewry, where he established a congregational presbytery. In 1647, he signed the *Testimony* of the London Presbyterian ministers against the toleration of heresy. Wherever he went, he was esteemed as an eminent preacher as well as a solid divine.

After the Westminster Assembly finished its work in 1649, Burgess returned to Sutton Coldfield. Noting his potential to be a university professor, Bishop Hacket of Lichfield supposedly begged Burgess to give up his nonconformist views. Hacket was familiar with Burgess through his writings, which thoroughly analyze each subject he addressed. During a fifteen-year span (1646-1661), Burgess wrote at least a dozen books, based mainly on his sermons and lectures. His writings reveal a scholarly acquaintance with Aristotle, Seneca, Augustine, Aquinas, Luther, and Calvin. He made a judicious use of Greek and Latin quotations, while he still reasoned in the plain style of Puritan preaching. In Burgess, cultured scholar and experimental preacher combined to produce astute, warm, devotional writing.

Several of Burgess's major works have a strong polemic emphasis. His first major treatise, *Vindiciae Legis* (1646), based on twenty-nine lectures given at Lawrence Jewry, vindicated the Puritan view of the moral law and the covenants of works and grace in opposition to Roman Catholics, Arminians, Socinians, and especially, Antinomians. Two years later, Burgess wrote against the same opponents, plus Baxter, in his first volume on justification. He refuted Baxter's work for its Arminian tendencies that promoted a process of justification involving the cooperation of divine grace and human works. His second volume on justification, which appeared six years later (1654), discusses the natural righteousness of God and the imputed righteousness of Christ. Those two volumes contain seventy-five sermons. His 555-page *Doctrine of Original Sin* (1659) drew the Anabaptists into the fray.

Burgess wrote as a faithful steward of the mysteries of God. In addition to being a formidable polemicist, he excelled as an experimental writer. He masterfully separated the precious from the vile in *The Godly Man's Choice*, based on thirteen sermons on Psalm 4:6-8. His detailed exegesis in his 145-sermon work on John 17, his 300-page commentary on 1 Corinthians 3, and his 700-page commentary on 2 Corinthians 1 are heart-warming and heart-searching. They fulfill Burgess's goal to "endeavour the true and sound Exposition...so as to reduce all Doctrinals and controversials to practicals and experimentals, which is the life and soul of all" (Burgess, *Second Corinthians 1*, intro.).

Burgess was ejected by the Uniformity Act of 1662. Resisting a desire to form a conventicle, he retired to Tamworth, Staffordshire, where he attended the parish church of his friend, Samuel Langley, a godly but conformist minister, until his death in 1664.

Burgess has been seriously underestimated in church history. He is one of only a few of the main Puritan authors who did not have a nineteenth century reprint of their works. Many of his books are worthy of being reprinted today.

———◆◆◆———

Spiritual Refining: The Anatomy of True and False Conversion (IO; 2 vols., 1,100 pages; 1986-96). IO has recently done two 2-volume editions of Burgess's *Spiritual Refining* (1652-54). The first edition, a facsimile, contains the complete unabridged text of 1658. The second edition of *Spiritual Refining*, an abridged edition, is worth the investment for those who have difficulty reading facsimile print, though choice sections have been removed.

Burgess's *magnum opus* has been called an "unequaled anatomy of experimental religion." The first volume, subtitled *A Treatise of Grace and Assurance*, contains 120 sermons; the second, subtitled *A Treatise of Sin, with its Causes, Differences, Mitigations and Aggravations*, contains 42 sermons.

In the first section of the first volume, Burgess discusses assurance and refutes the antinomian error that internal marks of grace in a believer are no evidence of his justification. In our opinion, the first sixty pages of the facsimile edition is the best treatment on assurance in all Puritan literature. Here is one choice quotation in which Burgess shows the need to give priority to Christ and His promises rather than to the marks of grace in ascertaining one's assurance:

> We must take heed that we do not so gaze upon ourselves to find graces in our own hearts as thereby we forget those Acts of Faith, whereby we close with Christ immediately, and rely upon him only for our Justification.... The fear of this hath made some cry down totally the use of signs, to evidence our Justification. And the truth is, it cannot be denied but many of the children of God, while they are studying and examining, whether grace be in their souls, that upon the discovery thereof, they may have comfortable persuasions of their Justification, are very much neglective of those choice and principal Acts of Faith, whereby we have an acquiescency or recumbency upon Christ for our Acceptation with God. This is as if old Jacob should so rejoice in the Chariot Joseph sent, whereby he knew that he was alive, that he should not desire to see Joseph himself. Thus while thou art so full of joy, to perceive grace in thee, thou forgettest to joy in Christ himself, who is more excellent than all thy graces (1:41).

Sections two and three describe numerous signs of grace. The remaining nine sections of this volume discuss grace in terms of regeneration, the new creature, God's workmanship, grace in the heart, washing or sanctifying grace, conversion or turning unto God, taking away the stony heart, God's Spirit within us, and vocation or calling. Throughout, Burgess distinguished saving grace from its counterfeits.

In the second volume of *Spiritual Refining*, Burgess focuses on sin. He addresses the deceitfulness of the human heart, presumptuous and reigning sins, hypocrisy and formality in religion, the misguided conscience, and secret sins that often go unrecognized. Positively, he explains the tenderness of a gracious heart, showing "that a strict scrutiny into a man's heart and ways, with a holy fear of sinning, doth consist with a Gospel-life of faith and joy in the Holy Ghost." His goal, as stated on the title page, is to "unmask counterfeit Christians, terrify the ungodly, comfort and direct the doubting saint, humble man, [and] exalt the grace of God."

Speaking of regeneration, Burgess writes: "If God work (this) in you, you will be astonished to see the difference between yourself now and once; all that you have heard, read, or preached, is nothing to that you feel; but how is it to be feared, that many have seen godliness but in the *map* only, they never had experience of the thing itself."

Cotton Mather writes in his *Student and Preacher*: "Of A. Burgess, I may say, he has written for thee excellent things."

Jeremiah Burroughs

——◆◆◆——

(c. 1600-1646)

J eremiah Burroughs (or Burroughes) was baptized in 1601 and admitted as a pensioner at Emmanuel College, Cambridge, in 1617. He graduated with a Bachelor of Arts degree in 1621 and a Master of Arts degree in 1624. His tutor was Thomas Hooker.

Burroughs's ministry falls into four periods, all of which reveal him as a zealous and faithful pastor. First, from about 1627 until 1631, he was assistant to Edmund Calamy at Bury St. Edmunds, Suffolk. Both men became members of the Westminster Assembly. Both men strongly opposed King James's *Book of Sports.* Both refused to read the king's proclamation in church that dancing, archery, vaulting, and other games were lawful recreations on the Lord's Day.

Second, from 1631 to 1636, Burroughs was rector of Tivetshall, Norfolk, a church that still stands today. Despite the best efforts of his patron, Burroughs was suspended in 1636 and deprived in 1637 for refusing to obey the injunctions of Bishop Matthew Wren, especially regarding the reading of the *Book of Sports,* and the requirements to bow at the name of Jesus and to read prayers rather than speak them extemporaneously.

Third, from 1638 to 1640, Burroughs lived in the Netherlands, where he was teacher of a congregation of English

Independents at Rotterdam, formerly ministered by William Ames. William Bridge was the pastor and Sidrach Simpson had established a second like-minded church in the city. Thus, three future dissenting brethren were brought together, all of whom would serve as propagandists for congregationalism later in the 1640s.

In the final period from 1640 to his death in 1646, Burroughs achieved great recognition as a popular preacher and a leading Puritan in London. He returned to England during the Commonwealth period and became pastor of two of the largest congregations in London: Stepney and St. Giles, Cripplegate. At Stepney, he preached early in the morning and became known as "the morning star of Stepney." He was invited to preach before the House of Commons and the House of Lords several times. Thomas Brooks called him "a prince of preachers."

As a member of the Westminster Assembly, Burroughs sided with the Independents, but he remained moderate in tone, acting in accord with the motto on his study door: *Opinionum varietas et opinantium unitas non sunt hasustata* ("variety of opinion and unity of opinion are not incompatible"). Richard Baxter said, "If all the Episcopalians had been like Archbishop Ussher, all the Presbyterians like Stephen Marshall, and all the Independents like Jeremiah Burroughs, the breaches of the church would soon have been healed."

In 1644, Burroughs and several colleagues presented to Parliament their *Apologetical Narration*, which defended Independency. It attempted to steer a middle course between Presbyterianism, which they regarded as too authoritarian, and Brownism, which they regarded as too democratic. This led to division between the Presbyterians and Independents. Burroughs served on the committee of accommodation, which tried to reconcile the differences, but on March 9, 1646, he declared on behalf of the Independents that presbyteries were "coercive institutions." Burroughs said he would rather suffer or emigrate than submit to presbyteries. Ultimately, the division between Presbyterians and Independents helped promote the cause of prelacy after the death of Oliver Cromwell.

Burroughs pursued peace to the end. He died in 1646, two weeks after a fall from his horse. The last subject on which he preached became his *Irenicum to the Lovers of Truth and Peace*, an attempt to heal divisions between believers. Many of his friends believed that church troubles hastened his death.

Burroughs was a prolific writer, highly esteemed by Puritan leaders of his day, some of whom published his writings after his death. Nearly all of his books are compilations of sermons.

The Evil of Evils, or The Exceeding Sinfulness of Sin (SDG; 345 pages; 1999). This book, first printed in 1654, consists of sixty-seven short chapters that expose sin and urge believers to choose affliction over sin. Burroughs organizes his material around seven major thoughts: (1) there is more evil in the least sin than in the greatest affliction; (2) sin and God are contrary to each other; (3) sin is directly against our good; (4) sin opposes all that is good; (5) sin is the evil of all other evils; (6) sin has infinite dimension and character; and (7) sin makes us comfortable with the devil. *Evil of Evils* is invaluable for sensitizing our consciences to the "exceeding sinfulness of sin" (cf. Rom. 7:13).

The Excellency of a Gracious Spirit (SDG; 260 pages; 1995). Based on Numbers 14:24 ("Caleb was of another spirit; he followed God fully"), this book is divided into two parts: (1) what this gracious spirit is, and (2) what it means to follow God fully. Burroughs says we must strive to live in the fear of the Lord to depart from evil and draw closer to Him. Living out of godly fear is the sum and substance of a gracious spirit.

An Exposition of the Prophecy of Hosea (SDG; 699 pages; 1990). This mammoth exposition of Hosea is one of Burroughs's finest works. This edition is a facsimile reprint of the 1863 James Sherman edition. Burroughs died before finishing the work, but two of his closest friends, Thomas Hall and Edward Reynolds, finished the commentary. Spurgeon called this work "masterly," noting that it is "a vast treasure-house of experimental exposition." No work on Hosea has since superseded this commentary.

Gospel Conversation (SDG; 310 pages; 1995). This masterful treatise deals with the right living of believers. It includes seven sermons on Philippians 1:27 ("Let your conversation be as becometh the gospel of Christ"), three on John 18:36 ("My kingdom is not of this world"), and a sermon on Exodus 14:13, titled "The Saints' Duty in Times of Extremity."

Burroughs moves the reader to mourn his alienated state and yearn for the spring of holiness, union, and communion with Christ. He stresses there can be no works of sanctification before union with Christ. But once in Christ, the Christian must give evidence of that union by fervently pursuing the pious life to which God calls him. Good works are dangerous if they are made the foundation of justification, but are necessary and useful in sanctification. The conversation and conduct of believers must be on a higher plane than that of unbelievers.

Gospel Fear: Developing a Tender Heart that Trembles at the Word of God (SDG; 147 pages; 2001). The concept of reverence has nearly been forgotten in our day, even by many who regard themselves as Christians. We are irreverent because we are ignorant of God and His holiness. As Burroughs writes, "The reason men worship God in a slight way is because they do not see God in His glory." These sermons (on Isaiah 66:2, "he that trembleth at my word" and on 2 Kings 22:19, "because thine heart was tender") are a corrective to prevailing ignorance. The entire volume shows our need for reverence and awe towards God and His Word.

Gospel Reconciliation (SDG; 379 pages; 1997). There is no more important issue for any one than how to be right with God. In this treatise of eighty-one chapters on 2 Corinthians 5:19, 20 ("God was in Christ reconciling the world unto himself"), Burroughs answers questions about reconciliation. Christ's atoning work is the only way for fallen sinners to be reconciled with God, for a finite creature can never satisfy the justice of an infinite God. Burroughs explains the consequences of our reconciliation in Christ, showing that this reconciliation is a deep mystery, that it is free, sure, full, honorable, firm, and eternal, but also a difficult work, for we are only saved by divine accomplishment, not by human achievement.

Gospel Remission (SDG; 310 pages; 1995). Subtitled *True Blessedness Consists in Pardon of Sin*, this first-time reprint consists of a series of sermons on Psalm 32:1, which Burroughs preached after finishing his masterpiece on sin, *The Evil of Evils*. As a tender pastor, Burroughs knew that after hearing about the deadly nature of sin, his congregation would need to hear about the remission of sins offered in the gospel. Burroughs covers five areas of forgiveness: (1) the many gospel mysteries in remission; (2) the glorious effects proceeding from remission; (3) the great mistakes made about remission; (4) the true signs and symptoms of remission; and (5) the ways and means to obtain remission. Burroughs stresses the dishonor done to God by not resting on the mercy of His remission.

Gospel Worship (SDG; 400 pages; 1990). Subtitled *The Right Manner of Sanctifying the Name of God in General*, this treatise on Leviticus 10:1-3 is a call to propriety and sobriety in the worship of God. It deals with the believer's sanctification through "three great ordinances": (1) hearing the Word, (2) receiving the Lord's Supper, and (3) prayer. In a day that promotes man-made forms of worship, *Gospel Worship* is a call to biblical worship of the Triune God through the means that He has instituted. Burroughs shows how important worship is to God and teaches us how to "give unto the Lord the glory due unto his name" (Ps. 29:2). He makes plain that we do not need new forms of worship to be relevant, but to renew old forms of worship.

Hope (SDG; 150 pages; 2005). This treatise on 1 John 3:3, "And every man that hath this hope in him purifieth himself," first establishes that every believer is a hopeful person; second, explains that where true hope resides, it will purge the heart; and third, provides ten ways in which believers can purify themselves by hope. Burroughs also shows the origin, object, and ground of hope. The book concludes with an exhortation to put away sin. This is a timely, succinct masterpiece for our impure world, lost in sin and full of despair.

Appendixed to *Hope* is a 63-page sermon by Burroughs on the misery of those who have hope only in this life, based on Psalm 17:14b, "From men of the world, which have their portion in this life."

Irenicum to the Lovers of Truth and Peace (SDG; 440 pages; 1998). Subtitled, *Heart-divisions opened in the causes and evils of them, with cautions that we may not be hurt by them, and endeavors to heal them,* this volume contains the last sermons Burroughs preached before his death. Burroughs pleads for unity among his brethren, addresses the issues that seriously divided believers in his day, and offers practical ways to promote unity. He explains when one should plead his conscience, provides rules to know in what areas we are to bear with our brethren, and shows that "every difference in religion is not a differing religion." He discusses the role of pride, self-love, envy, anger, rigidity, rashness, willfulness, inconsistency, jealousy, contentiousness, covetousness, and gossip in division. He concludes that the answer for division does not lie in blanket tolerance of all religions nor in a compromising attitude towards sin, but in a biblical striving for peace. Given the divisiveness of Christians in all generations, this treatise is extremely applicable.

The Rare Jewel of Christian Contentment (BTT; 228 pages; 2000). In this book on contentment (Philippians 4:1, "I have learned in whatsoever state I am, therewith to be content"), Burroughs presents two major themes: (1) peace among believers of various persuasions, and (2) peace and contentment in the hearts of believers during "sad and sinking times."

Burroughs expounds what Christian contentment is (chap. 1), unveils its mystery (chaps. 2-4), shows how Christ teaches it (chaps. 5-6), and describes ten of its fruits (chap. 7). He then addresses the evils and aggravations of discontentment (chaps. 8-11). He concludes by showing how to attain contentment (chaps. 12-13). This classic provides numerous practical remedies for the spiritual disease of discontent.

The Saints' Happiness (SDG; 264 pages; 1988). This book offers a detailed exposition of the Beatitudes in forty-one sermons. Though Burroughs does not match Thomas Watson in popular appeal or Robert Harris in exegetical skill on the Beatitudes, his work is a significant contribution for proper understanding of these important marks of spiritual life.

The Saints' Treasury (SDG; 175 pages; 1994). This is a compilation of five sermons on the holiness of God, Christ as all in all, faith's enjoyment of heavenly things, the natural man's bondage to the law and the believer's liberty by the Gospel, and preparation for judgment.

A Treatise of Earthly-Mindedness (SDG; 220 pages; 1998). A timely reprint for our earthly-minded age, this book contains two treatises: a serious warning against the evils of being earthly minded; an explanation on how to "get our hearts free from earthly-mindedness"; and a discussion on what it means to be heavenly-minded, with an accent on living godly in Christ Jesus. Several chapters deal with how to foster heavenly conversation and a heavenly walk.

Nicholas Byfield

(1579-1622)

Nicholas Byfield was born in 1579 in Warwickshire, the son of Richard Byfield, who later became vicar of Stratford-upon-Avon. He entered Exeter College, Oxford, in 1596, where he studied for four years without taking a degree. Eventually, he determined to secure a living in Ireland; on his way there, he stopped to preach at St. Peter's in Chester. After preaching there, he accepted an invitation to become lecturer, and in 1608, became curate. His ministry there was highly esteemed, despite opposition from the bishop of Chester.

About this time, Byfield married Elizabeth Tomkyns, who bore him ten children, the last of whom he did not live to see. In 1615, Byfield was presented with the living as vicar of Isleworth, Middlesex, where he labored diligently with considerable fruit until his death. He preached there twice each Lord's Day and on Wednesdays and Fridays in the summer, despite chronic problems with kidney stones for fifteen years. He died on September 8, 1622, from a huge kidney stone.

In addition to his massive work on Colossians noted below, Byfield wrote at least sixteen books, including classic Puritan devotionals, such as *The Pattern of Wholesome Words* (1618), *The Marrow of the Oracles of God* (1627), and an extensive commentary on First Peter, finally published in its full form in 1637. His *The Beginning of the Doctrine of Christ, or, A Catalogue of Sins* (1619) furthered the conviction among many Puritans that a knowledge of oneself is prerequisite to a knowledge of Christ. In response to challenges presented against Byfield's strict

Sabbath views by Edward Brerewood, an astronomer and mathematician, Byfield wrote one of the earliest of several Puritan apologies for the keeping of a Sunday Sabbath (1626).

Byfield was a moderate Puritan and "a nonconformist at heart who conformed for the sake of the gospel and for the sake of the church, disapproving of the 'contentious zeal' of those who 'make needless rents in the church' (*Exposition upon Colossians*, 1628 edition, p. 194), and advising his parishioners to conform as long as the required ceremonies and customs were not in opposition to the word of God" (*Oxford DNB*, 9:305). Byfield was known for his excellent scholarship, judgment, and aptitude, in addition to his ministerial skills. William Gouge wrote of him as a pastor, "When he had to do with tender and troubled consciences, he was a Barnabas, a son of comfort; but when he had to do with impudent and obstinate sinners, he could make his face hard and strong, and show himself like a Boanerges, the son of thunder" (preface to sermons on 1 Peter 2).

An Exposition upon the Epistle to the Colossians (TENT; 413 pages; 2002). For nearly seven years Byfield preached every week from Colossians. This massive commentary is based on those 300-plus sermons. It was first published in London in 1615 and reprinted in 1617, 1627, 1628, and 1649. In 1869, the book was included in Nichol's series of standard divines. Byfield's contemporaries considered the work a clear and faithful exposition of Paul's epistle.

Spurgeon wrote of Byfield: "The author lived in intense pain and died at 44, yet he produced quite a mountain of literature. He writes like an earnest, faithful man, resolved to keep back nothing of the counsel of God; but he too little studies brevity, and consequently he wearies most readers, but is always worth consulting."

Thomas Cartwright
(1535-1603)

Thomas Cartwright, leader of the Elizabethan Presbyterian movement and an early English Puritan, was probably born in Royston, Hertfordshire, in 1535. He was educated at Clare Hall, and then at St. John's College, Cambridge, where he was elected a scholar in 1550, and graduated with a Bachelor of Arts degree in 1554. He probably left the Marian university in 1556 to earn his living as clerk to a counselor-at-law.

After Elizabeth came to the throne in 1558, Cartwright returned to St. John's, Cambridge; he was admitted to a fellowship in 1560. In June he commenced a Master of Arts program at Trinity College, and became a fellow there in 1562. When Elizabeth visited the college in 1564, she supposedly listened to a debate in which Cartwright argued that God's sovereignty did not need the support of a monarchical form of government. The Queen was not pleased, though she took no action against him.

The return of the Marian exiles generated considerable agitation as many of them sought for further reformation of the Church of England. Questions about worship and the polity of the Church of England moved Cartwright to preach in the college chapel three sermons that promoted further reform. Three hundred of the scholars and fellows of St. John's and Trinity attended those services without their surplices—a bold and dangerous move in those days.

Partly because of the tense atmosphere that ensued, Cartwright left Cambridge in 1565 to serve as chaplain to Adam Loftus, the new archbishop of Armagh, in Ireland. He returned to Cambridge in 1567, where he took the degree of Bachelor of Theology and became a renowned university professor. Two years later, he was appointed Lady Margaret Professor of Divinity. He promptly provoked controversy with his lectures on the Book of Acts, in which he argued from New Testament principles that Presbyterianism should replace the prelatic system of the Church of England. He said that prelates such as archbishops and archdeacons should be removed and a Presbyterian form of church government should be adopted. Every church should be governed by its own minister(s) and elders, who should be chosen by the church rather than the state. Moreover, ministers should be responsible for only one church. He also said that observance of Lent, signing with the cross at baptism, and kneeling at the Lord's Supper should be abolished, since they were remnants of popish superstition. Until these kinds of reforms were implemented, he concluded, the reformation of the church in England would remain incomplete.

John Whitgift, master and vice-chancellor of Trinity and a notorious foe of Puritanism, opposed Cartwright from the pulpit. Other authorities censured Cartwright, in part to avoid further disruption of the peace. Cartwright lost his professorship in 1570, and when Whitgift became vice-chancellor in 1571, he lost his fellowship as well. The stated reasons for his expulsion were that he maintained (1) it was necessary to reduce all things to the apostolic institution; (2) only ministers ought to pray publicly in the church and administer sacraments; (3) only canonical Scripture ought to be read publicly in the church; (4) all worshipers should attend to the prayers of the minister and not their own; and (5) standing or bowing when the Scriptures were read was superstitious.

The Elizabethan Puritans viewed Cartwright as a hero of their cause and pressed for the implementation of his reform program. Meanwhile, expelled from Cambridge, Cartwright traveled to Geneva, where Theodore Beza said of him, "I think the sun does not see a more learned man."

When Cartwright returned to England a year later, he again faced the wrath of Whitgift when he espoused the cause of the writers of *An Admonition to the Parliament*, John Field and Thomas Wilcocks, two young Puritan ministers who had been cast into prison. He also published *A Second Admonition*, which asked for relief from the subscription required by the ecclesiastical commissioners. Cartwright engaged in a pamphlet war with Whitgift, which eventually led to the issuing of a warrant for his arrest in 1573.

Forced into exile again, Cartwright went abroad once more, first to Heidelberg and then to Basel. From there, he went to Antwerp, where he served as a minister in an English church structured along Presbyterian lines and founded by a company of English merchants, and then followed the merchants to Middelburg when they moved there. In the midst of all these moves and trials, Cartwright married Alice Stubbs, the sister of a friend, who served him as a godly helpmeet for the remainder of his life.

Though he remained a Presbyterian by conviction until the end of his life, Cartwright did not separate from the Church of England. During his time abroad, he acquired distaste for the separatism and sectarianism that he encountered. He still regarded the Church of England as a true church, and by 1576 he held that ministers should not abandon their posts for the sake of offensive ceremonies, since preaching is always more important than rituals or ceremonies. To the end, he sought to balance the local church's autonomy with the need for wider and more visible unity without resorting to a prelatic system.

In 1582, Robert Dudley, Earl of Leicester, upon the advice of Theodore Beza, commissioned Cartwright to write a critique of the Douai New Testament, the Roman Catholic translation published that year. Cartwright went as far as Revelation 15 before his death. His work was eventually published posthumously in 1618 as *A Confutation of the Rhemist's Translation.*

Cartwright returned to England without Elizabeth's permission in 1585 because of ill health and was briefly imprisoned. After Cartwright's release, the earl of Leicester appointed him master of a new hospital at Warwick. He preached frequently in the area and remained there until Whitgift's final crackdown on Presbyterians in 1590. Imprisoned again (1591-1592), Cartwright's release was secured by King James and Lord Burghley. He apparently returned to the Warwick area, but also preached in various places, including Cambridge, where he brought God's Word to large congregations.

In 1595, Lord Zouche of Guernsey invited Cartwright to accompany him to the Channel Islands, which were amenable to Presbyterianism. There Cartwright became acquainted with William Bradshaw. He also corresponded with numerous Puritan divines, including Laurence Chaderton.

Cartwright returned to Warwick, where he spent his final days. On December 25, 1603, he preached from Ecclesiastes 12:7, "Then shall the dust return to the earth as it was; and the spirit shall return unto God who gave it." Two days later, after spending two hours in prayer, he told his wife moments before he died that he found "wonderful and unutterable joy and comfort, for God had given a glimpse of heaven." Of his sixty-eight years, Cartwright spent twenty in exile and three in prison.

Cartwright's influence was foundational for Presbyterianism and Puritanism. Charles Briggs wrote, "Thomas Cartwright is the hero of Presbyterianism in England, laying the foundations of Puritanism broad and deep, upon which a great structure was subsequently erected." John Strype said, "Cartwright was the head and most learned of that sect of dissenters then called Puritans." And Patrick Collinson concludes that Cartwright "was the true progenitor of English Presbyterianism" (*Oxford DNB*, 9:413).

———◆◆◆———

A Commentary on the Epistle to the Colossians [Bound with Henry Airay's commentary on Philippians] (TENT; 67 pages; 2001). Though small in size and compiled from a listener's notes on thirty-one sermons, it contains, as Spurgeon says, "the true ring" of rich spirituality. Unfortunately, the collection was never read by the preacher and thus lacks refinement. Nevertheless, Alexander B. Grosart, a later editor of Cartwright, said the commentary was "well put and suggestive."

Joseph Caryl

(1602-1673)

Joseph Caryl was born in London in 1602 to aristocratic parents. He was educated at Exeter College, Oxford, where he became a noted debater, earning his Bachelor of Arts degree in 1625 and a master's in 1627. He first served as curate of Battersea, Surrey. From 1632 to 1648, he served as lecturer at Lincoln's Inn, London, an appointment he received because he was "puritanically affected," and was received with "good liking and applause" (Wood, *Athenae Oxonienses*, 3:979).

Caryl preached before the Long Parliament fourteen times in the 1640s. He was second only to Stephen Marshall in the number of times he appeared before that body. In April 1642, Parliament called an assembly of divines to decide the faith, government, and liturgy of the national church. The Independents hesitated, fearing their consciences would be bound. Thomas Goodwin and Joseph Caryl even used the pulpit of Parliament to preach against the adoption of a church polity that would threaten their beliefs concerning the true worship and service of God.

Caryl was appointed a member of the Westminster Assembly of Divines. He became known as a zealous supporter of the Solemn League and Covenant, a moderate Independent, and a defender of the view that there should be an office of church teacher ("doctor") alongside of and distinct from the office of pastor. He was the only Independent asked by Parliament to serve on a committee to check the rise of antinomianism. Caryl became one of the triers responsible for approving ministers to fill vacant churches. He also became a licenser to approve theological material for the press.

In 1645, Caryl succeeded Cornelius Burgess as minister of St. Magnus the Martyr, near London Bridge, where he served for seventeen years. During those years, he undertook an impressive number of tasks. He published a Greek grammar in 1658, and three years later, was the principal author of an English-Greek lexicon. From 1649 to 1660, he served as one of the preachers of Westminster Abbey. He also served Parliament in a variety of ways, and became a friend of Oliver Cromwell. After the restoration of the monarchy, Caryl was ejected from his living in 1662 for his nonconformist views. For the last decade of his life, he served an Independent congregation in London. In 1672, he was licensed to preach for a congregation of 136 communicants in Leadenhall Street, London.

Caryl died peacefully, in full assurance of faith, on February 25, 1673, and was buried at College Hill. In his last moments, he asked to be alone. After his death, his congregation merged with John Owen's in Leadenhall Street. David Clarkson and Isaac Watts succeeded him. Henry Dorney, author of *Divine Contemplations*, said of his colleague, "He lived his sermons."

———◆◆◆———

Bible Thoughts (SDG; 252 pages; 1995). Caryl is best known today for his preaching on Job. Those sermons were published over a sixteen-year period (1651-66) in twelve volumes of more than eight thousand pages. In the nineteenth century, Ingram Cobbin chose excerpts from Caryl's sermons of Job and arranged them under scriptural headings. *Bible Thoughts* is the result of that work.

For 1 Corinthians 13:7 ("Charity believeth all things"), Caryl writes, "Not that charity is so credulous as to take up every thing for truth which is scattered by any common and ungrounded report; that is no commendation in any man, much less is it the commendation of a godly man. The meaning is, charity interprets every thing in the best sense which it will bear; and makes the fairest construction which every man's case and condition will admit."

An Exposition of Job (SGP; 367 pages; 1959). This is a one-volume abridgement of the 12-volume work below. Like most abridgements, it is helpful for core thoughts but is no substitute for the larger work.

An Exposition upon the Book of Job (RHB and DA; 12 vols., 8,000 pages; 2001). This facsimile reprint is the first time Caryl's mammoth work on Job has been reprinted since the seventeenth century. The first ten volumes of Caryl's work are sermons that he preached at St. Magnus; the last two were completed after the Act of Uniformity. Believing that the Book of Job was relevant to the times, Caryl preached from it 424 times over a period of twenty-four years, averaging ten sermons per chapter.

It has been said that his congregation dwindled significantly during that time. History, however, affords no evidence to confirm this report. Besides, one must bear in mind that, over those twenty-four years, Caryl preached an average of three sermons on Job every two months.

Caryl's sermons are full of exegetical insights, experiential descriptions, and poignant applications. In true Puritan style, he brings all of Scripture and Reformed doctrine to bear on a text. His work is thus commentary combined with a comprehensive work on practical Christian living; it is a treasure of practical divinity. Because of its exposition, doctrinal content, organization, and Christ-centered focus, Caryl's work on Job has been called "the crown jewel of Puritan preaching."

His prefaces are also invaluable. They summarize the chapters explained in the volume and shed light on his hermeneutics and pastoral perspectives. For example, in the first preface, Caryl explains the contemporary relevance of the Book of Job. In the preface of the sixth volume, he stresses that preachers must promote righteousness by expounding true doctrine, reproving error, correcting evil habits, and promoting holiness. He stresses the need to compare Scripture with Scripture and refutes the notion that God does not use commentators and preachers to shed light on His Word throughout the generations. He acknowledges that human expositors, by no means infallible, are no better than spectacles for the vision-impaired compared to the clear view of truth that saints will enjoy in the coming glory. But, he argues, "'Tis no wisdom for a dim-sighted man presently, to throw away his spectacles, though he be assured that within a while his eye-sight shall be cleared."

In the preface of the tenth volume (Job 32-34), Caryl defends Elihu and asserts that his address, as well as the entire Book of Job, may be summarized in six propositions:

1. No man can stand before God in his own righteousness.

2. God may afflict people, no matter how godly they may be, in whatever way and to whatever degree He deems fitting.

3. God's goals in afflicting believers are always wise and gracious.

4. Believers may not complain against God, as if He were "rigorous or unrighteous in the least," no matter how much or how long they are afflicted.

5. Complaining under or fighting against the afflicting hand of God yields no profit.

6. We should possess our souls with patience by glorifying God as just and good, even when everything seems to be going terribly wrong for us. We must wait by faith upon God until He grants a fresh experience of His goodness, either by "sweetening our troubles" and supporting us under them, or by bringing us out of them at His time.

Here's what others have said about Caryl's work on Job:

Spurgeon: "Caryl must have inherited the patience of Job to have completed his stupendous task. It would be a mistake to suppose that he is at all prolix or redundant; he is only full. In the course of his expounding he has illustrated a very large portion of the whole Bible with great clearness and power. He is deeply devotional and spiritual. He gives us much, but none too much. His work can scarcely be superseded or surpassed."

James Reid, an early nineteenth-century historian: "The whole work is strongly marked [by] sound judgment, extensive erudition, and genuine piety." In a memoir of Caryl, Reid said he had seen both editions of Caryl's commentary in the libraries of gospel ministers in various parts of Scotland and in many families. He recommended that it be included in the library of every minister and student of theology.

James I. Packer: "Caryl's control of his vast and complex canvas is masterly; he never loses the threads of the argument himself, nor permits his readers to lose sight of it, nor, in all his microscopic study of verbal detail and his proliferation of edifying inferences, does he go beyond the scope of his text. His analyses of the debate between Job and his friends in particular are models of lucid exposition."

Thomas Case
(1598-1682)

Thomas Case was born in 1598 in Boxley, Kent. His father, George Case, was vicar of Boxley. Thomas began praying for salvation in earnest when he was six years old. In 1616, he began his studies at Christ Church College, Oxford, where he earned a Bachelor of Arts degree in 1620 and a master's degree in 1623. He stayed at the university a few more years, preaching in the vicinity of Oxford and then in Kent.

In 1626, Case was ordained in the diocese of Norwich. He then took up a curacy in Northrepps, Norfolk, with Richard Heyrick, a close friend from Case's Oxford days who would also become a member of the Westminster Assembly. In 1629, Case moved six miles away to become rector at Erpingham, Norfolk. He served there for nearly ten years. In his last years there, he encountered considerable opposition from Bishop Matthew Wren, who started proceedings against Case in the High Commission Court. That court was abolished while charges against Case were still pending.

While at Erpingham, Case married Ann Pots. She died after a few years, before bearing children. In 1635, Case became minister of the collegiate church of Manchester. Many churches opened their pulpits to him in that area; large crowds attended his preaching. In 1637, he married Ann Mosley, who came from a family of considerable Puritan influence in the northwest of England. Through his wife he came into even wider circles of influence, though he also encountered more persecution.

The House of Commons recommended Case as lecturer of St. Martin's-in-the-Fields in 1641. He preached there for nearly twenty years on Sabbath afternoons and Thursday evenings. He was also appointed lecturer at St. Mary Aldermanbury, where Edmund Calamy served as rector. In those positions, Case zealously promoted the Solemn League and Covenant. He often preached before the Long Parliament, stressing the need for laws in the church and commonwealth that were consistent with God's laws.

Case served in the Westminster Assembly, where he played a major role in the discussions, especially in promoting Presbyterianism. From the beginning of the assembly, he was one of the most ardent of the English Puritans for Presbyterianism.

In 1645, Case became rector in neighboring Stockport, Cheshire, his wife's hometown. The appointment lasted only nine months, however; he was asked to be rector of St. Mary Magdalene Church in Milk Street, London, where he had preached occasionally. Case became more opposed to episcopal government during that time. He was convinced that the Church of England was the Babylon of Revelation 18:4, with all its "idolatrous bowings, cringings, altars, crosses, and cursed ceremonies, false worship, [and] false doctrine."

During the Civil War, Case received more prayer requests from church members for relatives and friends of the earl of Essex's army than he could fulfill in regular services. So he began an early morning service for this purpose. The services soon multiplied and spread to other parts of London. Ministers accompanied these "Morning Exercises," as they came to be called, with fervent prayer for soldiers and their families. After the war was over, the services continued, but focused on eminent ministers offering spiritual counsel on pertinent questions by means of preaching or lecturing. Eventually the Morning Exercises were moved to Cripplegate, where they were continued by Samuel Annesley, grandfather of John and Charles Wesley. Later, they were published and have recently been republished in six volumes by Richard Owen Roberts as *Puritan Sermons* (see below).

In 1648, Case spoke out strongly against the Independents both in the army and in Parliament. He signed a document titled, *A Vindication of the Ministers of the Gospel in and about London*, which opposed the actions of the army that led to the trial and execution of the king. In 1651, he was imprisoned in the Tower of London for five months for preaching against the proceedings of Parliament and because of his perceived association with Christopher Love. His property was also seized. His wife was given permission to live with him in the tower. Just before his trial date, Case addressed Parliament, and what he said was deemed "sufficiently submissive" to earn his discharge. His prison meditations were published as *Correction, Instruction* the following year.

Upon his release, Case became lecturer at the large church of St. Giles in the Fields. When the rector, Abraham Molyne, died in 1654, Case succeeded to the rectorship, a position that he held until he was ejected in 1662 for Nonconformity. While still at St. Giles in 1660, Case went with Edmund Calamy, Thomas Manton, Edward Reynolds, and William Spurstowe as part of the Presbyterian delegation to Charles II in the Netherlands. They were well received, and Case became one of the Presbyterian ministers appointed as a royal chaplain.

Case was also a member of the Savoy Conference (1661). After his ejection from the pulpit, he remained in London, preaching whenever he had the opportunity and promoting the Puritan and Presbyterian causes. In 1676, Case was among the signers of Richard Baxter's *The Judgment of Nonconformists of the Interest of Reason in Matters of Religion*, which appealed for unity among the brethren.

Case outlived all the members of the Westminster Assembly except one, dying on May 30, 1682, at the ripe age of 84. He was buried at Christ Church in London, near Richard Baxter, who called Case an "old faithful servant of God."

Edmund Calamy described Case as "one of a quick and warm spirit, an open plain-hearted man, a hearty lover of God, goodness, and all good men." He added, "He was a scriptural preacher, a great man in prayer, and one who brought home many souls to God" (*Nonconformist's Memorial*, 1:154).

⇒◆◆◆⇐

The Select Works of Thomas Case (SDG; 432 pages; 1997). Case's two major works, *A Treatise of Afflictions* and *A Prospect of Heaven*, were reprinted and updated in 1836 by the Religious Tract Society of London. Soli Deo Gloria has combined those works in one volume, which is a photolithograph of the 1836 editions. *A Treatise of Afflictions* is based on Psalm 94:12: "Blessed is the man whom thou chastenest, O Lord, and teachest him out of thy law." The theme of the book is, "that man is a blessed man, whose chastisements are joined with divine teachings; or, it is a blessed thing when correction and instruction go together. The rod and the Word make up a complete blessing" (p. 14). Case penned this treatise while imprisoned in the Tower of London. Believing that experience was greatly used by God for his own soul, Case preached about it so convincingly upon his release that Thomas Manton wrote in the preface to the book: "I could even envy your prison comforts."

A Prospect of Heaven is based on 1 Thessalonians 4:13-18 and is subtitled *Mount Pisgah; or, Words of Comfort on the Death of our Gracious Relations*. After explaining the foundations of a believer's prospects for heaven in the soul's vital union with Christ (pp. 13-36), which alone is worth the price of the book, Case offers valuable instruction on Christ's second coming, the resurrection of all people, the final judgment, and the comfort of believers in heaven.

Stephen Charnock

(1628-1680)

Stephen Charnock was born in 1628, the son of Richard Charnock, an attorney in the parish of St. Katharine Cree, London. After preparatory studies, Charnock entered Emmanuel College, Cambridge, in 1642 under the tutorship of William Sancroft, who later became archbishop of Canterbury. While at Cambridge, Charnock experienced new birth in Christ and was imbued with the desire to spread the gospel to all people. He earned a Bachelor of Arts degree in 1646. In the late 1640s, he spent some time as chaplain in a private family and undertook a ministry in Southwark, London.

Charnock moved to Oxford to become a fellow at New College (1650), where he graduated with a Master of Arts degree in 1652 and was appointed proctor in 1654. He was a diligent student, specializing in biblical languages, Reformed and scholastic theology, patristics, and philosophy. While in Oxford he belonged to a church gathered within the university by Thomas Goodwin.

In 1655, Charnock accompanied Henry Cromwell (Oliver Cromwell's son and the governor of Ireland) to Ireland as a chaplain, where, Calamy writes, he had "all the gentry and persons of quality in the city for his auditors." His sermons, delivered without notes, made a profound impact.

Charnock returned to England in 1660. He lost his post during the Restoration and lived for fifteen years in the London area without a pastoral charge, reportedly providing an income by practicing medicine. He made occasional preaching itineraries in the Netherlands and France, possibly in part to elude arrest due to the government's insinuations that he was involved in a conspiracy to seize Dublin Castle. In 1666, Charnock lost his entire library in the great fire of London. Throughout these years, however, he continued to study and write, becoming, in the words of Calamy, "a very considerable scholar and an eminent divine," noted for his personal piety and his extraordinary command of the original languages of Scripture.

In 1675, Charnock became co-pastor with Thomas Watson of a nonconformist congregation at Crosby Hall, Bishopsgate Street, London. He remained there until his death in 1680. During his last years, his ministry faltered as his memory and sight failed. He resorted to using extensive notes on the pulpit and had to use a magnifying glass to read them. His sermons also became difficult for ordinary people to follow. Ministers and discerning laypeople, however, continued to benefit from his sermons to the end.

The only work that Charnock published in his lifetime was the sermon "The Sinfulness and Cure of Evil Thoughts." It was included in the Cripplegate Exercises, republished by Richard Owen Roberts as *Puritan Sermons*. After Charnock's death, his Oxford friends, Richard Adams and Edward Veal, prepared his manuscripts for publishing. They filled two large folio volumes, which subsequently became five octavo volumes in reprint.

Christ Crucified: A Puritan's View of Atonement (CFP; 207 pages; 1996). Edited and introduced by Maurice Roberts, this edition is easier to read than the original work. Linking the Old and New Testaments, Charnock explains how Christ's sacrifice fulfills the Old Testament requirements. He particularly illustrates the importance of the Passover and shows how Christ is *the* Passover for believers. These sermons focus on the Lord's Supper (its end, subjects, unworthy receiving, and self-examination) and Christ's death (its voluntariness, acceptableness, and necessity).

Divine Providence (IO; 150 pages; 2005). Based on 2 Chronicles 16:9, Charnock explains God's providence with depth of insight, and presents its various uses with pastoral and experiential care. This is a standard Puritan treatment of providence, second only to that of John Flavel's *Mystery of Providence*. This present reprint is taken from the 1864 James Nichol edition of Charnock's *Complete Works*.

The Doctrine of Regeneration (GM; 306 pages; 2000). This treatise proceeds from the necessity of regeneration to its nature, its author (God as the sufficient author and sole agent), and its instrument, the gospel. Charnock closes the book with these words: "Before you wait upon God in any ordinance, plead with him as Moses did in another case, to what purpose should I go, unless thy presence go with me?"

The Existence and Attributes of God (Baker; 1,149 pages; 2000). Originally a private journal, this voluminous and magisterial work was first published in 1681-1682 as volume 1 and 2 of his works in the Nichol series (without Charnock's essay on providence). It is a treasure of sound theology, profound thinking, and humble adoration of God. The following discourses are included: the existence of God, practical atheism, God as Spirit, spiritual worship, the eternity of God, the immutability of God, God's omnipresence, God's knowledge, the wisdom of God, the power of God, the holiness of God, the goodness of God, God's dominion, and God's patience.

J. I. Packer writes of this classic, "The discourses are the product of a big, strong, deep, reverent mind; they are in every way worthy of their sublime subject and are one of the noblest productions of the Puritan epoch. Charnock displays God's attributes as qualities observable in the concrete actions of the living God of which the Bible speaks. The technical terms, and sometimes, arguments of scholastic theology are employed, but always with a biblical orientation. Charnock has no desire to speculate but only to declare the works and ways, the nature and character, of the God of the Bible" (*Encyclopedia of Christianity*, 2:411).

This is *the* work on the character and attributes of God. It should be read by every serious Christian. The twelfth discourse on the goodness of God, covering nearly 150 pages, is unsurpassed in all of English literature.

This edition is prefaced with an interesting account of Charnock's life and character by William Symington. Charnock spent the last three years of his life writing his *magnum opus*. Apparently, he intended to preach an entire "body of divinity" but he came no further than the attributes of God before being translated to glory at the age of fifty-two.

The Knowledge of God (BTT; 604 pages; 1995). This fourth volume of Charnock's works contains the following discourses: the knowledge of God, the knowledge of God in Christ, conviction of sin, unbelief, the misery of unbelievers, signs of unbelievers, the end of the Lord's Supper, the subjects of the Lord's Supper, unworthy receiving of the Lord's Supper, self-examination, the knowledge of Christ crucified, Christ our Passover, the voluntary death of Christ, the acceptableness of Christ's death, and obedience. This volume is weighty and a bit tedious, yet is eminently scriptural and experiential.

The New Birth (BTT; 544 pages; 1996). Originally the third volume of Charnock's works, this collection contains discourses on regeneration, the Word as instrument of regeneration, God as author of regeneration, and the cleansing virtue of Christ's blood. Though repetitive, this volume provides a first-rate exposition of one of Christianity's most fundamental doctrines.

Truth and Life (BTT; 592 pages; 1997). This fifth and concluding volume of Charnock's works contains discourses on the necessity of Christ's death, Christ's exaltation, Christ's intercession, the object of faith, afflictions, the removal of the gospel, mercy received, mortification, proving weak grace victorious, the sinfulness and cure of thoughts, the church's stability, the fifth of November (an anniversary of English deliverance), delight in prayer, mourning for other men's sins, comfort for child-bearing women, the sins of the regenerate, the pardon of sin, man's enmity to God, and chief sinners as the objects of God's choicest mercy. Also included is an index to Charnock's works in the Nichol series.

David Clarkson

(1622-1686)

Richard Baxter commended David Clarkson for "solid judgment, healing moderate principles, acquaintance with the Fathers, great ministerial abilities, and a godly upright life" (*Reliquiae Baxterianae*, 1696, 3:97). Born at Bradford, in Yorkshire, Clarkson was educated at Trinity College, Cambridge (1641-45), and became a fellow of Clare Hall, Cambridge, in 1645. One of his pupils was John Tillotson, later the archbishop of Canterbury.

Clarkson served as rector of Crayford, Kent from 1650 to 1655, and of Mortlake, Surrey, from 1656 to 1661. For about a year, he served as assistant to Samuel Clark at St. Benet Fink, London, until he was ejected for Nonconformity in 1662. For the next decade, he ministered quietly wherever he could and continued studying and writing. Finally, in 1672, after the Declaration of Indulgence, he became pastor of a combined Presbyterian and Independent congregation at Mortlake. In 1682, he became co-pastor with John Owen in Leadenhall Street, London. Upon Owen's death the following year, Clarkson became sole pastor. He died June 14, 1686. His funeral sermon was preached by William Bates.

The Works of David Clarkson (BTT; 3 vols., 1,400 pages; 1988).
This reprint of the 1864-65 edition is filled with biblical and
practical sermons covering a wide variety of topics. Volume 1
contains sermons on such themes as sin and repentance, the
work of Christ, the nature of faith, prayer, living as strangers,
bearing the cross, and knowing Christ. Volume 2 covers the
depravity, inability, and guilt of man, as well as rich expositions on the new creature (Gal. 6:15), God's purposes in the
afflictions of the believer (Isa. 27:9), and how to be free from
anxiety. Volume 3 contains outstanding sermons on the love,
humanity, sacrifice, and intercession of Christ, and a polemical treatise against Roman Catholicism (*The Practical Divinity of
the Papists discovered to be the destruction of Christianity and men's
souls*), which Barry Till asserts is Clarkson's most important
book: "The work eschews the normal doctrinal issues between Protestants and Roman Catholics. Rather it is an
elaborate attack on Roman Catholic casuistry which 'strikes
at the heart of Christianity'" (*Oxford DNB*, 11:933).

　　Throughout, Clarkson's style is clear, vigorous, and evangelical, though not as warmly experiential as some of his
colleagues. He focuses on the large themes of the gospel: sin,
Christ as Mediator, justification, faith, and repentance. He ca-
pably handles the great texts of Scripture and the central
matters of living the Christian life.

　　Clarkson's *Sermons and Discourses on Several Divine Subjects*,
published after his death, could often be found chained to
reading desks in dissenting chapels in the eighteenth century.
His sermons titled "Christ's Gracious Invitation to Sinners"
(on Rev. 3:20) provide a clear Puritan view on the offer of
grace (3:34-100). One of his most striking writings is a sermon
titled "Public Worship to be Preferred before Private" (3:187-
209), which stresses God's great delight in communing with
His people in corporate worship.

Thomas Cobbet
(1608-1686)

Thomas Cobbet was born at Newbury, Berkshire, in 1608. He was an Oxford scholar for a few years, then was a pupil of William Twisse, prolocutor of the Westminster Assembly. Cobbet was ordained to the ministry in Lincolnshire, England, but was driven from his flock when he refused to conform to the established usages of the Church of England. He sought refuge in America, sailing there in 1637 on the same ship as John Davenport.

In America, Cobbet and his friend, Samuel Whiting, served as pastor and teacher at a church in Lynn, Massachusetts. The two men served there harmoniously for several years, furthering the cause of pure religion. Cobbet then accepted the pastorate at Ipswich, Massachusetts, succeeding Nathaniel Rogers, who died in 1655.

In 1657, Cobbet and twelve other pastors met in Boston to discuss various questions proposed by the legislature of Connecticut. The main subject for their deliberation was the baptism of children. Cobbet's book, *A Defense of Infant Baptism,* was a great help in resolving issues raised by the Baptists. The General Court then appointed Cobbet as one of five ministers to debate several Baptists in Boston.

Cobbet served the congregation of Ipswich until his death in 1686. Throughout the three decades of that pastorate, he endeared himself to the flock. He was an able preacher, conscientious pastor, and skillful writer. Many people were converted under his ministry. God's people trusted his judgment in and beyond Ipswich; his writings also spread his fame throughout New England.

Today, Cobbet is the least known of five leading New England Puritan pastors of his day, the others being Thomas Shepard, Thomas Hooker, John Cotton, and Peter Bulkeley. Nonetheless, he was highly regarded by them in his own day. His epitaph reads: "Stop, traveler! A treasure lies here, Thomas Cobbet: whose effectual prayers and most exemplary life, thou, if thou art a New Englander, must have known. Admire, if you revere piety: follow, if you long for happiness!"

⸺◆⸺

Gospel Incense, or A Practical Treatise on Prayer (SDG; 436 pages; 1997). This book is a masterful, practical treatment of the doctrine and benefits of prayer. It deals with subjects such as family prayer, private prayer, importunity in prayer, constancy in prayer, humility and sincerity in prayer, distractions in prayer, the use of means with prayer, time spent in prayer, soul "enlargements" and "meltings" in prayer, and how to think of God in prayer.

Cobbet was known for his prayer life. Cotton Mather wrote: "Of all the books written by Mr. Cobbet, none deserves more to be read by the world, or to live till the general burning of the world, than that of prayer; and indeed prayer, the subject so experimentally and therefore, judiciously, therefore profitably, therein handled, was not the least of those things for which Mr. Cobbet was remarkable. He was a praying man, and his prayers were not more observable throughout New England for the argumentative, the importunate, and I had almost said, filially familiar strains of them than for the wonderful successes that attended them" (*Magnalia*, 1:520).

Elisha Coles

(c. 1608-1688)

Elisha Coles was a native of Northamptonshire. He received some training in Calvinist tenets in his youth, but received no formal university training. Originally a trader in London, Coles moved to Oxford in 1651, having been appointed deputy registrar of the university. In 1657, he became steward of Magdalen College through the influence of Thomas Goodwin, president of the college during the years of the Commonwealth. Coles also served as a member of the Commission for the Ejection of Scandalous Ministries in Oxfordshire.

After the Restoration, however, Coles was forced to quit his position as steward on the grounds that he had been improperly admitted. He spent the remainder of his working life as a clerk in the East India Company.

Coles married and had one son, Elisha. He died at his home in London on October 28, 1688. He is best known for his book on God's sovereignty, one of the most popular seventeenth century books written by a lay theologian.

A Practical Discourse of God's Sovereignty (GM; 298 pages; 1999). Written in response to discussions the author had with some Arminians, and originally intended as a legacy for his children, this book was first published in 1673. Over the centuries, it has gone through more than fifty editions. It was popular among the dissenters and was promoted by Thomas

Goodwin, John Owen, and Samuel Annesley in the preface to its third impression (1678).

The work, which heavily relies on Scripture, explains the doctrinal and practical implications of the sovereignty of God. Its premise is that "the great God, blessed for ever, hath an absolute power and right of dominion over his creatures, to dispose and determine them as seemeth him good" (p. 20). Coles discusses sovereignty in its practical workings, namely, the creation of the world (which Coles calls the "great act of sovereignty"), the universal providence by which creation is sustained, and the redemption of the world through the merits of Jesus Christ.

Coles also discusses the righteousness of God, election, redemption, effectual calling, and perseverance of saints as they relate to God's sovereignty. His treatment is sound, careful, and exhaustive. He cautions against schemes that would "make God the author of sin" or lead to licentious living. His running polemic against Arminianism is skillfully conducted.

The current edition of this work is reprinted from a nineteenth century edition, with a recommendation by William Romaine, who writes, "In the practical view of [the doctrines of grace], Elisha Coles is singularly excellent. He has brought these deep things into daily use, and has proven them to be absolutely necessary in daily experience." This is suitable reading for both the beginning and the advanced reader.

John Cotton
(1584-1652)

John Cotton is remembered as "the patriarch of New England." He was born in Derby on December 4, 1584, the son of a lawyer, Roland Cotton, and Mary Hurlbert. His parents were sympathetic to Puritanism. Cotton entered Trinity College, Cambridge, at the age of thirteen, graduating with a bachelor's degree in 1603. He was not yet converted. He said later that he inwardly rejoiced when he heard death bells toll for William Perkins, for Perkins's strong preaching on human sin and divine judgment "laid siege to and beleaguered [Cotton's] heart."

Cotton became a fellow in the more Puritan-minded Emmanuel College, Cambridge, under Laurence Chaderton, where he earned his master's degree in 1606. During the next six years, according to his friend and biographer, Samuel Whiting, Cotton was "head lecturer and dean, and catechist," and "a diligent tutor to many pupils." In the midst of those years, Cotton was converted under the ministry of Richard Sibbes, whose sermons convinced him that he had been building his salvation on intellectual prowess rather than on Christ alone. Through Sibbes's sermons on regeneration, Cotton embraced God's promises of salvation.

Cotton's conversion had private and public consequences, for he could no longer use the elegant pulpit style that had impressed others. Denying his natural inclinations, he opted for Perkins's method of plain style preaching.

JOHN COTTON

Cotton obtained a Bachelor of Divinity degree from Emmanuel College in 1610, and later that year was ordained at Lincoln. In 1612, he became vicar of the large parish church of St. Botolph's in Boston, Lincolnshire, at the age of twenty-seven, and remained there for twenty-one years. According to Cotton Mather, Cotton was brought to full assurance of faith on the day he married Elizabeth Horrocks, shortly after his installation at St. Botolph's. On that day, Mather said, Cotton "first received that assurance of God's love unto his own soul, by the Spirit of God, effectually applying His promise of eternal grace and life unto him which happily kept with him all the rest of his days; for which cause, he would afterwards often say, 'God made that day, a day of double marriage to me!'" (*Magnalia*, 2:237).

During his years at St. Botolph's, Cotton's nonconformity cost him brief suspensions from his ministry in 1615 and 1621, but his supportive relations with his diocesan bishops and the Boston community helped lift those suspensions. Cotton's preaching (twice on the Sabbath as well as in the early morning on Thursdays and Fridays and on Saturday afternoons) and ministry defeated the local Arminian faction, helped Reformed believers grow in the grace and knowledge of Christ, and assisted numerous colleagues and theological students who were vexed by the bishops' policies or were seeking deeper insight into various doctrines. For example, James Ussher spoke at length with Cotton about the doctrine of predestination. John Preston had his theological students complete their ministerial preparation under Cotton. William Ames sent some German students to Cotton from Franeker. Other students from the continent, such as Maximiliaan Teellinck (the oldest son of Willem Teellinck, father of the Dutch Further Reformation), came to live with and study under Cotton. John Norton, who would later be Cotton's successor in Boston, New England, and his first biographer, said

that "Cotton answered many letters that were sent far and
near, wherein were handled many difficult cases of conscience, and many doubts by him cleared to the greatest
satisfaction" (*Abel being Dead yet Speaketh*, 1658).

Anthony Tuckney, a cousin of Cotton's wife, was appointed assistant to Cotton in 1629. Tuckney would
eventually succeed Cotton at St. Botolph's and would also
serve as a member of the Westminster Assembly. The timing
was providential, for the following year, both Cotton and his
wife were disabled for a year from malaria. Elizabeth died
from it in 1631.

Theophilus Clinton, fourth earl of Lincoln, hosted the
Cottons while they were sick. At his manor, Cotton became
well informed about the colonization of New England. His interest had already been piqued, as can be seen in the farewell
sermon he preached to John Winthrop's company just before
they departed for America.

After his wife's death, Cotton traveled extensively
throughout Europe while recuperating. Increasingly, he realized how good he and his church had it in the midst of
growing ecclesiastical persecution of nonconformity. But
Cotton's turn to suffer oppression would soon come. Shortly
after he married Sarah Hawkridge, widow of John Story, in
1632, Cotton was summoned to appear before William Laud's
Court of High Commission. He escaped, however, to London,
where he remained in hiding for several months, as he contemplated his future. On the way to London, he consulted the
venerable John Dod, who said, "I am old Peter, and therefore
must stand still, and bear the brunt; but you, being young
Peter [Cotton was already forty-seven years old], may go
whither you will, and ought, being persecuted in one city, to
flee unto another."

Thomas Goodwin and John Davenport tried to persuade
Cotton that conforming was not an evil, but in their discussions

Cotton actually persuaded them that conformity was no longer an option. Cotton was deeply interested in the colonization of New England from its beginnings through his friendship with John Davenport and John Winthrop. Eluding the watch set for him at various English ports, he immigrated to the colony of Massachusetts Bay in July 1633 with his colleague, Thomas Hooker. He arrived in Boston early in September.

Cotton was joyfully received in New England and was quickly given the most important position in the largest church of the colony. On October 10, he was chosen to be teacher of the First Church of Boston, of which John Wilson (1588–1667) was pastor. In the first year of Cotton's ministry, the church took in 117 new members. Winthrop commented, "More were converted and added to that church than all the other churches in the Bay" (*Journal of John Winthrop*, p. 106).

Cotton was very popular in Boston. His influence, both in ecclesiastical and in civil affairs, was probably greater than that of any other minister in New England at the time. According to the historian William Hubbard, "Whatever he delivered in the pulpit was soon put into an order of court, if of a civil, or set up as a practice in the church, if of an ecclesiastical concernment." Vernon Parrington commented, "The New England which the immigrant generation bequeathed to its sons bore upon it the marks of John Cotton's shaping hand more clearly than those of any other minister" (*Main Currents in American Thought*, p. 27).

Cotton took an active part in three major theological and political controversies of his time. First, he was at the center of the antinomian controversy that swirled around Anne Hutchinson. Hutchinson, who had followed Cotton to the New World and to Boston, claimed to adhere to Cotton's emphasis on the primacy of grace and divine sovereignty in conversion, and accused all the other New England ministers (except her newly arrived brother-in-law, John Wheelwright) of preaching a covenant of works rather than the covenant of grace. Enthusiastically embracing the doctrine of immediate revelation, she asserted that assurance of faith is experienced by inner feelings of the immediate testimony of the Holy Spirit rather than by the evidence of good works. She thus downplayed the need for sanctification and for the law as a rule of life. This gifted woman attracted many believers into her fellowship and managed to cause friction between Cotton and other ministers, even to the point that some of the ministers, particularly Thomas Shepard, began to question Cotton's orthodoxy. Cotton initially seemed to support Hutchinson and a few of her ideas, particularly her criticism of a clerical overemphasis on sanctification as evidence of election and on preparationism. Cotton clearly embraced both of these doctrines, but felt uncomfortable with the amount of emphasis they were receiving among the New England clergy.

Hutchinson's aberrational views were gradually brought out into the open, however, and when she openly lapsed into mysticism, Cotton sided with the other ministers against her. That became evident when Cotton's fellow clergymen presented him with a list of questions to clarify his views in relation to Hutchinson, after which the synod detailed a list of Hutchinsonian errors. The controversy ended dramatically with Hutchinson's trial and conviction both by the colony's general court and by the Boston church, which led to her banishment from the colony.

Second, Cotton debated extensively with Roger Williams on such issues as the separation of church and state and the liberty of individual conscience. Williams maintained that the biblical precedent for the spiritual authority of the state was no longer valid after the coming of Christ because it had only been symbolic. Cotton responded that such an argument could be used to deny divine sanction of all civil government. Cotton also rejected Williams's attempt to deny the religious power of the state, because he believed that without that power there could be no reformation. If Williams had his way, Cotton reasoned, there would be no ecclesiastical means to root out heresy, which would tempt God to destroy all of society. Cotton believed that punishment for false doctrine, however sincerely that doctrine was believed, was permissible after several admonitions, for then one, having been better instructed, "is not persecuted for cause of conscience, but for sinning against his own conscience." Cotton tried to fend off Williams's banishment, yet ultimately approved of it as "righteous in the eyes of God." His banishment was a great relief for nearly all concerned.

Third, in 1646, Cotton was one of a committee of three chosen to frame a model of church government. The choice was no surprise, for he had already written *The Way of the Churches of Christ in New England* (1641) and *The Keys of the Kingdom of Heaven, and the Power Thereof* (1644). These books, which went through several printings, were used extensively by the Independents at the Westminster Assembly. After being attacked by Robert Baillie, a Scottish attendee who advocated a Presbyterian settlement for England, Cotton responded in 1648 with his *The Way of Congregational Churches Cleared*, in which he presented New England Congregationalism as steering between strict Independency and Presbyterianism. All of these writings were followed up with a final call to accommodation in Cotton's *Certain Queries Tending to Accommodation* (1655). No New England minister was as influential as Cotton in promoting Congregational church practice.

Cotton wrote nearly forty works in his lifetime, many of which have never been reprinted. His catechism, *Milk for Babes* (1646), bound with the New England Primer, became standard fare for New England children until the late nineteenth century. His *Exposition upon the Thirteenth Chapter of Revelation* (1655) dealt with millennial issues and, together with *The*

Pouring Out of the Seven Vials (1642) and *The Churches Resurrection* (1642), strongly opposed Roman Catholicism. These writings and others often touched on issues transpiring in England with which Cotton always stayed abreast.

Cotton was equally known for his Christ-like humility. For example, when one of his parishioners admonished him that his preaching had become dark or flat, Cotton responded, "Both, brother, it may be both: let me have your prayers that it may be otherwise." That kind of humility sustained him in many conflicts. It also helped him maintain peace among his colleagues and made him very influential in fostering the New England way. Whether as an overseer of Harvard College, or writing on issues of the day in New England, as in *The Grounds and Ends of the Baptism of Children* (1647) and *Singing of Psalms a Gospel Ordinance* (1646), Cotton was a leader among leaders and a towering force to be reckoned with by any who opposed his views.

Cotton remained at First Church until his death on December 23, 1652. John Wilson was at his side in his last moments, praying that God would lift up the light of His countenance upon his dying colleague. Cotton replied, "He hath done it already, brother." He then committed his children to God's gracious covenant as their never-failing portion, after which he requested to be alone. He died a few hours later.

Cotton was survived by his second wife, Sarah (who subsequently married Richard Mather), and several children. One son, Seaborn, so named because he was born on their voyage to America, graduated from Harvard and became a minister at Hampton, New Hampshire, for twenty-six years. Another son, John, Jr., became minister at Plymouth, Massachusetts and Charleston, South Carolina. He preached to the Indians and revised John Eliot's Bible translation. A daughter, Mariah, married Increase Mather, and was the mother of Cotton Mather. Increase and Cotton Mather, both noted New England theologians, took up Cotton's mantle.

Christ the Fountain of Life (Arno; 256 pages; 1972). First published in 1651, these sermons based on 1 John 5:12-17 focus on Jesus Christ's fullness and life for believers. About two-thirds of the book expounds verse 12, "He that hath the Son, hath life, and he that hath not the Son, hath not life." These sermons are heavily condensed and are taken up in outline form in Cotton's larger sermonic commentary on 1 John (see below).

The Correspondence of John Cotton (UNC; 688 pages; 2001). This volume consists of 125 letters to and from Cotton, more than fifty of which have never before been printed. They cover the years 1621-1652, a period of great change and activity in the progress of English Puritanism. Carefully edited, annotated, and contextualized, the letters chart Cotton's career and revive many voices from the troubled times of the reign of Charles I, including those of Oliver Cromwell, Bishop John Williams, John Dod, and Thomas Hooker, as well as others who wrote to Cotton for advice and guidance.

Ecclesiastes & Song of Solomon (TENT; 198 pages; 2005). This volume, combined with Peter Muffet on Proverbs, is a reprint of an 1868 edition done in the Nichol's series of commentaries. Cotton's helpful work on Ecclesiastes runs 135 two-column pages, and is packed with good homiletical insights. Spurgeon writes, "Ecclesiastes is not a book to be expounded verse by verse; but Cotton does it as well as anyone."

Cotton's work on Song of Solomon, which is only 63 pages, was subtitled in the original 1652 edition: "Describing the estate of the Church in all ages thereof, both Jewish and Christian, and modestly pointing at the gloriousness of the restored state thereof." It is one of Cotton's inferior books. He approaches the Song of Songs from a historical perspective, viewing Solomon as "a type of Christ, admitting the Gentiles into the fellowship of his marriage bed" (p. 2). Spurgeon comments that by using this approach, he loses "much of its sweetness."

An Exposition of First John (SGP; 586 pages; 2001). Cotton preached through 1 John while he was still in England, partly in response to the death of his bosom friend, John Preston, a famous convert of Cotton's. The sermons were published after Cotton's death as *A Practical Commentary, or, An Exposition with Observations, Reasons, and Uses upon the First Epistle General of John* (1656). It is the largest collection of Cotton's extant sermons. The manuscript was first given to Christopher Scott, who then gave it to the famous London printer, Thomas Parkhurst. The commentary was confirmed genuine by Thomas Oresby, who had heard Cotton preach on the subject on several occasions. In the preface to the first impression, Scott recommended the author as "a burning and shining light, famously eminent abroad and at home."

The commentary, approved for publication by Edmund Calamy, Sr., deals primarily with the practical teachings of 1 John. Cotton carefully addresses all kinds of readers, including those who are weak in faith. For example, after explaining God's love as the foundation of reconciliation and showing how to experience that love, Cotton tells how new believers might know that their experience is worked by the Holy Spirit. His answer sounds much like Preston's: "Just as a woman that is breeding a child feels such qualms and distempers that she knows thereby she is with child; so they that have the breeding of the Spirit in their hearts, and have perceived his motions, they know more clearly than any other, [for they have] a scientifical instruction about certain experimental things." Cotton stressed that when God crowned "love with experience" and made a believer know that he had been saved, He did so according to principles and marks of grace that could be "scientifically" studied. Assurance flows out of right knowledge known in the mind, experienced in the heart, and witnessed to by the Spirit (pp. 176, 311).

Cotton's exegesis is sound and reliable. His experiential and practical emphases are authenticated by God's dealings with His people. Spurgeon wrote that Cotton "in doctrine and in experience" was a noble teacher. Parts of this book remind us that Cotton's parishioners thought that listening to him was, as someone said, "like hearing the Lord Jesus Christ Himself speaking in my very heart."

Two Sermons: God's Mercy Mixed with His Justice, and The True Constitution of a Particular Visible Church (Arno; 150 pages; 1972). First printed in London in 1641 and 1642 respectively, these two sermons show Cotton's views of God's attributes and of the local church with clarity. In *The True Constitution*, Cotton argues his case from Scripture, citing numerous texts for support. These two sermons are among the most influential that Cotton preached.

Tobias Crisp
(1600-1643)

Tobias Crisp, "a Church of England clergyman and stimulator of religious controversy" (*Oxford DNB*, 14:215), was born in Bread Street, London, in 16 00. He was the third son of Ellis Crisp, a wealthy merchant and alderman of the city. Crisp's elder brother, Nicholas, also a wealthy merchant, was knighted by King Charles I. Tobias Crisp was educated at Eton College and then at Cambridge University, where he graduated with a bachelor's degree in 1624. In 1627, he was incorporated at Balliol College, Oxford, and received his Master of Arts degree that same year. A few months later, he became rector of Newington, Surrey, and two years later, of Brinkworth, Wiltshire. Later, in the late 1630s, he earned a Bachelor of Divinity degree from Oxford and a doctorate in divinity from Cambridge.

Crisp's wife, Mary Wilson, was the daughter of Rowland Wilson of London, a merchant who sat in Parliament during the Civil War. They had thirteen children, two of whom died before Tobias. Crisp had a large income of his own and was known as a liberal host to strangers. He reportedly had a hundred people in his house at one time, providing for both them and their horses.

After a period of delivering legalistic Arminian sermons, Crisp became a strong Calvinist. To avoid the insolence of

Cavalier soldiers in the Civil War, Crisp left Brinkworth and retired to London, where several of his later-reprinted sermons were preached. He was much opposed by the divines in the city, and was baited by fifty-two opponents in a dispute concerning the freeness of grace in Jesus Christ. He vigorously defended the doctrine of Christ's graciousness.

Crisp contracted smallpox and died on February 27, 1643, at age forty-three. He was buried in the family vault at St. Mildred's Church in Bread Street, London. His son and editor, Samuel, wrote of his death, "As he had lived in the free grace of God, through Christ, so he died, with confidence and great joy, even as much as his present condition was capable of. [He] resigned his life and soul into the hands of his dear Father."

<hr/>

Christ Alone Exalted (GM; 4 volumes; 888 pages; 1998). This collection of fifty-two sermons, reprinted from a nineteenth century edition, contains all of Crisp's sermons as well as John Gill's explanatory notes. Crisp handles such topics as the preeminence of Christ, forgiveness of sins, the covenant of free grace, Christian liberty, the free offer of the gospel, good works, Christ's righteousness, the imputation of sin to Christ, the assurance of faith, good works, and the use of the law. Unfortunately, the memoir in the original edition was omitted in this reprint.

Historically, Crisp's posthumously published sermons provoked fierce debates, first, between evangelicals and Grotians, who adhered to the atonement views of Hugo Grotius, a Dutch jurist and theologian. Grotius rejected both the orthodox and the Socinian positions of the atonement, advocating the cross as a penal example by which God revealed both the inviolable nature of the law and His own displeasure against sin. In a public lecture at Pembroke-Hall, Richard Baxter, who favored the Grotian theory of the atone-

ment, branded Crisp as a "Jezebel" for believing that justification precedes faith. William Twisse, who had read Crisp's
sermons, confessed that he "could give no reason why they
were so opposed, but because so many were converted by his
preaching, and so few by ours." The Westminster Assembly in
general, however, regarded Crisp as heterodox. Nevertheless,
few of Crisp's opponents attacked him personally, since he
was known for his humility, quietness, and good works.

Second, anomalies in Crisp's sermons moved some Puritans
to charge him with antinomianism in doctrine (the belief that
the law is abolished for the Christian as a rule of life), though he
was not antinomian in practice. Crisp refused to believe that his
theology was antinomian, and his son, Samuel Crisp, in a
lengthy refutation of Baxter's charges, titled *Christ Made Sin*
(1691), refused to accept the term in reference to his father.

Third, Samuel Rutherford and others accused Crisp of
being a hyper-Calvinist because he taught the doctrine of
actual justification of the elect from eternity. These concerns
led to much confusion surrounding Crisp's preaching in the
seventeenth century. Some Westminster Assembly divines
even proposed to have his sermons burned. Other divines,
such as Johannes Hoornbeek, a Dutch Further Reformation
theologian, and later, John Gill, strongly supported Crisp.

Finally, Crisp's sermons continued to provoke periodic
religious controversy throughout the seventeenth and eighteenth centuries. Some have blamed these sermons for the
failure of the London nonconformist congregations to unite in
the 1690s. A booklet titled, *Doctor Crisp's ghost...being a bridle for
antinomians and a whip for Pelagians and Arminian-Methodists*, published in 1773, shows that his sermons continued to stir up
controversy some 135 years after they were preached.

How should Crisp be viewed? The charges of being a
doctrinal antinomian and a hyper-Calvinist are quite understandable, though strictly speaking, are only partially true.

Though Crisp emphasized that the law is "cruel and tyranni-cal," he maintained that the moral law is the Christian's rule of life (*Christ Alone Exalted*, 2:124, 526ff.) and, in contrast to hyper-Calvinism, he unreservedly proclaimed the free offer of the gospel (1:112ff, 213f). On the other hand, Crisp made some unguarded, even extreme, statements about the one-sided-ness of the freeness of sovereign grace that understandably provoked other divines to write and preach against him. For example, Crisp states: "There is not one sin you commit, after you receive Christ, that God can charge upon your person" (1:73); "before a believer confesses his sin, he may be as certain of the pardon of it, as after confession" (1:359); and "they that have God for their God, there is no sin that ever they commit, can possibly do them any hurt" (2:171).

Crisp's sermons must therefore be read with caution, rec-ognizing, as Spurgeon rightly noted, that they include some careless statements that could lead to serious doctrinal error. That is particularly true of his convictions on how a believer's sins are laid on Christ. Crisp wrote that the "sins of the elect were so imputed to Christ as that, though he did not commit them, yet they became actually his transgressions, and ceased to be theirs." Rutherford preached strongly against Crisp's doctrine of laying not only the guilt of sin but sin itself upon Christ and the resulting confusion of justification and sancti-fication that can ensue.

Finally, we should remember that many believers have been richly edified through Crisp's sermons. Samuel Crisp re-lates the story of an older gentleman who "wrung [him] by the hand, and with tears in his eyes, thanked [him] for assisting to reprint [his father's sermons], and said that he had been a poor creature full of doubts for ten years" until reading Crisp's sermons, which gave him liberty. James Hervey wrote that Crisp's sermons were of special use for the "distress of con-science." He confessed, "I know not any treatises more proper,

or more excellently calculated, to administer solid consolation; they are, under the divine influence, one of my first
counselors, and principle comforters."

Crisp is not easy to assess. Nearly everyone who reads
him reacts strongly, whether it be positively or negatively.
There is no agreement among scholars as to whether he can
even be classified as a Puritan. We do well to remember John
Flavel's modest approach to the works of Crisp when he
states that "there are many things said in them with good
savor, quickness, and spirit, as to be very apt to make good impressions upon men's hearts," but that whereas many parts of
his works are "deep," others run "shallower" (*Works* 3:413-18;
cf. 6:353-54).

John Davenant

(1572-1641)

John Davenant was born to an eminent merchant on May 20, 1572, in Watling Street, London. When he was fifteen years old, Davenant entered Queens' College, Cambridge, where he earned a Bachelor of Arts degree in 1591 and a master's degree in 1594. In 1597, he was elected a fellow. He graduated with a Bachelor of Divinity degree in 1601, and a doctorate in divinity in 1609. That same year he was appointed as Lady Margaret Professor of Divinity, a position that he held for twelve years.

In 1609, Davenant was instituted as rector of Fleet, Lincolnshire, and in 1612, of Leake, Nottinghamshire. Cambridge remained his home, however, and especially there he became known as a defender of Calvinist orthodoxy.

Davenant served in a variety of important posts. In 1613, a royal party visiting Cambridge for the marriage of Princess Elizabeth and Frederick V elected Davenant moderator for the theological disputation that customarily occurred on such occasions. In 1614, he was elected president of Queens' college. He presided over the building work at the college, but was increasingly drawn away from college affairs by his growing reputation as a theologian and his duties at court.

In 1618, Davenant became a royal chaplain. That same
year, King James I chose Davenant along with three other delegates to represent the Church of England at the Synod of
Dort. Davenant, a moderate Calvinist, took an active role in
synodical deliberations. John Hales said Davenant defeated
"learnedly and fully...certain distinctions framed by the
[Arminian] remonstrants." Johannes Bogerman, chairman of
the synod, said that Davenant's experience and skill in the
"laws and histories" helped the delegates "better order their
debates and votes."

Regrettably, Davenant held to "hypothetical universalism," a mild form of universal redemption, attested to not only
by James Ussher and Richard Baxter but also by Davenant's *A
Dissertation on the Death of Christ*, which he finished shortly after
leaving Dordrecht. This treatise presents the view that Davenant defended at the synod. Ultimately, Davenant and the
English delegates won synod over to the view that the debate
on redemption must be worked out in terms of both sufficiency and efficiency, i.e., that Christ's death was sufficient in
terms of its intrinsic worth to save a thousand worlds, but
was efficient or efficacious only for the elect. Davenant's views
went further, however, claiming that the Father and the Son
had a conditional intention to save all, though that condition
was not absolutely efficacious (see W. Robert Godfrey, "Tensions With International Calvinism: The Debate on the
Atonement at the Synod of Dort" [Ph.D. dissertation, Stanford
University, 1974], pp. 179-88).

In 1620, Davenant received the rectory of Cottenham,
Cambridgeshire, and the following year, he was elected
bishop of Salisbury, a position left vacant by the death of his
brother-in-law, Robert Townson. Davenant held this post
until his death in 1641, though not without times of difficulty.
In 1630, he preached before the court on predestination; after
the sermon, he was summoned before the privy council. The

archbishop of York spoke strongly against him. Davenant defended himself and was dismissed without sentence, but the king privately forbade him to preach anymore on such a subject in the court's presence.

For the most part, however, Davenant was quite amenable to the state authorities. He even acquiesced to Archbishop Laud's high-church commands in ecclesiastical matters such as ordering the Communion table to be placed back in the chancel in the position of an altar.

Davenant retained strong ties with the English church. On occasion, he offended staunch Puritans when he wrote that the Roman Catholic Church, though miserably corrupt, was still a true, visible church. However, friends and opponents alike were impressed by Davenant's profound learning, acute intellect, catholic spirit, and benevolent meekness. He was referred to as "the good Bishop Davenant," "the excellent Bishop Davenant," "the learned Bishop Davenant," and "the jewel of the Reformed churches."

———◆◆◆———

An Exposition of the Epistle of St. Paul to the Colossians (BTT; 2 vols. in 1, 856 pages, 2005). This classic on Colossians, which includes a biography of Davenant and copious notes by Josiah Allport, minister of St. James's, Birmingham (who also translated it from Latin in 1831), is based on lectures given to students at Cambridge. The first edition was published in Cambridge in 1627, the second in 1630, and the third in 1639. It reveals Davenant's fluency in Greek and Latin and his knowledge of the church fathers and the Reformers. James Ussher said that Davenant understood the ancient controversies better than any man since Augustine.

This book is extensive, insightful, practical, and Christ-centered. For example, on the phrase *in Him* (Col. 2:10), Davenant writes: "We are declared to be complete not from him, or by him only, but in him: that we may understand that we have that aforesaid wisdom, righteousness, and holiness, not as far as we look to Christ, as though he were distant from us; but as far as we are incorporated into Christ, as far as we have Christ dwelling and abiding in us" (1:426).

James Hervey said of this commentary, "For perspicuity of style and accuracy of method; for judgment in discerning and fidelity in representing the Apostle's meaning; for strength of argument in refuting errors, and felicity of invention in deducing practical doctrines, tending both to the establishment of faith and the cultivation of holiness, it is inferior to no writing of the kind; and richly deserves to be read, to be studied, to be imitated, by our young divines." Charles Bridges said, "I know no exposition upon a detached portion of Scripture (with the single exception of Owen on the Hebrews) that will compare with it in all points."

Arthur Dent

(1553-1607)

Arthur Dent was born at Melton Mowbray, Leicestershire. He earned a bachelor's degree from Christ's College, Cambridge, in 1576, and a master's degree in 1579. In 1577, he was ordained as deacon at Peterborough. The following year, he was ordained at the age of twenty-four as priest by John Aylmer, bishop of London.

In 1580, Aylmer installed Dent as rector of South Shoebury, Essex, where he served for twenty-seven years until his death. In 1582, he was one of the witnesses summoned to support charges against Robert Wright, a noted Puritan minister. In 1584, Archdeacon Walker and others began harassing Dent for refusing to wear a surplice and for omitting the sign of the cross in baptism. That harassment continued for at least five years, but, apart from a short period of suspension, Dent was able to continue his work, due in part to his irenic temperament and Aylmer's leniency.

By the mid-1580s, Dent was appointed to several positions of leadership, including being involved in discussions about the Book of Discipline, and being nominated as "one of seven Essex delegates to the proposed provincial synod designed to follow the setting up of 'presbytery in episcopacy'" (*Oxford DNB*, 15:844). But most of all, Dent became known as a great preacher; "his ability to edify rural congregations was legendary," Brett Ussher writes (ibid.).

Dent's *The Ruin of Rome, or, An Exposition upon the Whole Revelation*, which was reprinted about twenty times over the centuries, was at the printer's when he contracted a fever and died on January 10, 1607, after only three days of illness. On his deathbed, he said of the Reformed faith, "This faith have I preached; this faith have I believed in; this faith I do die in; and this faith would I have sealed with my blood, if God had so thought good; and tell my brethren so." His last words were, "I have seen an end of all perfection, but thy law is exceeding broad." Dent left seven manuscripts that were published after his death.

———◆◆◆———

Christ's Miracles (PP; 20 pages; 2000). This sermon, preached at South Shoebury, is based on John 9:16, containing the comments of the Pharisees regarding Christ's miracles. Dent expounds his text beautifully and offers compelling applications. The sum of his sermon, according to Dent, is "to lead us unto God, to acknowledge Him to be our only Lord and Saviour, and to embrace the Son of God, as our King."

The Plain Man's Pathway to Heaven (SDG; 332 pages; 1997). This was one of the most popular Puritan devotional classics ever written. It went through twenty-five editions by 1640 and fifty editions by 1860. Richard Baxter recast the book in 1674 as *The Poor Man's Family Book*, "abandoning Dent's homely dialogue for connected prose" (ibid.). John Bunyan was also profoundly influenced by it. Like *Pilgrim's Progress*, this book uses the pilgrimage motif with dialogue. It features four characters: Theologus, a pastor; Philagathus, an honest, God-fearing man; Asunetus, an ignorant man; and Antilegon, a caviler.

On their journey, these men discuss religious topics including the misery of man by nature, the corruption of the world, the marks of the children of God, the difficulty of entering into life, the ignorance of the world, and the sweet promises of the gospel "with the abundant mercies of God to all that repent, believe, and truly turn unto Him." Individual dialogues address subjects such as regeneration, pride, adultery, covetousness, contempt of the gospel, swearing, lying, drunkenness, idleness, oppression, effects of sin, predestination, hindrances to salvation, and Christ's second coming. The book teaches much about God, sin, and salvation.

A Sermon of Repentance (PP; 38 pages; 1996). This sermon, preached at Leigh in 1582, was reprinted at least twenty-two times by 1638. It teaches with great clarity the nature and results of turning to God. Dent reminds us that everything in this life calls us to repentance: God's mercy, God's judgments, God's Word, our sins, the shortness of life, the small number of the saved, the day of judgment, and hell's torments.

Edward Dering

(c. 1540-1576)

Edward Dering was born into an ancient, distinguished family. He was educated at Christ's College, Cambridge, where he earned bachelor's (1560) and master's (1563) degrees, as well as a Bachelor of Theology degree (1568). He also served there as a fellow from 1560 to 1570, and was ordained deacon by Bishop Cox of Ely in 1561.

In 1564, Queen Elizabeth visited Cambridge and toured its colleges. At Emmanuel College, Dering, who had already gained a reputation as a Greek scholar, presented the queen with a congratulatory copy of Greek verses he had written. This was only one evidence of the kind of scholarship that eventually led Matthew Parker, archbishop of Canterbury, to call him "the greatest learned man in England."

In 1566, Dering was appointed university proctor. The following year he preached before the university as Lady Margaret preacher, and was appointed rector of Pluckley by Archbishop Parker. At that time, Dering was still an Anglican; later, he would reveal that, in his own estimation, he was still unconverted. Meanwhile, he was chosen to refute various statements advancing Presbyterian views supposedly written by Thomas Cartwright. He also became one of the chaplains to England's premier nobleman, Thomas Howard, the fourth duke of Norfolk, and held a chaplaincy in the Tower of London.

Early in 1569, Dering began leaning toward the Puritan views that were current in Cambridge. His first public espousal of them appears to have been on February 25, 1570, when he preached a strong sermon on Psalm 78:70 before the royal court, reproving Queen Elizabeth to her face for tolerating clergy whose practices and lives were objectionable. He described the ministers as "ruffians and dizers," blind guides and foolish dogs that will not bark. "And yet you," he told the queen, "sit still and are careless, and let men do as they will." Not surprisingly, the queen suspended him from preaching, but failed to remove him as lecturer because her deputies could not agree on how to compose the charge brought against him. Patrick Collinson notes, "No Elizabethan sermon was more often reprinted, with sixteen editions by the year of Elizabeth's death, 1603" (*Oxford DNB*, 15:873).

On December 20, 1571, Dering was restored to the pulpit in Salisbury Cathedral, probably in an effort to win him back to the Anglican cause. In 1572, Dering pleaded before Lord Burghley that Cartwright receive permission to return to Cambridge and lecture there. The same year, Dering became reader of the divinity lecture at St. Paul's Cathedral, where he lectured on the Epistle to the Hebrews. These lectures attracted large numbers of "the godly in London" with whom he "enjoyed a huge reputation" (*Oxford DNB*, 15:873). Before lecturing, Dering would often pray: "O Lord God, which hast left unto us Thy holy Word to be a lantern unto our feet, and a light unto our steps, give unto us all Thy Holy Spirit, that out of the same Word we may learn what is Thy eternal will, and frame our lives in all holy obedience to the same, to Thy honor and glory, and increase of our faith, through Jesus Christ our Lord. Amen."

After lecturing on Hebrews, Dering published his *A Brief and Necessary Catechism*. In the preface, he renewed his attacks on the clergy, saying that there was never a nation that had such ignorant ministers and that parsons and vicars disputed among themselves "all for the belly." That preface, among other attacks on the clergy, such as his prediction that Parker would be the last archbishop of Canterbury, resulted in his suspension from the lectureship and a summons to appear before the Star Chamber. Upon examination, however, Dering was cleared of all charges and his suspension was lifted, despite the queen's dislike of him.

Dering was a great man with a remarkable command of language. Despite his attacks on the clergy of the Church of England, he was reverenced as a gentleman with a sound theology and a warm and affectionate disposition. Samuel Rutherford listed Dering alongside Calvin, Cartwright, and Beza as one to whose judgment he would readily bow.

Dering's health failed in 1575. He suffered from bouts of "blood spitting and difficulty of breathing." Among his last words were: "Dally not with the Word of God, make not light of it; blessed are they that use their tongues well when they have them." He died at age thirty-six on June 26, 1576, in Thoby, in the parish of Mountnessing, surrounded by preachers and friends who faithfully recorded his last words. Essex mourned for him.

M. *Dering's Works* (WJ; 800 pages; 1972). Dering was one of the first Puritan-minded divines to have his collected writings printed. First printed in 1572, this facsimile begins with Dering's sermon on Psalm 78:70, "He chose David also his servant, and took him from the sheepfolds," preached before the queen (referenced above). Dering considers three issues: the mercy of God in calling David, the purpose and intent of God in calling David, and the character of David in obeying his call. The next work, also a sermon, was preached at the Tower of London on December 11, 1569. It is based on John 6:34, "Then said they unto him, Lord, evermore give us this bread." Dering reproves those who would take the Bread of Life for selfish reasons, saying they are infatuated with "transitory vanities."

He then presents the beauty of God's kingdom and the preciousness of eating and drinking Christ, which, he says, is synonymous with coming to Christ and believing in Him.

Dering's third work, consisting of twenty-seven lectures on Hebrews, was published in London in 1590. It is Dering's best work, full of timely, practical exhortations. Dering systematically expounds the text, making ample references to church history. When considering the authorship of Hebrews, Dering says that it does not matter since the whole epistle was inspired and directed by God.

The rest of the volume contains "certain godly and comfortable letters," written by Dering throughout his life to console believers; *A Brief and Necessary Catechism* (co-authored with his friend, John More, called the "apostle" of Norwich), which includes scathing statements against the episcopacy; and a collection of prayers and speeches, most notably, Dering's deathbed prayer.

Thomas Doolittle
(1630-1707)

Thomas Doolittle was born at Kidderminster, Worcester-shire. While at the grammar school in Kidderminster, Doolittle heard Richard Baxter preach sermons that were later published as *The Saints' Everlasting Rest* (1653). Those addresses led to Doolittle's conversion in the early 1640s; thereafter, he called Baxter his "father in Christ."

Shortly after conversion, Doolittle left his occupation as assistant to a county lawyer, who had demanded that he work on the Sabbath. Baxter encouraged Doolittle to enter the ministry. To prepare himself, Doolittle studied at Pembroke Hall, Cambridge, earning a Bachelor of Arts degree in 1653 and a master's degree in 1656. His tutor was William Moses, who was later ejected from Pembroke.

Doolittle quickly earned a reputation as a great preacher. In 1653, he received Presbyterian ordination but committed himself to St. Alfege, London Wall, a Church of England congregation that he served until he was ejected for Nonconformity in 1662. His ministry there was eminently successful. In 1657, he wrote to Richard Baxter, whom he continued to consult for counsel and theological questions, "God hath given me abundant encouragement in my work, by giving me favor in the hearts and affections of the people...& others in the city" (*Oxford DNB*, 16:561).

Doolittle married Mary Gill in 1655. They had three children and were expecting a fourth when Doolittle was ejected from his living. After the ejection, they had five more children. Reduced to poverty, Doolittle moved to Moorfields, where he organized a children's boarding school in his home, called the Pioneer Nonconformist Academy. When the school grew, Doolittle took on as his assistant, Thomas Vincent, who had been ejected from St. Mary Magdalene, Milk Street.

In 1665, the year of the great plague, Doolittle and his pupils moved to Woodford Bridge, near Chigwell. Vincent remained behind to minister to the dying. When Doolittle returned to London, he was one of the nonconformist ministers who defied the law by erecting meetinghouses in place of churches that were lying in ruins after the Great Fire of 1666. The first of these was in Bunhill Fields, where he served without disturbance. When this building proved too small for a growing congregation, a larger one was built on Monkwell Street. Doolittle preached twice each Lord's Day and, on Wednesdays, delivered his exposition of the Westminster Assembly's Shorter Catechism. Those talks were published posthumously in 1723 as *A Complete Body of Practical Divinity*. He also urged other ministers to catechize in order to promote knowledge, establish young people in the truth, and prepare them to better read and listen to sermons.

When Doolittle was serving at Monkwell Street, the authorities took action. The lord mayor urged Doolittle to cease preaching, but he declined. On the following Saturday soldiers broke down Doolittle's door and burst in to arrest him. Doolittle escaped by climbing over a wall. Several of his friends persuaded him not to preach the next day. Thomas Sare, an ejected minister, took his place. His sermon was interrupted by troops who ordered him to stop preaching. When Sare stood his ground, the commanding officer ordered the troops to fire. "Shoot, if you please," Sare replied. Great confusion resulted, though no blood was spilt. The king's forces seized the building.

When Charles II issued his Declaration of Indulgence in 1672, Doolittle applied for a license for his meetinghouse. Meanwhile, Pioneer Nonconformist Academy had expanded into a school that prepared students for university. When Charles revoked his indulgence in 1673, Doolittle moved his school to Wimbledon, where he cautiously carried on his work. He was nearly arrested again.

In 1680, Doolittle returned to Islington. After being fined several times for preaching, he was forced to leave there in 1683. He went to Battersea, where all his possessions were seized and sold by authorities, and from there, moved on to Clapham. In 1687, persecution compelled him to move yet again—this time to St. John's Court, Clerkenwell, Middlesex.

The moves so ruined his academy that Doolittle was forced to close it temporarily in 1687. After the Toleration Act of 1689, he re-established both his school and his ministry. He led services at the Monkwell Street church twice on Lord's Days and lectured on Wednesdays. During the next eighteen years, he was assisted by John Mottershead, Samuel Doolittle (his son), and Daniel Wilcox, who later succeeded him.

Doolittle's wife of forty years died in 1692. About that time, Doolittle apparently stopped taking on students. In its approximately thirty-five years of operation, the school had a great impact on hundreds of students, including such notables as Matthew Henry, Edmund Calamy, and John Kerr, who would follow in Doolittle's footsteps by becoming influential nonconformist ministers.

A few years later, Doolittle married another Mary, who lovingly assisted him in the ministry and survived him by only five months. After a relatively short illness, Doolittle died May 24, 1707, and was buried in Bunhill Fields, London. He was the last of the ejected London clergy to die.

Doolittle wrote twenty-three edifying treatises. His five works on catechizing were the most highly praised by his peers. Many of his books, all of which were typically Puritan, went through numerous printings.

➤◆◆◆◄

Love to Christ Necessary to Escape the Curse of His Coming (SDG; 216 pages; 1997). This work is a series of sermons based on 1 Corinthians 16:22, "If any man love not the Lord Jesus Christ, let him be *anathema maranatha.*" Doolittle explains why sinners should hate sin and love Christ supremely. He encourages readers to love Christ, and shows the consequences of not loving Him. He concludes with ten directives on how to obtain sincere love for Christ, and "ten springs of spiritual comfort flowing into the hearts of the lovers of Christ." Doolittle's book is a powerful evangelistic treatise for the unconverted and a heart-warming hortatory treatise for the believer.

A Treatise Concerning the Lord's Supper (SDG; 200 pages; 1998). This book was first published in 1665 as *A Treatise Concerning the Lord's Supper with Three Dialogues for the More Full Information of the Weak, and in the Nature and Use of this Sacrament.* It was so popular that it went through at least twenty-eight English editions, twenty-two Scottish editions, and twenty-six New England editions, as well as translations into German and Welsh. The book discusses twenty properties of the blood of Christ. Doolittle urges his readers to examine themselves before and after receiving the Lord's Supper. The purpose of the work, as Doolittle notes in his "Epistle to the Reader," is to promote assurance "of the love of God, and eternal life." Many believers have been helped by reading this book before or after Communion.

George Downame

(c. 1563-1634)

George Downame (or Downham), brother of John Downame (see below), was born in Chester, Ireland, where his father was a bishop. He was educated at Christ's College, Cambridge. He became professor of logic at the college in 1585, and was later granted a Doctor of Divinity degree.

Downame, described by Thomas Fuller as an excellent Aristotelian, was made prebendary of Chester in 1594, of St. Paul's in 1598, and of Wells in 1615. His sermon at the consecration of James Montague, bishop of Bath and Wells, on April 17, 1608, provoked a controversy on the divine institution of episcopacy.

James I made Downame a court chaplain in 1603 and appointed him bishop of Derry, Ireland, on September 6, 1616. Downame was installed on October 6. He presided over his diocese eighteen years until his death. His appointment was partly due to his strong Calvinist sentiments, which made him acceptable to Scottish settlers in Ulster. He was also a most zealous signer of the protest against the toleration of popery, issued on November 26, 1626, by some of the Irish hierarchy.

On April 11, 1627, Downame preached before the lord deputy at Dublin, reading the protest during his sermon and adding, "and let all the people say, Amen." The response was so enthusiastic that it shook the building. The lord deputy disapproved of the reading and sent copies of it to the king.

Some time before, Downame had preached a sermon at St. Paul's Cross against the tenets of Arminianism, which was later printed in Dublin in 1631. When copies reached William Laud, then bishop of London, Laud urged the king to forbid publishing the document, but by the time the royal letter reached James Ussher, archbishop of Armagh, nearly all of the published edition had been distributed.

Downame was given a cathedral in 1633. He died at Derry on April 17, 1634, and was buried either in the cathedral or at the old Augustinian church.

Downame wrote several influential books, including treatises on the Lord's Prayer, the Ten Commandments, the covenant of grace, perseverance, the Antichrist, and the episcopacy. Perhaps his most outstanding work is *A Treatise of Justification*, in which he refutes Robert Bellarmine's arguments for the Roman Catholic doctrine of justification by inherent righteousness. Downame argues that since man is corrupt because of imputed sin, only the imputation of Christ's righteousness can make him righteous. He believed the doctrine of imputation made it imperative to embrace the federal headship of Adam (see Edward Hindson, ed., *Introduction to Puritan Theology*, pp. 197-217).

The Christian's Freedom (SDG; 144 pages; 1997). Subtitled *The Doctrine of Christian Liberty*, this book is based on John 8:36, "If the Son therefore shall make you free, ye shall be free indeed." Downame explains the doctrine of Christian freedom in twenty-six sections under four headings: what Christian liberty is; the author of this liberty; the persons on whom this liberty is conferred; and the genuineness of this liberty.

Downame says Christian liberty is the freedom to do what is right, not what is wrong. It is the law of liberty, meaning there are constraints, but these constraints must be from God, not from the narrow mind of man. Downame steers between legalism (too little freedom) and antinomianism (too much freedom). He argues against Epicureanism, which promotes surrendering to one's passions, and against Roman Catholicism, which confuses liberty by confounding justification and sanctification. In classic Puritan style, Downame argues that the true Christian enjoys true liberty because he is fully justified and becomes progressively sanctified. Nevertheless, this liberty does not abrogate his moral duties to the law as a rule of life.

Downame's work is deep and precise and well represents the Puritan view of Christian freedom, which will be fully realized in the believer's glorification. Downame writes, "The right use of the doctrine concerning the liberty of glory, is, truly to believe it, and to live as in expectation of it" (p. 124).

John Downame
(d. 1652)

John Downame, the second son of Bishop William Downame, was born in Chester, Ireland. He received his education at Christ's College, Cambridge, where he earned a Bachelor of Divinity degree. On August 4, 1599, Downame was installed as vicar of St. Olave, Jewry; in 1601, he moved to the rectory of St. Margaret, Lothbury, where he succeeded his brother George as vicar. He resigned from this post in 1618.

In 1623, Downame married Thomas Sutton's widow, Catherine. They had three sons, William, Francis, and George, and several daughters. In 1630, Downame became rector of Great Allhallows, Thames Street. He held that position until his death.

In the late 1630s, Downame began giving lectures on Tuesdays in St. Bartholomew's Church. The lectures were very popular. In 1640, Downame joined the Puritan ministers of the city in presenting a petition against Laud's *Book of Canons* to the privy council. In 1643, Downame was appointed as a licenser of the press. The following year, he was chosen to examine and ordain public preachers.

While a licenser, Downame printed Thomas Sutton's *Lectures on the Eleventh Chapter to the Romans* (1632). In the preface to that work, Downame promised more publications from Sutton. He also edited his brother's *Treatise of Prayer* and Archbishop James Ussher's *Body of Divinity*. With other divines, he wrote *Annotations upon all the books of the Old and New Testament*

(1645). He also wrote ten books himself, of which the best known are *The Christian Warfare* (1609-18, see below), *A Guide to Godliness, or a Treatise of a Christian Life* (1622), *The Sum of Sacred Divinity* (1630), and *A Treatise tending to direct the Weak Christian how he may rightly Celebrate the Sacrament of the Lord's Supper* (1645). In those books, Downame develops typical Puritan themes, such as how to engage in Christian warfare, exercise self-discipline, live by faith in Christ, gain assurance, and live to God's glory in every sphere of life.

Downame died in 1652. He was buried at his parish church. Historians of the time considered him to be a "learned and laborious divine." J. I. Packer wrote, "Downame stands with Perkins, Greenham, and Richard Rogers as one of the architects of the Puritan theology of godliness."

⟶◆◆◆⟵

The Christian's Warfare (WJ; 674 pages; 1974). With the possible exception of Gurnall's *Christian Armour*, this book is the finest Puritan work on the theme of Christian warfare. It is also Downame's best work. Each of the book's four parts was published separately between 1609 and 1618. (This reprint contains the 1609 edition of *Warfare*, containing the first three books). The first part is about the threat of the devil; the second and third parts, the threat of the world; and the final part, the threat of the flesh. Several editions of the book were printed in London, culminating in the definitive four-volume edition of 1634, which contains one of the most extensive Scripture and subject indexes of the period. The entire work contains 1,164 pages (plus the indexes) in double-columned print.

As noted by the printer in the 1634 edition, the intent of *The Christian's Warfare* was to "instruct...in military discipline for [the] better enabling to stand in the day of battle as a valiant soldier." Downame himself said the book aimed to do three things: to "relieve and comfort those who are poor in spirit and humbled in the sight of sin"; to "lead the Christian in an even course, unto the haven of eternal happiness"; and "to give solid and substantial consolations, which are firmly grounded upon God's undoubted truth."

An interesting story is told about Downame's book. In 1637, John Harvard moved from England to Charlestown, Massachusetts. Harvard died a year later and donated all of his books to Harvard College, the newly founded college named after him. Downame's *The Christian Warfare* was one of the few that survived a massive fire that destroyed most of Harvard's library in 1763. Apparently, the book had been checked out of the library on October 14, 1763 for three weeks and was long overdue. Ephraim Briggs, a senior at the college, had the book. Unintentionally, he had preserved Downame's book for a future generation of readers.

Daniel Dyke

(d. 1614)

Daniel Dyke was born in Hempstead, Essex, where his father, William Dyke, served as vicar. Dyke was educated at Cambridge; he earned a bachelor's degree at St. John's College in 1596, and a master's degree at Sidney Sussex College in 1599. Around 1606, he became a fellow and earned a Bachelor of Divinity degree.

Dyke was ordained at Coggeshall, Essex, where he served as minister until 1583, when John Aylmer, bishop of London, suspended him from the ministry. Aylmer had infuriated the Puritans by bowling on Sundays and promoting lax Sabbath observance. His grounds for dismissing Dyke were that Dyke refused to be ordained as a priest, resisted wearing the surplice, promoted conventicles, and pushed for further reformation in the church.

Aylmer hounded Dyke relentlessly, such that Collinson describes Dyke as "a puritan stormy petrel whose repeated brushes with the ecclesiastical authorities took him from Great Yarmouth to Coggeshall in Essex, St. Michael's at St. Albans, and, finally, to Hemel Hempstead" (*Oxford DNB*, 17:495). When Aylmer suspended Dyke for the second time in 1589 at St. Albans, the parishioners petitioned Lord Burghley (William Cecil) to intervene for Dyke. They pleaded that Dyke's work had reduced disorder and promoted godliness. Indeed, he "had carried himself so peaceably and dutifully among them, both in his life and doctrine, that no man could justly find fault with him, except of malice." Their letter concluded: "There were some, indeed, who could not bear to hear their faults reproved; but through his preaching many had been brought from their ignorance and evil ways to a better life."

Lord Burghley's defense did not move Bishop Aylmer. Rather, he intensified his investigation of Dyke's character. He even persuaded the elders at Dyke's church to bring forward a woman charging Dyke with sexual unfaithfulness. Happily, before Dyke's reputation was permanently damaged, the woman confessed that her claim was contrived and begged forgiveness. Even after Dyke was cleared, however, Aylmer refused to lift his censure. Eventually, the influence of Lord Burghley and others secured for Dyke the safe living of Hemel Hempstead, in the Lincoln diocese, where Thomas Wilcox was his neighboring pastor.

All of Dyke's treatises were published posthumously by his brother, Jeremiah Dyke, vicar of Epping, mostly from 1614 to 1618. About twenty years later, Jeremiah published his brother's collected works in two folio volumes. Daniel Dyke's most frequently reprinted book, *The Mystery of Self-Deceiving*, based on Jeremiah 17:9, is a detailed anatomy of the "gospel-hypocrite," i.e., one who claims to know Christ but whose life reveals little self-knowledge and no fruit. Thomas Fuller, a noted historian and a younger contemporary of Dyke, said the book "will be owned for a truth, whilst men have any badness [in them], and will be honored for a treasure, whilst men have any goodness in them."

Dyke died in 1614. He was highly respected among the Puritans as a solid, educated divine. He preached soundly and experientially, aiming to promote biblical, Reformed piety. John Wilkins, born the year of Dyke's death and later the bishop of Chester, regarded Dyke's sermons as "among the most excellent in his day."

Michael and the Dragon; or, Christ Tempted and Satan Foiled
(OP; 253 pages; 1996). This work was first published in 1616
as part of *Two Treatises, the one of Repentance, the other of Christ's
Temptations.* It was reprinted by John Beale in 1635. It contains
three parts: preparation to combat the devil, the combat itself,
and Christ's answer to Satan's temptations.

In the first part, Dyke shows how the Lord fits true believers for the battle against Satan and how the Word of God and
the sacraments enable us to progress. Dyke explains fourteen
doctrines in this preparation for battle. In the second part,
Dyke shows how the devil attempts to discredit God's Word
and our trust in that Word. The last part provides believers
with numerous ways on how to handle Satan and his devices.

Though not as detailed as Thomas Brooks's *Precious Remedies against Satan's Devices,* Dyke's treatise is nearly as helpful. In
one way it surpasses Brooks, for it sets the believer's temptation in a Christ-centered context, teaching from Scripture
that we must handle Satan as Christ handled him.

The language of this book is old, but the matters it addresses are relevant for today. Dyke argues that it is
impossible to be a Christian without encountering Satan and
daily waging war with temptation. When God becomes real
in the soul, Satan becomes real as well. Satan will not easily
release his prey.

Though many modern scholars claim that scholastic and
Ramist methodology result in coldness and impracticality,
Dyke's writings are warm and practical. *Michael and the Dragon*
must be read slowly and digested with prayer. Here is practical divinity at its best.

Jonathan Edwards
(1703-1758)

Jonathan Edwards, often called America's greatest theologian and philosopher and the last Puritan, was a powerful force behind the First Great Awakening, as well as a champion of Christian zeal and spirituality. Both Christian and secular scholarship concur on his importance in American history. The treasures from Edwards's pen have been mined, pondered, and evaluated to the present day. His famous sermon, "Sinners in the Hands of an Angry God," is still being read and studied in America's public schools as a specimen of eighteenth-century literature. Students of American history pay much attention to Edwards's scientific, philosophical, and psychological writings; theologians and church historians regard Edwards's work on revivals as unexcelled in analysis and scope. Christians continue to read his sermons with great appreciation for their rich doctrine, clear and forceful style, and powerful depiction of the majesty of God, the sinfulness of sin, and Christ's power to save.

Still, not everyone agrees about Edwards's place in the history of Christian thought. Scholars continue to debate his philosophical musings, his fidelity to certain historic Calvinist doctrines, and his influence upon subsequent generations. As Iain H. Murray notes, "Edwards divided men in his lifetime and to no less degree he continues to divide his biographers" (*Jonathan Edwards: A New Biography*, p. xix).

JONATHAN EDWARDS

As the huge body of his writings shows, Edwards was intellectually brilliant, multifaceted in his interests, and abundantly creative. Spiritually, he was profound, reflective, experiential, and intense. Early on, he developed the habit of self-mastery and a capacity for unremitting toil. Though laboring in places far from the cultural centers of his society, Edwards influenced many people while he lived and greatly impacted the generations to follow.

Jonathan Edwards was born October 5, 1703, in East Windsor, Connecticut. He was the only son of eleven children born to Timothy Edwards and Esther Stoddard, daughter of Solomon Stoddard. Both Edwards's father and maternal grandfather greatly influenced his education and career. Solomon Stoddard served for sixty years as minister of the parish church of Northampton, Massachusetts. He was a powerful force in the pulpit, a leader in the churches of western Massachusetts and along the Connecticut River, and a stirring writer. Timothy Edwards was highly educated and also well known as a preacher, and, like Stoddard, no stranger to religious revivals.

Like many other ministers in that day, Timothy Edwards conducted a grammar school in his home, preparing boys for Connecticut's Collegiate School, known as Yale College after 1718. The school was founded in 1701 as an orthodox Congregationalist alternative to Harvard College, where the prevailing parties were hostile to the ideas proposed in John Cotton's *Way of the Churches of Christ in New England*, or, at least, favorable to Episcopalianism.

Edwards received his early education in his father's school, where he was nurtured and instructed in Reformed theology and the practice of Puritan piety. At age thirteen, he went on to the Collegiate School, which as yet had no permanent home. Several towns were competing for the honor of playing host to the fledgling institution. Edwards went to the nearest location, downriver from Windsor at Wethersfield, to begin his studies with Elisha Williams. When the college finally located at New Haven in 1716 under the rectorship of Timothy Cutler, Edwards went to New Haven, where the course of study included classical and biblical languages, logic, and natural philosophy. He was awarded the Bachelor of Arts degree in 1720, finishing at the top of his class, and then stayed at Yale to study for a master's degree.

Edwards's spiritual life was influenced by various factors. His parents, vibrant and intelligent Christians, offered a godly example and nurtured Edwards toward godliness. He went through several periods of spiritual conviction in his childhood and youth, which culminated in his conversion in 1721 after being impacted by the words of 1 Timothy 1:17, "Now unto the King eternal, immortal, invisible, the only wise God, be honour and glory for ever and ever. Amen." He later wrote,

> As I read [these] words, there came into my soul…a sense of the glory of the Divine Being; a new sense quite different from anything I ever experienced before…. I kept saying and as it were singing over those words of Scripture to myself and went to pray to God that I might enjoy Him…. From that time I began to have a new kind of apprehensions and ideas of Christ, and the work of redemption, and the glorious way of salvation by him. And my mind was greatly engaged to spend my time in reading and meditating on Christ, in the beauty of his person and the lovely way of salvation by free grace in Him (from Jonathan Edwards, *A Personal Narrative*).

Edwards's ministerial career began in 1722 with a brief sojourn of eight months in New York City. Frictions had arisen between the English members of the First Presbyterian Church and the Scots-Irish majority, led by Scottish minister James Anderson. The English eventually withdrew and began meeting separately. Edwards accepted their invitation to preach for

them. Later he wrote: "I went to New York to preach and my
longings after God and holiness were much increased. I felt a
burning desire to be in everything conformed to the blessed
image of Christ...how I should be more holy and live more
holily.... The heaven I desired was a heaven of holiness, to be
with God and to spend my eternity in holy communion with
Christ" (ibid.).

In April 1723, Edwards was persuaded by his father to return to Connecticut. After he had completed work for a
master's degree at Yale, he spoke at commencement exercises.
The title of his address was "A Sinner is Not Justified before
God except through the Righteousness of Christ obtained by
Faith." That November, Edwards took a call to the parish
church at Bolton, about fifteen miles east of Hartford.

The following year, Edwards returned to New Haven to
serve as tutor at the college. Yale was in upheaval due to the
decision of rector Timothy Cutler in 1722 to abandon Congregationalism and revert to the Church of England. No suitable
candidate would agree to take his place, so the college was in
the hands of a temporary rector. Each local minister served for
a month in rotation, while the forty or so students were left in
the care of two tutors. The students were a disorderly lot,
adding discipline to the heavy burden of Edwards's teaching
duties. Edwards remained there until 1726, when he received
a summons from the people of Northampton, Massachusetts,
to come upriver and serve as assistant to his aged grandfather,
Solomon Stoddard. Edwards was installed there on February
15, 1727, and became sole minister of the parish church upon
the death of Stoddard in 1729.

While at New Haven, Edwards had befriended Sarah
Pierrepont, whom he met when he was sixteen years old and
she was only thirteen. Friendship blossomed into romance,
and the two were wed eight years later in 1727 after Edwards
was settled at Northampton. Edwards later described his wife

as a model of true conversion in *Some Thoughts Concerning the Present Revival of Religion* (1743). Their eleven children were the beginning of a large progeny that greatly affected the life and history of New England.

Edwards's spiritual life was developed by various testings and difficulties. Sometimes he agonized over decisions; sometimes he suffered spells of exhaustion, depression, and serious illness; and often he faced problems and challenges in the pastorate as well as in his personal and family life. As a true Puritan, Edwards sought to discern the message of Providence in every event and to improve spiritually on all that befell him, good or bad.

Edwards's first publication, based on a lecture given at Boston in 1731, was titled *God Glorified in the Work of Redemption, by the Greatness of Man's Dependence upon Him in the Whole of It*. Edwards there spoke of faith as "a sensibleness of what is real," and as an "absolute and universal" dependence on God. Three years later, his *Divine and Supernatural Light, Immediately Imparted to the Soul by the Spirit of God* described the work of true regeneration as producing a new "sense of the heart...above all others sweet and joyful." This "new sense," apprehended by faith, would become a key to Edwards's theology.

People who heard Edwards's sermons undoubtedly appreciated them, yet Edwards was still left with the problem of promoting godliness in a congregation that seemed to be lapsing into spiritual indifference. To correct the errors into which some had fallen during the last years of Stoddard's pastorate, Edwards focused his preaching in the early 1730s on common, specific sins. He urged people to repent and to embrace the gospel by faith. That theme was repeated in a series of sermons Edwards preached on justification by faith in 1734 (published in 1738 as *Five Discourses on Important Subjects*), which prompted a significant awakening at Northampton.

Those sermons also set the stage for the forthcoming revival known as The Great Awakening.

In *Faithful Narrative of Surprising Conversions*, Edwards describes how, in the winter of 1734-1735, the young people and their parents responded to his preaching with renewed interest, wishing a genuine examination of their public and private behavior. People who visited Northampton noticed the change of spiritual climate and returned to their homes bearing Edwards's message. Meanwhile, independently of Northampton, the Holy Spirit brought revival to other places as well.

After a lull in the late 1730s, Edwards was caught up in the Great Awakening, which began in 1740; he became one of the ablest instruments and defenders of the revival. He preached "Sinners in the Hands of an Angry God" (Deut. 32:35) at Enfield, Connecticut, on July 8, 1741. The congregation was profoundly moved. A witness wrote, "Before the sermon was done, there was a great moaning and crying out throughout the whole house. What shall I do to be saved? Oh, I am going to hell! Oh, what shall I do for Christ?" Edwards asked for silence, but the tumult increased until Edwards had to stop preaching. A monument to the sermon stood until the twentieth century on the site of the Enfield meeting house ("The Diary of Stephen Williams" in Oliver Means, *A Sketch of the Strict Congregation Church of Enfield, Connecticut* [Hartford, 1899]).

Edwards worked hard to correct false notions of piety. His aim was twofold: he cared immensely about the spiritual welfare of his congregation's souls, and he wanted to save the Awakening from disrepute. But when prominent church leaders denounced the revival, Edwards felt compelled to defend the Spirit's authentic work in it. In September of 1741, Edwards explained the revival in a sermon titled "The Distinguishing Marks of a Work of the Spirit of God." He insisted that non-traditional church services, unusual body movements, and strange fancies among the seemingly pious neither proved nor disproved claims of grace. After testing the revival for evidences of true piety, which essentially involved devotion to Jesus as Savior, reverence for and sound interpretations of Scripture, Edwards concluded that it indeed was the work of the Spirit of God. He cautioned that the devil could and would counter this work, however, using men's own imaginations to produce irrational behavior.

By late 1742, New England Congregationalism was divided into two camps: the "Old Light" anti-Awakening group and the "New Light" pro-Awakening party. Colonial Presbyterians were also of two minds about the Awakening; "New Side" Presbyterians promoted the Awakening against the objections of "Old Side" traditionalists. In an effort to make peace within the clerical community, Edwards wrote *Some Thoughts Concerning the Present Revival of Religion* (1742), taking pains to denounce extremists on all sides. He even suggested that the remarkable outpouring of the Spirit in this Awakening could be ushering in the millennium. Pushing the argument from *Distinguishing Marks* a step further, he insisted that true spiritual life was a matter not only of intellectual assent, but also of the affections. "Now if such things are enthusiasm," he wrote, "let my brain be evermore possessed of that happy distemper! If this be distraction, I pray God that the world of mankind may be all seized with this benign, meek, beneficent, beatifical, glorious distraction!"

The Old Lights, however, were not persuaded. Charles Chauncy, one of the greatest opponents of the revival, wrote *Seasonable Thoughts on the State of Religion in New England* (1743), denouncing affections as carnal passions and necessarily profane. In response, Edwards published the *Treatise Concerning Religious Affections* (1746), which distinguished between true and false religious experience. It has long been regarded by many historians as his most influential work.

Edwards's 1749 edition of the diary of a young missionary named David Brainerd was perhaps his most moving publication. Brainerd had been expelled from Yale for slandering a tutor during the Awakening. He was denied reinstatement despite Edwards's support. He began working among the Delaware Indians in New Jersey and Pennsylvania, but tuberculosis forced him to come home. He spent his final days at the home of Edwards, constantly attended by Edwards's daughter, Jerusha. The loss of this young man, who was like a son to Edwards, moved him deeply. His *Life of Brainerd* was a tribute to true piety, and it also became a model for missionaries.

Meanwhile, in the late 1740s, Edwards became embroiled in controversy over who should partake of the sacraments. Solomon Stoddard had taught that the Lord's Supper could be a "converting ordinance" to which any baptized person of blameless life should be admitted. Edwards opposed this view, saying that only people who professed to be converted and who were bringing forth the fruits of conversion in their lives should be received at the Lord's Table. As a corollary, Edwards said that baptism ought to be administered only to the children of believers who had made a credible profession of faith. That was contrary to the long-established practice of the so-called "Half-Way Covenant," a modified form of church membership used in some New England Congregational churches. Baptized adults who professed a historical faith without claiming to be converted and who lived uprightly would be regarded as "half-way" church members, so that they could therefore present their children for baptism, though they themselves could not participate in the Lord's Supper or vote in church matters.

A moment of crisis was reached in 1748 when Edwards told two applicants that they lacked the saving grace necessary to partake of the Lord's Supper. At the same time, Edwards published his *An Humble Inquiry into the Rules of and*

Qualifications for Communion, which insisted that genuine conversion bears visible fruit and is essential for sacramental privileges. Many townspeople and ministers objected to *The Humble Inquiry,* concluding that Edwards had gone too far. When these objections were combined with false rumors of Edwards's treatment of some young people and other complications resulting from several discipline cases, the members of Northampton voted to eject him from the Northampton pulpit. In his farewell sermon on June 22, 1750, Edwards suggested that the discipline cases had turned the town against him. Privately, however, he told a friend that he suspected the real issue was his refusal to baptize infants of members who could not profess saving grace. By a large majority, the Northampton church voted not to change its sacramental practices.

The following year, Edwards left Northampton with his family, taking refuge in the frontier settlement of Stockbridge, near the western border of Massachusetts, where he served as pastor to a small congregation and as a missionary to the Housatonic Indians. He learned to accommodate himself well to the level of understanding of the Native Americans. Here is a simple outline of a sermon preached to them on Hebrews 11:14-16: "(1) This world is an evil country; (2) Heaven is a better country." His years in Stockbridge were complicated, however, by the outbreak of the French and Indian War, which reached the village in 1754, when several inhabitants were killed.

Though Edwards's desire to witness revival among the Indians did not materialize, from another perspective these were his most fruitful years. Edwards is often remembered for spending thirteen hours a day in study. Modern readers may be inspired or appalled by that, but we should realize that most workers in those times spent nearly as much time pursuing their callings. Under such circumstances, Edwards would have appeared diligent and faithful to his calling, not over-committed to study or unbalanced in his use of time. Out of those long hours in the study, and especially from the period of relative isolation at Stockbridge, came a vast body of Edwards's writings. His greatest literary achievement from this period was *Freedom of the Will* (1754), in which Edwards argues that only the regenerate person can truly choose the transcendent God; that choice can be made only through a disposition that God infuses in regeneration. In this, Edwards rejected the materialism of the British philosophers along with the utilitarianism of free-will advocates. Logically, Edwards succeeds in making Arminianism an impossibility. Other important works completed during his Stockbridge years include *Concerning the End for which God Created the World* and *The Nature of True Virtue* (both published posthumously in 1765), and *The Great Christian Doctrine of Original Sin* (1758)—a *tour de force* against Pelagianism.

In 1758, Edwards agreed to become president of the College of New Jersey at Princeton. He left his family that January, as "affectionately as if he should not come again," one of his daughters wrote; as he departed, he turned back to his wife and said, "I commit you to God" (Karlson and Crumpacker, eds., *The Diary of Esther Edwards Burr: 1754-1757*, 1984, p. 302).

Edwards preached his inaugural sermon at Princeton on Hebrews 13:8, "Jesus Christ the same yesterday, today, and for ever." The sermon was two hours long and made a great impact on its hearers. While at Princeton, Edwards hoped to complete two major treatises, one showing the harmony of the Old and New Testaments, and the other, a much-expanded treatise on *The History of the Work of Redemption*. However, Edwards did not live to complete these works. On March 22, 1758, after only a few months in Princeton, he died of complications from a smallpox inoculation.

The effect of this spiritual giant's theological insight on New England Christianity has been immense and is often debated. Some say Edwards provided the impetus to move New England beyond the thought of its founders. In that sense, Edwards was a true philosopher. Others say Edwards was the last representative of Puritan theology and thought in the New World, where Puritanism would later be disdained. A third group finds little fault with Edwards or his theology, but accuses his followers of veering from the truths that inspired Edwards. Though Edwards himself stressed godly living, some of his successors discarded the biblically Reformed base which supported that godliness in their attempt to adopt Edwards's more speculative views and methods. That, in turn, fostered a decline of both doctrinal and experiential Calvinism in New England. This group maintains that Edwards was a theologian-philosopher whose vision died with him, but that is certainly not true. Edwards's vision continued at Princeton and many other places, and was alive in the Second Great Awakening.

Perhaps the most accurate assessment of Edwards is a combination of several views. Edwards was a profound theologian, as readers of *The End for Which God Created the World* can attest. Edwards was also a minister with great pastoral sensitivity—consider his *Religious Affections*. Recent scholarship has focused on Edwards's metaphysics, gleaning primarily from his philosophical and scientific writings (e.g., Sang Hyun Lee's *The Philosophical Theology of Jonathan Edwards* [2000] and Paul Helm's *Jonathan Edwards: Philosophical Theologian* [2003]). Whatever view one may hold, all agree that his writings, specifically his sermons, are profitable specimens of one of America's best and last Puritans.

＞◆◆＜

The Works of Jonathan Edwards (BTT; 2 volumes; 1,900 pages; 1974). This is the standard reference edition for pastors and laymen, while specialized scholars prefer the Yale edition, prompted by the work of Perry Miller in the 1950s (see below). The Hickman edition, from which the BTT edition is printed, contains most of Edwards's published writings. The first volume offers "Freedom of the Will," "Original Sin Defended," "Religious Affections," "Narrative of Surprising Conversions," "Thoughts on the Revival of Religion in New England," "Qualifications for Communion," "History of the Work of Redemption," "Five Discourses on the Soul's Eternal Salvation," a few minor treatises, and a 230-page biography of Edwards. The second volume contains "Life and Death of David Brainerd," several dozen sermons, and some shorter theological works.

The Works of Jonathan Edwards (Yale; 23 volumes at present; 1957–). Perry Miller (1905-1963), historian and literary scholar, proposed the Yale Edition of *The Works of Jonathan Edwards* in 1953 after examining all of Edwards's manuscripts. He wanted to offer a collection that could foster further inquiry into the mind of this eighteenth-century genius. Both conservative and liberal scholars continue to acknowledge their debt to Miller as hundreds of manuscripts come to press, which otherwise might have remained in the archives of Yale University.

Each volume in the Yale series has been thoroughly edited by scholars, and includes, on average, 35 to 150 pages of introduction. This series is essential for aspiring scholars of Edwards. Those interested in reading Edwards for devotional benefit could better purchase the two volume edition of his *Works*, since the Yale volumes are expensive.

Presently, twenty-three of the twenty-eight projected volumes have been published. Here is a summary of the set, volume by volume, adapted from Yale's descriptions:

1. *Freedom of the Will* (494 pages; 1957, 1985), edited by Paul Ramsey (see below).
2. *Religious Affections* (526 pages; 1959, 1987), edited by John E. Smith (see below).

3. *Original Sin* (448 pages; 1970), edited by Clyde A. Holbrook. The controversy over human depravity that raged during the eighteenth century was an important phase of America's philosophical understanding of human nature and its potential. In defending the hated doctrine of original sin, Edwards battled a heresy that had already engulfed much of Europe and was now threatening America. The Enlightenment, hailed as man's greatest achievement, had nearly eradicated the notion of original sin.

John Taylor's treatise, perhaps the most impressive assault on the doctrine of original sin, haunted Edwards throughout his years at Stockbridge. Ultimately, he wrote this rebuttal to Taylor, focusing on three major issues: the fact and nature of original sin, its cause and transmission, and God's responsibility for humanity's sinfulness.

First published in 1758, *The Great Christian Doctrine of Original Sin Defended* went through at least thirteen editions and was later included in all collections of Edwards's works. The text of the first edition has been adapted to the standards of the Yale series in making full use of all relevant manuscript materials. Holbrook's introduction and notations provide detailed information about the sources, development, and reception of the work.

4. *The Great Awakening* (595 pages; 1972), edited by C.C. Goen. These writings on the Great Awakening theologically defined the revival tradition in America. Moving from descriptions of "the surprising work of God" in conversion to a quest for the essence of true religion, Edwards threads his way through increasing controversies over "errors in doctrine and disorders in practice." He looks for an authentic core of evangelical experience, then examines it in light of biblical faith and experiential insight to defend it against overheated zealots and rationalistic critics. His writings (with related correspondence), presented here for the first time in accurate critical text, document a move-

ment so significant that it has been called the American "national conversion."

In the introduction, Goen explains the Arminian
threat to which Edwards responded at the onset of
the Awakening, and traces Edwards's understanding
of vital religion as it developed in the context of re-
vivalism. Goen also sheds light on little-known
aspects of "A Faithful Narrative" and describes the
haphazard way in which that important work
reached its audience.

5. *Apocalyptic Writings* (501 pages; 1977), edited by
Stephen J. Stein. This is the first published text of
Edwards's private commentary on the book of Revelation. Written over a period of thirty-five years,
Edwards's notebook reveals his lifelong fascination
with apocalyptic speculation (including its bizarre
aspects) and his conviction about the usefulness of its
visions in the life of the church. It was no small wonder, then, that Edwards viewed the sinking of several
Spanish ships in the Atlantic as foreshadowing of the
demise of the papal Antichrist.

This volume also contains the first complete edition
since the eighteenth century of "Humble Attempt"
(1748), which was Edwards's response to the decline
in religious fervor after the Great Awakening. In his
introduction and commentary, Stein examines the
development of Edwards's apocalyptic interest in the
events of his time, showing how Edwards's private
judgments on the book of Revelation affected his
pastoral and theological activity. The texts and the introduction present a much-ignored facet of Edwards's
thought.

6. *Scientific and Philosophical Writings* (433 pages; 1980), edited by Wallace E. Anderson. This volume contains
two notebooks by Edwards titled "Natural Philosophy" and "The Mind," as well as a number of shorter
manuscripts on science and philosophy. Several of the
shorter papers have not previously been published,
notably Edwards's letter on the flying spider, an essay

on light rays, and a brief but important set of philosophical notes written near the end of his life.

Each major work in this volume and group of related writings are preceded by a detailed discussion of
manuscript sources and dates. Anderson makes these
the basis for a revised account of the chronology of
Edwards's early writings and a deeper investigation of
their biographical and historical context. Also included are a new appraisal of Edwards's efforts and
achievements in science and an analysis of the development of his philosophical views. Anderson
concludes that Edwards was an enthusiastic, though
untrained, investigator in the Newtonian tradition
who grappled with the major metaphysical problems
raised by this tradition. The papers reveal Edwards's
fertile mind that earned him recognition as the leading eighteenth-century philosopher-theologian.

7. *The Life of David Brainerd* (620 pages; 1985), edited by
   Norman Pettit (see below).

8. *Ethical Writings* (791 pages; 1989), edited by Paul
   Ramsey. In this comprehensive theological and philosophical work, Ramsey includes the two major ethical
   writings of Edwards. The series of sermons Edwards
   preached in 1738, known as "Charity and Its Fruits,"
   and "Two Dissertations: I. Concerning the End for
   Which God Created the World; II. On the Nature of
   True Virtue," provide the principles of Edwards's ethical reflections.

9. *A History of the Work of Redemption* (594 pages; 1989), edited by John F. Wilson. In 1739, Edwards preached a
   series of thirty sermons based on Isaiah 51:8. He intended to develop these into a major work explaining
   God's progressive redemption of the world. This modern, authoritative text of those sermons is based on a
   new transcript of Edwards's preaching booklets.

   The first sermon deals with the doctrine and design
   of the work of redemption. The next eleven sermons
   show how God's redemption became increasingly clear
   throughout the Old Testament era. Sermons 13-17 trace

redemption in Christ's life and ministry, and the next three sermons follow redemption through the rest of the New Testament era. Sermons 21-25 show God's redemptive work through church history, from Constantine until Edwards's day, focusing on Christ's battles with the Antichrist. Sermons 26-29 offer Edwards's eschatological views of what will happen until the fall of the Antichrist. The concluding sermon focuses on the character of God, the happiness of the church, and the misery of the wicked. The work as a whole is reminiscent of Augustine's *City of God.*

10. *Sermons and Discourses, 1720-1723* (670 pages; 1992), edited by Wilson H. Kimmach. This work contains the complete texts of twenty-three sermons preached by Edwards during the first years of his career. The previously unpublished sermons reveal one of the least explored periods of his life and thought. These fully annotated manuscripts include an editor's preface that combines new information with fresh readings of related texts. The sermons cover topics such as man's slavery to sin, poverty of spirit, and the necessity of true repentance as well as Christian happiness, Christian holiness, and Christian liberty.

11. *Typological Writings* (349 pages; 1993), edited by Wallace E. Anderson and Mason L. Lowance, Jr. This volume offers a comprehensive, readable, and annotated text of Edwards's notebooks titled "Images of Divine Things," "Types Notebook," and "Types of the Messiah" (no. 1069 of the "Miscellanies"). These works show how Edwards developed his theory of typological exegesis. That theory helped him understand the relationship between the Hebrew Bible and the New Testament as well as correspondence between the natural and the spiritual worlds.

Edwards's theories of typology have fascinated scholars from a variety of fields. These documents clearly show Edwards's epistemology and his involvement in contemporary philosophical and exegetical trends. Introductions to the documents explain Edwards's typology within the context of his period, and clarify some of the problems caused by his use of the types throughout his career. They also discuss his philosophical defenses of types against the claims of materialists, deists, and rationalists.

12. *Ecclesiastical Writings* (596 pages; 1994), edited by David D. Hall. This volume includes four documents of Edwards on the nature of the church. They show his views on ecclesiology, congregational autonomy, ordination, and admission to church membership and the sacraments. The first document, reprinted here for the first time since the eighteenth century, is Edwards's defense of fellow Hampshire County ministers in the Robert Breck controversy of 1735-36.

The other three documents relate Edwards's efforts to restrict admission to the sacraments at Northampton in 1749-50. Those actions ultimately led to his dismissal as pastor. "An Humble Inquiry" explains Edwards's reasons for refuting the open admission policy of his grandfather and predecessor, Solomon Stoddard. "Misrepresentations Corrected" is Edwards's response to the criticisms of his cousin Solomon Williams on *Humble Inquiry*. The third work is Edwards's untitled narrative, available before only in Sereno Dwight's 1829 edition. It offers details on Edwards's final conflict with his Northampton congregation.

The introduction by Hall puts these writings in their theological and historical contexts, highlighting Edwards's Puritan, Congregational heritage and the tensions between lay and clerical piety. It also reassesses Edwards's relationship with Stoddard in light of Edwards's experience during and after the Great Awakening.

13. *The Miscellanies a–500* (596 pages; 1994), edited by Thomas A. Schafer. This is the first published collection of Edwards's theological notebooks, called the "Miscellanies" or "commonplace books." Throughout his ministerial career, Edwards filled private notebooks with writings on a variety of theological topics, numbering his entries—some 1,360 of them—in sequence. The entries in volume 13 were written

during the early years of Edwards's ministry (1722-31) and cover a variety of subjects. They reveal Edwards's initial thoughts on topics such as original sin, free will, the Trinity, and God's purpose in creation. Many entries also cover subjects not included in the main body of Edwards's published writings. This volume includes Edwards's index to the entire "Miscellanies." This becomes a theological document in its own right in showing the relationship between the various components of Edwards's theological system.

The editor's introduction includes an essay linking Edwards's growing body of entries in the "Miscellanies" with the main events in his life and career. It shows how, even before tutoring at Yale in 1724, Edwards had developed certain fundamental positions and distinctive elements in his theology. The introduction ends with an explanation of the methodology used to establish the chronology of the "Miscellanies." The conclusions of this research are summarized in a chart that shows the chronological order of the miscellanies from "a to 500," as well as the sermons, essays, and other manuscripts that Edwards wrote prior to 1731.

14. *Sermons and Discourses, 1723-1729* (575 pages; 1996), edited by Kenneth P. Minkema. This book includes previously unpublished manuscript sermons from a crucial period in Edwards's life: the years between the completion of his master's degree at Yale College and the death of Solomon Stoddard. These sermons show the intellectual and professional development of young Edwards during his pastorate at Bolton, Connecticut; his Yale tutorship; and his work at Northampton. The sermons cover themes such as the pleasantness of religion, nobleness of mind, hearing the Word profitably, the threefold work of the Holy Spirit, and the torments of hell.

In his introduction, Minkema links the details of Edwards's emerging career with concerns expressed in the sermons. He shows how Edwards addressed local and provincial concerns as well as the great theological debates of his day. He also shows how

Edwards struggled to work out his innovative concept of "excellency" and to develop his definition of conversion as "spiritual light."

15. *Notes on Scripture* (674 pages; 1998), edited by Stephen J. Stein. This is the first complete edition of the private notebooks on Scripture that Edwards compiled over a period of nearly thirty-five years. *Notes on Scripture* confirms the centrality of the Bible in Edwards's thought. It balances earlier writings that appeared to emphasize scientific and philosophical elements while overlooking Scripture. In this critical edition, entries appear in the order that Edwards wrote them, beginning with a short commentary on Genesis 2:10-14 that he wrote in 1724, and ending with his last entry (on the Song of Solomon), written two years before his death.

Edwards's entries cover the whole Bible, revealing his creativity in interpreting the text as well as his fascination with typology. The notebook also documents Edwards's relationship with the intellectual trends of his day, particularly his response to the challenge of the Enlightenment regarding biblical revelation. Stein's introduction reveals Edwards as a true exegete in biblical commentary within the world of eighteenth-century Western thought.

16. *Letters and Personal Writings* (854 pages; 1998), edited by George S. Claghorn. This volume contains all the letters of Edwards along with his personal writings. For more than three decades, Claghorn scoured America, Great Britain, and Scotland for these letters and documents. The result is a fascinating compendium of 235 letters, including 116 never before published or reprinted since Edwards's death, and four autobiographical texts—Edwards's meditation "On Sarah Pierpont," his future wife; "Diary"; "Resolutions"; and "Personal Narrative."

These writings reveal the private side of Edwards: his relations with parents, siblings, college classmates, friends, and family, as well as interactions with the political, religious, and educational leaders of his day. Included are letters that he wrote to Samuel

Hopkins, Benjamin Colman, George Whitefield, Isaac Chauncy, Joseph Bellamy, Thomas Clap, Thomas Gillespie, John Brainerd, Thomas Foxcroft, Timothy Dwight, and Aaron Burr. The new documents include Edwards's only known statement on slavery as well as letters showing Edwards's interest in Native Americans and his efforts on their behalf.

17. *Sermons and Discourses, 1730-1733* (480 pages; 1999), edited by Mark Valeri. When he became pastor of the Northampton church, Edwards turned his attention to the religious and social activities of his congregation, shaping his preaching to practical, everyday occurrences in the lives of his congregants. This volume contains eighteen sermons that Edwards delivered in Northampton from 1730 through 1733, including such classics as "God Glorified in Man's Dependence" and "A Divine and Supernatural Light," along with many previously unpublished sermons.

The sermons show Edwards's development as a preacher and theologian. They provide unique insights into the development of themes that would one day develop into mature theological thought, such as the viciousness of the unregenerate life, the importance of evangelical humiliation as a religious exercise, and the necessity of a genuine conversion from worldliness to godliness.

18. *The Miscellanies, 501-832* (578 pages; 2000), edited by Ava Chamberlain. This book, the second of four volumes devoted to "Miscellanies," contains his entries from July 1731 to approximately January 1740, the eve of the Great Awakening. They record Edwards's thoughts as he defended orthodox Calvinism, took a leadership role in colonial church politics, and became a crusader for revival in the Connecticut River Valley of 1734 and 1735.

Edwards used "Miscellanies" to jot down ideas that he intended to develop in future sermons and treatises. These entries thus contain the seeds of such contemporaneous works as *Justification by Faith Alone* and *The History of the Work of Redemption*. They also show

how the Connecticut Valley revivals influenced Edwards's thoughts on such important theological topics as perseverance, the nature of spiritual knowledge, justification by faith, rationality in the Christian religion, and the history of redemption, conversion, and the religious life.

19. *Sermons and Discourses, 1734-1738* (849 pages; 2001), edited by Ava Chamberlain. According to Chamberlain, Edwards mastered his preaching style and content between 1734 and 1738, while experiencing the first revival of his ministry and its aftermath. Edwards delivered probably four hundred sermons and lectures during that time. Less than half of those have survived, but the ones we have cover various theological doctrines, pastoral life, conversion, and, in due time, declension.

This volume also includes Edwards's account of the Northampton revival, *A Faithful Narrative of the Surprising Work of God*, published in 1737 in London and Edinburgh. Within a year, the work was reprinted, issued in Boston in three printings, and translated into German. Finally, this volume also includes Edwards's *Discourses on Various Important Subjects*, based on five sermons about the Awakening.

20. *The Miscellanies, 833-1152* (592 pages; 2002), edited by Amy Plantinga Pauw. These are the notebook entries Edwards wrote during the tumultuous years of 1740-1751. During this time, Edwards led his congregation through the Great Awakening, which resulted in a series of controversies with his Northampton congregation that eventually led to his dismissal.

21. *Writings on the Trinity, Grace, and Faith* (592 pages; 2003), edited by Sang Hyun Lee. In this collection of writings drawn from his essays and topical notebooks, Edwards deals with key Christian doctrines. The volume includes long-established treatises of Edwards, newly edited from the original manuscripts, as well as several smaller documents never published before; in

some cases, these documents reveal new aspects of his theology that still need to be studied.

22. *Sermons and Discourses, 1739-1742* (608 pages; 2003), edited by Harry S. Stout, Nathan O. Hatch, and Kyle P. Farley. The sermons and discourses in this volume, preached from 1739 to 1742, chart the rise and decline of the Great Awakening in Northampton and beyond. Several sermons included in this volume have never been printed before; also, the transcript of the original manuscript of "Sinners in the Hands of an Angry God" is reproduced for the first time, along with the text of its first printed edition.

23. *The Miscellanies, 1153-1360* (776 pages; 2004), edited by Douglas A. Sweeney. This fourth and final volume of miscellanies cover Edwards's final years, from 1751 to 1758, a period when Edwards faced the challenges of ministering at the Stockbridge Indian mission and made his transition to the presidency at Princeton. In these entries, Edwards responds to modern naturalism and the Enlightenment, showing us how to make reason subservient to the Scriptures.

Altogether Lovely: Jonathan Edwards on the Glory and Excellency of Jesus Christ (SDG; 231 pages; 1998). These sermons, collected from Edwards's *Works*, focus on the beauty and excellence of Christ. They are comforting and uplifting. They include "God the Best Portion of the Christian," "The Excellency of Jesus Christ," "Christ Exalted," and "Praise One of the Chief Employments of Heaven."

The Blessing of God, edited by Michael D. McMullen (B&H; 390 pages; 2003). This volume consists of twenty-two previously unpublished sermons transcribed from a collection of Edwards's papers held at the Beinecke Rare Book Room and Manuscript Library of Yale University. They cover a broad range of topics such as confessing and forsaking sin, delighting in exalting God, knowing the Redeemer, true conversion,

and the way to receive God's blessing. One remarkable sermon is titled, "In True Conversion Men's Bodies Are in Some
Respect Changed as Well as Their Souls."

A Call to United, Extraordinary Prayer (CFP; 165 pages;
2003). Historically, this little paperback proved to be a very
important book. It was first published by Edwards in 1747 as
*An Humble Attempt to promote an explicit agreement and visible union
of God's people through the world, in extraordinary prayer, for the revival of religion and the advancement of Christ's kingdom on earth.*
Edwards said he was motivated to write on "a concert of
prayer" for two reasons: first, he realized that the revivals of
the mid-1730s and the early 1740s would not recur until God's
people engaged in earnest prayer for revival. Second, he
wanted to provide additional theological support for a document simply called *Memorial*, written by some Scottish pastors.

In a helpful preface, David Bryant tells us the story of
Memorial: "Rising out of scores of prayer societies already func-
tioning in Scotland around 1740, especially among young
people, by 1744 a committee of ministers determined it was
time to do more. They decided to try a two-year 'experiment,'
uniting all prayer groups and praying Christians in their
nation into a common prayer strategy. They called for focused
revival prayer on every Saturday evening and Sunday morning, as well as on the first Tuesday of each quarter. By 1746
they were so gratified by the impact of their experiment that
they composed a call to prayer to the church worldwide, especially in the colonies. However, this time the 'concert of
prayer' was to be for *seven* years" (*Memorial*, pp. 16-17).

Citing Zechariah 8:20-22, Edwards says that God's rich
promises encourage us to expect great success from corporate prayer: "That which God abundantly makes the subject
of his *promises*, God's people should abundantly make the
subject of their *prayers*." He concludes that when believers
persevere in united, concerted prayer, God will grant a fresh

revival, which "shall be propagated, till the awakening reaches those that are in the highest stations, and till whole nations be awakened" (p. 18).

Edwards's book had a limited influence during his lifetime. Republished late in the eighteenth century in England, it influenced William Carey (1761-1834) and his prayer group. It also affected John Sutclif (1752-1814), a well-known Baptist pastor in Olney, who led weekly prayer meetings for revival in the Baptist churches of the Northamptonshire Association, to which his church belonged. Those prayer meetings spread throughout the British Isles, particularly impacting eighteenth century revivals in Wales. Heman Humphrey writes in his *Revival Sketches and Manual*, "One of the most important revivals of religion, when the effects are considered, is that which occurred in the 'Principality of Wales' under Howell Harris and Daniel Rowlands; and this was carried forward and fostered by means of private societies for prayer and religious conference" (pp. 55-56). In the end, tens of thousands were converted throughout Britain from the 1790s to the 1840s (Erroll Hulse, *Give Him No Rest: A call to prayer for revival*, pp. 78-79).

Edwards's treatise became a major manifesto for the Second Great Awakening around the beginning of the nineteenth century. It also fueled other awakenings in the late 1850s. Samuel Prime's *The Power of Prayer* explains how corporate prayer ushered in the famous 1857-1859 revival (sometimes called the Third Great Awakening) along the eastern coast of the United States, then spread west, resulting in the conversion of hundreds of thousands of people.

In sum, Edwards's book is a powerful call for united prayer in the worldwide church. It could have a powerful effect if church members would study it together and implement its suggestions in dependency on the Spirit.

Charity and Its Fruits (BTT; 368 pages; 1988). Originally given in Northampton in 1738, these sixteen sermons on

1 Corinthians 13 were prepared for the press by Edwards. They were not published until 1851, however, under the editorship of Edwards's great-grandson, Tryon Edwards. Edwards preached these sermons between the 1734 and 1740 revivals, shortly after a series on the wise and foolish virgins. To Edwards, the biblical principle of his text was clear: "By their fruits ye shall know them." Edwards shows the nature and virtue of love as *the* distinguishing mark of a true Christian—love, which manifests itself in preferring others before self. Throughout, he navigates skillfully between Arminianism and antinomianism. The series concludes with one of Edwards's most popular sermons, "Heaven is a World of Love," which has been called the most beautiful of all his writings.

Though somewhat repetitious, this work is among the best of Edwards's practical writings. Richard Allen said Edwards repeated himself so often because he was "knocking on closed doors."

Day by Day with Jonathan Edwards, edited by Randall J. Pederson (HP; 398 pages; 2005). Featuring 365 thought-provoking reflections accompanied by Scripture, this collection offers readers a daily measure of penetrating insight and thoughtful encouragement from the writings of Edwards. This book serves both as an introduction to the thought of Edwards and as a glimpse into a heart consumed by passion for God's glory. Includes an introduction on Edwards's life and ministry.

Devotions from the Pen of Jonathan Edwards (SDG; 120 pages; 2003). First compiled by Ralph G. Turnbull and published in 1959 as *Devotions of Jonathan Edwards*, this expanded reprint includes 120 excerpts from Edwards's writings. Notations at the bottom of each section inform the reader where the readings were taken from. The purpose of this small book is to "get people to read Jonathan Edwards," says Don Kistler in the preface. The only downside of this book is that it only includes four months' worth of daily readings, rather than a full year.

The Freedom of the Will (SDG; 325 pages; 1998). Many scholars believe this work, published in 1754, is the most important argument against Arminianism published in America. *Freedom of the Will* is divided into four parts. The first deals with terminology; the nature and determination of the will; the meaning of necessity, impossibility, and contingency; the distinction between natural and moral necessity; and the nature of moral agency and liberty. The second considers the possibility of self-determination. The third analyzes divine agency regarding human beings and the world. In the conclusion, Edwards anticipates the reception the work will receive.

Noteworthy is Edwards's essential agreement with the empiricist John Locke that the question of whether or not the will was "free" was badly posed; the real issue, he said, is whether the *person* is free. The majority of the work, however, deals with the will's freedom (in contrast to the freedom of the whole person) as it seeks to refute the Arminian notion of the will. For Edwards, the errors of the Arminians essentially resulted from denying God's absolute sovereignty; in contrast to Calvinist orthodoxy, Arminians insisted that secondary causes could operate in the individual apart from the influence of the divine will. This notion of the will's freedom had Pelagian roots, which Edwards rightly exposed. Furthermore, the refusal of the Arminians to acknowledge the individual's total corruption promoted further error. The will cannot be free as the Arminians would have it, Edwards argued, for true freedom can only belong to God, who is self-sustaining and therefore free from other influences.

*The Glory and Honor of God (B&H; 387 pages; 2004). This is the second volume in a series of unpublished sermons by Jonathan Edwards, all taken from the Beinecke Rare Book

Room and Manuscript Library of Yale University. There are twenty sermons: "That Wicked Men's Sins Lie at Their Door" (Gen. 4:7); "The Glory and Honor of God Requires That His Displeasure Be Manifested Against Sin" (Num. 14:21); "'Tis a Blessed Thing to Some Persons That God Is to Be Their Judge" (Ps. 7:8); "That Wicked Men Be Not Apt to Be Sensible but That It Will Always Be with Them as It is Now" (Ps. 10:6); "God's Manner Is First to Prepare Men's Hearts and Then to Answer Their Prayers" (Ps. 10:7); "That This Present World Shall One Day Come to an End" (Ps. 102:25-26); "It's a Very Decent and Comely Thing That Praise Should be Given to God" (Ps. 147:1); "Faith Renders Those Things That Are Most Terrible in Their Own Nature Harmless to Believers" (Dan. 6:23); "It Is What May Well Make Us Willing and Desirous to Go with God's People, That God Is with Them" (Zech. 8:23); "When a Company or Society of Christians Have Christ Present with Them, 'Tis the Greatest Cause of Joy to Them" (Matt. 9:15); "That the Son of God by Appearing in Our Nature Laid a Glorious Foundation for Peace to the Inhabitants of This World" (Luke 2:14); "That Hearing and Keeping the Word of God Renders a Person More Blessed Than Any Other Privilege That Ever God Bestowed on Any of the Children of Men" (Luke 11:27-28); "Even As I Have Kept My Father's Commandments" (John 15:10); "Jesus Christ Is the Shining Forth of the Father's Glory" (Heb. 1:3); "Those Who Love Christ Shall Receive of Him a Crown of Life" (James 1:12); "It Would Have Been Better for Some Persons If Christ Never Had Come into the World to Save Sinners" (1 Pet. 2:8); "That a Christian Spirit Is of Great Price in the Sight of God" (1 Pet. 3:4); "The Spirit of the True Saints Is a Spirit of Divine Love" (1 John 4:16); "Christ Was Worthy of His Exaltation upon the Account of His Being Slain" (Rev. 5:12); "In Hell Is Inflicted the Fierceness of the Wrath of a Being That Is Almighty" (Rev. 19:15).

Growing in God's Spirit (P&R; 160 pages; 2003). This is the inaugural volume in a series devoted to bringing Jonathan Edwards's works to today's reader in an easy-to-read format. It includes three of his greatest sermons, divided into selections of thirteen chapters. "A Divine and Supernatural Light" teaches what the divine work of the Holy Spirit is in the heart of man and the spiritual light He imparts through the Word of God. "Christian Knowledge" shows man's responsibility in pursuing divine knowledge as his daily calling. "The Christian Pilgrim" calls the believer to live more in the prospect of eternity.

A History of the Work of Redemption (BTT; 448 pages; 2003). In this classic, consisting of thirty sermons preached in Northampton in 1739, Edwards reviews the whole panorama of human history from the fall of man to the end of time, concluding that everything in human history is subservient to Christ's work of redemption. Here we catch Edwards's optimistic vision of the irresistible advance of the cause of Christ in the world and gain encouragement for gospel labors.

Jonathan Edwards on Revival (BTT; 140 pages; 1984). This book contains "Narrative of Surprising Conversions," "Distinguishing Marks of a Work of the Spirit of God," and "An Account of the Revival in Northampton in 1740-42." The first is Edwards's early assessment of the 1735 revival. It includes a fascinating account of several conversions, including those of young children. The second, written several years later, examines the saving marks of grace according to 1 John 4:1. The final piece was initially a letter written to a minister in Boston in 1743 during the Great Awakening.

This is a good book to begin a study of Edwards's view of revival, but it should be followed with a reading of *Religious Affections*, which is a more mature and realistic assessment of spiritual experience.

A Jonathan Edwards Reader, edited by John R. Smith, Harry S. Stout, and Kenneth P. Minkema (Yale; 335 pages; 1995). The selections in this book are divided into two major categories. The first tracks the public development of Edwards's thinking from his early days as a Yale student to the end of his life and ministry. These writings consist of treatises and sermons he published, including *Faithful Narrative, Religious Affections,* and *Freedom of the Will,* as well as notes that remained in manuscript form until after his death.

The second category shows the personal side of Edwards in autobiographical writings, correspondence, and family papers. The family papers include a letter from Edwards to his daughter, Esther, who became the mother of Aaron Burr, Jr., vice president of the United States. Edwards expresses his hopes that "Mr. Burr and you would be frequent in counseling Timmy [Edwards's eldest son] as to his soul concerns" (p. 313).

Jonathan Edwards's Resolutions and Advice to Young Converts (P&R; 37 pages; 2001). Edited and introduced by Stephen J. Nichols, this small paperback contains Edwards's personal resolutions for daily living as well as his lesser-known work, *Advice to Young Converts. Resolutions* shows a mature Edwards (though he was only age nineteen when he wrote most of this) reflecting the Puritan piety of the era. This small piece reveals what spiritual giants the Puritans were, even as young adults.

Justification by Faith Alone (SDG; 154 pages; 2000). This book is the substance of two lectures that Edwards delivered in 1738 to refute Arminianism, which was affecting Northampton, as well as antinomianism, which had persisted in the colonies since the days of Anne Hutchinson. With solid, scriptural reasoning, the work stresses that God justifies *the ungodly* (Rom. 4:5). John H. Gerstner wrote of Edwards: "More sharply than any he saw the sense in which justification by faith alone rested ultimately on justification by works—the works of Christ."

On Knowing Christ (BTT; 280 pages; 1991). This book contains ten sermons explaining the Spirit's work in the conviction of sin and leading believers into an experiential acquaintance with Christ and the marvels of the Christian life. It includes several famous sermons, such as "God Glorified in Man's Dependence," "Pressing into the Kingdom of God," "Sinners in the Hands of an Angry God," and "Safety, Fullness, and Sweet Refreshment, to be Found in Christ." In these sermons, Edwards is clearly evident as a God-centered thinker, searching preacher, precise theologian, and earnest pastor. This is a good book for those who wish to be introduced to Edwards.

*Knowing the Heart: Jonathan Edwards on True and False Conversion (IO; 441 pages; 2003). This volume consists of thirteen of Edwards's sermons never before published, with one exception on the theme of the heart of man. Edwards shows that the natural heart of man is at enmity with God: depraved, deceitful, and proud. William Nichols, as editor, premises that effective evangelism is dependent upon a knowledge of how the heart works and understanding the signs of true and false conversion. Chapters particularly relevant for today include: "A Pretence of Trusting in Christ is Vain as Long as Men Live Wicked Lives"; "Particular Repentance is Necessary to Salvation"; and one that may surprise many in our prosperous day, "God gives Plenty of Earthly Things to Those He Hates."

The Life and Diary of David Brainerd (Baker; 385 pages; 1989). This biography depicts life in pre-Revolutionary America, when religious revival swept the colonial frontier. From 1743 to 1747, Brainerd was a missionary to the Indians. Riding thousands of miles on horseback, he kept a journal of daily events until the week before he died at age twenty-nine at Edwards's house. In the journal are entries professing Brainerd's love for Edwards's daughter, Jerusha. When Jerusha is frightened about moving among the Indians, Brainerd advises her, "If God would have you die by an arrow, you would want it no other way."

Published in 1749, *Life of Brainerd* became a spiritual classic in its own time. It was the first popular biography to be published in America. It went through numerous editions and has been reprinted more times than any other work by Edwards. Recently scholars have suggested that Edwards substantially altered Brainerd's original diary (cf. vol. 7 of the Yale Edition of Edwards's works, where a surviving copy of Brainerd's diary is compared with Edwards's manuscript).

Regardless, Brainerd's diary, which is on a par with Augustine's *Confessions*, reveals the spiritual growth and intense personal struggles of a young man with great zeal for God. Both teenagers and adults should read this moving account. Brainerd's selfless life of prayer and zeal is convicting and inspiring.

Our Great and Glorious God (SDG; 212 pages; 2003). This book is a compilation of material from Edwards's sermons and "Miscellanies" on the existence and character of God, particularly His attributes of grace, sovereignty, wisdom, and justice. There are also chapters on God's decrees and God's glory. One of many savory quotations from the chapter on God's glory is as follows: "God is glorified not only by His glory being seen, but by its being rejoiced in. When those who see it delight in it, God is more glorified than if they only see it. His glory is then received by the whole soul, by both the understanding and by the heart."

The closing chapter, "Heaven is God's House," is a fitting capstone to the book. Edwards movingly raises our conceptions of God to higher levels, which is sorely needed in our day when most professing Christians are woefully deficient in understanding God's nature and character.

Pressing Into the Kingdom (SDG; 350 pages; 1998). This volume contains many of Edwards's sermons on seeking salvation. The eleven sermons include: "Pressing into the Kingdom of God" (Luke 16:16); "Preciousness of Time" (Eph. 5:16); "Procrastination" (Prov. 27:1); "Ruth's Resolution" (Ruth 1:16); "The Folly of Looking Back in Fleeing Out of Sodom" (Luke 17:32); "God Makes Men Sensible of Their Misery" (Hos. 5:15); "Sinners in Zion Tenderly Warned" (Isa. 33:14); "The Manner in Which the Salvation of the Soul is to be Sought" (Gen. 6:22); "The Vain Self-Flatteries of the Sinner" (Ps. 36:2); "Christ's Agony" (Luke 22:44), and "The Christian Pilgrim" (Heb. 11:13-14).

These sermons leave no excuse for spiritual slothfulness. Tender warnings combined with urgent exhortations are well designed to press sinners into the kingdom of God.

*The Puritan Pulpit: Jonathan Edwards (1703-1758) (SDG; 285 pages; 2004). This book is comprised of sixteen sermons by Edwards. Fourteen of these sermons have never been published before in any edition. Some of the sermon titles are: "It is Good for Us that God is Not as We are," "God Doesn't Thank Men for Doing Their Duty," "God Never Changes His Mind," "Men's Addiction to Sin is No Excuse, but an Aggravation," "There is a Mutual Abhorrence Between God and Wicked Men," and "Christ is the Christian's All."

Pursuing Holiness in the Lord (P&R; 215 pages; 2005). Holiness is something to be pursued, though never in our own strength. The three sermons of Edwards made accessible in this volume in thirteen chapters guide us past the rival pitfalls of lawlessness and works-righteousness to explore the believer's role in God's work of sanctification.

The Religious Affections (BTT; 382 pages; 2001). This work is often regarded as the leading classic in American history on spiritual life. Edwards here presents a more mature reflection of revival than in his *Faithful Narrative*, reflecting upon the strengths and weaknesses of the Great Awakening after it crested. Fundamentally, Edwards grapples with the questions: What makes a person a Christian? What is it about a person that would move others to recognize him as a Christian? What is the difference between true and false Christian experience? Edwards first considers the nature of affections and their importance in religion, answering the charges of Charles Chauncy. He views affections as the desires of the heart based upon intellectual reflections, and argues that true religion consists in the affections.

In the second part of his work, Edwards describes twelve signs of gracious affections that may not necessarily indicate saving faith. These include intense feelings; experiences that produce physical effects; fluency in spiritual matters; not causing one's own affections; having verses of Scripture impressed upon the mind; the appearance of being loving; experiencing a variety of affections; being moved by affections to spend much time in religious matters; affections that move one to praise God; affections that lead to a strong sense of assurance of salvation; affections that lead one to act in ways that are accepted by the godly. Edwards goes on to argue that external signs motivated by religious affections neither deny nor confirm genuine religious experience. He takes a middle position between those who claimed the phenomena that took place in Northampton proved the revival true and those who said the phenomena showed it to be false.

In the final section, Edwards explains the true marks of genuine conversion, noting that they all arise from the illumination of God's Spirit. He describes twelve true signs of gracious affections:

- A new birth, or regeneration
- A new transcendental perspective in daily life that focuses on God's glory
- A love for the loveliness of divine things
- A "new taste" that combines "heat with light"; understanding is essential but insufficient by itself
- A deep conviction of an immediate sense of divinity and total control of self by the truths of the gospel
- An evangelical rather than legal humiliation
- A radical change of nature that results in conversion
- A genuine love for and meekness toward others
- A Christian tenderness toward others
- A kind of symmetry or proportion of all the foregoing affections
- A desire for a growing relationship with God
- A gracious love that manifests itself in behavior

The Salvation of Souls: Nine Previously Unpublished Sermons by Jonathan Edwards on the Call of Ministry and the Gospel (Crossway; 190 pages; 2003). In this new collection of sermons, Edwards calls ministers to focus on the salvation of souls. They must not shrink from this important task but must persevere in denouncing sin and calling sinners to repentance and faith in Christ. They should not depend on their own wisdom but on the Holy Spirit as they faithfully preach the Word. This challenging yet comforting book is designed for ministers of the gospel.

Sermons include: "The Death of Faithful Ministers a Sign of God's Displeasure" (Isa. 3:12); "Ministers Need the Power of God" (2 Cor. 4:7); "The Kind of Preaching People Want" (Micah 2:11); "The Minister Before the Judgment Seat of Christ" (Luke 10:17-18); "Deacons to Care for the Body, Ministers for the Soul" (Rom. 12:4-8); "Ministers to Preach Not Their Own Wisdom but the Word of God" (1 Cor. 2:11-13);

228   MEET THE PURITANS

"Pastor and People Must Look to God" (Acts 14:23); and "The Work of the Ministry is Saving Sinners" (Acts 20:28).

Seeking God: Jonathan Edwards' Evangelism Contrasted with Modern Methodologies, ed. William C. Nichols (IO; 564 pages; 2001). This book reprints sixteen of Edwards's evangelistic sermons and treatises. Each document is accompanied with a detailed editorial analysis of Edwards's evangelistic methods in contrast to modern Arminian and naturalistic evangelistic methods. The editor repeatedly concludes that modern evangelism deceives the unsaved, for it does not tell impenitent sinners the truth about themselves as God's enemies or about their impending eternity in hell if they fail to repent. By contrast, Nichols stresses Edwards's stark biblical realism which focuses on the dreadfulness of man's natural state as essential to God-honoring evangelism.

The goal of Edwards's evangelistic method is to call people to seek God. Nichols concludes that Edwards's concept of "seeking God"—which stresses waiting on God in His appointed means of grace such as reading, hearing, crying for mercy, praying for a new heart, and forsaking every known sin—appears in almost every sermon he preached. Though this book serves as a helpful antidote to much of modern evangelism, it needs to be balanced with Edwards's equal emphasis on the Triune God seeking and finding sinners by means of His gracious invitations and glorious promises.

The Selected Writings of Jonathan Edwards (Waveland Press; 190 pages; 1992). Edited by Harold P. Simonson, this collection of essays and sermons demonstrates Edwards's perspectives in theology, ethics, psychology, and aesthetics. Included are "Personal Narrative," "God Glorified in Man's Dependence," "A Divine and Supernatural Light," and "A Farewell Sermon." Edwards's interpretations address current philosophical questions about the natural goodness of people and the growing need for accurate theology to inform philosophical musings.

Selections from the Unpublished Writings of Jonathan Edwards, edited by Alexander Grosart (SDG; 212 pages; 1997). In 1854, Grosart, editor of the Nichols Series of Puritan reprints, began working with the unpublished manuscripts of Jonathan Edwards. Some of this material was published in 1865 as *Selections.* This work includes "A Treatise on Grace," "Annotations on the Bible," "Directions for Judging Persons' Experiences," and sermons on Matthew 7:14, 2 Timothy 3:16, Romans 6:1, Acts 24:25, and 1 Peter 3:19-20.

Sermons of Jonathan Edwards (HP; 400 pages; 2005). This is a collection of twenty of Edwards's most famous sermons, many of which focus on the majesty and grandeur of God and the hopelessness of man's spiritual reformation and revival apart from God's grace. It includes "God Glorified in Man's Dependence," "Wicked Men Useful in Their Destruction Only," "Pressing into the Kingdom of God," "The Excellency of Christ," "Pardon for the Greatest Sinners," "Christ's Agony," and "Sinners in the Hands of an Angry God." This book would be a wise purchase for those who desire to be introduced to Edwards's sermons.

The Sermons of Jonathan Edwards: A Reader (Yale; 281 pages; 1999). This anthology shows Edwards addressing a great variety of Christian experiences. The collection contains fifteen sermons (of the more than 1,200 that Edwards preached), including five that were not previously published. An introduction describes the sermons' historical context (some were preached to predominantly English congregations, others to Native Americans; all were delivered in the period between the Salem witch trials and the American Revolution) and their literary structure. Each sermon starts with a Scripture text and brief interpretation; states a doctrine that will be explained; then proceeds with various defenses, applications, and uses of the doctrine in the lives of listeners.

One of the most interesting sermons, titled "The Way of Holiness," was preached when Edwards was a teenager. It explains each step in the soul's pilgrimage and urges believers to live in such a way that deepens the "likeness in *nature* between God and the soul of the believer." Edwards's personal journey, described in *Resolutions*, reveals his commitment to live as a teenager with all his might in the way of holiness he here preaches about.

Standing in Grace (SDG; 70 pages; 2002). In this work, Edwards examines the difference between common grace and saving grace. He shows the nature and qualities of saving grace, emphasizing how grace is given by the Spirit of God. Edwards also explains the nature of the Holy Spirit's relationship to grace. This work was first published in 1865 by Alexander Grosart as *A Treatise on Grace*. It is a part of *Selections from the Unpublished Writings of Jonathan Edwards*.

Thoughts on the New England Revival: Vindicating the Great Awakening (BTT; 294 pages; 2005). D. Martyn Lloyd-Jones advises, "If you want to know anything about true revival, Edwards is the man to consult." Edwards was uniquely qualified to write on the subject of revival because of his theological grasp and his first-hand experience of spiritual awakenings. In this volume, first published as *Some Thoughts Concerning the Present Revival of Religion in New England* (1742), he expresses his thoughts on "the glorious work of God" in the Great Awakening, and shows why the Awakening should be promoted. Edwards defends this revival against its critics and the excesses of its friends. What is a revival? How is it to be recognized? Is it a genuine work of the Spirit of God? If it is, then how is revival to be guarded against the spurious errors and unscriptural tendencies of its over-zealous promoters? What are we to make of "outcries and bodily effects" in revival? How can spiritual pride, immediate revelation, and unjust censuring of others be avoided in revival? All these questions and more are ably answered by Edwards.

To All the Saints of God: Addresses to the Church (SDG; 401 pages; 2003). This collection of twelve sermons explains the role of the church and its relationship to God. Edwards considers the issues of ecclesiology and membership from a practical standpoint. He also focuses on personal duties in the church. Such topics as prayer, dependence on God, bereavement, self-examination, and hope for the penitent are addressed with biblical fidelity and keen pastoral insight. Particularly helpful are "The Church's Marriage to Her Sons and to Her God" (Isa. 62:4-5) and "The Nature and End of Excommunication" (1 Cor. 5:11). Edwards shows us that solutions to all church problems are always available by God's gracious kindness but need to be practiced if the church is to be "fair as the moon, clear as the sun, and terrible as an army with banners" (S.S. 6:10).

*To the Rising Generation: Addresses Given to Children and Young Adults (SDG; 183 pages; 2005). During his Northampton tenure, Edwards preached thirty sermons to children and young adults. This new book contains thirteen of those addresses (nine of which are published for the first time), plus a letter to a young convert and a list of 115 Bible questions for children. For the most part, these messages focus on the importance of obedience, discipline, and seeking God. Chapter titles include: "Early Piety is Especially Acceptable to God," "The Sudden Death of Children," "The Sins of Youth Go With Them to Eternity," "The Most Direct Way to Happiness," "Children Ought to Love the Lord Jesus Christ above All

Things in this World," "Corrupt Communications," "The Danger of Sinful Mirth," and more.

Throughout this book, Edwards impresses on young people the constant need to repent of sin and live faithfully to the Lord. He stresses that when young people devote themselves to following Christ, they are able to serve the purposes of the kingdom for the majority of their years. "There is a peculiar honor done to God," he writes, "when persons devote their youthful age to God."

Treatise on Grace and Other Posthumously Published Writings (JC; 144 pages; 2000). This collection contains Edwards's famous work on grace, which shows how saving and common grace differ in nature and in fruits (see above). It also contains "Observations Concerning the Trinity and the Covenant of Redemption" (Edwards's *Miscellanies*, pp. 573-88, prepared for publication by Edwards's son), and "An Essay on the Trinity" (first published in 1903 and edited by G.P. Fisher), which provides an *a priori* argument for the existence of the Trinity. The book is edited by Paul Helm, who provides a succinct introduction to the work (23 pages), viewing Edwards from the perspectives of history, theology, and philosophy.

The True Believer: Sermons by Jonathan Edwards on the Marks and Benefits of True Faith (SDG; 315 pages; 2003). This anthology of eight sermons distinguishes between the marks of true and false converts. Included are "Pardon for the Greatest of Sinners," "True Grace Distinguished from the Experience of Devils," "Hypocrites Deficient in the Duty of Prayer," "A Warning to Professors of Religion," "Christians a Chosen Generation, a Royal Priesthood, a Peculiar People," "The Peace which God Gives His True Followers," "True Saints, when Absent from the Body, are Present with the Lord," and "The Portion of the Righteous."

Unless You Repent (SDG; 232 pages; 2005). Jonathan Edwards is famous for sermons such as "Sinners in the Hands of an Angry God," which vividly portray the reality of hell. But Edwards was no mere "hellfire and brimstone" preacher; he spoke of divine judgment because of his desire to see many come to Christ and be spared from God's wrath. This volume contains fifteen previously unpublished sermons on the judgment awaiting the impenitent. Sermon titles include: "Vengeance for Sin Properly Belongs to God," "All Wicked Men Shall Go to Hell," "The Torments of Hell are Exceedingly Great," etc. We know of no more solemn volume ever published than this.

The Wrath of Almighty God: Jonathan Edwards on God's Judgment Against Sinners (SDG; 390 pages; 1998). This contains eleven sermons and treatises from *The Works of Edwards* dealing with some aspect of hell or God's judgment against sin. The sermons include "Sinners in the Hands of an Angry God," "The Justice of God in the Damnation of Sinners," "Wrath to the Uttermost," "The Eternity of Hell's Torments," and "The End of the Wicked Contemplated by the Righteous."

When reading these sermons, keep in mind that Edwards should not be classified as a "hell-fire and brimstone" preacher. While he did preach regularly on hell, he did so not to scare people into the kingdom but to awaken slumbering sinners. If this book fails to make its unconverted reader tremble, despair of self-righteousness, and take refuge in Christ, the fault lies wholly with the reader.

John Eliot

(1604-1690)

John Eliot, missionary to Native Americans, was born in England, the son of Bennett Eliot, a prosperous yeoman, and Lettice Aggar. He was baptized at Widford, Hertford-shire, on August 5, 1604. Before John was six years old, the Eliots moved to Nazeing, Essex, where Bennett Eliot owned considerable property. John enjoyed studying classical litera-ture and Hebrew. He went to Jesus College, Cambridge, in 1619, where he earned a Bachelor of Arts degree in 1622. While at college, both of his parents died—his mother in 1620 and his father in 1621.

Eliot was ordained in the Anglican Church, but he soon became dissatisfied with its rules and policies. Instead of searching for a parish, he chose to teach at the grammar school in Little Baddow, Essex, where Thomas Hooker was master.

Eliot lived for some time with Hooker and was strongly influenced by him. He later explained how this teaching expe-rience brought him to conversion: "To this place I was called, through the infinite riches of God's mercy in Christ Jesus to my poor soul: for here the Lord said unto my dead soul, live; and through the grace of Christ, I do live, and I shall live for ever! When I came to this blessed [Hooker] family I then saw, and never before, the power of godliness in its lively vigour and efficacy." Soon after his conversion, Eliot decided to devote himself to the ministry.

In 1630, Hooker left England, where nonconformist pastors were being persecuted, and went to the Netherlands. With the closing of Hooker's school and increasing pressures for conformity, Eliot chose to immigrate to Massachusetts. He arrived in Boston on November 3, 1631. He was soon asked to serve as a substitute pastor for John Wilson, who had gone to England. Eliot's preaching and pastoral work so impressed the congregation that when Wilson returned in May 1632, Eliot was asked to stay on as "the teacher of the congregation." He declined the offer because he had agreed to serve the people of Nazeing (England) who had settled in Roxbury, Massachusetts. Roxbury became Eliot's home for the remainder of his life.

Shortly before Eliot was ordained, his fiancée, Hannah Mumford, arrived in New England. Theirs was the first wedding in Roxbury. Hannah soon became known for her holiness and service.

The Eliots were blessed with five sons and one daughter. Two sons died in their youth. The remaining three sons—John, Joseph, and Benjamin—lived to become missionaries to the Native Americans. Only Joseph and his sister, Hannah, outlived their father, however. Cotton Mather recalled Eliot saying about his sons, "My desire was that they should have served God on earth; but if God will choose to have them rather in heaven, I have nothing to object against it, but his will be done!" (*Magnalia Christi Americana*, 1:530).

Eliot served the Roxbury church as teacher and later as pastor for more than fifty years. The first fifteen years, he devoted himself wholly to the work of the church, and the next thirty-five to pastoring the congregation and working among Native Americans. Eliot became widely known as a skilled preacher and counselor. His fluency in Hebrew earned him a position on the translation team of the Bay Psalm Book, published in 1640. Three years later, he began studying the

Algonquian language. He began preaching to the natives in their own language in 1646.

Eliot undertook the task of convincing philanthropists in England about the necessity of converting the Native Americans. He first appealed to individuals for support, but after the Puritan Commonwealth was approved, Eliot began working with the Corporation for The Promoting and Propagating the Gospel of Jesus Christ in New England. Over the next twenty years, Eliot wrote or sponsored a great many works that became known as the Eliot Indian Tracts. These tracts were published in London as aids in fundraising. Eliot soon had the support he needed to work among the native people of America.

Eliot began to set up towns of "praying Indians." Natick was the first (1651). By 1674, there were fourteen praying towns, with an estimated population of 3,600; approximately 1,100 had been converted. In each town, the natives made a solemn covenant to give themselves and their children "to God to be His people" as the basis of the new civil government. Eliot organized the new government following Jethro's advice to Moses in Exodus 18; he appointed rulers over hundreds, fifties, and tens in each town to keep law and order. These towns were almost entirely self-governing, though major issues could be referred to the Massachusetts General Court. For the most part, the natives were expected to adopt the Puritan lifestyle along with the Christian faith.

After organizing the civil government, Eliot started establishing churches with the Congregationalist form of government. After overcoming numerous difficulties in a fifteen-year period, the first native church was officially established in 1660 at Natick. The establishment of other churches in praying towns soon followed.

In the meantime, Eliot had been working hard since 1653 on translating the Bible into the Native American language. One of the most difficult tasks was inventing a vocabulary as well as grammar to express the relationships of time and space that were missing from the native language. With the help of English supporters, Eliot established a printing press in Cambridge. In 1661, Marmaduke Johnson printed the first New Testament in the Massachusett language. The Old Testament with metrical psalms followed in 1663, making it the first complete Bible printed on the American continent. The Algonquian Bible is considered by many to be Eliot's greatest accomplishment, but for Eliot, that Bible was simply an aid to the conversion of Native Americans.

Eliot translated more works into Massachusett, ranging from classics of Puritan piety to primers and one-page catechisms. By this time, Eliot had some co-workers. They kept the society's printing press busy until King Philip's War. They also founded schools in the native towns. To help in the schools, Eliot published *The Indian Grammar Begun* (1666), *The Indian Primer* (1669), and *The Logic Primer* (1672). A building was even put up for an "Indian college" at Harvard. Few natives went to the college, however, due to a scarcity of teachers and students.

The souls of natives so dominated Eliot's thinking that he did not fear for his life. When once challenged by a Native American sagamore with a knife, Eliot said, "I am about the work of the great God, and He is with me, so that I fear not all the sachems of the country. I'll go on, and do you touch me if you dare" (Ola Winslow, *John Eliot: Apostle to the Indians*, p. 1).

Eliot's work prospered until the onset of King Philip's War in 1675. Fearing for their lives, numerous native converts moved to an island in the Boston harbor. Many died there. That pattern was repeated in other towns, where praying Indians were destroyed by either warring tribesmen or angry colonists. Unfortunately, the praying Indians were considered enemies of both the English and native Indians; only Eliot and a few others stood by them during the war. In the end, the fourteen praying towns were wiped out.

After the war, the surviving Native Americans returned to Natick. Eliot attempted to start over, rebuilding Natick and three other towns despite the distrust of the English. It seemed at first that Eliot's experiment in the New World might still be successful, but that effort never recovered. By the nineteenth century, not one convert remained who could read the Bible in the Massachusett language.

Cotton Mather wrote Eliot's first biography, titled *The Life and Death of the Renowned Mr. John Eliot, who was the first preacher of the Gospel to the Indians in America with an account of the wonderful success which the Gospel has had amongst the heathen in that part of the world, and of the many strange customs of the pagan Indians in New-England* (1691). He portrays Eliot as a man of great piety and single-hearted dedication. "He was one who lived in heaven while he was on earth," Mather writes. Eliot encouraged others to pray. His charity to Indians and the English was limited only by his resources; he pleaded with his congregation to help others. He often attended lectures in surrounding towns to "feed his own soul." He labored to form a "well-principled people" through preaching, catechizing, and the founding of schools; he established the first free school in America (Sidney Rooy, *The Theology of Missions in the Puritan Tradition*, p. 158). He also served as overseer of Harvard for more than forty years, bringing a strong Puritan presence to the college even though he never taught there.

In the last days of his life, Eliot was in much physical pain. However, all he could focus on was Christ and his beloved Native Americans. "There is a cloud, a dark cloud among the poor Indians," he said. "The Lord revive and prosper that work, and grant it may live when I am dead. It is a work, which I have been doing much and long about. But what was the word I spoke last? I recall that word, 'my doings.' Alas, they have been poor and small and lean doings, and I'll be the man that shall throw the first stone at them all" (p. 127).

Mather describes how that concern kept Eliot going: "For many months before he died, he would often cheerfully tell us that he was shortly to go to heaven, and that he would carry a deal of good news thither with him; he said he would carry tidings to the Old Founders of New England, which were now in glory, that church-work was yet carried on among us, that the number of our churches was continually increasing, and that the churches were still kept as big as they were, by the daily additions of those that shall be saved" (p. 130).

Eliot died May 20, 1690, at the age of eighty-six. His last words, as recorded by Mather, were, "Welcome joy!"

<hr/>

The Eliot Tracts: with Letters from John Eliot to Thomas Thorowgood and Richard Baxter (Greenwood; 175 pages; 2003). This collection contains the complete set of tracts—eleven in all—that were published in London between 1643 and 1671. Written by John Eliot, Thomas Shepard, and other leaders among the colonists, these tracts offer the most detailed record of missionary activity by the English in the New World. They are also a rich source of ethnographic information about the Native Americans of Southern New England in the seventeenth century. The volume also contains two letters in which Eliot argues for the significance of mission work.

The Indian Grammar Begun: Or, an Essay to Bring the Indian Language into Rules, for Help of Such As Desire to Learn the Same, for the Furtherance of the Gospel among Them (Applewood; 146 pages; 2001). Originally published in 1666, this edition of Eliot's grammar contains both facsimile and reset editions of Eliot's work.

Edward Fisher

(d. 1655)

E dward Fisher of London, of whom little is known, must be distinguished from Edward Fisher of Mickleton. He was probably a member of the guild of barber surgeons in London, attended a Presbyterian church there, and was converted to Puritan thinking after a conversation with Thomas Hooker. Though lacking a formal education, and remaining a layman, Fisher was apparently well versed in theological issues. He described himself as "a poor inhabitant of London," but acquired a goodly number of books for writing his controversial *Marrow of Modern Divinity*, the history of which is told below. That book overshadows his other works, such as *A Touchstone for the Communicant* (1647) and *London's Gate to the Lord's Table* (1648), both of which concern the question of exclusion from the sacrament, and *Faith in Five Fundamental Principles* (1650), which was a strong defense against the "diabolical, atheistic, blasphemous batteries [i.e. assaults of the truth]" of those times.

The Marrow of Modern Divinity (SWRB; 370 pages; 1991). First published in 1645, this work was considerably revised in the next two years and passed through seven editions by 1650. It is written in the form of a dialogue in which Evangelista plays the major role. His responses to questions and objections of others present the "marrow" or chief tenets of

Reformed theology. Other characters include Neophytus (a young Christian), Nomista (a legalist), and Antinomista (an antinomian). Fisher's goal was to mediate between legalists and antinomians, pointing out "the middle path, which is Jesus Christ received truly and walked in answerably."

Fisher's dialogues addressed issues of his day, such as the offer of grace, assurance and saving faith, the covenant of grace and faith, preparation for grace and evangelical repentance, the necessity of holiness, and good works to salvation. Thomas Boston's extensive notes and an appendix of questions and answers submitted by the twelve Marrowmen are priceless.

This work played an important role in the so-called Marrow Controversy among Scottish divines (1717-1723). In 1717, William Craig, a divinity student, issued a complaint to the General Assembly of the Church of Scotland against one of the propositions which the Presbytery of Auchterarder required ministerial candidates to sign as "the Auchterarder Creed." The proposition, which was intended to guard against preparationism, said: "I believe that it is not sound and orthodox to teach that we must forsake sin in order to our coming to Christ, and instating us in covenant with God." The General Assembly sided with Craig, declaring the proposition to be "unsound and most detestable." It said the statement tended to "encourage sloth in Christians and slacken people's obligation to gospel holiness."

The assembly's commission softened the harshness of the General Assembly's pronouncement by stating in its report to the 1718 assembly that the Presbytery was sound and orthodox in its intent, though the word choice was "unwarrantable" and should not be used again. In the context of that debate, Thomas Boston told John Drummond of Crieff that he had received help on the disputed issue from a relatively unknown book titled *The Marrow of Modern Divinity*. Drummond mentioned the book to James Webster of Edinburgh, who told James Hog of Carnock about it. Hog wrote a preface to a new edition of the book in 1718.

With the exception of its sympathy for Amyraldism, Fisher's book largely reflects the orthodox Reformed thought of the time in which he wrote it. It emphasizes an immediate offer of salvation to sinners who looked to Christ in faith. That was avidly supported by Boston and the Erskines, who were leaders among the church's evangelical minority. Fisher's emphasis, however, raised objections from the controlling party of the church who, as neonomians, held that the gospel is a "new law" (*neonomos*) (see above on Richard Baxter). They said the gospel replaced the Old Testament law's legal conditions of faith and repentance, which had to be met before salvation could be offered. These neonomians, who became known as the Moderates, maintained the necessity of forsaking sin before Christ could be received, whereas the Erskines and their evangelical friends said that only union with Christ could empower a sinner to become holy.

The Moderates said a call to immediate trust in Christ and full assurance was dangerously antinomian. James Hadow of St. Mary's College in St. Andrews found a number of supposed antinomian statements in Fisher's book. He said one suggested that the believer is not subject to the divine law as a rule of life, and another that holy living was not essential to salvation. Hadow also said the book taught that assurance is of the essence of faith, and that the fear of punishment and the hope of reward are not proper motives for a believer's obedience. Finally, Hadow claimed that Fisher's book taught universal atonement because it asserted that Christ's death was "the deed of gift and grant to mankind lost."

Led by Hadow, the General Assembly condemned *The Marrow of Modern Divinity* in 1720 and required all ministers of the church to warn their people against reading it. The Erskines, Boston, and nine of their colleagues, who became

known as the Marrowmen or Marrow Brethren for their defense of Fisher's book, protested this action but without avail.
They were formally rebuked by the General Assembly in 1722.

The Marrow Controversy quieted down by 1723, but its
effects lingered. The Marrow Brethren suffered continuing rejection in the Church of Scotland. They lost many friends and
opportunities to move to important parishes. In some presbyteries, approval of assembly acts against Fisher's book became
a requirement for ordination.

The Erskines and other Marrow Brethren continued to
teach and write on the doctrines the assembly had condemned.
Thomas Boston published copious notes on *The Marrow of
Modern Divinity* in the 1726 edition, and Ralph Erskine wrote
several tracts defending Marrow theology. The Marrow
Brethren also presented formal protests to the assembly to
reverse its judgment on Fisher's book.

The Marrowmen were convinced that in condemning
Fisher's book, the assembly condemned gospel truth. Doctrinally, the controversy centered on various aspects of the
relationship between God's sovereignty and human responsibility in the work of salvation. The Marrow Brethren
emphasized God's grace, and the assembly insisted on what
must be done in order to obtain salvation. The Marrow
Brethren described the covenant of grace as a testament containing God's promises of grace in Christ, which is freely
offered to all. Assurance is found primarily in Christ and His
work. A believer's response to this is love and gratitude, they
said. Their opponents viewed the covenant as a contract with
mutual obligations. The gospel is offered only to the prepared
or "sensible" sinner, and assurance focuses on the good works
of the believer. Obedience is a response to threats of God's
wrath as much as it is to His love.

Theological divisions in the Marrow controversy
reflected similar divisions in Reformed thought. Still, the

Marrow Brethren were more in harmony with the Reformed orthodoxy of the sixteenth and early seventeenth centuries, codified in the Westminster Confession of Faith and catechisms. Marrow opponents, though representative of the majority of ministers in the early eighteenth-century Church of Scotland, reflected, among other things, the legalistic tendencies of the Reformed theology that developed in the late seventeenth century, though they no doubt did have some grounds to be critical of parts of Fisher's work, particularly his tendency to Amyraldism.

John Flavel

(1628-1691)

J ohn Flavel (or Flavell) was born in 1628 in Bromsgrove, Worcestershire. He was the son of Richard Flavel, a minister who died of the plague in 1665 while in prison for nonconformity. John Flavel was educated by his father in the ways of religion, then "plied his studies hard" as a commoner at University College, Oxford. In 1650, he was ordained by the presbytery at Salisbury. He settled in Diptford, where he honed his numerous gifts.

He married Joan Randall, a godly woman, who died while giving birth to their first child in 1655. The baby died as well. After a year of mourning, Flavel married Elizabeth Stapell and was again blessed with a close, God-fearing marriage, as well as children.

In 1656, Flavel accepted a call to be minister in the thriving seaport of Dartmouth. He earned a smaller income there, but his work was more profitable; many were converted. One of his parishioners wrote of Flavel, "I could say much, though not enough of the excellency of his preaching; of his seasonable, suitable, and spiritual matter; of his plain expositions of Scripture; his talking method, his genuine and natural deductions, his convincing arguments, his clear and powerful demonstrations, his heart-searching applications, and his comfortable supports to those that were afflicted in conscience. In short, that person must have a very soft head, or a

JOHN FLAVEL

very hard heart, or both, that could sit under his ministry un-affected" (Erasmus Middleton, *Evangelical Biography*, 4:50-51).

Flavel was ejected from the pulpit in 1662 for nonconfor-mity, but he continued to meet secretly with his parishioners in conventicles. On occasion, he would preach for them in the woods, especially on days of fasting and humiliation. Once he even disguised himself as a woman on horseback in order to reach a secret meeting place where he preached and adminis-tered baptism. At another time, when pursued by authorities, he plunged his horse into the sea and managed to escape arrest by swimming through a rocky area to reach Slapton Sands.

In 1665, when the Five Mile Act went into effect, Flavel moved to Slapton, which was beyond the five-mile limit of legal disturbance. There he ministered to many people in his congregation. At times, he would preach secretly in the woods to larger numbers of people, sometimes as late as midnight. Once, soldiers rushed in and dispersed the congregation. Sev-eral of the fugitives were apprehended and fined, but the remainder brought Flavel to another wooded area where he continued his sermon.

Flavel preached from other unique pulpits, such as Sal-stone Rock, an island in the Salcombe Estuary that is submerged at high tide. In that refuge, the congregation would "linger in devout assembly till the rising tide drove them to their boats."

In 1672, King Charles II issued the Declaration of Indul-gence, giving Nonconformists freedom to worship. Flavel returned to Dartmouth, licensed as a Congregationalist. When the indulgence was canceled the following year, Flavel once more resorted to preaching secretly in private homes, secluded neighborhoods, or remote forests. Flavel's second wife died during this time and he married Ann Downe, a min-ister's daughter. They were happily married for eleven years, and had two sons.

In the late 1670s and early 1680s, Flavel carried on his ministry mainly by writing. He published at least nine books in this period. In the summer of 1682, he was forced to seek safety in London, where he joined the congregation of his friend, William Jenkyn, known today for his commentary on Jude. In 1684, soldiers interrupted a prayer service Flavel was conducting with Jenkyn. Flavel narrowly escaped arrest. During his stay in London, Flavel's third wife died. He married Dorothy, a widowed daughter of George Jefferies, minister of Kingsbridge; she survived him.

In 1685, Flavel returned to Dartmouth, where his ministry was confined to his home. He preached every Sunday and on many weekday evenings to people who crowded into his home. That same year he was burned in effigy by a mob, but he pressed on, praying for his beloved Dartmouth, "O that there were not a prayerless family in this town!" In 1687, King James II issued another indulgence for Nonconformists that allowed Flavel to preach publicly once again. This freedom was later augmented with the coming of William of Orange and the Glorious Revolution in 1688.

Flavel's congregation built a large church upon his return to the pulpit. His last four years of public preaching, which began with his sermons on Revelation 3:20, "Behold I stand at the door and knock," were greatly blessed. Yet he was aging rapidly. Speaking for himself and his colleagues, he wrote, "We have long borne the burden and heat of the day; we are veteran soldiers almost worn out." While visiting Exeter to preach on June 6, 1691, Flavel suffered a massive stroke and died that same evening at the age of sixty-three. His final words were, "I know that it will be well with me."

Flavel was humble, godly, and learned. He spent much time in study and prayer. One of his children wrote, "He was always full and copious in prayer, seemed constantly to exceed himself, and rarely made use twice of the same expressions." He was well versed in church discipline, infant baptism, and a number of Oriental languages.

Flavel's preaching was blessed by the Spirit. Robert Murray M'Cheyne tells about an American immigrant, Luke Short, who remembered listening to Flavel preach in England when he was fifteen years old. The text was, "If any man love not the Lord Jesus Christ, let him be *anathema maranatha*." Eighty-five years after hearing Flavel preach on the horror of dying under God's curse, the Spirit of God effectually converted him at the age of one hundred as he meditated on that sermon!

Flavel's power as a preacher came out of his depth of spiritual experience. He spent many hours in meditation and self-examination. As Middleton writes, "He [Flavel] attained to a well-grounded assurance, the ravishing comforts of which were many times shed abroad in his soul; this made him a powerful and successful preacher, as one who spoke from his own heart to those of others. He preached what he felt, and what he had handled, what he had seen and tasted of the word of life and they felt it also" (ibid., p. 58).

While meditating on heaven on one occasion, Flavel was so overcome with heavenly joy that he lost sight of this world. Stopping his horse by a spring, he viewed death as the most amiable face he had ever seen, except that of Christ's, who made it so. When he finally arrived at an inn, the innkeeper said to him, "Sir, what is the matter with you? You look like a dead man." "Friend," Flavel replied, "I was never better in my life." Years later, Flavel said that he understood more of heaven from that experience than from all the books he had ever read and all the sermons he had ever heard on the subject.

———◆◆◆———

The Works of John Flavel (BTT; 6 vols., 3,600 pages; 1968). Flavel's complete works were printed five times in the eighteenth century, three times in the nineteenth century, and several times in the twentieth century. Repeated printings of his writings (also in individual paperback editions) testify to their sound doctrinal instruction and spiritual application. They have been used by the Spirit to influence many people, including notable divines such as Jonathan Edwards and George Whitefield, and Scottish evangelical leaders such as Robert Murray M'Cheyne and Andrew Bonar. Archibald Alexander, the first professor at Princeton Seminary, read Flavel when he was a teenager. He later wrote, "To John Flavel I certainly owe more than to any uninspired author." Edward Bickersteth wrote, "There are few writers of a more experimental, affectionate, practical, popular, and edifying character than Flavel" (cf. Iain Murray, "John Flavel," *Banner of Truth*, no. 60 [September 1968]: 3-5).

The first volume of Flavel's *Works* describes the life of John Flavel and includes "The Fountain of Life." Volume 2 contains "The Method of Grace" and "Pneumatologia: A Treatise of the Soul of Man." Flavel deals with the origin, nature, and capacities of the soul and its union with the body. He proves the immortality of the soul and shows how it loves and "inclines" to the body.

Volume 3 contains the remaining part of "Pneumatologia," in which Flavel stresses that we ought to think often of death, particularly our own, before it comes. As believers, we should strive to begin to be what we expect to be, realizing there is nothing between us and those who have died but a breath and moment of time. Thoughts of hell can also benefit us by making us more aware of the horrifying end of sinners. These thoughts can also make us more conscious of the purpose of our existence. More than a hundred pages describe the souls of believers in the intermediate state, and twenty pages deal with souls of unbelievers in the intermediate state. Flavel concludes by stressing the value of our souls and our need to redeem time. "A Practical Treatise on Fear," based on Isaiah

8:12-14, focuses on fear and how one's own fears are the cruelest tormentors. "Some fear more than they ought, and some before they ought, and others when they ought not at all," Flavel writes. "The Righteous Man's Refuge," based on Isaiah 26:20, stresses how God's people rest in God and how His attributes of wisdom, faithfulness, unchangeableness, and love are revealed when He pours out His wrath upon a nation. "The Causes and Remedies of Mental Errors" stresses the differences between matters of faith and human opinion. Flavel exposes the dangers of errors that creep into the church. This volume concludes with "Gospel Unity," a sermon based on 1 Corinthians 1:10, which promotes unity in the church of Christ.

In addition to "England's Duty Under the Present Gospel Liberty [1689]" and "The Mystery of Providence," volume 4 includes "Mount Pisgah," a thanksgiving sermon based on Deuteronomy 3:24-25; "A Narrative of Some Late and Wonderful Sea Deliverances"; "*Antipharmacum Saluberrimum*" ["A Most Wholesome Antidote to Poison"], a short treatise providing eight ways that believers should respond to temptation and trial, particularly the special pressures of the moment exerted by Roman Catholicism; and "Tidings from Rome, or England's Alarm," which stresses the need to oppose the papacy and prepare for a time when Roman Catholicism might prevail in England.

Volume 5 contains "A Saint Indeed," "The Touchstone of Sincerity," and "A Token for Mourners," as well as the impressive "Husbandry Spiritualized," which illustrates spiritual truths through various aspects of farming. It also includes three treatises written primarily for sailors: "Navigation Spiritualized," which spiritualizes life at sea; "A Caution to Seamen," which warns against "several horrid and detestable sins"; and "The Seaman's Companion," subtitled "Six Sermons on the Mysteries of Providence as Relating to Seamen."

Volume 6 contains an excellent question-and-answer exposition on the Westminster Assembly's Shorter Catechism, as well as twelve helpful meditations to prepare believers for the Lord's Supper, followed by a dialogue between a minister and a doubting Christian on attending the Lord's Supper. The volume also includes several additional sermons and three minor treatises on preparing for suffering, defending infant baptism, and the need for personal reformation and conversion.

Flavel's work includes catchy titles, striking sayings, apt quotations, and simple illustrations. We know a pastor who has profited greatly from reading a sermon or chapter of Flavel every morning for decades. When he finishes volume 6, the pastor begins over again with volume 1. If you can afford only a few sets of Puritan works, Flavel's should be included.

Christ Knocking at the Door of the Heart (GM; 400 pages; 1978). Originally titled *England's Duty Under the Present Gospel Liberty* (1689), this book contains eleven sermons on Revelation 3:20. It explains God's offer of Christ to sinners, the natural heart that resists that offer, and Christ's patience in persisting with the offer. Flavel suggests that every conviction of conscience is Christ's knocking for entrance into the soul. Christ is an "earnest suitor for union and communion with the souls of sinners," Flavel says. Christ will not refuse the vilest sinner who is willing to open to Him; rather, His own quickening voice enables the sinner to receive Christ by faith and to commune with Him. That is the great goal of the gospel. The last sermon on the "mutual, sweet, and intimate communion between Christ and believers in this world" is worthy of repeated reading. This book is particularly helpful for convicted sinners who are struggling to find liberty in Christ.

The Fountain of Life (GM; 556 pages; 1977). This book, subtitled *A Display of Christ in His Essential and Mediatorial Glory*, contains forty-two sermons on the riches of Christ's offices and states. The book offers a comprehensive Christology with a devotional accent. Chapter 3 alone, on the covenant between the Father and the Son, is worth the price of the book. The book also contains fifteen sermons on Christ's sufferings, from the Garden of Gethsemane until His burial. It rivals Friedrich W. Krummacher's *Suffering Savior* for experiential warmth and depth. Flavel says this book was written "in a time of great distractions [persecutions]." No doubt his faith was greatly strengthened by his reflections on the great sufferings of his glorious Savior.

Keeping the Heart (SDG; 170 pages; 1998). In this work, originally titled *A Saint Indeed*, Flavel examines how to keep the heart and why this is the great calling of every believer. He suggests six ways to keep the heart before God: (1) converse with your heart, (2) let the evils of your heart humble you, (3) pray for grace, (4) resolve to walk more carefully with God, (5) be jealous for holiness and afraid of sin, and (6) be aware of God's omniscience.

Flavel provides powerful motives for keeping our hearts. He says that will help us understand "the deep mysteries of religion" and preserve us from dangerous errors. It will prove our faith as real and sincere. It will maintain joy through the means of grace, such as praying, worshiping, and listening to sermons. It will furnish grist for prayer and make us strive more for revival. It will help keep us from falling into sin, promote better fellowship among believers, and enable us to preserve our impressions of spiritual truth.

God has used this book to convert many. For example, a gentleman from London tried to purchase some plays at a bookshop. The owner had none in stock, but recommended Flavel's *Keeping the Heart*. The man from London swore and threatened to burn the book. Still, he bought it. He returned a month later, saying that God had used it to save his soul. "Can I purchase one hundred copies?" he asked.

Included in the SDG edition are a helpful introduction, outline, and study guide written by Maureen Bradley, making this an excellent book for adult study groups.

The Method of Grace (GM; 560 pages; 1977). In five sections, this book describes the work of the Spirit in applying Christ's redemption to sinners. It consoles the weak believer and exposes the dangers of false comfort. In the first section, beginning with union with Christ (John 17:23), Flavel shows how the Holy Spirit applies Christ to the soul (John 6:44) so that faith can receive and fellowship with Him (John 1:12; Ps. 14:7).

In the second section, Flavel invites sinners to come to Christ by means of His titles and benefits. Those titles include Physician, Mercy, Altogether Lovely, Desire of All Nations, Lord of Glory, and Consolation of Israel. The benefits include forgiveness of sin, acceptance with God, Christian liberty, reconciliation, and glorification. Flavel shows in the third section how coming to Christ implies true conviction of sin, "being slain by the law" (Rom. 7:9), and being "taught of God" (John 6:45).

Section four describes evidences of union with Christ, including the indwelling of the Spirit (1 John 3:24), becoming a new creature (2 Cor. 5:17), mortifying sin (Gal. 5:24), and imitating Christ (1 John 2:6). The last section shows "the lamentable state of unbelievers" in their spiritual death and misery (Eph. 5:14), their condemnation (John 3:18), and their unbelief (2 Cor. 4:3-4). This book searches the believer's heart, challenges faith, and enriches love.

The Mystery of Providence (BTT; 221 pages; 1963). First published in 1678 as *Divine Conduct or the Mystery of Providence Opened*, this frequently reprinted book is based on Psalm 57:2, "I will cry unto God most high; unto God that performeth all things for me." It explains the following doctrine: "It is the duty of the saints, especially in times of straits, to reflect upon the performances of Providence for them in all the states and through all the stages of their lives" (p. 20).

The BTT edition divides this book into three sections. In the first, Flavel explains the evidence of providence in the birth and upbringing of believers, in their conversion and employment, in their family affairs, and in their sanctification and preservation from evil. In the second, he instructs believers on the art of meditating on the providence of God, explaining the duty of such meditation, how to do it, and the benefits of doing it. Such meditation promotes communion with God, the endearment of Christ, and delight in the Christian life. It supports the life of faith and provides matter for praise. If we don't meditate on providence, we will minimize God's benefits, slight God, and harm our prayer life, for we cannot pray intelligently unless we are in tune with God's providence. Finally, Flavel applies the doctrine of providence by showing its practical implications for believers and the problems of wrestling with it. The book concludes with a chapter titled "The Advantages of Recording our Experiences of Providence."

Flavel's book is rich with illustrations. For example, when dealing with the difference between what Flavel calls "our time" and "God's time," Flavel concludes that our time is not the proper season for us to receive our mercies, since God's delay "is nothing else but the time of His preparation of mercies for you, and your heart for mercy, so that you may have it with the greatest advantage of comfort. The foolish child would pluck the apple while it is green; but when it is ripe it drops of its own accord and is more pleasant and wholesome" (p. 139).

This excellent book on providence opens avenues of spiritual knowledge and experience that few believers have probed. It is invaluable for understanding God's purposes for our lives.

Flavel teaches us how to find delight in discerning how God works all things in the world for His glory and our good.

True Professors and Mourners: Two Works by John Flavel (Rhwym; 176 pages; 1996). This small book contains two works: *The Touchstone of Sincerity* and *A Token for Mourners*. The first book, based on Revelation 3:17-18, probes the sincerity of one's Christianity and ruthlessly exposes hypocrisy. The second, based on Luke 7:13, discusses Christ's advice to the widow of Nain who is mourning the death of her only son. Flavel warns against immoderate sorrow and presents ways of curing that problem. The language of this book has been updated for modern readers, but the binding and formatting quality are seriously deficient.

Thomas Ford

(1598-1674)

Thomas Ford, minister at Exeter and member of the Westminster Assembly of Divines, was born at Brixton, Devon. He attended school at Plympton and matriculated at Magdalen Hall, Oxford, earning his Bachelor of Arts in 1625 and Master of Arts in 1627. He was ordained a deacon at Salisbury in 1631 and priest at Bristol the following year. Due to his sermonic attacks on church liturgy, Ford was censured and forced to resign from a lectureship at Oxford. He returned to Devon where he was well received by the magistrates of Plymouth, who chose him as their vicar and lecturer, but the king intervened and forbad the appointments.

Ford was associated with the Fleetwood family for a time and served as chaplain to Colonel George Fleetwood. Ford returned to England in 1637 and was offered the living of Aldwincle All Saints, Northamptonshire, by Sir Miles Fleetwood, father of his former colonel. In 1640, Ford was one of the representatives of the diocese of Peterborough. His first publication, *Reformation Sure and Steadfast,* was printed in 1641 by order of the House of Commons. Throughout the following years, Ford shared different livings. His most notable achievement during the 1640s, aside from his published work *The Times Anatomized,* was his continued involvement with the Westminster Assembly.

In 1648, Ford revealed his Presbyterianism by endorsing *The Joint Testimony of the Ministers of Devon* in support of the Solemn

League and Covenant. Ford became vicar of St. Lawrence, Exeter, where he had much influence with the clergy of that city. He was able to arrange a Tuesday lecture with each minister participating by turn and to hold a communion service every two weeks, alternating between the churches.

For the next few years, Ford was involved in ecclesiastical conflict. He engaged in a conflict with Lewis Stuckley over the excommunication of two women, and eventually was deprived of his post at St. Lawrence in 1657.

After the Restoration, Ford remained in Exeter and preached a farewell sermon at St. Mary Major on August 13, 1662, the day before being ejected for nonconformity. He moved to Exmouth after the enactment of the Five Mile Act and busied himself with writing. In 1667, he published *Scriptures' Self-Evidence*, a defense of the Protestant position, followed the next year by *The Sinner Condemned of himself*, arguing that unbelievers merit their own condemnation, and *The Bishops condemned Out of Their Own Mouths*, showing the tragic consequences of a restored Episcopal government.

Ford returned to Exeter after the 1672 Declaration of Indulgence. Under the terms of indulgence he was able to minister at his home but only preached twice before ill-health consumed him. He died in 1674 and was buried in St. Lawrence.

⇒◆◇◆⇐

Singing of Psalms: The Duty of Christians under the New Testament (PA; 121 pages; 2005). Using Ephesians 5:19, Ford considers the duty, matter, manner, and goal of the church's singing, stressing the suitability of the Psalms as a means of instruction and admonition in the Christian life. He often pauses to reflect on the message of individual Psalms and to show how they may be sung with heartfelt conviction by those who are exercised in spiritual matters. The book serves not only to point out the Christian's duty of singing Psalms, but also provides practical help towards fulfilling that duty. It also contains a memoir of the author by James Reid.

William Gearing

(c. 1625-c. 1690)

Little is known about William Gearing. He seems to have served as a minister in Lymington in the 1650s and later at Christ Church in Surrey. He preached a sermon at St. Mary Le Bow on September 3, 1688, in commemoration of the Great Fire in London.

Gearing published several works that reveal intimate awareness of the church fathers, experiential Calvinism, and the spiritual need of believers. His meditative treatise on prayer, *A Key to Heaven* (1683), is among the finest examples of seventeenth-century piety. He was also active in publishing some of the writings of John Maynard, a member of the Westminster Assembly.

The Glory of Heaven (SDG; 304 pages; 2005). This work was first published in 1673 as *A Prospect of Heaven: Or, A Treatise of the Happiness of the Saints in Glory*. In expounding Romans 8:18, Gearing raises the reader's contemplation to heaven and to the blessedness of living there. Gearing examines the nature, quality, excellence, and certainty of heaven. He describes in some detail the misery of those who forfeit heaven, the blessedness of those who attain it, and the disparity between present sufferings and future glory.

Gearing reminds us that heaven will be a place of enduring blessedness not only because of the presence of God, but also because of the absence of evil. He ably explains how God will show us that He has worked all things together for good. In the final section, he discusses offering violence for heaven, and concludes: "God hath not appointed heaven for idle droans, and loiterers, but for such as labor for it; heaven is a crown or garland, win it and wear it; it is an harvest, labor for it, if thou wilt enjoy it; it is a field of treasure, thou must purchase it, if thou wilt possess it; it is a strong city, and must be taken by force and violence."

Though Gearing has received little attention by scholars, his work on heaven has drawn some attention in scholarly literature (e.g., Philip C. Aland comments on Gearing's view of the heavenly body and its physical perfection in *Heaven and Hell in Enlightenment England* [Cambridge University Press, 1994], p. 108).

Richard Gilpin
(1625-1700)

Richard Gilpin was a descendant of Bernard Gilpin (1517-1583), a Church of England minister often called "the Apostle of the North" due to his many evangelistic tours of remote northern dales where the Reformation had made little progress. Richard was born in 1625 at Strickland in Westmorland. He matriculated at the University of Edinburgh, where he first studied medicine, then theology, earning a master's degree in 1646.

Gilpin began his ministry at Lambeth. Next, he became an assistant to John Wilkins, later bishop of Chester, at the Savoy in London. In 1652, Gilpin became rector of the large parish of Greystoke, Cumberland, including four chapels. Though Gilpin preferred the Presbyterian system of church government, he organized his parish along Congregational lines in accord with local custom. In 1653, he organized a voluntary association of ministers and churches in the counties of Cumberland and Westmorland, similar to Baxter's Worcestershire association, though he gave the clergy more power than Baxter had approved. Gilpin vocally opposed the Quakers, who heavily populated his district and occasionally interrupted his services.

Gilpin was married twice. His first wife died soon after they were married. He had thirteen children with his second wife, Susanna, daughter of William Brisco of Crofton, Yorkshire.

After the ejection of 1662, Gilpin first retired to his residence at Scaleby Castle, then moved to Newcastle in 1668 to minister for thirty-two years to a nonconformist congregation. On several occasions in the 1660s, he was fined for leading secret worship services, but he escaped more serious prosecution. By 1670, he seems to have been left alone.

Gilpin continued to practice medicine on a part-time basis and graduated with a medical degree from Leiden, the Netherlands, in 1676. He specialized in the medical understanding of enthusiasm and melancholy. Some of his work has recently been reprinted in Timothy Rogers's *A Discourse on the Trouble of the Mind and the Disease of Melancholy.*

In 1681, following the death of William Durant, an Independent preacher, Gilpin merged Durant's congregation with his own. The challenge of merging two groups "of very different opinions and tempers," as Calamy put it, was great. Gilpin accepted King James II's 1687 Declaration of Indulgence and happily addressed the king. In the early 1690s, Gilpin threw his support behind the Happy Union of Congregationalists and Presbyterians, begun in London. After the breakdown of that union in 1695, Gilpin's congregation experienced considerable tension, which ultimately led to a painful secession that burdened Gilpin until the end of his life.

Gilpin was a popular preacher. A born orator, his sermons were well organized and were delivered extemporaneously with passion and pathos, pleading with sinners to turn to Christ. "In prayer he was solemn and fervent, using Scripture language extensively and with a flood of affection which often forced him to silence until he had vented it in tears" (quoted in *Oxford DNB*, 22:321).

Gilpin's assistant from 1694 to 1698 was William Pell, followed by Timothy Manlove (d. 1699) and Thomas Bradbury. Gilpin died February 13, 1700, of pneumonia. It was said that his last sermon, based on 2 Corinthians 5:2 ("For in this we groan, earnestly desiring to be clothed upon with our house which is from heaven") was "groaned rather than spoke."

Bradbury was not able to hold the congregation together; within three years, a major split, which Gilpin had so feared, took place. Gilpin's memory lingered on long, however. His contemporaries viewed him as "the most significant Protestant dissenting minister in the four northern counties in the period 1660-1700" (ibid.).

<hr>

A Treatise of Satan's Temptations (SDG; 480 pages; 2000). First published in London in 1677, this book on spiritual warfare clearly illustrates the Puritan approach to the devil—that he is dangerous and that Christians must defend themselves against his attacks. As Peter Lewis said, "The Puritans knew their worst enemy better than most people know their best friend." In forty-four chapters, Gilpin details the devil's devices, much as Brooks does in *Precious Remedies Against Satan's Devices.* Gilpin's work, however, surpasses Brooks's work in size.

Gilpin's book has three parts. The first deals with Satan's malice, power, knowledge, cruelty, diligence, craftiness, and deceitfulness. Gilpin shows numerous ways that Satan uses to entice, hinder, and discourage believers. He addresses lusts that darken our minds and pervert our reason. He explains how Satan feigns his departure, keeps a sinner's conscience quiet, and spoils church services and spiritual duties.

In the second part, Gilpin describes how Satan corrupts people's minds through their understanding and affections. He shows how Satan robs believers of inner peace through personality, fears, and spiritual sorrows.

In the last part, Gilpin shows how Christ encountered Satan's temptations and what we can learn from that. He concludes with five practical antidotes to Satan's attacks: resolve to resist temptation; don't dispute with the tempter or his temptations; repel temptation immediately; resist temptation with scriptural arguments; and use prayer to beat back temptation.

After reading this book, John Ryland wrote, "If ever there was a man that was clearly acquainted with the cabinet councils of hell, this author is the man." Edward Bickersteth said the book was "full of Christian experience."

Thomas Goodwin

(1600-1679)

Thomas Goodwin was born October 5, 1600, in Rollesby, near Yarmouth in Norfolk, an area known for Puritan resistance to government persecution. This climate influenced Thomas Goodwin's God-fearing parents, Richard and Catherine Goodwin. They did their best to train their son to become a minister through personal example as well as by providing him with the best classical education offered by local schools.

When he was only a child, Goodwin had a tender conscience. From the age of six, he had such vivid impressions of the Holy Spirit that he wept for his sin and had "flashes of joy upon thoughts of the things of God." By age thirteen, Goodwin was enrolled at Christ's College, Cambridge, a "nest of Puritans." The memory of William Perkins still permeated Cambridge. Richard Sibbes, the "sweet dropper of Israel," was also a strong influence. Sibbes regularly preached at Trinity Church, attracting those who yearned for spiritual edification rather than fancy rhetoric.

At age fourteen, Goodwin looked forward to Easter, when he hoped to partake of the Lord's Supper. When the day arrived, however, his tutor, William Power, lovingly restrained the boy from receiving Communion because of his age and spiritual immaturity. Feeling rejected, Goodwin stopped attending Sibbes's sermons and lectures, ceased praying and reading the Scriptures and Puritan literature, and set his heart on becoming a popular preacher. He determined

THOMAS GOODWIN

to study the rhetoric of preachers who cared more for style than substance and were inclined to embrace the Arminianism that was coming in from the Netherlands.

Goodwin graduated from Christ's College with a bachelor's degree in 1616. In 1619, he continued his studies at St. Catherine's Hall in Cambridge, probably in hopes of obtaining early promotion. He graduated with a master's degree in 1620 and became a fellow and lecturer. Other fellows who served there were John Arrowsmith, William Spurstowe, and William Strong. All would one day serve with Goodwin in the Westminster Assembly. Several of these Puritans tried to persuade Goodwin that rhetoric and Arminianism were not edifying and did not serve the truth. In addition, Goodwin could not shake the influence of Sibbes's preaching and the sermons of John Preston in the college chapel. His interest in Puritanism fluctuated for another year, often rising just prior to the Lord's Supper.

Finally, God brought Goodwin to a profound conviction of sin. He was converted October 2, 1620, just after his twentieth birthday. On that afternoon, he met with some friends to have a good time. One of the friends convinced the group to attend a funeral. Thomas Bainbridge preached at that service on Luke 19:41-42, focusing on the need for personal repentance. God used the message to show Goodwin his dreadful sins, the essential depravity of his heart, his averseness to all spiritual good, and his desperate condition, which left him exposed to the wrath of God. A few hours later, "before God, who after we are regenerate is so faithful and mindful of his word," Goodwin received a "speedy word" of deliverance from Ezekiel 16. As he describes the experience, Goodwin was told:

> 'Live, yea, I said unto you, Live'— so God was pleased on the sudden, and as it were in an instant, to alter the whole of his former dispensation towards me, and said of and to my soul, 'Yea, live; yea, live,' I say, said God: and as

he created the world and the matter of all things by a
word, so he created and put a new life and spirit into my
soul, and so great an alteration was strange to me....

God [then] took me aside, and as it were privately
said unto me, 'Do you now turn to me, and I will pardon
all your sins though never so many, as I forgave and pardoned my servant Paul, and convert you unto me'
(*Works*, 2:lxi-lxii).

After his conversion, Goodwin aligned himself with the
theological tradition of Perkins, Baynes, Sibbes, and Preston.
He resolved not to seek personal fame, but "to part with all for
Christ and make the glory of God the measure of all time to
come." He abandoned the polished style of preaching favored
by Anglican divines, since it served only to call attention to
the preacher, and adopted the Puritan "plain style of preaching," which sought to give all glory to God. His preaching
became earnest, experimental, and pastoral.

From 1620 to 1627, Goodwin sought personal assurance of
faith. Through letters and conversations with a godly minister,
Rev. Price of King's Lynn (who Goodwin said "was the greatest man for experimental acquaintance with Christ that ever
he met"), he was led to see his need to "live by faith in Christ,
and to derive from him life and strength for sanctification, and
all comfort and joy through believing." Later, he said about this
time of spiritual struggle: "I was diverted from Christ for several years, to search only into the signs of grace in me. It was
almost seven years ere I was taken off to live by faith on Christ,
and God's free love, which are alike the object of faith."

Goodwin's soul finally found rest in Christ alone. His
preaching became more Christ-centered. He could agree
with Sibbes's advice: "Young man, if you ever would do good,
you must preach the gospel and the free grace of God in
Christ Jesus."

Shortly before this time, in 1625, Goodwin had been
licensed as a preacher. The following year, he helped bring

Sibbes to St. Catherine's Hall as master. In 1628, Goodwin was appointed lecturer at Trinity Church, succeeding Sibbes and Preston at age twenty-seven. From 1632 to 1634, Goodwin served as vicar of the church. Then, because he was unwilling to submit to Archbishop William Laud's articles of conformity, Goodwin was forced to resign his offices. He left Cambridge, although many people, including several who later became influential Puritan pastors, were converted under Goodwin's preaching and lecturing there.

During the mid-1630s, largely under the influence of John Cotton, Goodwin adopted Independent principles of church government. From 1634 to 1639, he was a Separatist preacher in London. In 1639, because of increasing restrictions against preaching with threats of fines and imprisonment, Goodwin took refuge in the Netherlands. He worked in Arnhem with other well-known Independent ministers, serving more than a hundred people who had fled from Laud's persecution. For two years, Goodwin exchanged ideas with his Dutch colleagues. He soon realized that the divines of the Dutch Further Reformation (*Nadere Reformatie*) were emphasizing the same kind of truths in preaching and pastoring that the English Puritans were, and with the same kind of responses from colleagues. Just as some orthodox Dutch Calvinists looked askance at the piety of Gisbertus Voetius, so some Calvinist clergy in England viewed the Puritans with suspicion. In Holland, however, there was more freedom to experiment with church government among the refugee congregations. Goodwin thus explored the "Congregational Way," knowing that Independency was a minority view among the Puritans in England as well as among the Reformed in the Netherlands.

In 1641, after Laud was impeached, Goodwin responded to Parliament's invitation to Nonconformists to return to England. Goodwin preached before Parliament on April 27, 1642. He was subsequently appointed as a member of the

Westminster Assembly. There he is said to have been "the most decisive figure and the great disturber of the Westminster Assembly," due to his continual promotion of Independent church government. Records of the 243 sessions of the assembly indicate that Goodwin gave more addresses than any other divine—357 in all. Goodwin, Philip Nye, Sidrach Simpson, William Bridge, and Jeremiah Burroughs became known as the five "Dissenting Brethren." They presented their views on Independency to the Westminster Assembly in their *Apologetical Narration* (1644).

Despite Goodwin's prolonged debate on church government, he retained the respect of the Presbyterian majority as a capable and irenic Puritan. He was chosen to pray in the solemn seven-hour meeting prior to the assembly's discussion on church discipline. He was also asked in 1644 to present *The Directory for the Public Worship of God* to Parliament. That was one of several times that Goodwin preached before Parliament. Goodwin and Jeremiah Whitaker were also asked by the House of Lords to oversee the papers that would be printed for the assembly.

After the assembly recessed, Goodwin received additional appointments. In 1649, Goodwin, Joseph Caryl, and Edward Reynolds were appointed as lecturers at Oxford. On June 7, 1649, both Goodwin and Owen preached before the House of Commons on a special day of public thanksgiving. The next day their names were put forward by the House for promotion to the presidency of two Oxford colleges. In 1650, Goodwin became president of Magdalen College, Oxford, and Owen became dean of Christ Church. The pair must have had considerable influence, since Cromwell soon yielded his power as chancellor to a commission headed by Owen. Goodwin was made a close adviser to Cromwell and the Lord Protector's Oxford commissioner.

Goodwin helped shape Magdalen College into an institution that adhered to scriptural truth and experimental Calvinistic doctrine. He demanded such academic excellence and dealt so plainly with the spiritual lives of the students that he was accused of operating a "scruple shop" by those who did not appreciate his Puritan emphasis. It was during those years, however, that, as Lord Clarendon later pronounced, "The University of Oxford yielded a harvest of extraordinary good and sound knowledge in all parts of learning."

When he began his college presidency, Goodwin married for the second time. In 1638, he had married Elizabeth Prescott, the godly daughter of a London alderman, but she died in the 1640s, leaving him with one daughter. In 1649, he married Mary Hammond, "of ancient and honorable Shropshire lineage." Goodwin was forty-nine and Mary Hammond seventeen, but she was wise beyond her years. The Goodwins had two sons, Thomas and Richard, and two daughters, both of whom died in infancy. Richard died as a young man on a voyage to the East Indies. Thomas followed in his father's footsteps as an Independent pastor and later established a private academy for training ministers.

Goodwin's years at Oxford were productive. He and John Owen lectured on Sunday afternoons to students, and both were chaplains to Cromwell. Spiritual fervor spread among the students. Philip Henry, father of Matthew Henry, the famous Bible commentator, attended Oxford in those days. He said, "Serious godliness was in reputation and beside the public opportunities they had, many of the scholars used to meet together for prayer and Christian conference, to the great comforting of one another's hearts in the fear and love of God, and the preparing of them for the service of the church" (J.B. Williams, *The Lives of Philip and Matthew Henry*, p. 19).

Goodwin also started an Independent church, preaching to a unique congregation that included Stephen Charnock, fellow of New College, and Thankful Owen, president of St. John's. In 1653, Goodwin was awarded a doctorate in divinity at Oxford University. The following year, he was chosen by Cromwell to sit on the board of visitors of Oxford University, as well as to be one of the triers on the board for the approbation of public preachers, which examined men for pulpit and public instructional work. Goodwin was next appointed to the Oxfordshire commission for the ejection of scandalous ministers. During this decade, Goodwin was probably closer to Cromwell than any other Independent divine. He attended the Lord Protector on his deathbed.

Before Cromwell died on September 3, 1658, Goodwin secured his permission to hold a synod of Independents and to draft a confession of faith. On September 29, 1658, Goodwin, Owen, Philip Nye, William Bridge, Joseph Caryl, and William Greenhill drew up the Savoy Declaration of Faith and Order, an edited version of the Westminster Confession of Faith, for some 120 Independent churches. Owen almost certainly wrote the lengthy introduction, but Goodwin was probably responsible for most of the first draft. The document was presented for approval to representatives from the Independent churches and was unanimously approved on October 12, 1658. On October 14, Goodwin led a delegation to present the declaration to Richard Cromwell; the document became the confessional standard for British congregationalism. With slight changes, it was adopted by American congregational churches at Boston, on May 12, 1680.

With the accession of Charles II in 1660 and the accompanying loss of Puritan power, Goodwin felt compelled to leave Oxford. He and most of his Independent congregation moved to London, where they started another church. Despite assurances to the contrary, the new king enacted strict acts of conformity. In 1662, two thousand godly ministers were ejected from the national church. Since he was in an Independent church and held no government-appointed offices, Goodwin did not suffer from the ejection. He continued preaching through many years of persecution under Charles II. He also stayed with his London congregation through the dreaded plague, when most clergy of the established church abandoned the city. He devoted his last years to preaching, pastoral work, and writing.

Goodwin died in London at age eighty. His son wrote of his godly father:

> In all the violence of [his fever], he discoursed with that strength of faith and assurance of Christ's love, with that holy admiration of free grace, with that joy in believing, and such thanksgivings and praises, as he extremely moved and affected all that heard him.... He rejoiced in the thoughts that he was dying, and going to have a full and uninterrupted communion with God. 'I am going,' said he, 'to the three Persons, with whom I have had communion: they have taken me; I did not take them.... I could not have imagined I should ever have had such a measure of faith in this hour.... Christ cannot love me better than he doth; I think I cannot love Christ better than I do; I am swallowed up in God....' With this assurance of faith, and fullness of joy, his soul left this world (*Works*, 2:lxxiv-lxxv).

Goodwin attained recognition as a leader of Independency during the Civil War and Interregnum period, and was also known among the Puritan divines of the seventeenth century as an eminent believer, an able preacher, a caring pastor, and a profoundly spiritual writer. Buried in Bunhill Fields, his epitaph, written in Latin, is most moving when read in full. It summarizes well his most important gifts, stating that he was knowledgeable in the Scriptures, sound in judgment, and enlightened by the Spirit to penetrate the mysteries of the gospel; he was a pacifier of troubled consciences, a dispeller of error, and a truly Christian pastor; he edified many souls whom he

had first won to Christ. Indeed, the closing section of his epitaph is being fulfilled today by the reprinting of his works:

> His writings..., the noblest monument of this great man's
> praise, will diffuse his name in a more fragrant odour
> than that of the richest perfume, to flourish in those dis-
> tant ages, when this marble, inscribed with his just
> honour, shall have dropt into dust.

The Works of Thomas Goodwin (RHB; 12 volumes; 2006).
Goodwin was a prolific author and editor. During the 1630s,
he and John Ball edited the works of John Preston and
Richard Sibbes. Goodwin began to publish his own sermons
in 1636. By the time he died, he had published at least twelve
devotional works, most of which were collections of sermons.
They were reissued forty-seven times, indicating a great demand for his publications.

Most of Goodwin's theological writings were written
when he was older and were published after he died. His large
corpus reveals a pastoral and scholarly zeal that is rivaled by
few Puritans.

The first collection of Goodwin's works was published in
five folio volumes in London from 1681 to 1704, under the editorship of Thankful Owen, Thomas Baron, and Thomas
Goodwin, Jr. An abridged version of those works was later
printed in four volumes (London, 1847-50). This reprinted
twelve-volume edition was printed by James Nichol (Edinburgh, 1861-66) in the Nichol's Series of Standard Divines. It is
far superior to the original five folio volumes.

Goodwin's exegesis is massive; he leaves no stone un-
turned. His first editors (1681) said of his work: "He had a
genius to dive into the bottom of points, to 'study them down,'
as he used to express it, not contenting himself with superficial
knowledge, without wading into the depths of things." Edmund Calamy put it this way: "It is evident from his writings,

he studied not words, but things. His style is plain and familiar; but very diffuse, homely and tedious." One does need patience to read Goodwin; however, along with depth and prolixity, he offers a wonderful sense of warmth and experience. A reader's patience will be amply rewarded.

How should a beginner proceed in reading Goodwin's works? Here is a suggested plan. Note: Books marked by † have been printed at least once since the 1950s.

1. Begin by reading some of the shorter, more practical writings of Goodwin, such as *Patience and Its Perfect Work*,† which includes four sermons on James 1:1-5. This was written after much of Goodwin's personal library was destroyed by fire (2:429-467). It contains much practical instruction on enhancing a spirit of submission.

Read *Certain Select Cases Resolved*, which offers three experimental treatises. They reveal Goodwin's pastoral heart for afflicted Christians. Each addresses specific struggles in the believer's soul: (a) "A Child of Light Walking in Darkness" is a classic work of encouragement for the spiritually depressed based on Isaiah 50:10-11 (3:231-350). The subtitle summarizes its contents: "A Treatise shewing The Causes by which, The Cases wherein, and the Ends for which, God leaves His Children to Distress of Conscience, Together with Directions How to Walk so as to Come Forth of Such a Condition." (b) "The Return of Prayers,"† based on Psalm 85:8, is a uniquely practical work. It offers help in ascertaining "God's answers to our prayers" (3:353-429). (c) "The Trial of a Christian's Growth" (3:433-506), based on John 15:1-2, is a masterpiece on sanctification. It focuses on mortification and vivification. For a mini-classic on spiritual growth, this gem remains unsurpassed.

You might also read *The Vanity of Thoughts*,† based on Jeremiah 4:14 (3:509-528). This work, often republished in paperback, stresses the need for bringing

every thought captive to Christ. It also describes ways
to foster that obedience.

2. Read some of Goodwin's great sermons. Inevitably,
they are strong, biblical, Christological, and experimental (2:359-425; 4:151-224; 5:439-548; 7:473-576;
9:499-514; 12:1-127).

3. Delve into Goodwin's works that explain major doctrines, such as:
• *An Unregenerate Man's Guiltiness Before God in Respect of
Sin and Punishment* [†] (10:1-567). This is a weighty treatise
on human guilt, corruption, and the imputation and
punishment of sin. In exposing the total depravity of
the natural man's heart, this book is unparalleled. Its
aim is to produce a heartfelt need for saving faith in
Christ rather than offer the quick fix of superficial
Christendom.

• *The Object and Acts of Justifying Faith* [†] (8:1-593). This is
a frequently reprinted classic on faith. Part 1, on the
objects of faith, focuses on God's nature, Christ, and the
free grace of God revealed in His absolute promises.
Part 2 deals with the *acts of faith*—what it means to believe in Christ, to obtain assurance, to find joy in the
Holy Ghost, and to make use of God's electing love.
One section beautifully explains the "actings of faith
in prayer." Part 3 addresses the *properties of faith*—its
excellence in giving all honor to God and Christ; its
difficulty in reaching beyond the natural abilities of
man; its necessity in requiring us to believe in the
strength of God. The conclusion provides "directions
to guide us in our endeavours to believe."

• *Christ the Mediator* [†] (2 Cor. 5:18-19), *Christ Set Forth*
(Rom. 8:34), and *The Heart of Christ in Heaven Towards
Sinners on Earth* are great works on Christology (5:1-
438; 4:1-92; 4:93-150). *Christ the Mediator* sets forth
Jesus in His substitutionary work of humiliation. It
rightly deserves to be called a classic. *Christ Set Forth*
proclaims Christ in His exaltation, and *The Heart of
Christ* explores the tenderness of Christ's glorified
human nature shown to His people on earth. Good-

win is more mystical in this work than anywhere else in his writings, but as Paul Cook has ably shown, his mysticism is kept within the boundaries of Scripture. Cook says Goodwin is unparalleled "in his combination of intellectual and theological power with evangelical and homiletical comfort."

• *Gospel Holiness in Heart and Life* (7:129-336) is a convicting masterpiece, based on Philippians 1:9-11. It explains the doctrine of sanctification in every sphere of life.

• *The Knowledge of God the Father, and His Son Jesus Christ* (4:347-569), combined with *The Work of the Holy Spirit* [†] (6:1-522), explore the profound work in the believer's soul of each of the three divine persons. *The Work of the Spirit* is particularly helpful for understanding the doctrines of regeneration and conversion. It carefully distinguishes the work of "the natural conscience" from the Spirit's saving work.

• *The Glory of the Gospel* (4:227-346) consists of two sermons and a treatise based on Colossians 1:26-27. It should be read along with *The Blessed State of Glory Which the Saints Possess After Death* (7:339-472), based on Revelation 14:13.

• *A Discourse of Election* [†] (9:1-498) delves deeply into issues such as the supralapsarian-infralapsarian debate, which wrestles with the moral or rational order of God's decrees. It also deals with the fruits of election (e.g., see Book IV on 1 Peter 5:10 and Book V on how God fulfils His covenant of grace in the generations of believers).

• *The Creatures and the Condition of Their State by Creation* (7:1-128). Goodwin is more philosophical in this work than in others.

4. Prayerfully and slowly digest Goodwin's 900-plus page exposition of Ephesians 1:1 to 2:11 [†] (1:1-564; 2:1-355). Alexander Whyte wrote of this work, "Not even Luther on the Galatians is such an expositor of Paul's mind and heart as is Goodwin on the Ephesians."

5. Save for last Goodwin's exposition of Revelation[†] (3:1-226) and his only polemical work, *The Constitution, Right Order, and Government of the Churches of Christ* (11:1-546). Independents would highly value this polemic, while Presbyterians wouldn't, probably saying Goodwin is trustworthy on every subject except church government. Goodwin's work does not degrade Presbyterians, however. One of his contemporaries who argued against Goodwin's view on church government confessed that Goodwin conveyed "a truly great and noble spirit" throughout the work.

Goodwin represents the best of Puritanism in addressing the intellect, will, and heart. His writings reveal the vigor of earlier Puritans such as William Perkins and Richard Sibbes as well as the mature thought of later Puritan divines, supremely represented by Owen.

Later men influenced by Goodwin's writings include John Cotton, Jonathan Edwards, George Whitefield, and John Gill. Alexander Whyte confessed: "I have read no other author so much and so often. And I continue to read him to this day, as if I had never read him before." Whyte said Goodwin's sermon titled "Christ Dwelling in Our Hearts by Faith" was one of the "two very greatest sermons in the English language." He added:

Goodwin is always an interpreter, and one of a thousand.... All his work, throughout his twelve volumes, is just so much pulpit exposition and pulpit application of the Word of God.... Full as Goodwin always is of the ripest scriptural and Reformation scholarship; full as he always is of the best theological and philosophical learning of his own day and of all foregoing days; full, also, as he always is of the deepest spiritual experience—all the same, he is always so clear, so direct, so non-technical, so personal, and so pastoral (*Thirteen Appreciations*, pp. 158ff.).

J. I. Packer concurs. "Whyte called Goodwin 'the greatest pulpit exegete of Paul that has ever lived,' and perhaps justly," he says. "Goodwin's Biblical expositions are quite unique [i.e., extraordinary], even among the Puritans, in the degree to which they combine theological breadth with experimental depth. John Owen saw into the mind of Paul as clearly as Goodwin—sometimes, on points of detail, more clearly—but not even Owen ever saw so deep into Paul's heart."

Thomas Gouge
(1605-1681)

Thomas Gouge, the eldest son of William Gouge (see below), was born in 1605 at Stratford-le-Bow, Middlesex. His father trained him in the knowledge and fear of God; at a very early age, Thomas devoted himself to the service of the Redeemer. He was educated first at Eton, then at King's College, Cambridge, where he became a fellow in 1628, and earned a bachelor's degree in 1629 and a master's degree in 1633.

In the midst of his studies, he became curate and lecturer at St. Anne Blackfriars, where his father ministered. In 1632, he accepted an appointment at Sion College. In 1637, he was admitted as perpetual curate of Teddington, Middlesex, and the following year moved to London to become rector at St. Sepulchre's, Holborn. Shortly after his arrival, he married Anne Darcy, the daughter of Sir Robert Darcy. They were married thirty-two years and had several children.

Gouge's twenty-four-year ministry at St. Sepulchre's was greatly blessed. He was known for his faithful attendance of the sick and his generosity to the poor, distributing alms among them once a week. He provided hemp and flax for the unemployed to spin, and even sold their products for them! Every morning he taught the children of his parish. Gouge excelled in modesty, humility, cheerfulness, kindness, and charity.

In 1661, Gouge's important sermon on charity, "After what manner must we give alms?" was published by Samuel Annesley in *The Morning Exercise at Cripple Gate* (now reprinted by Richard Owen Roberts as *Puritan Sermons*). That same year, Gouge published his *Christian Directions: Showing How to Walk with God All the Day Long,* an influential guide to prayer, Bible reading, Sabbath observance, and Christian conduct. In the last section, he argued against gambling, cock-fighting, and dangerous sports. He provided a free copy to every family in his parish.

Gouge was ejected for Nonconformity in 1662. An old university license enabled him to preach periodically, but being a moderate Nonconformist, he did not attempt to form a nonconformist congregation. Had it not been for Thomas Manton's dissuasion, Gouge would have taken the oath in the Five Mile Act of 1665, which commits to do nothing that challenges the existing government of church or state. Though he appears to have ministered for a time to a congregation of two hundred that worshipped near St. Sepulchre in the late 1660s, and was licensed to preach as a Presbyterian at Snow Hill, London, in 1672, Gouge spent most of the last twenty years of his life in evangelism and acts of charity. He raised considerable funds for nonconformist ministers who had been ejected from their pulpits.

Gouge lost many possessions to London's Great Fire, but he bore the loss with patience and humility. He had a large estate from his father, which he used to help the poor. After giving portions of the estate to his children, he was left with an income of 150 pounds per year. Of that amount, he gave two-thirds to charity and lived on 50 pounds.

Following his father's footsteps, Gouge published additional handbooks of practical Christianity, including *A Word to Sinners, and a Word to Saints* (1668), which prods the consciences of the saved and unsaved to perform their moral duties, and *The Young Man's Guide through the Wilderness of this Word to the Heavenly Canaan* (1670), a primer on behavior and spiritual duties for apprentices. In 1672, he published *The Principles of the Christian Religion Explained to the Capacity of the Meanest*, a practical catechism based in part on the Westminster Shorter Catechism.

That same year, Gouge decided to pursue Joseph Alleine's plan for evangelizing Wales; he spent most of the last nine years of his life working there. The misery and ignorance of the people roused his compassion. He had two goals. First, he wanted to teach poor children to read and write English and to instruct them in the Shorter Catechism and the principles of the Reformed faith. He thus set up schools, hired teachers, and educated thousands of children. By 1675, he had established eighty-seven new charity schools throughout Wales, only one county excepted. Second, he wanted to provide edifying books for poor adults. To implement that, he founded the Welsh Trust in 1674, together with Stephen Hughes and Charles Edwards, through which he raised funds from affluent gentry and merchants in London and Wales to print and distribute thousands of Welsh Bibles, tracts, and books by himself and such authors as Richard Baxter, Lewis Bayly, and Arthur Dent.

After having complained of heart problems for a few weeks, Gouge died in his sleep on October 29, 1681, at age seventy-six. He was buried in his father's vault at St. Anne Blackfriars. John Tillotson, then dean of St. Paul's, preached at the funeral.

Gouge's distribution of Welsh books continued for decades after his death, but his Welsh schools did not survive. His complete works were published in 1706 in one large folio volume. Several of his books were translated into Welsh.

Riches Increased by Giving (SPR; 234 pages; 1992). Based on Matthew 10:41-42 and subtitled "the right use of mammon: being the surest and safest way of thriving," this book reveals the importance of giving from the heart. The first part offers an exhaustive discussion on true giving; the second part provides Scripture references on giving. This edition, prefaced with a brief life of the author, contains recommendations by such divines as John Owen, Thomas Manton, and William Bates.

William Gouge

(1575-1653)

William Gouge was born in Bow, near Stratford, in Middlesex County. He received a classical education at St. Paul's School in London and at Felsted in Essex. He was converted under the ministry of his uncle, Ezekiel Culverwell, a well-known Puritan. He then went to Eton College, where he gave himself to study, prayer, and searching God's Word. In his years at King's College, Cambridge, Gouge became known as an excellent logician and defender of Ramism. He was called an "arch-Puritan" by some students because of his strict godliness. He apparently never missed one of the chapel prayer services conducted every morning at 5:30. He read fifteen Bible chapters daily—five in the morning before chapel, five after dinner, and five before going to bed.

Gouge graduated from King's College with a bachelor's degree in 1598 and a master's degree in 1602. He became a fellow and a leading Hebrew scholar, and was appointed as a lecturer in logic and philosophy. In 1603, his father persuaded him to travel from Cambridge to London to meet Elizabeth Caulton, the God-fearing daughter of Henry Caulton, a former London merchant. The couple were soon married, and had thirteen children, eight of whom reached maturity. Gouge's biographer details the care Gouge took in conducting family worship.

In 1608, Gouge became a lecturer at the parish church of St. Anne Blackfriars, London, where he served for forty-five years until his death. He was appointed rector upon the death of Stephen Egerton in 1621. He preached regularly twice on the Lord's Day and once every Wednesday. After his sermons on Sunday mornings, he invited poor people from the neighborhood to his house for dinner, after which they would discuss his sermon. His lectures on Wednesdays drew such large crowds that, according to his biographer, "When the godly Christians of those days came into London, they considered their business unfinished, unless they attended one of the Blackfriars lectures." Hundreds of people were converted and nurtured in the faith through his ministry. Brett Usher concludes, "Gouge's pulpit became the most celebrated in London" (*Oxford DNB*, 23:37).

Gouge was a hard worker, cheerful philanthropist, meek friend, great peacemaker, and earnest wrestler with God. He wrote eleven treatises, some of which were extensive. He supported poor students at the university and contributed generously to the poor. He had such a meek disposition that his biographer wrote, "No one, his wife, nor children, nor servant with whom he lived and worked all those years ever observed an angry countenance, nor heard an angry word proceed from him toward any of them."

Gouge was "a sweet comforter of dejected souls, and distressed consciences," according to his biographer. He became a spiritual mentor to many ministers in London, helping many keep peace in their congregations. His confessions of sin were accompanied with "much brokenness of heart, self-abhorrency, and justifying of God." In prayer, he was "pertinent, judicious, spiritual, seasonable, accompanied with faith and fervor, like a true Son of Jacob wrestling with tears and supplications."

A contemporary wrote of Gouge: "He studied much to magnify Christ, and to debase himself." Gouge said of himself,

"When I look upon myself, I see nothing but emptiness and weakness; but when I look upon Christ, I see nothing but fullness and sufficiency."

Throughout his pastoral years, Gouge continued his studies. He earned a Bachelor of Divinity degree at Cambridge in 1611, and eventually, a doctorate in divinity in 1628. His wife Elizabeth did not live to witness this occasion, however, as she died in 1625 while giving birth to their thirteenth child. Gouge never remarried.

For the most part, Gouge worked without interference from the government. However, he was harassed by authorities because of his Puritan sympathies in opposing new ceremonies ordered by Bishop Laud and for opposing Arminianism. He once spent two months in prison for republishing Finch's *The Calling of the Jews*.

Gouge was a prolific writer. In addition to his two massive works that have been reprinted, he published a diversity of titles, ranging from *The Whole Armour of God* (1616)—a major work on the Christian armor of Ephesians 6:10-20, overshadowed only by William Gurnall's even more massive masterpiece—to *A Short Catechism*, which was printed six times by 1636. Other titles include an exposition of John's gospel (1630), *God's Three Arrows* (1631), and *The Saint's Sacrifice* (1632).

In 1643, Gouge was nominated to the Westminster Assembly. He took turns with Cornelius Burgess leading the sessions when the moderator or prolocutor, William Twisse, was not present. In 1644, Gouge was appointed to the committee that examined ministers; in 1645, he was assigned to the committee that drafted the Confession of Faith; and in 1647, he was elected as assessor after the death of Herbert Palmer. In 1648, he was on the committee that supported the Presbyterian system *de jure divino*, or divine right, which held that Presbyterian church government is commanded by God ("by divine law") in Scripture. Later that year, Gouge was asked to contribute notes on 1 Kings through Esther for what would become the second edition of the Westminster Assembly's *Annotations on the Bible*.

Gouge suffered from asthma and kidney stones in his later years. His faith held firm, however, through acute suffering until death. He would say, "[I am] a great sinner, but I comfort myself in a great Savior." Often he repeated Job's words: "Shall we receive good from the hand of God, and shall we not receive evil?" When a friend tried to comfort him by pointing to the grace he had received or the works he had done, his response was, "I dare not think of any such things for comfort. Jesus Christ, and what He hath done and endured, is the only ground of my sure comfort." As he approached death, he said, "Death, next to Jesus Christ, you are my best friend. When I die, I am sure to be with Jesus Christ. Jesus Christ is my rejoicing."

Gouge died December 12, 1653, aged seventy-eight. His funeral sermon was preached by William Jenkyn, his friend, pastoral assistant, and successor. According to William Haller, Gouge ranked with Sibbes and Preston among the influential Puritan ministers of London of the previous generation.

———◆◆◆———

A Commentary on the Epistle to the Hebrews (Kregel; 1,148 pages; 1980). This massive book, originally published in three volumes, contains the notes of more than a thousand sermons given over a thirty year period at Blackfriars. The first volume was published in 1655; Gouge was still working on the last half of the last chapter of Hebrews when he died. His son, Thomas, completed it, using his father's notes. It is a golden exposition of the fullness of Christ, second only to Owen on Hebrews.

Gouge's work abounds in helpful application. For example, in commenting on Hebrews 11:17, which describes Abraham offering up Isaac, Gouge, who buried several of his own children (including a murdered daughter), has a section on "yielding the dearest to God." He writes, "The grounds of our yielding our dearest to God are such as these: 1. The supreme sovereignty of God, whereby he hath power to command us and all ours; and what he may command we must yield. 2. The right that God hath to all we have. 3. The might and power that God hath to take away all. Willingly to yield what he will have, is to make a virtue of necessity. 4. The due, which, in way of gratitude, we owe unto God. They that hold anything too dear for God are not worthy of God. 5. The bounty of God, who can and will beyond comparison recompense whatsoever is given to him. None shall lose by giving to God" (p. 806).

Of Domestical Duties (WJ facsimile; 693 pages; 1976). First published in 1622, this penetrating analysis of the godly household for which Gouge became best known is divided into eight sections dealing with the duties of family life. In the first part, Gouge explains the foundation of family duties, based on Ephesians 5:21-6:9. The second part deals with the husband-wife relationship. The third focuses on the duties of wives, and the fourth with the duties of husbands. The fifth examines the duties of children, and the sixth, the duties of parents. The final parts examine the relationships and duties of servants and their masters.

While some of Gouge's material is outdated, his emphasis and advice are timeless on the whole. Usher claims that Gouge is finally being "recognized as one of the subtlest of early modern writers to articulate the concept of 'companionable' marriage—his own was regarded as exemplary—and of considerate, rather than merely prescriptive, parenthood. His psychological insights into the nature of childhood and adolescence can be breathtaking in their modernity. He even touches on the question of child-abuse, a subject effectively taboo until the 1970s" (*Oxford DNB*, 23:38).

Gouge is a skilled expositor who draws practical applications from the Epistles in instructing families how to walk in a manner worthy of their Lord. As a father of seven sons and six daughters, Gouge knew whereof he spoke.

The Sabbath's Sanctification (PA; 34 pages; 2002). Gouge originally wrote this brief treatise for his family's use. After touching briefly on the grounds for the morality of the Sabbath, he provides judicious directions for sanctifying the Sabbath, carefully outlining the distinction between works of piety, mercy, and necessity. These directions are followed by some proofs that the Lord's Day is the Christian's Sabbath, with pertinent remarks on the time of day when the Sabbath begins. The subsequent section on aberrations of the Sabbath exposes the ungodly opinions and practices of those who desire to sanctify the Sabbath in name only. Gouge concludes his work with a number of motives which encourage Christians to keep this day holy to the Lord.

Richard Greenham

(c. 1542-1594)

Richard Greenham matriculated as a sizar at Pembroke Hall in Cambridge in 1559. He earned a Bachelor of Arts degree in 1564 and a master's degree in 1567. That same year he was elected a fellow. In 1570, he became the rector in the small farming village of Dry Drayton, five miles northwest of Cambridge. Upon his arrival, the congregation numbered thirty-one households, with about 250 people.

In 1573, Greenham married Katherine Bownd, a physician's widow, who brought four children with her into the marriage. At times Greenham seemed to have an antipathy toward marriage, seeing it almost as a last resort against fornication ('*Practical Divinity*,' pp. 77-79); on the other hand, his extensive pre-marital counseling sessions indicate that he had a high regard for marriage.

Greenham had his work cut out for him at Drayton. The people had little understanding or even interest in Reformed piety and in the differences between Romanism and Protestantism. Greenham complained about those "profaning the holy exercises," shortcomings in prayer and hearing the word, superstition in the use of the sacraments, and Sabbath neglect (*The Works of M. Richard Greenham*, p. 54).

Greenham soon became known for devotion to God in his life, ministry, and writings. He was especially known for his defense of keeping the Sabbath holy. His treatise on the Sabbath was published posthumously in 1599, but it circulated in unpublished form while he was alive (Richard L. Greaves, "The Origins of English Sabbatarian Thought," *Sixteenth Century Journal* 12, no. 3 [1981]: 27).

Teaching was an important part of Greenham's ministry. For two hours every Thursday and on Sundays between the two services, he catechized his flock. He was convinced that teaching prepared the hearts of the people for public preaching, since they would not otherwise understand it clearly. He viewed the purpose of the catechist as making doctrine easy to understand, and the role of the pupil as internalizing it through repetition. Greenham adapted the 1549 Prayer Book catechism to the needs of his own parishioners (Greenham's "A short form of Catechising" is published in *'Practical Divinity,'* pp. 265-97). Following Luther rather than Calvin, Greenham placed the Decalogue first because he believed its principal purpose was to make sinners aware of their sinfulness to drive them to Christ. Although he followed Luther's order, his content was much different. His catechism had many questions followed by very short answers.

Greenham was a tireless preacher. He preached six times each week: twice on Sunday and four early morning sessions during the week. To accomplish that, he rose every day at four a.m. He describes preaching as a painful and fearful experience. He was so energetic in the pulpit that he often drenched his shirt in sweat. Friends at times advised him to remain more calm.

Greenham was a pioneer. First, he was the pioneer of Reformed and Puritan casuistry. He became best known as a spiritual counselor dealing with afflicted consciences and answering people's various questions. These discussions were collected in a group of writings known as "tabletalk" and published as Rylands English Manuscript 524 (republished in *'Practical Divinity,'* pp. 129-259). The writings address spiritual and practical rather than doctrinal matters. John Primus writes that "Greenham's style, when dealing with sinners, was honest confrontation tempered by gentleness" (*Richard Greenham*, p. 41).

Greenham was also a pioneer in establishing a rectory seminary. A goodly number of men trained for the ministry under him. Some of them, like Arthur Hildersham and Henry Smith, became well-known Puritan preachers and authors. As his lecture notes were copied and circulated widely by his students, his practical, winsome approach to theological study became highly respected in the early Puritan movement.

Greenham was also sensitive to the material concerns of the community. When food was scarce, he encouraged the rich to establish a community granary where poor people could buy grain at a reduced price. Greenham himself generously contributed to the effort. He was so open-handed in donating money wherever he went that sometimes he had to borrow money to fulfill his committed donations.

In 1591, Greenham moved to London. Before moving there, however, he was influential in selecting Richard Warfield as his successor in Dry Drayton. Greenham's parting words to Warfield were: "God bless you, and send you more fruit on your labors then I have had, for I perceive no good wrought by [my] ministry on any but one family" ('*Practical Divinity*,' p. 23). Samuel Clarke reports that Greenham left because of "the untractableness and unteachableness of that people among whom he had taken such exceeding great pains." History has shown, however, that though Greenham was discouraged by the lack of fruit on his ministry in Dry Drayton and no doubt hoped that he would be more useful in London, his Dry Drayton ministry was far more successful than he made it out to be.

Greenham initially did not have a parish in London, but he eventually settled as lecturer in Christ Church Greyfriars, Newgate. By September of 1593, the black plague had erupted in the parish. Greenham preached a number of well-attended fast sermons and continued to work diligently among the people, preaching and visiting. Thomas Fuller thinks that he succumbed to the plague in 1594, but most modern scholars think it more probable that he died from a combination of various health problems—"including severe toothaches, a fistula, and stomach problems"—which he had been battling for at least a decade.

Greenham's legacy as a physician of souls continued after his death. In 1599, Henry Holland likened him to Elijah, and said that for "practical divinity he was inferior to few or none in his time" (*Works*, 1605, p. 724). Thomas Fuller said that Greenham's "masterpiece was in comforting wounded consciences; many, who came to him with weeping eyes, went from him with cheerful souls" (*The Church History of Britain*, 1655, pp. 219-20). Joseph Hall called him "that saint of ours." This impression of him continued, especially through his collected sayings, which have been said to resonate "with a truth and force that gave Greenham a place among English divines which was second to none" ('*Practical Divinity*,' pp. 35-36). His writings were often quoted by later Puritans, and Puritan diaries reveal that his *Works* were owned and read by many.

——◆◆◆——

'*Practical Divinity*': The Works and Life of Revd Richard Greenham** (Ashgate; 410 pages; 1998). This book contains several important writings drawn from Greenham's 1599 *Works*. It focuses particularly on Greenham's earliest compositions, including his unfinished catechism, treatises on the Sabbath (abridged) and marriage, and advice on reading Scripture and educating children. This volume also includes "the sayings of Richard Greenham," which, modeled after Luther's *Table Talk*, contain numerous paragraphs on various practical subjects that Greenham commented on from 1581 to 1584.

Nearly every one of Greenham's treatises deserve mention, but we limit ourselves to commenting on "A Profitable Treatise,

Containing a Direction for the reading and understanding of
the holy Scriptures." After establishing that the preaching and
reading of God's Word are inseparably joined together by God
in the work of the believer's salvation, Greenham focuses on our
duty to read the Scriptures, gleaning support from Deuteronomy 6:6, 11:18; Nehemiah 8:8; Psalm 1:2; Acts 15:21; and 2 Peter
1:19. He suggests eight ways to read Scripture:

1. *With diligence.* We must be more diligent in reading the
   Scriptures than anything else—more than men dig for
   hidden treasure. Diligence makes rough places plain;
   makes the difficult, easy; makes the unsavory, tasty.

2. *With wisdom.* We must be wise in the choice of matter,
   order, and time. In terms of matter, we must not try
   to move from the revealed to that which is not revealed, nor spend more time on the most difficult
   portions of Scripture. In terms of order, the wise
   reader of Scripture must be firmly grounded in all the
   major points of doctrine. Moreover, Scripture reading
   must follow some semblance of order, for a whole
   Bible makes a whole Christian. In terms of time, the
   entire Sabbath should be devoted to such exercises as
   the reading of Scriptures. On other days, a portion of
   Scripture should be read in the morning, at noon, and
   in the evening.

3. *With preparation.* In desiring to learn of God, we must
   approach Scripture with a reverential fear of God and
   His majesty, with faith in Christ, and with sincerity.

4. *With meditation.* This is as critical as preparation before
   reading Scripture. Reading may give some breadth, but
   only meditation will offer depth. "Meditation without
   reading is erroneous, and reading without meditation
   is barren," Greenham writes. "Meditation makes that
   which we have read to be our own." It helps transfuse
   Scripture through the entire texture of the soul.

5. *With conference.* This means godly conversation with
   ministers or other believers. The godly must share
   with others what they learn from the Scriptures, not
   in a proud manner but with humility, trusting that

where two or three are gathered together for spiritual conversation, God will be among them.

6. *With faith.* As Hebrews 4:2 says, faith is the key to profitable reception of the Word. Through reading the Word by faith, our faith will be refined. Scripture reading ought to try our faith, not only in the generalities of our lives, but also in particular afflictions. As gold is tried in the fire, so faith will abide the fire of affliction.

7. *With practice.* Practice will "bring forth increase of faith and repentance," Greenham writes. Practice is the best way to learn; the more we put the Word into practice in the daily obedience of faith, the more God will increase our gifts for His service and for additional practice.

8. *With prayer.* Prayer is indispensable in the reading of Scripture. It must precede, accompany, and follow our reading. Prayer also necessarily involves thanksgiving: "If we be bound to praise God when he hath fed our bodies, how much more when he hath fed our souls?" Greenham asks.

In short, if the Bible is to get into us, we must get into it. To neglect the Word is to neglect the Lord, but those who read Scripture "as a love letter sent to you from God" will experience its warming and transforming power.

Kenneth L. Parker and Eric J. Carlson ably edited this volume, which includes a scholarly 126-page introduction of Greenham, covering his life and legacy. They show the place that Greenham had in the development of Elizabethan Reformed parochial ministry. Particularly helpful are their analysis of Greenham's pastoral style and their study of his approach to curing cases of conscience.

The Works of the Reverend and Faithful Servant of Jesus Christ M. Richard Greenham (Da Capo; 500 pages; 1973). This book is a facsimile of the 1599 edition of Greenham's *Works*, published by Henry Holland. In addition to the titles listed in

'*Practical Divinity*' (see above), this work includes Greenham's unabridged treatise on the Sabbath, one of the most profoundly influential early works supporting strict observance; sermons on murmuring, zeal, a good name, humility, repentance, and not quenching the Spirit; some meditations on Proverbs 4; and a treatise and several letters to the spiritually afflicted, for which he deservedly became famous.

These writings reveal the practical and experimental divinity of early Puritanism. They show why Greenham was a respected figure, a model pastor, and an important casuist among the Elizabethan clergy.

Eric Josef Carlson notes of Greenham's *Works* that "additional sermons, letters, and collections of sayings were incorporated into later editions. After Holland's death in 1603, Stephen Egerton took over editorial duties, and in 1612 produced a fifth and final edition, more rationally organized and with a superb index" (*Oxford DNB*, 23:595).

William Greenhill

⟫•◆•⟪

(1598-1671)

William Greenhill was probably the son of John Greenhill, husbandman of Harrow on the Hill, Middlesex.
He entered Gonville and Caius College, Cambridge, at the age
of seventeen. In 1619, he earned a bachelor's degree, and in
1622, a master's degree, having attained proficiency in the
classical languages and history. He was ordained in 1628 and
the following year became rector of Oakley, Suffolk. John
Preston, with whom he remained friends until Preston's death
in 1628, was the primary influence in shaping his Puritan convictions. In the early 1630s, Greenhill participated in
lectureships at Mendlesham, Suffolk, and at St. George's
Tombland, Norwich, together with Jeremiah Burroughs and
other Puritans. All of this came to a sudden halt in 1636, when
Bishop Matthew Wren of Norwich deprived Greenhill for refusing to read the *Book of Sports*.

Greenhill and Burroughs took refuge in Rotterdam, where
they worshipped in the Independent church pastored by William Bridge. By 1641, Greenhill and Burroughs had returned to
England and settled in London, where they became lecturers at
Stepney, Middlesex. Burroughs lectured at 7 a.m. and Greenhill at 3 p.m. Due to their preaching gifts, the two became known
respectively as "the morning star" and "the evening star."

After civil war erupted in England, Greenhill preached
several fast sermons before Parliament, urging the enforce-
ment of justice and the implementation of reforms. He

defended the Magna Carta and parliamentary privileges. When the breakdown of royal authority promoted more Separatist congregations, Greenhill joined several Presbyterians and Independents in writing *Certain Considerations to Dissuade Men from Furthering Gathering Churches* (1643), yet the following year he accepted the pastorate of a newly gathered congregation in Stepney, becoming its first minister.

Greenhill served as a divine at the Westminster Assembly. He opposed the Presbyterian majority and sided with the minority of Independents, though unlike Burroughs, Bridge, Thomas Goodwin, and others, he did not sign the *Apologetical Narration* (1643). He did join the Independents the following year, however, when they published *A Copy of a Remonstrance Lately Delivered in to the Assembly,* which, as Richard Greaves writes, "explained why they would not provide an alternative model of congregational church government. Not only had parliament by this time already implemented a form of Presbyterian polity, but the Remonstrants also felt the assembly had not seriously considered their previous reports" (*Oxford DNB,* 23:601-602).

While serving in the assembly, Greenhill dedicated the first volume of his massive commentary on Ezekiel to Princess Elizabeth, daughter of Charles I and queen of Bohemia, in 1645. After Charles's execution in 1649, Parliament appointed Greenhill chaplain to three of the royal children: James, duke of York (later James II); Henry, duke of Gloucester; and Henrietta Maria. The remaining four volumes of Greenhill's *magnum opus* on Ezekiel appeared between 1649 and 1662.

Greenhill was a lover of Reformed literature and wrote numerous commendations of treatises for colleagues in the ministry, such as Burroughs, Bridge, and Thomas Shepard. In prefacing Burroughs's *The Excellency of a Gracious Spirit* (1657), he says that books "are more needful than arms; the one defends the body, the other the soul" (ibid., p. 602).

Greenhill was involved in numerous kinds of activities in the late 1640s and throughout the 1650s. To mention only a few, he and others, including Goodwin and Simpson, urged Parliament in writing to support mission work among Native Americans. The letter was later published as *The Day Breaking, if not the Sun Rising of the Gospel with the Indians in New England.* In 1652, Greenhill was involved with nine other divines, including Owen and Bridge, in drafting a statement on behalf of Parliament condemning the Racovian catechism, a Socinian document. That same year, Cromwell made Greenhill a commissioner, or trier, for the approbation of preachers, and also appointed him as vicar of St. Dunstan's-in-the-East, the old parish church of Stepney. Meanwhile, Greenhill continued to serve as pastor for the Independent congregation. With Owen, Goodwin, Nye, Caryl, and Bridge, Greenhill drafted the document of faith and order that the Savoy Conference approved in 1658.

Greenhill was ejected from his parish church in 1660 after the Restoration, but managed to continue to serve his gathered Independent church at Stepney—sometimes meeting in his house adjacent to the church and sometimes in a concealed attic—until his death. In 1669, when the congregation numbered five hundred, he took on Matthew Mead as his assistant. Mead became his successor upon Greenhill's death in 1671. By that time, the two preachers were also serving a conventicle of three hundred in Meetinghouse Alley, Wapping.

Having established a large network of ministerial contacts over the decades, Greenhill's loss was mourned throughout England and even in America. A few years before his death, he was still in active correspondence with the governor of Massachusetts, urging him to stop persecuting Baptists. He worked hard even until the end. Only weeks before Greenhill died, a group of magistrates and ministers in

Massachusetts wrote to him requesting assistance for Harvard College (ibid., p. 603).

John Howe referred to Greenhill as "that eminent servant of God whose praise is still in the churches." James Reid, in *Memoirs of the Westminster Divines*, described Greenhill as "a zealous Puritan, greatly against the Prelates, the superstitious ceremonies, and corruptions, of the Church of England."

An Exposition of Ezekiel (BTT; 860 pages; 1995). One of the foremost Puritan works in Old Testament exposition, this book remains one of the most helpful sermonic commentaries on Ezekiel in English. Here Greenhill shows his skill as a popular preacher. This edition is a reprint of the 1863 Nichol edition. Spurgeon said about this work, "We always get something out of Greenhill whenever we refer to him. He had not, of course, the critical skill of the present day, but his spiritual insight was keen. He rather commented on a passage than expounded it."

Christ's Last Disclosure of Himself (SDG; 211 pages; 1999). This work, based on Revelation 22:16-17, examines the last invitation of the Bible in twelve sermons. Greenhill shows Christ as the root and offspring of David as well as the bright and morning star, revealing the heart of Christ towards sinners. These sermons offer some fine material on spiritual thirsting, the willingness of Christ to save sinners, and the free offer of the gospel. Here's one example:

> Suppose that a man is in a rotten boat at sea. There is a great storm rising and many pirates abroad. And the admiral of the sea, seeing his condition, sends to him, saying, "Friend, friend, come in to me and I will secure you." But the man refuses, and soon he is taken by the pirates, carried away, and put into a dungeon. Now

what is it that troubles this man so? The admiral's kindness which he spurned. So it will be with sinners. Christ, the Admiral of the sea, calls to poor sinners, "Come in to Me, I will save you from the storm. I will save soul and body for all eternity." But you refuse, and at last you are taken and cast into hell; and there you lie with this upon your souls: that you might have had mercy and would not. Oh, therefore, come in to Jesus Christ! Stand out no longer, but come and give yourselves up to Him. Live like Christ, and you shall have a heaven here, and a heaven hereafter (pp. 161-62).

Obadiah Grew

(1607-1689)

O badiah Grew was born on November 1, 1607, and baptized three weeks later at Mancetter, Atherstone, Warwickshire. He was the third son of Francis Grew and Elizabeth Denison. After being educated by his uncle, John Denison, a schoolmaster in Reading, he was sent to Balliol College, Oxford, where he earned both a Bachelor of Arts degree in 1629 and a Master of Arts degree in 1632. After graduation, he served as principal of the grammar school in Mancetter for three years and was ordained into the ministry in 1635. He married Ellen Vicars on Christmas Day, 1637. They had two children, Mary and Nehemiah, and the latter became a distinguished botanist, authoring *The Anatomy of Plants* in 1682.

In 1642, Obadiah Grew moved to the parliamentary stronghold of Coventry and, along with Richard Vines, preached to the troops. By 1644 he had become the vicar of St. Michael's, replacing William Panting, a royalist minister. In the next decade, Grew established himself as a pious and orthodox pastor, debated such noted Baptists as Hanserd Knollys and Benjamin Cox on baptism and church polity, and was influential in Presbyterian circles, serving on a variety of committees to promote the well-being of Presbyterianism. Grew received Bachelor of Divinity and Doctorate of Divinity degrees from Oxford in 1651.

Grew was ejected from his living for nonconformity in 1662, but remained in the Coventry area preaching privately wherever opportunity afforded. He established a conventicle by 1665. Later that year when the Great Plague struck, and many ministers vacated their flocks, Grew preached freely in many areas. He was one of four preachers at the Presbyterian Great Meeting of 1669. Three years later, he was licensed as a Presbyterian preacher, but faced persecution again later in the 1670s.

In 1682, Grew, who had nearly lost his eyesight, was convicted of breaching the Five Mile Act and was imprisoned, for six months in a Coventry prison. While imprisoned, he dictated several sermons to an assistant; so many copies were made available that conventicles were held. Nearly two hundred people were arrested for attending meetings where Grew's sermons were read aloud.

After the indulgence of James II in 1687, Grew preached regularly, despite his blindness and old age, to his old, large congregation at Coventry's Leather Hall. He ministered until September 1689, when his health failed. He died on October 22, 1689, and was buried in the chancel of St. Michael's.

Grew published three works during his lifetime: *A Farewell Sermon* (1663), *A Sinner's Justification* (1670), and *Meditations upon Our Saviour's Parable of the Prodigal* (1678). His work on the prodigal was reprinted several times in the late seventeenth century.

The Lord Our Righteousness: The Old Perspective on Paul (SDG; 102 pages; 2005). First published in 1670 as *A Sinner's Justification*, this treatise was compiled as personal reflections and later published at the nudging of friends. The work is divided into eight chapters and in typical Puritan fashion states the doctrine, exegetes it, and then closes with application. Grew's work is important because it gives a sound exposition of the doctrine of justification by faith alone. "A man is not justified *for* faith, but *by* it," Grew says.

With zeal and clarity, Grew shows from Scripture that man's justification before God is not dependent on any righteousness inherent in him, but is wholly dependent on the righteousness of Christ credited to the believer. He provides a solid Reformed emphasis on Christ's imputed righteousness, concluding, "Oh, let this doctrine of Christ's righteousness feed us with admiration that the Lord should give His dear and only Son this name: 'The Lord our Righteousness!'"

William Gurnall

(1616-1679)

William Gurnall was born in St. Margaret's parish, King's Lynn, and was baptized on November 17, 1616. He was the second son of Gregory Gurnall and Catherine Dressyt. His father was an alderman in Lynn when William was born, and became mayor when William was age eight. William was educated at the free grammar school in Lynn, then went to Emmanuel College, Cambridge, "nursery of the Puritans." He earned a bachelor's degree in 1635 and a master's degree in 1639.

Gurnall probably began his ministry at Sudbury, Suffolk. In 1644, he was asked to serve as curate of Lavenham, the largest church in West Suffolk. He became rector upon the death of the incumbent, Ambrose Copinger. Despite poor health, Gurnall spent the next thirty-five years ministering there.

In 1646, Gurnall married Sarah Mott, the daughter of vicar Thomas Mott of Stoke by Nayland, Suffolk. The couple had at least fourteen children, six of whom survived them.

Gurnall did not receive episcopal ordination until the Restoration. He was Puritan in doctrine, but was willing to stay in the Church of England, especially under Bishop Edward Reynolds of Norwich, who professed Puritan sympathies. Reynolds finally ordained Gurnall in 1662 after he submitted to the Act of Uniformity; consequently, Gurnall was not ejected from the pulpit in 1662. Although Gurnall's parish ministry appeared unaffected by that submission, his

reputation among Puritans suffered. In 1665, he was denounced in an anonymous pamphlet titled *Covenant Renouncers,
Desperate Apostates*, which stated that he was not "alone in
these horrible defilements, hateful to the soul of God and his
saints" (p. 6; quoted in *Oxford DNB*, 24:271).

Gurnall published a few sermons in 1660, but is best
known for his massive *The Christian in Complete Armour*. He died
October 12, 1679, at the age of sixty-three, and was buried in
the Lavenham church or churchyard. Shortly after the funeral,
William Burkitt, rector of neighboring Milden, preached a
sermon on Hebrews 13:7, urging his congregation to follow
Gurnall's example in soundness and steadfastness of faith,
and to imitate his walk of humility, love, charity, diligence,
and sympathy with the afflicted church of Christ.

<hr />

The Christian in Complete Armour (BTT; 1,189 pages; 1995).
This commentary on Ephesians 6:10-20, was first published in
three parts in 1655, 1658, and 1662, and was reprinted many
times throughout the centuries. It was translated into several
languages; the translation into Welsh alone underwent four
reprintings in a thirty-five year period around the turn of the
nineteenth century. An edition with a biographical introduction by J. C. Ryle first appeared in 1844, and was reissued in
1865, which BTT reprinted. It is the most well-known of the
Puritan manuals on spiritual warfare, and has provided much
spiritual comfort for beleaguered saints over the centuries.

Gurnall said of this treatise, "The subject is solemn: A war
between the saint and Satan, and that so bloody a one, that
the cruellest which was ever fought by men will be found but
sport and child's play [compared] to this. It is a spiritual war
that you shall read of, that concerns thee and every one that
reads it. The stage whereon this war is fought is every man's
own soul. There is no neuter in this war. The whole world is

engaged in the quarrel, either for God against Satan, or for Satan against God."

The work has two parts: "A Short but Powerful Encouragement to the War," and "Directions for Managing the War Successfully." After describing the believer's spiritual enemies, Gurnall details the work of Satan in temptation, depression, and discouragement. The last half of the work tells how to use all of the Christian armor listed in Ephesians 6:10-20.

Gurnall's *magnum opus* is doctrinally balanced and packed with practical guidelines for Christian living. It is remarkably free of repetition. J.C. Ryle wrote of it, "You will often find in a line and a half some great truth, put so concisely, and yet so fully, that you really marvel how so much thought could be got into so few words." Spurgeon said Gurnall's work "is peerless and priceless; every line is full of wisdom; every sentence is suggestive. The whole book has been preached over scores of times, and is, in our judgment, the best thought-breeder in our library." John Newton added, "If I might read only one book beside the Bible, I would choose *The Christian in Complete Armour*."

In 1986, BTT published a three-volume paperback abridgment of *The Christian in Complete Armour*. It is helpful for readers unfamiliar with Gurnall's style and vocabulary.

The Christian's Labor and Reward (SDG; 180 pages; 2004). In this volume, first published in 1672, Gurnall expounds 1 Corinthians 15:58 and encourages Christians by assuring them, "Your labour is not in vain in the Lord." He analyzes the nature and quality of this labor, as well as of the reward. Appended is his sermon, "The Civil Magistrate's Portrait Drawn from God's Word," along with a biographical sketch of Gurnall by J. C. Ryle.

Gleanings from William Gurnall (SDG; 147 pages; 1996). First published in 1914 as *Gleanings from the Past: Extracts from the*

Writings of William Gurnall, this collection of extracts, selected by Hamilton Smith, highlights choice sayings from *The Christian in Complete Armour*. Such nuggets as this warm the heart and search the conscience: "Most men are more tender of their skin than of their conscience, and had rather the gospel had provided an armor to defend their bodies from death and danger, than their souls from sin and death." This book is excellent for daily devotions.

Joseph Hall

(1574-1656)

The respected English bishop, Joseph Hall, was born July 1, 1574, at Bristow Park, near Ashby-de-la-Zouch, Leicestershire. His father, John Hall, was the town agent for Henry, earl of Huntingdon. His mother, Winifred Bambridge, was a godly woman, comparable in Hall's mind to Augustine's mother, Monica. Hall was privately tutored for several years by William Pelsett, rector of Market Bosworth, then sent to Emmanuel College, Cambridge, in 1589. There he gained a life-long love for Puritan piety though he supported Anglican rather than Presbyterian ecclesiology. In 1595, he became a fellow of the college; the following year he earned a Master of Arts degree and was elected as a university lecturer in rhetoric. During his time at Cambridge, Hall wrote *Virgidemiarum* (1597; "A Collection of Sound Thrashings"), a collection of satires in Latin verse. In 1599, the archbishop of Canterbury ordered that Hall's satires be burnt because they were licentious, but that order was soon reversed.

In 1601, Hall became rector of Hawstead, Suffolk, under the sponsorship of Sir Robert and Lady Anne Drury. Here he wrote *Contemplations*, which, being printed scores of times, memorialized him to future generations. In 1603, he received a Bachelor of Divinity degree. That same year he married Elizabeth

Winiffe; together they had six sons and two daughters. Four of the sons followed their father in serving the church.

In 1605, Hall accompanied Sir Edmund Bacon to the Netherlands, in part to learn about the condition and practices of the Roman Catholic Church. Hall took part in debates at Jesuit College in Brussels on the authenticity of modern miracles. When his debating skills became too convincing, his patron asked Hall to abstain from further discussions.

Hall's devotional writings impressed Henry Frederick, eldest son of King James I of England and later Prince of Wales. Henry appointed Hall as one of his chaplains in 1608. Two years later he received his doctorate in divinity. In 1612, Lord Denny, later earl of Norwich, gave Hall the curacy of Waltham Holy Cross, Essex. That same year he became a prebend of Willenhall in the college church of Wolverhampton.

In 1616, Hall accompanied James Hay, Lord Doncaster, later earl of Carlisle, to France, to congratulate Louis XIII on his marriage. Illness forced him to return early. In his absence, King James nominated him dean of Worcester. In 1617, Hall went with the king to Scotland, where he defended the five points of ceremonial worship that the king wanted to impose upon the Scots. Though the king became very unpopular for his efforts to build Episcopacy on the ruins of Presbyterianism, Hall's reputation did not suffer. His character earned the respect of the most eminent Scotsmen of the day.

In 1618, King James asked Hall to be an English deputy at the Synod of Dort, where he "worked for an amicable confessional settlement between the Reformed and the Arminians, albeit from a distinctly Reformed perspective, resting on the theology of Musculus, Zanchius, Polanus, and other Reformed theologians of the age" (Richard Muller, in *Solomon's Divine Arts*, p. 14). The long meetings affected his health, however, so after some months he returned to England.

In 1627, Hall was appointed bishop of Exeter, where he continued to take an active part in the Calvinist-Arminian controversy in the English church. He did his best in his *Via media: The Way of Peace* (*via media*, literally, "The middle way") to persuade the two parties to compromise. His Calvinistic convictions notwithstanding, he maintained that acknowledging the errors that had risen in the Roman Catholic Church did not necessarily negate her catholicity. He also said that the Church of England, having repudiated those errors, should not deny the claims of the Roman Catholic Church to be a true church. This was also the view of Charles I (who had married a Roman Catholic) and his Episcopal advisers. However, Archbishop Laud, a staunch Arminian, sent people to Hall's diocese to investigate the Calvinistic tendencies of the bishop and his toleration of Puritans and low-church clergy. Hall says he was often on his knees before the king responding to Laud's accusations. In time, he grew so tired of the criticism that he threatened to "cast up his rochet" (the surplice-like vestment worn by bishops) rather than submit to them.

Hall was generally patient with criticism, however. His defense of the English church, *Episcopacy by Divine Right* (1640), was twice revised under Laud's direction. He then wrote *An Humble Remonstrance to the High Court of Parliament* (1640-41), a forceful defense of episcopacy. Five Puritan divines writing under the name of "Smectymnuus" responded to the book, in which they accused Hall of trying for twelve years to avoid being called a Puritan even when he really was a Puritan in "all but episcopacy" (*Oxford DNB*, 24:636). A long controversy ensued. John Milton alone wrote five pamphlets attacking Hall and his satires.

In 1641, Hall served on the Lords' committee on religion. Late that year, he and other bishops were brought before the bar of the House of Lords to answer a charge of high treason. They were convicted, asked to forfeit their estates, and incarcerated. After several months of imprisonment, they were finally released on bail.

Hall paid a bond of 5000 pounds to secure his release and transfer to the see of Norwich. As bishop of Norwich, he seems to have received revenue from the see for a time, but in 1643, the property of the "malignants," including Hall, was sequestered under the Act of Sequestration. Hall's wife had difficulty securing a fifth of the maintenance assigned to her husband by Parliament. Eventually the Halls were ejected from the palace about 1647, and the cathedral was reduced to a parish church. Hall's house, library, and some of his possessions were sold for the Parliamentary cause.

Hall retired to the nearby village of Higham, where he spent time preaching and writing until he was too ill to continue. As he said, "He was first forbidden by man, and at last disabled by God." He bore his troubles, poverty, and suffering patiently, dying September 8, 1656, at the age of eighty-one.

Thomas Fuller wrote of Hall: "He was commonly called our English Seneca, for the pureness, plainness, and fullness of his style. [He was] not unhappy at controversies, more happy at comments, very good in his characters, better in his sermons, best of all in his meditations." Hall's polemical writings, although vigorous and effective, were of passing interest, but many of his devotional writings have often been reprinted. He is also known for his early work censoring morals and his criticism of literary extravagance. In this he and the Puritans were like-minded, comparing fine words to fine clothes: the more ornamental they are, the more wicked they must be. In his Puritan-minded convictions, he strove for peace, edification, and conservatism in his commentaries, contemplations, and polemical pamphlets.

———◆◆◆———

Contemplations on the Historical Passages of the Old and New Testament (SDG; 3 vols., 1,600 pages; 1995). This three-volume reprint is taken from a ten-volume set of Hall's *Works* published in 1837. Though Hall did not associate with the Puritans, he did share their experiential heritage. That is clearly exemplified in this work, which took him twenty years to complete.

The twenty-five books of *Contemplations* include numerous historical narratives of Scripture. Hall uses simple, precise prose to make his points, moving readers to adore scriptural truths and the God of Scripture. To read Hall's *Contemplations* is to "read the narrative passages of the Bible through the eyes of a delightful saint and veteran pastor. It is to accompany the great man on a walk through the lanes and byways of all the events in the sacred record, and to hear his reflections, and the responses of his own heart. Seldom did anyone combine such easy prose with so many profound comments."

Contemplations has been prized throughout the centuries. For example, in the nineteenth century, Charles H. Spurgeon wrote: "Need I commend Bishop Hall's *Contemplations* to your affectionate attention? What wit! What sound sense! What concealed learning! His style is as pithy and witty as that of Thomas Fuller, and it has a sacred unction about it to which Fuller has no pretension." A century earlier, George Whitefield wrote, "Though weak, I often spent two hours in my evening retirements, and prayed over my Greek Testament and Bishop Hall's most excellent *Contemplations*."

Solomon's Divine Arts, ed. Gerald T. Sheppard (Pilgrim; 374 pages; 1991). This book conveys Hall's rather unique approach in commenting on Proverbs, Ecclesiastes, and Song of Solomon. Instead of expounding each text separately, Hall selects biblical texts under a given theme, often grouping texts together and then addressing issues of ethics, economics, and politics.

George Hamond

(c. 1620-1705)

George Hamond entered Trinity College, Dublin, in 1637, and graduated with a Bachelor of Arts degree. Recognizing his talents at an early age, Archbishop James Ussher remarked that Hamond would become "a considerable man." In 1639, Hamond entered Exeter College, Oxford, where he earned a Master of Arts in 1641. He was ordained at Exeter on October 26, 1645, and became the rector of Mamhead, Devon.

In 1648, Hamond signed a testimony that supported Presbyterianism, together with seventy-two other Devon ministers. That same year, he became curate at the parish of Kenton, Devon, and then in 1654, lecturer and minister of Totnes. In 1658, he became the rector of Bigbury, Devon, and two years later, the rector of the joint parish of Holy Trinity and St. Peter, Dorchester. He was ejected from his pulpit by the Act of Uniformity but remained in office until 1663. He subscribed to the Oxford oath in 1665 and so avoided the consequences of the Five Mile Act. In 1672, he was licensed as a Presbyterian teacher.

In 1677, Hamond became co-minister with George Newton in Taunton. While ministering there, Hamond kept a boarding school. Though several counties allowed tolerance for nonconformists, ministers of dissent in Taunton were severely persecuted. Both Hamond and Newton were brought before the Somerset assizes in 1680 and ordered to stop nonconformist activities. Newton died several months later, but

Hamond continued to defy the order. Their church, Paul's Meeting Presbyterian Church, was eventually destroyed in 1683 by order of the town mayor. Hamond struggled to keep the congregation together, but later moved to London to avoid persecution.

In London, Hamond became the colleague of Richard Steele at Armourers' Hall, Coleman Street. He was certified as a minister in 1689. Steele died on November 16, 1692; Hamond preached his funeral sermon the next day (later published as *A Good Minister of Jesus Christ* [1693]) and became the sole pastor. At the request of colleagues, he wrote *A Discourse on Family Worship* (1694), which in many respects was a conciliatory work, attempting to unite increasing factions between united Presbyterian and Independent ministers.

In 1699, Hamond succeeded William Bates as one of the Tuesday lecturers at Salters' Hall. He died in 1705, survived by two sons and a daughter.

◆

The Case for Family Worship (SDG; 130 pages; 2005). First published in 1694 as *A Discourse on Family Worship*, Hamond's book included an appendix by the Independent minister Matthew Barker. The appendix in this SDG edition has been relabeled as chapter 12 and misleadingly presents itself as Hamond's work. The effect of uniting Barker's thoughts on family worship to Hamond's larger work was to further unite ministers on the common ground of sincere worship of God in one's home. Sadly, this endeavor was too late as the union between Presbyterian and Independent ministers dissolved prior to its publication.

Hamond's presentation of the Bible's case for family worship is still relevant today. Arguing from both the Old Testament examples of Abraham, Job, and Joshua, and the New Testament examples of Christ and Cornelius, he shows that if we are not spending time in worship at home, our children will be more likely to find corporate worship irrelevant. Positively, as we take the time to catechize our families and worship with them beyond Sundays, they will understand how worship is to be found in all of life.

Nathanael Hardy

(1619-1670)

Nathanael Hardy, a prolific writer, was born September 14, 1619, and baptized in the church of St. Martin's, Ludgate. He was educated in London, and became a commoner of Magdalen Hall, Oxford, in 1633. He earned a bachelor's degree in 1635 and a master's degree at Hart Hall in 1638. He was twenty years old when he was ordained, becoming one of the youngest preachers of his time.

Hardy became a popular preacher in the early 1640s, known for his Puritan sentiments until Henry Hammond persuaded him of the merits of Episcopalian government. That happened during a meeting between royalists and parliamentarians in Uxbridge in 1645. Two years earlier, Hardy had been appointed lecturer at St. Dionis Backchurch, in Fenchurch Street. The congregation included mostly Presbyterians. After the meeting with Hammond, Hardy preached a sermon renouncing Presbyterianism and endorsing the Episcopalian system.

Hardy was not silenced during the Commonwealth years, even though at times he publicly questioned the legitimacy of the protectorate. He was appreciated by both royalists and parliamentarians for his solid biblical preaching and experiential emphasis.

After the restoration of Charles II, Hardy was given a chaplaincy and frequently preached in the royal chapel. Awarded a doctor's degree from Oxford in 1660, he was made rector of St. Dionis, where he had preached for several years. Later that year he became dean of Rochester. He was installed as archdeacon of Lewes in the diocese of Chichester in 1667 and held a rectory in Leybourne, Kent, for a short time. After a severe illness, he died in his home on June 1, 1670.

———◆◆◆———

Commentary on 1 John (TENT; 390 pages; 2002). This commentary, as the editor of the 1865 edition notes, "was intended to consist of five parts, corresponding to the five chapters of the epistle," but only two chapters were finished. The editor introduced the sermons as evangelical in subject matter, earnest and affectionate in spirit, and eloquent and impressive in manner. Since its first publication, the commentary was so prized by students of John's first epistle that it was hard to find. Still, the book had critics. In the nineteenth century, Charles Spurgeon remarked that the editor's praise was "too ardent a commendation."

Robert Harris
(1581-1658)

Robert Harris was born at Broad Campden, Gloucester-shire, in 1581. He was educated at the free schools of Chipping Campden and Worcester. At age sixteen, he entered Magdalen Hall, Oxford, where his relative Robert Lyster was principal. Harris had a great thirst for knowledge and soon became known as an excellent scholar and logician. Because his parents were too poor to pay for higher education, Harris taught Greek and Hebrew to finance his study of philosophy. He earned a bachelor's degree in 1600, but decided to pursue the pastoral ministry rather than to become a lawyer, as his father had wished.

When the university closed in 1604 because of the plague, Harris went home and preached his first sermon at Chipping Campden. The low ebb of spiritual life there was graphically displayed by the lack of a single Bible at the church. Finally, after a vain search in surrounding homes, a Bible was located in the parish vicar's home. Harris preached from Romans 10:1, and the sermon was so well received that many urged him not to pursue any further education. Harris returned to Oxford, however, where he studied theology for ten years, graduating with a Bachelor of Divinity degree in 1614. Shortly afterward, Sir Anthony Coke offered Harris the living of Hanwell, Oxfordshire, which was vacant because of the ejection of John Dod. Archbishop Richard Bancroft, however, had his own nominees. It wasn't until Harris had been thoroughly examined in theological matters by William Barlow, bishop of Rochester, that Harris's appointment was confirmed.

The Hanwell vicarage became a favorite gathering place for students. Harris became a popular preacher at St. Paul's, St. Saviour's Southwark, and other London churches, as well as in his own neighborhood. A staunch Puritan and parliamentarian, he was in wide demand as a visiting preacher. In 1642, he became one of the Puritan divines consulted by Parliament and preached before the House of Commons on the occasion of a public fast day.

Harris lived a disciplined lifestyle, fearing the face of no man. He worked hard every day, but allowed himself Saturday afternoon for recreation. Of alcohol, he said that he would rather pour it into his boots between meals than into his mouth. Once, in 1642, after preaching on James 5:12, "Swear not at all," some Royalist soldiers warned him they would shoot him if he ever preached on that text again. Undismayed, he did just that the following Sabbath. When he noticed a soldier preparing his weapon to shoot him, he preached on and completed his sermon without any digression.

Later the same year, Royalist soldiers in Hanwell ejected Harris and his family from the church and burned their possessions. The Harrises fled to London, where Robert was given the living of St. Botolph's, Bishopgate, in 1644.

The following year, Harris was called as a delegate to the Westminster Assembly of Divines, and was soon appointed as one of seven theologians to frame what became known as the Westminster Confession of Faith. It was said that while Harris was in the assembly he "heard all, and said little." During those years, he was frequently invited to preach before Parliament.

In 1646, the committee of Hampshire appointed Harris to Petersfield. Before he could go there, he was ordered to Oxford as one of the six divines commissioned to preach in any pulpit they pleased. From 1647 to 1658, he was visitor to the university. In his first visitation sermon, he defended himself against the charge of pluralism. In 1648, the chancellor, Lord Pembroke, awarded Harris with a doctorate in divinity and appointed him president of Trinity College, Oxford.

Though elderly by this time, Harris diligently performed his duties as president for the last ten years of his life. He also lectured once a week at All Souls' College, in both English and Latin, and preached on Sundays at Garsington. Harris was a good Hebrew scholar and well versed in church history. Bishop John Wilkins, who married Oliver Cromwell's sister, said Harris was one of the most eminent divines in preaching and in practical theology.

Harris died in December of 1658, at the age of seventy-seven. Prior to his death, he confessed: "It is all one to me whether I am kept alone, or have my friends with me. My work is now to arm myself for death, which assaults me, and to apply myself unto that great encounter." As he was dying, Harris told his friends, "I am now going home, even quite spent. I am now at the shore, but leave you still tossing on the sea. Oh, it is a good time to die in! I never in all my life saw the wrath of Christ, nor tasted the sweetness of God's love in that measure as I do now."

Harris left several letters of advice to his wife and children, encouraging them to hope and trust in the Lord. Upon his request, he was buried in the graveyard at Trinity College.

———◆◆◆———

The Way to True Happiness (SDG; 450 pages; 1998). First published in London (1653), this work on the Beatitudes contains twenty-four sermons full of practical depth and insight. Harris shows that true happiness can come only from true blessedness, which can flow only from God Himself. If God is infinitely blessed, then knowing Him must bring the happiness for which man eternally seeks. Knowing God offers not only eternal life, but also eternal happiness.

This book on how to find true happiness is marked by careful exposition and solid comfort. It rightfully takes its place among other major Puritan works on the Beatitudes, such as those by Thomas Watson and Jeremiah Burroughs.

Matthew Henry

(1662-1714)

M atthew Henry, the celebrated Bible commentator, was
born at Broad Oak, Flintshire, on October 18, 1662, less
than two months after his father, Philip Henry, was ejected
from the ministry in the Church of England. Born prema-
turely, he was a frail child, yet was spiritually robust and
gifted in learning. He was educated primarily by his father,
with the assistance of tutors.

Henry entered Thomas Doolittle's academy at Islington in
1680. He studied there under Doolittle and Thomas Vincent
for two years; then, when persecution forced the academy to
relocate, Henry moved to the estate of Bronington, Flintshire,
which he inherited from Daniel Matthews, his maternal
grandfather. Realizing his chances of being called to the ministry were remote, Henry decided to enter the legal profession.
On the advice of Rowland Hunt, he was admitted to Gray's
Inn in 1685 to study law, while continuing theological study
in private.

In 1686, Henry began to preach in his father's neighborhood. Because of business matters, he moved to Chester in
1687. He preached there in private houses until he was asked
to become the local minister. On May 9, 1687, he was privately
ordained in London by six ministers at the house of Richard
Steele. Then he returned to Chester to begin his ministry.
Within a few years, the number of communicants in his congregation grew to 250.

MATTHEW HENRY

In September, James II visited Chester to hear the non-conformists of the city give public thanks "for the ease and liberty they then enjoyed under his protection." A new charter was granted to the city (the old one was repealed in 1684), which gave power to the crown to displace and appoint magistrates. Henry refused to consent to the terms of the new charter, and, along with others, demanded the restoration of the old one. That demand was finally granted.

In 1687, Henry married Katherine, the only daughter of Samuel Hardware of Bromborough, Cheshire. She died in childbirth in February of 1689, at the age of twenty-five. In 1690, Henry married Mary Warburton. They had one son, Philip, and eight daughters, three of whom died in infancy.

A meetinghouse built for Henry in Crook Lane was opened in 1700. In 1706, a gallery was added to accommodate another congregation that joined Henry's. The number of communicants rose to 350. In addition to his congregational work, Henry held monthly services at five neighboring villages and regularly preached to prisoners in the castle.

Henry's study was a two-story summerhouse in the back of his residence in Bolland Court, Whitefriars, Chester. In 1704, at the age of forty-two, Henry began work on a Bible commentary, based on his system of expository preaching and the copious notes and writings on the Bible that he had compiled during his ministry. He had learned Latin, Greek, and Hebrew as a child, and also had a working knowledge of French; this gave him a wide range of reading. Additionally, he had a keen spirit of inquiry, profound knowledge, and the ability to convey doctrinal matters in a simple yet profound way.

In 1710, Henry was invited to Hackney, one of the most important congregations near London. He agreed to move, though not immediately. He finally preached his farewell sermon at Chester on May 11, 1712, amid many tears. His ministry at Mare Street, Hackney, began the following week.

In May of 1714, Henry revisited Cheshire. As he rode back to London, he fell from his horse at Tarporley and was taken to the house of a neighboring nonconformist minister, Joseph Mottershead. He died the following day. He was buried in the chancel of Trinity Church, Chester; Peter Withington, John Gardner, Daniel Williams, William Tong (Henry's first biographer), Isaac Bates, and John Reynolds preached at the funeral.

Though Matthew Henry is most remembered for his commentary on the Bible, he wrote thirty additional works, focusing primarily on practical piety. He kept a diary from 1690 until he died, but only the latter portion, from 1705 to 1714, survives. He also was a zealous preacher and a devoted husband, father, and friend. Henry's first biographer said, "Those who knew him coveted his company and were delighted with it." The message that Henry stressed to his friends and family was simple: "A life spent in the service of God, and communion with him, is the most comfortable life anyone can live in this world."

<hr />

The Complete Works of Matthew Henry (Baker; 2 vols., 1,392 pages; 1997). This reprint contains all of Henry's treatises, sermons, tracts, and biographies. Excluded are his *Commentary*, *Covenant of Grace*, and private diaries.

In 1690, Henry published his first book, *A Brief Inquiry into the True Nature of Schism*. After proving from Scripture that schism signifies "an uncharitable distance, division, or alienation of affections among those who are called Christians, and agree in the fundamentals of religion, occasioned by their different apprehensions of little things," Henry explains how there may be schism where there is no separation of communion, and that there may be separation of communion where there is no schism.

In 1694, Henry published *Family Hymns*, a compilation of works by various authors, prefaced by his brief essay on psalmody. This selection of metrical versions of Psalms and other passages of Scripture were omitted from various editions of Henry's *Works*, but they were included in the definitive 1855 edition, from which this set is reprinted.

In 1698, Henry published *An Account of the Life and Death of Philip Henry*. Thomas Chalmers called this biography of Henry's father "one of the most precious religious biographies in our language." In 1974, The Banner of Truth Trust reprinted this work along with J. B. Williams's *Memoirs of the Life, Character, and Writings of the Rev. Matthew Henry* (1828).

One of Henry's best works, not reprinted elsewhere, is *A Church in the House: Family Religion* (1704). It contains the sermon Henry preached in London based on 1 Corinthians 16:19, "With the church that is in their house." Henry outlines the great necessity and duty of family religion, stressing how families may be called "churches." He then urges family members to turn their homes into little churches. The house "must be consecrated to God" as a society that is called out of the world, Henry says.

Henry did this with his own family. Each day he rose early to pray with his family, and reviewed parts of the sermons the family had heard the previous Sabbath. In the afternoons, he catechized his younger children. At night, when the small ones were in bed, Henry taught his older children. He put together *Family Hymns* primarily for use by his own family. Fathers would do well to use this excellent book.

Other works of Henry's not reprinted elsewhere include: *Against Vice and Profaneness*; *Self-Consideration and Self-Preservation*; *The Right Management of Friendly Visits*; *Great Britain's Present Joys and Hopes*; *England's Hopes*; *The Work and Success of the Ministry*; *Baptism*; *The Catechizing of Youth*; *A Scripture Catechism*; *Faith in Christ and Faith in God*; *Hope and Fear Balanced*; *The Forgiveness of Sin as a Debt*; *Popery: A Spiritual Tyranny*; *The True*

Nature of Schism, several funeral sermons, and biographies of lesser-known individuals.

*Commentary on the Whole Bible (HP; 6 vols., 2,485 pages; 1991). Henry began his *magnum opus* in November 1704. After ten years of diligent study, he was able to finish expository comments on Genesis through Acts. The first volume of *Commentary* (published as *Exposition of the Old and New Testaments*), which covered the Pentateuch, was published in 1707. That, plus four more volumes, together covering Genesis through the Acts, were completed by his death. After his death, thirteen of Henry's fellow ministers compiled a commentary primarily from Henry's notes and writings on Romans through Revelation. The six-volume 1811 edition, edited by George Burder and John Hughes, contains additional material from Henry's manuscripts.

Henry's *Commentary*, though superseded to some degree in the area of exegesis, has never been surpassed in its practical emphasis. Its divisions, main points, and practical applications are invaluable. Interestingly, some of the quaint sayings and pithy remarks sprinkled throughout the text were based on what Henry's father said during family worship.

By 1855, Henry's popular commentary had been reprinted twenty-five times, and has been reprinted numerous times since then, sometimes by more than one publisher at a time. It remains an indispensable reference tool for pastors, students, and theologians, as well as for families in devotions. It is available in a variety of editions: the complete six-volume edition (1811), an unabridged single volume, and several abridged editions, most of which strip Henry's work of its Calvinistic emphasis.

Scores of ministers have praised Henry's *Commentary*. Here's a sampling:

- Philip Doddridge, who educated Henry's grandson, Charles Bulkley: "Henry is, perhaps, the only commentator, so large, that deserves to be entirely and attentively read through."
- Charles Spurgeon: "First among the mighty for general usefulness, we are bound to mention the man whose name is a household word, *Matthew Henry*. He is most pious and pithy, sound and sensible, suggestive and sober, terse and trustworthy."
- William Romaine: "There is no comment upon the Bible, either ancient or modern, in all respects equal to Mr. Henry's."
- William Tong: "As long as the Bible continues in England, Mr. Henry's admirable *Expositions* will be prized by all serious Christians; in them his clear head, his warm heart, his life, his soul appears."

The Covenant of Grace (CFP; 420 pages; 2003). For fifty years, Allan Harman, a research professor at Presbyterian Theological College, Melbourne, had a copy of Matthew Henry's hand-written sermon notes on the covenant of grace, comprising twenty-eight sermons preached at Chester in 1691 and 1692. Convinced of their worth, Harman began the laborious task of transcribing the notes into printable form. The resulting work, *The Covenant of Grace*, offers a deeply spiritual look at one of the most fundamental doctrines—God's promise of unmerited favor to humanity.

The book explains covenant themes such as pardon, peace, grace, access, ordinances, providences, angels, creatures, afflictions, death, and heaven. The last sermon, titled "Repetition," is a summary of the sermons. We highly recommend this book for its depth, practical worth, and ability to inflame the heart.

How to Prepare for Communion (SGT; 128 pages; 2001). Originally titled *The Communicant's Companion; or Instructions and Helps*

for the right receiving of the Lord's Supper (1704), this small work
was popular from the start. In his diary of December 31, 1705,
Henry confessed, "I desire, with all humility, to give God
praise for what acceptance my book on the sacrament has met
with; the intimations I have had thereof from diverse people, I
desire may never be the matter of my pride (the Lord mortify
that in me), but ever, ever, the matter of my praise."

Henry provides several helps for the serious communicant: a description of the ordinance, qualifications
prerequisite to it, helps for self-examination, helps for meditation and prayer, the proper frame of mind, the precious
benefits received, helps for devout affections, and, finally,
ways to "improve the sacrament" (i.e., to derive the greater
profit from receiving the sacrament).

A Method for Prayer (RAP; 390 pages; 1994). Edited and revised by J. Ligon Duncan III, this magnificent work on prayer
was originally titled *A Method for Prayer with Scripture Expressions
proper to be used under each head.* Finished before Henry left
Chester, it reflects a lifetime of prayer, ministry, and Christian
experience.

For those who lead the church in public prayer or who
want to be more faithful in their prayer lives, this book provides the order, proportion, and variety that are necessary.
This edition of *A Method for Prayer* contains two parts: the
entire text of Henry's original work, and three of Henry's sermons on prayer given shortly after his arrival in London in
1712. It also includes an outline of Henry's plan for prayer,
guidelines for public prayer (drawn from Samuel Miller's
Thoughts on Public Prayer), and a short version of Henry's outline, perforated for easy removal.

Overall, this edition is impressive. The type is large and
readable, and the divisions are easy to follow. Henry's plan
for prayer (adoration, confession, petition, thanksgiving,

intercession, and conclusion), should enrich the life of the serious follower.

Christian Focus Publications printed a shorter edition of this work (1994) in its Christian Heritage series.

The Pleasantness of a Religious Life (SDG; 192 pages; 1996). Printed in London in 1714, and in New York by Robert Carter in 1847 (from which this edition is reproduced), Henry's work on the pleasantness of the religious life is a treasure. In six chapters on Proverbs 3:17 ("Her ways are ways of pleasantness, and all her paths are peace"), Henry proves and illustrates the doctrine of religious pleasantness, saying the religious life is the *only* life worth living. "What was the fall and apostasy of man, and what is still his sin and misery, but the soul's revolt from the divine life, and giving up itself wholly to the animal life?" Henry writes.

In an age when the temptations of a transient world afflict travelers to heaven, we cannot recommend this work enough, for Henry clearly shows how pleasant, desirable, and worthwhile a God-fearing life is. He writes, "We are not yet home, but we should long to be there, and keep up holy desires of that glory to be revealed, that we may be quickened, as long as we are here, to press 'toward the mark for the prize of the high calling'" (p. 192).

Many ministers, including James Hervey, have recommended this book to young people. It is a great help in demolishing Satan's insinuation that true religion is boring and burdensome.

The Quest for Meekness and Quietness of Spirit (SDG; 144 pages; 1996). First published in 1699 with *A Sermon on Acts 28:22 showing that the Christian Religion is Not a Sect*, this work explains the nature of meekness and quietness of spirit (contentment) in three chapters, describing its nature, excellence, and application. Meekness impacts our entire life, governing even our greatest character flaws, Henry asserts.

Henry says Paul offers two goals of contentment: (1) to wean Christians from the vanity of excessive concern for outward appearance instead of issues of the heart, and (2) to help Christians love the treasures of godliness. In his closing application, Henry notes the purpose of his work: "That which I have been so intent upon in this discourse, is only to persuade you not to be your own tormenters, but to govern your passions so that they may not be furies to yourselves" (p. 143).

This modern edition contains only Henry's *Quest for Meekness*. Originally, the work included a preface written by the Puritan John Howe, who wrote: "It was with real difficulty, through the not easily vincible aversion of the Reverend author, that these two discourses are now at length brought together, into public view." Apparently, the modest Henry did not consider the work to be worth the paper it was printed on. But Howe said the book had "true value in it, and so real usefulness unto common good." Several individuals thus wrestled it out of "the hands that penned it" and published it.

Howe is most complimentary of the work, saying, "Were it a common design to have minds habited and clothed according to it [Christian meekness], what a blessed calm would it introduce into our world! How serene and peaceful a region would it make every man's soul to himself, and to all about him! It would then be truly said of the Christian church, 'this is the house of God; this is the gate of heaven.'"

Revelation (Crossway; 191 pages; 1991). The book of Revelation poses a serious interpretive challenge for any writer. Full of vivid imagery and symbolism, it ultimately reminds the church of God's sovereignty in accomplishing His purposes regardless of opposition.

Edited and abridged for modern readers, this commentary on Revelation provides classic insights into this rather intimidating book of the Bible. It portrays the last battle of human history, the career and defeat of the Antichrist, Christ's millennial reign, and Christ's judgment of the wicked and the righteous.

The Secret of Communion with God (Kregel; 123 pages; 1991). This small work shows how to begin the day with God, how to spend it with God, and how to end it with God. It was first published in 1714 under the title *Directions for Beginning, Spending, and Closing Each Day with God*, being the written version of three addresses that Henry gave at the morning lectures held at Bednal Green (now Bethnal Green), London. This handbook is helpful for the practice of daily piety.

The Young Christian (CFP; 64 pages; 1993). Published for the first time in 1713 as *Sober-mindedness Pressed upon Young People*, this small book urges young Christians to be considerate, cautious, humble, self-denying, gentle, chaste, composed, content, and serious. Henry explains the necessity for spiritual cultivation and closes his work with several benefits of sober-mindedness, such as a useful life and a happy death. He includes practical ways to promote sober-mindedness in one's life.

One of the best ways to cultivate this grace, says Henry, is to choose carefully what to read. "Read sober books," he says. "Those that are given to reading are as much under the influence of books they read, as of the persons they converse with, and therefore in the choice of them you need to be very cautious, and take advice. Nothing more prompts vanity, especially among the refined part of mankind, than romances and plays, and loose poems.... Inquire not for merry books, songs, and jests, but serious books, which will help you to put you into, and keep you in a serious frame" (p. 63).

Philip Henry

(1631-1696)

Philip Henry was born in Whitehall on August 24, 1631, to John and Magdalen Henry. His father, of Welsh descent, settled in England early in life. He entered the service of the earl of Pembroke and then of Charles I, who became his close friend. As a child, Philip was playmate to Prince Charles (later Charles II) and Prince James. Later, Henry thanked God for delivering him from the snares of the court.

After preliminary studies that focused on Latin, Philip was admitted in 1643 to Westminster School, where he studied under Thomas Vincent and later became the favorite pupil of Richard Busby, a Puritan. Henry's mother, a zealous Puritan, obtained permission for Henry to attend the early lecture at Westminster Abbey. Through the influence of his parents, Busby's lectures, and the preaching of Stephen Marshall, Henry was converted and became a Puritan.

Henry was admitted to Christ Church, Oxford, in 1647, shortly before his tutor was ejected. When Henry was home in January 1649, he watched as Charles I, who "went by our door on foot each day," went on trial before Parliament, and then was executed.

Henry earned a bachelor's degree in 1651 and a master's degree in 1652. His father's death in 1652 left the family in great financial distress, which was relieved only by the occasional gifts of friends.

Henry preached his first sermon at South Hinksey, Oxfordshire, on January 9, 1653. For several months he tutored the sons of John Paleston, a judge at Emral Hall, Flintshire, while serving as a preacher at the prosperous Worthenbury Chapel, in the parish of Banger-is-y-coed. In 1654, he worked with pupils at Oxford, but from 1655 on, he worked exclusively at Worthenbury.

After a thorough examination in 1657 by the local presbytery (which included Richard Steele), Henry was ordained at Prees, Shropshire. He made a strong Calvinistic confession, although he did not support the Presbyterian system. In 1658, Henry helped organize a North Wales association of clergymen, consisting of Episcopalians, Presbyterians, and Independents. He authored the section of the association's agreement that dealt with worship.

Henry appears to have been sympathetic with the royalist uprising under Sir George Booth in August 1659. At the Restoration, Henry welcomed the political change as a "public national mercy." In 1660, however, he was called before the Flint assizes for not reading *The Book of Common Prayer*. He was chastised again at the spring assizes, but without effect. He had taken the oath of allegiance but refused reordination. On October 24, 1661, Henry was ejected from his pulpit; he preached his farewell sermon three days later.

Meanwhile, in 1660, Henry married Katherine, the only daughter and heir of Daniel Matthews of Broad Oak and Bronington, Flintshire. The marriage would be blessed with six children.

Henry's seven years at Worthenbury yielded numerous conversions. His ministry was earnest and loving. His son Matthew Henry wrote, "He adapted his method and style to the capacities of his hearers, fetching his similitudes for illustration from those things which were familiar to them. He did not shoot the arrow of the word over their heads in high notions, or the flourishes of affected rhetoric; nor under their feet by blunt and homely expressions; but to their hearts in close and lively applications. His delivery was very graceful and agreeable, neither noisy and precipitate on the one hand, nor dull and slow on the other. His doctrine dropped as the dew, and distilled as the soaking rain, and came with a charming, pleasing power, such as many bore witness to, that have wondered at the gracious words which proceeded out of his mouth."

When the Act of Uniformity took effect on St. Bartholomew's Day, August 24, 1662, Henry was silenced as a minister. "Our sins have made Bartholomew-day, in the year 1662, the saddest day for England since the death of Edward the Sixth, but even this [is] for good," he wrote. He gave up his house and left Worthenbury, moving his family to property inherited by his wife at Broad Oak, Flintshire. With some brief intervals, the Henrys remained there for the next thirty-four years.

In 1663, Henry and thirteen other preachers were imprisoned for four days at Hanmer, Flintshire, on suspicion of insurrection. In 1665, Henry was summoned to Malpas, Cheshire, for baptizing one of his own children. At the end of the month, he was treated as a layman and made sub-collector of taxes for the township of Iscoyd. The Five Mile Act of 1665 placed him in a quandary, for Broad Oak was only four miles away from Worthenbury. Henry thus moved to Whitchurch, Shropshire, where he regularly attended the local churches. In 1668, he preached in the parish church of Betley, Staffordshire; distorted accounts of that event were reported to the House of Commons, and Henry had to wait until 1672 before he was allowed to resume public ministry in his own house. After the indulgence was withdrawn, he preached without interference until 1681, when he was fined for holding unauthorized meetings for worship.

Henry was publicly vocal on contemporary issues. In 1682, he engaged in public discussion with Quakers at Llanfyllin, Montgomeryshire. He participated in a debate on ordination at Oswestry, Shropshire, with William Lloyd, then bishop of St. Asaph, and Henry Dodwell. At the time of the Monmouth rebellion, Henry was confined in Chester Castle for three weeks under a general order from the lord-lieutenant. He added his name to a cautiously-worded address to James II in 1687.

With the accession of William and Mary and the passing of the Act of Toleration, Henry was able to preach openly again. He accepted the terms of the Act of Toleration, but he would have preferred toleration without subscription. He frequently preached at Broad Oak near his home and in neighboring towns, but he did not accept another pastoral call.

Henry continued to work hard, but his health was declining. He died of colic at Broad Oak on June 24, 1696. His last words were, "O death, where is thy sting?" He was buried in Whitchurch, where a marble tablet was erected to his memory. He was survived by his wife, Katherine Matthews, with whom he had two sons, John and Matthew, and four daughters, all of whom professed salvation in Christ alone.

Henry was noted for his exemplary, Christ-centered worship and godly conduct. "See your need of Christ more and more," he once wrote to his son, "and live upon Him. No life like it; so sweet, so safe. My Savior is mine in all things. We cannot be discharged from the guilt of any evil we do, without His merit to satisfy; we cannot move in the performance of any good required, without His Spirit and grace to assist and enable for it; and when we have done all, that all is nothing, without His meditation and intercession to make it acceptable, so that, every day and in everything, He is All in All."

Henry was deeply committed to seeking peace among his brethren at all personal cost. He loved the truth and died in the assurance of it.

Though not as prolific an author as his son, Philip Henry's most famous book, *Christ All in All*, has been reprinted several times. John B. Williams published Henry's other works from his manuscripts: *Eighteen Sermons* (1816), *Skeletons of Sermons* (1834), *Expositions upon Genesis* (1839), *Remains* (1848), and *Diaries and Letters* (1882).

———————

Christ All in All (Reiner; 380 pages; 1976). Henry did not publish any books during his lifetime. However, he bequeathed several handwritten manuscripts to his children, each of whom was to select one to be "transcribed into their hearts and lives." Of these, Mrs. Savage, a God-fearing daughter, selected forty-one sermons titled *What Christ is Made of God to True Believers in Forty Real Benefits* (based on Colossians 3:11, "Christ is all and in all"). That work was not published until 1830. Savage wrote in her autobiography that the "sweet wholesome truths" of this book are "food for my poor soul. He being 'dead yet speaketh.' And what is it he says, but that which his heart was always full of? Christ—Christ—Christ. Methinks I hear him still: Oh, make Christ your all!"

This remarkable exposition of Colossians 3:11 considers Christ in forty offices: the foundation, food, root, raiment, head, hope, refuge, righteousness, light, life, peace, passover, portion, propitiation, freedom, fountain, wisdom, way, ensign, example, door, dew, sun, shield, strength, song, horn, honor, sanctification, supply, resurrection, redemption, lesson, ladder, truth, treasure, temple, ark, altar, and all. It is a compelling work on Christ's sufficiency for the believer in all stations of life.

Each chapter is based on the notes of a sermon. The chapters are pungent, edifying, and experiential. The Reiner edition of this work includes a brief memoir of Henry.

Oliver Heywood
(1630-1702)

Oliver Heywood was the third son born to Richard and Alice Heywood in Little Lever, near Bolton, Lancashire, in 1630. His parents brought him up under a continual round of sermon attendance characteristic of the most zealous Puritans, and with a library of godly Reformation and Puritan writers. They sent Oliver to Bolton's grammar school to study with William Rathband, the suspended curate at Little Lever, and then with George Rudhall, schoolmaster of Horwich in the adjacent parish of Deane, whose spirituality profoundly impacted him. Heywood matriculated at Trinity College, Cambridge, in 1647, where he was greatly influenced by the preaching of Samuel Hammond at St. Giles's Church. He also enjoyed spiritual fellowship with other students. He later wrote of his university years, "My time and thoughts were most employed on practical divinity, and experimental truths were most vivifying to my soul: I preferred Perkins, Bolton, Preston, and Sibbes far above Aristotle [and] Plato."

After earning a Bachelor of Arts degree in 1650, Heywood began to preach. His uncle, Francis Critchlaw, recommended him as preacher for Coley Chapel, near the village of Northowram, in the parish of Halifax, West Riding. Heywood accepted the position and was ordained at the age of twenty-one at Bury, Lancashire. His younger brother,

Nathaniel, was a pastor at Illingworth Chapel, in the same parish of Halifax. The two lived together for about a year.

In 1655, Heywood moved to Northowram after marrying Elizabeth, the daughter of John Angier. She died after giving birth to three sons. One of the sons died as an infant; the other two, John and Ebenezer, became ministers.

Heywood introduced Presbyterian church order to his congregation in 1657, including the setting up of an eldership, church discipline, and monthly communion. These changes roused considerable opposition, particularly from the more prosperous members of the church who opposed his ministry, but Heywood persevered despite the ensuing split in his congregation.

Heywood was a Royalist as well as a Presbyterian. Though he took no part in the insurrection led by George Booth in 1659, Heywood disobeyed the order requiring public thanksgiving for its suppression. Consequently, he was apprehended and threatened with sequestration. Upon hearing the news that General Monck had sided with the king, Heywood privately rejoiced. He wrote a psalm of praise in his diary.

With the Restoration, Heywood's real troubles began. Richard Hooke, the new vicar of Halifax, prohibited baptism in the remote chapels. Heywood continued to baptize, however, hoping to maintain peace by sending periodic gifts to the vicar. On January 23, 1661, authorities stopped his "private fast" against church practices that violated his Presbyterian principles. Stephen Ellis, a wealthy parishioner who, along with others, favored the restoration of the prayer book, laid a copy of The Book of Common Prayer in the pulpit on August 25, 1661. Heywood quietly moved it to one side.

Ellis reported the matter, and Heywood was ordered to report to York on September 13. After several hearings, he was suspended from ministering in the diocese of York. He continued to preach for some weeks, but within a month of the Act of Uniformity (August 24, 1662), he was excommunicated. That sentence was read publicly in several churches over the following months. Attempts were even made to forbid him from attending church. Meantime, Ellis, who served as church warden, demanded that Heywood pay fines for failing to attend services at Coley Chapel.

Though by law Heywood was now a "silenced" minister, he regularly led secret worship services at the houses of Presbyterian landowners and farmers. His sermons drew large crowds, attracting all kinds of people. When the Five Mile Act went into effect, Heywood became an itinerant evangelist in the northern counties. He gave thanks for his new work, believing that the act of forcing ejected ministers into new localities promoted rather than hindered the nonconformist cause.

In 1667, Heywood married Abigail, daughter of James Crompton of Breightmet in the parish of Bolton, Lancashire. Three years later, he was arrested after preaching at Little Woodhouse, near Leeds. He was released after two days, but his goods were seized to meet the fine under the new Conventicle Act.

During his years of roving ministry, Heywood wrote a number of books on practical divinity, which he distributed freely among his friends and wherever he preached. The most important of these were *Heart Treasure* (1667), *Closet Prayer, a Christian Duty* (1671), and *Life in God's Favour* (1679). He also became well-known for his pastoral heart and as a man of prayer, both of which are reaffirmed in his diary.

When the royal indulgence of 1672 went into effect, Heywood applied for two licenses as a Presbyterian teacher: one for his own house at Northowram and the other for the house of John Butterworth at Warley, in the parish of Halifax. More than a hundred of his former parishioners entered with him into a church covenant. When the licenses were revoked in 1675, Heywood became an itinerant preacher again.

In 1685, Heywood was fined at the Wakefield sessions for "a riotous assembly" in his house, but he refused to pay the fine. Consequently, he was imprisoned in York Castle for nearly a year. He approved of King James II's declaration for liberty of conscience in 1687 and immediately built a meeting-house at Northowram, to which he later added a school.

The agreement between Presbyterians and Congregation-alists in London (1691), known as the "happy union," was introduced to Yorkshire mainly through Heywood's influence. On September 2, 1691, Heywood preached at a house in Wake-field to twenty-four preachers of the two denominations, where the agreement was adopted. The meeting was the first of several assemblies of nonconformist divines of West Riding, which granted preaching licenses and arranged ordinations.

For the last ten years of his life, Heywood was greatly dis-tressed by the gradual decline in orthodoxy in some of his colleagues. He kept up his evangelistic work with unimpaired vigor till the end of 1699.

In 1700, Heywood's asthmatic condition worsened, so that his ministry was confined to the area in and around Northowram. Nevertheless, his diary for 1700 records that, in addition to his regular Sabbath ministry, he still managed to preach forty-five weekday sermons, conduct twenty-two fasts, and attend eight ministers' conferences. By the end of 1701, he had to be carried to his meetinghouse in a chair—"as had Calvin," he notes in his diary. He wrote to a friend: "I have now been above fifty years laboring in the Lord's vineyard, studying, praying, and preaching both at home and abroad, wherever the providence of God called me. I have reached nearly two years beyond the age of man, and am, as may be supposed, incapaci-tated for traveling. A very sore asthma, or difficulty of breathing, adds considerably to the weight of my other infirmi-ties, so that I am mostly confined to my own house, and can only study, preach in my chapel, and exercise myself in writing books and sermons for those that desire them."

Heywood died at Northowram on May 4, 1702. He was buried in a chapel of Halifax Church, in his mother's grave. Throughout nearly half a century of ministry, Heywood held the ministerial office in high esteem. "To be instrumental in converting a sinner is to do more than Alexander did in conquering the world," he said.

Richard Slate compiled Heywood's *Works* in the early nineteenth century and published them in 1825 in five volumes. While Heywood is not greatly known today, he had a solid influence in Lancashire. His diaries, printed in four volumes, offer an excellent account of Lancashire history. They reveal their author to be a man of feeling, depth, and commitment to hard work. Heywood preached 3,027 sermons, kept 1,256 fasts, observed 314 thanksgiving days, and traveled 31,345 miles during the course of his ministry. Looking back on his own life, Heywood records his indebtedness to God's grace in this way: "That I should be a public preacher above 44 years, have such measure of health, liberty, opportunities, more than most of my brethren, some good success and fruit of my poor labours, marry famous Mr. Angier's daughter, print so many books, enjoy so many comforts of life, bring up two sons to be ministers, build a chapel, help so many ministers and Christians in their necessities by myself and others,...I record not for ostentation but to set off the riches of grace" (*The Rev. Oliver Heywood...his autobiography, diaries, anecdote and event books*, ed. J. H. Turner, 3:297).

William Sheils concludes: "Heywood's life formed a bridge between the Puritan tradition of early and mid-century England, the years following the Restoration when dissent was outlawed and many ministers, Heywood included, suffered imprisonment as a result of their preaching, and the years after the revolution of 1688 when toleration was granted and dissenting ministers could operate from settled congregations with their own chapels." Throughout these years, Heywood was "the pre-eminent figure in northern nonconformity" (*Oxford DNB*, 26:975).

———◄♦►———

The Family Altar (SDG; 568 pages; 1999). In this extensive work (volume 4 of his *Works*), Heywood deals primarily with the family. He begins with the personal covenant made with God in baptism, then describes the importance and duty of family worship. He addresses the ways God dealt with families throughout Scripture and history, then closes with the relationship between those who remain on earth while their loved ones are in heaven.

John Howe wrote of this work: "The design is to persuade and engage those that are heads and governors of families, to take up Joshua's resolution; that whatever others do, yet 'they and all their house will serve the Lord; in daily, faithful, fervent prayer, with thanksgiving."

Heart Treasure (SDG; 528 pages; 1997). In this treatise on Matthew 12:35 ("A good man out of the good treasure of the heart bringeth forth good things," pp. 1–245), Heywood describes the inward dispositions of the heart, then shows how to cultivate them for godliness. He tells how to acquire Christian treasure; how to store it up in various thoughts, truths, graces, experiences, and comforts; and how to bring "forth good things out of the believer's good treasure."

An appendix to the first part of *Heart Treasure* offers an excellent essay on the use of meditation (pp. 246–82). It includes twenty subjects to meditate on, plus instructions on how to do so. It also offers thirty practical items to meditate on during a typical day. The essay concludes with twenty motivations for meditating on profitable subjects.

The second part of *Heart Treasure*, titled "The Sure Mercies of David," is based on Isaiah 55:3. After explaining the mercies of God's covenant with His people (pp. 283-500), Heywood shows how those mercies are made sure, how they are confirmed and conveyed, and how God uses mercies to instruct, refute error, and encourage self-examination, conviction, and encouragement. This is the second of the five-volume set of Heywood's *Works*.

Arthur Hildersham

(1563-1632)

Arthur Hildersham was born on October 6, 1563, at Stetchworth, Cambridgeshire, and baptized as a Roman Catholic. His parents, Thomas and Anne, were devout Roman Catholics who taught him in the Catholic faith, but Hildersham was influenced by a godly and staunch Protestant school teacher at the grammar school in Saffron Walden, Essex, to embrace Protestant principles. In 1576, he entered Christ's College, Cambridge, where he probably came under the influence of Laurence Chaderton, a prominent proponent of Puritanism. Due to Arthur's increasing Puritan sentiments, his father forced him to return to London, hoping that Catholic friends would convince him to go to Rome and be reclaimed for the Catholic faith. When these efforts failed, he was disinherited. He was able, however, to finish his studies at Christ's College with the assistance of a relative, Henry Hastings, third earl of Huntingdon. He graduated with his Bachelor of Arts in 1581 and Master of Arts in 1584. He was appointed divinity reader at Trinity Hall by Lord Burleigh around this time.

Hildersham was disciplined for preaching before his ordination and had to recant on January 10, 1588, but soon after took up the lectureship at Ashby-de-la-Zouch, Leicestershire. In 1593, Hildersham succeeded Thomas Wyddowes as vicar of

St. Helen's, Ashby. His assize sermon at Leicester on 1 Kings 18:17-18, preached in 1596, offended Judge Sir Edmund Anderson; though threats of indictment by the grand jury were made, nothing came of it.

Ties to Puritanism did not favor Hildersham's position ecclesiastically. In 1603, he was one of the promoters of the millenary petition to James I. This petition sought further reforms in church polity and liturgy. Two years later, William Chaderton, bishop of Lincoln, deprived him for Nonconformity. He was favored, however, by William Overton, bishop of Coventry and Lichfield, and was allowed to preach at the godly exercises that were held at Burton upon Trent and Repton. He was later restored to his position in Ashby, but in 1613 he was suspended for supposedly encouraging the deviant thoughts of Edward Wightman, a man infamous for being the last person burned in England as a heretic. Two years later, Hildersham was confined in the Fleet prison and then King's Bench prison for refusing to take an official oath. He was also accused of refusing to kneel for communion and on November 28, 1616, was sentenced once again to imprisonment, but this time he was also sentenced to be degraded from the ministry and to pay a large fine. He eluded capture, however, and after the death of James I, was licensed to preach by Sir Thomas Ridley, the vicar-general of Canterbury.

Hildersham returned to Ashby and began a series of sermons in 1625 on Psalm 51, which lasted several years. In 1630, he was suspended for failure to wear a surplice and hood for public worship but was restored the following year.

Hildersham's last sermon was preached on August 27, 1631. He contracted scorbutic fever and died at Ashby on March 4, 1632. He requested that there be no funeral sermon and was buried in the chancel of Ashby church.

Dealing with Sin in Our Children (SDG; 29 pages; 2004). Three years after Hildersham's death, his son Samuel published the 152 sermons his father had preached on Psalm 51. Several of those sermons were based on verse 7, where David focuses on his conception as a sinner. This booklet is taken from those sermons, with the goal that God might bless a proper biblical response to children's sin, such that they might be born again and become stalwart sons and daughters in the church of Jesus Christ.

Robert Hill

(d. 1623)

Robert Hill was born in Ashbourne, Derbyshire. He matriculated as pensioner at Christ's College, Cambridge, in 1581, and graduated with a Bachelor of Arts degree in 1585 and a Master of Arts degree in 1588. He was admitted a fellow of St. John's College in 1589, and showed definite Puritan sympathies, probably due to the influence of William Perkins. While at St. John's, Hill was associated with several young men who would later become noted Puritans, such as William Crashawe and Abdias Ashton.

In 1596, Hill engaged in a brief controversy over a sermon preached by regius professor John Overall, who had apparently made questionable statements about the extent of the atonement. Hill responded by taking the matter up with Richard Bancroft, bishop and overseer of London.

Hill served as curate of St. Andrews, Norwich, from 1591 to 1602, and remained a fellow at St. John's until 1609. That same year, he was awarded a doctorate in divinity. From 1602 to 1613, he was lecturer at the parish of St. Martin-in-the-Fields. Meanwhile, he obtained a living at St. Margaret Moses in 1607, but remained financially insecure for many years. Finally, he obtained a more financially stable living at his final post in St. Bartholomew by the Exchange, London, where he remained until his death in 1623.

Hill was a promoter of piety in several ways. First, he was committed to writing works of practical piety. In 1606, while preacher at St. Martin's, he published *Christ's Prayer Expounded*, in which he directs the Christian in the proper path of communion, such as prayer and thanksgiving. Three years later he greatly expanded this work in his *Pathway to Prayer and Piety*. Second, Hill was an avid translator and promoter of both British and continental Protestant divines. In 1591, he translated William Perkins's *A Golden Chain* into English (at Perkins's request); in 1596, he published *The Contents of Scripture*, an explanation of the Bible that compiled comments from such men as Isaac Tremelius, Francis Junius, Theodore Beza, Johannes Piscator, and John Calvin; in 1604, he published Perkins's *Lectures upon the First Three Chapters of Revelation*; and in 1620, he edited the works of Samuel Hieron.

━━━◆◆◆━━━

The Pathway to Prayer and Piety (WJ; 350 pages; 1972). Hill gives a catechetical exposition of the Lord's Prayer, a preparation for the Lord's Supper, direction for the Christian life, and instruction for dying well. Diverse prayers and thanksgivings are added. J. F. Merritt writes, "This catechism displays Hill's pastoral abilities to best advantage, and it is distinguished by its clarity of exposition, use of homely similes, and willingness to tackle difficult pastoral issues" (*Oxford DNB*, 27:174).

This 1972 reprint is a facsimile of the 1613 edition. It was by far Hill's most popular work, being reprinted eight times in English as well as being translated into Dutch.

Thomas Hooker

(1586-1647)

Thomas Hooker was born in 1586 in Leicestershire. His father was a yeoman. Hooker entered Queen's College at age nineteen, then transferred to Emmanuel College, regarded by many as a nursery for Puritans. He earned a Bachelor of Arts degree in 1608, became a fellow in 1609, and graduated with a master's degree in 1611.

While at Emmanuel, Hooker became acutely afflicted by "the spirit of bondage" (Rom. 8:15). He was so distressed by thoughts of the just wrath of heaven that he cried out, "While I suffer thy terrors, O Lord, I am distracted!" Simeon Ash, Hooker's sizar and later a member of the Westminster Assembly, spent many nights trying to console Hooker by directing him to the Savior. Hooker clung to the promises of Scripture until he was soundly converted. With a certainty born of experience, he would later say to others, "The promise of the gospel was the boat which was to carry a perishing sinner over into the Lord Jesus Christ" (Mather, *Great Works of Christ in America*, 1:334). His experiences gave him an abiding sympathy for others involved in similar struggles of the soul.

After his conversion, Hooker served as lecturer and catechist at Emmanuel where many of England's spiritual leaders (including Stephen Marshall, Anthony Burgess, Jeremiah Burroughs, and William Bridge) listened to him preach. Hooker emphasized the application of salvation, which, wrote Cotton Mather, was a natural fruit of the "storm of soul that had helped him unto a most experimental acquaintance with the truths of the gospel." His students preserved many notes of those sermons, some of which were later printed without Hooker's approval.

In 1619, Hooker accepted a call to serve as rector of St. George's, a small parish in Esher, Surrey, about fifteen miles from London. Francis Drake, Hooker's patron and a relative of the famous Elizabethan seaman with the same name, gave Hooker a small salary. He also invited Hooker to stay at his home. There Hooker ministered at length to Drake's wife, Joan, who feared she was a reprobate and had committed the unpardonable sin. Just prior to her death on April 18, 1625, Hooker's efforts bore fruit; she died at peace in the Lord.

In 1621, Hooker married Mrs. Drake's servant, Susannah Garbrand. He and his bride moved to Essex in 1625. The Hookers had five children, two of whom died in infancy. They named their first child, Johanna, after Mrs. Drake; she would later marry Thomas Shepard.

Hooker served as lecturer and curate at St. Mary's in Chelmsford, about thirty miles east of London, where his work was greatly blessed. Morality and Sabbath-keeping improved in the community during that time. People flocked to hear him, even though he challenged their consciences with penetrating "uses," or applications. One listener said, "He was the best at a Use that ever he heard." Mather said, "There was a great reformation wrought, not only in the town, but in the adjacent country, from all parts whereof they came to hear."

"If any of our late preachers and divines came in the spirit and power of John Baptist, this man did," wrote Thomas Goodwin and Philip Nye. Giles Firmin, a fellow Puritan, said that Hooker's sermons were so powerful that he could "put a king in his pocket" (The Real Christian, p. 38).

In 1629, however, Hooker's preaching against some Anglican rituals brought him into conflict with Archbishop

William Laud of Canterbury. After several disputes, Hooker was ejected from his lectureship in Chelmsford. He started a grammar school in nearby Little Baddow with the help of John Eliot, a convert of Hooker's ministry who would one day become a famous missionary to the North American Indians.

Hooker's academy became influential, and thus it wasn't long before the Court of High Commission summoned him to appear before them. On the fixed date, Hooker was in bed with a fever. The Court set another date. Hooker barely escaped to the Netherlands before that date. The ship on which he sailed was barely out of sight when the court officers pursuing Hooker were on the pier inquiring about his whereabouts.

Hooker went first to Amsterdam, where he had been invited by several elders to serve a Presbyterian Church of English refugees pastored by John Paget. Paget did not concur with his elders, however. He was a staunch Presbyterian who brought Hooker's views of non-separating Congregationalism to his classis. Hooker occupied a middle ground between Presbyterianism and the Brownists, who represented an extreme form of Congregationalism. After interviewing Hooker, the classis refused to let him be installed as Paget's assistant because Hooker believed that a classis did not have the power to call ministers. Classis also said Hooker was too tolerant in accepting ex-Brownists into a congregation, even though he repudiated their separation from the Church of England.

From Amsterdam, Hooker went to Delft, where he was welcomed by the minister of the Scottish Presbyterian Church, John Forbes, who worked with English-speaking merchants in the Prinsenhof Church. He worked so harmoniously with Forbes that an observer said the two ministers were like "one soul in two bodies."

After two years, Hooker accepted a call to Rotterdam to work as an associate with William Ames. Hooker deeply respected Ames, saying, "If a scholar was but well studied in Dr. Ames's *Marrow of Theology* and *Cases of Conscience*, so as to understand them thoroughly, he would make a good divine, though he had no more books in the world." Hooker wrote a complimentary preface for Ames's *A Fresh Suit against Human Ceremonies in God's Worship.* Ames, in turn, wrote of Hooker that though he had been "acquainted with many scholars of diverse nations, yet he never met with Mr. Hooker's equal, either for preaching or for disputing" (Mather, "Piscator Evangelicus," in *Johannes in Eremo*, pp. 20-21).

Hooker soon became distressed with Rotterdam's failure to be receptive to "heart-religion." His participation in the Congregational experiment there helped mature him as a non-separatist, but he did not feel at home. When some merchants told Hooker that some of his former parishioners from Chelmsford were planning to immigrate to North America and wanted him to accompany them, Hooker joined them.

By 1633, the Puritan exodus to Massachusetts was well under way. Hooker sailed for America on the *Griffin* along with Samuel Stone (1602–1663), a close friend and colleague; John Cotton; and two hundred others, many of whom were believers. During the eight-week voyage, the people enjoyed three sermons nearly every day. They heard Cotton in the morning, Hooker in the afternoon, and Stone in the evening. People in Massachusetts were overjoyed to receive such noted ministers. They quipped that they now had "Cotton for their clothing, Hooker for their fishing, and Stone for their building."

Shortly after arriving in Boston, Hooker and Stone were asked to serve at the first church of Newtown (now Cambridge). Preaching, weekly lectures, pastoral duties, counseling "cases of conscience," and advising in political and civil affairs kept Hooker busy. The church in Newtown was greatly blessed under his leadership. One of its key members, John Haynes, was elected governor of Massachusetts Bay.

In time, Hooker's desire for more and better land, growing discontent with the political situation at Massachusetts Bay Colony, and strained relationships with John Cotton and John Winthrop led him to consider moving. Hooker also had serious differences with several Massachusetts leaders on civil government. As Iain Murray writes, "The counsel which prevailed in Boston, influenced by the assumption that at various points a Christian state should follow the Old Testament theocracy, restricted suffrage to church members and was ready to deal with differences of religious opinion by force of law" ("Thomas Hooker and the Doctrine of Conversion," *Banner of Truth*, no. 195 [Dec. 1979]: 29). Advocates of that position, led by Winthrop, were vehemently opposed to the democratic political theory that Hooker favored. Winthrop and Hooker debated this issue at great length, personally and in written correspondence.

Ultimately, Hooker and thirty-five families—the majority of his congregation—left the colony and settled in the Connecticut valley at Hartford. They sold their homes to the latest arrivals from England, who were led by Thomas Shepard.

Though Hooker had opposed the chief leaders of the Bay Colony and had led a seceding group, he still had a good reputation in Massachusetts. In 1637, he returned to Boston to serve as one of the moderators of the synod that condemned the teachings of Anne Hutchinson and her followers.

Hooker devoted considerable time to political matters. As Albert Hart wrote, "He was to Connecticut what John Winthrop was to Massachusetts, and what Roger Williams was to Rhode Island—the grand old man, the trusted leader" ("Thomas Hooker," in Charles Perry, *Founders and Leaders of Connecticut, 1633-1783*, pp. 52-53). When the General Court of Connecticut began drafting a constitution, Hooker preached a sermon on Deuteronomy 1:13, which advocated democratic principles. The constitution that Connecticut adopted in

1639, called the *Fundamental Orders*, embodied those demo-cratic views. Still, it is extravagant to call Hooker, as some have done, "the father of American democracy."

In 1642, Hooker, John Davenport, and John Cotton were invited to represent New England at the Westminster Assembly of Divines. Hooker declined the offer, but sought to influence the assembly by publishing three books in London, two on the Lord's Prayer (*A Brief Exposition of the Lord's Prayer* and *Heaven's Treasury Opened*), and a catechism on the funda-mental principles of religion (*An Exposition of the Principles of Religion*). Though these books agree with the Westminster Standards at nearly every point, there is no evidence that the Westminster Divines were greatly impacted by them. All three of these books, together with Hooker's *The Immortality of Man's Soul* and *The Saint's Guide in Three Treatises*, were published in London in 1645.

Meanwhile, Hooker was fully involved in leading his own congregation and contributing to the ecclesiastical life of the colonies. In 1643, he served as moderator of a conference assem-bled to combat Presbyterian tendencies, which were beginning to show up in some churches. He wrote a book to refute those tendencies and to promote Congregationalism; it was a point-by-point refutation of Samuel Rutherford's 800-page *The Due Right of Presbyteries* (1644). The book was sent to England, but the ship carrying the original manuscript was lost at sea. Reluc-tantly, Hooker rewrote his book. It was not published until after Hooker's death (*A Survey of the Sum of Church Discipline*, 1648). It has been described as the most profound and "rea-soned statement of the practical program of New England Puritanism" (Miller and Johnson, *The Puritans*, p. 802).

In the thirty-six publications of 5,000 pages of sermons and treatises that he wrote, Hooker dealt primarily with the doctrine of salvation; his favorite themes were regeneration and experiential grace or, as he called it, the application of redemption. His major series of books, drawn from a lengthy series of sermons preached in Cambridge, Chelmsford, and Hartford, traces the experiential work of the Holy Spirit in the soul from the preparatory stages of conviction through the entire order of salvation to glorification. The sermons were first published from auditors' notes as *The Soul's Preparation* (1632), *The Soul's Humiliation* (1637), *The Soul's Effectual Calling* (1637), *The Soul's Implantation* (1637), *The Soul's Exaltation* (1638), and *The Soul's Possession of Christ* (1638). In New England, Hooker revised these sermons for publication as *The Application of Redemption*. They were published in two volumes after his death in 1656, as was his treatise on glorification, the final step in the soul's ascent to heaven.

Hooker promoted covenant or federal theology with its ethical and social implications. He taught that the covenant of grace, entered upon savingly in regeneration, provides a basis for ethical motivation. Consequently, he strongly supported both the church covenant that became the Congregational polity of New England and the social covenant that became the basis of a political system that subjugates magistrates and citizens to the demands of God's righteousness.

In 1647, Hooker became ill during an epidemic that was spreading across the country. On his deathbed, he communicated to Thomas Goodwin that his "peace was made in heaven and had continued for thirty years without alteration." A close friend said to him just before he died, "You are going to receive the reward of all your labors." Hooker responded, "Brother, I am going to receive mercy." He died on July 7, 1647, his sixty-first birthday.

Hooker's contemporaries often called him "The New England Luther." Hooker was a man of many gifts: an astute statesman, a dedicated churchman, a sound theologian, a voluminous writer, and a beloved pastor. He played a formative role in the development of religion in the New World. It was as a preacher that Hooker rose "to his grandest stature," however. His sermons were peppered with colorful illustrations that brought the truths of the gospel home to his hearers.

Hooker was a strong leader, gifted with grace and humility. He was an able debater, but he was also artful in reconciling differences. His influence has been considerable in experiential Christianity, homiletics, evangelism, colonization, political philosophy, and church polity. "The fruits of his labors in both Englands," wrote John Winthrop in his *Journal*, "shall preserve an honorable and happy remembrance of him forever."

⇒✦⇐

The Christian's Two Chief Lessons: Self-Denial and Self-Trial (IO; 174 pages; 1997). In this book, Hooker searches the inner recesses of the human heart. He explains the nature of a sound resolution and its duty, the meaning of self-denial, and the necessity of cross bearing. He also describes the civil man, the formalist, the temporary professor, essential Christian graces, and adoption.

The Poor Doubting Christian Drawn to Christ (SDG; 129 pages; 2001). This first published work of Hooker's was largely drawn from his pastoral experience dealing with the wife of Francis Drake. Hooker spent many hours counseling Joan Drake in her extreme melancholy. For anyone who struggles with doubts and perplexities, this volume is a treasure. It has been used for centuries to encourage believers to take refuge by faith in Christ.

Redemption: Three Sermons, 1637–1656 (SF; 160 pages; 1977). This facsimile consists of three sermons drawn from three volumes: "No Man by Nature Can Will Christ and Grace" (1638); "The Heart Must be Humble and Contrite," from *The Application of Redemption* (1656); and "The Soul's

Ingrafting into Christ," from *The Soul's Implantation* (1637). The sermons explain how God converts His people.

The Soul's Humiliation (IO; 167 pages; 2000). In this work, Hooker explains the necessity of humbling the soul before conversion can take place. Hooker writes about the humiliation of the heart, the soul's remedy, inward trials, true humiliation, God's dealing with the soul, personal trials, and the consciousness of misery.

The Soul's Preparation for Christ (IO; 204 pages; 1994). This book, originally printed in 1632, grew out of a lengthy series of sermons that Hooker preached on Acts 2:37. It describes the soul's preparation for grace, examining such concepts as brokenness of heart, true sight of sin, the means by which sin is seen, the evil of particular sins, meditation on sins, soul-piercing sorrow, heart preparation, Christ's supports, and sound contrition.

Though Hooker's books offer teaching of great spiritual value, some of his writings on how the soul is led to Christ (such as *The Soul's Preparation*) can be overwhelming to new believers. Giles Firmin says in *The Real Christian*, "When Mr. Hooker preached those sermons about the soul's preparation for Christ, and humiliation, my father-in-law, Mr. Nath Ward, told him, 'Mr. Hooker, you make as good Christians before men are in Christ, as ever they are after'; and wished, 'would I were but as good a Christian now, as you make men while they are but preparing for Christ'" (p. 19).

Thomas Hooker, Writings in England and Holland, 1626-1633, eds. George H. Williams, Norman Pettit, Winfried Herget, and Sargent Bush, Jr. (Harvard; 445 pages; 1975). This major text of Hooker's early work contains ten of his writings composed before his departure for America in 1633. This collection includes two prefaces to the works of

Hooker's contemporaries (John Rogers and William Ames), the fragment of a letter, a first draft of Hooker's theory of church organization, and six sermons, including a funeral sermon, and a farewell sermon on Hooker's departure from England to Holland. To facilitate the reading of these documents, the editors provide helpful, extensive essays that (1) place the writings in their historical setting, (2) address Hooker's order of salvation in relation to Puritan theology, (3) describe the transcription of Hooker's sermons, and (4) provide a survey of the problems encountered in deciding what Hooker actually wrote. The book concludes with a detailed bibliography of Hooker's writings.

Ezekiel Hopkins

(1634-1690)

E zekiel Hopkins was born December 3, 1634, in Sandford, in the parish of Crediton, Devonshire. His father, John Hopkins, had ministered there as a curate for many years. Ezekiel was educated at Merchant Taylors' School (1646-48) and Magdalen College, Oxford, where he earned a bachelor's degree in 1653 and a master's degree in 1656.

Hopkins became a chaplain at Magdalen College and continued to study there until the Restoration (1660). He then became assistant to William Spurstowe at St. John's, Hackney, near London. Complying with the Act of Uniformity in 1662, he lost his position when Spurstowe refused to conform and was ejected, and his successor did not care for Hopkins. Hopkins was then elected preacher of either St. Edmund's, Lombard Street or St. Mary Woolnoth.

In 1666, Hopkins returned to Devonshire. He became a minister at St. Mary Arches, Exeter, where he attracted the attention of Lord Roberts (later the earl of Radnor and Hopkins's father-in-law). When Lord Roberts became Lord Lieutenant of Ireland in 1669, he appointed Hopkins as his chaplain. Later that year, Hopkins became archdeacon and treasurer of Waterford and prebendary of Rathmichael,

Dublin. The following year, Hopkins was appointed dean of
Raphoe, and, in 1671, he was consecrated as bishop of Raphoe.

Hopkins was married twice—first to Alice, the only
daughter of Samuel Moore of London, and a niece of Thomas
Vyner, former mayor of London. They had two sons, Charles
and John. After his wife died, Hopkins married Lady Araminta
Roberts, daughter of the earl of Radnor.

When Michael Ward, the bishop of Derry, died in 1681,
Hopkins was translated to the bishopric of Derry, Ireland.
Religion had declined in this large city when Hopkins arrived.
He preached against lawlessness in his sermons on "Practical
Christianity" and "The Almost Christian Discovered," both of
which are contained in the second volume of his *Works*. After
the outbreak of rebellion in 1688, when many Roman Catholic
Irish forces supported James II, Hopkins offended people
in his diocese by advocating non-resistance. Like many
Protestants at that time, he took refuge in England from
threatened persecution.

In 1689, Hopkins was elected preacher of the small parish
church of St. Mary Aldermanbury in London. He soon became
very ill, however, and died on June 19, 1690, only nine months
after his installation. Richard Tenison, bishop of Clogher,
spoke at Hopkins's funeral, praising him for his keen judgment, humility, and charity.

Despite retaining the Church of England view on church
government, Hopkins's books, several of which were published during his lifetime, convey a strong sense of Puritan
piety. These and other volumes were published in a first edition of his works in 1701. In a 1712 edition, his *Doctrine of the
Two Covenants, Doctrine of the Two Sacraments*, and *Death Disarmed
of Sting* were added. Josiah Pratt published a four-volume
edition in 1809.

The Works of Ezekiel Hopkins (SDG; 3 vols., 2,076 pages; 2001). The first volume of *Works* offers a brief biographical sketch of Hopkins, followed by major treatises on the Lord's Prayer, the Ten Commandments, and several sermons on the law and on sin. Volume 2 concludes Hopkins's discourses on sin and offers teaching on the covenants, regeneration, sacraments, and God's attributes. It also includes sermons on assurance of faith, practical Christianity in working out salvation, the sufficiency of Christ, and the excellence of heavenly treasures. Volume 3 contains treatises on the conscience, mortification of sin, and facing death; miscellaneous sermons; and a complete Scripture and subject index.

Hopkins's writings are very readable; he is clear, persuasive, personal, and experimental. He offers a simple, compelling writing style without sacrificing depth. His books on the Ten Commandments and the covenants are of great value. He plumbs the depths of the soul. For example, in dealing with the sixth commandment, he looks at pride as one of its motivating sins, then says, "Pride is the fruitful mother of many vices, but it nurseth none with more care and tenderness than it does anger. The proud man is the greatest self-lover in the world; he loves himself without a rival."

Charles Spurgeon said of these books, "Hopkins searches the heart thoroughly, and makes very practical application to the situations and circumstances of daily life. His homely eloquence will always make his works valuable."

John Howe
(1630-1705)

John Howe was born on May 17, 1630, in Loughborough, Leicestershire. His father was a minister with Puritan sympathies who, in 1634, was suspended from the ministry by the High Commission Court for praying publicly "that God would preserve the prince in the true religion, of which there was cause to fear" that such would not be the case and that "the young prince might not be brought up in popery." The Howes fled to Ireland in 1635, lived there through the Irish rebellion of 1641, then returned to England in the early 1640s to settle in Lancashire.

Howe earned a bachelor's degree in 1648 at Christ's College, Cambridge. He was influenced there by the Puritan Henry Field, and by Henry More and Ralph Cudworth, who were Cambridge Platonists. Howe then went to Brasenose College, Oxford, where he earned a master's degree in 1652. That year he was also elected a fellow at Magdalen College, where Thomas Goodwin was president. He became a member of the Congregational church that Goodwin pastored. During those years, he outlined a book of divinity for his private use, and deviated little from its emphases throughout his life.

At the age of twenty-three, Howe returned to Lancashire. He was ordained there by Charles Herle, the rector of

Winwick who had embraced Presbyterian convictions. The next year, Howe was asked to be minister of the parish church of Great Torrington, Devonshire. He joined a ministerial fraternal there and became close friends with George Hughes of Plymouth, a minister known for his piety and learning. Howe maintained weekly correspondence in Latin with Hughes; he also met Hughes's daughter, Catherine, and married her a year later. They were blessed with four sons and a daughter.

When the Puritans held fast days, Howe worshipped with his flock from 9 a.m. to 4 p.m. He began with a fifteen-minute prayer, then spent forty-five minutes reading and expounding Scripture. After that, he prayed for an hour, preached for an hour, and prayed again for half an hour. After a half-hour break, he prayed and preached for another three hours.

In 1656, Oliver Cromwell asked Howe to be one of his chaplains. Howe undertook that task with a profound understanding of the prophetic responsibilities of his ministry. For example, he wrote to Richard Baxter, "I should be exceeding desirous to hear from you, what you understand to be the main evils of the nation that you judge capable of redress by the present government? What [do] you conceive one in my station obliged to urge upon them as matter of duty?"

Howe was a great peacemaker. He did everything he could to reconcile the Presbyterians and the Congregationalists. Yet he did not fear to speak out against wrongdoers, including Cromwell. After one particularly pointed sermon, someone told Howe that he feared Howe might have irrecoverably lost Cromwell's favor. Howe replied, "I have discharged my duty, and will trust the issue with God." Cromwell worked through his resentment, and Howe remained with him until Cromwell died in 1658.

Cromwell's son, Richard, could not successfully fill his father's place. For eighteen months after Cromwell's death, one crisis followed upon another. Richard eventually resigned, and the Presbyterians joined Monk's army in inviting Charles II to return. A brokenhearted Howe wrote to Baxter, "Religion is lost out of England, further than it can creep into corners.... I am returning to my old station, being now at liberty beyond dispute."

Howe returned to his former pastorate at Torrington until the Act of Uniformity passed in 1662. Then he left his congregation, saying, "I have consulted my conscience, and cannot be satisfied with the terms of conformity settled by law." In 1665, he took the oath of passive obedience prescribed by the Five Mile Act. For several years he continued to preach in private houses. Life was difficult for him, as it was for many Nonconformists. Howe wrote, "Many of them live upon charity, some of them with difficulty getting their bread." Unable to preach publicly, Howe prepared for publication sermons he had preached at Torrington. In 1668, he published *The Blessedness of the Righteous.*

In 1671, Lord Massereene of Antrim Castle invited Howe to become his chaplain in Ireland. On the journey to Ireland, high winds drove the ship off course to Holyhead. Having reached land, Howe received an unusual invitation from a stranger on horseback to preach the next Sunday. He preached two times that Sabbath. The ship could not sail the next week because of high winds. A much larger crowd gathered the following Sunday to hear Howe, but Howe was sick in bed. The local minister was so astonished to see so many people that he immediately sent for Howe, who got out of bed and went to preach two more sermons. He preached without notes—as a dying man to needy sinners. Howe later said, "If my ministry was ever of any use, it must have been then."

Howe found the Irish church less hostile to Nonconformists than was the English church. Bishop Down gave him permission to preach in any of the parish churches of his diocese. The

Presbyterian ministers valued Howe's presence so highly that he was asked to help preside over their theological seminary.

In 1674, Howe published *Delighting in God*, written from notes of sermons preached at Torrington twenty years before. Two years later, he published the first part of *The Living Temple*, which would become his best-known book.

In 1676, Howe accepted a call to the Silver Street Presbyterian Church in London. At first, all went well. He preached to large numbers of people and was esteemed by both Anglicans and Dissenters. Gradually, however, persecution of the Dissenters intensified. In 1683, when the bishop of Lincoln wrote a pastoral letter urging that penal laws against Dissenters be activated, Howe protested.

By 1685, Howe's life was in such danger that he could not walk openly in the streets of London. His health suffered. The ascent of James II to the throne promised even worse things, so Howe accepted an invitation from Philip, Lord Wharton, to tour Europe with him. The arrangements were made in such secrecy that he could say farewell to his congregation only by letter, in which he exhorted them not to become bitter under persecution.

After traveling in Europe for a year, Howe realized he still could not return to England, so he settled in Utrecht, the Netherlands. He preached occasionally in the English church in Utrecht and oversaw the theological studies of several English students at the University of Utrecht. Bishop Burnet, the historian, visited Howe in Utrecht. William of Orange, who later became king of England, also befriended Howe. The prince admired Cromwell and wanted to hear everything that Howe could tell him about the Protector.

In 1687, James II published the Declaration of Indulgence, suspending penal laws against Roman Catholics and Protestant Dissenters. Howe's congregation sent him letters, pleading with him to return, but William warned Howe that this was another strategy for the Roman Catholics to gain influence. Howe returned home, only to discover that William was right. The king would have been greatly strengthened if Howe had been willing to declare the legality of the royal dispensing power, but Howe refused to do that. He and the majority of the Dissenters saw that toleration based upon the king's overruling of Parliament would have no lasting force. Soon, the king offended the majority of his subjects by attacking the liberty of the church and the prerogatives of Parliament. Leading men of the kingdom invited William to occupy the throne. On November 5, 1688, William landed at Torbay. Howe led the deputation of dissenting ministers who greeted William, and, in a moving address, assured him of their support.

Howe hoped that a ruling would be passed granting toleration to dissenters within the Church of England, but the House of Commons threw out the bill. Howe published his concerns in *The Case of the Protestant Dissenters Represented and Argued*, emphasizing agreement in doctrine between church and dissent, and how it was wrong to impose uniformity of worship upon those whose consciences led them in another direction.

Despite their efforts, the Dissenters gained minimal toleration. The Act of Toleration exempted them from persecution for not attending their parish churches. They could build meetinghouses and use them for worship, provided they registered them with the authorities. Dissenters, however, were still barred from state or municipality offices, and universities were closed to them. Nevertheless, they were grateful for the relief offered by the act. In response, Howe published *Humble Request to both Conformists and Dissenters touching their temper and behaviour towards each other upon the lately passed Indulgence*, showing that he was more concerned with the fellowship of Christians than with the advantage of any ecclesiastical party.

Howe was fifty-nine years old when the Act of Toleration was passed. In 1690, he and others drew up "Heads of Agreement between Presbyterians and Congregationalists," but it was in vain. Disputes between Calvinists and Arminians and arguments about the writings of Tobias Crisp complicated the situation. Theological pamphlet wars and debates entered the fray. Howe remained on the cutting edge of current discussions on predestination, the Trinity, and conformity, often writing books or lecturing at the weekly Broad Street Merchants' Lecture on such subjects. His last book, *Of Patience in Expectation of Future Blessedness,* was published in 1705, the year of his death.

Meantime, Howe continued preaching twice each Sabbath at Silver Street. The closer he came to death, the more his fellowship with God increased. At the last Communion that he administered, he so dwelt on heaven that some people were afraid that he would die during the service.

Like many Puritans, Howe was blessed with the presence of God in the midst of excruciating pain. "I expect my salvation," Howe said, "not as a profitable servant, but as a pardoned sinner." Once he told his wife that though he thought he loved her as well "as it was fit for one creature to love another," yet if he had to choose whether to die that moment or live for another seven years, he would choose to die. After a temporary respite, he pointed to his body and said, "I am for feeling that I am alive, and yet I am most willing to die and to lay aside this clog."

Before he died, Howe made his son George promise that he would burn all his private papers, except for his sermons and manuscripts, "stitched up in a number of small volumes." Consequently, few of Howe's numerous letters survived. Those that did survive are printed in Henry Rogers's *Life and Character of John Howe* (London: Religious Tract Society, 1863), the definitive biography on Howe.

Howe's dying words were those of one who already belonged to another world. As one biographer says, "He dwelt with great frequency, and almost superhuman eloquence, upon his favorite theme, the happiness of heaven, and spake as

if he were already in the veil." Howe had several remarkable
visits with Richard Cromwell, in which the tears of both men
flowed freely as they conversed about the glory of the life to
come. On April 2, 1705, God granted Howe his wish; he died
without a struggle.

Howe was a prolific writer, publishing more than thirty
treatises during his lifetime. Scores of additional lectures and
sermons were published posthumously in Edmund Calamy's
edition of Howe's collected works first published in 1724. Several more multi-volume editions were published in the
nineteenth century.

The Works of John Howe (SDG; 3 vols., 1,950 pages; 1990).
This set includes most of Howe's prose. Treatises worthy of
comment are:

The Living Temple (1:1-344). This is Howe's largest, most
profound book. It was originally published in two parts (1676
and 1702). Its goal, Howe writes, is to show how "a good man
is the temple of God." The book offers a miniature system of
theology that expounds many of the great truths of Christianity. Since the idea of the believer as a temple presupposes an
object of worship, Howe devotes the first part to demonstrating the existence and perfections of God and His willingness
to commune with worshipers. He refutes Hobbes and others
who published heretical speculations about God and biblical
worship. In the second part, Howe opposes Spinoza's attempt
to deify everything. After establishing the authority of Scripture, Howe presents man as a "temple in ruins," then spends
the remainder of the book explaining the great doctrine of reconciliation with God. The most striking portions of these
chapters are his description of the incarnate Messiah, his defense of the doctrine of substitutionary atonement, and his
delineation of the character of Christ, which every believer
must ultimately reflect. The temple of believers' hearts must

correspond to Christ, the perfect temple. Howe concludes by referring readers to his sermons on "Self-Dedication" (1:345-78) and "Yielding Ourselves to God" (1:378-405), which further explain the subject.

Delighting in God (1:474-664) is based on Psalm 37:4, "Delight thyself also in the Lord, and he shall give thee the desires of thine heart." It has two parts: "The import of the precept" and "The practice of the precept." In the first part, Howe shows that God is "a Lord to be obeyed, and a Portion to be enjoyed." By His very nature, God yearns to communicate goodness to His people, making God an object of delight. Howe then discusses divine communication under three main headings: an inward, enlightening revelation of God to the mind; a transforming impress of His image; and the manifestation of divine love to the soul. In the second part, Howe explains the exercise of delighting in God that, first, relates to all other duties of the Christian life, and second, is a duty in itself. Throughout this part, Howe challenges believers to aspire to a more heartfelt enjoyment of God in Christ. Believers should not settle for half-hearted devotions but should pursue the rapture of communion with God that saints of former ages experienced. The remainder of volume 1 contains sermons on man's creation, his natural enmity against God, and his reconciliation with God by grace. It also includes a 30-page memoir of Howe by J. P. Hewlett.

Volume 2 begins with Howe's third major work, *The Blessedness of the Righteous* (pp. 1-260), which was first published in 1668 with a preface by Richard Baxter. It is based on Psalm 17:15, "As for me, I will behold thy face in righteousness: I shall be satisfied, when I awake, with thy likeness." The introductory chapter reflects on the foolishness of supposing that man was created only for the present life. After examining the text, Howe introduces the glorious doctrine of heaven in chapter 2, the character of its inhabitants, their preparations for entering glory, and heaven's occupations and enjoyments. Chapters 3 and 4 show the blessedness of heaven as "the vision of God's face, in the assimilation to the character of God, and the satisfaction resulting" from that assimilation. Chapters 5 through 9 show the happiness of heaven that flows from the "vision of the divine glory." Howe shows how contemplating divine glory causes the soul to resemble God's character, which, in turn, enriches eternal communion with God. Chapter 10 proves from Scripture that the believer's soul enters immortal felicity at the moment of physical death. The last ten chapters are packed with applications.

The next treatise, *The Vanity of Man as Mortal*, is a more extensive treatment of Howe's introductory chapter in *The Blessedness of the Righteous*. That is followed by *The Redeemer's Tears Wept over Lost Souls* (see paperback edition below), several smaller pieces on the Trinity, and a few miscellaneous sermons. "Charity in Reference to Other Men's Sins" is particularly enlightening.

The Redeemer's Dominion over the Invisible World is Howe's most important treatise in volume 3. Founded on Christ's words, "I have the keys of death and of hell" (Rev. 1:18), Howe shows that the word *death* should be translated as "the invisible world," and then describes the invisible world. Howe has incredibly beautiful passages on the ultimate purpose of the gospel in delivering sinners from sin, the composure with which the Christian should consign himself to the disposal of Him "who liveth" and has "the keys of Hades and death," and on the Redeemer's dominion of the vast, invisible world of Hades.

The remainder of volume 3 contains minor treatises on patience in expecting future blessedness, the carnality of religious contention, union among Protestants, deliverance from Satan, true peace, the duty of civil magistrates, and how one can know if he truly loves the Lord. Also included are funeral sermons, papers on Nonconformity, prefaces to the works of others, and comforting letters packed with wise counsel. The works conclude with John Spademan's funeral sermon for Howe.

Howe's writings show an original, contemplative, discrim-
inatory mind. They lack terseness, and are a move away from
the older Puritan style, but in some areas they are exceedingly
valuable. He provides numerous quotable statements, such as:

- To be much taken with empty things betokens an
  empty spirit.
- Your delight in God can find no way into your hearts
  but by the introduction of your exercised minds.
- Is it reasonable one should be a child and a minor in
  the things of God and of religion all his days—always
  in nonage?
- The more there is of light, unaccompanied with a
  pious inclination, the higher, the more intense and fervent, the finer and more subtle is the venom against
  Christ and real Christianity.
- Christians ought not to have their souls ruffled or put
  into disorder, nor let any cloud sit on their brow,
  though dark and dismal ones seem to hang over their
  heads.
- The judgments of God are audible sermons: they have
  a voice.

The Redeemer's Tears Wept Over Lost Souls (Baker; 120 pages;
1978). First printed in 1683, this reprint contains Howe's essay
on Luke 19:41-42, telling how Jesus wept over Jerusalem because the city didn't recognize what belonged to its peace in its
day. It begins with a long exposition on the great gospel truths
that "belong to men's peace." It then focuses on the short "day"
we have in this life, which will decide our eternal destiny. It
admonishes readers to flee to the willing, yearning Savior.

This is Howe's most searching and compelling book for
wooing a sinner to Christ. He stresses the responsibility of
man within the framework of divine sovereignty. Also included is a 53-page essay on Howe's life by William Urwick
(1791-1868), a Congregational minister from Dublin.

Thomas Jacomb

(1623-1687)

Thomas Jacomb was born in 1623, near Melton Mowbray, Leicestershire. He was educated at Magdalen Hall, Oxford, and St. John's, Cambridge, receiving a bachelor's degree in 1644. He was elected to a fellowship at Trinity College, where he earned a master's degree in 1647. That same year, he received Presbyterian ordination and moved to London to become chaplain for Elizabeth Cecil, the Countess of Exeter. He continued in this pious woman's service for forty years.

Jacomb became pastor of St. Martin Ludgate, London, in 1650. Four years later, he married Phebe Mellar at St. Bride's, London. In 1659, he was appointed as advisor to a commission to eject "insufficient and ignorant ministers." Later that year and early in 1660, he was one of the London ministers who welcomed the prospect of returning the king to the throne. The following year, he was awarded a doctorate in divinity at Cambridge by royal mandate, and was appointed to review the Book of Common Prayer. Since he was a devout Presbyterian, Jacomb raised many objections against the prayer book. His comments were received with respect even by those who disagreed with him. That same year, he served as a commissioner at the Savoy Conference.

Jacomb was ejected from the ministry in 1662 because of his Nonconformity. His two farewell sermons, preached on St. Bartholomew's Day, were later printed in *The London Ministers' Legacy* (1662) and *The Farewell Sermons of some of the most eminent of the Nonconformist Ministers* (1816).

Like other Puritan ministers, Jacomb continued to preach. In 1672, he received a licence to preach for the Presbyterian congregation meeting in Haberdashers' Hall, Staining Lane, Cheapside, in association with its pastor, Lazarus Seaman. After Seaman's death in 1675, he continued to preach there for Seaman's successor, John Howe. He also continued to give a weekly Thursday evening sermon in the home of his aged patroness, the Countess of Exeter, who protected him from imprisonment.

Jacomb died of cancer in 1687. His "incomparable library" of over 5,000 books was sold for 1,300 pounds. In conducting his funeral, William Bates said Jacomb was "a servant of Christ in the most peculiar and sacred relation; and he was true to his title, both in his doctrine and in his life. He was an excellent preacher of the gospel, and had a happy art of conveying saving truths into the minds and hearts of men."

Jacomb was a man of exemplary life and great learning. He was one of the eight nonconformist ministers who helped complete *Annotations on the Bible*, begun by Matthew Poole.

———⇒◆◆◆⇐———

Romans 8 (BTT; 392 pages; 1998). This collection of sermons was first preached by Jacomb in the home of the Countess of Exeter. It was published in 1672 at her request and dedicated in her honor. The BTT edition is a reprint of the Nichol's edition, first published in 1868.

Jacomb provides an outstanding exposition of Romans 8:1–4. All the major truths of the gospel are here in a remarkably clear manner. His work grips the heart and understanding. The purpose of this book is clearly stated in the preface: "If thou wilt forget me, I trust that I shall not forget thee in my poor prayers, that God will bless thee in the clearer revealing of gospel mysteries to thee, the fuller illumination of thy understanding in spiritual things, the confirming and stablishing of thee in the great truths of God, the daily heightening and perfecting of thy graces, the sanctifying of all helps and means, public and private, to the furtherance of thy salvation; in a word, that thou mayest be the person in Christ Jesus, living the spiritual life, and thereby that the 'no condemnation,' and all the other branches of the precious grace of God spoken of in these verses, yea, in the whole chapter, may be thine."

Thomas Smith, general editor of the Nichol's series, said of Jacomb's book, "We know few books in which there is a finer blending of the doctrinal with the practical, a richer exhibition of the fullness of the grace that is in Christ." Sadly, Jacomb died before he could revise his sermon notes for additional volumes on Romans 8.

James Janeway

(1636-1674)

James Janeway was born in Lilley, Hertfordshire. He was the fourth of nine sons of a minister, William Janeway, and the younger brother of John, who also became a Puritan minister. He was educated at Christ's Church, Oxford, where he earned a bachelor's degree in 1659. He then spent some time tutoring at Windsor.

Ordained a deacon in 1661, Janeway was ejected in 1662 for Nonconformity. He ministered on in conventicles, however, through national disasters such as the plague and the great fire of London in 1666. After Charles II issued his Declaration of Indulgence, Janeway was licensed as a Presbyterian minister in 1672.

Janeway's last years as preacher in Rotherhithe were his most fruitful and yet most difficult. In 1672, his supporters built a large meetinghouse for him in Jamaica Row, Rotherhithe, Surrey. Janeway's popularity so enraged Anglicans that several times they threatened to shoot him and actually attempted to do so twice. One time, a bullet pierced his hat. Another time, soldiers destroyed Janeway's church building. His congregation replaced it with a larger building.

After struggling several years with depression, Janeway contracted tuberculosis. He died when he was thirty-eight. At least five of his brothers also died of tuberculosis before reaching the age of forty.

Janeway's experience with suffering, persecution, and death is reflected in much of his work. His acute awareness of the mortality of man charges his work with spiritual intensity and eternal focus.

───◆◆◆───

The Saints' Encouragement to Diligence in Christ's Service (SDG; 140 pages; 1994). This treatise on 2 Peter 1:11, first published in 1674, is "an admonition to sinners to reform and an exhortation to zealous conscientiousness in the converted, in their performance of duties, in introspective scrutiny of their spiritual condition, and in meditation upon God's providences" (*Oxford DNB*, 29:782). The book powerfully exhorts believers not to grow weary in pursuing good, but to be diligent in the service of Christ. It is full of practical suggestions and applications. "Time is short," writes Janeway. "Our work, our Master, our wages are great, and, not to mince the matter, we have yet done little. Instead of creeping, let us run; instead of sleeping and dreaming, let us awake and work diligently."

An appendix to the book describes the Christ-centered deathbed experiences of a godly woman (named Mrs. B.) to enrich the book's theme of persevering in Christian diligence. In his preface, Richard Baxter says that such testimonies "help to confirm the reader's faith."

A Token for Children (SDG; 176 pages; 2001). Janeway here compiled numerous accounts of the conversions of young children and their testimonies prior to their early deaths, with the purpose of rescuing children from their "miserable condition by nature" and "from falling into everlasting fire" (preface). Next to the Scriptures and Bunyan's *Pilgrim's Progress*, Janeway's book was the most widely read children's book in the seventeenth century.

Cotton Mather wrote his own account of children converted by God and called it *A Token for the Children of New*

England. That book plus Janeway's are printed together in this volume. They are most effective in showing how Puritan parents evangelized their children in the home.

John Gerstner says in the foreword to this book, "If we contemporary 'Christians' want to know what Christian experience is, we can do no better than to let these little children of centuries ago teach us. Every modern Christian parent ought to buy and study this book before making it required reading for all his/her offspring."

William Jenkyn
(1613-1685)

William Jenkyn was born in 1613 into a staunchly Puritan family in Sudbury, where his father, William Jenkyn, was vicar; he was disinherited for his Puritan convictions. His mother was the daughter of Richard Rogers, the godly preacher of Wethersfield in Essex, and the granddaughter of John Rogers, the Protestant martyr under the reign of Mary Tudor.

At the age of fifteen, William, Jr. went to St. John's, Cambridge, to study under Anthony Burgess. After earning a bachelor's degree in 1628, he moved with Burgess in 1634 to Emmanuel College, earning a master's degree there in 1635. In 1639, he became lecturer at St. Nicholas Acons in London, then minister of St. Leonard's, Colchester. In 1643, he was appointed vicar of Christchurch, Newgate Street.

Jenkyn was one of the most zealous Presbyterians in London. His congregation soon became a center of Presbyterian fervor. His parish elected five elders, including William Greenhill, a godly publisher, and John Vicars, a Puritan activist.

Jenkyn was also one of the London ministers who, along with Christopher Love and Thomas Watson, were imprisoned in 1651 for their attempts to assist in restoring Charles II to the throne via the power of the Scots army. Parliament used the plot's failure to silence the London Presbyterian ministers that supported it. Although Love was executed, Jenkyn escaped with his life because he signed a submissive recantation. After he was restored to his ministry at Christchurch, Jenkyn preached for a few years about the names of Christ.

Under the Cromwellian protectorate, Jenkyn's reputation was publicly restored. In 1654, he replaced William Gouge as minister at St. Anne Blackfriars. His first task was to preach Gouge's funeral sermon. Jenkyn returned to Christchurch a few years later, and was officially reinstituted there in 1658. About that time, he preached his renowned series of sermons on Jude.

Though Jenkyn probably welcomed the restoration of Charles II, he soon lost the favor of the new regime and was ejected from the pulpit in 1662 as a Nonconformist. He settled in a home he owned in Hertfordshire where he held conventicles, preaching privately to his neighbors in the vicinity until he was restored to public ministry in 1672. He then returned to London, where his friends built a chapel for him in Jewin Street. He preached to a large congregation there and also served as lecturer at Pinner's Hall. However, in 1682, the rights of nonconformist preachers were revoked, and Jenkyn was deprived of his ministry. He continued to meet with congregants in private houses to proclaim the truths of the gospel.

In September 1684, officers stormed the house where Jenkyn was preaching. All the other ministers escaped, including John Flavel and Edward Reynolds. However, Jenkyn did not escape because he was busy helping a lady out of the house. At age seventy-one, Jenkyn was imprisoned at Newgate under severe restrictions. He was forbidden to pray with any visitors, even his own daughter, and was not allowed to leave prison even to baptize his own grandchild. He lamented, "A man might be as effectively murdered in Newgate as at Tyburn."

Jenkyn's health rapidly deteriorated in prison. The royal court showed no mercy. "Jenkyn shall be a prisoner as long as he lives," was the response to the petition sent to the court for his release.

Four months after his imprisonment, Charles playfully asked his musicians to play *Jenkyn's Farewell* one evening at Whitehall Palace. "Please, your majesty," said a nobleman, "Jenkyn has got his liberty." Surprised, the king responded, "Aye, and who gave it to him?" The man replied, "A greater than your Majesty, the King of kings—Jenkyn is dead." The date was January 19, 1685.

More than 150 coaches accompanied Jenkyn's body to the nonconformist cemetery at Bunhill Fields. There, Jenkyn's daughter Elizabeth gave out mourning rings with the inscription: "William Jenkyn, murdered in Newgate." The Latin inscription on Jenkyn's grave is translated:

> *Sacred to the remains of WILLIAM JENKYN,*
> *Minister of the Gospel,*
> *who during the heavy storms of the Church*
> *was imprisoned in Newgate.*
> *Died a martyr there in 72nd year of his age*
> *and 52nd of his Ministry, 1685.*

Jenkyn's wife, Elizabeth Lovekin, preceded him in death by ten years. Together, they had ten children.

———◆◆◆———

Exposition of the Epistle of Jude (SDG; 367 pages; 1990). This work best exhibits Jenkyn's piety and learning. It includes a series of sermons he preached at Christchurch, Newgate Street. Spurgeon says of it: "Earnest and popular, but very full, and profoundly learned. A treasure-house of good things."

Here is one sample of Jenkyn's writing: "None are such enemies to unbelievers as themselves; nor is any folly so great as infidelity. The business and very design of unbelief, and all that it has to do, is to stop mercy, and hinder happiness. Every step which an unbeliever takes is a departing from goodness itself" (p. 123).

Thomas Manton said that the "elaborate commentary of [his] revered, Mr. William Jenkyn" was done so well, that for some time he regarded the publication of his own work on Jude as unnecessary.

Edward Johnson

(1598-1672)

Edward Johnson was born in 1598 at Canterbury, Kent, son of William Johnson, clerk of St. George's parish in Canterbury. William trained his son as a furniture maker. Edward Johnson married Susan Munnter about 1620; they would have eight children. In 1637, Johnson traveled with his wife and children to New England.

Johnson soon became a leader of the Massachusetts Bay Colony, living first in Charlestown, near Boston, then in 1642, moving to Woburn, Massachusetts, where he helped establish the town and the local church. He held the town clerkship from 1642 until his death thirty years later. For most of his life, he was busy with government affairs; in his spare time, he studied history. He was a deputy to the general court and, for a time, captain of the local militia company. He was also a printer; he published the 1648 document known as the Cambridge Platform, the church order of the Congregationalists. He died in 1672.

Johnson became known as a Puritan historian. Like the accounts written by Winthrop and William Bradford, Johnson's narratives reveal his involvement in government affairs. He wrote *A History of New England from the English Planting in the Year 1628, until the Year 1652* (1653; retitled as *Johnson's Wonderworking Providence* in the reprint below), which, together with Winthrop's *Journal* and Bradford's *History of Plymouth Plantation*, share a common vision of the early Massachusetts Bay

Colony. Likening the experience of the early colonists to that of the ancient Israelites, Johnson, Winthrop, and Bradford endeavor to show how the people left Egypt (England) in a divinely ordained migration across the Atlantic wilderness to settle in the promised land of the New World and to build the New Jerusalem.

———◦⟨⟩◦———

Johnson's Wonder-Working Providence (SF; 284 pages; 1974). In this work, Johnson shows how God established the New World as a city on a hill. Johnson views America as God's new Israel. Unlike Winthrop and Bradford, who tell their stories through the lives of eminent men, Johnson relates the experiences of an entire group. His book's subtitle, *Wonder-Working Providence of Sion's Saviour in New England*, reflects this emphasis. Although the work is written in prose, it includes verses that are used as epigraphs or division headings. The style is somewhat stilted, but the book is worth reading. It is the earliest published history of New England (Winthrop's *Journal* was not published until 1790, and Bradford's *Plymouth Plantation* until 1856). Johnson's work contains some historical errors, yet it gives the reader what neither Bradford nor Winthrop could: the history of the Massachusetts colony seen through the eyes of an ordinary citizen.

Johnson's *Wonder-Working Providence* influenced later Puritan histories, such as Cotton Mather's *Magnalia Christi Americana* (1702). Johnson's chronicle provided the model of recounting a history that reflected the early colonists' sense of divine mission in the New World.

Benjamin Keach
(1640-1704)

B enjamin Keach, a Particular Baptist minister of Puritan persuasion, was born on February 29, 1640. His parents were unable to afford schooling, so he was apprenticed as a tailor. Nevertheless, Keach studied the Bible and educated himself rigorously. Although baptized as an infant, Keach came to Baptist convictions at a young age, and was subsequently re-baptized at age fifteen. Before long, he became distinguished as one gifted for gospel ministry, and became a non-ordained preacher at age eighteen in a General Baptist church in Winslow, Buckinghamshire. After the Restoration, Keach was frequently arrested for his unlicensed activities. In 1664, he scarcely escaped being trampled on as soldiers interrupted one of his meetings. He was saved by an officer's intervention and was subsequently imprisoned.

Sometime in 1664 Keach published an anonymous book, *The Child's Instructor*, which attacked paedobaptism, endorsed lay preaching, and expressed millenarian convictions. The book was discovered by a local Anglican minister and Keach was brought to trial for sedition. He refused to renounce the book's tenets and was therefore imprisoned and pilloried. The pillory was designed as harsh punishment and consisted of the criminal being bound, head and arms, through a wood-like structure. Crowds were encouraged to throw items, which often caused permanent damage; the usual fare was vegetables, dead animals, and stones. But Keach used this occasion to preach before a supportive crowd. When Daniel Defoe was placed in the pillory at Charing Cross for writing a satire, public sympathy won out and the crowds threw flowers instead of stones. In both instances, the purpose of the pillory was defeated. In Keach's case, however, public officials decided to execute the pillory more strictly and at Winslow, a week after his first pillory, Keach was humiliated with the burning of his book by the hangman. Of all the copies printed, some 1500, none survived. Keach was finally released and was bound to good behavior.

Being unable to settle in Buckinghamshire, Keach preached in other counties on an itinerant basis from 1664 to 1668. During those years, he was imprisoned at least once more. He moved to London in 1668 and was ordained as an elder of a General Baptist congregation based in Tooley Street, Southwark. Being influenced there by William Kiffin and Hanserd Knollys, Keach's theological convictions became increasingly Calvinistic.

A breach occurred in 1672 when Keach declared himself a Calvinist and founded a Particular Baptist church in Horselydown, Southwark. After the Declaration of Indulgence, which allowed limited freedom for dissenting ministers, Keach facilitated a meeting house in Goat Street, Horselydown. The congregation grew rapidly in subsequent decades, and later came under the pastoral ministry of such famous pastors as John Gill and Charles Spurgeon.

Keach's subsequent years were marked by his involvement in various disputations, leadership among Particular Baptist churches, and pastoral labors among his flock. Concerning disputations, Keach entered into numerous debates against paedobaptists, Quakers, Seventh-Day Baptists, and even some among his own Particular Baptist circles, particularly through his promotion of hymn-singing, which he had advocated in his rewritten edition of *The Child's Instructor*. While he deviated from the characteristically Puritan doctrines of infant baptism and exclusive psalmody, he stood among other Puritans as a staunch defender for gospel truth against Richard Baxter's unorthodox views on justification. As a leader among Particular Baptists, he pushed for a ministry that had studied to show itself approved. By signing on to the Second London Confession of 1689 and through his association with a Baptist catechism, Keach advocated a creedal tradition highly modeled after the Westminster Standards. As to his pastoral ministry, his experiential preaching and promotion of catechetical training were markedly within the Puritan tradition and served to win many to Christ.

Keach's last years were spent ministering and publishing a variety of practical, theological, and seminal works (he seems to have run a printing and bookselling business from his house in Horselydown). The most noted of these works are: *War with the Devil* (1673); *The Glorious Lover* (1679); *Tropologia: Or, A Key to Open Scripture Metaphors* (1681), his famous work on types and metaphors of the Bible, coauthored with Thomas Delaune—something modern reprints fail to mention; *The Travels of True Godliness* (1684), an allegory of similar vein to Bunyan's *Pilgrim's Progress*; *The Marrow of True Justification* (1692); *The Display of Glorious Grace* (1698), containing fourteen sermons on the covenant of grace; and *Spiritual Songs* (1700).

Keach died in London in 1704, and was buried in Southwark Park. According to relatives, Keach was a kind, gentle, and temperate man but was prone to outbursts of temper. He was said to be intolerant of alternative viewpoints and prone to single-mindedness, which, in some sense, was useful for establishing the Particular Baptists in the latter half of the seventeenth century.

=◆=

Exposition of the Parables (Kregel; 918 pages; 1974). Keach introduces this work with guidelines and principles for distinguishing parabolic passages in Scripture and explaining them effectively. He then embarks on 147 messages, covering forty-eight different passages from the gospels where our Lord makes use of similitude and parable in His teaching. Keach carefully determines the scope of each parable, draws out appropriate doctrines revealed, and makes fruitful application. This work provides great insight into preaching the parables, and remains a valuable resource for ministers to this day.

Preaching from the Types and Metaphors of the Bible (Kregel; 1034 pages; 1972). Originally published as *Tropologia: Or, A Key to Open Scripture Metaphors*, the first part of Keach's classic work distinguishes and describes the various figures of speech used in Scripture. By defining and demonstrating uses of such literary elements as metaphor, synecdoche, hyperbole, types, and parables, Keach helps his readers navigate through the vivid imagery of sacred Scripture. In the second part, he catalogues numerous elements of figurative language in Scripture, showing their proper significance and experimental value.

The Travels of True Godliness (SG; 210 pages; 2005). After defining godliness and showing its worthy pedigree and antiquity, "the excellent Benjamin Keach" (as he was fondly called) allegorically personifies "Godliness," much as Bunyan did "Christian." He introduces us to more than two dozen enemies of godliness, then details Godliness's encounters with several of them, including apostasy, hypocrisy, legalism, antinomianism, worldliness, and Satan. We meet in graphic detail the temptations of youth and old age, of riches and poverty, as well as the joys of contentment, thoughtfulness, kindness, and love. This is a fascinating book by one of the most important late seventeenth-century Baptist thinkers, designed to stir us up to a greater pursuit of godliness.

Edward Lawrence
(1627-1695)

Edward Lawrence was born in 1627 at Moston in Hawkstone, Shropshire. He was educated at the school in Whitchurch, then went to Magdalene College, Cambridge, where he earned a Bachelor of Arts degree in 1648 and a Master of Arts in 1654. While in college, he distinguished himself as a scholar.

In 1648, having received Presbyterian ordination, Lawrence was made vicar of Baschurch, Shropshire. Lawrence had several offers to serve elsewhere, but he stayed in Shropshire until he was ejected from the pulpit by the Act of Uniformity in 1662.

After ejection, Lawrence lodged with a gentleman in his parish until 1666, when the Five Mile Act forced him to move out of the parish. He settled in Tilstock, a village in Whitchurch, a nearby parish, where he had numerous friends. The next year, he and his friend, Philip Henry, were invited to Betley in Staffordshire, where they resumed preaching. This was reported to the House of Commons along with a plea that King Charles II would indict all Nonconformists for disobedience.

In 1670, while preaching at a neighbor's house, Lawrence was arrested and charged with defying the second Conventicle Act, which prohibited groups of more than five persons from assembling for worship that was not prescribed by the Established Church. Lawrence's conviction led to the confiscation of his goods. He appealed the ruling without success. When asked how he would support his wife, Deborah, and their nine children, Lawrence replied that they had to live out of the sixth chapter of Matthew, trusting God's providence for their welfare.

The Lawrence family moved to London in 1671, where Lawrence would spend his last twenty-five years. After being licensed in 1672 as a Presbyterian minister under the Declaration of Indulgence, he became pastor of a congregation meeting near the Royal Exchange. Despite periodic fines, he continued to preach there and in that vicinity until 1685, when he was arrested at Middlesex for attending a conventicle. After the Act of Toleration of 1689, Lawrence was licensed as a preacher at his house in Moorfields. He died in 1695, greatly mourned and respected by his parishioners.

Nathaniel Vincent preached at Lawrence's funeral a sermon later published as *The Perfect Man Described in His Life and End* (1696). He said, "I do believe there was not a man upon earth that better deserved to be called a perfect man, than our Mr. Edward Lawrence." Elsewhere Vincent wrote: "I never heard any one speak ill of Mr. Edward Lawrence, but all that knew him were ready to acknowledge that he was a man of eminent godliness, of a most peaceable temper, and of a very great integrity." Richard Baxter described Lawrence as "solid, calm, peaceable, a godly man, and a good preacher" (*Reliquiae Baxterianae*, 3:94).

———◆◆◆———

Parents' Concerns for their Unsaved Children (SDG; 68 pages; 2003). Published in London, 1681, as *Parents' Groans over Their Wicked Children*, this small booklet is drawn from several sermons Lawrence preached on Proverbs 17:25. In seven short chapters, Lawrence explains the duties of parents and children towards one another. He urges parents to raise their children in the Lord, relying on God's covenantal faithfulness to convert their children. He advises unrepentant children to remember the bonds they have broken and to return to covenant fellowship. Lawrence ends his work with these words: "And now, children, I will take my leave of you, and shall leave you to the God with whom you have to do, and with whom you must have to do forever" (p. 68).

Lawrence wrote out of personal experience. The conduct of two of his children caused him such grief that he said they made him "the father of fools." Yet, like so many faithful servants of past generations, he could not abandon his call to ministry. Rather, he prayed earnestly that God would use him mightily as a broken vessel, both in the pulpit and in pastoral counseling. That prayer was richly answered.

John Lightfoot
(1602-1675)

John Lightfoot, Hebraist and biblical scholar, was born in 1602 in Stoke-on-Trent. He was the son of Thomas Lightfoot, who served as vicar for thirty-six years in Uttoxeter, Staffordshire. His mother, Elizabeth Bagnall, came from a prominent family at Newcastle-under-Lyme. In 1617, Lightfoot entered Christ's College, Cambridge, where he gained an immense appreciation for ancient languages and excelled in oratory.

After receiving his bachelor's degree in 1621, Lightfoot served for two years as an assistant at a school in Repton, Derbyshire. He was then ordained deacon at Lichfield, and received a Master of Arts degree the following year. In 1626, he was installed in the curacy of Norton-in-Hales, Shropshire, where Sir Rowland Cotton appointed him as his domestic chaplain. Cotton encouraged Lightfoot to study Hebrew and related languages.

Lightfoot became rector of Stone, Staffordshire, about 1627. He began his writing career while there. He also married a widow, Joyce Copwood, in 1628, with whom he had four sons and two daughters, in addition to the three children she brought into the marriage.

In 1628, Lightfoot accepted a call to Hornsey, Middlesex, partly because it gave him access to secure rabbinical material at the library of Sion College in London. Two years later, he moved to Uttoxeter; he then spent twelve years (1631 to 1642) in the rectory of the Staffordshire town of Ashley, where he devoted himself to pastoral work and rabbinical studies.

In 1643, he was appointed to the Westminster Assembly of Divines. He was very active in the debates, often giving lengthy, scholarly addresses on various points. He was one of the few delegates who sided with the Erastians on issues of church government. He considered himself a moderate Presbyterian, strenuously resisting what he called the "vehemence, heat, and tugs" of the Independents. He was an influential voice on the sacraments and on ministerial training and preaching. He kept a record of minutes; these minutes are still extremely helpful in studying the proceedings of that assembly (see volume 13 of John Rogers Pitman's edition of *Works* [1825]). They give "his personal account and must be supplemented by the letters of Robert Baillie and the notes of George Gillespie as well as the official Minutes, but for some sessions when the Minutes are missing, they give us our only reliable information" (Barker, *Puritan Profiles*, p. 62). Lightfoot was frequently invited to preach before the House of Commons. Many leaders there appreciated his Presbyterian convictions.

Meanwhile, in 1643, Lightfoot was given the rectory of St. Bartholomew's in Moor Lane, London, where he lived briefly until he moved in 1644 to the rectory of Great Munden, in Hertfordshire, succeeding Samuel Ward. Here he continued his writing career and his ministerial duties.

In 1650, Lightfoot was appointed master of St. Catherine Hall, Cambridge, succeeding the ejected William Spurstowe. In 1652, the university awarded him a Doctor of Divinity degree. Two years later, he was appointed vice-chancellor of the University of Cambridge.

After his wife died in 1656, Lightfoot married another widow, Anne Brograve. She died in 1666. For the last ten years of his life, Lightfoot remained a widower.

Lightfoot took part in the Savoy Conference in 1661, siding with the Presbyterians. He acquiesced to the Act of Uniformity in 1662, but was quite loose in adhering to its demands. In 1668, he was appointed as a prebend at Ely.

Lightfoot was tireless in all his responsibilities. He was a man of great learning, humility, candor, and gratitude. He died at Eby in 1675, leaving behind a sizeable collection of works, which were later published as *The Whole Works of the Rev. John Lightfoot, D.D.*, ed. John Rogers Pitman, 13 volumes (London: J.F. Dove, 1822-1825; see 1:43–62 for a biographical summary). He also contributed extensively to the writings of other projects, such as Brian Walton's *Polyglot Bible*, Edmund Castell's *Lexicon Heptaglotton*, and Matthew Poole's *Synopsis Criticorum* (5 volumes). Lightfoot left his impressive collection of Oriental books to Harvard College, but those books were lost in the fire in 1769 that destroyed most of Harvard's library.

Archibald Alexander wrote, "That the learning of Dr. Lightfoot was profound and extensive, is a thing so fully established by his writings, and so well known through the Christian world, that it would be superfluous to say anything on the subject. In all departments of biblical learning, he was richly furnished; but in Hebrew and rabbinical learning, it is doubtful whether he had a superior in the world" (cited in Barker, *Puritan Profiles*, p. 64). Modern Hebraic scholarship has been said "to date from Lightfoot" (*Oxford DNB*, 33:756).

A Commentary on the New Testament from the Talmud and Hebraica (HP; 5 vols., 1,675 pages; 1985). This classic work, first published in English in four volumes in 1859, explains the New Testament from the perspective of rabbinic tradition, furnishing colorful background for the biblical text. Lightfoot covers Matthew through 1 Corinthians, devoting one volume alone to the names of places in the gospels. This work, written more for the specialist than for the general reader, offers a wealth of information and remains the only work of its kind in English.

Christopher Love
(1618-1651)

C hristopher Love was born in Cardiff, Wales, in 1618. At
the age of fourteen, he went to hear William Erbury,
vicar of St. Mary's in Cardiff, who would later stray into mysticism. His wife later wrote how Love reacted to that sermon:
"God met with him and gave him such a sight of his sins and
his undone condition that he returned home with a hell in his
conscience." His father noticed his son's depression and
locked him in a room on the second floor of the house to prevent him from attending church the next Sabbath. Love tied a
cord to the window, slid down it, and went to church. His
earlier convictions deepened and he was soon converted.

Against the wishes of his father but with the encouragement of Erbury, Love was admitted to New Inn Hall, Oxford,
in 1635, and earned a bachelor's degree in 1639. Love then
moved to London and became chaplain to Sheriff Warner. He
met the sheriff's ward, Mary Stone, the daughter of a London
merchant; he married her, and the Loves had five children:
two girls who died early in life, and three boys. The last son
was born thirteen days after Love's death.

Love was the first clergyman to refuse subscription to
the canons of Archbishop Laud (1640). That action resulted
in his suspension, but just prior to the suspension going into

effect, Love received the call of the parish of St. Anne and St. Agnes within Aldersgate, London. The bishop of London, however, would not allow Love to accept this call because Love had not been ordained. A staunch Presbyterian, Love declined Episcopal ordination. He went to Scotland to seek Presbyterian ordination, but was refused because he had no call to a church there.

Returning from Scotland in 1641, Love was put in prison because of the sermon he preached at Newcastle denouncing the errors of *The Book of Common Prayer* and superstitious ceremonies in the Church of England. For some months, Love preached to large crowds through his prison bars. Eventually, he was moved to London, tried in the king's court, and acquitted.

Love then returned to Oxford in 1642 to acquire a Master of Arts degree, but was expelled from the university for his Nonconformity. At the outbreak of the Civil War, he was made chaplain to Colonel John Venn's regiment. He became preacher to the garrison of Windsor Castle, ministering to many people during the plague. Some political leaders were offended by Love's sermons, though those of Puritan persuasion were usually impressed. William Twisse, later prolocutor of the Westminster Assembly, was so moved by Love's preaching that he invited Love to live in his home and use his library, although that never materialized.

Love was finally ordained as a Presbyterian in 1645, at St. Mary's Aldermanbury, London, which enabled him to work as a pastor at St. Ann and St. Agnes, Aldersgate. After preaching there for three years, Love became minister of St. Lawrence Jewry (about 600 feet from St. Ann's). He earned a great reputation for his eloquence and vigor in preaching, though he continued to offend Independents.

Love was one of the youngest members of the Westminster Assembly, but he was not very active in the proceedings. His attendance there was sporadic.

Love was arrested on May 14, 1652, by Oliver Cromwell's forces for alleged involvement with the Presbyterians of Scotland who were raising money for the restoration of the monarchy under Charles II. Love denied the charge, but he was tried and convicted of treason for what has become known as "Love's plot." Love's wife and numerous friends, including several prominent ministers in London, interceded on his behalf, but to no avail. Ardent republican Independents were determined to destroy him. Love was beheaded on Tower Hill, London, on August 22, 1651, at the age of thirty-three. Presbyterians were divided on the issue. Some were incensed, and regarded Love as a heroic martyr. Others were less sympathetic to Love's cause. In the end, the Scots and some English, like Love, were badly deceived by Charles II's supposed adherence to the "Covenant." Even Thomas Watson, who was involved with Love in the plot to some degree, later had second thoughts about the affair.

In a moving address from the scaffold, Love answered the charges made against him and urged citizens of London to heed and love their godly ministers. Sheriff Tichburn granted him permission to pray. He prayed:

> Most Glorious and eternal Majesty, Thou art righteous and holy in all Thou dost to the sons of men, though Thou hast suffered men to condemn Thy servant, Thy servant will not condemn Thee. He justifies Thee though Thou cuttest him off in the midst of his days and in the midst of his ministry, blessing Thy glorious name, that though he be taken away from the land of the living, yet he is not blotted out of the Book of the Living....
>
> O Thou blessed God, whom Thy creature hath served, who hath made Thee his hope and his confidence from his youth, forsake him not now while he is drawing near to Thee. Now he is in the valley of the shadow of death; Lord, be Thou life to him. Smile Thou upon him while men frown upon him. Lord, Thou hast settled this

persuasion in his heart that as soon as ever the blow is given to divide his head from his body he shall be united to his Head in heaven. Blessed be God that Thy servant dies in these hopes.

We entreat Thee, O Lord, think upon Thy poor churches. O that England might live in Thy sight! And O that London might be a faithful city to Thee! That right-eousness might be among them, that peace and plenty might be within her walls and prosperity within their habitations. Lord, heal the breaches of these nations; make England and Scotland as one staff in the Lord's hand, that Ephraim may not envy Judah, nor Judah vex Ephraim, but that both may fly upon the shoulders of the Philistines. O that men of the Protestant religion, en-gaged in the same cause and covenant, might not delight to spill each other's blood, but might engage against the common adversaries of our religion and liberty! God, show mercy to all that fear Thee. The Lord think upon our covenant-keeping brethren of the Kingdom of Scot-land; keep them faithful to Thee, and let not them that have invaded them overspread their whole land. Prevent the shedding of more Christian blood if it seems good in Thine eyes....

After the public prayer, Love thanked the sheriff, and said, "I go from a block to the bosom of my Savior." Love called for the executioner and tipped him to encourage a beheading with one blow. He fell on his knees and said, "I lie down with a world of comfort as if I were to lie down in my bed. My bed is but a short sleep, and this death is a long sleep where I shall rest in Abraham's bosom and in the embraces of the Lord Jesus." His last words, just before he put his head on the block, were, "Blessed be God for Jesus Christ."

Thomas Manton, a fellow Presbyterian and Love's good friend, preached at Love's funeral to a huge audience. Love's wife wrote 140 pages of memoirs about her husband. "His family looked upon him as a Moses for meekness and a Job for patience," she wrote. "He lived too much in heaven to live long out of heaven."

Fifteen volumes of Love's sermons were published by Edmund Calamy, Matthew Poole, and others shortly after Love's death. For a detailed account of his life, see Don Kistler's *A Spectacle unto God: The Life and Death of Christopher Love.* The title is drawn from Love's response to the clerk's charges at his trial: "I am this day made a spectacle to God, angels, and men, and singled out from among my brethren to be the object of some men's indignation and insultation."

———◆◆◆———

The Dejected Soul's Cure (SDG; 306 pages; 2001). True believers struggle with sin and its devastating effects. This can lead to what the Puritans called "the soul's melancholy," a deep depression in which the light of God's countenance has seemingly been removed. In seventeen sermons on Psalm 42:11, "Why art thou cast down, O my soul," Love examines various reasons for spiritual desertion and provides pastoral solutions. He shows that Satan will do all he can to distance believers from their Savior, even if that means a morbid preoccupation with sin and self.

This book gives scriptural guidelines for recovering a sense of God's love, convicts those who may be falsely comforted, and provides comfort for the convicted. Also included is Love's work, "A Treatise of Angels," based on Hebrews 1:14.

Grace: The Truth, Growth, and Different Degrees (SDG; 173 pages; 1997). This extensive work on grace contains Love's sermons on the examples of Abijah (sermons 1-5) and Timothy (sermons 6-13). The fourteenth sermon refreshingly shows what Christ is for all believers, and the concluding message exhorts us to glorify God and abase ourselves.

Five sermons show how God notices the least degree of grace in His people, and ten sermons encourage Christians to grow in grace. The following subjects are addressed: the beginnings of grace, the least measure of true grace, God's notice of grace in His people, laboring in grace, the marks of strong Christians, strong temptations and strong grace, the comforts of grace, and applications. "Nothing is so free as grace," Love concludes.

Love's work is practical and encouraging; he applies doctrine with pastoral warmth. As a skilled spiritual physician, he shows how a gracious God loves even the weak but sincere grace of His children. He explains how true grace is not inconsistent with strong temptations and weak affections. This study of God's grace in the believer deals with issues that lie at the root of every true Christian's experience.

The Mortified Christian: A Treatise on the Mortification of Sin (SDG; 148 pages; 1998). This insightful work on mortification contains ten sermons on Romans 8:13, "For if ye live after the flesh, ye shall die, but if ye through the Spirit do mortify the deeds of the body, ye shall live." Love shows the nature, signs, necessity, and difficulty of true mortification. He explains the Spirit's work in mortification and deals with several cases of conscience. The last sermon, "Special Helps for Special Corruptions," reveals some of Love's personal experience with mortification. As he writes, "These sermons concern mortification, in which the author's judgment is more to be valued because his heart was a commentary upon his text, and his own experience was a seal to his doctrine."

Two appended sermons by Love on how to profit from listening to God's Word are also noteworthy. They illustrate the Puritan concern for not only preaching well but also listening well.

The Penitent Pardoned (SDG; 144 pages; 2002). This compelling exposition of Psalm 32:5 urges readers to confess their sins (chapter 1), and describes the faithfulness of God in forgiving them (chapter 2). Love answers objections against forgiveness (chapter 3), presents the riches of God's pardoning grace (chapter 4), and deals with various cases of conscience (chapter 5).

These cases deal with such questions as: Can God forgive a believer without his being aware of his sin? Can God afflict and punish a believer after forgiving that sin? Does pardon precede or follow repentance? Can those who are pardoned repeatedly commit the same sins? Should the godly who are pardoned pray for pardon? When we come to God for pardon, should we make a distinction between great and small sins?

This book offers much comfort for those struggling with indwelling and repeated sin. Much like Bunyan's *Jerusalem Sinner Saved*, it clearly sets forth God's amazing and inestimable forgiveness upon confession, for Christ's sake. "Let your sin be ever so great," Love concludes, "yet the mercies of God are greater."

Preacher of God's Word: Sermons by Christopher Love (SDG; 178 pages; 2000). This book contains the following sermons: "Christ's Prayer the Saint's Support" (John 17:15), "A Divine Balance to Weigh all Doctrines By" (1 Thess. 5:21), "Directions Concerning Immoderate Joy for Worldly Comforts," "Directions Concerning the Nature and Ends of Sorrow and Affliction" (1 Cor. 7:30), "A Christian's Great Inquiry" (Acts 16:30-31), "A Description of True Blessedness" (Luke 11:28), and "Wrath and Mercy" (four sermons on 1 Thess. 5:9). They reveal Love's gift of applying doctrinal truth practically and experientially.

A Treatise of Effectual Calling and Election (SDG; 300 pages; 1998). The goal of these sixteen sermons on 2 Peter 1:10 is to awaken people from false security and to stir them to strive to make their calling and election sure. Seeing there is such glory prepared for the elect and such torment for the reprobate, ought not everyone strive to be prepared for glory?

In this book, Love handles many practical cases for the comfort of sincere believers and for the discomfort of those who are not true believers. He excels in showing believers how they may unadmittedly oppose assurance and how they may obtain it. He provides striking illustrations, such as comparing a believer's refusal to receive God's free offer of His Son to a sick man throwing a glass of medicine against a wall (p. 215).

The Works of Christopher Love, Volume 1 (SDG; 720 pages; 1995). This volume contains three sets of sermons: "The Combat between the Flesh and the Spirit" (twenty-seven sermons on Gal. 5:17); "Heaven's Glory" (ten sermons on Col. 3:4); and "Hell's Terror" (seven sermons on Matt. 10:28). The weighty subject matter is presented in such a lively style and is so carefully applied that readers cannot help but be edified.

Most of the remaining books of Love, originally intended to be collected in a second and third volume of his works, have been published as individual titles by Soli Deo Gloria.

The Zealous Christian (SDG; 137 pages; 2002). Love explains in thirteen sermons how the Christian must wrestle with sin and fight by prayer. The work is divided into two parts: "Taking Heaven by Holy Violence in Wrestling" (five sermons on Matt. 11:12), and "Holding Communion with God in Importunate Prayer" (eight sermons on Luke 11:8).

Like Thomas Watson's *Heaven Taken by Storm*, Love insists that the believer must take the kingdom of heaven by a kind of holy violence or persistence. Zealous, fervent prayer and diligent reception of the preached Word are the best weapons for exercising this holy violence. Love writes, "The longer you continue in sin, the longer will God keep you under suspension; and it will be long before he vouchsafes the comforts of His Spirit. He will fill you with indignation and horror. Though great sins cannot lay waste the grace of God, yet they may lay waste the peace of conscience. Though they will not put you into a state of ejection, they will bring you into a state of dejection. If you are not cast off, yet you shall be cast down. Therefore, take heed you do not abuse this precious doctrine."

William Lyford
(1597-1653)

William Lyford was born in 1597 at Peasemore, Berkshire, where his father was rector of the parish church.
He entered Magdalen College, Oxford, in 1615, where he earned
a bachelor's degree in 1618, a master's degree in 1621, and bachelor of divinity degree in 1631. He became a fellow both at
Magdalen College (1620) and at Pembroke College (1624).

Following the death of his father in 1632, Lyford became
rector of his home parish of Peasemore. He gave up his fellowship at Magdalen in 1633, and then soon married his wife,
Elizabeth, who outlived him. In 1642, Lyford published his
Principles of Faith and a Good Conscience, a thorough catechism designed to prepare people for communion over a three-year
period of study. Seven years later, he abridged this work for
young people.

In 1643, Lyford was called to be one of the Westminster
Assembly of Divines, but he chose to stay home to fulfill his
pastoral duties. It appears that he suffered few repercussions
from rejecting this summons. In 1647, he was appointed as a
member of the committee of triers of ministers. Later that
year, he preached a sermon of traditional Puritan thought on
regeneration and sanctification which he turned into a book
titled *The Translation of the Sinner from Death to Life* (1648).

In the late 1640s, Lyford also became increasingly involved
in the controversies revolving around toleration. He aimed to
steer his people toward "what he hoped was a moderate and

sober course between the magistrate's duty to promote preaching and restrain idolatry and the people's liberty not to be forced into a particular act of worship" (*Oxford DNB*, 34:859).

Lyford died in 1653 and was buried under the communion table in the chancel of his church. Lyford was a faithful minister. Wood, the Oxford historian, described Lyford as one whose labors "savour much of piety, zeal and sincerity, and show him to have been a zealous Calvinist." He was a devoted catechizer and wholly dedicated to the duties of his pastoral office. His joy, cheerfulness, and devotion in his Master's service were much admired.

⟫◆⟪

The Instructed Christian (SDG; 345 pages; 1999). Lyford wrote this book to help laymen discern truth from error. He was once asked how he could be so steadfast in his doctrine when so many around him were altering their opinions. He answered, "Because I ground myself upon the Word of God, which is not altered."

This book, reproduced from an 1847 American edition, was originally published in 1655 as *The Plain Man's Senses Exercised to Discern Both Good and Evil*. It exposes error on topics such as the divine authority of Holy Scripture, the nature and essence of God, the deity of the Son of God, the union between God and Christ, God's eternal decrees of election and reprobation, original sin, universal and particular redemption, the issue of free will, and justification by faith. Lyford scripturally answers practical objections at every turn, illustrating and applying truth to the mind and conscience.

THOMAS MANTON

Thomas Manton
(1620-1677)

Thomas Manton was baptized on March 31, 1620 at Lydeard St. Lawrence, Somerset, where his father, Thomas Manton, was probably curate. The young Thomas was educated at the free school in Tiverton, Devon; then, at the age of sixteen, he went to study at Wadham College, Oxford. He graduated from Oxford with a Bachelor of Arts degree in 1639, a Bachelor of Divinity degree in 1654, and a Doctorate of Divinity degree in 1660.

Manton was ordained to the diaconate in 1640 at age twenty by Joseph Hall, and served for three years as lecturer at the parish church of Sowton, near Exeter, Devonshire, where he married Mary Morgan of Sidbury in 1643. Through the patronage of Colonel Popham, he obtained the living of St. Mary's, Stoke Newington, London, where his pastorate became a model of consistent, rigorous Calvinism. He soon became a leading Presbyterian in London, and used his influence to encourage ministers to establish Presbyterian church government and to promote public tranquility in troubled times. He was appointed one of three clerks at the Westminster Assembly and preached many times before Parliament during the Commonwealth.

Once, after Manton chose a difficult text to preach before the Lord Mayor, a needy believer rebuked him, complaining that he came for spiritual food but had been disappointed. Manton replied, "Friend, if I did not give you a sermon, you have given me one; and by the grace of God, I will never play the fool to preach before my Lord Mayor in such a manner again" (Hulse, *Who are the Puritans?*, p. 93).

Manton provided spiritual counsel to Christopher Love prior to his execution for insurrection in 1652, and was with Love when he was beheaded. Despite threats of being shot by soldiers from the army who were present that evening, Manton preached a funeral message to a large midnight audience at Love's parish of St. Lawrence Jewry.

Despite his strong disapproval of the king's execution, Manton retained the favor of Cromwell and his Parliament. In the mid-1650s, he served several important commissions, including being a commissioner for the approbation of public preachers, or "triers." He served with Edmund Calamy, Stephen Marshall, and other Presbyterians in holding talks of accommodation with Congregationalists such as Joseph Caryl and Sidrach Simpson. He served on a committee to help resolve the division in the Church of Scotland between the Resolutioners and the Remonstrants. Then, too, he served on a committee with Thomas Goodwin, John Owen, Henry Jessey, and Richard Baxter for composing articles on the "fundamentals of religion" essential for subscription to the protectorate church.

In 1656, Manton was chosen as lecturer at Westminster Abbey and became rector of St. Paul's, Covent Garden, London, as Obadiah Sedgwick's successor. Manton desired to establish Presbyterian discipline at St. Paul's, but was prevented from doing so by his assistant, Abraham Pinchbecke, and his parishioners. He accepted this graciously, and was ever the gentleman, showing charity to all, including ministers of other persuasions.

When Oliver Cromwell was offered the crown by Parliament in 1657, Manton was chosen, as were John Owen, Joseph Caryl, Philip Nye, and George Gillespie, to pray with the Lord

Protector for divine guidance. After Cromwell finally refused the crown, Manton delivered the public blessing at the inauguration of the second protectorate Parliament (*Oxford DNB*, 36:366).

After the failure of Richard Cromwell's protectorate, Manton favored the Restoration of Charles II. He accompanied Charles at Breda and swore an oath of loyalty to the king. Manton was appointed one of twelve chaplains to King Charles II, though he never performed the duties or received the benefits of this office. All the while, Manton remained firmly Presbyterian in his convictions and warned against the restoration of episcopacy and the Anglican liturgy.

After Manton was ejected from the Church of England pulpits for nonconformity in 1662, he preached at his house in King Street, Covent Garden, and other private places. Attendance kept increasing until he was arrested in 1670 and imprisoned for six months. When the Declaration of Indulgence was granted in 1672, Manton was licensed as a Presbyterian at his home in Covent Garden. He also became lecturer for London merchants in Pinner's Hall and preacher at the revival of the Presbyterian morning exercises.

When the king's indulgence was annulled in 1675, Manton's congregation was torn apart. He continued to preach to his aristocratic followers at Covent Garden, however, until his death in 1677. William Bates preached at Manton's funeral.

Manton was remembered at his funeral as "the king of preachers." Bates said that he never heard him deliver a poor sermon and commended his ability to "represent the inseparable connection between Christian duties and privileges." Archbishop James Ussher described Manton as "a voluminous preacher" and "one of the best in England." That is certainly evident from Manton's many writings, most of which are sermons.

The Complete Works of Thomas Manton (MP; 22 vols., 10,500 pages; 1975). Manton's sermons fill twenty of his twenty-two volumes. They are the legacy of a preacher devoted to the systematic teaching and application of God's Word. Manton presents us with the best that English Puritans had to offer in careful, solid, warmhearted exposition of the Scriptures.

Manton's *Works* include expositions of the Lord's Prayer, Isaiah 53, James, and Jude. These volumes offer numerous treatises on scores of subjects, such as the life of faith and self-denial. Their sermons provide detailed exposition of such passages as Psalm 119, Matthew 25, John 17, Romans 6 and 8, 2 Corinthians 5, and Hebrews 11. It also has a number of sermons preached on public occasions, including those preached before Parliament. A memoir on Manton by William Harris is in the preface to the first volume; an essay on Manton by J.C. Ryle is in the preface to the second. The first eight volumes, as well as most of volumes 13-15, were republished by the Banner of Truth Trust in the 1990s.

By Faith: Sermons on Hebrews 11 (BTT; 712 pages; 2001). Taken from volumes 13-15 of Manton's *Works*, this volume contains every sermon (sixty-five in total) that Manton preached on Hebrews 11, the "heroes of faith" passage. This gifted preacher's treatment of such a practical, experiential subject cannot help but benefit a reader. Spurgeon said, "Manton is not brilliant, but he is always clear; he is not oratorical, but he is powerful; he is not striking, but he is deep."

The Epistle of James (BTT; 481 pages; 1998). First published in 1653, Manton's commentary is one of the best expositions ever written on James. Manton provides sound exegesis, searching applications, and wise spiritual guidance.

Spurgeon said Manton was at his best in this commentary. J.C. Ryle said, "Every verse and every sentence [of James is] explained, expounded and enforced, plainly, clearly and usefully and far more fully than in most commentaries."

The Epistle of Jude (BTT; 380 pages; 1989). When William Jenkyn published his commentary on Jude, Manton first hesitated to publish his own. He then decided to go ahead with a volume that complemented Jenkyn's. Manton wrote, "I consulted with my reverend brother's book, and when I found any point at large discussed by him, I either omitted it or mentioned it very briefly; so that his labours will be necessary to supply the weaknesses of mine."

Originally published in 1658, this commentary abounds with exegetical insights and practical observations. Manton thoroughly covers the problems of pride, the angelic guardianship of believers, right behavior under oppression, idolatry and worship, Christian reverence, unworthy passions in preachers, the right methods of rebuke, and apostate lawlessness.

Manton probes each verse—sometimes each word. For example, he devotes eleven pages of text to explain the meaning of the word *called*, then twenty-four pages on the result of being called.

Historically, this book preceded the infamous Act of Uniformity and sheds light on how the church ought to defend the faith in times of growing crises. Manton's exhaustive study highlights the special relevance of this epistle in situations that still challenge the church today.

An Exposition of John 17 (SGP; 550 pages; 1958). This work, drawn from volumes 11 and 12 of Manton's *Works*, explains the fruits and benefits of Christ's intercession for believers. Manton shows how this intercession secures the justification and pardon of believers' sins, moves God to accept their persons and their works, and encourages them to come to the throne of grace with the boldness of Christ.

The book is vintage Manton. The pastoral and doctrinal observations he derives from a single, glorious Bible chapter offer an education on how to use a text.

One Hundred and Ninety Sermons on Psalm 119 (BTT; 3 vols., 1,475 pages; 1991). This collection of sermons, which fills most of volumes 6-9 of Manton's *Works*, was first published three years after the author's death. In them, Manton demonstrates the blessings of living in the light of God's Word and strongly urges fidelity to this Word. The sermons are faithful to the text of Scripture and never abandon well-balanced Calvinist views. They are cogently outlined, simply written, and profoundly deep. Spurgeon said of them, "There is not a poor discourse in the whole collection: he is evenly good, constantly excellent."

Temptation of Christ (CFP; 176 pages; 1996). This work consists of a number of discourses originally prepared by Manton as sermon outlines. Manton looks at the temptation of Christ in the wilderness, then shows the origin and purpose of temptation. He examines how Jesus can be God and yet be tempted, and demonstrates how temptation exists for our good and God's glory. He also explains how to combat temptation, describing the roles angels and we ourselves play in overcoming temptation. The relevance of the subject and the gift of the author for explaining and applying it make it very useful for today's Christian.

A Treatise of Self-Denial (PA; 219 pages; 2005). In this book, reprinted from volume 15 of his *Works*, Manton shows that the duty of self-denial is applicable to everyone, whatever their age or condition. He expounds seven means of self-denial and describes various kinds of self-denial toward God, our neighbor, and ourselves.

Manton stresses that self-denial involves the "whole self," including all that a man is, has, and does—not just some prohibitions. Following Christ means obeying Him as Lord, which means that we must deny our wills when they would encroach upon the Lord's prerogative to rule our lives. This practical treatise provides sound advice for carrying out the work of self-denial as well as signs by which believers may examine whether or not they are exercising this essential grace.

The Works of Thomas Manton, volumes 1-3 (BTT; 1,500 pages; 1993). Volume 1 of this collection includes Manton's exposition of the Lord's Prayer, seven sermons on Christ's temptation, seven on His transfiguration, and eight on His redemption and eternal existence. Volume 2 includes sermons "tending to promote peace and holiness among Christians," twenty miscellaneous sermons, a farewell sermon, the funeral message for Christopher Love, a sermon on the saint's triumph over death, and a sermon on the blessed future of those who die in the Lord. Volume 3 contains eighteen sermons on 2 Thessalonians 2 and a detailed exposition of Isaiah 53.

Edward Marbury

(d. 1655)

Little is known of Edward Marbury. He became rector of St. James, Garlickhithe, London, in 1613, and later served as rector of St. Peter's, Paul's Wharf. He retired from public ministry during the Rebellion. His commentaries on Obadiah and Habakkuk were written near the end of his life (1649-1650). He died in 1655.

Obadiah and Habakkuk (TENT; 763 pages; 2002). These commentaries on Obadiah and Habakkuk are exhaustive, homiletical, and practical. They contain extensive outlines and applications for pulpit use. For example, in explaining Habakkuk 2:4, Marbury admonishes sinners to fly to "evangelical righteousness." That righteousness includes the righteousness of faith and the righteousness of a good conscience. He goes on to explain the benefits of each, telling how the righteousness of a good conscience gives strength to ward off temptation, helps make our calling and election sure, honors God in this world, shows our sincerity in the love and service of God, and provides comfort in death's hour. Striving for a good conscience out of Christ's righteousness becomes a winsome task rather than one of drudgery and legalism.

Spurgeon says of Marbury: "His spirituality of mind prevents his learning becoming dull.... Marbury holds the field among the old English authors, and he does so worthily. There is about him a vigorous, earnest freshness which makes his pages glow."

Walter Marshall
(1628-1680)

Walter Marshall was born in 1628 at Bishops Wearmouth in Durham, England. At age eleven, he went to study at Winchester College. He then became a fellow at New College, Oxford, from 1648 to 1657. He graduated with a Bachelor of Arts degree in 1652. Two years later, he was approved for the living of Fawley, Hampshire. In 1656, he was appointed to the vicarage of Hursley, Hampshire, four miles from Winchester. From 1657 to 1661, he served as a fellow at Winchester College. He married and had two daughters.

When the Act of Uniformity passed in 1662, ministers of the Church of England were asked to give proof of Episcopal ordination and their conformity to the Book of Common Prayer. Like hundreds of his Puritan colleagues, Marshall decided on the basis of conscience not to conform. He and other Nonconformists were ejected from their parishes on St. Bartholomew's Day, August 24, 1662. In the preface to Marshall's work on sanctification, a friend said, "He [Marshall] was put under the Bartholomew Bushel with near two thousand more lights whose illumination made the land a Goshen."

Soon after that, Marshall was installed as minister of an Independent congregation at Gosport, Hampshire, where he served the last eighteen years of his life. At Gosport, he wrote a book on sanctification, titling it *Gospel Mystery* from Paul's statement in 1 Timothy 3:16: "Great is the mystery of godliness."

During this time, Marshall experienced bouts of deep spiritual depression. For years he sought holiness and peace.

He read Richard Baxter extensively, then questioned Baxter, who said that Marshall had taken him too legalistically. He went to Thomas Goodwin next, telling him about the sins that weighed heavily on his conscience. Goodwin's response was that Marshall had forgotten to mention the greatest sin of all: not believing on the Lord Jesus Christ for the remission of his sins and the sanctifying of his nature.

Marshall began to focus more on studying and preaching Christ. He realized that he had been trying to make personal righteousness the basis of his dealings with God and the ground of his peace. Consequently, he had not submitted to the righteousness of God in Jesus Christ. When he focused upon Christ, he found holiness, peace of conscience, and joy in the Holy Ghost. *The Gospel Mystery of Sanctification* was the fruit of that experience. Of this book, James Hervey stated that if he were banished to a desert island and could take only a Bible and two other books, Marshall's classic would be one of them.

Marshall's preaching was edifying, though it did not win him great recognition. Still, he preached in many places in the last years of his life, including Winchester, Alton, Winton, Taunton, and Crewekerne.

Marshall died at Gosport in 1680. Before he died, he said to his visitors, "I die in the full persuasion of the truth, and in the comfort of that doctrine which I have preached to you." He then offered his last words, "The wages of sin is death; but the gift of God is eternal life through Jesus Christ our Lord" (Rom. 6:23). Samuel Tomlyns of Andover preached at Marshall's funeral. In the preface to the sermon, Tomlyns said of his friend, "He wooed for Christ in his preaching, and allured you to Christ by his walking."

The Gospel Mystery of Sanctification (RHB; 247 pages; 1999). First published posthumously in 1692 and then many times thereafter, this classic Puritan work on sanctification also deals with justification. It is divided into fourteen sections that Marshall called "directions." In the first direction, Marshall asserts that "sanctification, whereby our hearts and lives are conformed to the law, is a grace of God that He communicates to us by means." Holy Scripture is the means. We must sit at Christ's feet to learn from Him the way of holiness. The second direction stresses that if our works are not motivated by God's love to us and do not flow out of reconciliation with Him, then we are still at enmity with Him. The third direction says that just as we are justified by Christ's righteousness worked out by Him and imputed to us, so we are sanctified by holiness accomplished in Christ, and imparted to us. We put holiness into practice by using what we already had received from being in union with Christ.

The fourth direction says, "The Means or Instruments whereby the Spirit of God accomplishes our Union with Christ, and our Fellowship with him in all holiness, are the Gospel, whereby Christ enters into our hearts to work faith in us; and faith, whereby we actually receive Christ himself, with all his fullness, into our hearts." Without saving faith, no human endeavor can produce any true holiness (directions five and six).

In the seventh direction, Marshall deals with what comes prior to faith. He argues that what people think of as preparation for faith is either faith itself or the result of faith. To try to make ourselves fit for Christ is to be led away from Christ by a satanic delusion.

After emphasizing the importance of getting faith and holiness in the right order, Marshall issues a stern warning in the eighth direction against antinomianism. The best way to oppose antinomianism is "not to deny as some do that trusting on Christ for salvation is a saving act of faith, but rather to show that none do or can trust on Christ for true salvation, except they trust on him for holiness; neither do they heartily desire true salvation if they do not desire to be made truly righteous in their hearts and lives."

The ninth direction says, "We must first receive the comforts of the gospel, that we may be able to perform sincerely the duties of the law." To reach that purpose, we must get some assurance of salvation in that very faith whereby Christ Himself is received into our hearts; therefore, we must endeavor to believe on Christ confidently, "persuading and assuring ourselves, in the act of believing, that God freely giveth to us an interest in Christ and his salvation, according to his gracious promise" (tenth direction). To believe on Christ rightly, the eleventh direction says, means to receive Him as a free gift with ardent affection, trusting in Him alone for salvation. We must not delay but come to Christ with assurance of faith for a new heart and a holy life.

Believers should strive to obey the law by "gospel principles and means," Marshall says in the twelfth direction. He goes on to explain in the thirteenth direction how we must use the means of grace to strive after holiness. We must endeavor diligently to know the Word of God, to examine our state and daily life by it, and to meditate on it regularly. We are to use the sacraments as spiritual feasts to promote the life of faith. We are to pray in such a way that we can live by faith in Christ, according to the new man. All of that must be accompanied by heartfelt singing of the Psalms, periodic fasting, and frequent fellowship with the saints. In all those means, however, we must take care that we *use* them without *abusing* them by putting them in the place of Christ.

Marshall concludes in the last direction that holiness, grounded in union with Christ and combined with the diligent use of the means of grace, will result in a fruitful and blessed life. Such a pursuit will abase our flesh, exalt God, and coalesce with all the doctrines of grace. This is the only pleasant and sure way to attain true holiness.

In summary, Marshall's book teaches us the inseparability of union with Christ and sanctification, the inseparability of justification and sanctification, and the inseparability of Christ and His Word.

Cotton Mather

(1663-1728)

Cotton Mather, born in Boston, Massachusetts, on February 12, 1663, was destined to become the most renowned member of the Mather family. He was the eldest son of Increase Mather and grandson of Richard Mather and John Cotton, after whom he was named. Both his grandfathers were founding ministers of Massachusetts.

Mather mastered Hebrew, Greek, and Latin as a child, then entered Harvard at the unprecedentedly early age of eleven, where he exhibited seriousness, a keen mind, and a capacity for strict self-examination. He graduated from Harvard with a Bachelor of Arts degree in 1678 at age fifteen and a Master of Arts degree in 1681.

Mather was converted as a teenager. He overcame a speech impediment and began to preach in Dorchester and Boston at age seventeen. He was ordained in 1685 and began working with his father at North Church, Boston. His father served as preacher and Cotton Mather served as teacher, but this also involved regular preaching. He also served as pastor during his father's absences.

Cotton Mather's first wife, Abigail, to whom he was married for sixteen years, died after a miscarriage and a long illness in 1702. The next year, Mather married Elizabeth Clark, daughter of a Boston physician, with whom he had six children, of which one died in infancy. Elizabeth herself and three more children died in a short space of time from measles

COTTON MATHER

and smallpox in 1713, plunging Mather into profound grief. In 1715, Mather married Lydia, daughter of a well-known Puritan, Samuel Lee, and widow of a wealthy Boston merchant. Lydia proved to be emotionally unstable. Her wild mood swings tormented Mather until his dying day.

Upon his father's death in 1723, Cotton Mather became the primary pastor at North Church, Boston, a position he held until his own death five years later. He wrote a large biography of his father, titled *Parentator*, in imitation of his own father Increase's biography of his father, Richard. The books are very different in style, however: Increase's is short, modest, and anonymous; Cotton's is effusive, ornate, and bulky. Later, Cotton Mather's son Samuel would publish a biography of his father Cotton himself, *The Life of the Very Reverend and Learned Cotton Mather* (1729), to complete the trilogy of the Mathers' father-son biographies.

Cotton Mather shared his father's commitment to promote orthodox and evangelical Calvinism and to oppose its detractors. Yet father and son were very different. Increase Mather focused on preaching and corporate worship; Cotton Mather focused on outreach, going door to door in Boston, evangelizing the unchurched. He also organized small group lay societies for Bible study and spiritual fellowship. Unlike his father, Cotton never gave up the vision of a restored and renewed nation. Instead, the idea of a faithful, covenanted nation lifted his hopes and kept him going. Cotton also traveled far less than his father, who spent a considerable amount of time in England.

Then, too, Cotton Mather, unlike his father, dabbled with mysticism. Those mystical tendencies, recorded in Mather's diaries, became somewhat strange at times. For example, he wrote that he had meetings with angels, and even claimed that one angel told him that Christ would return in 1716.

Despite those mystical tendencies, Mather was a talented preacher and a zealous pastor. Every Lord's Day he asked himself, "What shall I do, as pastor of a church, for the good of the flock under my charge?" However, it was his indefatigable writing that made Mather one of the most celebrated New England ministers. As a scholar of considerable learning, Mather gathered an impressive library, was a voracious reader, and wrote 469 published works on biblical subjects, theology, church history, biography, science, and philosophy. His theological writings, now largely forgotten, were greatly influential in his time. They abounded with quotations from patristic and Reformation scholarship, as well as from Greek and Roman literature.

Today, Mather is generally regarded as the archetype of the narrow, intolerant, severe Puritan who took part in the Salem witch trials of 1692. Although Mather did not approve of all the trials, he did help stir up the wave of hysteria with his *Memorable Providences Relating to Witchcraft and Possessions* (1689). Later, he looked further into satanic possession with *Wonders of the Invisible World* (1693, new ed. 1956), in which he defended the judges in the Salem witchcraft trials as well as the use of spectral (unseen) evidence.

Nonetheless, Mather was remarkably broadminded. He operated in a much less diverse Protestant world than we know today, so we must appreciate his openness in relating to colleagues from other denominations. For example, in 1718, he participated in the ordination of a Baptist minister. For most Congregationalists, that was scandalous; for Mather, it was an act that signified unity in Christ beyond church differences. He also thought it was unethical that Puritans had persecuted Quakers.

Mather tried to focus on the essentials of faith. He said that ultimately, the three things necessary for a Christian are fearing God, accepting the righteousness of Christ to justify sinners by faith, and honoring God by loving one's fellow man. By expressing briefly and simply what was essential, he tried to encourage ways of showing Christian unity. Thus, he corresponded with August Hermann Francke, a leading pietist in Germany, and was delighted at some of the stories of Christian progress that Francke sent him.

Mather also tried to simplify church membership requirements, while maintaining the purity of the church. He did not require assurance of faith in someone who wanted to join the church or partake of the Lord's Supper; rather, he felt it was sufficient for that person to abhor his sin and have some hope in Christ.

Christianity had to have an impact on society through the good works of Christians, Mather believed. One writer said the "great ambition" of Mather's whole life was "to do good." He was an avid philanthropist and advocated improvements for Massachusetts, including taking care of orphans and homeless women, preventing public drunkenness, and suppressing dueling. Mather's benevolence was reflected in his writings, such as *Essays to Do Good* (1710).

Mather promoted learning and education, too, and worked hard to make New England a cultural center. He was disappointed in his hopes of being president of Harvard but was influential in the founding of Yale. He was deeply interested in science and was the first native-born American to be a fellow of the Royal Society. He persuaded Zabdiel Boylston to inoculate against smallpox, supporting the unpopular procedure even when it was life-threatening.

For a time, Mather stressed the reasonableness of Christianity, but later in life he became alarmed by the deism that was affecting the church in England. So, while continuing to say that reason could be a great help and support to one's faith, he was careful to subordinate reason to Scripture.

Mather was a minister of ministers. His *Manuductio ad min-
isterium: Directions for a Candidate to the Ministry* (1726), a
standard work for theological students, advises young men to
carry out a consistent evangelical ministry, studying faithfully
and widely, and "doing good" in their talk and walk. In addition to theology, Mather urges theological students to study
languages, history, sciences, poetry, philosophy, and mathematics—in short, to imitate himself.

Mather often dabbled in millenarian thinking. Michael
Hall notes: "Between 1720 and 1726 he broke away from his father's literalist interpretations to a preterite position similar
to the new philological interpretations in Europe. This decisive break with his father's generation and his own earlier
thinking provides a link to Jonathan Edwards's postmillenar-
ianism of the 1740s" (*Oxford DNB*, 37:268).

Mather was influential in the state as well as in the
church; he helped lead the revolt against the rule of Sir Edmund Andros. Then he supported the new charter and the
royal governor of Massachusetts Bay Colony, Sir William
Phips (1692–1702).

On February 13, 1728, Cotton Mather, aged sixty-five, died
peacefully at home surrounded by family and friends, and survived by two children. He was buried in the family crypt on
Copp's Hill in Boston's North End.

Mather was easily the most influential writer of his generation in America. He became well-known for his many
books, covering an amazing diversity of subjects. Thomas
James Holmes's *Cotton Mather: A Bibliography of His Works* (1940;
reprint Newton, Mass.: Crofton, 1974) is a helpful and massive three-volume work that annotates Mather's books and
shows most of his books' original title pages.

The three generations of Mathers were strong Puritan
leaders in Massachusetts. From Richard Mather's arrival in
1635 until Cotton Mather's death in 1728, the Mathers formed

a spiritual dynasty concerned with the spirituality, faithfulness, and purity of the church, although they differed about how much the interests of the church were tied to the success of New England as a colony and as a holy community. Cotton Mather, in particular, earnestly prayed throughout his life that God would do a great and reviving work in New England that would have worldwide ramifications. He believed that through spiritual awakening, New England could become a model of faithfulness and devotion to the world.

Only twelve years after Cotton Mather's death, great revival did come to New England. The Great Awakening that followed extended Mather's vision into all the colonies.

The Angel of Bethesda (AAS; 384 pages; 1972). This book is the colonies' first complete medical guide; it is full of interesting speculations. In addition to providing reviews of the work of scores of European scientists and offering medical advice, Mather recounts tales of several people who had remedies presented to them in dreams as they slept, or of men and women so miserably ill that doctors could do nothing more for them, yet who achieved full and dramatic recoveries due to "the wonderful work which He had wrought" upon them.

Mather cautiously suggests the possibility of the direct involvement of angels, though he fears arousing "unwarrantable *superstitions,* or *affectations.*" Nevertheless, he concludes that "it is possible there may be more of the *angelical ministry*, than we are *ordinarily* aware of." He suggests that angels operate covertly, or "behind the curtain," leaving "impressions on the mind" of physicians, providing them with information about available cures. He even hints that his own book, *The Angel of Bethesda*, might in fact have been a product of the guiding hand of angels.

Bonifacius: An Essay To Do Good (SF; 220 pages; 1967). This facsimile of Mather's most widely read book, first published anonymously in Boston in 1710, is a guide for ordinary men. It is written in the Puritan "plain style" and promotes what is good in private circumstances (husband and wife, children, relatives, servants, neighbors) and in public circumstances (the minister, the teacher, the public office holder, the physician, the lawyer). It helped Benjamin Franklin and others develop practical ideas for humanitarian work. Michael Hall notes: "It was the perfect book to introduce the new century of pietism and experiential religion" (*Oxford DNB*, 37:267).

The Christian Philosopher (UIP; 632 pages; 2000). In this lengthy study, originally published in 1721, Mather examines Scripture and nature—the two great books of God—to show how they are not at odds with the science of Newton and his contemporaries. Theodore Hornberger says that Mather's chapter on astronomy in this book is "the finest example of how Newtonian Science came to America and was disseminated" (*Oxford DNB*, 37:267). While parts of this book are outdated, it is still appealing because of Mather's observations, particularly on the flora and fauna of New England, as well as his facts and lessons on how the work of God shines through the work of nature.

The editor provides notes identifying Mather's sources of classical quotations as well as a biographical register. His introductory essay explains Mather within the context of his time.

Cotton Mather on Witchcraft (Dorset Press; 172 pages; 1991). First published in Boston in October 1692, this strange volume contains Mather's reflections on witchcraft. Highly speculative, this work should be read with the utmost care and discretion. While Mather had a heart for sound piety, he often indulged in speculation. This is Mather at his worst.

Days of Humiliation, Times of Affliction and Disaster (SF; 9 vols. in 1, 400 pages; 1970). This book of facsimiles contains nine sermons, preached from 1696 to 1727, on how to restore favor with an angry God, emphasizing lessons drawn from the afflictions of fires and storms. Sermon titles include: "Things for a Distressed People to think upon," "Humiliations followed with Deliverances," "Advice from Taberah," "Advice from the Watch Tower," "The Saviour with His Rainbow," "A Voice from Heaven," "The Voice of God in a Tempest," "The Terror of the Lord," and "Boanerges."

The Diary of Cotton Mather (FUP; 2 vols., 1,504 pages; 1957). Mather's diary unveils the work of a man of massive attainment and is an important contribution to the history of colonial Massachusetts. It was hastily edited by Mather before his death, so what remains is what he would have wished to preserve. While different editions of Mather's diary have appeared in the last century, the 1957 Ungar edition is the best and most complete.

The Diary shows Mather as enigmatic. He loved his Savior, fought to preserve Puritan orthodoxy, and yet, at times, ventured from it in mystical ways. While many gems can be gleaned from Mather's private prose, his mystical bent and strict asceticism, which, at times, almost ended his life, are certainly deviances from the mainstream of Puritan thought. Here, too, we meet a man of stern principles and restless self-abasement, assiduous in promoting his astonishing output of books. For today's reader, the *Diary* provides a fascinating glimpse into the heart and mind of one of early America's Puritan giants.

A *Family Well-Ordered* (SDG; 53 pages; 2001). Published in Boston in 1699, this brief essay on the family considers the duties of parents to their children (based on Genesis 18:19) and the duties of children to their parents (based on Deuteronomy 27:14, 16). The emphasis throughout is how to make a family well-ordered and pleasing to God.

Mather views the family in a typically Puritan way. As Don Kistler writes, "The Puritans saw the family as a little church. As there must be order in the church, so there must be order in the family. And, for the Puritans that order was set down in Scripture, and therefore, being of divine inspiration, was infinitely binding on parents and children alike."

The Great Works of Christ in America (BTT; 2 vols., 1308 pages; 1979). Begun in 1690, completed in 1700, and first published in 1702 as *Magnalia Christi Americana, or, The Ecclesiastical History of New England*, this massive history of early America in seven "books" is replete with historical nuances, biographical memoirs, and compelling insights into the work of God in America. The work is disparate in character, including "important biographies of governors and ministers, histories of Harvard College, the conflicts with the American Indians, and selected churches, and an engraved 'Ecclesiastical map of the country'" (*Oxford DNB*, 37:266).

Mather's intent is to show how the colony of Massachusetts demonstrated the working of God's will. In essence, this is a Puritan church history, covering much of the seventeenth century and supplying a unique commentary on many of its Christian leaders. Barrett Wendell has described this book as one of "the great works of English literature in the seventeenth century."

Mather's *magnum opus* was immediately controversial. Some reviewers focused on Mather's historical errors, convoluted style, and overblown prose. Others admired it for its coherence, detail, and zeal. Among nineteenth-century American writers, Ralph Waldo Emerson, Nathaniel Hawthorne, and Harriet Beecher Stowe were inspired by the "influence and power of its vision" (ibid.).

Help for Distressed Parents (SDG; 36 pages; 2004). In this booklet, based on Proverbs 10:1, "A wise son maketh a glad father, but a foolish son is the heaviness of his mother," Mather seeks to accomplish two important things: first, to give counsel and comfort for godly parents afflicted with ungodly children; and second, to persuade children not to entertain those evil ways which would bring misery to their parents. This is a most helpful booklet for parents who are grieved over rebellious, prodigal sons and daughters.

Ornaments for the Daughters of Zion; or, The Character and Happiness of a Virtuous Woman (SF; 128 pages; 1978). This facsimile is taken from the third edition of Mather's influential treatise. It seeks to prescribe scriptural modes of dress, makeup, attitudes, and social behavior for women in colonial America.

Paterna: The Autobiography of Cotton Mather (SF; 504 pages; 1978). Mather wrote this autobiography to record "a number of those experiences and contrivances, which I have had, in my own poor walk with God," so that his sons, Increase and Samuel, and other friends might receive instruction from it, and to promote his own self-examination and meditation. Remarkably, this is the first time that the complete text has been printed. Scholars have generally underestimated its value.

Like Mather's other extensive autobiographical work, *The Diary*, specificity concerning major events during his life is often absent. The editor, Ronald A. Bosco, has compensated for Mather's unwillingness to keep his reader informed of significant dates and events in his life by providing a chronological chart of Mather's life in the preface and by detailed annotations that accompany the text of *Paterna*.

Selected Letters of Cotton Mather (LUP; 446 pages; 1971). Edited by Kenneth Silverman, this collection of letters presents Mather as a man, a clergyman, and a father. While there is a high devotional tone to the letters, they are perhaps best used to help us better understand Mather himself.

The Threefold Paradise of Cotton Mather: An edition of "Triparadisus" (UGP; 526 pages; 1995). This edited edition of *Triparadisus*, the largest colonial work on the millennium, contains Mather's ideas on the last days and the reign of Christ. In a critical introduction, Reiner Smolinski shows that Mather's hermeneutical defense of revealed religion seeks to negotiate between the orthodox literalist position of his New England forebears and the new philological challenges to the Scriptures by men as diverse as Hugo Grotius, Thomas Hobbes, Isaac de la Peyrere, Benedict Spinoza, Richard Simon, Henry Hammond, Thomas Burnet, William Whiston, Anthony Collins, and Isaac Newton.

Triparadisus shows Mather's hermeneutics undergoing a shift from a futurist interpretation of the prophecies to a semi-preterist position as he joins the somewhat allegorical camp of Grotius, Hammond, Lightfoot, and Baxter. It provides important biographical insight into Mather's last years and serves as an important link between Mather's premillennialism in the late seventeenth century and Jonathan Edwards's postmillennialism in the Great Awakening.

Increase Mather

(1639-1723)

Increase Mather was born June 21, 1639, in Dorchester, Massachusetts. He was raised according to the strict Puritanism of his father, Richard Mather. He studied under John Norton in Boston, then entered Harvard College at the age of twelve, and graduated with a Bachelor of Arts degree in 1656. Some months prior to his graduation, his dying mother begged him to become a minister; about the same time, he came to assurance of faith. Following his mother's wishes, he preached his first sermon on his eighteenth birthday. Weeks later, he went to England and began studying at Trinity College in Dublin. He earned a master's degree in 1658, and then preached in England and Guernsey until the Restoration.

Mather returned to Boston, Massachusetts, in 1661. Six churches asked him to be their pastor, but he chose to work with his father in Dorchester. In March of 1662, Mather married Maria, daughter of John Cotton, bringing two influential Puritan families closer together. They had seven daughters and three sons that survived childhood. One son, Nathaniel, died at the age of nineteen; the other two, Cotton and Samuel, became ministers.

Mather served as a delegate to the "Half-Way" Synod of 1662. There he opposed his father and other ministers by arguing against the Half-Way Covenant, which he thought weakened Congregationalism by lowering standards for church membership. By the 1670s, however, he was convinced that churches would not prosper unless their standards granted membership to people who could not give a clear testimony of their conversion experience. In 1675, he published two books defending the Half-Way Covenant.

In 1664, Mather was called to pastor Second Church ("Old North") in Boston, a large congregation of 1,500 members. He served there for nearly sixty years until his death in 1723, becoming one of the leading ministers of his generation. For decades, he had a leading role in various synods that sought to reform the church. He presided at the Boston Synod of 1680 and wrote the preface to the Confession of Faith, which was their version of the Savoy Declaration that was agreed upon at that synod.

In the early days of his ministry, Mather believed that New England had a crucial role in the anticipated growth of God's kingdom. In addition to the church, New England itself was important, for only New England had the opportunity to do what God wanted done and to serve as an inspiration to the world. Mather and others had an eschatological fervor in this belief. So when things did not go right in New England and churches began to decline spiritually, Mather was deeply distressed and greatly feared that New England would cease to exist as a godly and covenanted nation. In his preaching, he frequently compared New England with Israel, arguing that as God's covenant with Israel did not fail, so God's covenant with New England would not fail.

In the 1670s, Mather's jeremiads, i.e., sermons of warning and calls to repentance, became more specific. In the 1660s, he had tended to criticize the colony as a whole for its failure, but in the 1670s, he focused on particular elements within the colony that he thought were responsible for spiritual decline, such as merchants, sailors, and young people, who were least likely to honor the covenant.

Mather's son Cotton joined his father in pastoral ministry in 1683. Together they upheld the old Puritan theocracy and the established order in church and state. This conservatism led to trouble with the government during the Restoration period. Increase Mather favored the government of Sir William Phips and became a bitter opponent of Edward Randolph and Sir Edmund Andros over the revocation of the Massachusetts charter and the conduct of the royal government. In 1688, Mather went to England to present the grievances of Massachusetts. After the Glorious Revolution and the subsequent revolt in Massachusetts against Andros, he obtained a new charter in 1691 that united Plymouth Colony with Massachusetts Bay Colony.

Mather opposed what he saw as liberalism creeping into the church through Solomon Stoddard's idea that communion could be a converting ordinance. Mather felt that opening the Lord's Supper to unconverted people would undermine the purity of the church. He also viewed restricting church membership as the central way for maintaining the Puritan experiment in New England. After 1691, when the new charter redefined citizenship no longer in terms of church membership but in terms of property, he was deeply distressed. He spoke to young people, warning them about not living up to their responsibility to join the church. These young people were not usually riotous in their living, but they were simply not coming forward to join the church because they could not give testimony of their conversion experience.

In 1692, Mather played a key role in reducing the public hysteria that accompanied the Salem witch trials. One of the important decisions that Mather and other Puritan ministers made was not to allow people's testimony about having seen ghosts to be used as evidence against the accused. Officials needed more concrete evidence to convict anyone of the practice of witchcraft.

Mather and other ministers did believe in the possibility of witchcraft and were willing to see people tried as witches, but they disapproved of the hysteria that was generated by the trials. Mather felt that it was better for a guilty witch to escape than to risk putting to death an innocent person. During the year of the witch trials, he published *Cases of Conscience Concerning Evil Spirits* (1692), in which he denounced "spectral evidence" in witch trials. The book played a key role in bringing the trials to a close, and, according to Cotton Mather, was instrumental in ending executions for witchcraft in Massachusetts.

After 1692, Mather's influence declined because many colonists opposed the new charter he had recommended. Nevertheless, Mather remained powerful to the end. He became president of Harvard College in 1685. While in that role, he reorganized and revitalized the college; he pushed to expand the study of science at Harvard, which broadened the scope of the school beyond training for the ministry. In 1701, liberal forces that rejected Calvinist orthodoxy successfully compelled his ouster.

Late in his ministry, Mather began focusing his preaching more on the elect and less on the nation. He returned to his father's emphasis on the importance of the church rather than of the nation as he became increasingly discouraged about prospects for national renewal. He regretted that his earlier preaching had been too moralistic and had not been sufficiently focused upon Christ.

Mather died in 1723 at the age of eighty-four. Many mourned his passing, including Benjamin Colman, a former enemy, who said of Mather, "He was the patriarch and prophet among us, if any one might be so called" (*The Prophet's Death*, 1723, p. 32). George Harper rightly notes, "Increase Mather was a dominant figure and the leading voice for orthodox Calvinism in an era when rationalism was beginning to undermine the Bay Colony's religious foundations" ("New England Dynasty," *Christian History*, no. 41, p. 21).

Mather wrote 175 books and pamphlets on a variety of subjects. He published a biography of his father in 1670 and *A History of the War with the Indians* (1676) just after King Philip's War. He also wrote *Remarkable Providences* (1684), based on an earlier work by other writers, and several works on the decline of New England.

―――――◦◆◦―――――

Departing Glory: Eight Jeremiads by Increase Mather (SF; 8 vols. in 1, 328 pages; 1987). The term *jeremiad* refers to a sermon or another work that accounts for the misfortunes of an era as a just penalty for great social and moral evils, but holds out hope for changes that will bring a happier future. It derives from the prophet Jeremiah, who attributed the calamities of Israel to its abandonment of the covenant with Jehovah and its return to pagan idolatry, denounced its religious and moral iniquities, and called on the people to repent and reform in order that God might restore them to His favor and renew the ancient covenant.

The term has also been used more broadly, according to Emory Elliott: "Taking their texts from Jeremiah and Isaiah, these orations followed—and reinscribed—a rhetorical formula that included recalling the courage and piety of the founders, lamenting recent and present ills, and crying out for a return to the original conduct and zeal. In current scholarship, the term 'jeremiad' has expanded to include not only sermons but also other texts that rehearse the familiar tropes of the formula such as captivity narratives, covenant renewals, as well as some histories and biographies" (*Cambridge History of American Literature*, 1:257).

The facsimiles of this volume include "The Day of Trouble is Near" (1674), "An Earnest Exhortation" (1676), "Heaven's

Alarm to the World" (1682), "Renewal of Covenant" (1682), "Returning unto God" (1684), "Ichabod" (1702), "Burnings Bewailed in a Sermon" (1711), and "Advice to the Children" (1721).

A History of God's Remarkable Providences in Colonial New England (Back Home Industries; 262 pages; 1997). This work on providence, first published in 1684 and enlarged in 1856, covers the following topics: sea-deliverances, preservations, stories of thunder and lightning, philosophical meditations, preternatural events, accounts of demons and possessed persons, apparitions, cases of conscience, tempests, and judgments. This book originated in the mind of Matthew Poole, who suggested that there be such a work to set down rules and guidelines for recording God's marvelous wonders. Mather responded with this book, which not only sets down certain rules, but applies them to various examples. At times, Mather seems to stretch facts and becomes somewhat hagiographical.

Jeremiads (AMS; 320 pages; 1985). These jeremiads of Increase Mather include "The Day of Trouble Is Near"; "Renewal of Covenant"; "A Call From Heaven"; "The Greatest Blessing of Primitive Counselors"; "David Serving His Generation"; and "The Surest Way to the Greatest Honor."

Two Mather Biographies: Life and Death and Parentator, ed. William J. Scheick (LUP; 241 pages; 1989). This work contains the first modern edition of Increase Mather's biography of his father, Richard Mather. It also contains Cotton Mather's biography of Increase Mather. The two works have been carefully edited and provide invaluable insight into the lives of two of New England's Puritan patriarchs.

Richard Mather

(1596-1669)

Richard Mather was born in Lowtown, near Liverpool. At age fifteen he was ready for Oxford, but his parents could not afford to send him there. Instead, Mather became master at a new grammar school at Toxteth Park. While teaching, he lived with a cultured Puritan farmer, Edward Aspinwall. He listened to Puritan sermons and read the writings of Puritan divines, and, over a three-year period (age fifteen to eighteen), he experienced an intense, lengthy conversion "in the classic Puritan mold: self-righteous attempts to obey God's law, despair as he compared his feeble efforts to those of seasoned saints, and finally a breakthrough" when the Holy Spirit poured evangelical promises into his soul (George W. Harper, "New England Dynasty," *Church History*, no. 41, p. 20).

In 1618, Mather went to study at Brasenose College, Oxford, but his education was cut short when the people at Toxteth begged him to return to minister to them. So, in 1619, Mather was ordained in the Church of England by Thomas Morton, bishop of Chester. He preached at Toxteth for fifteen years with growing success. William Gellibrand, Puritan minister of Warrington, said after he heard Mather preach, "Call him Matter; for, believe it, this man hath substance in him."

In 1624, Mather married Katherine Hoult of Bury, Lancashire. They had six sons. One died in childbirth, and four became ministers. The two oldest, Samuel and Nathaniel, returned to England after graduating from Harvard, while

Eleazer and Increase became well-known preachers in Massachusetts.

Thomas Morton's successor, John Bridgeman, suspended Mather in 1633 for denigrating the Church of England's ceremonies, but Mather was restored to the pulpit after several months. Mather had developed nonconformist views and supported Congregational views of church government. After he was suspended from preaching a second time in 1634 for refusing to wear a surplice, there was little hope of his being restored to the pulpit. So John Cotton, Thomas Hooker, and other Nonconformist leaders persuaded Mather to immigrate to America.

In 1635, Mather sailed to America and settled in the Massachusetts Bay Colony. The following year, he helped found the church of Dorchester, Massachusetts, where he ministered until his death in 1669. As was true of many first-generation immigrants, Mather saw himself as an Englishman living in exile because of problems in England. He did not come to New England because he disliked England; he only disliked certain practices that made it difficult for him to remain there. To him, New England was the church rather than a geographical location.

Mather helped produce *The Bay Psalm Book* (1637), but he was best known for his defense of "the Congregational Way" of church government in the 1640s during debates with Samuel Rutherford, a staunch Scottish Presbyterian. Mather drafted a form of church government for the Massachusetts Bay Colony, which, after modification by the Cambridge Synod, emerged as "The Cambridge Platform of Church Government" (1648).

Mather was convinced that New England would become an inspiration and a model to the world. He became a close friend of John Cotton, another first-generation Puritan minister in New England. But unlike Cotton, Mather firmly opposed what he saw as antinomian tendencies in the church. He supported a visibly pure church and defended a restrictive church membership requiring a testimony of religious experience.

Cotton thought that Mather's position was extreme. Cotton once told Mather that it was better to admit ten hypocrites to the church than to exclude one Christian; Mather responded that it was better to keep out many Christians than to admit one hypocrite. For Mather, the visible purity of the church was synonymous with the Puritan experiment. If the purity of the church could not be maintained, then the whole experiment would fail.

Shortly after his wife died in 1655, Mather married Sarah Cotton, widow of John Cotton. In the late 1650s, Mather became deeply involved in the baptismal controversy that engulfed the New England churches. He participated in the "Half-Way" Synod of 1662 and wrote a tract defending its conclusions. He also wrote ten works, mostly on issues of ecclesiology.

Mather was a powerful preacher. "His way of preaching was very plain," wrote Cotton Mather of his grandfather's preaching, "aiming to shoot his arrows, not over the *heads*, but into the *hearts* of his hearers. Yet so scripturally and powerfully did he preach his plain sermons, that...he saw a great success of his labours in both Englands [Old and New], converting many souls to God" (cited in Harper, p. 20).

While presiding at a council of churches in Boston in 1669, Mather had a kidney stone attack. He returned to Dorchester, where he died a week later.

———◆◆◆———

Church Covenant: Two Tracts (Arno; 162 pages; 1972). Mather was not ordinary, as a man or as a minister. One remarkable thing he did was taking the lead in establishing Congregationalism in Massachusetts and defending it against critics.

Many Puritans in Massachusetts considered their churches to be part of the Church of England; they were thus non-separating Congregationalists. They formed their churches by covenants, or agreements, among members who had given evidence of their conversion experiences. As "a company of the faithful gathered out of the world," a Congregational church administered the sacraments only to those who were deemed qualified. The church also disciplined members who fell into sin. Each church was quite autonomous; there was no hierarchy of bishops over them. New Testament churches did not have such a hierarchy, the Puritans said; thus, neither would they.

Mather defended this system whenever it was challenged. Some of the most outstanding critics were Samuel Rutherford and Charles Herle, Presbyterians who attacked the autonomy of Congregationalism, saying each church should be put under the authority of a synod. Their model was the Presbyterianism of Scotland.

Mather responded to both critics in works published in London titled *A Reply to Mr. Rutherford* (1647), and *A Modest and Brotherly Answer to Mr. Charles Herle* (1644). He offered further expositions of Congregationalism in two powerful works (here reprinted) published in 1643: *An Apology for Church Covenant and Church Government* and *Church Covenant Discussed in Answer to Two and Thirty Questions*. In these works, Mather explains the scriptural basis for Congregational churches, while insisting that the New England churches remained within the great tradition of the Church of England before it began its downward slide.

Samuel Mather
(1626-1671)

Samuel Mather was born at Much Woolton, Lancashire, on May 13, 1626. He immigrated to New England with his parents, Richard (see above) and Katherine, and his three younger brothers when he was nine years old. He graduated from Harvard College with a Master of Arts degree in 1643, and was the first graduate who became a fellow.

Mather preached for several years in New England, especially for the Second Church of Boston (North Church). Eventually the congregation called him as their pastor, but he declined, choosing instead to return to England, where, in 1650, he was made chaplain of Magdalen College, Oxford, under the presidency of Thomas Goodwin.

In 1654, Mather was sent on a mission to Ireland with Oliver Cromwell's son, Henry, and subsequently was appointed as senior fellow at Trinity College, Dublin. Two years later, he accepted a ministerial call to co-pastor with Samuel Winter the church of St. Nicholas, Dublin, where most of the Dublin aldermen worshipped. Upon his request, he was ordained as a Congregationalist minister, which certainly indicates his acceptance as a Puritan preacher. In addition to preaching each Sunday morning at St. Nicholas's church, he preached every six weeks before the Lord Deputy Cromwell and became one of the leading Puritan clergy in Ireland. During the Protectorate, he maintained cordial relations with Anglican divines, but after the Restoration he became increasingly impatient with the Anglican ceremonies. In 1660, he preached two strong sermons calling for reform of several Anglican rites, including the use of the clerical surplice, sign-ing with the cross at baptism, kneeling at communion, and bowing to the altar. As a result, he was dismissed from his pulpit and ordered to surrender his sermon notes. Instead, he sent his notes to New England where they were eventually published in 1670 through the influence of his brother In-crease. These sermons show his developing conception of typology that was later documented in his influential work, *The Figures or Types of the Old Testament*, published posthumously by his brother Nathaniel in 1683.

Mather returned to Lancashire and preached in the area of his homeland until he was ejected in 1662. Hearing that Ire-land was tolerating dissent better than England, he returned to Dublin where he preached for a congregation on New Row. In 1664, he was imprisoned briefly for holding conventicles. A few years later, he preached a sermon vindicating withdrawal from the Church of Ireland, which he called "the wicked party," and called for Congregationalist, Baptist, and Presby-terian dissenters to co-labor for orthodox Reformed faith. These convictions were published posthumously in his *Irenicum, or, An Essay for Union* (1680).

Mather died on October 29, 1671, aged forty-six, survived by his second wife, Hannah, and his daughter, Catherine, who was a fruit of his first marriage to a sister of Sir John Stevens. Three or four children preceded him in death.

———◆◆◆———

The Figures or Types of the Old Testament (Johnson; 585 pages; 1969). In the opening sermons of this facsimile reprint of the second edition of this work (1705), Mather shows why some scriptures should be read typologically. He then dis-cusses the origins and value of exegesis through typology, unveiling the distinctions between the revelation of the old and new covenants, and showing the superiority of the gospel to the law. Christ, he says, was "partially though not fully revealed" in the "legal types and shadows" and other Old Testament modes of revelation.

In the main section of his book, Mather discusses the Old Testament types under two major divisions, "personal types" and "real types." Personal types include such figures as Adam, Noah, Melchizedek, Abraham, Isaac, Jacob, and Joseph. This section includes discussion of "collective types," such as the nation of Israel, the Nazarites, prophets, priests, and kings. Under the real types, Mather distinguishes "occasional types" (such as Noah's ark, Jacob's ladder, the burning bush, and manna) from "perpetual types," which "had a more lasting value and were epitomized by the Old Testament ceremonial law." Mather goes on to show how moral principles and examples that still have relevance for us today can be gleaned from types and figures instituted in Old Testament times (pp. xvi-xix).

Mason Lowance concludes, "While Mather, like Thomas Shepard, has done much to minimize the differences between the dispensations, he has also raised some serious questions about the abrogation of the types which Shepard had treated more thoroughly in the *Theses Sabbaticae* a generation earlier" (p. xix).

Matthew Mead

(1629-1699)

M atthew Mead was born in 1629 to Richard and Joanne Mead, at Leighton Buzzard, Bedfordshire. After studying at Eton College (1645-48), Mead was elected as a scholar at King's College, Cambridge (1649), but resigned in 1651, probably "to avoid expulsion for refusing to take the engagement to the Commonwealth."

Mead married Elizabeth Walton of All Hallows parish, London, in 1655. That same year, he became morning lecturer at St. Sunstan and All Saints, Stepney, where William Greenhill was vicar. The following year, he joined the gathered congregation that Greenhill pastored.

During the time of Oliver Cromwell's rule, Mead identified with the Independents. In 1658, Cromwell appointed Mead curate of New Chapel, Shadwell, near Stepney; however, Mead lost that position after the Restoration. In 1659, Mead became lecturer at St. Bride's, Fleet Street.

Mead and seven other nonconformist ministers published *An English-Greek Lexicon* in 1661. That summer, as lecturer at St. Sepulchre, Holborn, Mead preached seven sermons to unmask hypocrites and awaken drowsy professors. The following year they were published as *The Almost Christian Discovered*, which became Mead's most popular work; it has been reprinted numerous times until the present day. A few months after printing this classic, Mead was ejected from all his lectureships and positions because of his nonconformity. His farewell sermon, *The Pastor's Valediction*, exhorted his audience to suffer rather than conform.

In 1663, Mead was working again in Stepney, probably assisting Greenhill. The Conventicle Act and the Five Mile Act forced him to leave Stepney. He visited the Netherlands, preaching on several occasions in Utrecht, before returning to England. In 1669, he formally became William Greenhill's assistant pastor at Stepney. Shortly after Greenhill's death in 1671, Mead was asked to succeed Greenhill as pastor. He was installed by John Owen on December 14.

For the last twenty-eight years of his life, Mead preached to an Independent congregation at Stepney that was reportedly the largest in London. His preaching was highly regarded, but he faced his share of trials. In 1682, Sir William Smith invaded the Stepney church with a strong guard, pulled down the pulpit, and broke up the pews. The following year, Mead was arrested on suspicion of being involved with the Rye House plot. Along with John Owen, he was brought before the Privy Council. Mead's answers were so satisfactory that the king ordered his release. But when King James II acceded to the throne, the old charges were resurrected. Eventually they were dismissed.

Mead succeeded Owen in 1683 as a Tuesday morning lecturer at Pinner's Hall, a position he held until his death. He wholeheartedly supported John Howe's attempt in 1690 to unite Presbyterians and Congregationalists. Mead was asked to preach for the service inaugurating "the Happy Union of Independents and Presbyterians" in Stepney on April 6, 1691. He preached perhaps his most famous sermon, *Two Sticks Made One* (1691), from Ezekiel 37:19, in which he stressed that nonessential divisions are very dishonorable to Jesus Christ.

When the union dissolved in 1694, largely due to the alleged heresies of Daniel Williams, Mead kept a neutral role. He continued lecturing at Pinner's Hall after the Presbyterians seceded.

Mead died at the age of seventy on October 16, 1699. John Howe, who preached at Mead's funeral, called his friend a "very reverend and most laborious servant of Christ."

Mead wrote several books that were published posthumously, most notably *The Young Man's Remembrancer, and Youth's Best Choice* (1701), and *Original Sermons on the Jews; and on Falling into the Hands of the Living God* (1836), now reprinted as *The Sermons of Matthew Mead*. Mead also remained very busy as the father of thirteen children. His eleventh child, Richard Mead, became a well-known physician and political activist.

=◆=

The Almost Christian Discovered (SDG; 186 pages; 1993). This work shows twenty ways that a person can be deceived into thinking he is a Christian when he really is an "almost Christian" (Acts 26:28). Mead explains the need for self-examination (pp. 126-34), signs of the unpardonable sin (pp. 142-46), and reasons for a believer's lack of comfort (pp. 155-63). He concludes with three matters that every reader must be convinced of: the evil and filthy nature of sin, the misery and desperate danger of the unregenerate, and "the utter insufficiency and inability of anything below Christ Jesus to minister relief" (pp. 163-64).

The two-fold purpose of this short, readable classic is to shake nominal believers out of their complacency and to comfort true believers. Caution should be exercised in giving this book to new converts because its contents could discourage them.

A Name in Heaven the Truest Ground of Joy (SDG; 144 pages; 2001). This reprint contains two discourses: "A Name in

Heaven the Truest Ground of Joy," on Luke 10:20 ("Rejoice because your names are written in heaven"), and "The Power of Grace in Weaning the Heart from the World," on Psalm 131:1 ("My soul is even as a weaned child"). Augustus Toplady, who abridged this work, says of it: "Nothing so effectively tends to *wean the soul* from every undivine attachment, as the knowledge that our *names are written in heaven.*" The practical substance and style of this work should be most helpful to readers.

The Sermons of Matthew Mead (SDG; 435 pages; 1997). This rare collection includes five sermons on the restoration of Jews from Ezekiel 37, twelve sermons on "Falling Into the Hands of the Living God" from Hebrews 10:31, and a farewell sermon from 1 Corinthians 1:3. Some of the sermons were transcribed from Mead's own handwriting and "bear the stamp of the vigorous, enlarged, and devout mind of the author."

Christopher Ness

(1621-1705)

Christopher Ness (Nesse) was an Independent minister born at North Cave, Yorkshire, on December 26, 1621. After some time spent at John Seaman's grammar school, Ness was admitted to St. John's College, Cambridge, from which he graduated with a Bachelor of Arts degree in 1642. He became curate to his uncle at South Cliff and preached at Holderness and Beverley, where he was later appointed as head of the grammar school in 1649.

In 1651, Ness became the rector of Cottingham and, in 1656, the preacher at Leeds. He was ejected in 1662 by the Act of Uniformity and engaged in controversy with noted Arminians of the day. No doubt the seeds of his last publication, *An Antidote Against Arminianism* (1700), were planted at this time.

For the remainder of the 1660s, Ness served as a school teacher and tutor in Yorkshire at Clayton, Motley, and Hunslet. He was licensed as an Independent minister in Leeds on 1672, where he opened a church two years later; he was, however, excommunicated four times and convicted for promoting schismatic assemblies. Ness fled to London in 1675 to avoid arrest and preached there to a private congregation in Salisbury Court, Fleet Street. He published several works of practical divinity, such as *The Crown and Glory of a Christian*

(1676) and *A Christian's Walk and Work on Earth until He Attain to Heaven* (1678), as well as several anti-papal works. Perhaps the most noted of these was a biography of Pope Innocent XI, *The Devil's Patriarch* (1683), of which the entire printing, according to the publisher, John Dutton, was sold in two weeks.

After some persecution following the Whig defeat, Ness fled London for a time. When he returned in 1690, he established a meeting place at Woodmonger's Hall, Duke's Place. He published a four-volume commentary on the Bible, *A Complete History and Mystery of the Old and New Testaments* (1690-96). He died on his birthday in 1705 and was buried in Bunhill Fields cemetery.

———◆◆◆———

An Antidote Against Arminianism (SWRB; 130 pages; 1988). Frequently reprinted over the centuries, this little book has become a classic defense of Calvinism. Its four sections cogently defend the doctrines of sovereign predestination, limited atonement, irresistible grace in conversion, and the final perseverance of the saints. Ness marshals more than 450 texts to support his case in the compass of this short work. The book was commended warmly by his friend, John Owen, as well as by Matthew Henry.

John Norton

(1606-1663)

John Norton was born in 1606 in Bishop's Stortford, Hertfordshire. He was the son of William Norton and Alice Browest. He entered Peterhouse College, Cambridge, in 1620, earning a Bachelor of Arts degree in 1624 and a Master of Arts degree in 1627. After graduation he served as usher at the grammar school and as a curate at the Stortford church. During that time the preaching of Jeremiah Dykes and other Puritans led to his conversion. As a result of his new Puritan convictions, he declined the generous support of his uncle, a fellowship at Cambridge, and a church benefice, and chose instead to study theology and become a chaplain at the house of Sir William Masham of High Lever, Essex.

England's increasing intolerance of dissenters led Norton to immigrate to the New World. He and his bride prepared to sail to Massachusetts Bay in America on the same ship as Thomas Shepard. A severe storm thwarted their attempt to leave England in 1634, but the next year their ship set sail without incident. Norton and his wife landed at Plymouth in October of 1635. Throughout the winter, he served as minister of the church in Plymouth Colony, but a year later the Nortons settled in Boston.

Norton's arrival in Massachusetts coincided with the antinomian crisis that centered around Anne Hutchinson. She advocated that one's election should be mystically apprehended and contended that the region's clergy, including

Norton, erroneously taught that people's works and fruits are a means of determining whether they are among the elect; consequently, she said, Norton and his colleagues were preaching an Arminian brand of the covenant of works. Hutchinson furthermore questioned the authority of the ministers, claiming that ordinary people could receive special revelations directly from God. Such beliefs threatened the foundation of Puritan theology, and, indeed, the social structure of early America.

Norton was a member of the Synod of 1637, called by the colony's leaders to deal with the controversy. The Synod denounced the religion that she and her followers espoused, and exiled her, with Norton's support.

In 1638, Norton was installed as teacher of the church at Ipswich, where Nathaniel Rogers was pastor. In the mid-1640s, Norton became involved in the Westminster Assembly church polity debates. Some of the Westminster Divines solicited support from various continental theologians, such as William Apollonius, minister in Middelburg, who wrote in defense of Presbyterianism. Independents such as Thomas Goodwin and Philip Nye cited the New England way, and turned to its ministers for support. Norton wrote a Latin tome, *Responsio ad totam questionum* (1648), which answered Appolonius. Printed in London and prefaced by Goodwin, Nye, and Sidrach Simpson, Norton demonstrated the consistency of Congregational polity with continental belief and practice and supported the dissenting brethren.

Norton preached the election sermon for the colony in 1645. He participated in the Synod of 1648 that adopted the Cambridge Platform, the church order for congregations in Massachusetts. That same year, Norton published *A Brief and Excellent Treatise Containing the Doctrine of Godliness*, one of his most useful books.

Before John Cotton died in 1652, he said that Norton should succeed him as minister of the First Church at Boston after his death. After more than three years of controversy between the congregations of Boston and Ipswich, both of which wanted Norton as pastor, Ipswich relented, and Norton was ordained at the Boston church on July 23, 1656. On the same day, Norton, whose first wife had died, married Mary Mason, who outlived him.

After the Restoration in 1660, Norton called for reconciliation with the crown in his election sermon, "Sion the Outcast Healed of her Wounds." In 1662, Norton and Governor Simon Bradstreet (Anne Bradstreet's husband) went to England as deputies of Massachusetts to petition Charles II to reconfirm their charter and to answer questions about the colony's treatment of Quakers. Although the king assured them that the charter would remain, the conditions of the agreement made the colonists think that Norton and Bradstreet had conceded too much and thereby had forfeited the rights of the colony. King Charles wanted to reestablish England's control over the colony's legal and religious practices, so he required court proceedings to be held in the king's name, made property the voting qualification instead of church membership, enforced tolerance for religious dissenters, and implemented the Navigation Acts.

Six months later, on April 5, 1663, Norton died, apparently from a stroke, after preaching on a Sunday morning. The sermon titled "The Believer's Consolation in the Remembrance of His Holy Mansion Prepared for Him by Christ," taken from John 14:3 and delivered just prior to his stroke, was somewhat prophetic of Norton's departure. Near the end of the sermon, he said, "I have not so lived that I am ashamed to live any longer, nor am I afraid to die." Some claimed that his anguish over the colonies' criticisms contributed to his death, but there is no evidence to support that.

Norton was well-known for his orthodoxy, his writings, and his persecution of Quakers. He even supported the death penalty for Quakers who violated an order of banishment from the colony. Norton also wrote official theological tracts for the general court, most notably, "The Heart of New England Rent at the Blasphemies of the Present Generation, Or a Brief Tractate Concerning the Doctrine of the Quakers" (1659)—a major critique of Quakerism. His treatise, *The Orthodox Evangelist* (1654), was a critical and technical explanation of Puritan theology, providing insight into the Puritan faith and into Norton's own beliefs. It powerfully taught the "inefficacy of man's work" in salvation as well as the inevitable fruits of divine love in the lives of God's elect. He also wrote *A Catechistical guide to sinners, and to such converts that are babes in Christ* (1680), a compendium of Puritan doctrine.

Norton fought for the heart of worship: fidelity to the Bible. He was suspicious of the trends influencing early America, especially the mounting "evidences" of premonitions and revelations. He said these would undo the country and undermine God's work in the city that he and others had worked so hard to advance.

———◆◆◆———

Abel Being Dead, Yet Speaketh (SF; 80 pages; 1978). This book, credited with being the first biography written in America, is a short history of the life of John Cotton. Norton was a close friend of Cotton, Puritan minister and author of more than forty works. Cotton, along with Thomas Hooker and Thomas Shepard, was on the front line of first-generation Puritan theology. Norton began his work with these words: "It is the privilege of those who lived in heaven while they lived on earth that they may live on earth while they live in heaven." This was a reference to Cotton's piety and prolific writing; though Cotton had departed to his rest, he still spoke to New England from the grave in his prose. Thus the title infers that Cotton, being dead, like Abel, still speaks.

JOHN OWEN

John Owen

(1616-1683)

John Owen, called the "prince of the English divines," "the leading figure among the Congregationalist divines," "a genius with learning second only to Calvin's," and "indisputably the leading proponent of high Calvinism in England in the late seventeenth century," was born in Stadham (Stadhampton), near Oxford. He was the second son of Henry Owen, the local Puritan vicar. Owen showed godly and scholarly tendencies at an early age. He entered Queen's College, Oxford, at the age of twelve and studied the classics, mathematics, philosophy, theology, Hebrew, and rabbinical writings. He earned a Bachelor of Arts degree in 1632 and a Master of Arts degree in 1635. Throughout his teen years, young Owen studied eighteen to twenty hours per day.

Pressured to accept Archbishop Laud's new statutes, Owen left Oxford in 1637. He became a private chaplain and tutor, first for Sir William Dormer of Ascot, then for John Lord Lovelace at Hurley, Berkshire. He worked for Lovelace until 1643. Those years of chaplaincy afforded him much time for study, which God richly blessed. At the age of twenty-six, Owen began a forty-one year writing span that produced more than eighty works. Many of those would become classics and be greatly used by God.

Though he embraced Puritan convictions from his youth, Owen lacked personal assurance of faith until God directed him in 1642 to a church service at St. Mary Aldermanbury,

London. He expected to hear Edmund Calamy preach, but a substitute was in the pulpit. Owen's friend urged him to leave with him to hear a more famous minister some distance away, but Owen decided to stay. The substitute preacher chose as his text, "Why are ye fearful, O ye of little faith?" God used that sermon to bring Owen to assurance of faith. Later, Owen tried in vain to learn the identity of the preacher.

In 1643, Owen published *A Display of Arminianism*, a vigorous exposition of classic Calvinism that refuted the Arminians by examining the doctrines of predestination, original sin, irresistible grace, the extent of the atonement, and the role of the human will in salvation. This book earned Owen nearly instant recognition as well as a preferment to the living of Fordham, a pastoral charge in Essex. His ministry was well-received in Fordham, and many people came from outlying districts to hear him. He also excelled in catechizing his parishioners and wrote two catechism books, one for children and one for adults.

At Fordham, Owen took the Solemn League and Covenant. There, too, he took Mary Rooke as his bride. Of the eleven children born to them, only a daughter survived into adulthood. After an unhappy marriage to a Welshman, the daughter returned to live with her parents. She died of consumption shortly afterwards.

When the sequestered incumbent of Fordham died, the rights of presentation reverted to the patron, who dispossessed Owen and appointed Richard Pulley instead. Owen became vicar of the distinguished pulpit of St. Peter's, Coggeshall (1646), where his predecessor, Obadiah Sedgwick, had ministered to nearly two thousand souls. At Coggeshell, through John Cotton's *Keys of the Kingdom of Heaven* (1644) and other political influences, Owen openly converted from Presbyterianism to Congregationalism. He wrote about this change in *Eshcol; or Rules of Direction for the Walking of the Saints in*

Fellowship. He also began remodeling his church on Congregational principles.

Owen's fame spread rapidly in the late 1640s through his preaching and writings, gradually earning him a reputation as a leading Independent theologian. While he was still in his early thirties, more than a thousand people came to hear his weekly sermons. Yet Owen often grieved that he saw little fruit upon his labors. He once said that he would trade all his learning for John Bunyan's gift for plain preaching. Clearly, he underestimated his own gifts.

Owen was asked to preach before Parliament on several occasions, including the day following the execution of King Charles I. The sermon he preached before Parliament on Hebrews 12:27 greatly impressed Oliver Cromwell. The next day Cromwell persuaded Owen to accompany him as chaplain to Ireland to regulate the affairs of Trinity College in Dublin. Owen traveled with 12,000 psalm-singing, Puritan soldiers who descended upon Ireland. Though he spent most of his time at Trinity College reorganizing it along Puritan lines, he also did considerable preaching. He ministered to the troops during the terrible massacre at Drogheda. That dreadful event so stirred his soul that, upon his return to England after a seven-month stay, Owen urged Parliament to show mercy to the Irish.

In 1650, Owen was appointed as an official preacher to the state. The position provided lodgings in Whitehall. The duties consisted primarily of preaching on Friday afternoons in Whitehall Chapel and offering daily prayers at the meetings of the Council of State.

In the summer of 1650, Owen accompanied Cromwell on his Scottish expedition. He assisted Cromwell in trying to convince Scottish leaders and people of the rightness of cutting off the monarchy.

The 1650s were Owen's most productive years. In 1651, he became dean of Christ Church College, Oxford and eighteen months later was made vice-chancellor of Oxford University, under the chancellorship of Cromwell. He replaced Daniel Greenwood, who, being a Presbyterian, was not considered to be sufficiently supportive of the government. Owen presided at most university meetings, served as administrator, and restrained worldly students from excesses. Through his lectures in theology, he promoted Reformed theology and Puritan piety. He set up several boards to regulate the religious life of the university. Undergraduates were required to repeat Sunday sermons to "some person of known ability and piety." They were to have private evening prayers with their tutors, and every home where students lodged was to offer frequent preaching.

Owen himself preached regularly at Christ Church in Oxford and on alternate Sundays with Thomas Goodwin at St. Mary's. Those sermons were the seeds of later treatises on mortification and temptation. Owen was a good manager; under his leadership, the university's treasury "increased tenfold, its salaries were restored, its rights maintained, its studies and its discipline improved" (Mallet, 2:396). Owen's godly leadership brought peace, security, and spiritual growth to the university during the difficult recovery from the chaotic civil war years.

In 1653, Owen was granted a Doctor of Divinity degree by the university. According to his own testimony, this was against his wishes. Throughout the 1650s, Owen was frequently called to London by Cromwell to settle a variety of disputes and to participate in various attempts at church settlement.

Owen published numerous books in the 1650s, including major works on the perseverance of the saints, Christ's satisfaction, mortification of sin, communion with the Trinity, schism, temptation, and the authority of Scripture. In 1658, Owen helped write *The Savoy Declaration*. He was probably the primary author of its lengthy preface.

Owen lost favor with Cromwell in the Protector's last year when he opposed Cromwell's becoming king. Owen's stature diminished further when Cromwell resigned from the chancellorship and his son, Richard, was appointed to succeed him. Under Richard Cromwell's leadership, Owen and his group soon lost their ecclesiastical positions to Presbyterian divines. Within two months, Richard Cromwell had replaced Owen as vice-chancellor with John Conant, Presbyterian rector of Exeter College. The Sunday afternoon sermons of Owen and Goodwin at St. Mary's Church were abolished soon after that.

In 1660, Owen was replaced as Dean of Christ Church by Edward Reynolds. Owen apparently then retired to his small estate at Stadhampton, where he continued to preach despite the Great Ejection of 1662. He lived there in relative seclusion. Every position of influence had been taken from him. He was offered a bishopric as well as a call to John Cotton's church in Boston, Massachusetts, but he declined both.

In 1665, Owen was indicted at Oxford for holding religious conventicles in his home. He escaped without imprisonment. However, like many other Puritan pastors, he returned to London to preach after the Plague and the Great Fire. He started a small congregation, engaged in ongoing theological battles against the Arminians, and wrote several anonymous tracts on behalf of religious liberty as well as numerous edifying treatises for the spiritual growth of believers. His *Indwelling Sin, Exposition of Psalm 130,* and the first volume of his massive commentary on Hebrews were written during this period.

In 1673, Owen's congregation in London merged with a group that Joseph Caryl had served as pastor. David Clarkson and other Puritans assisted him. He devoted much time to helping Independent ministers such as Robert Asty and John Bunyan, offering them financial assistance as well as spiritual advice. This earned him the title of "prince and metropolitan of Independency."

In 1674, Owen published *Pneumatologia*, a classic on the work of the Holy Spirit. Two years later, his wife died. Within eighteen months, he married Dorothy, the widow of Thomas D'Oyley of Chislehampton near Stadham.

Owen suffered much from asthma and gallstones in his last years, both of which often kept him from preaching. He kept writing, however, producing major works on justification, spiritual-mindedness, and the glory of Christ. The day before his death, Owen wrote to a friend, "I am going to Him whom my soul has loved, or rather who has loved me with an everlasting love—which is the whole ground of my consolation.... I am leaving the ship of the church in a storm; but whilst the great Pilot is in it, the loss of a poor under-rower will be inconsiderable. Live, and pray, and hope, and wait patiently, and do not despond; the promise stands invincible, that He will never leave us, nor forsake us."

On August 24, 1683, William Payne, a Puritan minister of Saffron Waldon, arrived to tell Owen that the first sheets of *Meditations on the Glory of Christ* had passed through the press. With uplifted eyes and hands, Owen replied, "I am glad to hear it; but, oh brother Payne, the long wished for day is come at last, in which I shall see that glory in another manner than I have ever done, or was capable of doing, in this world." Owen was buried in Bunhill Fields beside many of his Puritan contemporaries.

———◆◆◆———

The Works of John Owen (BTT; 16 vols., 9,000 pages; 1996). The contents of these volumes, reprints of the 1850–55 Goold edition, include the following:

Doctrinal (volumes 1-5). Of particular value in this section are: *On the Person and Glory of Christ* (vol. 1); *Communion with God* (vol. 2); *Discourse on the Holy Spirit* (vol. 3); *Justification by Faith* (vol. 5). To master such works as these, Spurgeon wrote, "is to be a profound theologian."

Practical (volumes 6-9). Especially worthy here are *Mortification of Sin, Temptation, Exposition of Psalm 130* (vol. 6); and *Spiritual-Mindedness* (vol. 7). Volumes 8 and 9 are comprised of sermons. These volumes are suited for the average layperson and have immense practical benefit.

Controversial (volumes 10-16). Noteworthy are *The Death of Death in the Death of Christ* and *Divine Justice* (vol. 10); *The Doctrine of the Saints' Perseverance* (vol. 11); *True Nature of a Gospel Church* and *The Divine Original of the Scriptures* (vol. 16). Several volumes in this section are of great historical value (particularly those written against Arminianism and Socinianism) but tend to be tedious for the non-theologian.

The wide range of subjects treated by Owen, the insightfulness of his writing, the exhaustive nature of his doctrinal studies, the profundity of his theology, and the warmth of his devotion explain the high regard he has among those acquainted with his works. On occasions Owen may be prolix, but he is never dry. These volumes provide an invaluable resource for all who wish to discover and explore the rich legacy left by one of the greatest British theologians of all time. Helpful indices conclude the last volume.

Dozens of Owen's treatises have been published individually in the past half century, but we would advise serious readers of Puritan literature to forego these and purchase the sixteen-volume set of Owen's works. For those who have difficulty reading Owen, we recommend R. J. K. Law's abridged simplifications of *Communion with God* (1991), *Apostasy from the Gospel* (1992), *The Glory of Christ* (1994), and *The Holy Spirit* (1998), all published by the Banner of Truth Trust.

Unabridged paperbacks of the last two titles, with helpful introductions by Sinclair Ferguson, were published in 2004 by Christian Focus.

Biblical Theology (SDG; 912 pages; 1994). Owen wrote twenty-four volumes on biblical and devotional themes, including his sixteen-volume *Works*, his seven-volume exposition on Hebrews, and the single-volume *Biblical Theology*. This book was finally translated from Latin by Stephen Westcott in 1994. *Biblical Theology* includes six books that trace biblical theology from Adam to Christ. It includes an appendix with Owen's *Defense of Scripture against Fanaticism*, affirming that the Bible is the perfect, authoritative, and complete Word of God. Though Owen considered this work his *magnum opus*, it has become one of his least-known works.

Still, as J. I. Packer writes of this book: "All the qualities we expect of Owen—the focus on God, the passion for Christ, the honoring of the Holy Spirit, the shattering depth of insight into human sinfulness and perversity, the concern for holiness, the radical view of regeneration, the vision of the church as a spiritual fellowship that worships, the distrust of philosophical schemes and styles for dealing with divine things, the celebration of God's wisdom in giving the Scriptures in the form in which we have them—all are seen here. The present treatise is vintage Owen, searching and spiritual, devotional and doxological, the product of a masterful mind and a humble heart."

The Correspondence of John Owen, 1616-1683 (JC; 190 pages; 1970). Until this book was printed, very few of Owen's letters were known; assumedly, no more existed. Peter Toon here presents much of Owen's correspondence, including letters and responses to Oliver Cromwell. Though they are not useful for devotional use, those who study Owen will appreciate their historical value. The book also includes an essay on Owen's life and work.

An Exposition of the Epistle to the Hebrews (BTT; 7 vols., 4,000 pages; 1985). This exposition of Hebrews is a definitive commentary on the epistle. As Thomas Chalmers noted: "A work of gigantic strength and size; he who hath mastered it is very little short, both in respect to the doctrinal and practical of Christianity, of being an erudite and accomplished theologian." Bogue and Bennett, in *History of Dissenters*, also highly commend the work, saying, "If the theological student should part with his coat or his bed to procure the works of Howe, he that would not sell his shirt to procure those of John Owen, and especially his Exposition, of which every sentence is precious, shows too much regard to his body, and too little for his immortal mind."

Edward Pearse
(c. 1633-1673)

Edward Pearse earned a Bachelor of Arts degree from St. John's College in 1654. In 1657, he was appointed preacher at St. Margaret's, Westminster, the historic church adjacent to Westminster Abbey in London. The following year he was appointed lecturer at Westminster Abbey.

Ejected from office in 1660, Pearse probably continued to live in London. There is some evidence that Pearse may have resumed preaching as minister of a dissenting congregation at or near Hampstead.

Pearse died of tuberculosis at about age forty. When he knew that death was imminent, he fretted that he had done so little of what he intended for the Lord, and prayed that some of his work might be useful after his death.

Little is known of Pearse's family. His wife's name was Grace, and he left provision in his will for a daughter, Sarah, then about nine years of age.

A *Beam of Divine Glory* (SDG; 190 pages; 1998). This is Pearse's masterpiece on divine immutability. In it he shows that the unchangeableness of God is the greatest comfort to saints and the greatest terror to sinners. Attached to this work is a treatise on the soul's rest in God, based on Ps. 116:7. That subject naturally proceeds from and beautifully harmonizes with Pearse's study on the unchanging nature of God. God's immutability is the wellspring of the comfort that believing souls find in Him.

In the foreword to this work, John Howe writes of Pearse: "While he lived here on earth, he saw many changes passing over himself, both as to his person and condition. This put him upon the contemplation of the unchangeableness of God, and caused him to seek for that rest in God which he could not find in himself, nor in anything here below. Those who observed his spirit clearly perceived that he was much quickened and helped, as to his spiritual state, by meditating much on a holy rest in God."

The Best Match (SDG; 216 pages; 2001). Subtitled "The Soul's Espousal to Christ," this is Pearse's best-known work. It shows how Christ woos His bride, the church; what it means to be espoused to Christ; and how Christ is a great Husband to His bride. Pearse treats this subject with warmth. The work is charged with experiential vitality and liberally sprinkled with gospel exhortations. It is a work of great spiritual value.

William Pemble

(1591-1623)

William Pemble, a learned Calvinistic theologian and author, was born to a poor clergyman in 1591 at Egerton, Kent. He was educated at Magdalen College, Oxford, where Richard Capel, a Puritan, was his tutor. Pemble earned a Bachelor of Arts degree in 1614, then moved to Magdalen Hall, where he became a noted divinity reader and tutor. He took his Master of Arts degree in 1618.

Pemble was a gifted Hebrew scholar. He used that knowledge to great advantage in explaining difficult passages of Scripture, such as *Solomon's Recantation and Repentance* (1627), a commentary on Ecclesiastes; *A Short and Sweet Exposition upon the First Nine Chapters of Zachariah* (1629); and *The Period of the Persian Monarchy* (1631), an explanation of the most challenging parts of Ezra, Nehemiah, and Daniel.

He was also a famous preacher and an excellent writer. In *An Introduction to the Worthy Receiving the Sacrament* (1628), Pemble argues for frequent communion and careful, personal examination. In *Tractatus de providential Dei* (1631), Pemble explains providence as "God's action in preserving, governing, and disposing everything, including their intermediate as well as ultimate ends."

Because of his emphasis on God's eternal justification of the elect sinner, Pemble has sometimes been called a "high" or "hyper" Calvinist. Those tendencies appear most clearly in his *Vindiciae gratiae* (1627), in which he espouses a supralapsarian view of predestination, asserts that justification precedes faith, and argues that sanctification operates without any assistance from the believer because of his corrupt nature. Richard Baxter later criticized Pemble in his writings for these high Calvinist views.

Philosophy and geography were other interests of Pemble, to which he devoted several books. His exertions in preaching and his extreme devotion to his studies and writings took their toll on his body. While visiting the home of Capel, his former tutor, Pemble came down with a fever and died on April 14, 1623.

All of Pemble's writings were published posthumously through the efforts of Capel. These were then collected and published in one volume in 1635 as *The Works of William Pemble*, which was reprinted several times in the seventeenth century. They influenced Richard Baxter away from Arminianism, and helped shape the high Calvinist tendencies of John Gill and John Brine.

⇒◆◆◆⇐

The Justification of a Sinner: A Treatise on Justification by Faith Alone (SDG; 257 pages; 2002). First published in 1625 as *Vindiciae Fidei*, this book contains writings that were originally delivered as lectures at Magdalen Hall, Oxford. In them, Pemble shows how faith in the finished work of Christ is what justifies the sinner. "Who satisfies God's justice for sin, Christ or us?" he asks. He asserts that the Protestant understanding of justification is irreconcilable with Roman Catholic and Arminian positions. He refutes the position of Robert Bellarmine (1542–1621), the Roman church's champion of that era, calling him "the rotten pillar of the antichristian synagogue" (p. 167).

But he also challenges the Arminian position as espoused by Socinus, Servetus, and Arminius.

All the essential biblical truths about justification are here. Pemble proves that justification is by faith alone, solidly refuting the Arminian notion that faith itself is imputed to believers rather than the righteousness of Christ. He shows that faith has no merit to deserve or earn justification, correctly distinguishes between justification and sanctification (p. 21), and ably grapples with differences between Paul and James on justification. He affirms that good works are in part sinful (p. 134), and reminds us of the Puritan emphasis that the inclination or proneness to sin is sin. The guilt of original sin is imputed to us through Adam as our covenant head, and its pollution is passed on to us from Adam as the father of us all.

Although Pemble confronts the erroneous doctrines of justification existing in his own day, the work is still valuable for today since no biblical treatment of the doctrine of justification could ever be wholly outdated. Furthermore, the errors refuted by Pemble have not disappeared. We stand greatly in need of a biblical arsenal of spiritual weapons to battle modern heresies that besiege the church. Pemble's work will amply reward the careful reader with such weapons.

William Perkins

(1558-1602)

William Perkins was born in 1558 to Thomas and Hannah Perkins in the village of Marston Jabbett, in Bulkington parish, Warwickshire. As a youth, he indulged in recklessness, profanity, and drunkenness. In 1577, he entered Christ's College in Cambridge as a pensioner, suggesting that socially he nearly qualified as gentry. He earned a bachelor's degree in 1581 and a master's degree in 1584.

While a student, Perkins experienced a powerful conversion that probably began when he overheard a woman in the street chide her naughty child by alluding to "drunken Perkins." That incident so humiliated Perkins that he gave up his wicked ways and fled to Christ for salvation. He gave up the study of mathematics and his fascination with black magic and the occult, and took up theology. In time, he joined up with Laurence Chaderton (1536–1640), who became his personal tutor and lifelong friend. Perkins and Chaderton met with Richard Greenham, Richard Rogers, and others in a spiritual brotherhood at Cambridge that espoused Calvinist and Puritan convictions.

Cambridge was the leading Puritan center of the day. Perkins's formal training was Calvinism within a scholastic framework. The strict scholastic training at Cambridge was modified somewhat, however, by Peter Ramus's influence. Ramism had won the support of the Puritans, due to its practicality. Ramus, a converted Roman Catholic, had reformed

WILLIAM PERKINS

the arts curriculum by applying it to daily life. He proposed a method to simplify all academic subjects, offering a single logic for both dialectic and rhetoric to make them understandable and memorable. Chaderton first introduced Ramus's *Art of Logick* to Cambridge students, particularly to Gabriel Harvey, a lecturer who used Ramus's methods for reforming the arts of grammar, rhetoric, and logic.

Perkins was impressed with Harvey's presentation and applied it to his manual on preaching titled *The Art of Prophesying, or a treatise concerning the sacred and only true manner and method of preaching.* Perkins's training in Ramus's method oriented him toward practical application rather than speculative theory, and gave him skills for becoming a popular preacher and theologian.

From 1584 until his death, Perkins served as lecturer, or preacher, at Great St. Andrew's Church, Cambridge, a most influential pulpit across the street from Christ's College. He also served as a fellow at Christ's College from 1584 to 1595. Fellows were required to preach, lecture, and tutor students, acting as guides to learning as well as guardians of finances, morals, and manners.

On July 2, 1595, Perkins resigned his fellowship to marry a young widow. That motivated Samuel Ward, later Lady Margaret Professor of Divinity, to respond in his diary, "Good Lord, grant...there follow no ruin to the college." Men such as Ward counted it a great blessing to sit under Perkins's teaching and to witness his exemplary living.

Perkins served the university in other capacities. He was dean of Christ's College from 1590 to 1591. He catechized the students at Corpus Christi College on Thursday afternoons, lecturing on the Ten Commandments in a manner that deeply impressed the students. On Sunday afternoons, he worked as an adviser, counseling the spiritually distressed.

Perkins had exceptional gifts for preaching and an uncanny ability to reach common people with plain preaching and theology. He pioneered Puritan casuistry—the art of dealing with "cases of conscience" by self-examination and scriptural diagnosis. Many people were convicted of sin and delivered from bondage under his preaching. The prisoners of the Cambridge jail were among the first to benefit from his powerful preaching. Perkins "would pronounce the word *damn* with such an emphasis as left a doleful Echo in his auditors' ears a good while after," wrote Thomas Fuller. "Many an Onesimus in bonds was converted to Christ" (*Abel Redevivus*, 2:145-46).

Samuel Clarke offers a striking example of Perkins's pastoral care. He says a condemned prisoner was climbing the gallows, looking half-dead, when Perkins said to him, "What man! What is the matter with thee? Art thou afraid of death?" The prisoner confessed that he was less afraid of death than of what would follow it. "Sayest thou so," said Perkins. "Come down again man and thou shalt see what God's grace will do to strengthen thee."

When the prisoner came down, they knelt together, hand in hand, and Perkins offered "such an effectual prayer in confession of sins...as made the poor prisoner burst out into abundance of tears." Convinced the prisoner was brought "low enough, even to Hell gates," Perkins showed him the gospel in prayer. Clarke writes that the prisoner's eyes were opened "to see how the black lines of all his sins were crossed, and cancelled with the red lines of his crucified Savior's precious blood; so graciously applying it to his wounded conscience, as made him break out into new showers of tears for joy of the inward consolation which he found." The prisoner rose from his knees, went cheerfully up the ladder, testified of salvation in Christ's blood, and bore his death with patience, "as if he actually saw himself delivered from the Hell which he feared before, and heaven opened for the receiving of his soul, to the great rejoicing of the beholders" (*The Marrow of Ecclesiastical History*, pp. 416-17).

Perkins's sermons were of many "colours," writes Fuller. They seemed to be "all Law and all gospel, all cordials and all corrosives, as the different necessities of people apprehended." He was able to reach many types of people in various classes, being "systematic, scholarly, solid and simple at the same time." As Fuller says, "His church consisting of the university and town, the scholar could have no learneder, the townsmen [no] plainer, sermons." Most importantly, he lived his sermons: "As his preaching was a comment on his text, so his practice was a comment on his preaching," Fuller concludes (*Abel Redevivus*, 2:148, 151).

Perkins aimed to wed predestinarian preaching with practical, experiential living. He refused to see the relationship between God's sovereignty and man's responsibility as antagonistic but treated them as "friends" who need no reconciliation.

Like Chaderton, his mentor, Perkins worked to purify the established church from within rather than joining Puritans who advocated separation. Instead of addressing church polity, he focused on addressing pastoral inadequacies, spiritual deficiencies, and soul-destroying ignorance in the church.

In time, Perkins as rhetorician, expositor, theologian, and pastor became the principle architect of the Puritan movement. His vision of reform for the church, combined with his intellect, piety, writing, spiritual counseling, and communication skills, enabled him to set the tone for the seventeenth-century Puritan accent on Reformed, experiential truth and self-examination, and their polemic against Roman Catholicism and Arminianism. Fuller said of Perkins, who was disabled in his right hand, "This Ehud, with a left-handed pen did stab the Romish cause." By the time of his death, Perkins's writings in England were outselling those of

Calvin, Beza, and Bullinger combined. He "moulded the piety of a whole nation," H.C. Porter said (*Reformation and Reaction in Tudor Cambridge*, p. 260).

Perkins died from kidney stone complications in 1602, just before the end of Queen Elizabeth's reign. His wife of seven years was pregnant at the time; she was caring for three small children as well as sorrowing over three children recently lost to various diseases. Perkins's closest friend, James Montagu, later bishop of Winchester, preached the funeral sermon for Perkins from Joshua 1:2, "Moses my servant is dead." Ward, deeply distressed, wrote on behalf of many: "God knows his death is likely to be an irrevocable loss and a great judgment to the university, seeing there is none to supply his place" (M. M. Knappen, ed., *Two Elizabethan Puritan Diaries*, p. 130). Perkins was buried in the churchyard of Great St. Andrews. His sizable library was purchased by William Bedell, one of Perkins's students who became bishop of Kilmore and Ardagh.

Eleven editions of Perkins's writings, containing nearly fifty treatises, were printed after his death. His major writings include expositions of Galatians 1-5, Matthew 5-7, Hebrews 11, Jude, and Revelation 1-3, as well as treatises on predestination, the order of salvation, assurance of faith, the Apostle's Creed, the Lord's Prayer, the worship of God, the Christian life and vocation, ministry and preaching, the errors of Roman Catholicism, and various cases of conscience. His writings, popularized for lay readers, are Bible-based in accord with the principles of literal and contextual interpretation established by the Reformers. They are practically and experientially Calvinistic, continually focusing on motives, desires, and distresses in the heart and life of sinners, ever aiming at finding and following the path of eternal life. For pietistic emphasis, Perkins usually uses a Ramistic method that presents the definition of the subject and its further partition, often by dichotomies, into progressively more heads or topics, applying each truth set forth.

Perkins's influence continued through such theologians as William Ames (1576-1633), Richard Sibbes (1577-1635), John Cotton (1585-1652), and John Preston (1587-1628). Cotton considered Perkins's ministry the "one good reason why there came so many excellent preachers out of Cambridge in England, more than out of Oxford." Thomas Goodwin (1600-1680) wrote that when he entered Cambridge, six of his instructors who had sat under Perkins were still passing on his teaching. Ten years after Perkins's death, Cambridge was still "filled with the discourse of the power of Mr. William Perkins' ministry," Goodwin said.

The translation of Perkins's writings prompted greater theological discussion between England and the Continent. J. van der Haar records 185 seventeenth-century printings in Dutch of Perkins's individual or collected works, twice as many as any other Puritan (*From Abbadie to Young: A Bibliography of English, mostly Puritan, Works, Translated i/o Dutch Language,* 1:96-108). He and Ames, his most influential student on the continent, influenced Gisbertus Voetius (1589-1676) and numerous Dutch *Nadere Reformatie* (Further Reformation) theologians. At least fifty editions of Perkins's works were printed in Switzerland and in various parts of Germany. His writings were also translated into Spanish, French, Italian, Irish, Welsh, Hungarian, and Czech.

Nearly one hundred Cambridge men who grew up in Perkins's shadow led early migrations to New England, including William Brewster of Plymouth, Thomas Hooker of Connecticut, John Winthrop of Massachusetts Bay, and Roger Williams of Rhode Island. Richard Mather was converted while reading Perkins, and Jonathan Edwards was fond of reading Perkins more than a century later. Samuel Morison remarked that "your typical Plymouth Colony library comprised a large and a small bible, Ainsworth's translation of the Psalms, and the works of William Perkins, a favorite theologian" (*The Intellectual Life of New England*, 2nd ed., p. 134).

"Anyone who reads the writings of early New England learns that Perkins was indeed a towering figure in their eyes," wrote Perry Miller. Perkins and his followers were "the most quoted, most respected, and most influential of contemporary authors in the writings and sermons of early Massachusetts."

The Works of William Perkins (Sutton Courtenay Press; 646 pages; 1970). Edited and introduced by Ian Breward, this volume contains five hundred carefully selected pages extracted from the writings of Perkins. It is divided into four sections: theological writings, worship and preaching, practical writings, and polemical writings. The whole is prefaced with a masterful 131-page introduction, covering five topics: Perkins's life, Perkins and the Elizabethan church, the ministry of the gospel, the direction of conscience, and grace and assurance. Breward is highly qualified to write this introduction since his doctoral dissertation was on the life and theology of Perkins. Breward seeks to "illustrate something of the range of Perkins's activity and the structure of his divinity" by the works that he includes. For this reason, anyone wishing to appreciate the significance of the work of William Perkins will find this a helpful place to start, though this volume is no substitute for reading Perkins's complete works in the original.

*The Art of Prophesying (BTT; 191 pages; 1996). This provides a classic exposition of the Puritan practice of "prophesying," i.e. preaching, or "speaking forth the truth of God's Word." Three things prompted Perkins to write it: the dearth of able preachers in Elizabethan England, the inadequate provision for the training of ministers, and his distaste for the sermonic style and structure of the "High-Church Anglicans."

Perkins explains how preaching should be done. He presents the method by which Scripture must be interpreted, sets forth the principles by which Scripture must be expounded, and describes various ways in which Scripture must be applied to various kinds of hearers. Perkins divides listeners into seven categories:

(1) *Ignorant and unteachable unbelievers.* They need to be prepared to receive the doctrine of the Word by clear, reasonable teaching as well as by reproof and pricking of their consciences.

(2) *Ignorant but teachable unbelievers.* Perkins says these must be catechized in the foundational doctrines of the Christian religion. He recommends his book written for that purpose, *Foundations of the Christian Religion,* which covers the subjects of repentance, faith, the sacraments, the application of the Word, the resurrection, and the last judgment.

(3) *Those who have some knowledge but remain unhumbled.* To them the preacher must especially proclaim the law to stir within them sorrow and repentance for sin, followed by the preaching of the gospel.

(4) *The humbled.* The preacher must not give comfort to such people too soon, but must first determine whether their humility results from God's saving work rooted in faith or from mere common conviction. To the partly humbled who are not yet stripped of their righteousness, Perkins says that the law must be propounded yet more, albeit tempered with the gospel, so that "being terrified with their sins, and with the meditation of God's judgment, they may together at the same instant receive solace by the gospel." To the fully humbled, "the doctrine of faith and repentance, and the comforts of the gospel ought to be proclaimed and tendered."

(5) *Those who believe.* Believers need to be taught the key doctrines of justification, sanctification, and perseverance, along with the law as the rule of conduct rather than as a sting and curse. "Before faith, the law with the curse is to be

preached; after conversion, the law without the curse," Perkins writes.

(6) *Those who are fallen, either in faith or in practice.* Those who backslide in faith fall in knowledge or in apprehending Christ. If they fall in knowledge, they are to be instructed in the particular doctrine from which they have erred. If they fail to apprehend Christ, they should examine themselves by the marks of grace, then fly to Christ as the remedy of the gospel. Those who fall in practice are those who fall into some sinful behavior. They need to be brought to repentance by the preaching of the law and the gospel.

(7) *A mixed group.* These people are not easy to categorize because they are a combination of the first six kinds of listeners. Much wisdom is needed to know how much law and how much gospel to bring to them.

The practical nature of this work, the plain language in which the subject matter is presented, and the depth of insight possessed by its author are all reasons why the modern reader should acquaint himself with this valuable work.

This edition has been extensively edited by Sinclair Ferguson for modern readers. Attached is a tract titled *The Calling of the Ministry.* This tract offers expositions of Job 33:23-34 and Isaiah 6, in which Perkins directs the reader to the duties of the minister of the gospel.

*A *Commentary on Galatians,* edited by Gerald T. Sheppard (Pilgrim; 700 pages; 1989). This volume contains a facsimile of the last book Perkins wrote, a massive work on Galatians (1617 edition). Ralph Cudworth, Perkins's posthumous editor, added commentary on the last chapter of Galatians.

The volume includes four introductory essays, two of which ably reflect on Perkins's expositional skills. The essay by John H. Augustine, "Authority and Interpretation in Perkins' *Commentary on Galatians*" (pp. xvii-xlvii) is particularly insightful.

*A Commentary on Hebrews 11, edited by John H. Augustine (Pilgrim; 300 pages; 1991). This volume contains a facsimile of Perkins's sermons on Hebrews 11 (1609 edition) and includes four introductory essays. Most helpful is Richard Muller's "William Perkins and the Protestant Exegetical Tradition: Interpretation, Style and Method" (pp. 71-94).

Perkins's work on Hebrews 11 serves as a window as to how the Puritans effectively used biographical illustration and exemplary preaching in both England and New England. Throughout, Perkins merges the Reformed doctrine of divine justification with sanctified living.

*The Foundation of Christian Religion, Gathered into Six Principles (PA; 40 pages; 2004). This work was written to combat ignorance of the essential teachings of Christianity so that church members might be fit, as Perkins writes on the title page, "to hear sermons with profit, and to receive the Lord's Supper with comfort." The first part of the work states six plain and easy principles in question-and-answer format, and briefly gives proof for each answer out of God's Word. The six principles treat God, man's fallen condition, Jesus Christ, the way of salvation by faith, the means of grace, and the state of men after death. The second part, also arranged catechetically, investigates the principles more fully.

*William Perkins, 1558-1602: English Puritanist. His Pioneer Works on Casuistry: "A Discourse of Conscience" and "The Whole Treatise of Cases of Conscience," edited by Thomas Merrill (DeGraaf; 242 pages; 1966). In this volume, Merrill includes two works of Perkins on casuistry (i.e., dealing with "cases of conscience"). The former is theoretical in nature. Its full title is *A Discourse of Conscience Wherein is Set Down the Nature, Properties, and Differences thereof: as also the Way to Get and Keep a Good Conscience.* This was written largely to help those struggling with the question of assurance.

The second work focuses more on Perkins's concern for the individual and social aspects of Christian morality. As Merrill notes, "It is concerned with presenting guidelines for the resolving of typical moral dilemmas that confront Christians in all phases of their lives. Since it was generally acknowledged that man was a member of three societies: the family, the church and the commonwealth, the work is divided into three books, the first concerning 'Man simply considered in himself without relation to another,' the second, 'Man as he stands in relation to God,' and finally, 'Man as he stands in relation to other men.'" In this last section, Perkins discusses at length current issues of his day, such as "the right use of money, truth and falsehood, the right use of leisure, the Christian attitude toward war, vows and promises, proper dress, the lawfulness of recreation, policy and prudence."

The art of casuistry has been much neglected by the modern church. Many who claim to be firmly committed to the authority of the Word of God will nonetheless espouse the use of subjective, situational, and autonomous ethics in specific cases of conscience. However, for Christians who wish to be faithful to God in the details of life without losing sight of the "weightier matters of the law," Perkins's work is a good place to start.

Edward Polhill

(c. 1622-c. 1694)

Edward Polhill was probably born in 1622 in Burwash, Sussex. He was the son of Edward Polhill, Sr., rector of the neighboring parish of Etchingham, by his second wife, Jane, the daughter of William Newton of Lewes. The young Edward entered Gray's Inn in 1638 to study law, but he afterward spent much of his time caring for his family's estate in Burwash, Sussex, and being active in local legal and civil affairs. In 1653, he was appointed as a Sussex county judge, overseeing relief for creditors and prisoners. He probably also served as justice of the peace for some years.

Polhill devoted most of his private hours to reading, analyzing, and writing religious treatises. Though he felt affinity with Puritan theology and sympathized with nonconformist ministers following the Restoration, Polhill seems to have remained a conforming member of the Church of England.

Polhill's first treatise, *The Divine Will* (1673), included a preface by the Independent leader, John Owen. In his *An Answer to the Discourse of William Sherlock* (1675), Polhill defended Owen's position on the sufficiency of faith for salvation. Seven years later, in his *The Samaritan* (1682), Polhill wrote that "the Church of England had only herself to blame for the ongoing divisions with moderate nonconformists by insisting on unreasonable conditions for communion." His *Discourse of Schism* (1694) explicitly defends Nonconformists from the charges of schism (*Oxford DNB*, 44:742-43).

In his final years, Polhill became blind. He died in late 1693 or early 1694. Lazarus Seaman, who claimed to have known Polhill from his childhood, testified to Polhill's intense, Puritan-minded piety.

—◆◆◆—

The Works of Edward Polhill (SDG; 359 pages; 1998). No collected edition of Polhill's works existed until 1844, from which this edition is reprinted. *The Works* contains four of Polhill's writings. "A View of Some Divine Truths," published in 1678, is Polhill's elaborate defense of evangelical divinity. He discusses God's nature, justice, love, power, truth, providence, and the Christian's duty towards a holy life. In the preface to the work, Polhill wrote: "The devout Father could not relish any thing but Jesus Christ; may our hearts ever burn and be inflamed with love to him, in whom are hid all the treasures of wisdom and knowledge."

The second work, "The Divine Will Considered in Its Decrees," printed in 1673, explains the nature of God's will and the eternal decrees of election and predestination. In this treatise Polhill unfortunately argues for some form of universal redemption, much the same as John Davenant and John Preston do. John Owen, who read Polhill's work, critiqued him on this point, but still highly commended the book.

The third work, "Precious Faith Considered in its Nature, Working, and Growth," was published in 1675. It contains some of Polhill's best work. In fourteen chapters, Polhill chronicles the life of faith, culminating in a discussion of the assurance of faith and how it is attained. He offers thirteen practical helps to his readers. Polhill concludes by writing, "The believer having arrived at assurance, which is the highest step on this side of heaven, may sit down with joy upon his head, and begin that song of free grace and the Lamb; which is sung above, though in higher tune, in the heavenly quire of angels and glorified saints for ever and ever" (p. 324).

The fourth work, "A Preparation for Suffering in the Evil Day in an Evil Day, Showing How Christians are to Bear Sufferings, and What Graces are Requisite Thereunto," was printed in 1682. In this most comforting writing, Polhill notes that he has no other purpose but to show how Christians are to bear suffering, and what graces are required to do it.

Cotton Mather wrote: "Everything of Polhill is evangelical and valuable."

MATTHEW POOLE

Matthew Poole

(1624-1679)

Matthew Poole, famous for his concise commentary on the Bible, was born at York in 1624. After earning a Bachelor of Arts degree from Emmanuel College, Cambridge, in 1649, he accepted a call to the ministry at a Presbyterian parish, St. Michael le Querne, in London, where he succeeded Anthony Tuckney. In 1657, Poole earned a Master of Arts degree from Oxford.

In 1658, Poole published *A Model for the Maintaining of Students of Choice Abilities at the University, and principally in order to the Ministry*, in which he advocated that certain ministerial students should receive aid from a permanent fund. The plan drew considerable attention. It was supported by John Arrowsmith, Ralph Cudworth, and other divines. Though it was cut short by the Restoration, it gave Poole recognition throughout England, paving the way for acceptance of his later writings.

After the Restoration in 1660, Poole published a sermon that he had preached before the mayor of London, in which he argued that the liturgy of the Church of England should not be reinstituted. In 1662, Poole refused to comply with the Act of Uniformity and was ejected from his pastorate. For the next twenty years, he apparently made no attempt to gather a congregation, but instead worked mostly in solitude.

During that time, Poole wrote prolifically. His first major work was *Synopsis Criticorum aliorumque Sacrae Scripturae*

Interpretum (1669-1676), a five-volume work that compiled and abridged the work of biblical commentators from all ages and nations. The first four thousand sets sold quickly, and by 1712 it had gone through five printings. The merit of this work is partly its wide range of contributors, including rabbinical sources and even some Roman Catholic commentators. The other strength is Poole's skill in condensing lengthy comments into crisp, helpful notes. This work, though famous in its day, was never translated from Latin into English.

Poole began compiling *Synopsis Criticorum* in 1666 and worked on it every day for ten years. His plan was to study from 4 a.m. until supper, stopping only to eat a raw egg at 8:30 a.m. and another egg at noon. In the evening he visited friends.

After completing the *Synopsis*, Poole began a smaller series of annotations in English. Today that commentary, first published as *Annotations Upon the Holy Bible* in 1683-85, is second only to Matthew Henry's in fame among Reformed ministers and lay people.

Poole frequently wrote against Roman Catholicism, particularly in *The Nullity of the Romish Faith concerning the Church's Infallibility* (1666) and *Dialogues Between a Popish Priest and an English Protestant* (1667). Not surprisingly, his name was added to the list published in 1679 by Titus Oates of those that Rome wished to destroy in the Popish Plot.

Later that year, Poole and a companion left a friend's house late one evening. On the way home, in a narrow lane, two men were waiting to ambush him. When one cried out, "Here he is!" the other responded, "Leave him alone, for someone is with him." Upon arriving home, Poole said to his friend, "I would have been murdered tonight, if you had not been with me." Having narrowly escaped assassination, Poole decided to move to the Netherlands. He died soon after in Amsterdam, possibly from being poisoned.

Poole was known for the depth of his learning, his skilled biblical commentary, and his gifts in casuistry. Calamy wrote that Poole was "very true to his friend, very strict in his piety, and universal in his charity."

———◆◆◆———

A Commentary on the Whole Bible (BTT; 3 vols., 3,000 pages; 1983). Poole's commentary is clear and concise. He is an excellent exegete. Spurgeon comments: "Poole is not so pithy and witty by far as Matthew Henry, but he is perhaps more accurate, less a commentator, and more an expositor." Like Henry, Poole did not live to complete his work. He died after working through Isaiah 58. Happily, Poole left behind many notes as well as his *Synopsis Criticorum*, from which material was gleaned to finish the commentary.

Poole's commentary is somewhat shorter than Henry's and somewhat longer than *The Dutch Annotations*, which are well known in the Netherlands. Richard Cecil observed, "Commentators are excellent where there are but few difficulties; but they leave the harder knots still untied; but after all, Poole is incomparable."

In our opinion, this is the best basic Puritan commentary for daily Bible study.

John Preston

(1587-1628)

John Preston was born on October 27, 1587, at Upper Hey-
ford in the parish of Bugbrooke, Northamptonshire. His
father, a farmer, died when Preston was twelve years old. A
maternal uncle provided for Preston's training at King's
College (1604-1606) and Queen's College, Cambridge (1606-
1607), where he primarily studied philosophy. After earning a
Bachelor of Arts degree in 1607, Preston became a fellow of
Queen's (1609) and prebendary of Lincoln Cathedral (1610).
About that time, he decided to study medicine and
astrology [i.e., astronomy], which was then valued as a handmaid to medicine.

In 1611, Preston took a Master of Arts degree. Shortly after
that, God brought Preston to conversion under the preaching
of John Cotton. Preston, along with other students, came to
hear Cotton to ridicule his plain style of exposition. During
this time, Cotton felt led by God to proclaim a simple, pointed
sermon even though he knew it would not gain much applause. He sighed to the Lord: "Lord, I have counted the cost,
let me count it loss for Thee." Later that evening, Preston
knocked at his door. God had told him that one thing was
needful—not an oratorical appointment at court or some lu-
crative practice as a physician, but the salvation of his soul. He

came to Cotton with searching questions. The two became lifelong friends.

In due season, the Lord provided comfort in Christ for the young Preston. He changed his course of study to divinity, specializing in Thomas Aquinas, Duns Scotus, and William of Ockham, followed by the Reformers, especially Calvin. After his conversion, Preston became a great influence in various notable ways.

Preston first of all became a valued politician. He first gained the attention of the king's court in 1615 through the Duke of Buckingham, who wanted to strengthen the Puritan influence at court. As court chaplain, Preston often called believers to "plotting"—that is, to prayer and fasting in times of political crisis, particularly on issues fought between Puritans and High Church men. He also used his influence to promote the appointment of Puritans in public offices. Until that time, the Puritans had failed to establish Presbyterian church government and were disappointed in their political efforts. Many of the strongest Puritans had gone into exile. But under the influence of Preston, the Puritan spirit revived politically. In *Prince Charles's Puritan Chaplain*, Irvonwy Morgan stated that Preston's real importance to the Puritan movement was in the sphere of politics (p. 206).

Preston also became an influential teacher. As a fellow at Queen's, he tutored numerous men who would become influential preachers or politicians. In 1622, two years after earning a Bachelor of Divinity degree, Preston became master of Emmanuel College in Cambridge, taking with him twelve students from Queen's who were frequently referred to as the "twelve disciples." The following year, he was awarded a doctorate in divinity by royal mandate.

Preston's work at Emmanuel became part of the ongoing conflict between Calvinism and Arminianism. In 1626, Richard Montague, an Arminian, influenced the court to convene a conference to discuss the doctrines of the Church of England in relation to the Canons of Dort. Despite Preston's efforts, the conference decided that the Church of England should not "borrow a new faith from any village in the Netherlands." In response, Preston motivated a number of Puritans to begin a significant pamphlet war condemning Arminianism, which was very much on the rise.

Preston trained his students to begin their studies of theology by reading modern theologians such as Calvin and his own *Sum of Theology*, then broaden their study by reading the Schoolmen and the Fathers, thus reversing the chronological order commonly pursued in his day.

In theology Preston stressed the covenant (see his *The New Covenant, or The Saint's Portion*) and assurance of faith. He taught that the most important mark of grace was zeal, which he defined as "the intention of all holy affections and holy actions." The supreme "intention" is to know Christ and to live for Him by love, Preston said. Such zeal differentiates the living Christian from the formal Christian by its inward motions of life. In *The New Covenant*, Preston explained: "A woman many times thinks she is with child, but if she find no motion or stirring, it is an argument that she was deceived. So, when a man thinks he hath faith in his heart, but yet he finds no life, no motion, no stirring, there is no work proceeding from his faith, it is an argument he was mistaken, he was deceived in it; for if it be a right faith, it will work, there will be life and motion in it."

Preston also became a great preacher. About 1618, he was appointed dean and catechist of Queen's College. He preached a series of sermons there that would later be the foundation of his body of divinity. These sermons became so popular that anyone who was not a faculty member or the student of the college was forbidden to attend. Preston then began an afternoon lecture at St. Botolph's, which brought him into conflict with Dr. Newcombe, a commissary to the chancellor of Ely, who denounced him as a Nonconformist. At the suggestion of Lancelot Andrewes, then bishop of Ely, Preston explained how he felt about form prayers in a sermon at St. Botolph's. That silenced the complaints.

In 1622, Preston succeeded John Donne (1573-1631) as preacher at Lincoln's Inn. As chaplain, he preached often before the king and the court. In 1624, he was offered the lectureship at Trinity Church. That appointment won back for the Puritans the most influential preaching position in Cambridge, which had originated with Sibbes. It was one of the last victories of the Puritans at court.

Preston was in the mainstream of the Puritan "spiritual preachers" who aimed for saving souls and sanctifying believers rather than theorizing about theology. Richard Sibbes and John Cotton were Preston's mentors. In turn, his preaching influenced such men as Thomas Goodwin and Thomas Shepard.

Some have called Preston the leading Puritan of the 1620s, primarily because of his preaching. After hearing Preston's sermon before the king, Bishop Neile complained: "He talked like one that was familiar with God."

Finally, Preston became an author of renown. His numerous books became extremely popular. Eleven volumes of his sermons were published within a decade after his death; some of these were reprinted ten or more times. Surprisingly, no publisher has reformatted his books and issued a multi-volume set of his works.

Preston's intense labors were hard on him; he died in 1628 at the age of forty. John Dod, minister at Fawsley, preached his funeral sermon; Preston was buried in Fawsley Church. Many who had benefited from his various ministries mourned him.

Preston espoused a modified and moderate form of Calvinism. Especially his later sermons reveal that he embraced the system of English hypothetical universalism, teaching that Christ died for all without exception and placing great stress on human responsibility in the covenant relation-ship. He also stressed more traditional Puritan themes such as assurance of faith and the need for self-examination prior to partaking of the Lord's Supper. On his deathbed, Preston chose four men to be the editors of his writings, none of which were yet published: Richard Sibbes, John Davenport, Thomas Goodwin, and John Ball. Unquestionably, Preston's greatest legacy "was the subsequent flood of published editions of his sermons, through which he continued to have a great influence on 'the godly' in England and New England. His works...were critical in establishing a new spiritual genre of protestant devotional publication, through Dutch-language editions among others" (*Oxford DNB*, 45:263).

The Breastplate of Faith and Love (BTT; 560 pages; 1979). Preston's written sermons became nearly as popular as his preached sermons. This book consists of eighteen sermons (expounding Romans 1:17; 1 Thessalonians 1:3; Galatians 5:6) and is rich in spiritual instruction for those who are willing to read a facsimile.

The Golden Scepter Held Forth to the Humble (SDG; 248 pages; 1990). Based on 2 Chronicles 7:14, this work discusses affliction, humiliation, seeking God's face, turning from evil, forgiveness, and sin. Preston concludes, "Whatsoever a man's sins, if he be truly humbled for them and forsake them, they shall be forgiven him" (p. 216).

Preston's work excels in illustrations. Here's one example: "Learn to see sin in its own colors. Sin is a secret and invisible evil, and in itself, is difficult to be seen even by the most experienced. Therefore, look upon sin as it is clothed with calamities; and when you view it under the clothing, you will have another opinion of it than you had before" (p. 240).

Irresistibleness of Converting Grace (PA; 26 pages; 2005). Preston gives a defense of the Reformed teaching that God "turneth sinners unto Himself after an irresistible manner." After explaining both the Arminian and Reformed views, Preston shows that the Reformed view of the irresistibility of saving grace is scriptural.

The Saint's Daily Exercise (WJ; 150 pages; 1976). The subtitle on the 1629 London printing of this work is "A Treatise concerning the whole duty of prayer. Delivered in five Sermons upon 1 Thessalonians 5:17." Though this is a facsimile reprint, its practical instruction is worth the effort to read. Let one example suffice in which Preston answers the objection of one who feels unfit to pray and therefore tries to fit himself for prayer by meditation. He advises that the best preparation for prayer is simply to pray immediately:

> The very doing of the duty is the first preparation to it. For example, if a man were to run a race, if he were to do any bodily exercise, there must be strength of body, he must be fed well, that he may have ability, but the use of the very exercise itself, the very particular act, that is of the same kind with the exercise, is the best to fit him to for it; so in this duty of prayer, it is true, to be strong in the inward man, to have much knowledge, to have much grace, makes a man able, and fit for duty; but, if you speak of the immediate preparation for it, I say, the best way to prepare us, is the very duty itself; as all actions, of the same kind, increase the habits, so prayer makes us fit for prayers; and that is a rule, the way to godliness is in the compass of godliness itself, that is, the way to grow in any grace is the exercise of that grace.

Nathanael Ranew

(c. 1602-1677)

Nathanael Ranew was admitted to Emmanuel College, Cambridge, in 1617. He graduated with a Bachelor of Arts degree in 1621 and a Master of Arts degree in 1624. Three years later, he was ordained at Peterborough, and became the minister of St. Andrew Hubbard, Little Eastcheap, London, about 1644. The following year he became rector of West Hanningfield, Essex. In 1648, he was instituted under parliamentary order to the vicarage of Felsted, Essex, filling the vacancy left by the death of Samuel Wharton.

That same year Ranew subscribed to the Solemn League and Covenant. Two years later, the triers reported that he was "an able, godly minister."

After being ejected from Felsted in 1662 for nonconformity, Ranew settled in Billericay. In 1672, he was licensed locally as a teacher in the house of a Mr. Finch, which was licensed the same day as a Presbyterian meeting house.

Ranew died in Billericay in 1677 and was buried there. Edmund Calamy wrote of him: "He was a judicious divine, and a good historian, which made his conversation very pleasant. He was generally esteemed and valued."

Solitude Improved by Divine Meditation (SDG; 350 pages; 1995). This treatise is based on the premise that time spent alone is profitable for meditation. Subtitled *A Treatise proving* *the Duty, and demonstrating the Necessity, Excellency, Usefulness, Natures, Kinds, and Requisites of Divine Meditation,* the book thoroughly explains what meditation is, why it is the believer's duty, and how to meditate for spiritual profit and pleasure.

Ranew's book is a typical Puritan work on meditation, though it is longer than most. He says that meditation exercises both the mind and the heart, for he who meditates approaches a subject with his intellect as well as his affections. Meditation is a daily duty that enhances every other duty of the Christian life. As oil lubricates an engine, meditation facilitates the means of grace, such as reading Scripture, listening to sermons, praying, and other ordinances of Christ. It deepens the marks of grace, such as repentance, faith, and humility; and it strengthens relationships with God, fellow Christians, and neighbors at large.

According to Ranew, there are two kinds of meditation: occasional and deliberate. Occasional meditation takes what one observes with the senses and raises up thoughts to heavenly meditation. It may be practiced at any time and any place. A spiritually minded man can quickly learn how to spiritualize natural things, for his desires run counter to the worldly minded who carnalize even spiritual things. The believer must be careful, however, to rein in his imagination by Scripture when engaged in occasional meditation, so as to avoid mysticism.

The most important kind of meditation is deliberate, daily meditation on sacred truth. Deliberate meditation draws from four sources: Scripture, practical truths of Christianity, providential occasions (experiences), and sermons. Ranew says the believer should deliberately meditate on topics such as the promises of God's Word, the Spirit's drawing power, self-denial, the heart's deceitfulness, death, judgment, hell, and heaven.

Finally, Ranew offers directives on how to improve one's meditative life. Particularly helpful are his specific directions to new converts, to young Christians, and to older believers.

Edward
Reynolds
(1599-1676)

E dward Reynolds, bishop of Norwich, was born in
Southampton in 1599. He was educated at Merton
College, Oxford, where he obtained a Bachelor of Arts degree
in 1618. He became a fellow in 1620, due to his ability in Greek,
debate, and oratory. Later, he received a Master of Arts degree
(1624) and a Doctor of Divinity degree (1648) from Cambridge.

Reynolds became a preacher at Lincoln's Inn, London, and
one of the king's chaplains in 1622. In 1628, he became vicar of
All Saints, Northampton; then, in 1631, rector of Braunston,
Northamptonshire, where he remained for nearly thirty years.
When civil war broke out, he earned a reputation as a voice of
moderation willing to accommodate his views on church
polity. A Presbyterian by conviction, he nonetheless wanted to
maintain the unity of the national church, and argued for a
milder form of episcopacy that would accommodate Presbyterian beliefs. He wrote out his convictions in *A Sermon Touching
the Peace & Edification of the Church* (1638).

In 1643, he was appointed to serve as a divine at the Westminster Assembly. Though he spoke little, Reynolds played a
major role in committee work on behalf of the assembly. He
was the only divine who was a member of all three major committees for the Confession of Faith: the large committee of

nineteen, with four later additions, appointed to set parameters; the drafting committee of seven for the first composition; and the committee of three, with four later additions, for proofing and final editing. More than anyone else, Reynolds provided continuity throughout the twenty-seven months it took to write the Confession. William Barker concludes, "It is ironic, however, that the one who seems to have contributed most of the Presbyterian doctrinal confession was the only Westminster divine to become a bishop after the Restoration and one of only four who were active in the Assembly who conformed" (*Puritan Profiles*, p. 180).

Reynolds also served on the "Grand Committee" that dealt with treaty obligations to the Scots, the committee that considered the "Reasons" offered by the Independents, and the committee appointed to respond to Parliament concerning the divine right of church government. Repeatedly, Reynolds's moderation compelled him to strive to accommodate different parties.

Reynolds was chosen dean of Christ Church College (1648-51, 1659) and vice-chancellor of the university (1648-50). From 1657 to 1661, he served as vicar of St. Lawrence Jewry, so he was again heard in London. After Cromwell's death in 1658, Reynolds became a leader of the Presbyterian clergy. He preached to Richard Cromwell's Parliament several times in 1659 and 1660, counseling that radical political and doctrinal opinions be suppressed but that differences on secondary issues be tolerated. At the Restoration, he and Edmund Calamy were appointed chaplains to the king.

Reynolds and other Presbyterian conformists became the propagators of a Low Church party, remaining loyal to Puritan ideals and tolerating dissenters within the Anglican Church. Paul Seaver concludes: "In an age of fierce partisanship his life presents rather an unheroic picture, but the popularity he enjoyed with his London vestrymen suggests that moderation in doctrine and action was regarded as a virtue by many of the laity" (*Puritan Lectureships*, p. 287).

In 1661, after consulting Calamy, Chalmers, and Baxter, Reynolds accepted the king's offer of the bishopric of Norwich, a position he retained until his death in 1676. Baxter thought he accepted this position too suddenly, while the historian Wood attributed it to the political maneuverings of his wife. Whatever the case may be, Reynolds's acceptance is not incon-sistent with his character and his desires for reconciliation.

Reynolds died of kidney stones in 1676 while at his bishop's palace. His wife, Mary, probably the daughter of John Harding, president of Magdalen College, Oxford, sur-vived him by seven years. They had at least two daughters and one son, Edward, who served nearly forty years as arch-deacon of Norfolk.

Reynolds was regarded by his contemporaries as a man of good judgment, a gifted preacher, a scholar of considerable talent, and a clear writer. He authored more than thirty books. Daniel Neal wrote of Reynolds: "He was reckoned one of the most eloquent pulpit men of his age, and a good old Puritan."

———◆———

The Works of Edward Reynolds (SDG; 6 vols., 2,875 pages; 1992–2000). Reynolds was highly regarded as a preacher. Many prized his written sermons and religious treatises. Col-lections of his works were first published in 1658 and 1679, followed by a complete six-volume edition in 1826. Volume 1 includes memoirs of the author and three treatises: "The Van-ity of the Creature," "The Sinfulness of Sin," and "The Life of Christ." Of the first two treatises, J. I. Packer writes, "The un-fashionable truth is that no discipline is so necessary for real godliness as facing up to one's own sinfulness in depth, which is what Reynolds makes us do."

Volume 2 offers a detailed exposition of Psalm 110. Reynolds explains the scepter of Christ's kingdom; the character of His subjects; His priesthood, victories, sufferings, and resurrection. Of this work, Spurgeon wrote, "Surpassingly clear and elaborate. Reynolds was a man of vast learning and thoroughly evangelical spirit."

Volume 3 contains seven sermons on Hosea 14, unfolding God's sovereign love to unworthy sinners, and "Meditations on the Holy Sacrament of the Lord's Supper." It is succinct and rich in explaining our communion with Christ and how believers partake of Christ in the Supper. Reynolds begins this section by saying, "First, we take Christ; and then we eat him. There are none that find any nourishment or relish in the blood of Christ, but those who have received him, and so have an interest, propriety, and title to him; ours, first, in possession and claim; and, after, ours, in fruition and comfort" (p. 37).

Volume 4 contains a 230-page commentary on Ecclesiastes, short meditations on Peter's fall and restoration, and eight sermons. The sermons on self-denial (Matt. 16:24), joy in the Lord (Phil. 4:4), and "Death's Advantage" (Phil. 1:21) are very practical.

Volume 5 offers twenty-two sermons that expose the sinfulness of man and exalt the righteousness of God. Some of these sermons were preached before the king or other political authorities. Worthy of mention are treatises on the preaching of Christ (2 Cor. 4:5), brotherly reconciliation (Phil. 3:15), and moderation (Phil. 4:5).

Volume 6 contains Reynolds's most theologically profound work, "Treatise on the Passions and Faculties of the Soul," which served as a common undergraduate text at Oxford until the early eighteenth century. In forty-two chapters, Reynolds first covers the human memory and its weaknesses; imagination and its relationship to the will and to reason; and passions and how they can be used to promote virtue. He then focuses upon human affections such as love, hate, desire, joy, delight, sorrow, hope, boldness, fear, and anger. He examines the image of God and the soul's immortality, then concludes by looking at faculties of the soul, such as understanding, will, and conscience. The volume concludes with a sermon preached at Reynolds's funeral by B. Riveley, a colleague in Norwich.

Thomas Ridgley
(1667-1734)

Thomas Ridgley was born in 1667 in London. He was trained at a private seminary in Wiltshire, "presumably at John Davison's academy at Trowbridge, and also at Islington under Thomas Doolittle" (*Oxford DNB*, 46:934). He then returned to London, where he was ordained into the ministry in 1695 as assistant to Thomas Gouge (c. 1665-1700), son of Robert Gouge. They ministered in an Independent church that met at Three Cranes, near Thames Street. In 1697, difficulties arose after a visiting minister made some political comments during weeknight lectures. Then, too, disagreements surfaced between Gouge and several members about receiving a particular person into church membership. Gouge's health was so affected by the controversies that he died in 1700 in his mid-thirties.

Ridgley became Gouge's successor and the congregation soon stabilized under his care. He remained at Three Cranes in London for nearly forty years. In his latter years, he had several assistants.

Shortly after becoming a minister, Ridgley was asked to give weekly lectures in various places. He was one of six ministers to deliver the Merchant's Lecture every Tuesday morning at Salters' Hall. He also gave the Thursday evening lecture at Jewin Street and, for much of his life, an evening lecture for young people on most Sabbaths at the Old Jewry.

When Isaac Chauncy, the first tutor of the oldest independent college in Britain, died in 1712, Ridgley succeeded
him as a theological tutor. The students met at Tenter Alley
in Moorfields. Here Ridgley delivered detailed lectures on the
Westminster Larger Catechism, the content of which became his *magnum opus* when published in 1731. During this
time, Ridgley became deeply involved in opposing the Arianism that was making its appearance in Presbyterian churches
at that time. Even when engaged in polemics, however, he exhibited the moderation and comprehensiveness that also
marked his writing.

Ridgley died March 27, 1734, at age sixty-seven, and was
buried at Bunhill Fields. By the time of his death, Ridgley had
become well-known for the depth and breadth of his thought,
and had published numerous theological works and sermons.
He was succeeded in the theological chair by John Eames, who
Isaac Watts said was "the most learned man" he ever knew.

A Body of Divinity on the Assembly's Larger Catechism
(SWRB; 4 vols. in 2, 1,350 pages; 1993). This was Ridgley's
major work, for which he was awarded a doctorate of divinity
by King's College, Aberdeen, in 1728. It is indisputably the
best work on the Larger Catechism. Ridgley does for the
Larger Catechism what Boston and Watson did for the
Shorter Catechism: taking hold of the reader's mind as they
aim for the heart.

Ridgley's work is superlative at times; for example, see
his masterful defense of limited atonement on the basis of
the names that Christ gave His people—"sheep," "friends,"
"children of God," and "church" (1:519-22). We heartily recommend this reprint, although the small type in parts of it is
somewhat difficult to read.

Ralph Robinson

(1614-1655)

R alph Robinson, born at Heswall, Cheshire, was educated
at St. Catharine's College, Cambridge. He graduated
with a Bachelor of Arts degree in 1639 and a Master of Arts degree in 1642. He was ordained at St. Mary Woolnoth,
Lombard Street, London, in 1643, by an *ad hoc* presbytery convened by London ministers for this purpose. A dedicated
Presbyterian, Robinson instituted the government of elders in
his congregation in 1646, and the following year, served as
clerk for the first assembly of provincial ministers in London.

Robinson united with the provincial ministers in the
protest against the king's death in 1649. Two years later he
was arrested for being involved with the conspiracy of
Christopher Love to return Charles II to the throne. He was
held for some weeks in the Tower of London but was released
before trial when he promised to submit to the government.
Though he returned to pastor St. Mary Woolnoth, he never
recovered fully from the effects of imprisonment. He died in
1655 at the age of forty-one and was buried in the chancel of
his church. Simeon Ashe preached his funeral sermon.

Robinson was a dedicated preacher, a faithful husband,
and a devoted father. He and his wife, Mary, had one daughter, Rebecca, who died at the age of seventeen.

Christ All and In All (SDG; 627 pages; 1992). This work was
first printed in 1660 after Robinson's death, under the

direction of Simeon Ashe, Edmund Calamy, and William Taylor. It was reprinted in 1834 and 1868.

The volume contains fifty-three sermons on Christ as the true believer's life, robe, protector, physician, light, shepherd, vine, horn of salvation, dew, chief cornerstone, sun of righteousness, precious ointment, consolation, and myrrh.

Robinson's exposition of this subject goes to the heart of the believer's faith and assurance. The editors write in their introduction: "By his opening the Scripture metaphors which familiarly reveal Christ, besides the many notions which shall be beamed into the understanding, the serious, musing Christian will be much advantaged in occasional meditations."

The sufficiency of our Lord and Savior is continually challenged today. Readers of Robinson's work should find their hearts warmed and lives challenged by its clear presentation of Christ. In viewing the all-sufficiency of Christ, the sinner cannot help but be struck by his own insufficiency and urged to cleave to the One who is all and in all.

Richard Rogers

(1551-1618)

R ichard Rogers was born in 1551, the son of a furniture maker at Chelmsford, Essex. In 1566, he was sent by a wealthy patron as a sizar to Christ's College, Cambridge. While there, Rogers experienced the excitement generated by the expulsion of Thomas Cartwright.

Rogers earned a Bachelor of Arts degree in 1571 and a Master of Arts degree from Caius College in 1574. The following year, he became curate of Radminster in Essex, and met with considerable success. In 1577, he was appointed lecturer at Wethersfield, Essex, where he stayed for the next forty years. He established a presbytery at Dedham, organized meetings in his neighborhood for prayer and spiritual fellowship, and ran a school in his own home to groom young men for Cambridge and the ministry.

Rogers was a man of considerable learning who led a humble, peaceable, and exemplary life. Yet he suffered greatly for his nonconformist views. When demands to conform became too strict in 1583, resulting from Archbishop Whitgift's efforts to enforce subscription to various articles of the Established Church, Rogers and twenty-six other ministers petitioned the government for relief. All were suspended from the ministry until they promised subscription and full conformity. Only after Sir Robert Wroth, a nobleman of influence, intervened was Rogers granted permission to preach again.

In 1603, Rogers was suspended again and told to appear before the archbishop. In his diary, Rogers wrote of his troubles: "It greatly troubles me that after laboring betwixt thirty and forty years in the ministry, I am now accounted unworthy to preach; while so many idle and scandalous people enjoy their ease and liberty." The archbishop died the day of that appointment, and Rogers was released.

Rogers married twice, first to a woman named Barbara (her family name is unknown), with whom he had at least seven children, six of whom survived him. Two of his sons, Daniel and Ezekiel, became Puritan ministers. His second wife was Susan Ward, the widow of a neighboring minister. He had no children with her but became stepfather to the six children she had by her first marriage. Of these children, three more sons—Samuel, John, and Nathaniel—became Puritan ministers. When Rogers died in 1618, John Knewstub delivered his funeral sermon. Stephen Marshall succeeded Rogers at Wethersfield.

Rogers's best known book, *Seven Treatises* (1604), was reprinted five times in the seventeenth century but never since. It is a pioneering work on practical, Puritan casuistry, showing how the Christian is to rule his life through seven means: exercising watchfulness, practicing meditation, using the Christian armor of Ephesians 6, engaging in prayer, reading Scripture and godly authors, offering thanksgiving, and practicing fasting. William Haller writes, "*Seven Treatises* was the first important exposition of the code of behavior which expressed the English Calvinist, or, more broadly speaking, the Puritan, conception of the spiritual and moral life. As such it inaugurated a literature the extent and influence of which in all departments of life can hardly be exaggerated" (*The Rise of Puritanism*, p. 36).

Rogers's *Diary*, used as a confessional to ward off the great adversary Satan and to commune with God, reveals his lament that he did not consistently exercise his daily directions. For example, his diary entry for September 12, 1587, says, "This noon I felt a strong desire to enjoy more liberty in thinking upon some vain things which I had lately weaned myself from" (M. M. Knappen, ed., *Two Elizabethan Puritan Diaries*, p. 59). Nevertheless, the diary affirms what Steve Egerton, the great Puritan preacher at Blackfriars, London, stated: Rogers "long labored [for] the conversion of many other[s]; but especially [for] the mortification and quickening of his own soul and conscience." Giles Firmin, another contemporary, said that Rogers was not "John Chrysostom" (i.e., a golden-tongued orator) and was too austere with the profane. Yet he concluded that "God honored none more in these parts of England with conversion of souls."

Rogers's grandson, William Jenkyn, called Rogers "the Enoch in his age," in that he walked with God and was often sorry that each day was not his last day. In a well-known tale about Rogers, a gentleman once said to him, "Mr. Rogers, I like you and your company very well, only you are too precise." Rogers's response was, "Oh, sir, I serve a very precise God."

━━◆◆◆━━

Judges (BTT; 990 pages; 1983). This massive folio on Judges, published in 1615, was formed from a collection of 103 sermons that Rogers preached to his congregation at Wethersfield in Essex. Spurgeon wrote about this work: "This for the Puritan period is *the* work upon Judges. It is thoroughly plain and eminently practical."

Rogers's sermons on Judges are classically Puritan. He offers teaching, then hastens to apply it. For example, in his sermon on Judges 13:25-14:4, Rogers establishes the doctrine that a man should solicit the advice of his parents when choosing a mate. He then immediately condemns the current heedlessness of children in this matter.

Some of Rogers's doctrines are so practical that they can hardly be distinguished from the Puritan "uses" of a later day.

For example, when Rogers offers his doctrine in discussing how Samson's parents opposed his proposed marriage to a Philistine, he gives this exhortation to duty: "And their example ought to be our instruction, that as they have done, so we should know we ought to do, that is to say, that we follow the light and knowledge which we have of the will of God" (*Commentary on Judges*, p. 661).

Rogers also brings the doctrine of assurance to bear upon people, pointing them to the "golden chain" of Romans 8:29-30 (p. 656). Citing Samson's filling with the Spirit, Rogers notes that God's people may gain an assurance of their spiritual condition as elect "by the means which serve to our calling. So that predestination itself is manifested in time, by the enlightening and opening of the heart to receive the glad tidings of the gospel." In this, Rogers takes his reader to the golden chain, described so eloquently by William Perkins. By ascertaining the evidences of the Spirit's effectual vocation, we may be assured of God's everlasting good pleasure towards us.

This beautifully produced facsimile edition will be greatly appreciated by all who love practical preaching.

Timothy Rogers
(1658-1728)

Timothy Rogers was the son of John Rogers, a nonconformist minister in the diocese of Durham. He was born
at Barnard Castle, Durham, on May 24, 1658. His father taught
him the principles of religion, then sent him to Glasgow University in Scotland, where he began to prepare for the ministry.
He also lived for some time in the house of the learned Edward
Veel, an eminent Puritan tutor. Veel resided in Wapping and
directed an academy for ministerial students.

Rogers entered the ministry as evening lecturer at Crosby
Square, Bishopsgate, a position he shared for several years
with Thomas Kentish, who later ministered to a congregation
in Southwark. Rogers acquired a solid reputation as a
preacher while lecturing at Crosby Square, which was supported by merchants and other respected leaders in the city.
He was comfortable in the pulpit, clearly articulated his
thoughts, and had a striking manner of address.

In 1683, Rogers published his first sermon, *Early Religion,
or, The Way for a Young Man to Remember His Creator.* The sermon
was prompted by the sudden death of Robert Linager, a fellow student training for the ministry in Veel's academy.
Rogers's words to those gathered at the funeral were sober:
"To you that were the acquaintances of the deceased, I shall

only say this: now you have stronger engagements upon you
to remember your Creator than you had before, for He has by
the death of your companion sent you a near and a loud warning to prepare for your own.'"

About this time, Rogers fell into a deep depression, which
lasted nearly two years. He gave up all hope of the mercy of
God and considered himself "a vessel of wrath fitted to destruction" (Rom. 9:22). He described the condition of his
mind as a land of darkness on which the sun never seemed to
shine. Nothing seemed to comfort Rogers; he felt trapped. He
later wrote, "Who can describe that anguish and tribulation,
which such apprehensions [of God's displeasure] cause in a
desolate and a mourning soul?" Another time he said, "It is impossible to relate the whole, for my sorrows were beyond
expression." The sufferings of his mind so weakened his body
that he could no longer lecture. Many of Rogers's relatives suffered from similar problems, prompting some to speculate
that his illness was hereditary.

Rogers's condition was well known to many God-fearing
people throughout the country, who were incessantly praying
for him. God heard their cries: the light of His countenance
was restored to Rogers, and he could see the Savior's love and
pleasure over his soul. "God...hath wrought a double salvation
for me," he said.

Rogers began to lecture again, gratefully acknowledging
God's goodness in restoring him. In his first sermon on Psalm
30:3-4 ("O Lord, thou hast brought up my soul from the
grave," etc.), Rogers declared, "I come to you as one from the
dead, to say no more." He preached four more sermons on the
same text and published them as *Practical Discourses on Sickness
and Recovery* in 1690. He dedicated the work to William
Ashurst and Thomas Lane, with whom he had stayed in the
country during his "troubled and uneasy times."

In *Practical Discourses*, Rogers deals primarily with the Christian's response to bodily ailments. He warns those who are healthy not to exult in that, for "he that is proud of his body is as foolish as if he should dote upon a flower, which in an unforeseen storm may be deprived of all its glory." He also reminds the sick to be thankful for God's mercy: "How many are dead since you were first ill? How many excellent ministers whom you must never hear again? How many of your dearest friends are now in the cold grave, with whom you cannot now discourse, and whose faces you shall never see till the Great Day.... This should engage us to make suitable returns to that God who has spared us when he hath taken them away." The following year, Rogers published *A Discourse on Trouble of Mind and the Disease of Melancholy*, in which he offered helps for the comfort of dejected souls.

In 1692, Rogers became assistant to John Shower, minister of the Presbyterian congregation in Jewin Street. They moved to a larger meetinghouse in Old Jewry in 1701. Shower was a brilliant Puritan orator who had preached at the funeral of Mary Doolittle, wife of Thomas Doolittle, in 1692. The two ministers highly respected each other.

For several years, Rogers, a pious, modest man much loved by his people, preached with great success. In 1692, he preached *Fall Not Out by the Way, or, A Persuasion to a Friendly Correspondence between the Conformists and Non-Conformists*, occasioned by the death of Anthony Dunwell. The discourse (consisting of two sermons on Genesis 45:24, "See that ye fall not out by the way") urged Christians to strive for unity. That same year, Rogers preached at the funeral of Edmund Hill. The sermon on 1 Corinthians 7:31 ("For the fashion of this world passeth away") was printed as *The Changeableness of this World with Respect to Nations, Families, and Particular Persons* (1692). It emphasized the fleetingness of the present world and the reality of the world to come.

Rogers published several more funeral sermons, including *The Character of a Good Woman, both in a Single and a Married State* (1697), based on Proverbs 31:10 ("Who can find a virtuous woman, for her price is far above rubies"), which he preached at the funeral of Elizabeth Dunton, daughter of Samuel Annesley. Rogers started the sermon with a history of notable women and finished it with an account of Mrs. Dunton's life, including extracts from her diary. The sermon is full of practical applications. For example, Rogers says that those who marry must do so out of love, but their prospective spouse must be judged by the understanding and the graces of the heart, not by physical attraction.

Rogers's proneness to despondency returned to hinder his usefulness in 1707. He became so depressed—looking upon himself "as a lamp despised, a broken vessel, and, as a dead man out of mind"—that he left the ministry and retired in Wantage, Berkshire. Though he spent his last twenty years in obscurity, he continued to justify God in all the dispensations of His providence, even in the midst of darkness. Rogers entered triumphantly into his Father's arms in November of 1728, and was buried in the Wantage churchyard. He never married.

———◆◆◆———

A Discourse on Trouble of Mind and the Disease of Melancholy (SDG; 441 pages; 2002). This work last appeared in print in 1808. The editor of that edition wrote, "Those who are acquainted with the distressing circumstances in which the pious Author was placed, previous to his writing the present Treatise, will readily grant that he was the fittest person to write upon such a subject. He had nothing to do, but to detail his own experience. In so doing, he has recorded the experience of many thousand persons, who, in all periods of the church, have been afflicted more or less with a *dejection of spirits*, which has very properly been termed religious Melancholy."

In the preface, Rogers offers thirteen directions to the family and friends of melancholic persons and discusses the best way of treating them. Several letters from ministers in the first edition of the book express gratitude for the author's recovery and strongly recommend the book. Among the letters is one from Joseph Hussey, who wrote, "Doubtless God hath thus clothed you with the garment of salvation, that you may encourage others to put on Christ, though hell is naked before them, and destruction hath no covering from those that are not hid in Him."

Many books have been written on religious melancholy, but most authors have not really experienced the condition. By contrast, Rogers wrote from the depths of his heart, expressing gratitude on every page and giving witness to the beauty of Christ, the best cure for spiritual depression. He had a unique perspective, for he lived through terrible darkness of soul to help others toward healing. He longed for the coming of his Deliverer and yearned for the heavenly places in Christ Jesus.

Rogers reminds us that in heaven "we shall feel the love of God in so sweet and transporting a manner that we shall never doubt whether He loves [us] or not." No longer will saints struggle with sin's decay, doubt their Savior's love, or despair of His mercy. We highly recommend this book for believers who struggle with depression.

Henry Scudder
(c. 1585-1652)

Henry Scudder received a Bachelor of Arts degree (1603) and a Master of Arts degree (1606) from Christ's College, Cambridge. Two years later he married Bridgett, daughter of George Hunt, rector of Collingbourne Ducis, Wiltshire, and sister-in-law of William Whately. She died in her early twenties, leaving behind one daughter.

Scudder then served as a minister in Drayton, Oxfordshire, for some years, where he was much appreciated for his exemplary piety. At Drayton, he became close friends with Robert Harris and William Whately. They met weekly for Bible study.

In 1631, Scudder published his most celebrated work, *The Christian's Daily Walk.* Two years later, following the death of his father-in-law, Scudder became rector of the large flock in Collingbourne Ducis, where he remained for twenty years until his death.

In May of 1642, Scudder was sanctioned by Parliament as lecturer for Warminster. The following month he was commissioned to be a member of the Westminster Assembly. He served there faithfully, chairing a committee that reviewed proof-texts for the Confession of Faith.

Scudder preached on Micah 6:9 before the House of Commons on a fast day in 1644. His sermon was later printed at the request of the House as "God's Warning to England by the Voice of His Rod." The following year, he served as interim rector of St. Mildred Poultry, London. About that time he signed "the petition addressed to the common council of the City by ministers who were dissatisfied with the proposed Presbyterian organization of London parishes" (*Oxford DNB*, 49:582).

Scudder died in 1652. He was buried at Collingbourne.

The Christian's Daily Walk, in Holy Security and Peace (SPR; 342 pages; 1984). Scudder is best remembered for this how-to manual of Puritan devotion. It addresses subjects such as walking with God, beginning the day with God, religious fasting, the Lord's Day, walking alone with God, rules for religious conduct in prosperity, directions for walking with God in adversity, uprightness, freedom from anxious care, the peace of God, impediments to peace, and false fears.

The book earned praise from numerous divines. Richard Baxter said it was the best Puritan devotional ever written. John Owen wrote of it, "I must say that I find in this [book] that authority and powerful evidence of truth, arising from a plain transferring of the sacred sense of the Scripture in words and expressions suited to the experience of gracious, honest, and humble souls, that the most accurate and adorned discourses of this age do not attain or rise up unto."

Theodore Haak translated *Christian's Daily Walk* into Dutch in 1636. It has been reprinted numerous times, both in English and in Dutch.

Obadiah Sedgwick

(c. 1600-1658)

Born about 1600, Obadiah Sedgwick was the son of Joseph Sedgwick, vicar of St. Peter's, Marlborough, Wiltshire. He entered Queen's College, Oxford, in 1619, but transferred to Magdalen Hall, where he received a bachelor's degree in 1620 and a master's degree in 1623. For a few years Sedgwick served as chaplain to Lord Horatio Vere of Tilbury, whom he accompanied to the Netherlands. In 1626, Sedgwick tutored Matthew Hale, who was to become one of the most respected lawyers of the time. Hale later defended Christopher Love before the high court.

After ordination, Sedgwick served as chaplain in 1628-29 to Horace, Lord Vere of Tilbury, in the Low Countries. In 1630, Sedgwick received a Bachelor of Divinity degree from Oxford. That same year he became curate and lecturer at St. Mildred, Bread Street, London, where he was a very popular preacher, but Bishop Juxon censured and suspended him in 1637 for nonconformity. Sedgwick took refuge at the earl of Warwick's house in Essex. In 1639, Sedgwick succeeded John Dod in the ministry at Coggeshall, Essex. With the opening of the Long Parliament, Sedgwick regained the lectureship at St. Mildred's.

In 1642, Sedgwick was commissioned as a member of the Westminster Assembly in which he played a prominent role. He was appointed to a committee of nineteen to work on the Confession of Faith, and to a committee of twenty to respond to the Independents' "Reasons." He supported the Presbyterians, but felt some sympathy for the Independents, though he strongly opposed rigid Independent views. When Philip Nye, an outspoken Independent, appealed for liberty of conscience from what he called the dangers of established Presbyterianism, Sedgwick requested that Nye be expelled from the assembly.

Robert Norris describes Sedgwick as one of the assembly's "liveliest and most colorful preachers" ("The Preaching of the Assembly," in *To Glorify and Enjoy God*, ed. John L. Carson and David W. Hall, p. 74). During the civil wars, he was called upon to preach before Parliament at least fourteen times—more than any other minister except Stephen Marshall. Five of those sermons were published. He was also asked to be a licenser of the press for books of divinity.

Sedgwick minced no words in preaching before Parliament. In *An Ark Against a Deluge* (1644), he told the House of Commons that they should abhor "the very thought of tolerating all opinions in the church. This was such a monstrous prodigy, such an intolerable way of confusion, such mocking of the people of God." The end result of such toleration, he concluded, would be that every person "makes an ark of his own fancy" (p. 19).

In 1645, Sedgwick resigned from Coggeshall, where he was succeeded by John Owen, and became rector of St. Andrew's, Holborn, London. The following year he moved to St. Paul's, Covent Garden, where he was instrumental in the conversion of many souls.

In 1651, Sedgwick petitioned Parliament for the release of his Presbyterian friend, Christopher Love. Two years later, he was appointed to the commission of triers to examine candidates for the ministry. Failing health forced him to resign from St. Paul's in 1656. He was succeeded by his son-in-law, Thomas Manton.

Sedgwick retired to Marlborough, where he died in 1658. He left each of his four children a sizable inheritance, and was buried beside his father at Ogbourne St. Andrew, Wiltshire. His older brother, John, was also a Puritan minister.

———◆◆◆———

The Anatomy of Secret Sins (SDG; 382 pages; 1999). This work is based on sermons Sedgwick originally preached to his congregation at St. Mildred's. Using Psalm 19:12-13 as his text, he shows how to identify the hidden sins of the heart and how to deal with them before they destroy one's soul. If we do not know our own depravity, we will be ill-equipped for the war that must be waged against the enemy in our own heart. Every believer who wishes to attack sin in his life will find this work helpful.

Sedgwick is eminently quotable. Here are a few samples:

- Beloved, the main battle of a Christian is not the open field. His quarrels are mostly within, and his enemies are in his own breast.
- If temptations do not drive you to your knees, they drive you to the ground.
- The least sin is further than a man should go, and the higher he mounts in sin, the deeper are his wounds.
- The way to be kept from a high sin is to fear the least sin.
- Men usually have been wading in lesser sins who are now swimming in great transgressions.

Along with this work are two sermons on Matthew 12:31, "The Throne of Mercy" and "The Tribunal of Justice," which deal with sinning against the Holy Ghost.

Christ's Counsel to His Languishing Church (SDG; 149 pages; 2001). Using Christ's words to the church at Sardis in Revelation 3, Sedgwick identifies the state of spiritual decay that may afflict negligent Christians. He then describes the means by which we may escape it and persevere in a state of spiritual health. He encourages Christians to repent and do their first works, thereby keeping aflame their love for Christ.

In an appendix to this work is a sermon titled *England's Preservation*, dealing with England's wandering from God and how she can be brought back to Him.

The Doubting Believer (SDG; 212 pages; 1997). The purpose of this work is to increase personal assurance of faith in believers. It explains fourteen reasons for a believer's doubts, then provides a cure for each. Subtitled *A Treatise containing the nature, the kinds, the springs, and the remedies of doubtings incident to weak believers*, this book offers doubting believers direction and encouragement.

In the dedication, Sedgwick writes: "In my weak judgment, it would be a great prudence to secure that which, being secured, now secures all. Nothing grows weak where faith grows strong. This poor treatise is like Aaron and Hur, who stayed up the hands of Moses. So does this treatise endeavor to stay the hand of faith in a weak believer who has an ample estate on the shore and at land, but those waves of doubtings too often make him to fall back and stagger."

The book's appendix includes a sermon Sedgwick preached before Parliament on the nature and danger of heresies.

Samuel Sewall

(1652-1730)

Samuel Sewall, a judge and diarist of high renown, is little known outside of literary circles and early American colonial history. Sewall was born at Bishop Stoke, Hampshire, England, in 1652. He was the son of Henry Sewall, a pastor, and Jane Dummer. Sewall's father had immigrated to Newbury, Massachusetts, in 1634. Though he was admitted to freemanship in 1637, he returned to England in 1646 and subsequently took the pulpit of North Baddesley. The Sewalls returned to Massachusetts when Samuel was seven years old.

Samuel attended grammar school in Romsey, Hampshire, England. He continued his schooling in Massachusetts with Thomas Parker, pastor of Newbury Church, who prepared him for Harvard College, from which he graduated with a Bachelor of Arts degree in 1671. Among his classmates were Edward Taylor, Samuel Mather, and William Adams. Undecided between a career in commerce and the ministry, Sewall was appointed a resident fellow, or tutor, of Harvard, where one of his duties was working in the library.

In 1674, he received a Master of Arts degree. That same year, Sewall declined a ministerial call to Woodbridge, New Jersey. That seemed to favor his bent toward business rather than the ministry. Another event influencing that decision was his preaching in Thomas Parker's pulpit. On one occasion, Sewall preached for two and a half hours, exceeding the one-hour limit because he was reluctant to watch the hourglass.

Sewall married Hannah Hull in 1676, the daughter of John Hull, the wealthiest man in New England. They had fourteen children, six of whom survived to adulthood. Sewall's wife brought a large dowry to the marriage, which influenced him to focus his calling on business, where he worked under the leadership of John Hull. Sewall soon took over many of his father-in-law's mercantile activities.

When the elder Hull died in 1683, Hannah Sewall received two-thirds of the estate, while her mother received one-third. Sewall became one of the wealthiest men in Boston, earning rentals from properties in the city and several other parts of the colony. He did not use his wealth frivolously, however. A diligent reader of the older Puritans, he purchased several copies of John Owen's works and distributed those to people he knew. He also gave Owen's works and other Puritan books to Samuel Willard, pastor of South Church, where Sewall was a member.

After 1683, Sewall became a major political force. He was elected to the General Court from Westfield in Hampden County and then to the Court of Assistants in 1684. With the revocation of the charter in 1684, he continued to serve as a justice of the peace and as an officer in the militia (he became a captain in 1701), though he was passed over for one of the new council appointments.

In 1688, his concern about his property titles in New England and the need to administer holdings in England took him to London. While in London, Sewall helped Increase Mather lobby for the old charter. During Sewall's absence from Massachusetts, Governor Edmund Andros and the Dominion of New England were replaced with an interim council. When he returned to Boston, Sewall became a member of that council. With the adoption of the new charter, Sewall was retained in the upper house in 1691, a post that he held until he declined to stand for election in 1725.

One of the first actions of Sir William Phips, the first governor under the new charter, was to appoint a special court to hear the witchcraft accusations that had accumulated in Salem over the winter of 1691. Phips asked Sewall to serve on the court. The court used spectral evidence—the "appearance" of the accused to the afflicted—as evidence in its condemnation of witches. This type of prosecution was unheard of and controversial, and eventually led Sewall to regret participating in the trials. He made a public apology in 1697, at the Old South Meeting House where Samuel Willard, a lifelong opponent of the trials, was pastor.

In addition to his activities as a justice of the peace and a member of the court, Sewall had a long career as a judge. In 1692, he was appointed to the Superior Court of Judicature, Massachusetts's highest court. He became chief justice of that court in 1718. In 1715, he had also become judge of the probate court of Suffolk County.

Sewall was a well-known philanthropist. In 1699, he became the treasurer and commissioner of the Puritan-minded Society for the Propagation of the Gospel (not to be confused with the more controversial Anglican-minded Society for the Propagation of the Gospel in Foreign Parts, founded in 1701). He was responsible for administering lands owned by the society and for supervising the disbursement of funds to Native American Christian churches. Sewall made extensive contributions to Native American Christians throughout his life. As early as 1691, he used an unpaid debt to procure land that was then turned over to a Native American ministry. He also donated land to a meetinghouse in Kingston and to Harvard for building expansion, and gave generously to a scholarship fund for Native American students at Harvard.

In 1700, Sewall wrote *The Selling of Joseph: A Memorial* (1700), opposing African slavery in the colony. Sewall's book described several cases in which freedom was promised by slave-owners, only to be denied later. Though Sewall's views were rejected by the society of the day, he did succeed in helping to enact a law legalizing marriages between African Americans.

Hannah Sewall died in 1717. Two years later, Sewall married Abigail, widow of James Woodmansy and William Tilley. In 1722, Sewall married Mary Gibbs, widow of Boston merchant Robert Gibbs.

Sewall died in Boston in 1730. In his public work, he always promoted Puritan ideals. When Harvard lost its conservative moorings in the early 1700s, Sewall helped establish Yale on Puritan principles. Among his last words was the desire that he might "follow the Captain of my salvation" to the end.

The Diary of Samuel Sewall (Farrar, Straus & Giroux; 1,254 pages; 1973). Sewall wrote many works, but this diary was his major literary accomplishment. Here Sewall reveals the complexities of his many activities and of the colony's affairs during a crucial time. Covering the period from 1674 to 1729 (with a gap between 1677 and 1684), the diary also provides an intimate look at his life and times. It is invaluable to see Sewall not only as a merchant and a politician at the center of the Massachusetts Bay Colony, but also as a grieving father, fearful city dweller, troubled sinner, and pious believer. The diary offers us a window into the world of early America's Puritan aristocratic laity.

The Diary and Life and Samuel Sewall (Bedford; 260 pages; 1998). An abridgment of Sewall's two-volume diary, this annotated work is the best place to begin studying the life of Sewall. The editor, Mel Yazawa, selects the best portions of Sewall's diary and adds notes for the reader. The result is a highly accessible volume that is historically faithful to Sewall's diary and reveals one of early America's greatest hearts.

Thomas Shepard

(1605-1649)

Thomas Shepard was born in Towcester, Northampton-shire, on Gunpowder Day, November 5, 1605. His father, William, an apprentice to a grocer, married the grocer's daughter. Thomas was the youngest of nine children. His mother died when Thomas was about four years old. His father remarried, but the stepmother had little time for children. Of her, Thomas wrote, "She let me see the difference between my own mother and a stepmother."

Thomas was educated at the Free School under a Welsh-man, who was exceedingly cruel and did much to discourage him from learning. When Shepard was age ten, his father died. His education became the responsibility of his stepmother, but she neglected to provide for his schooling. Later, Shepard was placed under the care of his older brother, John. Shepard said, "God made him to be both father and mother" to me (Shepard's *Autobiography* in Michael McGiffert, ed., *God's Plot: Puritan Spirituality in Thomas Shepard's Cambridge*, p. 41). Shepard's unkind schoolteacher died and was replaced by one who instilled in Shepard the desire to pursue further education.

Shepard was admitted at age fifteen to Emmanuel College, Cambridge, as a pensioner. During his first two years at Cambridge, he neglected God and prayer. At times he was affected by the preaching of men such as Laurence Chaderton, but this influence was short-lived. Shepard fell in with bad company, fellow scholars who were given to lust, pride, gambling, and drinking.

Shepard was eventually brought under profound conviction of sin, which at times moved him to contemplate suicide. The preaching of John Preston in particular was used to open "the secrets of my soul before me—the hypocrisy of all good things I thought I had in me—as if one had told him [i.e., Preston] of all that ever I did" (*Autobiography*, p. 44). Finally, when Preston preached from 1 Corinthians 1:30, opening up the fullness that lay in Christ's redemption, Shepard awoke to Christ's sweetness and embraced Him as his Savior and Lord.

Shepard earned a Bachelor of Arts degree in 1624 and a Master of Arts in 1627, then was ordained deacon and priest that same year in Peterborough. Meanwhile, he worked for some time (1626-27) under the tutelage of Thomas Weld, vicar at Terling, Essex, who gave him valuable pastoral and practical training. There, too, he came under the influence of Thomas Hooker, then preaching at Chelmsford.

Shepard became occasional lecturer in 1627 at Earls Colne, near Coggeshall, Essex, where he worked with great success until 1630. He desired to continue there, but, in December of 1630, he was summoned for nonconformity before William Laud, then bishop of London, and was forbidden to exercise ministerial duties in the diocese of London. In examining the ceremonies and duties to which he was required to conform, Shepard became increasingly disenchanted with the established church. He writes that he came to "see the evil of the English ceremonies, cross, surplice, and kneeling" (ibid., p. 52). When he was summoned a second time before Laud, he was asked to leave the diocese.

After a third encounter with Laud, Shepard took refuge in Yorkshire, where he was appointed chaplain to Sir Richard Darley, Knight of Buttercrambe in the North Riding of Yorkshire. In 1632, Shepard married Darley's cousin, Margaret

Tauteville. Shortly after, he accepted a call to the ministry at Heddon in Northumberland. When he refused to subscribe to the Thirty-Nine Articles, he was silenced by Archbishop Richard Neile of York, but continued to preach until John Cotton, Thomas Hooker, Thomas Weld, and Samuel Stone emigrated from England.

It was only with difficulty that Shepard, who suffered much from ill health, now avoided arrest for his nonconformist principles. In 1634, he sailed for Boston but was driven back by a storm. He remained in hiding in England until August of 1635, when he sailed again. Meanwhile, his first child had died, and a second, Thomas, had been born. The Shepards finally reached their destination on October 3, 1635. His wife became ill from tuberculosis and died four months later. Meanwhile, Shepard settled in Newtown (now Cambridge), Massachusetts, where he became pastor of the newly established Congregational church. There he remained until his death.

In Cambridge, Shepard acquired a reputation for effectiveness as an evangelist. Cotton Mather called him "Pastor Evangelicus" (*Magnalia Christi Americana*, 1:380) and Edward Johnson, the chronicler of early New England, memorialized him as "that gracious, sweet, heavenly-minded and soul-ravishing minister, in whose soul the Lord shed his love so abundantly that thousands of souls have cause to bless God for him" (*Wonder-Working Providence*, 201). According to the eighteenth-century preacher Thomas Prince, who published a portion of Shepard's *Journal*, it was not unusual when someone hearing Shepard preach, would cry out in agony, "What shall I do to be saved?" (cited by John A. Albro, "Life of Thomas Shepard," in *The Works of Thomas Shepard*, 1:clxxx).

Shepard was a friend of John Harvard and helped establish Harvard College in 1636. He was probably instrumental in securing its location at Cambridge.

Shepard was involved in the controversies of his day, arguing from his position as a Calvinist reflecting the doctrine of God's sovereignty. He defined Congregationalism as a *via media* between Brownism, which placed church government entirely in the hands of the members, and Presbyterianism, which gave that power to the presbytery of the local church. He was unswerving in opposing the antinomians and was one of the leaders in the synod at Cambridge that condemned them. He firmly maintained, as he wrote to Cotton, that one "cannot separate God's revelation in the Word (the Bible) from God's revelation in the Holy Spirit" (*Oxford DNB*, 50:233).

Shepard was particularly concerned with educating the young. In 1644, he approached the commissioners of the United Colonies of New England, asking them to approve a plan for every family in the colony to give to the college a quarter bushel of wheat, or its monetary equivalent, annually for needy students. That was the beginning of the scholarship program in America. Shepard also instituted public confession of faith and a plan of church government which, after some delays in the Synod of 1637, became part of the laws of the Commonwealth of Massachusetts and an important platform for Congregational churches in America. He was consistently interested in the conversion of Native Americans and kept friendly watch over the first Indian Mission in Cambridge, established by his friend John Eliot.

In 1637, Shepard married Joanna Hooker, daughter of Thomas Hooker. They had four children, one of whom died at birth and another in infancy. Samuel and John survived their father. After the death of his second wife, Shepard married Margaret Boradel in 1647, who bore him one son, Jeremiah. Shepard died in Cambridge on August 25, 1649, and was buried there. His influence lived on in the New World, particularly through Jonathan Edwards.

God's Plot: Spirituality in Thomas Shepard's Cambridge, revised, expanded edition, ed. Michael McGiffert (UMP; 237 pages; 1994). This contains Shepard's full autobiography and part of his *Journal.* Both are profoundly personal and spiritual. In a preface titled "Thomas Shepard: The Practice of Piety," McGiffert unfortunately suggests that Puritanism was the refuge that Shepard fled to in order to escape the anxieties and guilt of a troubled childhood, and to have his emotional needs met.

Of greater interest in this volume are the conversion accounts of prospective church members. These are simple accounts of saving faith and not a probing into the heart of the candidate in search of the leaven of hypocrisy, as those who have read much of the caricatures of Puritanism might expect.

The Parable of the Ten Virgins (SDG; 640 pages; 1994). This book, first published ten years after Shepard's death (1660), is the outgrowth of a series of sermons Shepard preached between 1636 and 1640, designed to squelch the antinomian error promoted by Anne Hutchinson and her followers that sanctification is not critical for assurance of faith. For example, Shepard writes, "The mighty working of Christ must conquer thy lusts; but must this put you to neglect striving?" (pp. 250-51).

The present edition of *Ten Virgins* is reprinted from Volume 2 of a three-volume set of Shepard's works published in 1853. In forty-one heart-searching sermons on Matthew 25:1-13, Shepard considers the difference between true and spurious conversions. This book is of particular importance today in confronting the prevailing climate of "easy believism."

Ten Virgins is not easy to read, however, and may discourage young believers who seek assurance. They might better first read *Religious Affections* by Jonathan Edwards. As Lloyd-Jones puts it: "Edwards...with all his analysis, negative and positive...never leaves us confused and despondent as Thomas Shepard does in his study on the Parable of the Ten Virgins" ("Jonathan Edwards And The Crucial Importance of Revival" in *The Puritan Experiment in the New World* [1976 Westminster Conference Papers], 117).

Interestingly, Jonathan Edwards in his *Religious Affections* quoted Shepard's *Ten Virgins* more than any other source. *Ten Virgins* does, however, remain a challenge by which the mature believer may chart growth in faith and grace, heeding the advice of John Gerstner in his foreword to the reprint: "This work is valuable in inverse proportion to its readability. Don't read it! Study it, a few pages at a time. Decipher it. Live with it, die with it. It may not save you, but it will leave you in no doubt whether you are saved or not."

The Sincere Convert and the Sound Believer (SDG; 543 pages; 1999). This book, reprinted from the first volume of the 1853 three-volume set, contains two of Shepard's best known works. *The Sincere Convert* shows the small number of true believers and the great difficulty of obtaining a saving conversion, while *The Sound Believer* demonstrates the work of Christ's Spirit in reconciling a sinner to God. This book also contains a 185-page biographical treatment of Shepard's life by John A. Albro.

Theses Sabbaticae (SDG; 1992; 540 pages). This book completes the trilogy of *The Works of Thomas Shepard.* In this work, Shepard defends the observance of the Sabbath as the Christian's reasonable act of worship and service to his God. He does this in four sections: the morality of the Sabbath, the change of the Sabbath, the beginning of the Sabbath, and the sanctification of the Sabbath. In the author's preface, we see some of the prevailing conditions and attitudes of his day that prompted him to write this volume: "It is easy to demonstrate by Scripture and argument, as well as by experience, that religion is just as the Sabbath is, and decays and grows as the Sabbath is esteemed: the immediate honor and worship of God which is brought forth and swaddled in the first three commandments is nursed up and suckled in the bosom of the Sabbath."

Shepard goes on to confront those in the church who "ceremonialized" and "spiritualized" the Sabbath out of the Decalogue. Could it be that the moral decline that we see today is related, at least in part, to Sabbath desecration? It is clear that exegetical antinomians have been around for quite some time.

The book contains a section titled "Meditations and Spiritual Experiences," which are extracts from Shepard's personal journal. Brainerd says of this journal record: "Whoever reads attentively...must own that he finds greater appearance of true humility, self-emptiness, self-loathing, sense of unfruitfulness, selfishness, exceeding vileness of heart and smallness of attainments in grace." At the end of the book is an account of work among Native Americans, revealing Shepard's longing for evangelism among the unsaved nations.

John Shower

(1657-1715)

John Shower was born at Exeter in 1657. He and his three brothers lost their father, a wealthy merchant, when John was about four years old. John was educated successively at Exeter and Otterford, Somerset, and then at the academy at Newington Green, Middlesex, prior to completing his course of ministerial training at Edward Veal's academy in Wapping.

Following the counsel of Thomas Manton, he began to preach before he was twenty years old. His first sermon was delivered at Thomas Vincent's church at Bishopsgate, London. His reputation for preaching grew, and in 1678 Shower was chosen as an evening lecturer in Exchange Alley. The following year, he was ordained by five ejected ministers, and became the assistant of Vincent Alsop in Tothill Street, Westminster. Shower assisted Alsop until 1683, when he was sent abroad as a companion to Samuel Barnardiston, Whig politician and deputy governor of the East India Company. They traveled with two other ministers and explored Europe, arriving in the Netherlands in 1684, where Shower remained for two years. He then returned to London and resumed his lectureship at Exchange Alley for one year before returning to the Netherlands, due to persecution of nonconformists. He joined John Howe at Utrecht for some months, then became a lecturer in Rotterdam at the Presbyterian Church of England, where Joseph Hill served as pastor.

Shower married Elizabeth Falkener, niece of Thomas Papillon, member of Parliament, in 1687. After her early death in 1691, Shower returned to London to serve as assistant to John Howe at Silver Street. After a few months, he accepted a call to serve the Presbyterian Church at Curriers' Hall, Cripplegate, where he remained for nearly twenty-five years until his death. His preaching was so well-received that the congregation had to build larger buildings in 1692 (Jewin Street) and again in 1701 (Old Jewry) to accommodate the people. Timothy Rogers and Joseph Bennet were among his assistants. In 1697, Shower was appointed as a Tuesday lecturer at Salters' Hall, succeeding Samuel Annesley.

Meanwhile, Shower married Constance White in 1692. In 1701, he was left a widower again. In 1706, Shower developed a high fever, which left him physically weak for his remaining years. He suffered a stroke in 1713, and died two years later at his home in Stoke Newington, Middlesex.

Shower wrote nine books and published twenty-one individual sermons. Among his best writings are *An Exhortation to Youth to Prepare for Judgment* (1681), which was reprinted twenty times by 1826, *Serious Reflections on Time and Eternity* (1689), *The Mourner's Companion* (1692), *Sacramental Discourses* (1693), and *Family Religion* (1694).

God's Thoughts and Ways are Above Ours: Especially in the Forgiveness of Sins (SDG; 127 pages; 2003). This moving book contains five sermons on the nature and virtue of pardoning mercy, based on Isaiah 55:7-9. Three concepts dominate Shower's thinking: the call to repentance, the promise of forgiveness to those who repent, and the effectualness of faith in pardoning mercy. Further, Shower shows that God's forgiveness differs from ours in its fullness and freeness. He then devotes a full sermon to the application of this doctrine. Reasoning from Isaiah 55:7 ("Let the wicked forsake his way, and the unrighteous man his thoughts, and let him return unto the Lord, and he will have mercy upon him; and to our God, for he will abundantly pardon"), Shower asserts that we must not abuse God's forgiveness, which is ready to pardon the worst offenses, and that we must be thankful to God for the gift of pardon itself. If there were no pardon, we would all be lost and undone.

In an age when the forgiveness of sins is frequently misunderstood and trivialized and when Christians themselves often do not truly and fully forgive, this title helps us see that God's stupendous forgiveness of sinners should be prized more than the healing of physical diseases, extraordinary signs and wonders, and the praise of others. Being truly forgiven reconciles us to a kind and loving Father, through His redeeming Son and applying Spirit, and moves us to wholeheartedly forgive those who have injured us wrongfully.

Richard Sibbes

(1577-1635)

Richard Sibbes was born in 1577 at Tostock, Suffolk, in the Puritan county of old England. He was baptized in the parish church in Thurston, and went to school there. As a child, he loved books. His father, Paul Sibbes, a hardworking wheelwright and, according to Zachary Catlin, a contemporary biographer of Sibbes, was "a good, sound-hearted Christian," but became irritated with his son's interest in books. He tried to cure his son of book-buying by offering him wheelwright tools, but the boy was not dissuaded. With the support of others, Sibbes was admitted to St. John's College in Cambridge at the age of eighteen. He received a Bachelor of Arts degree in 1599, a fellowship in 1601, and a Master of Arts degree in 1602. In 1603, he was converted under the preaching of Paul Baynes, whom Sibbes called his "father in the gospel." Baynes, remembered most for his commentary on Ephesians, succeeded William Perkins at the Church of St. Andrews in Cambridge.

Sibbes was ordained to the ministry in the Church of England in Norwich in 1608. He was chosen as one of the college preachers in 1609 and earned a Bachelor of Divinity degree in 1610. From 1611 to 1616, he served as lecturer at Holy Trinity Church, Cambridge. His preaching awakened Cambridge from the spiritual indifference into which it had fallen after the death of Perkins. A gallery had to be built to accommodate visitors in the church. John Cotton and Hugh Peters were converted under Sibbes's preaching. During his years at Holy Trinity, Sibbes helped turn Thomas Goodwin away from Arminianism and moved John Preston from "witty preaching" to plain, spiritual preaching.

Sibbes came to London in 1617 as a lecturer for Gray's Inn, the largest of the four great Inns of Court, which still remains one of the most important centers in England for the study and practice of law. In 1626, he also became master of St. Catharine's College, Cambridge. Under his leadership, the college regained some of its former prestige. It graduated several men who would one day serve prominently at the Westminster Assembly: John Arrowsmith, William Spurstowe, and William Strong. Soon after his appointment, Sibbes received the Doctor of Divinity degree at Cambridge. He became known as "the heavenly Doctor," due to his godly preaching and heavenly manner of life. Izaac Walton wrote of Sibbes:

> Of this blest man, let this just praise be given,
> Heaven was in him, before he was in heaven.

In 1633, King Charles I offered Sibbes the charge of Holy Trinity, Cambridge. Sibbes continued to serve as preacher at Gray's Inn, master of St. Catharine's Hall, and vicar of Holy Trinity until his death in 1635.

Sibbes never married, but he established an astonishing network of friendships that included godly ministers, noted lawyers, and parliamentary leaders of the early Stuart era. "Godly friends are walking sermons," he said. He wrote at least thirteen introductions to the writings of his Puritan colleagues.

Sibbes was a gentle man who avoided the controversies of his day as much as possible. "Fractions breed fractions," he insisted. His battles with Archbishop Laud, Roman Catholics, and Arminians were exceptions. He also remained close friends with many pastors and leaders who wanted more radical reform than he did for the Church of England.

Sibbes was an inspiration to many. He influenced Anglicanism, Presbyterianism, and Independency, the three dominant parties of the church in England at that time. He was a pastor of pastors, and lived a life of moderation. "Where most holiness is, there is most moderation, where it may be without prejudice of piety to God and the good of others," he wrote.

The historian Daniel Neal described Sibbes as a celebrated preacher, an educated divine, and a charitable and humble man who repeatedly underestimated his gifts. Yet Puritans everywhere recognized Sibbes as a Christ-centered, experiential preacher. Both learned and unlearned in upper and lower classes profited greatly from Sibbes's alluring preaching.

Sibbes wrote, "To preach is to woo.... The main scope of all [preaching] is, to allure us to the entertainment of Christ's mild, safe, wise, victorious government." He brought truth home, as Robert Burns would say, "to men's business and bosoms." Catlin wrote of Sibbes, "No man that ever I was acquainted with got so far into my heart or lay so close therein." In our day, Maurice Roberts says of Sibbes, "His theology is thoroughly orthodox, of course, but it is like the fuel of some great combustion engine, always passing into flame and so being converted into energy thereby to serve God and, even more, to enjoy and relish God with the soul."

David Masson, biographer of John Milton, wrote, "No writings in practical theology seem to have been so much read in the mid-seventeenth century among the pious English middle classes as those of Sibbes." The twentieth-century historian William Haller said Sibbes's sermons were "the most brilliant and popular of all the utterances of the Puritan church militant."

Sibbes's last sermons, preached a week before his death, were on John 14:2, "In my Father's house are many mansions...."

I go to prepare a place for you." When asked in his final days how his soul was faring, Sibbes replied, "I should do God much wrong if I should not say, very well." Sibbes began his will and testament, dictated on July 4, 1635, the day before his death, with "I commend and bequeath my soul into the hands of my gracious Savior, who hath redeemed it with his most precious blood, and appears now in heaven to receive it." William Gouge preached Sibbes's funeral sermon.

The Works of Richard Sibbes (BTT; 7 vols., 3,850 pages; 2001). These seven volumes, meticulously edited with a 110-page memoir by Alexander Grosart, were published by James Nichol of Edinburgh in the 1860s and reprinted by the Banner of Truth Trust in the 1970s. They reveal Sibbes's conviction that the best Christian counseling is done by the Holy Spirit through the patient and lively exposition of God's Word. This should surprise no one who is aware of Sibbes's subject matter in his sermons. J. I. Packer writes, "Sibbes concentrated on exploring the love, power and patience of Christ, and the riches of the promises of God. He was a pioneer in working out the devotional application of the doctrine of God's covenant of grace."

The first volume of *Works* contains "The Bruised Reed" (see below) and "The Soul's Conflict," a 175-page treatise on Psalm 42:11, showing how the believer can, by faith in Christ, gain victory over spiritual despair. The volume concludes with five sermons on 1 Peter 4:17-19 and four other sermons. The sermon "Christ is Best" (Phil. 1:23-24) alone is worth the price of the book.

The second volume in the set contains larger treatises from Old Testament passages, including "Bowels Opened" (expository sermons on Song of Solomon 4:16 to 6:13), "A Breathing after God" (Ps. 27:4), the well-known "Returning

Backslider" (Hos. 14), and "The Glorious Feast of the Gospel" (Isa. 25:7-9).

The third volume is devoted to Sibbes's exposition of 2 Corinthians 1. Solid doctrine, love for Christ, and warm pastoral applications abound in this commentary. Sibbes is full of Christ when he describes the Christian in his sufferings and the promised comfort of God, saying that sufferings precede comforts because that was the pattern Christ established for us. This work also contains Sibbes's notable teaching on the sealing of the Holy Spirit (vv. 22-23).

According to Sibbes, looking at the role of the Spirit in sealing the soul of believers is like examining His work in personal assurance of faith. Sibbes viewed the sealing of the Spirit as two distinct matters, however. He distinguished between the office or function of the Spirit as a seal given in regeneration to a sinner and the work of the Spirit in applying that seal to the believer's consciousness.

The once-for-all sealing of salvation is granted when a person first believes in Christ. Sibbes taught that as a king's image is stamped upon wax, so the Spirit stamps believers' souls with the image of Christ from the moment of believing. Such sealing produces in every believer a lifelong desire to be transformed fully into the image of Christ.

This seal, which every believer has whether he is conscious of it or not, is a mark of authenticity that distinguishes the believer from the world. As merchants mark their wares and herdsmen brand their sheep, so God seals His people to declare that they are His rightful property and that He has authority over them, Sibbes said.

The second kind of sealing is a process. It is the kind of assurance that can gradually increase throughout a believer's life through singular experiences and by daily, spiritual growth. This sealing can be observed in the fruits of sanctification, such as peace of conscience; the spirit of adoption whereby we cry "Abba, Father"; prayers of fervent supplication; and conformity with the heavenly image of Christ. Sibbes thus emphasized both the intuitive testimony of the Spirit and the sanctifying fruits of the Spirit.

The Spirit grants this special sealing to saints in times of great trial, Sibbes said. The Spirit gave such seals "even as parents [who] smile upon their children when they need it most." Such sealing was "a sweet kiss vouchsafed to the soul." Paul in the dungeon, Daniel in the lions' den, and his three friends in the fiery furnace experienced that kind of encouragement.

Volume 4 contains other sermons on texts or portions of the two epistles to the Corinthians, including "Glorious Freedom: The Excellency of the Gospel Above the Law" (see below) and an exposition of 2 Corinthians 4. This volume emphasizes the centrality of Christ and the role of the Spirit in the lives of believers. According to Sibbes, the Spirit must be an integral part of our lives, our churches, and our world. We must relish His indwelling and His comforting work, while striving not to grieve Him. We should walk in daily communication with the Spirit through the Word, relying upon every office the Holy Spirit provides, as described in Scripture. As Sibbes writes: "The Holy Spirit being in us, after he that prepared us for a house for himself to dwell in and to take up his rest and delight in, he doth also become unto us a counselor in all our doubts, a comforter in all our distresses, a solicitor to all duty, a guide in the whole course of life, until we dwell with him forever in heaven, unto which his dwelling here in us doth tend."

The fifth volume offers teaching on passages in Romans, Galatians, Ephesians, Philippians, Colossians, and 1 Timothy. They contain sermons on several of the richest and best known of all Paul's words, such as Romans 8:28 and Galatians 2:20, and address subjects such as the art of contentment, the life of faith, the power of Christ's resurrection, the Christian's end, Christian work, and the providence of God. Most well-known are Sibbes's "A Fountain Sealed" (Eph. 4:30) and "The Fountain Opened" (1 Tim. 3:16).

This volume stresses the privileges of believers, such as communion with Christ, the indwelling of the Spirit, assurance of faith, and future glory. Nearly two hundred pages are devoted to teachings on Philippians, which stress the believer's heavenly citizenship. Everywhere in this volume, Sibbes proves his reputation as "a Christ-preacher." He writes, "The special work of our ministry is to lay open Christ, to hold up the tapestry and unfold the mysteries of Christ. Let us labour therefore to be always speaking somewhat about Christ, or tending that way. When we speak of the law, let it drive us to Christ; when of moral duties, let them teach us to walk worthy of Christ."

The sixth volume contains eighteen sermons on a great variety of subjects, including faithful covenanting, Josiah's reformation, successful seeking of God, the saint's comforts, spiritual mourning, and Lydia's conversion. "A Heavenly Conference between Christ and Mary after His Resurrection" (John 20:16) represents Puritan divinity at its best. For example, when speaking of the constancy of Christ's love for Mary and for the church, Sibbes writes, "The whole chain [of God's love] so holdeth, that all the creatures in heaven and earth cannot break a link of it. Therefore never doubt of continuance, for it holds firm on God's part, not thine. God embraceth us in the arms of his everlasting love, not that we embraced him first. When the child falleth not, it is from the mother's holding the child, and not from the child's holding the mother. So it is God's holding of us, knowing of us, embracing of us, and justifying of us that maketh the state firm, and not ours; for ours is but a reflection and result of his, which is unvariable" (p. 439).

The final volume contains thirty-five sermons on practical themes such as recovery from discouragement, true happiness, prayer, the success of the gospel, the return of Christ, the danger of backsliding, and the resurrection. The sermon titled "The Matchless Mercy" (Micah 7:18-20) exalts the mercy of God. Sibbes's last two sermons on John 14:2 are also included.

The Bruised Reed (BTT; 128 pages; 1998). This treatise on the dejected sinner is one of the best works of its kind. In sixteen chapters, Sibbes expounds Isaiah 42:3, "A bruised reed shall he not break, and the smoking flax shall he not quench: he shall bring forth judgment unto truth." Richard Baxter said that God used the reading of this treatise to effect his own conversion. Martyn Lloyd-Jones wrote, "I shall never cease to be grateful to Richard Sibbes who was balm to my soul at a period in my life when I was overworked and badly overtired, and therefore subject in an unusual manner to the onslaughts of the devil.... I found at that time that Richard Sibbes, who was known in London in the early seventeenth century as the 'Heavenly Doctor Sibbes' was an unfailing remedy.... *The Bruised Reed* quieted, soothed, comforted, encouraged and healed me."

Glorious Freedom (BTT; 194 pages; 2000). This book was published under the supervision of Thomas Goodwin and Philip Nye four years after Sibbes's death. They said it shows "the liberty of the sons of God...the image of their graces here and glory hereafter" and it provides "much comfort and great encouragement to all [who] begin timely and continue constantly in the ways of God."

Glorious Freedom explains the believer's relation to the law based on 2 Corinthians 3:17-18. Sibbes describes the fuller revelation of God in the coming of Christ and its effect on those who behold that glory by the Spirit. The vitality of the new covenant results in spiritual liberty and likeness to Christ. The book addresses subjects such as the Spirit of Christ, liberty, the gospel beyond the law, communion with God in Christ, and conformity to the image of Christ. "Sibbes never wastes the student's time," Spurgeon wrote; "he scatters pearls and diamonds with both hands."

Henry Smith

(1560-1591)

Henry Smith, one of the most popular sixteenth-century preachers in England, was called "the silver-tongued Smith" by his contemporaries for his remarkable oratory. Born in Withcote, Leicestershire, about 1560, Smith was the eldest son of Erasmus Smith. He came from an honorable family line in Leicestershire and was heir to a considerable estate. In 1573, he was admitted as fellow commoner to Queens College, Cambridge, but he did not stay there long. Three years later, he moved to Lincoln College, Oxford, where he graduated with a Bachelor of Arts degree in 1579. He continued his studies under Richard Greenham, rector of Dry Drayton, Cambridgeshire, with whom he resided, and from whom he learned more fully the principles of Puritanism.

Smith initially became a minister in the Church of England, but became increasingly dissatisfied with various practices and ceremonies, soon settling for a lectureship. For some time, Smith was active in the Husbands Bosworth Church, which operated under his father's patronage, though it is uncertain whether he became rector there. While studying with Greenham, Smith's anti-Episcopal leanings intensified. Like Greenham, Smith took a strict stance against leaving the church, however, believing that the Church of

England should be reformed from within. He viewed separatists such as the Brownists and Barrowists as enemies of the true church and justly liable to persecution.

In 1582, Smith's uncle, Bryant Cave, High Sheriff of Leicestershire, became acquainted with Robert Dickons, an apprentice at Mansell in Nottinghamshire. Dickons, though intelligent and knowledgeable, believed that he was the prophet Elijah and that he had been visited by angels in a series of visions. Presumably, Cave arranged for Smith to counsel Dickons. Smith opened the Scriptures to Dickons and persuaded Dickons of his error. Fuller noted that Dickons "was reclaimed, renouncing his blasphemies by subscription under his own hand." Smith then preached the sermon "The Lost Sheep Is Found," on 1 John 4:1: "Try the spirits whether they are of God."

Smith's preaching in the London area was very successful. In 1587, upon Greenham's recommendation, he was elected lecturer at St. Clement Danes, London. Thomas Fuller noted that "persons of good quality brought their own pews with them, I mean their legs to stand there upon in the aisles, [and] their ears did so attend his lips, their hearts to their ears, that he held the rudder of their affections in his hand, so that he could steer them whither he pleased, and he was pleased to steer them only to God's glory and their own good." Smith became so popular that he was referred to as "the prime preacher of the nation." Wood said that he was "esteemed the miracle and wonder of his age, for his prodigious memory, and for his fluent, eloquent, and practical way of preaching."

The freedom that Puritan lecturers enjoyed in the early 1570s diminished in 1577 when Archbishop Grindal, who was somewhat sympathetic to the Puritan cause, fell into disfavor with the Queen. Consequently, the bishop of London, John Aylmer, made a series of investigations to ensure that preachers were adhering to "proper conformity." The Puritans suffered greatly under Grindal's replacement, the vigorous Archbishop John Whitgift, who opposed Puritanism in all its forms.

In 1588, Bishop Aylmer was erroneously informed that Smith had slandered *The Book of Common Prayer* in one of his sermons. Supposedly, Smith had refused to subscribe to Whitgift's articles, which insisted on the supreme authority under God of the monarchy, the use and promotion of the Prayer Book, and subscription to the Thirty Nine Articles. Accordingly, Smith was suspended from preaching.

Smith attempted to defend himself to Lord Treasurer Burghley, Elizabeth's most trusted adviser, stating that Aylmer had personally called him to preach at St. Paul's Cross. Smith also denied the accusation that he spoke against the Prayer Book; he said that he had subscribed to all the articles of "faith and doctrine" but had avoided the issue of discipline. The parishioners of St. Clement Danes sent a testimonial and supplication on his behalf. These efforts and Burghley's influence at court were effective in getting Smith restored to the lectureship.

In the late 1580s, the rector of St. Clement Danes, William Harward, became very ill. The parishioners of St. Clement Danes tried to obtain Smith as their rector, but he refused the position. Smith subsequently resigned his lectureship in 1590 because of failing health. He retired to Husbands Bosworth, Leicestershire, where he prepared his writings for the press and revised his sermons. He dedicated his collection of sermons to Lord Burghley but died at age thirty-one before the collection was published.

Smith was buried at Husbands Bosworth on July 4, 1591. Puritans and Anglicans alike mourned the loss of a great preacher and peacemaker. Even Thomas Nashe, known for his fierce opposition to the Puritans, saw Smith's death as an occasion for "the general tears of the muses."

Henry Smith promoted moderate Puritanism from within the Established Church, believing that, until the Church of England separated from Christ, no one should separate from it. He remained conscious of the church's faults until the end; yet, much like Greenham and Perkins, he sought first the reformation of individuals and then, secondly, the reformation of churches. This was the heart of moderate Puritanism during the reign of Elizabeth.

The Works of Henry Smith (TENT; 2 vols., 1,050 pages; 2002). Smith's sermons were so popular that by the early seventeenth century, collections of them had gone through more than eighty-five editions. While many of Smith's sermons were published in his lifetime (a few of them without his consent), a complete collection was not available until 1675 under Thomas Fuller's editorship. Fuller also supplied the first biography of Smith, drawing from Wood's history and correspondence with individuals who still remembered him. Thomas Smith reissued Fuller's edition in 1866 with minor changes and added several pages of commentary. This edition, printed in James Nichol's Series of Standard Divines in two volumes and now reprinted by Tentmaker, remains "the fullest, the most accurate, and the most elegant" edition published.

A similar edition was published in 1866 by William Tegg as "an exact reprint of the edition which was printed according to the Author's corrected copies in his lifetime." Since it was not under Thomas Smith's editorship, however, it does not contain the commentary on Fuller's biography. The editor of the Tegg edition, Edwin Davies, made minor linguistic changes in the text (for instance, "thorow" was changed to "thorough"), but left Fuller's archaisms alone.

Nichol's two-volume set contains all of Smith's extant works: fifty-six sermons with their original prefaces; an account to the Lord Justices concerning Robert Dickons; "God's

Arrow Against Atheism and Irreligion"; eight prayers for various occasions; "A Comfortable Speech, taken from a Godly Preacher lying upon his Deathbed, Written for the Sick"; "A Letter to One's Friend in Sickness"; eight epigrams; the poem "Microcosmographia: The Little World's Description; or, The Map of Man"; Fuller's original biography of Smith; eleven pages of notes by Thomas Smith, and extensive indices and textual references.

Smith's sermons discuss such subjects as the Lord's Supper, usury, the Christian's sacrifice, the trial of the spirits, the way to walk, dissuasions from pride, the young man's task, the trial of the righteous, the Christian's practice, the pilgrim's wish, the godly man's request, a mirror for Christians, the poor man's tears, the sinner's conversion, and the sinful man's search.

It is impossible to determine the exact dates or chronological order for all of Smith's sermons, though R. B. Jenkins, relying somewhat on the work of Thomas Ehret, attempts to do this. In brief, here is what he says:

1. "The Lost Sheep Is Found" is dated in 1582, shortly after Smith's examination of Robert Dickons, and deals directly with that event.

2. The two sermons on "The Art of Hearing" are dated 1587 by Ehret. Jenkins notes that it "is impossible to ascertain the year in which these sermons were preached, but certainly one followed the other."

3. "The Sinful Man's Search" is dated January 1, 1588 by Ehret, with Jenkins's affirmation.

4. "Satan's Compassing the Earth" and "The Trial of the Righteous" are dated some time in 1588 because of their seeming references to the Spanish Armada.

5. "The Dialogue between Paul and King Agrippa," "The Ladder of Peace," and the four sermons on Jonah were preached, presumably, after July 29, 1588, when the Armada was defeated, as they refer to that event.

6. "The Godly Man's Request," a New Year's sermon, was preached on January 1, 1589.

7. The series of sermons on Nebuchadnezzar are dated in close proximity to the Armada incident.

8. "The Christian's Sacrifice," which Smith called the sum of "all the lessons together which ye have heard since I came [to St. Clement Danes]," is dated just prior to Smith's retirement; its first printing was shortly after his retirement.

9. "The Petition of Moses to God" is classified as Smith's last sermon at St. Clement Danes, though it scarcely bears the mark of a farewell sermon. Near the end of the sermon, however, Smith says, "Now it resteth that I should encourage Joshua, which succeedeth me."

The remaining 39 sermons are impossible to date, and neither Ehret nor Jenkins attempt to do so. It is fairly certain they were preached during Smith's lectureship at Clement Danes, with the possible exception of "The Trumpet of the Soul Sounding to Judgment."

Smith's sermons should be studied for several reasons. First, for scholars, no book exists that exhaustively examines Smith's place within his Elizabethan context. Ehret's work, while critically examining four of Smith's sermons, does not deal with his entire corpus. The best work on Smith to date is by R.B. Jenkins (1983); it fills many gaps in Ehret's edition and supplements that work with a more inclusive grasp of Smith's place in Elizabethan England. But even Jenkins's work is sketchy at times and does not fully consider the intricacies of politics and religion in the 1580s.

Second, for pastors, Smith exemplifies an early Puritan ideal: simplicity and intelligence combined with heart appeal. Here is one example: "Nowadays," said Smith, "men take upon them to reprove others for committing such things as themselves have practiced, and do practice without amendment, notwithstanding their diligence in teaching others their duty; they can teach all the doctrine of Christ saving three syllables, that is, Follow me." Scores more of such examples could be given that could stimulate pastors in the challenging task of preaching.

Third, for laymen, Smith's sermons provide a treasure of inspiration and contemplation. For instance, in Smith's sermon "The Art of Hearing," he admonishes those who are quick to remember old tales and equally quick to forget sermons: "Therefore, that you may not hear us in vain, as you have heard others, my exhortation to you is, to record when you are gone that which you have heard." Also, in reference to conjugal love, Smith admonishes that "man must take heed that his love toward his wife, be not greater than his love toward God, as Adam's and Samson's were."

Smith called the masses to consider the world as a place of vanity and sorrow, and thus to fight their way towards the heavenly city, a place that contains true happiness. His listeners, from all stations in life, asserted that "his preaching, living, and sound doctrine had done more good among them than any other that had gone before or, which they doubted, could follow after." No wonder, then, that Richard Baxter recommends Smith's sermons in his *The Christian Directory* as essential even for the "smallest library that is tolerable."

William Spurstowe

(c. 1605-1666)

William Spurstowe was the son of a London merchant, William Spurstowe, and a descendant of the Spurstowes of Bunbury, Cheshire. William was admitted to Emmanuel College, Cambridge, in 1623, where he earned a bachelor's degree in 1627. He then moved to St. Catharine's College, Cambridge, where he received a master's degree three years later.

In 1638, Spurstowe entered the ministry at Great Hampden, Buckinghamshire, the church of the celebrated Parliamentary leader John Hampden. That same year he was also elected as a fellow of St. Catharine's College. A year or two later, he married a godly young woman named Sarah.

When the English civil war began, Spurstowe sided with Parliament and served as a chaplain (1642-43) in John Hampden's regiment, under the command of the Earl of Essex. Spurstowe, like Hampden, hoped to overthrow the king's forces in order to push the sovereign to a position more favorable to the Puritan conscience. Like most other royalist Puritans, neither Spurstowe nor Hampden was against the king himself—they never condoned his execution. After Hampden's untimely death in 1643, however, a process of events transpired that would culminate in the king's trial.

Spurstowe was one of five divines who wrote tracts against Episcopal church government in 1641 under the acronym *Smectymnuus*, the last three letters of this word forming his initials (VVS). The other authors were Stephen Marshall, Edmund Calamy, Thomas Young, and Matthew Newcomen. Reprinted at least four times by 1680, *Smectymnuus* contributed a note of conciliation into the ongoing debate between Episcopacy and Presbyterianism. Denying the apostolic origin of liturgies and the divine right of Episcopacy, its authors were willing to bear with the existence of bishops, if the office was reduced to its primitive simplicity. Furthermore, they were willing to allow liturgies on the condition that certain divines reform them according to God's Word. These conditions, however, were unacceptable to high churchmen.

Along with the other authors of *Smectymnuus*, Spurstowe was summoned to the Westminster Assembly of Divines. Shortly before the assembly convened on May 3, 1643, he succeeded Calybute Downing as preacher of St. John's, Hackney, Middlesex. The following year he subscribed to the Solemn League and Covenant. Spurstowe served the assembly faithfully for several years, except for brief excused absences in 1645 to attend to duties associated with his new appointment as master of St. Catharine's College, Cambridge, and, in 1646, for a preaching itinerary at Cambridge.

During his years with the Assembly, Spurstowe preached before Parliament on at least four occasions. On July 21, 1643, he preached a sermon titled *England's Pattern and Duty* to a joint session of Lords and Commons on 1 Samuel 7:6 for a day of fasting and humiliation. In this sermon, he stressed the need for monthly fasting; he asserted that true fasters should be weepers, and that fasting should involve acknowledgment and confession of sin. Second, he preached a sermon on Ezra 9:13-14, *England's eminent Judgments caused by the abuse of God's eminent Mercies*, before the House of Lords on November 5, 1644, the anniversary of the Gunpowder Plot of 1605. He admonished the House of Lords to show their zeal for reformation by living out their Christianity as a "seamless coat of Christ [rather than]" like a beggar's cloak, which hath a thousand patches in it." He encouraged them to view the church as "the enclosed garden of Christ," which must not be allowed to be overrun with many poisonous weeds that "in a short time will eat out [its] very life and power of holiness." He also preached to the House of Commons on June 24, 1646, and to the House of Lords on August 25, 1647, but the sermons were not printed.

Called a "grand Presbyterian" by his contemporaries, Spurstowe sat on the committee to consider the reasons given by the Independents for their views of church government. He was appointed a commissioner to Newport to confer with King Charles I in the Isle of Wight in 1648. Near the end of that year, he was one of the signers of a document drafted by Cornelius Burges (*A Vindication of the Ministers of the Gospel in, and about London*) vindicating the ministers of the gospel in London who opposed the anticipated trial of Charles I. Their pleas, however, were not heard; the king was executed for high treason in London on January 30, 1649.

Spurstowe was awarded a doctorate in divinity in 1649. The following year, he was deprived of his position as master of St. Catharine's for refusing allegiance to the existing government without a king or House of Lords. The renowned John Lightfoot succeeded him. After the Restoration, Lightfoot offered to resign in Spurstowe's favor, but Spurstowe declined.

In 1654, the Spurstowes lost their only son, William, at age nine to cholera. Simeon Ashe, a close friend, preached the funeral message, which was titled, "Christ: The Riches of the Gospel and the Hope of Christians." In the sermon, he describes how the young William was often much affected with heaven's glory and frequently spoke of the blessedness of being with Christ forever.

In the late 1650s, Spurstowe and a number of Presbyterian ministers supported Richard Cromwell. Spurstowe was appointed commissioner for the approbation of ministers in

1660, but that committee was soon disbanded with the Convention Parliament.

Spurstowe assisted in the negotiations with Charles II in Holland in May 1660. Afterward, he was appointed chaplain-in-ordinary to Charles II, together with about ten other Presbyterian ministers. Of these, the king selected Spurstowe as one of four ministers to preach before him; the others were Edmund Calamy, Edward Reynolds, and Richard Baxter.

Ezekiel Hopkins became Spurstowe's assistant at Hackney in 1660. The following year, Spurstowe served as a commissioner to the Savoy Conference. When the Act of Uniformity took effect on August 24, 1662, Spurstowe resigned his living at Hackney, which then went to Thomas Jeamson. Spurstowe retired to his home in Hackney, living off his own means.

Having survived the plague of 1665, Spurstowe died suddenly the following year. His widow married Anthony Tuckney, a colleague from the Westminster Assembly.

Richard Baxter described Spurstowe as "an ancient, calm, reverend minister." Edmund Calamy praised him as "a man of great humility and meekness; and great charity both in giving and forgiving." According to James Reid, Spurstowe was a man with a peaceable disposition.

Spurstowe wrote three books: *The Wells of Salvation Opened: Or, A Treatise Discovering the nature, preciousness, usefulness of Gospel-Promises, and Rules for the right application of them* (1655); *The Spiritual Chymist; or, Six Decades of Divine Meditations* (1666); and *The Wiles of Satan* (1666). Only *The Wells of Salvation* was reprinted in the seventeenth century (1659), and it may well be the best book ever written on God's promises. The book contains the content of several sermons, which Spurstowe introduces in a preface by saying: "The promises are a large field in which the wise merchant may find more pearls hidden, than are yet espied: A rich mine in which the diligent laborer may dig forth more fine gold, than any yet have taken from them."

The Wiles of Satan (SDG; 118 pages; 2004). Published posthumously as *Satana Nohmata; Or, The Wiles of Satan*, Spurstowe presents a fine discourse on 2 Corinthians 2:11: "Lest Satan should get an advantage of us, for we are not ignorant of his devices." He demonstrates the devil's abilities as a tempter, exposes a good number of his strategies, and furnishes the Christian with biblical antidotes for these various schemes.

Spurstowe is particularly powerful in enumerating six reasons Satan is so skillful at tempting us to sin: (1) Satan's spiritual being and intellectual power; (2) Satan's experience and work; (3) Satan's tireless energy for promoting evil; (4) Satan's kingdom of demons; (5) Satan's evil suggestions, which are nearly indistinguishable from our own corrupt desires; and (6) Satan's skill at matching his suggestions with our own corrupt reason.

Though not as exhaustive as other related Puritan classics such as Thomas Brooks's *Precious Remedies*, Richard Gilpin's *A Treatise on Satan's Temptations*, William Gurnall's *The Christian in Complete Armour*, and John Downame's *The Christian Warfare*, Spurstowe's little book is every bit as helpful. Its succinctness can be an asset to those heavily engaged in battling temptation, for the sorely tempted seldom are looking for a massive tome.

Spurstowe was halfway through editing chapter 4 of *The Wiles* when he died. The remainder of that chapter and the concluding chapter have been developed from his extensive notes.

Richard Steele
(1629-1692)

R ichard Steele, son of a farmer, Robert Steele, was born at Claycroft in Barthomley, Cheshire, in 1629. He was educated at the grammar school in Northwich and then admitted to St. John's College, Cambridge, in 1642, where he received a Bachelor of Arts degree in 1650 and a Master of Arts degree the following year. In 1656, he received a Master of Arts degree from Oxford.

Steele succeeded Thomas Porter as rector of Hanmer, Flintshire, in 1654. A Presbyterian in practice, Steele associated his parish with the fourth Shropshire classical presbytery, which enabled him to be among the presbyters who participated in the ordination of his lifelong friend, Philip Henry. Thirty years later, he also participated in the ordination of Philip's son, Matthew Henry.

In 1660, Steele was cited at the Flint Assizes with Philip Henry for not reading *The Book of Common Prayer*. The conviction was dropped the following month when Charles declared an indulgence of tolerance. The following spring, Steele was again brought before the Assizes, this time at Hawarden. He resigned his living due to the Act of Uniformity in 1662. At his farewell sermon, he stated that he was ejected for not subscribing to a prayer book that he had not yet had the opportunity to see.

Steele moved to Hanmer, where he continued to preach in private. In 1663, he was questioned for baptizing his own children. A few months later, he was arrested on suspicion of treason, but was soon released. Eighteen months later, when he was arrested again, passages from his pocket diary, which was taken from him, were twisted and used to accuse him falsely of an adulterous affair. After considerable gossip ensued "to his great reproach and injury" (Calamy, *Abridgement*, 2:708), the matter was dismissed.

In 1666, with the passing of the Five Mile Act, Steele was forced to leave Hanmer, and took up residence near Betley, Staffordshire. By 1672, he had moved to London, where he spent his remaining years as a minister of the gospel. He was granted a license to preach on Sabbath mornings at Armourers' Hall, Coleman Street, and in the afternoons at Hoxton. He also preached regularly at the nonconformist morning exercises. He registered as a preacher at Hoxton in 1688 when the Revolution brought toleration.

Steele suffered from tuberculosis for several years, but he kept working. On November 14, 1692, Steele visited several friends in London. That evening, his physical condition began to deteriorate; he was carried home in a coach and passed away two days later at age sixty-four. His last words were: "Ye cannot make a better choice [than God], and are eternally undone if ye make a worse." George Hamond, his colleague and successor, preached at the funeral a sermon printed as *A Good Minister of Jesus Christ* (1692), in which he urged Steele's congregation to live as their pastor had lived.

Prior to his death, Steele was preaching on the attributes of God. The Sabbath before he died, he offered a "rich mine of spiritual treasures" from the goodness of God. Steele's assistant wrote: "The contemplation of the attributes of God must needs have filled him with ravishment, while he viewed them, though but as in a glass, darkly; but now he is gone to those regions of light and love, where all mists are dispelled, and there he hath such a knowledge of them, as they who are muffled up with mortality, cannot comprehend."

Steele's character was like that of Caleb, "a man of another spirit." He was constant in preaching and disciplined in study. His manuscript notes were "exceedingly many," but most of them have been lost. In addition to his sermons, Steele compiled and edited several treatises (noted below). His writings show skill in expounding God's Word and rare insight into the human heart. He was a compassionate shepherd to his family of ten children (five of whom he buried) and his flock.

<hr/>

The Character of an Upright Man (SDG; 120 pages; 2004). Originally published as *A Plain Discourse upon Uprightness* (1670), this collection of sermons was originally written only for Steele's congregation, but in time its influence reached much further. The bishop of Chichester, Robert Grove (1634-1696), who opposed Nonconformity in nearly all forms, gave his *imprimatur* ("let it be printed") to Steele's treatise, showing how influential Steele's teaching had become.

Written for the advancement of the "vitals of genuine piety," Steele scorned controversies that "scorch up all true love and zeal, and greatly grieve such as love peace." If people could unite to promote the honor, love, and fear of God, and the furtherance of holiness, they would soon agree or at least indulge one another in the lesser things, said Steele. "'Tis hypocrites on all sides that make our wound incurable," he wrote. In many ways, this book sought to moderate the fiery debate between Conformists and Nonconformists.

The Character of an Upright Man has three chapters. The first addresses the uprightness of man, the second the uprightness of God, and the third applies the teaching of the earlier chapters to inform the mind and reform conversation. Characteristic of Puritan style, there is something for everyone in these pages. The faithful Christian will find a road map to godliness; the backsliding believer will see the danger of delaying repentance; and the unbeliever will be challenged by the integrity and compassion of the Christian life.

Steele argues that it is impossible to be a Christian and not strive to live uprightly. The hypocrite thus remains on slippery ground. Steele puts it this way: "You see a spider's web to be a very curious work, but its original is from a spider's bowels, and its design is to catch poor flies; and though she be as secure in it as in a castle, yet when the broom comes, down they go." When God comes in judgment, the hypocrite will be undone.

The Religious Tradesman (SPR; 216 pages; 1989). Originally printed as *The Tradesman's Calling* (1684), Steele addresses the duties of common shopkeepers in the midst of the bustle of daily life, showing how God-glorifying labor in their calling can serve as proof of the saving grace of God at work in their lives. After providing reasons for work and giving direction on pursuing and quitting a vocation, Steele elaborates on how prudence, diligence, justice, truth, contentment, and faith characterize the religious tradesman.

The Religious Tradesman is evangelical and practical throughout. Prefaced by Isaac Watts, it was one of the first books given away by the Society for Promoting Religious Knowledge. Recently, Randall Caldwell has reissued Steele's classic in a modern English version (VH; 159 pages; 2005).

A Remedy for Wandering Thoughts in Worship (SPR; 239 pages; 1988). First published in 1667 as *An Antidote against Distractions; or An Endeavor to Serve the Church in the Daily Case of Wanderings in the Worship of God*, this is Steele's most famous work. It is an extensive Puritan treatment on mental distrac-tions. Based on 1 Corinthians 7:35, it provides a much needed corrective to intrusive, unwanted, and distracting thoughts in public worship. Interestingly, this work was written while Steele was in a Welsh prison, suffering for nonconformity. Between writing and sleeping, he witnessed to the guards, zealous for their eternal welfare.

Characteristic of this work is its stress on the basics of religion and the heart piety of the Puritans. Steele's book is as probing and practical as Nathaniel Vincent's *The Cure of Distractions in Attending upon God* (1695). For those tormented by unruly thoughts, Steele's work is a great help.

Solomon Stoddard

(1643-1729)

Solomon Stoddard was born in Boston, Massachusetts, as one of fifteen sons to Anthony Stoddard, a prominent merchant, and Mary Downing, niece of Governor John Winthrop and sister of Governor Simon Bradstreet's wife. Stoddard graduated from Harvard College in 1662. He was appointed a fellow, or tutor, at the college in 1666 and became its first librarian. He then spent two years as a chaplain in Barbados.

Stoddard was about to leave by ship for England in 1669, when a delegation from Northampton, Massachusetts, persuaded him to succeed their recently deceased pastor, Eleazar Mather, brother of the well-known Increase Mather. Several months after arriving at Northampton, he married his predecessor's widow, Esther. She was a daughter of John Warham, an eminent minister in Connecticut. Together the couple raised twelve children, three of them from Esther's previous marriage.

During the sixty years that Stoddard was pastor, Northampton grew from a small community to a prosperous town. The town was blessed with excellent farmland in the Connecticut River floodplain and a strategic location at the crossroads of New England's inland travel routes. Delegates from Northampton became spokesmen for the western region in the Massachusetts General Court, and Solomon Stoddard's son, John, became the region's most prominent land speculator, magistrate, and military commander. Providentially, Stoddard was at the center of an enormous network of

influential people in New England. He used that position
to promote godliness and stand against growing practices
of impiety.

Stoddard's preaching made Northampton one of New
England's most famed towns. His church became known for
periodic revivals of piety (five "harvests," as he called them),
and his ecclesiology furthered the Puritan experiment in New
England communities. John Erskine wrote of Stoddard: "His
sermons were searching and experimental, yet rational and
argumentative; and often peculiarly suited for awakening the
secure, directing in the great work of salvation, and assisting
the doubtful in judging their spiritual state."

Upon arriving at Northampton, Stoddard accepted the
Half-Way Covenant that his predecessor had violently opposed. Pastorally, he saw that many of the children of the
founders were faltering in spiritual intensity. He offered full
membership rights of the church to any professing Christian,
even if that person had little or no assurance about being in a
state of grace. He preached God's love as well as God's wrath,
and he urged all who found in their hearts any ground of hope
for salvation to come into the church.

This was a substantial break with the practices of earlier
generations. It dismissed not only the testimony of experienced grace as the criterion for full church membership, but
also the second generation's compromise of "half-way" membership status for those who agreed to be governed by
Christian rules but lacked true religious experience. After
years of argument, Stoddard also persuaded his church to
open the Lord's Supper to all who were not living an openly
sinful life and to embrace that sacrament as a possible means
of receiving God's saving grace.

Stoddard's was an unprecedented approach, and soon the
majority of New England churches were moving in that direction. Called "Stoddardism" by modern scholars, critics rightly

argued that the practice lessened the sanctity of the sacraments as symbols and seals for God's covenantal people and opened the door to a generation of spiritually presumptuous individuals. Its long-term effects were disastrous, as Jonathan Edwards would later discover.

Stoddardism did not go unopposed. Increase and Cotton Mather vehemently resisted it in public and in print. Increase Mather denounced Stoddard for taking Congregationalism in the direction of Presbyterianism and for losing the distinction between the church as a community of regenerate persons and the secular community. Nonetheless, Stoddard was widely followed by ministers and churches in western Massachusetts and Connecticut. His influence spread in particular through the ministry of his eldest son, Anthony, in Connecticut, and through the work of the five pastors who married his daughters. Through these daughters, the Stoddard clan became the socio-religious elite of western New England in the first half of the eighteenth century. It was said that Stoddard's fame surpassed that of both Mathers. Timothy Dwight, Stoddard's grandson, said that Stoddard possessed "more influence than any other clergyman in the province." When Stoddard died, he was eulogized in his home region and in once-hostile Boston as a fallen patriarch.

Stoddard published vigorous arguments for his doctrinal innovations in two themes that reflect the two sides of his professional personality. One motif was evangelical: he exhorted laymen to trust in Christ's mercy and advised ministers to find Christ within their hearts, not just scholarship within their heads. The most significant publications addressing this motif were *The Safety of Appearing at the Day of Judgment in the Righteousness of Christ* (1687); *An Appeal to the Learned* (1709); *A Guide to Christ* (1714); and *The Defects of Preachers Reproved* (1724). The second motif, Stoddard's attraction to hierarchical church government and his disdain for laymen's presumptuousness as judges of souls, are evident in *The Doctrine of Instituted Churches* (1700) and *An Examination of the Power of the Fraternity* (1718).

In another work, *The Trial of Assurance* (1698), Stoddard deals extensively with the Lord's inquiry, "Simon, son of Jonas, lovest thou me?" This book shows Stoddard's pastoral care for perplexed souls, despite his flaws as a spiritual physician.

Stoddard's increasing emphasis on the governing power of the minister and elders within the congregation earned him the epithet "pope of the Connecticut River Valley." Some churches refused to support that form of church government and adhered to the more democratic Cambridge Platform of 1648, which gave lay members greater control over admissions of members and the discipline of sinners. One of the clearest arguments over these policies rose in East Windsor, Connecticut, where Stoddard's son-in-law, Timothy Edwards, tirelessly advocated Stoddard's system in its Connecticut manifestation as the Saybrook Platform against a resistant congregation.

Stoddard died in 1729. Within twenty years after his death, Stoddardism began to decline, although many of its elements continued in other theological systems. Ultimately, Stoddardism failed in its attempt to have a gathered and regenerate church that embraced the whole community.

⇒◆◆◆⇐

The Fear of Hell Restrains Men from Sin (SDG; 20 pages; 2003). In every revival of note, two themes have been common in preaching: justification by faith alone and the certainty of hell for the impenitent. Stoddard zealously desired to see souls saved by Jesus Christ, so he preached often about hell, saying, "If sinners don't hear often of judgment and damnation, few will be converted."

Originally published in 1713 as *The Efficacy of the Fear of Hell to Restrain Men from Sin,* this is a powerful sermon that explains how the fear of hell can benefit parents, ministers, magistrates, office-bearers, businessmen, and young people. He concludes by considering the great miseries of hell and the impossibility of the damned to escape from hell.

A Guide to Christ (SDG; 120 pages; 1997). This manual was written "to help young ministers guide seeking souls through the work of conversion." It is mainly a treatise that addresses the question, "What should a person do who desires salvation, but does not find it in his heart to believe on the Lord Jesus Christ and be saved?" Though much sound advice is given, Stoddard leans too heavily on preparationism in this book.

The book contains a preface by Increase Mather and two additional sermons by Stoddard on preaching the gospel to the poor and needy, both based on Luke 4:18.

The Nature of Saving Conversion (SDG; 180 pages; 1999). In sixteen chapters, Stoddard shows what conversion is, how it affects the soul, what its distinguishing marks are, and how a person may know if he has truly been converted. Stoddard is pastoral and comforting. Here's one example: "When you look into the Bible, there you may read your title. When you hear the Word, you will hear abundant matter of consolation. When you are exercised with your corruptions, you may comfort yourselves with the fact that after awhile Christ will present you without spot or blemish. When Satan is tempting, you may rejoice that God will tread Satan under your feet shortly. When you mourn under the withdrawings of God, you may be refreshed with the consideration that ere long you shall behold His face in righteousness."

An appendix to this work offers four sermons by Stoddard: "The Way to Know Sincerity and Hypocrisy Cleared Up"; "The Defects of Preachers Reproved"; "The Presence of Christ with Ministers of the Gospel"; and "The Duty of Gospel Ministers to Preserve a People from Corruption."

The Puritan Pulpit: Solomon Stoddard (1643-1729) (SDG; 315 pages; 2005). The material reprinted in this volume contains nearly all of Stoddard's remaining unpublished sermons, including seven excellent messages for "the benefit of the gospel to those who are wounded in spirit," as well as ten individual sermons that cover such subjects as the cleansing power of Christ's blood, the gospel as a means of conversion, how young people can praise the Lord, false hopes of salvation, the trial of assurance, and the danger of backsliding. This is the second volume in *The Puritan Pulpit: The American Puritans Series.*

The Safety of Appearing on the Day of Judgment in the Righteousness of Christ (SDG; 360 pages; 1997). First printed in 1729, this book was Stoddard's final statement on the imputed righteousness of Christ before his death. There is no more important question than how a man is made right with God. Is it through the merits of Christ or self-merit? Stoddard shows that at the end of our life we must be found "in the righteousness of Christ" because salvation is experienced through Christ's merits alone.

John Erskine writes in the preface: "It examines not learned, critical, or philosophical objections against the doctrine of imputed righteousness, but, in a plain and practical strain, opens the grounds and encouragements of faith, resolves the doubts of a jealous and unbelieving heart, and unfolds the subtle working of a self-righteous spirit. In these views, it is the best treatise I know on the subject, though those will think otherwise who relish the beauties of language and composition more than they regard the importance and justness of the sentiments."

Lewis Stuckley
(c. 1621-1687)

Born about 1621, Lewis Stuckley was a descendent of an honorable family in Devonshire. The family estate was quite large; thirteen manors could be seen from its gatehouse. One of Stuckley's ancestors, Lewis Stuckley of Affeton, was standard-bearer to Queen Elizabeth. Sir Thomas Stuckley, the English adventurer, was his brother.

In 1646, the standing committee of Devon appointed Stuckley to the rectory of Newton Ferrers, near Plymouth. It is uncertain whether he accepted it, for soon afterward he was appointed to the living of Great Torrington. From Great Torrington, Stuckley moved to Exeter, where he first preached in the cathedral, then formed his own Congregational church in 1650.

In 1658, Thomas Mall, Stuckley's assistant in Exeter, anonymously published *A True Account Of What was done by a Church of Christ in Exon* (*whereof Mr. Lewis Stuckley is Pastor*) *the eighth day of March, 1657, when two members thereof were Excommunicated.* In response, Toby Alleine, the brother of Joseph Alleine and husband of one of the excommunicated members, wrote *Truths Manifest* (1658). Stuckley responded with *Manifest Truth* (1658), after which Alleine reprinted his former treatise with added notations as *Truth Manifest Revived* (1659). Susanna Parr, the other woman who was excommunicated, printed her own defense in *Susanna's Apology against the Elders* (1659).

Stuckley was forced to quit his work at the cathedral after the Restoration of Charles Stuart. He was silenced with the rest of his nonconforming brothers on Saint Bartholomew's Day, 1662. Had Stuckley conformed, he could have had an illustrious state career, since he was a kinsman of George Monk, duke of Albemarle, and an influential supporter of the king. But Stuckley refused the preferment and chose instead to busy himself with preaching in private.

Stuckley married Susanna Dennis in 1672; they had five children. Some years later, the Stuckleys moved to Bideford. Stuckley became very ill in the summer of 1687 and died on July 21.

A Gospel Glass (Ebenezer; 306 pages; 2002). Aside from the piece on church polity mentioned above, Stuckley's *A Gospel-glass, Representing the Miscarriages of English Professors, both in their Personal and Relative Capacities; Or, A Call from Heaven to Sinners and Saints by Repentance and Reformation to Prepare to Meet God* (1667) was his only work. It became to the gospel hypocrite what Peter DuMoulin's *The Anatomy of Arminianism* (1619) was to the Arminian.

Presumably, the substance of this work was preached at the Congregational church in Exeter. Thomas Mall preached something similar to *A Gospel Glass* about the same time it was published, which seems to affirm this. Mall's *The Axe at the Root of Professors Miscarriages in a Plain Detection of, and a Wholesome Caveat against the Miscarriages Opposite to Faith in God* (1668) likewise reproved professors against the "miscarriage," or misuse, of the gospel.

Like many treatises of the period, Stuckley's *A Gospel Glass* aims at reproving, correcting, and changing the sinner's perception. Many times Stuckley tells his readers to consider who and what they *truly* are, and not to hide behind a cloud of self-deception. As he writes in the preface: "My design in this enterprise is to obviate this distemper and to bring you, all of you, to your own iniquity" (p. x). He would have the reader to see the "full catalogue" of his or her sins, which are "provocations in the eyes of the Lord."

The aim of this perception was not simply conviction of sin, but repentance and forgiveness: "I desire you would take this catalogue into your closets with you, and, as you read, set a special mark of observation on those sins, which are chiefly yours, in order to repentance and amendment, and then give the Lord no rest till he hath taken his pen, and dipped it in the blood of his Son, and blotted them out of his diary and remembrance" (p. xii). Contrary to popular modern opinion, the preparationists in England *did* have a theology of grace.

Many people admired Stuckley's work. John Ryland, Jr., for instance, wrote: "For many years past I have been accustomed to set a high value upon Mr. Stuckley's *Gospel-glass.* I find, by notes in the margin of my copy, that my dear and honored father began to read it, with much attention, in the year 1745, and gave it to me in 1771. In my youth I have often employed it in private, as a very valuable assistant in the duty of self-examination, and frequently read parts of it to my friends, or recommended it to their perusal."

George Swinnock

(c. 1627-1673)

Born at Maidstone in Kent, George Swinnock lost his father as a little boy. He was raised in the home of his uncle, Robert Swinnock, a staunch Puritan. He was educated at several colleges in Cambridge and Oxford, earning a Bachelor of Arts degree in 1648 and a Master of Arts in 1650.

The following year Swinnock was ordained and became vicar of Rickmansworth. In 1655, he was appointed to St. Leonard's Chapel at Aston Clinton in Buckinghamshire. In 1661, he became vicar of Great Kimble, Buckinghamshire. He was ejected from that post in 1662 for Nonconformity. For several years he preached in private houses in the surrounding area and prepared a collection of his works for the press (1665). He dedicated them to a local politician, Richard Hampden, whom he also served as chaplain intermittently until 1672. Then, availing himself of the Declaration of Indulgence, he returned to his native town of Maidstone to pastor a large flock until his death on November 10, 1673. He was survived by his wife and nine children.

Swinnock has been described as "a man of good abilities, and a serious, warm, and practical preacher."

The Works of George Swinnock (BTT; 5 vols., 2,500 pages; 1996). Weighty yet warm simplicity and numerous illustrations characterize Swinnock's writings. His major work, "The

Christian Man's Calling," contained in Volumes 1 and 2 and part of Volume 3 (more than a thousand pages), masterfully explores the calling of the true believer in "spiritual disciplines, personal lifestyle, relations in the home, marriage and daily work, in times of prosperity and adversity, in a hostile world, and at the time of death." The editors say this work "is one of the fullest and best exhibitions of the gospel in its application to the ordinary affairs of life."

Volume 3 also contains "Heaven and Hell Epitomized," and the first part of "The Fading of the Flesh," a judicious treatise on preparing for death. In Volume 4, "The Fading of the Flesh" is concluded, followed by three treatises on the work of magistrates and a rich, practical study on the divine attributes titled "The Incomparableness of God." Volume 5 contains "The Door of Salvation Opened by the Key of Regeneration" and "The Sinner's Last Sentence"—sermons on Matthew 25:41-42 with two hundred pages of counsel on the seriousness of sin.

Swinnock's works show keen sensitivity to the Scriptures and their applications to daily life. Our only criticism is that his larger treatises lack organization; his real strength is illustration. As Spurgeon wrote, "George Swinnock had the gift of illustration largely developed, as his works prove, [which] made his teaching attractive. There remains 'a rare amount of sanctified wit and wisdom.'"

Joseph Symonds

(d. 1652)

As a young man, Joseph Symonds was assistant to Thomas Gataker at Rotherhithe, near London. In 1632, he was appointed rector of St. Martin's, London. He adopted the views of the Independents on church government, for which he was persecuted by Archbishop Laud. Symonds took refuge in the Netherlands in 1639, where he was appointed pastor of an English-speaking congregation at Rotterdam, along with William Bridge and Jeremiah Burroughs. His work there was greatly blessed, but he did have some struggles. He wrote to his friends in England that he was "so pestered with Anabaptists, that he knew not what to do."

In 1647, Symonds returned to England to become vice president and fellow of Eton College. He held this office for five years until his death in 1652.

The Case and Cure of a Deserted Soul (SDG; 360 pages; 1997). According to J. I. Packer, Symond's work is *the* classic Puritan treatment on spiritual depression. In this book, Symonds describes the state of the deserted soul. He outlines the reasons for such a condition, the ways to recover from such a condition, and how to avoid falling into such a condition. Peter Lewis says that this book "shows a mind and heart replete with the best qualities of Puritan learning and devotion."

Edward Taylor

(c. 1642-1729)

E dward Taylor was born on a farm in Sketchley, Leicester-shire, most likely in 1642. He apparently studied at Cambridge University, then taught school in Bagworth, Leicestershire, for a short time. His grandson, Ezra Stiles, who served as one of Yale's early presidents, said that his grandfather was "a vigorous advocate of Oliver Cromwell." Taylor opposed the Restoration and had little sympathy for the Church of England. The 1662 Act of Uniformity, which also compelled schoolteachers to accept *The Book of Common Prayer* in its entirety and to reject the Solemn League and Covenant, left Taylor restless. But it was the Conventicle Act of 1664, de-claring conventicles illegal, that moved Taylor to begin considering immigration to the Massachusetts Bay Colony where he might worship in peace (*Oxford DNB*, 53:878).

Taylor left England for the Massachusetts Bay Colony in 1668. He spent the long voyage reading his Greek New Testa-ment, observing the beauty of birds and fish encountered by the vessel, and recording his bouts with seasickness in his diary, finally arriving at the home of Increase Mather in Boston. Within three weeks, and after conferring with Charles Chauncy, president of Harvard College, Taylor en-rolled in the school. He was given the position of college butler in recognition of his age and experience. His room part-ner was Samuel Sewall, who became a lifelong friend and correspondent. Taylor completed his studies of both medicine and theology, proving to be a distinguished scholar. He was one of four students asked to give speeches at his Bachelor of Arts commencement in 1671. Three years later, he received a Master of Arts degree from Harvard.

Although Taylor planned to stay on as a tutor at Harvard, a delegation from Westfield, Massachusetts, a village in the Connecticut Valley, asked him to be the minister of its congregation. Despite his fears, Taylor took on multiple roles as a farmer, rural physician, and minister. Little did he know that he would preside over this flock for more than fifty-seven years as a spiritual guide, and serve as a learned theologian and disciplinary statesman in the community.

Taylor preached his first sermon in Westfield on December 3, 1671. By 1673, a parsonage and a church, which also doubled as a fort for protection against the enemies, were built. Due to delays caused by the Indian wars and other hardships, the church at Westfield was not formally organized until 1679, shortly after Taylor was ordained. The gathering of elders and neighboring clergy at that service included Solomon Stoddard, with whom Taylor would later argue bitterly over differences regarding the Lord's Supper. Taylor's "Relation" and "Foundation Day," delivered on that occasion, are among his earliest extant prose. In them Taylor described his personal conversion.

Meanwhile, in 1674, Taylor married Elizabeth Fitch of Norwich, Massachusetts; he recorded his courtship with her in both a letter and a lengthy acrostic poem. She bore him eight children, five of whom died in infancy. His 1689 funeral elegy for her, titled "Only Dove," presents customary Puritan praise for a woman as wife, mother, and homemaker. His second wife, Ruth Wyllys, from Hartford, Connecticut, whom he married three years later, gave birth to six children. As a minister-poet, Taylor penned "Upon Wedlock, & Death of

Children," which resembles the elegies of Anne Bradstreet, whose poetry Taylor owned and appreciated.

During this early period, Taylor wrote metrical paraphrases of many Psalms. He transcribed a second version of different Psalms during the early 1680s. Taylor's private poetry, however, was hid from public view for 250 years. R.S. Clark writes, "In his will, he forbade the publishing of his poetry, and so his grandson, Ezra Stiles, kept his wishes and had them deposited inconspicuously at Yale library. Thomas H. Johnson's discovery of the material in 1937 ended the anonymity and Taylor emerged as America's great colonial poet, rivaled only by Anne Bradstreet (1612-1672). Since Johnson's discovery, Princeton University Press and Yale University Press have published authoritative editions of his poetry, and numerous scholarly students have followed" ("An Early Response to Open Theism," *Reformation and Revival* 12, 2 [Spr 2003]:119).

Taylor's first major collection of poems, written during the 1680s, was titled *God's Determinations Touching His Elect: and The Elect's Combat in their Conversion, and Coming up to God in Christ together with the Comfortable Effects thereof.* In this collection of thirty-five poems, Taylor unveils his view of salvation history and creation with a debate between Justice and Mercy over mankind's destiny. Taylor details Christ's warfare with Satan over the elect, and ends with the elect's joyful reception into church fellowship. God's eternal, sovereign will explains the why and how of all events, including those that are so difficult for the human mind to accept and understand. No stranger to sorrow, Taylor embraced his woes as messengers from heaven.

Karen Rowe, to whom we are indebted for much of this entry, says that Taylor had at least three stimuli for this work: first, his struggle to rescue his Westfield flock from Indian attacks; second, backsliding among the church's second generation; and third, the need to maintain doctrinal purity by admitting only true converts to the church and the Lord's Supper (*The Heath Anthology of American Literature*, 4th ed., ed. Paul Lauter, pp. 456-459). J. Daniel Patterson suggests that the structure of *God's Determinations* is patterned after the typical Puritan sermon. R. S. Clark thinks that Patterson's thesis is worth pursuing, as it reveals that Taylor's "abundant use of dialogue" reveals "the hopes and fears of those in his congregation" as reflected in the "use" or "application" section of Puritan sermons. Clark concludes that "this focus on application allows Taylor to express poetically his pastoral concerns for his congregants as they engage the sovereignty of God and his working in the world" (*Reformation and Revival* 12, 2 [Spr 2003]:120).

In 1682, Taylor began a sequence of Communion poems, called *Preparatory Meditations before my Approach to the Lord's Supper*, which eventually numbered 217. These poems were usually written after he had drafted or preached a sermon, and became one of his greatest poetic achievements. Characteristic of the Puritan minister, Taylor applied to his own soul the lessons gleaned from the sacramental text, always aiming to abhor sin, to love God the more, and to look forward to eternal communion with Christ Jesus as heavenly Bridegroom.

In 1720, Taylor suffered a severe illness. Upon recuperating, he wrote three poems renouncing worldliness and welcoming death. These poems harmonize well with his poetry based on the Song of Solomon, written about that time. Taylor also wrote *A Metrical History of Christianity* in 1692, as well as various paraphrases of Psalms and Job, and countless elegies, acrostics, love poems, allegorical histories, meditations, and lyrics. The volume of his writings is amazing considering his diligence in pastoral ministry.

Taylor was a voracious reader who copied books by hand for personal use. He also transcribed in 400 pages the poems "God's Determinations" and "Preparatory Meditations" and included them in the leather-bound "Poetical Works" to preserve them. Though they were never published, they are truly a rare find.

As Westfield's physician, Taylor was also interested in natural science, especially botany and medicinal herbs. He was also active in civic matters. He helped prepare Westfield's defense during King Philip's War.

Taylor died in 1729 at Westfield, Massachusetts, where he was buried. He was described by his grandson Ezra Stiles as a man "of quick passions, yet serious and grave. [He was] exemplary in piety, and for a very sacred observance of the Lord's Day" (Rowe, p. 459). John Shields concludes, "He left his parish the solid legacy of his orthodox, puritan theology, a tradition of thorough medical care, and a sizeable body of sensitive and intellectually challenging poetry" (*Oxford DNB*, 53:880).

⟫◆⟪

The Diary of Edward Taylor (CVHM; 40 pages; 1964). Taylor's diary comprises only sixteen pages; the rest is devoted to historical introduction and commentary. Taylor journalistically describes his voyage on the sea and his early years in school. Beyond that there is little here for the devotional reader.

Edward Taylor's Christographia, edited by Norman S. Grabo (Yale; 507 pages; 1962). In fourteen sermons, Taylor sets forth the two natures of Christ, providing a portrait of Christ as a model to be followed. He repeatedly informs us that "Christ is a perfect example for all to live up unto." It is impossible, he says, to attain to a higher pattern; there is fullness of life in Christ and nowhere else.

In this book, Taylor resembles his Anglican counterparts in England, who preached often on the theme of "the imitation of Christ." Early Puritan theology somewhat neglected this theme. In keeping with the Reformers, sermons focused most often on Christ's righteous imputation rather than on

Christ-like sanctification. Second and third generation Puritans like Taylor, however, focused more on the importance of imitating Christ. They differed from Roman Catholic and Anglican authors by stressing that all imitation of Christ is dependent upon the Spirit's enabling grace in a believer's heart. No one could live as Christ lived without being born again, Taylor said.

Upon the Types of the Old Testament (NUP; 2 vols., 1,005 pages; 1989). In 1977, one of Taylor's supposedly lost manuscripts, bound in vellum, was discovered in a relative's library in Lincoln, Nebraska. Over the next ten years, *Upon the Types of the Old Testament* was carefully edited. The work was published in 1989, revealing some of Taylor's finest work. In thirty-six sermons, Taylor chronicles Christological types such as Abraham, Isaac, Jacob, Joseph, Moses, Joshua, Solomon, and Samson. The sermons are excellent, both in prose and insight. As heir of the Puritan tradition, Taylor consulted the best sources available to him. He quotes Augustine, Matthew Poole, and Henry Ainsworth. Taylor also carefully annotated another work on types, *Christ Revealed, or, the Old Testament Explained*, written by Thomas Taylor in 1635.

Edward Taylor's theology, as revealed in *Types*, is a composite theology of Puritan thinking. He did not hesitate to modify the sources that he consulted, however. His great purpose in these sermons was to instruct his congregation how to read the Old Testament to see Christ.

Thomas Taylor
(1576-1632)

Thomas Taylor was born in 1576 in Richmond, Yorkshire. His father, a local magistrate, showed great kindness to Puritans and other ministers in the northern part of England who had been ejected from their pulpits. Thomas earned a Bachelor of Arts degree in 1595 and a Master of Arts in 1598 from Christ's College, Cambridge. He served as a fellow (1599-1604) and lecturer in Hebrew (1601-1604) prior to entering the ministry, though he had begun preaching at age twenty-one. He probably served as chaplain William, Lord Russell of Thornhaugh, to whom he dedicated his edition of William Perkins's *Exposition upon Jude*. Taylor was one of Perkins's most avid disciples.

When he was twenty-five, Taylor delivered a sermon before Queen Elizabeth that earned him the reputation as "a brazen wall against popery." In 1608, he denounced Archbishop Bancroft's severe treatment of Puritans. Taylor was silenced for some time by Samuel Harsnett, who conducted Bancroft's metropolitan visitation.

Taylor probably first served as a minister in Watford, Hertfordshire (1612), also preaching frequently in Reading, Berkshire. In addition, he formed and directed a Puritan seminary, described as a "nursery of young preachers." Among these preachers were Thomas's brother, Theophilus, who was pastor of St. Lawrence Church, Reading, from 1618 to 1640, and William Jemmat, who would later edit Thomas Taylor's works.

At some point in the 1620s, Taylor served as chaplain to Edward Conway, secretary of state and later first Viscount Conway. Taylor shared Conway's anti-Spanish outlook, which he detailed in his *Map of Rome* (1620) and in two sermons (1624) that thoroughly condemned all thought of allying England and Spain.

In 1625, Taylor was asked to be curate and lecturer at St. Mary Aldermanbury, London. Here, too, he established a Puritan seminary and worked hard for the Protestant cause. In 1627, he joined William Gouge, Richard Sibbes, and John Davenport in efforts to relieve the Palatinate's Calvinist ministers, for which they were condemned by William Laud, the new bishop of London, the following year. That same year, he was awarded a Doctor of Divinity degree from Cambridge, despite the opposition of the anti-Puritan Bishop Matthew Wren. Called "an illuminated doctor" by Wood, Taylor worked diligently in his spare time, writing seven books and numerous sermons and pamphlets.

Taylor opposed separatism and antinomianism as vigorously as he opposed Roman Catholicism and Arminianism. Whoever doubted the presence of God in the church's assemblies, he quipped, was "as blind as a mole, and palpably deluded" (*Oxford DNB*, 53:986).

Taylor retired in 1630 due to failing health. He had a blessed and prolonged deathbed. On his deathbed, he exclaimed: "In Christ, I am more than a conqueror. Oh, I serve a good God who covers all imperfections, and gives great wages for little; and in mercy has provided for me some of the greatest!"

He died of pleurisy in 1632 at Isleworth, survived by his wife, Anne, and at least six children. His funeral was led by William Jemmat, Taylor's former assistant at Reading and the editor of several of his books. In 1653, Edmund Calamy and eleven other leading Puritan colleagues readied for publication the first of several editions of Taylor's works.

Christ Revealed; or, The Old Testament Explained (SF; 384 pages; 1979). A facsimile reprint of the 1635 edition, this book was a most popular Puritan study on Christ-like types in Old Testament individuals, events, and ceremonies. Basing his work on John 14:6 ("I am the truth"), Taylor's stated purpose is to "demonstrate that Christ is Truth as opposed to the shadows and figures of the old law." The New Testament fulfills or manifests more perfectly the old Mosaic law, Taylor says.

In the first third of the book, Taylor shows how Adam, Noah, Melchizedek, Isaac, Joseph, Moses, Joshua, Samson, David, Solomon, and Jonah foreshadow Christ. He then considers other types of Christ: the firstborn, the priesthood, the Nazarites, clean persons, circumcision, the Passover, the pillar of cloud and fire, the Read Sea, manna, water that flowed out of the rock, and the brazen serpent.

Throughout this work, Taylor leans on few contemporary sources; he does not even quote Henry Ainsworth's annotations of the Bible or Thomas Goodwin's discussions of ceremonial laws. While one may not always agree with Taylor's exegesis, his practical instruction is very valuable.

An Exposition of Titus (K&K; 565 pages; 1980). First published in 1612, then reprinted in an enlarged edition in 1619, this book remains the most famous work and safest guide on Titus. Reprinted numerous times over the centuries, it is packed with valuable homiletical thoughts for ministers and, as Spurgeon says, "will well repay the reader."

Taylor's *Titus* is a massive work that aims to show that this short epistle is a sort of digest of the entire doctrine and practice of salvation. In the introduction, Taylor writes: "By the learned [this epistle] is called an abridgement of all Paul's epistles.... In this epistle, as in a map or model, he would deliver his whole spirit, style, and understanding in the doctrine of salvation, and would leave this to the church as a manual or compendious sum of all Christian religion, so that when Christians have been instructed in the matter of faith and manners, they might be made not only wise unto salvation, but profitable and fit for the place unto which God has assigned them, in church, commonwealth, or family."

Robert Traill
(1642-1716)

Robert Traill was born in 1642 in Elie, Fifeshire. His father, Robert, carefully supervised his son's early education. The elder Traill served first as minister of Elie, then went to Greyfriars Church in Edinburgh, pastoring there with fidelity and zeal. During the Civil War, he enlisted as chaplain with the Scottish army in England. He was later imprisoned for seven months, then exiled for reminding Charles II at the Restoration of his obligation to keep the Covenant. In 1662, Traill fled to the Netherlands, leaving behind his God-fearing wife, Jean Annan, and six children. Three years later, Jean was imprisoned for corresponding with her exiled husband.

Meanwhile, young Robert Traill studied at the University of Edinburgh, where he was a good scholar. William Guthrie of Fenwick, author of *The Christian's Great Interest*, became his mentor and close friend. At age nineteen, Traill was attendant to James Guthrie of Stirling, his father's friend and Cromwell's "short man who could not bow," when Guthrie went to the scaffold. Traill served briefly as chaplain to the Scotstarvet family and spent some time with John Welsh, minister of Irongray, who was first to hold "armed conventicles," i.e., spiritual fellowships where several attendees would bear arms to defend the group from arrest.

In 1666, agents of the prelatical party in Scotland discovered copies of the forbidden book *An Apologetic Relation* (1660) in the Traill home. The entire family was forced to become cautious. The crisis culminated during the Pentland Rising that same year, when young Traill was denounced as a "Pentland rebel." Anticipating arrest, he fled to the Netherlands, where his father and other British divines were taking refuge from Stuart absolutism. Young Traill continued his theological studies there, assisting Matthias Nethenus, professor of divinity at Utrecht, and helping to prepare Samuel Rutherford's *Examination of Arminianism* for print.

In 1669, young Traill returned to Britain and settled in London. The following year he was installed in a Presbyterian congregation in Cranbrook, Kent. In 1677, Traill was again arrested in Edinburgh, this time for preaching in private homes and assisting in conventicles. While imprisoned on the Bass Rock in Firth, he met James Fraser of Brea and Alexander Peden. He was released from prison a few months later and returned to his flock at Cranbrook. After a few years, he moved to a Scottish congregation in London, where he ministered for the remainder of his life. His Christ-centered approach to prayer and ministry is evident from his confession:

> I have no name to come to God but in Christ. My own name is abominable to myself. No other name is given under heaven, but that of Jesus Christ, in which a sinner may safely approach unto God. Since the Father is well pleased with this name, and the Son commands me to ask in it, and the Holy Ghost hath brought this name to me, and made it as ointment poured forth (Song of Sol. 1:3), and since its savor hath reached my soul, I will try to lift it up as incense to perfume the altar enthroned above; since all that ever come in this name are made welcome, I will come also, having no plea but Christ's name, no covering but His borrowed and gifted robe of righteousness. I need nothing, I will ask nothing, but what His blood hath bought (and all that I will ask); I will expect answers of peace and acceptance only in that blessed Beloved—beloved of the Father, both as His Son and our

Savior, and beloved of all that ever saw but a little of His grace and glory.

In 1682, Traill published a powerful sermon, "By what means can ministers best win souls?" (on 1 Tim. 4:16), which is still a "must read for soul-winners" today. Later, he published *Justification Vindicated* (see below), *Thirteen Sermons on the Throne of Grace* (on Heb. 4:16) and *Sixteen Sermons on the Prayer of Our Saviour* (on John 17:24). These books went through numerous printings, becoming very popular among the evangelicals of succeeding generations.

Traill died in 1716, at age seventy-four. He never married. He was a great contributor to the Puritan age; his name is linked to the best in Scotch, Dutch, and English Puritan traditions.

<hr/>

The Works of Robert Traill (BTT; 4 vols. in 2, 1356 pages; 1975). These works were first published in 1745 (Edinburgh, 4 vols.). Later, three different editions were printed in Glasgow (1776, 3 vols.; 1795, 4 vols.; 1806, 4 vols.). The 1975 edition of four volumes in two bindings is a reprint of the 1810 Edinburgh edition and is the fullest edition ever published. It contains: "An Account of the Life and Character of Robert Traill"; "Concerning the Throne of Grace"; "By What Means May Ministers Best Win Souls?"; "A Vindication of the Protestant Doctrine of Justification from the Unjust Charge of Antinomianism"; "Concerning the Lord's Prayer"; "Steadfast Adherence to the Profession of our Faith"—twelve sermons on Hebrews 10:20-24; "Eleven Sermons on Important Subjects" based on 1 Peter 1:1-4; "Righteousness in Christ"—six sermons on Galatians 2:21; and two letters to Traill's wife and children.

Although Traill had an excellent mind and received a thorough theological education, his sermons were not meant for academic readers. In all, he sought to promote popular, practical godliness. Readers will find him warm, instructive, spiritual, and encouraging. His sermons are compelling and forceful without being overbearing. He is an edifying Puritan for daily reading.

Justification Vindicated (BTT; 77 pages; 2002). In this short paperback, originally written in 1692 to his oldest brother, William, minister of Borthwick, Midlothian, Traill defends the doctrine of justification by faith alone. In eight chapters, he covers the rising controversy about justification; justification by faith alone, not lawlessness; real differences in justification; advantages of the true doctrine of justification; disadvantages of the true doctrine of justification; the charge of antinomianism misapplied; "the good old way of the Protestant doctrine"; and the vital importance of the doctrine of justification.

The book was occasioned by the controversy that broke out among dissenting ministers after the writings of Tobias Crisp were published. Traill opposes antinomianism on one side and Arminianism and neonomianism on the other. "All my design in publishing this is, plainly and briefly, to give some information to ordinary plain people who lack either time or judgment to peruse large and learned tractates about this point of justification, wherein every one is equally concerned," Traill wrote.

Traill's book became very popular in the 1720s in Scotland among the Marrowmen and their followers. Ralph and Ebenezer Erskine and others supported Traill's basic position on justification and gleaned considerable help from this little book. Thomas Boston did not agree with all that Traill wrote, however. Unlike Boston, who supported a two-covenant view (covenants of works and grace), Traill affirmed a three-covenant view (covenants of redemption, works, and grace). But like Boston, Traill avoided conditionalism in the covenant of grace, stressing its absolute freeness, despite the occasional use of mercantile language.

In the 1800s, J.C. Ryle quoted extensively from Traill's little book, using its clear distinctions between justification and sanctification to defend the church against the Holiness Movement led by Hannah Pearsall Smith. Today, justification by faith is once again under assault. We pray that Traill may still be used today to dispel much confusion in evangelical circles.

John Trapp

(1601-1669)

John Trapp was born in 1601 at Croome d'Abitot, Worcestershire. He was the son of Nicholas Trapp of Kempsey, Warwickshire. His uncle, Simon Trapp, and his pastor, John Ballam, were Trapp's first teachers. God used Ballam, whom Trapp later called "my spiritual father," as an instrument in Trapp's conversion.

Trapp went to Worcester as a king's scholar for his pre-university education. After being "foremost pupil of the school," he went on at age seventeen to Christ Church, Oxford. He earned a Bachelor of Arts degree in 1622 and a Master of Arts degree in 1624.

In 1622, Trapp became usher of the free school of Stratford-upon-Avon. Two years later, he became headmaster of the school. Trapp continued to serve the school in various capacities "unto his white-haired old age." He was deeply respected by many, including the son-in-law of William Shakespeare, who was one of Trapp's students. He described Trapp as "second to none for his piety and learning."

In 1624, Trapp married Mary Gibbard, with whom he had twelve children. Four of their children died during the first twelve years of their marriage. These losses moved Trapp to write his first book, *God's Love-Tokens* (1637). Alexander

Grosart described the work as an "uncommonly soft, sweet, soothing, gospel full little book."

Trapp became vicar at the Stratford chapelry of Ludding-ton about 1631. Five years later, he moved to Weston-on-Avon, Gloucestershire, situated within two miles of the school at Stratford-upon-Avon. He passed up more prestigious positions to labor with diligence in his beloved church and school. During these years, Trapp received treatment for depression for some time from a God-fearing neighbor, John Hall.

Trapp sided with Parliament at the outbreak of the civil war and subscribed to the Solemn League and Covenant in 1643. From 1644 to 1646, he served as chaplain to the parliamentary soldiers in the garrison at Warwick Castle. His position at times brought him into grave difficulties. He was once taken captive and set free only in an exchange of prisoners. Though he was no radical, he had to relinquish his work at the school after the restoration of Charles II because he had made himself "obnoxious to the Cavaliers."

These difficulties did not hinder Trapp's productivity. "I labored night and day," Trapp said of this period. "What hours I could then well spare, I gladly spent on these Notes upon the New Testament." He published ten commentaries on various books of the Bible (1646-1656) which are combined in the five-volume work, *A Commentary on the Old and New Testaments* (1662). Samuel Clark said Trapp's deep concern for the church was evident by his labors in church and school as well as in his commentaries, which he wrote "in the midst of the noises of guns and drums."

In the Great Ejection of 1662, Trapp, whose sentiments sided with those of the two thousand ministers who were ejected, nevertheless chose to conform. He was allowed to retain his manse and his ministries at Stratford and Weston.

Trapp died in 1669 and was buried at Weston. His friend, Thomas Dugard, said he was "one of the Age's greatest little men"—for he was small in stature yet great in godliness and in writing (ibid.).

———◆◆◆———

A Commentary on the Old and New Testaments (TP; 5 vols., 3,620 pages; 1997). Trapp's exegesis is orthodox but sometimes irregular. He excels, however, in using colorful paraphrases and captivating illustrations. His pithy style makes him very quotable. While his treatment of the Old Testament is superior to his treatment of the New, his comments are always worth reading, though, at times, his comments can be somewhat outdated, particularly when he enlarges on mid-seventeenth-century polemics.

Trapp is not as thorough as Henry and Poole. Spurgeon said that preachers should use Trapp for "spicing" sermons. "Trapp will be valuable to men of discernment," Spurgeon wrote.

With the exception of two sermons, Trapp's other writings are included in Tanski's edition of his commentaries. These include *God's Love-Tokens* (see above), which explains Revelation 3:19 to comfort believers in losses; *Theologia Theologiae* (1641), a discourse framed around Hebrews 1:1-3 on the Scriptures—their attributes, objections raised against them, and how we are to use them; *The Righteous Man's Recompense* (1654), which characterizes and encourages true believers and is based on Malachi 3:16-18; and *A Decade of Common Places* (1656), which treats the following subjects from a Christian perspective: abstinence, admonition, alms, ambition, angels, anger, apostasy, arrogance, arts, and atheism.

George Trosse

(1631-1713)

Apart from voyages abroad and a time at Pembroke College, Oxford, most of George Trosse's life was spent in Exeter. He was born there in 1631. His mother, Rebekah Burrow, was the daughter of a prosperous merchant and mayor. His father, a lawyer, left his son a library of law books, intending that he also become a lawyer.

After leaving grammar school, Trosse lived an ungodly life, often indulging in alcoholic excess. He was wealthy, yet he stole, drank, gambled, flirted, and spent his money on all sorts of self-indulgent frivolity. His addictions grew worse and his mental state failed. His strange sickness, called "*delirium tremens*" by his nineteenth-century biographer, was probably a form of hallucinations or schizophrenia. As Trosse confesses in his surprisingly frank autobiography, he often saw things that were not there and heard voices. He first thought the voices were from God, but later concluded they were from Satan. His suffering caused him immense spiritual pain and grief. His friends had to restrain him several times from harming himself and from attempting suicide. He was finally brought by friends to a caring physician at Glastonbury. He came to his senses several times, only to relapse into periods of insanity. Between these relapses, he listened to the Presbyterian preaching of Thomas Ford. Eventually, he found relief from his illness through Ford's sermons, counseling, and prayer.

With a substantial sum of money from his mother, Trosse entered Pembroke College in 1657. His tutor was Thomas Cheeseman, a blind scholar. Trosse often attended the lectures of Robert Harris, president of Trinity College. He spent several years at Oxford, specializing in Greek and Hebrew.

Intending to go into the ministry, Trosse carefully studied the issue of conformity under Henry Hickman. However, he became increasingly more convinced of the validity of nonconformity. He returned to Exeter and began attending church with his mother. Privately, he began preaching to a growing crowd of listeners. Robert Atkins, the ejected minister of St. John's, Exeter, urged him to seek ordination. Trosse followed his friend's advice and was ordained in 1666 by Joseph Alleine in Somerset.

Trosse decided to conduct his ministry in Exeter because he wanted "to live as a reformed sinner in the very city where some of his worst outrages had been staged and where his reputation had been notorious" (A. Brink, *The Life of the Reverend George Trosse*, p. 6). For twenty years, he preached privately and secretly, usually several times a week. During the year of Charles II's indulgence, Trosse preached publicly in a licensed house. In 1673, he was fined three times for holding conventicles, but continued to preach unabated.

In 1680, Trosse married Susanna, daughter of Richard White, a rich merchant who greatly assisted Presbyterians in Exeter. In 1685, he was arrested for preaching at a conventicle. Imprisoned for six months, Trosse confessed, "I enjoyed a great measure of health during my imprisonment. I followed my studies, served and worshipped God with the rest of my brethren, and found opportunities frequently in secret to pay my devotions to the blessed God" (*Life*, pp. 127-28). When James II ascended the throne and declared liberty of conscience, Trosse declined to avail himself of it. He wrote: "At the end of six months I was discharged from my confinement, which was the place of my greatest enlargement."

After the Toleration Act was passed, Trosse succeeded Joseph Hallet as minister of James's Meeting in Exeter in 1689. He conducted services regularly and took a stipend that he later declined. He was assisted by the former pastor's son, also Joseph, who succeeded Trosse at his death, and later prepared Trosse's life story for publication.

In 1691, Trosse preached at the funeral of John Flavel and finished Flavel's exposition of the Shorter Catechism. The following year, he published his *The Lord's Day Vindicated*, challenging the Saturday Sabbath views of Francis Bampfield. For the remainder of the seventeenth century and well into the next, Trosse took a leading role in the formation of the union of Devonshire ministers. He often acted as moderator and submitted questions for discussion.

For nearly fifty years, Trosse preached the gospel, sometimes eight times a week at services that seldom lasted less than two hours. He rose at 4 a.m. and prayed six or seven times a day. Yet he viewed all that devotion as gifts from his Father's hand.

In his eighty-second year, Trosse preached the Sabbath morning service of January 11, 1713, returned home, and died two days later. Cotton Mather preached at the funeral to "a very great multitude, among whom were many of the gentry of the city and county" (I. Gilling, *The Life of Mr George Trosse, late minister of the gospel in Exon*, pp. 120-21). Trosse was buried in St. Bartholomew's churchyard, Exeter. Edmund Calamy, a close friend of Trosse, wrote: "Much was forgiven him, and he loved much."

———◆◆◆———

The Life of the Reverend Mr. George Trosse (MQ; 140 pages; 1974). Edited by A.W. Brink, this 1714 edition of Trosse's autobiography was published at the request of Trosse in his will. In the book, Trosse confesses his great struggles with sin, his quest for personal assurance, and his descent into schizophrenia. Alexander Grosart said Trosse's "narrative of his earlier years is one of the strangest pieces of realism in the language, entering into vicious details with extraordinary frankness."

The Life of Trosse offers first-person insights into the mind of a mentally ill patient in seventeenth-century England, but also displays the stupendous grace of God in saving a wretched sinner and provides valuable information on the political and religious atmosphere of the day.

Ralph Venning

(c. 1622-1674)

A minor ejection of Puritan ministers took place in 1633. Among those pastors who had to quit preaching for nonconformity was George Hughes, age thirty. Persuaded by John Dod not to immigrate to New England, Hughes moved to Devon, where he became rector of Tavistock. His first convert there was Ralph Venning. Venning later wrote that Hughes was "as gentle to me as a nurse which cherisheth her children" (Venning, *Mysteries and Revelations*, preface).

Born in Devonshire to Francis and Joan Venning, Ralph Venning was educated at Emmanuel College, Cambridge. He earned a Bachelor of Arts degree in 1646 and a Master of Arts degree in 1650.

Venning held a lectureship at St. Olave's, Southwark, for about twelve years, where he became known as an excellent preacher. Here he published several volumes, including *The New Command Renewed* (1650) and *Canaan's Flowings* (1653). In his ministry, he stressed practical Christian living, especially giving to the poor. He collected thousands of pounds for the needy.

During the Protectorate, Venning was appointed to examine candidates for chaplaincies in the navy. He also preached a number of sermons at St. Paul's before various mayors of London. In 1657, he became lecturer at St. Mary Magdalen.

In 1661, Venning married Hannah, widow of John Cope of London. They had at least two children. The following year, he was ejected for nonconformity. He became an assistant to Robert Bragge (1627-1704), pastor of an independent congregation at Pewterers' Hall, Fenchurch Street. Venning served there until his death in 1674. He was buried in Bunhill Fields among other nonconformists.

Venning spent much time writing. He published at least ten books as well as miscellaneous sermons and pamphlets. A book titled *Venning's Remains*, which contains some of his shorter writings, was published a year after he died, as was *Mr. Venning's Alarm to Unconverted Sinners*. His books rightly divide the word of truth; they are convicting, captivating, and witty. Venning excels in the use of epigrams and word play, which is shown most strongly in his *Orthodox Paradoxes* (1647). John Edwards said of Venning, "He turns sentences up and down, and delights in little cadences and chiming of words."

⇒◆◆⇐

Learning in Christ's School (BTT; 297 pages; 2000). This work, republished in the Puritan paperbacks series, is based on 1 John 2:12-14 as well as 1 Corinthians 3:1-2 and Hebrews 5:12-14. Venning describes four stages of growth in grace: babes, children, youth, and fathers. He writes to comfort, exhort, and stimulate the growing Christian. As Hywel Jones says in the publisher's foreword, "Noting the eagerness of the newborn, the delight of the little child, the vigor of the young, and wisdom of the mature, cannot but challenge mediocrity; seeing their foibles, weaknesses, and vulnerability will, on the other, challenge presumption. The book contains a much needed message for today."

The major weakness of this book is its brief discussion—less than two pages—of the fathers in grace. Venning's explanation of the other three stages, however, is superlative; he vividly shows how God leads His people through experience to rely more fully on Christ and to know more personally the Triune God. It is most instructive to compare Venning's treatment of 1 John 2:12-14 with Willem Teellinck's treatment in *The Path of True Godliness* (pp. 136-43).

The Sinfulness of Sin (BTT; 288 pages; 1996). This was first published as *Sin, The Plague of Plagues* in 1669, after the Great Plague of London. It is a practical, probing work based on Romans 7:13 ("That sin by the commandment might become exceedingly sinful"). It clearly explains what sin is, why it is so serious, and what its only remedy is. Venning says the worst physical pestilence is inconsequential when measured against the soul-destroying plague of sin.

Arguing that sin is always "against man's good and happiness," Venning appeals to the reader's self-interest. He justifies that approach by saying God "is so condescending that he is pleased to treat man as a self-lover, and so to gain him, and win him." Here is one example of how Venning confronts us with the deadliness of sin: "Shall I now entreat you to consider what has been said, and to think what an abominable and ugly thing sin is? It is the worst of evils, worse than the worst of words can express. I have shown you how it is contrary to God and man. For proof of this I have brought witness from Heaven, Earth, and Hell. I have shown you how dearly it cost Christ Jesus who died for it, and how dearly it will cost you, if you live and die in it. Therefore stand in awe and sin not. Lay up the Word of God's command, promise and threatening, that you may not sin against him. Take heed of sinning, for at once you sin against God and your own selves."

Nathaniel Vincent

(1638-1697)

Nathaniel Vincent was born in Cornwall to John Vincent, a nonconformist minister, and his wife, Sarah. He was the younger brother of Thomas (see below). A brilliant child, Nathaniel memorized and repeated sermons at age seven. He graduated from Christ Church, Oxford, with a Bachelor of Arts degree in 1656 and a Master of Arts in 1657. He was then appointed chaplain of the Corpus Christi College.

Vincent was ordained at age twenty-one and became rector of Langley Marish, Buckinghamshire. Ejected by the Act of Uniformity of 1662, he spent three years as a private chaplain to Sir Henry Blount and his wife, Hester, at Tittenhanger, Hertfordshire, before moving to London in 1666. A large meetinghouse was built in Farthing Alley, Southwark, to accommodate the crowds that came to hear him preach. That drew the attention of the authorities, who began to harass him. On one occasion, soldiers with muskets surrounded his pulpit. When Vincent refused to stop preaching, the soldiers pulled him out of the pulpit by his hair and dragged him through the streets. He was fined and sent to prison. After several months of imprisonment, he was sentenced to banishment from the country, but a flaw in the indictment prevented that sentence from being carried out.

In 1672, Vincent was licensed as a Presbyterian preacher. It was not long, however, before he was persecuted again for preaching. On one occasion in 1681, his meetinghouse was visited by "three justices with constables and other officers." Vincent continued to preach even though the uproar of the audience became so great that he could scarcely be heard. When the justices then commanded the people to disperse, the whole congregation broke out into singing, during which time Vincent managed to escape through a side exit. Two years later, Vincent was charged for conventicling and sentenced to a three-month prison term. Four years later, he was arrested and falsely accused of taking part in Monmouth's Rebellion.

Vincent's imprisonments left him so weak that for some time he was unable to preach, and resorted to writing. Most of his fourteen books were written in prison. His books reflect a warm, experiential piety expressed according to the Ramistic method of outlining. His love and concern for the body of Christ is evident in every book.

Vincent died suddenly in 1697, at age fifty-eight; he was survived by his wife, Anna, and six children. His funeral was conducted by Nathaniel Taylor. He was buried in the nonconformists' burial ground at Bunhill Fields. Even the anti-Puritan historian Anthony Wood had to confess of Vincent: "He was of smarter, more brisk, and florid parts than most of his dull and sluggish fraternity can reasonably pretend to; of a facetious and jolly humor, and a considerable scholar" (*Athenae Oxonienses*, 4:617).

———⇒◆◆⇐———

A Discourse Concerning Love (SDG; 113 pages; 1999). This includes seven chapters on the importance of love among Christians in the church. The subjects addressed include how the church is to edify itself by love, the properties of love, and how there is no excuse for lack of love in the church.

Vincent describes the properties of love in detail. Love must flow from a pure heart and be fervent. It must flow from faith, be mixed with a good conscience, be brotherly in nature, and embrace the entire body of Christ. The church should grow in love for the glory of the Father, the honor of Christ, the increase of the Spirit, the church's own advantage, and the benefit of the world. Vincent mourns the lack of love in the church: "O love! How much want is there of you in the Church of Christ! And how much does the Church feel for this want! It groans, it languishes, it dies daily because of your absence. Return, O love, return! Repair breaches, restore paths to dwell in, edify the old ways and places, and raise up the foundations of many generations, for after all the most politic contrivances; you will be found the master builder."

His chapter on "the vanity of excuses for the want of love" is convicting. How desperately the body of Christ still needs to read this chapter today, be convicted of its sin, and fly to the only remedy, Christ Jesus! Vincent goes on to offer hope in Christ, stressing that Christ is the head of the church and the source of love. He writes, "Though the case is deplorable, it is not desperate. Christ is the Church's Head and Healer; and were love revived it would quickly bring His body to a better and more healthy temper. Light may do much, but love will do more."

Vincent concludes with two comforts for those who are discouraged by the church's lovelessness. He advises us to remember that the love of Christ is unchangeable and that there will be no lack of love in heaven.

Thomas Vincent

(1634–1678)

Thomas Vincent was born in 1634 in Hertford, England. He was the second son of John Vincent and the elder brother of Nathaniel Vincent (see above). He was educated first at Westminster School, then at Felsted School, Great Dunmow, Essex, an institution of strong Puritan convictions. In 1648, he was elected to Christ Church, Oxford, where he earned a Bachelor of Arts degree in 1652 and a Master of Arts degree in 1654. He was chosen to be catechist to John Owen. After that, he served as chaplain to Robert Sidney, second earl of Leicester. In 1657, Vincent succeeded Thomas Case as rector of St. Mary Magdalen, Milk Street, London, where he remained until he was ejected for nonconformity in 1662.

Between his ejection and the Great Plague of 1665, Vincent assisted Thomas Doolittle in educating children at Doolittle's Nonconformist Academy at Islington. During the plague of 1665, Vincent showed great courage and godly zeal by serving the sick left behind by the conformist ministers who fled the city. God protected him during that year, for 68,000 people in London died of the plague, including seven in the home where Vincent lived, but he remained healthy throughout the ordeal. Due to a shortage of ministers, he was asked to preach every Sabbath to large crowds of needy people. God blessed that work; one biographer said of Vincent's preaching during the Great Plague, "It is remarkable that he did not preach one sermon in which there were not some seals to his ministry."

For the last twelve years of his life, Vincent preached to a large congregation gathered at Hand Alley, off Bishopsgate Street. He was fined and probably imprisoned at least once during those years. He devoted himself extensively to educating young people. Vincent also spent much time in Scripture —he supposedly memorized the entire New Testament and the book of Psalms. This close acquaintance with the Word of God is evident in his numerous books.

Vincent died in 1678, survived by his wife, Mary, and at least four children. Samuel Slater preached at the funeral, basing his message on Hebrews 13:7. Slater told the large audience that Vincent was "freely willing to venture his life for the salvation of souls." He said of Vincent's last hours: "The night before his death, he broke out in the following language, expressive of his comfort, peace and joy: 'Farewell the world, the pleasures, profits, and honors of the world; farewell sin, I shall ever be with the Lord. Farewell my dear wife, farewell my dear children, farewell my servants, and farewell my spiritual children.'"

According to the preface of Vincent's *The True Christian's Love to the Unseen Christ*, Vincent also had words for his congregation, "Be careful in your choice of a pastor; choose one who in his doctrine, life, and manners, may adorn the gospel. I shall be glad to meet you all in heaven."

As death drew near, Vincent cried out, "O noble death, welcome, welcome! Death hath wounded my head; death hath wounded my breast, but he hath not wounded my conscience, blessed be God." His final words expressed his longing to be with Christ: "Dear Jesus, come and take me away. I have no business here; my work is done, my glass is run, my strength is gone, why shall I stay behind? How long shall I be absent from Thee? Oh, come and take me to Thyself, and give me possession of that happiness which is above, the vision of Thyself, perfect likeness to Thyself, full fruition of Thyself, without any interruption or conclusion" (ibid., pp. ix-xi).

———◆◆◆———

Christ's Sudden and Certain Appearances to Judgment (SDG; 300 pages; 2001). Written after the Great Fire of London, this book is about the impending judgment awaiting impenitent sinners. Vincent's arguments are lucid, his thinking clear, and his message ominous. He earnestly begs sinners to come to Christ in love before He comes upon them in judgment. Vincent's preface succinctly states his purpose: "The design of these sheets is to set forth the glorious appearance of Christ with the certainty and suddenness thereof, that sinners might be awakened to repent, and believers might be comforted with hopes of it, and all might be in readiness for the day which is so sure and near."

Fire and Brimstone (SDG; 250 pages; 1999). As a classic Puritan, Vincent warns sinners to flee from the wrath to come. He presents the theme of fire and brimstone, showing first the punishment of wicked Sodom. He then cites a catastrophe that happened in his own day: the eruption of Mount Etna and how people were overtaken by that tragedy. Finally, he shows how insignificant those two events are compared to the coming judgment upon impenitent sinners.

The book concludes with two sermons that offer a much-needed promise of deliverance ("The Only Deliverer from Wrath to Come," on 1 Thess. 1:10) and sanctification ("Godliness in Principle and Conversation," on 2 Pet. 3:11).

God's Terrible Voice in the City (SDG; 236 pages; 1997). Vincent acted heroically during London's Great Fire and Great Plague. This is his eyewitness account of those horrible events and his spiritual analysis of how God judges wickedness in a city. First printed in 1667, this book was reprinted fifteen times in eight years.

God's Terrible Voice is packed with suitable applications for any city or nation that faces great tragedies, such as the September 11, 2001 bombing of the World Trade Center in New York City. Vincent urges people to hear the terrible voice of their Maker. The relevance of Vincent's work to the events of his day is a good pattern for modern preachers to follow.

The Good Work Begun: A Puritan Pastor Speaks to Teenagers (SDG; 150 pages; 1999). This work, fully titled as *The Good Work Begun in the Day of Grace Performed until the Day of Christ*, is intended to instruct young people and bring them to salvation. It tells how God saves sinners and preserves them for Himself.

Vincent met regularly with the young people of his church to teach them the ways of God. That experience is evident from his warm, practical approach in this book. In an appendix to the book are two sermons written for young people: "Christ the Best Husband: An Invitation to Young Women unto Christ," and "The Best Gift: God's Call upon Young Men for their Hearts."

The Shorter Catechism Explained from Scripture (BTT; 280 pages; 1991). When this explanation of Westminster's Shorter Catechism was first published in 1674, John Owen, Joseph Caryl, Thomas Manton, Thomas Brooks, and Thomas Watson, along with thirty-five other Puritans, declared that it would "be greatly useful to all Christians in general."

For over a hundred years, children committed "Vincent's Catechism" to memory. The work clearly exhibits Vincent's gifts in communicating with young people as well as his concern for their spiritual health and salvation. The neglect of catechism instruction in today's churches has sapped the people of God of much strength. Young minds, deeply rooted in the biblical soil provided by this work, will not so readily fall prey to unsound winds of doctrine.

The True Christian's Love to the Unseen Christ (SDG; 140 pages; 1994). This work is subtitled: *A discourse chiefly tending to excite and promote the decaying love of Christ in the hearts of Christians with an appendix concerning Christ's manifestation of Himself to them that love Him.* It focuses on 1 Peter 1:8, "Whom having not seen, ye love; in whom, though now ye see him not, yet believing, ye rejoice with joy unspeakable and full of glory." Love for Christ flows from every page of this treatise.

John MacArthur writes in the foreword to this work: "Secular history generally paints Puritanism as a rather unsophisticated form of religion. Puritans are usually caricatured as cold, austere, and simplistic, devoid of any appreciation for love and beauty, obsessed with law and judgment. This book surely debunks that myth. It reveals the Puritan passion for 'joy inexpressible and full of glory,' which grows out of a warm-hearted, fervent love for Christ." A biographical sketch of Vincent is included in the preface of this work.

THOMAS WATSON

Thomas Watson
(c. 1620-1686)

Thomas Watson was probably born in Yorkshire. He studied at Emmanuel College, Cambridge, earning a Bachelor of Arts degree in 1639 and a Master of Arts degree in 1642. During his time at Cambridge, Watson was a dedicated scholar. After completing his studies, Watson lived for a time with the Puritan family of Lady Mary Vere, the widow of Sir Horace Vere, baron of Tilbury. In 1646, Watson went to St. Stephen's, Walbrook, London, where he served as lecturer for about ten years, and as rector for another six years, filling the place of Ralph Robinson.

In about 1647, Watson married Abigail Beadle, daughter of John Beadle, an Essex minister of Puritan convictions. They had at least seven children in the next thirteen years; four of them died young.

During the Civil War, Watson began expressing his strong Presbyterian views. He had sympathy for the king, however. He was one of the Presbyterian ministers who went to Oliver Cromwell to protest the execution of Charles I. Along with Christopher Love, William Jenkyn, and others, he was imprisoned in 1651 for his part in a plot to restore the monarchy. Although Love was beheaded, Watson and the others were released after petitioning for mercy. Watson was formally reinstated to his pastorate in Walbrook in 1652.

When the Act of Uniformity passed in 1662, Watson was ejected from his pastorate. He continued to preach in private

—in barns, homes, and woods—whenever he had the opportunity. In 1666, after the Great Fire of London, Watson prepared a large room for public worship, welcoming anyone who wished to attend. After the Declaration of Indulgence took effect in 1672, Watson obtained a license for Crosby Hall, Bishopsgate, which belonged to Sir John Langham, a patron of nonconformists. Watson preached there for three years before Stephen Charnock joined him. They ministered together until Charnock's death in 1680. Watson kept working until his health failed. He then retired to Barnston, in Essex, where he died suddenly in 1686 while engaged in private prayer. He is buried in the same grave as his father-in-law who served as a minister at Barnston.

Watson's depth of doctrine, clarity of expression, warmth of spirituality, love of application, and gift of illustration enhanced his reputation as a preacher and writer. His books are still widely read today.

———◆◆◆———

All Things for Good (BTT; 128 pages; 1988). Watson once said he faced two great difficulties in his ministry: to make the unbeliever sad without grace and to make the believer glad with grace. In this study of Romans 8:28, formerly titled *A Divine Cordial* (first printed in 1663, one year after two thousand ministers were ejected from the Church of England), Watson encourages God's people to rejoice. He explains how the best and worst experiences work for good. He writes, "To know that nothing hurts the godly, is a matter of comfort; but to be assured that *all* things which fall out shall co-operate for their good, that their crosses shall be turned into blessings, that showers of affliction water the withering root of their grace and make it flourish more; this may fill their hearts with joy till they run over."

If someone asks, "Why do bad things happen to good people?" or "How can I know if I am called by God?," offer them this book. Its chapters on the love of God, effectual calling, and the purpose of God are especially helpful in understanding Romans 8:28. Chapter 5, on the "tests of love to God," is particularly searching.

The Art of Divine Contentment (SDG; 133 pages; 2001). Watson's works are all marked by profound spirituality, terse style, impressive remarks, and practical illustrations. This book, first printed in 1653, is no exception. Based on Philippians 4:11, "I have learned, in whatsoever state I am therewith to be content," Watson writes, "For my part, I know not any ornament in religion that doth more bespangle a Christian, or glitter in the eye of God and man, than this of contentment. Nor certainly is there any thing wherein all the Christian virtues do work more harmoniously, or shine more transparently, than in this orb. If there is a blessed life before we come to heaven, it is the contented life."

Godly contentment is a theme missing from many pulpits today. A serious reading of this treatise or Jeremiah Burroughs's *Rare Jewel of Christian Contentment* would do much to fill this void.

The Beatitudes (BTT; 307 pages; 1971). First published in 1660, this exposition of Matthew 5:1-12 is rich with instruction. For example, in explaining the blessedness of meekness (5:5), Watson explains meekness towards God as submission to His will and flexibility to His Word. Meekness towards man, he says, involves bearing injuries, forgiving injuries, and recompensing good for evil. In bearing injuries, meekness opposes a hasty spirit, malice, revenge, and speaking evil of others. In forgiving injuries, meekness forgives truly, fully, and often. In recompensing good for evil, Watson says, "To render evil for evil is brutish; to render evil for good is devilish; to render good for evil is Christian." He offers numerous reasons why Christians should be meek, such as: Jesus Christ is meek; meekness is a great ornament to a Christian; meekness is the way to be like God; meekness argues a noble and excellent spirit; meekness is the best way to conquer and melt the heart of an enemy; meekness contains great promises, for the meek shall inherit the earth; and an un-meek spirit hinders peace. All of this is cogently explained in a mere fifteen pages (pp. 105-119).

A Body of Divinity (BTT; 316 pages; 1998). This book, first published after Watson's death in 1692, was his *magnum opus* and became his most famous work. Following the question-and-answer format of the Westminster Shorter Catechism, it offers 176 sermons on the essential teachings of Christianity. It shows the author's deep understanding of spiritual truths and his ability to make them clear to anyone. Unlike most other systematic theologies, it weds knowledge and piety together, and can be used effectively in daily devotions. It is perhaps the most experiential systematic theology ever written, with the exception of Wilhelmus à Brakel's *The Christian's Reasonable Service.*

The Lord's Prayer and *The Ten Commandments* (cf. below) complete Watson's exposition of the Shorter Catechism. This trilogy on the Shorter Catechism has been reprinted often over the centuries in one or three volumes.

The Duty of Self-Denial and Ten Other Sermons (SDG; 210 pages; 2001). This book includes eight chapters on self-denial, based on Luke 9:23, and ten additional sermons, seven of which have not been reprinted since the seventeenth century. Watson teaches that "self-denial is the first principle of Christianity." He describes what self-denial is, then demonstrates the Christ-asserting nature of every self-denying act. The additional sermons in this volume are also valuable, particularly those on God as the reward of His people (Gen. 15:1), "kissing" the Son (Ps. 2:12), the comforting rod (Ps. 23:4), and the Judgment Day (Acts 17:31).

The Fight of Faith Crowned (SDG; 191 pages; 1996). This book contains six sermons that had not yet been reprinted in the twentieth century. They include "The Crown of Righteousness" (2 Tim. 4:8), "The Righteous Man's Weal and the Wicked Man's Woe" (Isa. 3:10-11), "Time's Shortness" (a funeral sermon for the Puritan preacher John Wells, based on 1 Cor. 7:29), "The Fight of Faith Crowned" (a funeral sermon for Henry Stubbs, based on 1 Tim. 4:7-8), "A Plea for Alms" (Ps. 112:9), and "The One Thing Necessary" (Phil. 2:12). The last sermon strips away every excuse for not seeking God and pleads that we bow to the demands of the gospel. Watson concludes by explaining six helps for working out one's salvation: Christ's strength, diligence, love, humility, hope, and prayer.

Gleanings from Thomas Watson (SDG; 144 pages; 2001). This work offers quotations from Watson's writings. It sorts them according to fifteen areas of the believer's walk with Christ, including contentment, persecution, temptation, preaching, prayer, and meditation. Watson had the gift of presenting profound doctrinal truth in vivid images and colorful metaphors that are particularly memorable.

Here are a few samples:

- He who is ashamed of Christ is a shame to Christ.
- Worldly sorrows hasten our funerals.
- They that bear the cross patiently shall wear the crown triumphantly.

The Godly Man's Picture (BTT; 252 pages; 1992). This work is subtitled *Drawn with a Scripture Pencil, or, Some Characteristics of a Man who is Going to Heaven.* After explaining the nature of godliness, Watson describes twenty-four marks of a godly man, including "moved by faith," "fired with love," "prizes Christ," "loves the Word," "is humble," "is patient," and "loves the saints." The concluding chapters offer helps to godliness, advice on how to persevere in godliness, counsel and comfort for the godly, and teaching on the mystical union between Christ and His people.

Harmless as Doves: A Puritan's View of the Christian Life (CFP; 188 pages; 1994). This book contains ten excellent sermons that provide a biblical picture of practical Christian living. They include "Christian Prudence and Innocency," "On Becoming A New Creature," "The Evil Tongue," "Not Being Weary in Well-Doing," "On Knowing God and Doing Good," "Christ All in All," "The Preciousness of the Soul," "The Soul's Malady and Cure," "The Beauty of Grace," and "The Trees of Righteousness Blossoming." These sermons reveal Watson's colorful and compelling style of preaching. They are experiential and practical and make excellent devotional reading.

Heaven Taken by Storm (SDG; 135 pages; 1992). This is an excellent handbook—perhaps the best ever written—on how to use the various means of grace. Based on Matthew 11:12, Watson describes how the Christian is to take the kingdom of heaven by holy violence through the reading and exposition of Scripture, prayer, meditation, self-examination, conversation, and keeping the Lord's Day. He explains how the believer is to battle against self, Satan, and the world, and counters objections and hindrances to offering such violence. An appendix to the book includes two additional sermons: "The Happiness of Drawing Near to God" and "How We May Read the Scriptures with Most Spiritual Profit."

This book helped lead Colonel James Gardiner (1688-1745) as well as many others to conversion. It is an excellent book to give to those who want to start reading the Puritans.

The Lord's Prayer (BTT; 332 pages; 1994). Originally produced as a companion to *A Body of Divinity* on the Shorter Catechism, Watson continues the question-and-answer format to explain the petitions of Jesus' model prayer. In our opinion, this book matches Herman Witsius's *The Lord's Prayer* in usefulness. Witsius's work is more deliberate and theological, while Watson's is more devotional and practical.

The Mischief of Sin (SDG; 176 pages; 1994). This is Watson's most definitive treatment of sin. It includes four parts: "The Mischief of Sin," "The Desperateness of Sinners," "An Alarm to Sinners," and "Hell's Furnace Heated Hotter." "The Mystery of the Lord's Supper" is included in an appendix.

John MacArthur writes, "Thomas Watson's study of sin is profound, convicting, thought-provoking, and filled with rich spiritual insight. It distills the best attributes of Puritan writing. As devotional as it is doctrinal, as practical as it is biblically sound, and as delightful as it is convicting, this books cuts to the very heart of the biblical issues regarding sin. You cannot read it and remain indifferent toward sin in your own life."

A Plea for the Godly and Other Sermons (SDG; 480 pages; 1997). This collection containing some of Watson's best work includes: "Comfort for the Church," "The Happiness of Drawing Near to God," "The Tongue, a World of Iniquity," "The Mystical Temple," "Christ All in All," "The Perfume of Love," "A New Creature," "The Heavenly Race," "The Fiery Serpents," and Watson's farewell sermon.

The Puritan Pulpit: Thomas Watson (c.1620-1686) (SDG; 233 pages; 2004). This book, the second in the Puritan Pulpit Series, is a collection of ten sermons not found in any other work of Watson's in print today: "A Christian on Earth Still in

Heaven," "Christ's Loveliness," "God's Anatomy Upon Man's Heart," "The Beauty of Grace," "The Preciousness of the Soul," "The Saint's Desire to be with Christ," "The Saint's Spiritual Delight," "The Soul's Malady and Cure," "The Tree of Right-eousness Blossoming and Bringing Forth Fruit," and "The Spiritual Watch." These sermons are vintage Watson—pastoral and easy to understand, rich with illustration and abounding in application.

Religion Our True Interest (BB; 144 pages; 1992). This work consists of Watson's notes on Malachi 3:16-18. It offers helpful teaching on religious conversation, God-centered thinking, God's disposition toward His people, and the fear of God, which Watson defines as "reverencing and adoring God's holiness, and setting ourselves always under His sacred inspection." Today, we're sorely in need of such teaching, for too many people who call themselves Christians lack this mark of grace, which Watson calls "the best certificate to show for heaven" though "the fear of God is not our plea, yet [it is] our evidence for heaven."

The covenant-keeping character of God is evident as Watson explains God's promise "They shall be mine" from the book of Malachi. Believers belong to God, Watson says, but God and all His riches also belong to believers. God says, "My wisdom shall be yours to teach you, my holiness shall be yours to sanctify you, my mercy shall be yours to save you," to which Watson responds, "What richer dowry than deity? God is a whole ocean of blessedness. If there is enough in Him to fill the angels, then surely He has enough to fill us." This book is rich fare for the encouraging, enlightening, and admonishing of believers.

Sermons of Thomas Watson (SDG; 745 pages; 1997). This work was originally titled *Discourses on Interesting and Important*

Subjects, being the Select Works of the Reverend Thomas Watson (2 volumes). With the exception of *The Beatitudes,* this reprint puts everything in the original two volumes under one cover. It includes "The Christian's Charter of Privileges," "The Saint's Spiritual Delight," "A Treatise Concerning Meditation," "The Upright Man's Character," and "The Godly Man's Picture Drawn with a Scripture Pencil." The treatise on meditation is particularly valuable. Edward Reynolds writes in the introductory epistle: "Meditation is the palate of the soul whereby we taste the goodness of God; the eye of the soul whereby we view the beauties of holiness; the *askesis* and *gymnasia,* whereby our spiritual senses are exercised,... it is the key to the wine-cellar, to the banqueting house, to the garden of spices, which letteth us in unto him whom our soul loveth; it is the arm whereby we embrace the promises at a distance, and bring Christ and our souls together."

The Ten Commandments (BTT; 245 pages; 1998). This third volume that Watson wrote on the Shorter Catechism examines the moral law as a whole as well as each of its commandments. Watson repeatedly shows the various ploys of indwelling sin. In view of the importance of law in Christian living, this is an extremely valuable work.

William Whitaker

(1548-1595)

William Whitaker was born in 1548 at Holme, near Burnley, Lancashire, the third son of Thomas Whitaker, the head of a gentry family rooted there since the fourteenth century. William was educated at St. Paul's School and at Trinity College, Cambridge, where he earned a Bachelor of Arts degree in 1568 and a Master of Arts degree in 1571. He was appointed a minor fellow in 1569 and a major fellow in 1571. He earned a divinity degree from Oxford in 1578. Whitaker was an indefatigable student of Scripture, Bible commentators, and medieval scholastics. He became professor of divinity at Cambridge in 1579, and the following year was appointed chancellor of St. Paul's. He became master of St. John's College, Cambridge, in 1586, and was awarded a Doctor of Divinity degree in 1587.

Whitaker was an able Calvinistic writer and a powerful Protestant champion against popery. As master of St. John's College, his scrupulous impartiality won the affection of members of the college, many of whom had opposed his appointment due to his Puritan convictions. Under his influence, the college increased in number and reputation, and the Puritan party gained power.

In 1593, Whitaker was nominated for but failed to receive the mastership of Trinity College. Two years later, he was appointed canon of Canterbury. He soon became seriously ill. His death on December 4, 1595, was a considerable loss to Cambridge University and to the Reformation cause in England.

Whitaker's first wife was a Culverwell, a sister-in-law of Laurence Chaderton, and his second wife was the widow of Dudley Fenner. Whitaker had eight children. One son, Alexander, became a well-known minister in Virginia; another, Richard, became a well-known printer and bookseller in London.

Whitaker wrote more than twenty books. He has been described as "the pride and ornament of Cambridge." Few English divines were held in higher esteem by their contemporaries. Even Robert Bellarmine, the Roman Catholic scholar, was so impressed by Whitaker's genius that he hung Whitaker's portrait in his study.

———◆◆◆———

Disputations on Holy Scripture (SDG; 718 pages; 2000). One of the key issues that divided Protestants from Roman Catholics was the role of Scripture in a believer's life. Protestants declared that Scripture alone was the rule of faith and practice, while Roman Catholics taught that Scripture as well as church traditions were equally authoritative. In this massive work, first printed in 1588, Whitaker argues the Protestant position. He deals with the number of canonical books, the authority of Scripture, the perspicuity of Scripture, the proper interpretation of Scripture (i.e., hermeneutics), and the perfection of Scripture.

Michael Wigglesworth

(1631-1705)

Michael Wigglesworth was a Puritan minister who became famous for his poetry. He was born in 1631 in Yorkshire, England, to Edward and Esther Wigglesworth, who were successful traders. In 1638, the Wigglesworths left Yorkshire because of religious persecution. They went to Charlestown, Massachusetts, where they stayed for a short time, then moved on to New Haven, Connecticut.

When he was seven years old, Wigglesworth's parents sent him to Ezekiel Cheever for formal training. He returned home after two years to assist his father, who had been injured on the farm. Farming did not suit him, however; he returned to Cheever in 1644, and studied until he could enter Harvard three years later. He initially wanted to be a doctor but, during his fourth year at Harvard, was converted and decided to study for the ministry. He graduated with a Bachelor of Arts degree in 1651, and served as a fellow at the college from 1652 to 1654. One of his pupils was Increase Mather, who became a lifelong friend. Wigglesworth was offered the pulpit in Malden, Massachusetts, shortly after that. Unsure of his calling, he preached in Malden for more than a year but refrained from committing himself.

While in Malden, Wigglesworth kept a diary documenting spiritual uncertainties brought about by illness (he was afflicted with various bodily ailments throughout his life), his sexual struggles, and doubts over his calling. A recurrent nightmare recorded in the diary showed God on His throne separating sheep from goats. That vision prompted such terror in Wigglesworth that it became the dominant image of his first major poem.

In 1655, Wigglesworth married Mary Reyner, a cousin, and settled in Malden with his mother and sister, Abigail. Mercy, the couple's only child, was born the following year.

Wigglesworth was not formally ordained until 1657. One year after that, illness prevented him from fulfilling his ministerial duties. For several years, Wigglesworth struggled with poor health and the pressure of parish duties. In 1659, his wife died, adding to his difficulties. By 1661, he was at such odds with his congregation and so depressed about the spiritual state of himself and his community that he wrote *The Day of Doom*, a poetic allegory describing Judgment Day.

The work, published in 1662, was an immediate success. The first edition of 1,800 copies sold out within a year. Clearly, the poetic allegory appealed to the needs and fears of its audience. Wigglesworth described the Last Judgment in graphic detail, relying upon familiar scriptural images as well as common meter and internal rhyme. The poetry was easy to memorize—and many people did so.

Three English editions and two American editions of *The Day of Doom* were published before the end of the seventeenth century. Wigglesworth's last edition (1701) was followed by eight more editions in the eighteenth and nineteenth centuries.

Wigglesworth's next poetic work was *God's Controversy with New England*. Using the language of Isaiah and Deuteronomy, the poem urges New Englanders to consider their behavior in light of "the years of many generations." Wigglesworth compares his community to that of the Israelites and the New England migration to the Exodus.

In 1663, Wigglesworth left Malden for Bermuda because of his health, but to little effect. He returned the following year to find that Malden had called an assistant minister, Benjamin Bunker. Wigglesworth served the medical needs of the community and began to tutor local boys for Harvard.

In 1669, Wigglesworth wrote *Meat Out of the Eater; or, Meditations Concerning the Necessity, End, and Usefulness of Afflictions unto God's Children*, which was published in 1670. Unlike *God's Controversy with New-England, Meat out of the Eater* emphasized the edification of individual souls. The poem consists of ten meditations and a concluding section on the purifying nature of afflictions for the individual. It combines biblical paraphrase and allusion in explaining the effect of afflictions upon the soul. It was printed four times during Wigglesworth's lifetime and again in 1717 and 1770.

Wigglesworth did not resume pulpit duties when Bunker died in 1670. Four years later, Benjamin Blackman arrived and ministered for four years, leaving in 1678. The following year, despite the objections of Increase Mather and others, Wigglesworth married his young, unbaptized housekeeper; they had six children. The scandal of the marriage moved Wigglesworth to resign as a pastor and teacher in Malden, but the town never officially accepted his resignation. Within a few years, Wigglesworth's health improved remarkably. Meanwhile, another minister, Thomas Cheever, served as minister in Malden from 1680 to 1686. After his departure, Wigglesworth resumed his duties as sole pastor and as teacher in Malden. When his young wife died in 1690, Wigglesworth augmented his duties. He became involved in the affairs of New England, joining the Cambridge Association of Boston ministers in their concern for the community's spiritual life.

In 1691, Wigglesworth married Sybil Avery Sparhawk, widow of Jonathan Avery. Their son, Edward, would become the first Hollis Professor at Harvard.

Until his death, Wigglesworth remained in Malden's pulpit. He was an active leader in the Bay Colony and, in 1697, once again took up the position of Harvard fellow and tutor, which he retained for the rest of his life. He also became close friends with Samuel Sewall and other important leaders.

Increase Mather was with Wigglesworth in his final hours. Wigglesworth reportedly said, "For more than fifty years together I have been laboring to uphold a life of communion with God, and I thank the Lord, I now find the comfort in it." When he died in 1705, he had outlived all his Harvard classmates except Isaac Chauncy, who lived in England. Early in his career, Wigglesworth was somewhat despised for his frequent ailments, but by the end of his life he was regarded as a New England patriarch.

Wigglesworth is mostly remembered today as a poet. His work does not demonstrate the poetic sensibility of Anne Bradstreet or Edward Taylor, but it does illustrate his Puritan ideals: love for God, community, and family. Because of *The Day of Doom*, Wigglesworth has often been regarded as a melancholic, joyless person. But Wigglesworth was no such man. He thoroughly enjoyed creation, edifying leisure, and the sublime beauties of life. He was even quite romantic. When he was courting Sybil, he gave her a locket inscribed with these words: "Thine forever."

<hr />

The Diary of Michael Wigglesworth, 1653-1657: The Conscience of a Puritan (Smith; 125 pages; 1970). Edmund Morgan discovered Wigglesworth's diary in the 1960s, carefully edited it, and then published this work. *Diary* records Wigglesworth's thoughts and communion with God during his tutoring years at Harvard, his marriage to Mary Reyner, and his agonizing decision to become pastor in Malden. It reveals his unceasing search for signs of God's favor or displeasure. He repeatedly returns to his most unrelenting sins: pride, lack of affection for his parents, especially his father, and attachment to things of the world rather than the heavenly. With emotional intensity, he describes worries about his sexuality and his frequent bouts of illness.

Poems of Michael Wigglesworth (UPA; 330 pages; 1989). Wigglesworth produced more than seventy poems. This collection presents all of his known poems. It includes a lengthy preface containing essays on his life as well as the historical and theological contexts in which he wrote.

John Winthrop

(1588-1649)

John Winthrop was born in Edwardstone, Suffolk, in 1588. He was the only son of Adam Winthrop, lord of Groton Manor, a small estate in the English countryside. John initially studied at home with a private tutor. At age fourteen, he went to Trinity College, Cambridge, where he studied for two years. He then returned to Groton to learn how to run his father's estate.

Back at home, Winthrop was introduced to Mary Forth, daughter of a distinguished Essex nobleman; he married her three weeks later. The young couple resided in Great Stambridge, and sat under the ministry of Ezekiel Culverwell, which God greatly blessed to Winthrop. His diary at this time records "intense experiences of union with God which periodically refreshed his faith and which he described in terms of conjugal union with Christ" (*Oxford DNB*, 59:802).

Just after his eighteenth birthday, Winthrop became a father. After bearing six children in ten years, Mary died in 1615. Winthrop married Thomasine Clopton of Groton six months later, but she died within one year. His diary shows that her lingering death greatly impacted him, emotionally and spiritually. In 1618, Winthrop married again, this time to Margaret, daughter of Sir John Tyndal of Great Maplestead, Essex. Margaret was a woman of great faith, and Winthrop loved her dearly. When he traveled, he sent her letters, expressing his deep love for her and encouraging her in the faith.

Winthrop studied law when he was in his twenties and early thirties. This equipped him with the legal expertise he needed to handle landlord-tenant disputes, collect rents, and deal with government authorities. He became an influential lawyer, frequently called on to draft petitions to Parliament. In due time, he would follow in his father's footsteps as lord of Groton Manor. Winthrop's father did his best to train his son as a country gentleman, but the son was never like his father. Sometime in those early years, Winthrop caught the fire of Puritanism. Here is a sample of one diary entry: "O Lord, crucify the world unto me, that though I cannot avoid to live among the baits and snares of it, yet it may be so truly dead unto me and I unto it" (cited in Mark Galli, "Gifted Founders," *Christian History*, no. 41, p. 29).

Winthrop decided to immigrate to America. The earliest indication of that decision is what he wrote in a letter to his wife on May 15, 1629. He writes, "My dear wife, I am verily persuaded God will bring some heavy affliction upon this land, and that speedily: but be of good comfort, the hardest that can come shall be a means to mortify this body of corruption, which is a thousand times more dangerous to us than any outward tribulation, and to bring us into nearer communion with our Lord Jesus Christ and more assurance of his kingdom." At that time, Winthrop was also preparing a statement of "Reasons to be considered for justifying the undertakers of the intended Plantation in New England, and for encouraging such whose hearts God shall move to join with them in it."

Winthrop shared this paper with his eldest son (who later became governor of Connecticut) in August 1629. The son responded, "For the business of New England I can say no other thing but that I believe confidently that the whole disposition thereof is of the Lord, who disposes all alterations by his blessed will, to his own glory and the good of his; and therefore do assure myself that all things shall work together for the best therein" (*Life and Letters*, 1:309-337).

The impetus for Winthrop and others leaving England was the religious and political condition of England. The king was systematically asserting his authority, reducing the power of Parliament to practically nothing. It became a time of high commissions, forced loans, and taxation without representation. Many distinguished men who opposed those policies were seized and imprisoned. Sir John Eliot, a friend of Winthrop's, was sent to the Tower after speaking out in Parliament. He died there after several years of suffering.

Puritan beliefs, which Winthrop strongly embraced, were also repressed. Laud, the bishop of London, was already showing the intolerance that he enforced a few years later as archbishop of Canterbury. Meanwhile, the New World was open to those seeking religious freedom. The Pilgrims especially were inviting Puritans to come. All of that encouraged the great Suffolk immigration that Winthrop led.

The Massachusetts Company had already established a plantation at Salem. John Endicott was appointed to govern that colony in subordination to the governor and company in London. But now the company wanted to transfer all of the government to the American soil, and thus asked Winthrop to carry out that transfer as the colony's newly appointed governor. Less than a year later, in April of 1630, Winthrop was on his way to Salem with a charter and a company of 700 people in a fleet of several ships. Winthrop gave his famous speech, "A Model of Christian Charity," on the ship *Arabella*. New England, he said, was called to be a "city upon a hill." When the ships reached the New World, Winthrop first went to what is now called Charlestown, but soon he settled in the area that would become Boston.

Winthrop governed the Massachusetts Bay Colony for twelve years with a firm hand, believing that liberty requires authority. To him, democracy was rule by the masses. He believed in representative rule, but those elected should rule primarily by Scripture and their consciences. The most difficult years were 1646 and 1647, due to contentions with Robert Childe and Samuel Gorton. Winthrop took strong measures against Childe and Gorton, which provoked more opposition. Winthrop also lost his third wife, Margaret, in 1647.

Later that year, Winthrop married Martha, daughter of Captain William Ransborough and widow of Thomas Coytmore of Boston. In 1649, Winthrop died in Boston at age sixty-one, after much hard work, anxiety, and sorrow. John Cotton, who was with Winthrop during his last hours, eulogized his friend as "a governor who has been unto us a brother."

Winthrop was a member of the Church of England while in England, but in the new country, he felt that Congregationalism was the best way to propagate Christianity. He became a Congregationalist until his death. Throughout his life, Winthrop endeavored to establish what he called "a city set on a hill." To that end, he opposed all forms of doctrinal deviance, including those of Roger Williams and Anne Hutchinson. Winthrop said true freedom could only be found in keeping those laws that God had ordained.

Winthrop had an outstanding influence on American ideals. He lived to see Boston, which he had founded, become a thriving and prosperous capital, and the state, of which he brought over the charter, extended by successive settlements over a wide territory and represented in its legislature by deputies from nearly thirty separate towns. Other colonies had planted themselves around Massachusetts, and a New England confederation, of which he was the first president, had been formed under his sponsorship. Free schools had been established and a college incorporated and organized. Above all, religion had taken deep root in all the settlements, and churches were gathered wherever there was an adequate population.

⇒◆◆◆⇐

The Journal of John Winthrop, 1630-1649 (Harvard; 704 pages; 1996). This journal has long been recognized as the central source for the history of Massachusetts in the 1630s and 1640s. Winthrop reported events, both religious and political, more fully and candidly than did any other observer. The journal has been edited and published three times since 1790, but those editions are outdated. Richard Dunn and Laetitia Yeandle offer this long-awaited scholarly edition, complete with introduction, notes, and appendixes. This unabridged edition uses the manuscripts of the first and third notebooks (both preserved at the Massachusetts Historical Society), retaining their spelling and punctuation, and James Savage's transcript of the middle notebook (accidentally destroyed in 1825).

Winthrop's narrative began as a journal and evolved into a history. Just before sailing, he began a daily account of the voyage. He continued his journal when he reached Massachusetts, at first making brief and irregular entries, but then settling into lengthier, more frequent reporting. From 1643 on, he went back to irregular writing sessions and retrospective reporting. Winthrop had intended to edit and revise his journal, but his health deteriorated before he could do so.

An abridged edition of the journal, published separately (Harvard; 354 pages; 1996), offers nearly half of Winthrop's text, with modern spelling and punctuation. Winthrop's sermon titled "A Model for Christian Charity" (1630) is included, along with an introduction and annotations. For those interested in studying Winthrop's life and writings, the abridged journal is the place to start. We also recommend Edmund Morgan's *The Puritan Dilemma*, which offers a fascinating look at the governor's life and times.

APPENDIX 1

Collections of Puritan Writings

[The Puritans] were great scholars, some of the greatest scholars that the Church of England has ever produced, outstanding scholars, godly, righteous and holy men. Here is a description of them in the words of the Rev. Robert Halley: "To praise the preaching of Baxter, the theology of Owen, the genius of Howe, the learning of Goodwin, the reasoning of Charnock, the sermons of Bates, the devotion of Flavel, the meditations of Isaac Ambrose, the expositions of Matthew Poole, the labours of Oliver Heywood, the life of Joseph Alleine! No, indeed! It is not for me to praise the men who have done much to make old England what it is.... They have left their deep and indelible impressions upon the history of our land, and upon all its institutions.... They have given to their country and its dependencies, in a language which, more than any other, promises to become universal, a religious literature, so thoughtful, so devout, and so practical, that pious Conformists as well as Nonconformists acknowledge it, as subordinate to Scripture, to be the wealth of our church, [and] the strength of our preachers."

Such were these men, great and mighty scholars, mighty preachers, men of character and of strength of conviction, men of courage. They proved that. When so many of the Episcopalians fled for safety, and for their lives, from the Plague and the Fire of London some three years later, these were the men who remained and preached to the people and gathered congregations round themselves, proving what wonderful and noble men they were.

—Martyn D. Lloyd-Jones
(1662-1962, Evangelical Library Lecture, 1962)

Collections of Puritan Writings

Worthy is the Lamb: Puritan Poetry in Honor of the Savior, compiled by Maureen Bradley (SDG; 380 pages; 2004). Here are hundreds of poems by some of Christ's choicest servants, many of which focus on Christ. The selections are arranged systematically and include numerous doctrinal themes not implied in the title, such as God the Creator, the sinfulness of man, God's sovereignty in salvation, the law of God, sanctification, the means of grace, prayer, the sacraments, self-examination, mortification, the Sabbath, death, and heaven.

Though a number of the authors included are Puritans, such as Richard Baxter, Mather Byles, John Flavel, Oliver Heywood, and Nathaniel Vincent, many of the poems are from men who lived a generation or two after the Puritan era but who convey the same experiential emphases as the Puritans, such as John Mason, John Newton, and Augustus Toplady.

Anthology of Presbyterian and Reformed Literature, Volume One, edited by Christopher Coldwell (NP; 326 pages; 1988). This includes three sermons by Alexander Henderson, preached on December 27, 1643, July 18, 1644, and May 28, 1645; two sermons by Samuel Rutherford; James Durham's *Sermon on Death*; a portion of Paul Bayne's *Commentary on Colossians*; and John Welsh's sermon on repentance.

Anthology of Presbyterian and Reformed Literature, Volume Two, edited by Christopher Coldwell (NP; 340 pages; 1989). Included are James Durham's *The Fourth Commandment*, Robert Harris's *Samuel's Funeral*, James Durham's *17 Sermons on Isaiah 53:1*, and Samuel Rutherford's *Separation from Corrupt Churches*.

Anthology of Presbyterian and Reformed Literature, Volume Three, edited by Christopher Coldwell (NP; 330 pages; 1990). This work contains David Calderwood's *Against Festival Days,* Alexander Henderson's *Communion at Leuchars,* Cornelius Burges's *A Chain of Graces,* Ralph Erskine's *A Short Paraphrase of Lamentations,* and the first part of Samuel Rutherford's *Trial & Triumph of Faith.*

Anthology of Presbyterian and Reformed Literature, Volume Four, edited by Christopher Coldwell (NP; 313 pages; 1991). This work contains John Sedgwick's *Antinomianism Anatomized,* George Gillespie's *Wholesome Severity Reconciled with Christian Liberty,* and David Hay Fleming's *Hymnology of the Scottish Reformation.*

Anthology of Presbyterian and Reformed Literature, Volume Five, edited by Christopher Coldwell (NP; 328 pages; 1992). This work includes Samuel Hudson's *The Doctrine of the Catholic Church Visible,* Samuel Rutherford's *The Last Heavenly Speeches of John Viscount Kenmure,* D. James Fisher's *Catechism on the Fourth Commandment,* and David Dickson's *Sermons Preached at a Communion in Irvine.*

These volumes are well-edited and typeset in an attractive two-column, large print format. We regret that the series did not continue beyond 1992.

The Valley of Vision: A Collection of Puritan Prayers and Devotions, edited by Arthur Bennett (BTT; 230 pages; 2002). First published in 1975, these prayers are taken from the works of Thomas Shepard, Thomas Watson, Richard Baxter, John Bunyan, and other Puritans. Bennett emphasizes that the book is not intended "to be read as a prayer manual." The prayers are best used as springboards for a believer's "communion with a transcendent and immanent God who on the ground of his nature and attributes calls forth all the powers of the redeemed soul in acts of total adoration and dedication" (Preface, page xi). The division of the prayers into categories, titles, and a kind of poetic structure promotes their meditative use.

A Golden Treasury of Puritan Devotion: Selections from the Writings of Thirteen Puritan Divines, compiled and edited by Mariano Di Gangi (P&R; 183 pages; 1999). From the doctrine of God to the practical aspects of life and death, Di Gangi supplies us with more than five hundred excerpts from the works of thirteen Puritans: Richard Baxter, John Bunyan, Stephen Charnock, William Gouge, William Gurnall, John Howe, James Janeway, Robert Leighton, Thomas Manton, John Owen, Richard Sibbes, Henry Smith, and Thomas Watson.

William S. Barker says of this work, "For anyone wanting a taste of the movement that emphasized 'a daring nonconformity to this present evil age, and complete conformity to God's beloved Son' (as Di Gangi put it in the epilogue), this book is a good place to start."

The Puritans in America: A Narrative Anthology, edited by Andrew Delbanco and Alan Heimert (Harvard; 456 pages; 2005). First published in 1985, this book, now released in paperback, contains a wide sampling of American Puritan literature from thirty-eight writers, such as John Cotton, Anne Bradstreet, Edward Taylor, and Cotton Mather. Many selections are reprinted for the first time since the seventeenth century, such as Peter Bulkeley's *The Gospel Covenant.* The book is divided into four sections: Loomings; The Migration; City on a Hill; and O New England. Unlike most modern scholarly anthologies, the texts have been modernized in punctuation and spelling.

The *Virginia Quarterly Review* notes that "by presenting Puritan sermons, reminiscences, poetry, and other writings in a chronological fashion, Heimert and Delbanco have captured the spirit of a vibrant New England, experiencing social, religious, and economic change. The editors' brief introductions to many of the selections make this volume especially attractive to students of Puritan history and literature."

Farewell Sermons (SDG; 465 pages; 1992). In 1662, more than two thousand Puritan ministers were ejected from their pulpits for refusing to submit to the Act of Uniformity, which required using *The Book of Common Prayer* and assenting to all the rites and ceremonies of the Church of England. Within two years, two volumes containing thirty-one farewell sermons of ejected divines were published. In 1816, Gale and Fenner printed eighteen of those sermons in London. This volume is a reprint of that edition.

A preface includes brief biographical notes on the eighteen pastors, including William Bates, Thomas Brooks, Edmund Calamy, Joseph Caryl, Thomas Jacomb, William Jenkyn, Thomas Manton, Matthew Mead, and Thomas Watson. Their remarkable sermons are firm yet tender pastoral charges to remain true to Scripture at all costs and to endure persecution for Christ's sake. Two notable portions are Thomas Watson's twenty points of "advice for your souls," and Thomas Brooks's twenty-seven legacies and reasons for his confidence that the gospel would not be removed from England despite the terrible darkness following the Act of Uniformity.

Fast Sermons to Parliament, 1640-1653: The English Revolution (CMP; 34 vols.; 1971). This is a collection of sermons preached to England's Parliament during the glory days of Puritan preaching on days of public humiliation under Oliver Cromwell's rule. In these volumes, the general editor, Robin Jeffs, has documented 448 sermons, the bulk of which are reproduced here by facsimile. The English government did not print the remaining sermons.

These sermons richly combine prayer and thanksgiving on England's behalf. They encourage and admonish Parliament to govern in the fear of God. The volumes include sermons of preachers who were frequently invited to Parliament, including William Ames, Samuel Bolton, William Bridge, Thomas Brooks, Anthony Burgess, Jeremiah Burroughs, Joseph Caryl, Thomas Goodwin, William Greenhill, Christopher Love, Thomas Manton, Stephen Marshall, Philip Nye, John Owen, Obadiah Sedgwick, and Ralph Venning.

The Godly Family: A series of Essays on the Duties of Parents and Children, by George Whitefield, Henry Venn, *et al.* (SDG; 360 pages; 1999). This is an outstanding compilation of fifteen essays and sermons from seventeenth- and eighteenth-century pastors, including several Puritans, on ordering a godly home. The work is divided into four sections: (1) The Importance of Family Religion; (2) The Duties of Parents; (3) The Duties of Children; and (4) The Eternal Family. The authors include Samuel Davies, Philip Doddridge, Arthur Hildersham, Thomas Houston, Samuel Stennett, Henry Venn, George Whitefield, and Samuel Worcester. Doddridge's sermons on educating children in the faith are particularly helpful. We know of no better volume in print today to promote family worship and godliness.

Jus Divinum Regiminis Ecclesiastici *or The Divine Right of Church Government,* edited by David W. Hall (NP; 285 pages; 1995). Subtitled *Originally asserted by the Ministers of Sion College, London, December 1646,* this work by London ministers on church government promotes a Presbyterian view of church government. Their writings were prompted by the Presbyterian opposition to the Erastians and Independents at the Westminster Assembly.

Puritans in the New World: A Critical Anthology, edited by David D. Hall (PUP; 392 pages; 2004). Hall's anthology captures a wide range of Puritan literature and helps the reader grasp the complexity of Puritan thought and practice. This anthology is different than others in that it approaches its subject historically rather than literarily. The overarching theme of the work is the Puritans' "errand into the wilderness" and the many trials and triumphs they experienced. The book is divided into seven main parts (I. From the Old World to the New; II. Theology in New England: The Plight of Sinners and the Stages of Redemption; III. Patterns of Piety and Devotion; IV. The Good Society; V. Dissenters; VI. Encountering the Native Americans; VII. Errand Into the Wilderness) with representative selections under each, such as William Bradford's *Of Plymouth Plantation* (I) and Mary Rowlandson's captivity narrative (VI).

Hall also provides scholarly chapter introductions that chronicle vital Puritan history and scholarship. Overall, this book is an important contribution to modern scholarship and provides accurate exposure to life in early New England.

Lessons for the Children of Godly Ancestors: Sermons for and about New England's Rising Generations, 1670-1750 (SF; 7 vols. in 1, 416 pages; 1982). This facsimile includes Increase Mather's "Pray for the Rising Generation" (1679), Cotton Mather's "The Best Ornaments of Youth" (1707), William Cooper's "How and Why Young People Should Cleanse Their Way" (1716), Benjamin Colman and William Cooper's "Two Sermons Preached in Boston, March 5" (1723), Charles Chauncy's "Early Piety Recommended and Exemplified" (1732), John Barnard's "A Call to Parents and Children" (1737), and Jonathan Todd's "The Young People Warned" (1740).

The Puritans: A Sourcebook of Their Writings, edited by Perry Miller and Thomas Johnson (Dover; 846 pages; 2002). First

635 when Puritan studies were a novelty, this collection includes some of the best prose in early America. In

printed in 1938 when Puritan studies were a novelty, this collection includes some of the best prose in early America. In addition to the writings, this book includes extensive bibliographies offering a comprehensive introduction to early American Puritanism. The writings are divided into nine sections: History; The Theory of State and Society; This World and the Next; Manners, Customs, and Behavior; Biographies and Letters; Poetry; Literary Theory; Education; and Science. While we do not agree with some of Miller's conclusions, we recommend this work as an overview to American Puritan society.

The Puritan Sermon in America, 1630-1750 (SF; 4 vols., 1,840 pages; 1978). This facsimile of four volumes, edited by Ronald A. Bosco, contains thirty-nine sermons.

Volume 1 titled *Sermons for Days of Fast, Prayer, and Humiliation, and Execution Sermons* contains:

- Thomas Shepard's "Wine for Gospel Wantons" (1668)
- Increase Mather's "The Day of Trouble Is Near" (1675)
- Increase Mather's "Pray for the Rising Generation" (1679)
- John Danforth's "The Vile Profanations of Prosperity by the Degenerate among the People of God" (1704)
- Thomas Prince's "Earthquakes the Works of God and Tokens of His Just Displeasure" (1727)
- John Webb's "The Duty of a Degenerate People to Pray for the Reviving of God's Work" (1734)
- Increase Mather's "The Wicked Man's Portion" (1675)
- Samuel Willard's "Impenitent Sinners Warned of Their Misery and Summoned to Judgment" (1698)
- John Williams's "Warnings to the Unclean" (1699)
- Cotton Mather's "The Valley of Hinnom" (1717)
- Benjamin Colman's "It is a Fearful Thing to Fall into the Hands of the Living God" (1726)
- Thomas Foxcroft's "A Lesson of Caution to Young Sinners" (1733).

Volume 2, titled *Connecticut and Massachusetts Election Sermons*, contains:

- John Whiting's "The Way of Israel's Welfare" (1686)
- William Burnham's "God's Providence in Placing Men in Their Respective Stations" (1722)
- Azariah Mather's "Good Rulers a Choice Blessing" (1725)
- Thomas Buckingham's "Moses and Aaron: God's Favour to His Chosen People" (1729)
- Isaac Stiles's "A Prospect of the City of Jerusalem" (1742)
- Jonathan Todd's "Civil Rulers the Ministers of God" (1749)

Volume 3, titled *Massachusetts Election Sermons*, includes:

- Increase Mather's "A Discourse Concerning the Danger of Apostasy" (1685)
- Samuel Torrey's "A Plea for the Life of a Dying Religion" (1683)
- Cotton Mather's "Things for a Distressed People To Think Upon" (1696)
- Samuel Belcher's "An Essay Tending to Promote the Kingdom of Our Lord Jesus Christ" (1707)
- Benjamin Colman's "The Religious Regards We Owe to Our Country, and the Blessing of Heaven Assured Thereunto" (1718)
- Thomas Prince's "The People of New-England" (1730)
- Samuel Wigglesworth's "An Essay for Reviving Religion" (1733)
- Charles Chauncy's "Civil Magistrates Must Be Just" (1747)

Volume 4, titled *New England Funeral Sermons*, includes:

- Samuel Willard's "The High Esteem which God Hath of the Death of His Saints" (1683)

- Benjamin Colman's "A Devout Contemplation on the Meaning of Divine Providence in the Early Death of Pious and Lovely Children" (1714)
- Cotton Mather's "Maternal Consolations" (1714)
- Cotton Mather's "Hades Looked Into" (1717)
- Benjamin Colman's "The Prophet's Death Lamented and Improved" (1723)
- Nathaniel Appleton's "A Great Man Fallen in Israel" (1724)
- Thomas Prince's "The Departure of Elijah Lamented" (1728)
- Thomas Prince's "A Sermon at the Public Lecture in Boston" (1730)
- Charles Chauncy's "Man's Life Considered under the Similitude of a Vapour" (1731)
- Jonathan Edwards's "The Resort and Remedy of Those That Are Bereaved by the Death of an Eminent Minister" (1741)
- Charles Chauncy's "The Blessedness of the Dead" (1749)

Puritan Sermons, 1659-1689 (ROR; 6 vols., 4,150 pages; 1981). This collection of Puritan sermons has been historically known as "The Morning Exercises," since most of them were preached at 5:30 or 6 a.m. Large crowds of people often gathered for these expositions of Scripture.

This six-volume set was published in London piecemeal from 1661 to the 1690s. James Nichols updated and republished the collection in 1844; Roberts's 1981 reprint is from that 1844 edition. The following summary of the contents of *Morning Exercises* is adapted from Nichols:

- The four volumes of sermons preached at Cripplegate were published separately. The first volume was published in 1661 as *The Morning Exercise at Cripplegate: or several Cases of Conscience practically resolved by sundry Ministers.* The second volume, *A supplement to the Morning Exercise at Cripplegate: or several more Cases of Conscience practically resolved,* was published in 1674. The third, published in 1682, was *A Continuation of Morning Exercise Questions and Cases of Conscience,* and the fourth, published in 1690, was *Casuistical Morning Exercises.* Each volume includes a preface and sermon by Samuel Annesley.

- Volume 5, titled *The Morning Exercise methodized; or certain chief Heads and Points of the Christian Religion opened and improved in divers Sermons,* includes sermons preached at St. Giles-in-the-Fields in 1659. They were originally published in 1660. Thomas Case wrote the preface and the first sermon in this volume. It is the best compilation of Puritan systematic theology ever written, but unfortunately is often overlooked in Puritan studies. The last six sermons begin to expose the doctrinal errors of Roman Catholicism.

- The last volume, titled *The Morning Exercise against Popery: or the principal Errors of the Church of Rome detected and confuted, in a Morning Lecture preached lately in Southwark* (1675), was edited by Nathaniel Vincent. Nichols wrote of it, "By competent judges it has always been deemed a standard book on that great controversy which is recently revived." Appended to volume 6 are excellent author, textual, and subject indices.

This six-volume set represents Puritan preaching at its best. *Morning Exercises* shows the care that Puritan pastors aimed for in preaching in the following ways:

1. *Balance.* The Puritans did not insist that every sermon balance doctrinal truths such as divine sovereignty and human responsibility. Rather, they allowed the text to dictate its particular emphasis. For example, when the Puritans preached on hell, they offered little mention of heaven, and when they preached on heaven, they did not dwell on hell. The Puritans fully preached the theme of each text. Over time, they addressed the major themes of Scripture.

COLLECTIONS OF PURITAN WRITINGS

2. *Appreciation.* The Puritan pastors tried to enhance appreciation for each scriptural doctrine. Listeners could relish a sermon titled "Make haste for thy life's sake" for its warning note of urgency and responsibility one Sabbath, and just as deeply savor the message the following week on "All that the Father giveth me shall come to me." The Puritans treasured the full scope of God's counsel.

3. *Variety.* Their appreciation for all scriptural doctrine allowed the Puritans to cover a wide variety of topics. For example, Volume 3 of *Puritan Sermons* contains "How May We Experience in Ourselves, and Evidence to Others, that Serious Godliness is more than a Fancy?" as well as:

- "What Are the Best Preservatives Against Melancholy and Overmuch Sorrow?"
- "How May We Grow in the Knowledge of Christ?"
- "What Must We Do to Prevent and Cure Spiritual Pride?"
- "How May We Graciously Improve Those Doctrines and Providences That Transcend Our Understanding?"
- "What Distance Ought We to Keep in Following the Strange Fashions of Apparel Which Come Up in the Days in Which We Live?"
- "How May We Best Know the Worth of the Soul?"

4. *Excellence.* Can you imagine an entire sermon on "the best Preservatives Against Melancholy and Overmuch Sorrow"? Without thorough research and excellent development, this topic would hardly hold the attention of listeners. Puritan pastors strove for such excellence. They also made their sermons practical enough to answer the questions of listeners in a thoroughly scriptural manner.

The Puritans on Conversion (SDG; 211 pages; 2002). This is a compilation of three Puritan treatises, each dealing with a different aspect of conversion:

- Samuel Bolton on the dread character of sin ("Sin the Greatest Evil")
- Nathaniel Vincent on the steps of conversion ("The Conversion of a Sinner")
- Thomas Watson on seeking God ("The One Thing Necessary").

Albert Martin writes in the foreword to this work: "The advantage of this trilogy is that each sermon has its own distinct areas of strength in setting forth both a sound theology of conversion as well as penetrating pastoral insights into the method of conversion. In contrast to much evangelical preaching and writing in our day, these three sermons are marked by the distinctive Puritan characteristics in the broad areas of the *content* of their doctrine of conversion, and in the *manner* in which they preached that doctrine."

The Puritans on the Lord's Supper (SDG; 196 pages; 1999). This work contains seven chapters on the theology and practical application of the Lord's Supper, including:

- Richard Vines on "The Passover" and "The Fruit and Benefit of Worthy Receiving"
- Edmund Calamy on "The Lord's Supper is a Federal Ordinance" and "The Express Renewal of Our Christian Vows"
- Thomas Wadsworth on "It is Every Christian's Indispensable Duty to Partake of the Lord's Supper"
- Joseph Alleine on "Self-Examination"
- Thomas Watson on "The Mystery of the Lord's Supper."

This outstanding anthology on the Lord's Supper brings together much scarce material. It shows how Puritan ministers balanced experimental and practical emphases in promoting Reformed spirituality regarding the Supper.

The Puritans on Loving One Another (SDG; 130 pages; 1999). This volume contains four treatises on the doctrine of loving one another:

- Ralph Venning's "The New Commandment Renewed," which stresses Christ's command to love our neighbor as ourselves
- Thomas Manton's "Love One Another," which expounds 1 John 3:11, stressing that he who does not love is not born of God
- Joseph Caryl's "The Nature and Principles of Love as the End of the Commandment," which explains how love flows out of a pure heart, a good conscience, and unfeigned faith (1 Tim. 1:5)
- John Ball's "The Holy Exercise of Love," which deals with what holy love is, how to stir it up, and signs that prove it is true love.

These Puritan writings show what true love consists of. Love flows like a golden chain: the Father loves the Son, the Trinity loves believers, and believers love one another and their neighbor.

The Puritans on Prayer (SDG; 300 pages; 1998). The Puritans wrestled with God in what they called "secret" or "closet prayer." This book offers practical advice on how to improve the quality and fervency of prayer in:

- "The Saints' Daily Exercise," by John Preston (five sermons on 1 Thess. 5:17)
- "The Spirit of Prayer," by Nathaniel Vincent (on Eph. 6:18)
- "Secret Prayer," by Samuel Lee (on Matt. 6:6).

If the kind of prayer described in these writings characterized believers today, the world would be a different place.

In an editorial note, Don Kistler writes: "Preston calls us to prayer and defines it. Vincent tells us to pray continually and gives instruction how to do that. Lee gives us the sweetness of secret prayer, then adds a section on sudden spontaneous prayers. Combined, these three treatises give us encouragement and instruction in the duty and privilege of prayer, that 'holy breathing of the soul.'"

Sermons and Cannonballs: Eleven Sermons on Military Events of Historic Significance during the French and Indian Wars, 1689-1760 (SF; 448 pages; 1982). This book packs eleven addresses into one, some of which are written by Puritans. They include:

- Cotton Mather's "The Present State of New-England" (1690)
- John Williams's "God in the Camp" (1707)
- Thomas Symmes's "Lovewell Lamented" (1723)
- William McClenachan's "The Christian Warrior" (1745)
- Gilbert Tennent's "The Necessity of Praising God for Mercies Received" (1745)
- Samuel Davies's "Virginia's Danger and Remedy" (1756)

Soldiery Spiritualized: Seven Sermons Preached before the Artillery Companies of New England, 1674-1774 (SF; 384 pages; 1979). This book puts seven volumes into one, some of which are written by Puritans. They include:
- Joshua Moodey's "Soldiery Spiritualized; or, the Christian Soldier Orderly, and Strenuously Engaged in the Spiritual War, and So Fighting the Good Fight" (1674)
- Samuel Nowell's "Abraham in Arms" (1678)
- Cotton Mather's "Military Duties, Recommended to an Artillery Company" (1687)

- Thomas Bridge's "The Knowledge of God, Secured from Flattery, and Strengthening to the Most Noble Exploits" (1705)

Daily Devotions from the Puritans, by I.D.E. Thomas (Gwasg Bryntirion Press; 383 pages; 2001). This book contains helpful daily devotional selections from both well-known and lesser-known Puritans. Each entry also quotes a verse from Scripture. A brief biographical note of the authors quoted would have been helpful. Nevertheless, this devotional will serve as a valuable introduction to Puritan literature and will also move the souls of those already familiar with the warmth and depth of Puritan writings.

A Golden Treasury of Puritan Quotations, by I.D.E. Thomas (BTT; 320 pages; 1977). This is a masterful selection of 1,500 quotations from Puritan writers. Each quotation is included under a topical heading. Large topics are broken into helpful subheadings. For example, the topic Conscience is broken into the subheads:
- Its excellency
- Its ministry
- Its limitations

The topic includes notable quotations such as "Conscience is God's spy and man's overseer" and "A good conscience and a good confidence go together."

These quotations are an ideal introduction to Puritan writings. They are excellent for devotions and will add color to sermons. We know of no other book of quotations as helpful as this one.

The Bible and the Closet, by Thomas Watson and Samuel Lee (SPR; 256 pages; 1998). This volume contains three parts:
- "How We May Read the Scriptures with Most Spiritual Profit" by Thomas Watson

- "Secret Prayer Successfully Managed," by Samuel Lee, a seventeenth-century Puritan
- "The Family Altar," a collection of helps and encouragements for conducting family worship given by Isaac Watts, Philip Doddridge, and others.

In the preface, George McCearmon says this work helps "believers develop and sustain effective and worshipful communion with God through the reading of the Bible and private prayer. [It] bears the marks of mature expression and deep spirituality. It is blessedly and distinctively different from the plethora of light and frothy devotional guides available in our day."

APPENDIX 2

Scottish Divines

I make no apology for treating the Scots under the general term "Puritan." It is sufficient justification that the word was used in reference to the Scots in the seventeenth century itself. For example, Robert Boyd, Principal of the Glasgow College, was charged with being a Puritan in 1621 and Samuel Rutherford preaching in Scotland, probably in the 1630s, says, "Many are ashamed to own Christ, and to profess him, they will not be called Puritans." Peter Heylyn was therefore not creating a precedent when in his History of the Presbyterians, published in 1670, he speaks of "the Presbyterians or Puritan Faction in the realm of Scotland."

—Iain H. Murray, *The Puritan Hope*, pp. xxiv-xxv

Introduction: England's Puritans and the Presbyterians of Scotland

Readers of this guide may be surprised to find that along with the Puritans of England and New England there are a significant number of Scottish Presbyterians included in this appendix. Though divided by lines of history, nationality, and race, and to some extent, language, England's Puritans and Scotland's Presbyterians were united by the closest spiritual bonds of doctrine, worship, and church order.

Most English Puritans were themselves Presbyterians, and they longed to see the imperfectly reformed Church of England brought into conformity with the faith and order of the Church of Scotland. Such was the express aim of the Solemn League and Covenant of 1643, which called for "the preservation of the reformed religion in the Church of Scotland, in doctrine, worship, discipline, and government," and "the reformation of religion in the kingdoms of England and Ireland, in doctrine, worship, discipline, and government, according to the word of GOD, and the example of the best reformed Churches."

For their part, the Scottish Presbyterians eagerly embraced the work of the Westminster Assembly of Divines. The Confession of Faith, the Larger and Shorter Catechisms, the Form of Presbyterial Church Government, and the Directory for the Public Worship of God were all carried home to Scotland and quickly approved as standards of the Church of Scotland. Just as important was the decision to adopt the assembly's new metrical version of the Psalms, which, after thorough review and amendment, appeared as the Scottish

Psalter of 1650, ever afterward published as "the version approved by the Church of Scotland, and appointed to be used in worship."

After the restoration of the monarchy, Puritanism was all but extinguished in the Church of England and compelled to live on in a humbler and often uncertain state in the conventicles and chapels of the Dissenters. It was not so in Scotland, where Presbyterians rose in defense of the faith, worship, and order of their national church. The Scots resisted, to the shedding of blood, the prolonged campaign of the Stuart kings to introduce Anglican ways and usages north of the border. When the smoke of battle cleared and blood had ceased to flow, Scotland's Presbyterians found they had prevailed in the great conflict and so determined that the faith of the Reformers and the Puritans would continue to be the faith of the Church of Scotland.

Later developments, such as the rise of the Cameronians, the Marrow Controversy, and the Secession of 1733, were only added chapters to the history of the faith of the Puritans in Scotland. In each case, the matters at issue were all central to the faith of the Puritans and their vision of what a national church should be.

When the great tide of Scottish emigration commenced, outward-bound Scots gladly carried the Westminster Standards first to North America, and then to the ends of the earth, founding Presbyterian churches everywhere. If Puritanism has been a force in the United States, Canada, Australia, and elsewhere, it is in very large part because of the tenacity of these Scottish migrants in maintaining the Puritan faith, worship, and order of the church of their homeland.

Hugh Binning
(1627-1653)

Hugh Binning was born in 1627 in Dalvennan, Ayrshire, the son of a wealthy landowner who gave him an excellent education. Alexander Grosart wrote, "He easily outstripped his schoolfellows of twice and thrice his years, and in his thirteenth and fourteenth years his gravity and piety were recognized with a kind of awe by all" (*DNB*, 2:521).

Binning entered the University of Glasgow at the age of thirteen, earning a Master of Arts degree in philosophy in 1646. At age nineteen, he was appointed professor of philosophy because the other applicant for the position was unwilling to face "such an able antagonist" as Binning. While teaching, he studied theology with the intention of entering the ministry of the Church of Scotland. By all accounts and despite undertaking two full-time careers simultaneously, Binning's lectures were both profound and practical. For Binning, philosophy was the handmaid of theology.

Ordained in 1650, Binning served as a minister in Govan, Scotland, for three years, quickly becoming known as a God-fearing, eminent preacher and able scholar. His sermons, which "regularly attracted vast crowds," were warm, pastoral, and experiential. He appealed to the conscience, urging sinners to come immediately to Christ. His style was quite unlike that of his contemporaries, for Binning did not approve of the "ordinary way of cutting [the word of truth] all in parcels and dismembering it by manifold divisions." James Durham said, "There was no speaking after Binning."

Shortly after he was ordained, Binning married Mary Simpson, daughter of James Simpson, parish minister of Airth, Stirlingshire. They had one son, John.

Binning was prominent in the 1651 debates between the Resolutioners and Protestors, siding with the Protestors; yet, he maintained an irenic spirit. His book *Treatise of Christian Love* illustrated that approach, and served as "a moving and compelling plea to Christians to overcome their differences and unite in the love of God and fellowship with one another" (*Oxford DNB*, 5:773).

Later that year, Binning took part in the Glasgow debates between Independents and Presbyterians in the presence of Oliver Cromwell. His theological knowledge and eloquent fervor bore down all opposition. Cromwell was deeply impressed at how thoroughly Binning embarrassed the party of Independents, particularly when he learned that Binning was only twenty-four years old. Making a pun of Binning as "Binding," Cromwell said, "He hath bound well indeed, but"—putting his hand on his sword—"this will loose all again" (ibid.).

Binning died from tuberculosis at Govan in 1653 at age twenty-six, and was buried in his churchyard. His writings were prolific for a young man; none were printed during his life, although most of them were published after his death.

———◄◆►———

The Works of the Rev. Hugh Binning (SDG; 659 pages; 1992). Binning's collected works were printed in five editions, ranging from one to three volumes, and were also translated into Dutch by Jacobus Koelman, minister at Sluys in Flanders, and published at Amsterdam in at least four editions.

This large, small-print volume is a photolithograph reprint of the 1851 edition edited by M. Leishman. It includes 133 sermons, divided as follows: (1) "The Common Principles of the Christian Religion," a series of twenty-five sermons on God and His glory, God's attributes, the Trinity, the decrees and predestination, creation, providence, the covenant of works, sin, and the way of deliverance; (2) "The Sinner's Sanctuary," a series of forty sermons on Romans 8:1-15, which are particularly powerful and comforting for believers; (3) "Fellowship with God," a series of twenty-eight sermons on 1 John 1:1-2:3; and (4) forty additional sermons. Two small treatises are also included: "An Useful Case of Conscience" and "A Treatise of Christian Love."

A *Treatise of Christian Love* (BTT; 106 pages; 2004). Binning shows that love is the badge of Christianity and should motivate all Christians to strive to demonstrate its presence in their lives. He describes how love works itself out practically in acts of righteousness and mercy, and shows humility and meekness to be its root and fruit. Also included in this book are three of his forty sermons on Romans 8:1-15, entitled *The Sinner's Sanctuary* (1670).

THOMAS BOSTON

Thomas Boston

(1676-1732)

Thomas Boston was born in Duns, Berwickshire, the youngest of seven children. His parents sent Boston from age nine to thirteen to the grammar school in Duns, where he loved reading the Bible and began studying Latin and New Testament Greek.

John Boston, Thomas's father, was a cooper by trade and a strict Presbyterian. He was imprisoned for a time for refusing to conform to the changes in worship and government that the Stuart kings imposed on the Church of Scotland. One of Thomas's earliest memories was visiting his father in prison. After the Act of Toleration in 1687 permitted non-conforming Presbyterians to hold services in private houses, John Boston began traveling with his family to Whitsome to hear the preaching of Henry Erskine, the father of Ebenezer and Ralph Erskine. Thomas Boston was spiritually awakened at age eleven while listening to Erskine's messages on John 1:29 and Matthew 3:7.

Erskine's ministry continued to influence the Boston family. Regardless of the weather, Thomas Boston would walk four or five miles each Sabbath to obtain food for his soul. He later wrote, "In the winter sometimes it was my lot to go alone, without so much as a horse to carry me through Blackadder water, the wading whereof in sharp frosty weather I very well remember. But such things were then easy, for the benefit of the Word, which came with power" (*Memoirs*, p. 10).

Boston's spiritual life grew during his teenage years with regular Bible study and spiritual conversations with two boys from school. Before long he felt convicted that God was calling him to the ministry. To meet the cost of further study, John Boston apprenticed his son to Alexander Cockburn, a notary in the town. Thomas Boston worked at that for two years. The training served him well in later years, both in disciplined study and in clerking for his presbytery and synod.

Boston became a student at Edinburgh University in 1691. In addition to Greek and Latin, he studied logic, metaphysics, ethics, and general physics. He studied incessantly and lived on such scanty fare that his health was impaired. After earning a Master of Arts degree in 1694, Boston received the bursary (a financial grant) from the Presbytery of Duns. He studied divinity on his own for one semester, then went back to Edinburgh to study theology under George Campbell. Boston spent one semester there, then completed studies under the oversight of his presbytery. During that time, he supported himself by working as a tutor in the home of Andrew Fletcher, stepson of Lieutenant Colonel Bruce of Kennet. This was good preparation for the ministry, as he "kept up family worship, catechized the servants, pressed the careless to secret prayer, reproved and warned against sinful practices, and earnestly endeavored the reformation of the vicious" (*Memoirs*, p. 25).

Boston was licensed in 1697 by the presbytery of Duns and Chirnside. The power and freshness of his preaching soon attracted attention. However, Boston did not immediately settle in a parish. Ordinary people who heard him would have called him, but the power to do so was in the hands of the principal heritor, or landlord. In seven parishes where people would have chosen Boston, the landlord intervened to prevent it. He thus remained a probationer for more than two years. Finally, in 1699, the landlord of Simprin, Berwickshire, a small parish eight miles southeast of Duns, agreed to call Boston. Prior to being ordained, Boston renewed his covenant with God, confessing that he was "utterly lost and undone" in himself, stood in "absolute need of a Savior," and "cordially received Him in all His offices, consenting to the terms of the covenant."

Boston's ministry at Simprin was challenging. The people of his congregation were ignorant of spiritual truth and needed to be taught the simplest things. They were more concerned about making a living than about their souls. Boston was dismayed to learn that only one household observed family worship. What's more, the Lord's Supper had not been administered for several years.

Within one year, Boston had reorganized his congregation. He reestablished two services on the Sabbath. He lectured on one chapter of the Bible in the morning and preached on various individual texts in the afternoon. In the evening, Boston taught people from the Shorter Catechism or expanded on sermons preached that day.

Boston also kept a rigorous schedule during the week. He rose early each Monday morning and devoted hours to prayer and reflection. He kept praying throughout the week. On nearly every page of his autobiography, Boston mentions laying one matter or another before the Lord in prayer. He established regular times for fasting. He set apart Tuesday evenings for prayer and praise. Every Thursday, he led public worship. He also called upon people in their homes, speaking intimately with them and urging the unconcerned to "close with Christ."

Boston kept studying theology and languages. He mastered the classical languages, French, and Dutch. He often consulted the *Statenbijbel*, the Dutch Bible translation ordered by the Dutch parliament, known as the *Dutch Annotations*. It contains helpful explanatory glossaries, notes, and cross references.

Boston's congregation outgrew its church building, especially on Communion Sabbaths. After seven years, not a single family neglected family worship. "Simprin! O blessed be the Lord for his kindness at Simprin," Boston wrote, "I will ever remember Simprin as a field which the Lord had blessed."

When Boston received a call from Ettrick, the poor spiritual condition of people there overcame Boston's reluctance to leave Simprin. Ettrick had less than four hundred people. The roads were nearly impassable. The parsonage was dilapidated. Church services were irregular. Spiritual barrenness, pride, deceit, swearing, and fornication abounded.

Boston had to rebuild and reorganize the parish. The first ten years were difficult. After eight years, he told his wife, "My heart is alienated from this place." Yet he couldn't leave. Gradually, the Spirit began to bless his work. His preaching attracted increasing numbers of people. After some of his sermons were published, people in Edinburgh began to take notice. When Boston received a call to Closeburn in 1716, the session at Ettrick called for a fast. That proved to be the turning point for Boston's ministry there. For the next sixteen years, he labored with new authority.

At both Simprin and Ettrick, Boston was cautious in administering the Lord's Supper. He waited more than three years at Ettrick, then privately interviewed each candidate before deciding whether that person should partake of the Supper. The first Communion service Boston led had fifty-seven participants; by the time Boston last celebrated it in 1731, there were 777 communicants, including all four of his surviving children.

Boston did not have an easy life. He lost his mother at age fifteen and his father a decade later. While in Simprin, Boston married Katharine Brown, the fifth daughter of Robert Brown of Barhill, Clackmannan, in whom Boston saw "sparkles of grace." Boston considered his marriage a gift of the Lord, even though his wife suffered repeated bouts of depression and insanity. From 1720 on, she was often confined to an apartment, which she called "the inner prison." She spent months and years without relief, "an easy target for Satan's onslaughts, both concerning her assurance of salvation and her peace with God." Boston had to bury six of ten children, two while in Simprin and four at Ettrick. Then, too, Boston himself was not a healthy man. He struggled often with pain and weakness.

Boston viewed these trials as discipline from his heavenly Father's hand. He continued to describe his wife as "a woman of great worth, whom I therefore passionately loved, and inwardly honoured: a stately, beautiful, and comely personage, truly pious, and fearing the Lord...patient in our common tribulations, and under her personal distresses" (Cook, *Singing in the Fire*, p. 122). He wrote to William Hog in Edinburgh, "It is a very sweet view of affliction, to view it as the discipline of the covenant; and so it is indeed; and nothing else to the children of our Father's family. In that respect it is medicinal; it shines with many gracious purposes about it; and, end as it will, one may have the confidence of faith, that it shall end well" (*Memoirs*, p. 499). Boston felt that God's gracious purposes included "more heavenliness in the frame of my heart, more contempt of the world, more carefulness to walk with God, and more resolution for the Lord's work over the belly of difficulties."

Philip G. Ryken says that Boston was "a preacher to his dying day" (*Thomas Boston as Preacher of the Fourfold States*, p. 1). Boston's entire life revolved around preaching. His goals in preaching were to assure the regenerate of salvation in Christ and to see the unregenerate converted to Christ. He thus preached a theology of "grace in its sovereignty; grace in its freeness, offered to all without money and without price; grace in its fullness, pardoning, adopting, sanctifying, glorifying; grace in its simplicity, without works of law; grace in its security, ratified by an everlasting covenant; grace in its appointed channels, coming mainly through word and ordinance; grace in its practical fruit," wrote William G. Blaikie (*The Preachers of Scotland*, pp. 201-202).

Boston was reluctant to engage in the theological controversies of his day; nevertheless, he was compelled at times to defend the truth. He preached several times against the errors of the Cameronians who willingly separated themselves from other Christians. In his sermon "The Evil and Danger of Schism," Boston pleaded for Christians to emulate Christ, who went to both temple and synagogue in spite of corrupt leaders.

Boston refused to sign the Abjuration Oath, which officers of church and state and others were required to sign, renouncing the claims of the Stuart pretender, James, to the British throne. The oath reaffirmed previous acts of Parliament requiring that the reigning sovereign belong to the Church of England. It was seen as an endorsement of episcopacy, or the government of the church by bishops. This prompted Boston to publish his pamphlet, *Reasons for refusing the Abjuration Oath in its latest form.*

The conflict that took most of Boston's time was the Marrow Controversy (1717-1723). This brought to a head differences between two schools of thought in Scottish theology. The legal strain, led by James Hadow (1670-1747), principal of St. Andrews, sought to discredit the "antinomian" teachings of *The Marrow of Modern Divinity.* That book, written by Edward Fisher in 1645, contained extracts from the works of Reformed and Puritan writers. The evangelicals, or "Marrowmen," sought to correct the legalistic tendency in Scottish preaching by emphasizing God's free offer of grace and Christ's meritorious work for the sinner.

Tension grew as the General Assembly of the Church of Scotland debated the action of the Auchterarder Presbytery requiring ministerial candidates to adhere to certain propositions known as the "Auchterarder Creed." One section reads: "I believe that it is not sound and orthodox to teach that we must forsake our sins in order to our coming to Christ." Boston saw these words as a muddled attempt to defend free grace rather than to promote antinomianism, but the Assembly condemned the proposition. Boston viewed its decision as a direct blow to the doctrine of free grace; he held that the Assembly's action endangered the doctrine of justification by faith alone.

Into this fray came a new edition of *Marrow*, printed by James Hog (1658-1734), minister of Carnock in Fife. It was immediately assailed by its opponents. Its wealth of paradoxical statements moved James Hadow, Alan Logan, and Robert Wodrow to speak out against it. They succeeded in convincing the General Assembly of 1720 that the book taught such errors as universal atonement, assurance as the essence of faith, holiness not implicit in salvation, and antinomianism.

At the Assembly of 1721, the Marrowmen responded with a document titled "The Representation." It argued against condemning *Marrow* and the prohibition imposed on ministers forbidding them to circulate anything in its favor. The assembly rejected the document and rebuked the Marrowmen. Boston wrote in his diary, "I received the rebuke and admonition as an ornament put upon me for the cause of truth."

Boston served as clerk of the Synod of Merse and Teviotdale and attended the General Assembly when needed. In 1728, he attracted attention at the Assembly when he stood to protest its leniency to John Simson; Boston said Simson deserved deposition rather than a brief suspension. Simson, professor of divinity at the University of Glasgow, had been involved in two heresy trials; the first (1715-1717) involving charges of Arminianism, and the second (1727-1729), charges of Arianism. Simson's family and friends shielded him from higher censure. Though he was permanently suspended in 1729, he remained on the Glasgow faculty until his death in 1740.

Boston's last sermons, preached from 2 Corinthians 13:5 on the first two Sabbaths of April 1732, were on self-examination. That was typical of his preaching as well as his personal life. Due to weakness, he preached them "from his deathbed, as the people of Ettrick gathered around the window of the manse to hear their beloved minister preach" for the last few times (*Oxford DNB*, 6:723). He died at age fifty-six on May 20, 1732. He was buried in the Ettrick churchyard.

After Boston's death, the growing hostility between legalists (known as "moderates") and evangelicals led to irreparable breaches in the Scottish church. In 1733, most of the Marrow-men left the Church of Scotland to join the Associate Presbytery, giving birth to the Secession Church.

The Complete Works of the Late Rev. Thomas Boston (TENT; 12 vols., 7,500 pages; 2002). Boston's works were first collected and published in 1767 and later reprinted in 1773. *The Complete Works*, edited by Samuel M'Millan and published in twelve volumes in 1853, have now been reproduced, thanks to Tentmaker Publications. We trust that Boston's writings will cause many to agree with John Duncan, who wrote, "Thomas Boston was a common place genius—not a common place man but a common place genius." Or with another writer who said that Boston did more "to fan the flame of true piety in Scotland than that of any other single minister in his generation."

The first two volumes contain Boston's sermons on the Shorter Catechism and "Forms of Personal Covenanting." Volume 3 contains thirty-seven sermons and two treatises: "The Crook in the Lot" and "The Unity of the Body of Christ, and the Duties the Members Owe One to Another" (on 1 Cor. 10:17). "Unity" is an excellent, 65-page treatment of the communion of saints, worthy of being printed alone.

Volume 4 contains forty miscellaneous sermons. The eight sermons on Philippians 3:8 are an outstanding exposition of the excellence of Jesus Christ and the duty of believers to esteem Him. It also includes a short treatise on "The Distinguishing Characters of Real Christians." Volume 5 expands this theme with two lengthy treatises: "The Distinguishing Characters of True Believers" and "The State and Character of Believers." Boston writes about the believer's relationship with God, the church, conversation, enemies, evil times, work, and the world to come. This volume also includes "The Art of Man-fishing."

Volume 6 contains 280 pages on "Miscellaneous Questions" and "Miscellaneous Tracts," of which nearly a hundred pages are devoted to the subject of baptism. This volume also includes sixteen sermons on various subjects; the sermons on self-denial and repentance are masterpieces.

Volume 7 includes Boston's brief "Explication of the First Part of the Assembly's Shorter Catechism," "The Marrow of Modern Divinity" by Edward Fisher with Boston's accompanying notes (see above), and nine sermons. Highly recommended are Boston's sermons "The Everlasting Espousals" (Hos. 2:19) and "The Mystery of Christ in the Form of a Servant" (Phil. 2:7).

Volume 8 contains "Human Nature" and "The Covenant of Grace" (see below); Volume 9, fifty-five miscellaneous sermons; Volume 10, eighteen sermons on the names and attributes of Christ, five sermons on the Christian life, and ten miscellaneous sermons. Volume 11 offers six discourses on prayer, a lengthy treatise on the covenant of works, and a treatise on fasting and humiliation in one's life and family. The concluding volume contains Boston's famous *Memoirs* (see below).

This is an excellent set of books to read, particularly for ministers of the gospel. Boston's sermons are models of sound exegesis combined with experiential piety and admonition.

The Art of Man-fishing: A Puritan's View of Evangelism (CFP; 110 pages; 1998). First published in 1773, this work was

written when Boston was twenty-two years old. It was a series of personal meditations on Christ as the model for
ministry in response to Matthew 4:19, "Follow me and I will
make you fishers of men." J. I. Packer wrote of this work,
"Boston's idea of the minister as a 'fisher of men' is that
through his public ministry in the pulpit and his private ministry of one-to-one admonition, God will work in people's
hearts to bring them to this place of settled commitment,
where they can confirm their assurance of being alive to God
by noting the ongoing change in their inner being" (pp. 8, 12).

This powerful little book will convict, humble, and encourage ministers of the gospel and those who engage in
evangelism. It challenges all to remain dedicated and persistent in presenting the gospel to the lost. Those who evangelize
are to follow Jesus' example in dealing with sinners, praying
earnestly that the Spirit will bless their efforts by driving sinners into the gospel net.

The Beauties of Thomas Boston: A selection of his writings
(CFP; 616 pages; 1979). Edited by Samuel M'Millan and first
published in 1831, these selections cover the following topics:
Scripture, prayer, God, public ordinances, God's decrees, the
Creator, Christ's priesthood, believing in Christ, God's providence, election, the covenant of works, the fall of man, the
judgment of the wicked, and the covenant of grace. This book
is no substitute for Boston's *Works*, but it is a handy reference
guide and can serve as a sound daily devotional.

Church Communion (PA; 111 pages; 2005). What is the communion of saints? How is the communion of saints shown in
partaking of the Lord's Supper? As members of one body,
what duties do the saints owe each other? Why should
admission to the Lord's Table be such a serious matter? In this
book Boston answers these questions and many more in a
thoroughly biblical manner. He stresses that believers in

Christ are united to one another and bear a responsibility for the welfare of other Christians. They have a duty to love each other sincerely, to bear with each other's weaknesses, to watch over and edify each other, to bear each other's burdens, and to fellowship with each other.

Commentary on the Shorter Catechism (SWRB; 2 vols., 1,350 pages; 1987). This reprinted work was first printed in three volumes as *An Illustration of the Doctrines of the Christian Religion* (1755) and is also contained in the first two volumes of Boston's *Works*. It contains ninety sermons expounding the Westminster Shorter Catechism. Here is Boston at his best— biblical, doctrinal, experiential, and practical. Of special mention are the chapters "The Divine Call to Leave the Devil's Family," "The Benefits Flowing from Justification, Adoption, and Sanctification," "The Duty of Ruling Elders and People," "The Danger of Not Complying with the Gospel Call," and "The Right Improvement of a Time of Sickness and Mortality." In these sermons, Boston fearlessly preaches the depths of man's depravity, the gracious sovereignty of God, the full responsibility of man, and the unconditional offer of grace. This work deserves to be much more of a classic than it is.

The Crook in the Lot (SDG; 168 pages; 2001). Boston finished this work in the final months of his life, subtitling it "The Sovereignty and Wisdom of God in the Afflictions of Men, together with a Christian Deportment under them." This book examines a believer's conduct under pressing circumstances. The three themes of the book are: whatever crook there is in one's lot, it is of God's doing; whatever God mars, no human will be able to mend; and, seeing the crook in one's lot as the work of God is the only way to true contentment.

Don Kistler writes of this work, "Boston does not commit the error of needlessly trying to protect God's reputation, nor does he go to the opposite extreme of making God a compassionate but helpless bystander. Rather, Boston brings God right into the mix, and shows how He is actively involved in both the events and their resolution." *The Crook in the Lot*, which contains a new study guide, would be an excellent gift for someone in troubled waters.

Human Nature in its Fourfold State (BTT; 506 pages; 1964). This book, first published in 1720 (a revised edition in 1729) as a "simple, practical, and memorable summary of Christian doctrine," became Boston's most influential treatise, going through a hundred editions in eighteenth-century Scotland alone. Consisting of sermons preached at Simprin and amplified at Ettrick, it traces man's condition through four states: his original state of righteousness or innocence; his state as a fallen creature; his state as a redeemed and regenerated being; and finally, his eternal state, be it heaven or hell. Boston abbreviated these as the states of innocence, nature, grace, and eternity.

Parts of this book are unparalleled. For example, Boston powerfully shows how Adam's sin imputed to us makes us guilty of sinning against all of the Ten Commandments. No other book so masterfully exposes our tragic fall in Adam. If someone you know doubts the pollution of original sin, give them this book. In addition, Boston's 68-page chapter on the mystical union between Christ and the believer has helped scores of believers over the centuries treasure their oneness with their Elder Brother.

The Fourfold State has been translated into several languages, including Gaelic and Welsh. John MacLeod wrote of it, "There is no book of practical divinity, not even William Guthrie's *Trial of Saving Interest in Christ*, nor Rutherford's *Letters*, which was more read in the godly homes of Scotland than this treatise. It did more to mold the thought of his countrymen than anything except the Westminster Shorter Catechism. It is of this work that Jonathan Edwards says that it 'showed Mr. Boston to have been a truly great divine'" (cf. *Works of Jonathan Edwards* [BTT], 2:489).

Phil Ryken has rightly noted: "*The Fourfold State*'s emphases on the totality of sin, the necessity of being born again, the desirability of being united to Christ, and the reality of the life to come also made it a central text for the rise of evangelicalism in Britain and America. It was a best-seller during the Great Awakening, in part because it came highly recommended by both John Wesley and George Whitefield" (*Oxford DNB*, 6:723).

Memoirs of Thomas Boston (BTT; 556 pages; 1988). This classic of Calvinist spiritual devotion was originally published in 1776 by Boston's grandson, Michael Boston, as *Memoirs of the Life, Time and Writings*. It reveals "a man earnest in ministry, melancholy in disposition, scholarly in interest, modest in aspiration, sober in judgment, sensitive in conscience, and devout in prayer" (ibid.).

Memoirs consists of two accounts written for Boston's posterity: *A General Account of My Life and Passages of My Life*. It tells much about Boston's life and is based, as William Blaikie wrote, "on a faith in the particular providence of God, in the intimacy of His fellowship with His children, and in the closeness of the connection between their spiritual and their natural life, the like of which perhaps no man of equal intellectual power ever attained."

Boston was hard on himself spiritually. A typical entry in *Memoirs* says: "Having allotted the morning entirely for prayer and meditation, some worldly thoughts crept in. In the afternoon I somewhat recovered my forenoon's loss" (p. 97). Such "lapses" led Boston to fasting, intense self-scrutiny, and passionate tears. "Oh, how my heart hates my heart!" he groaned.

But he also had moments of joy, which he describes as "outgates" from spiritual bondage. Once, in taking the words of Psalm 14 for his own, he wrote, "My soul blessed God for His word, and for that word in particular, that ever it was put in the Bible. It has loosed my bands, set me to my feet again, and put courage in my heart. My heart rejoiceth in His salvation and in Himself" (p. 115).

This edition is a reprint of the 1899 edition. It includes an introduction and notes by George H. Morrison of Dundee. Boston's memoirs rank with those of Augustine, Bunyan, and Halyburton as one of the church's most enduring spiritual autobiographies.

A View of the Covenant of Grace (FCM; 232 pages; 1994). Boston was a parish minister, but he was also a theologian. Perhaps his most significant contribution to theology was his clarification of the covenantal or "federal" (from the Latin *foedus*, meaning "covenant") theology of the Westminster Standards. He wrote his treatises on the covenants of works and of grace as correctives to the Pelagian and Arminian errors of his day. Proper understanding of the two covenants is necessary because of their role in man's salvation, Boston said. The first covenant shows our lost estate in Adam, and the second offers the remedy in Jesus Christ.

A *View of the Covenant of Grace* (1734), consisting of a series of sermons preached over two years on Psalm 89:3 and 1 Corinthians 15:45, was the first book published after Boston's death. Boston was led to preach on the covenant of grace after reading Herman Witsius's *Economy of the Covenants.* Boston divided his work into the following heads: the parties to the covenant; the making of the covenant of grace; the parts of the covenant; the administration of the covenant; the trial of a saving, personal "inbeing" in the covenant; and the way of "instating" sinners, personally and savingly, in the covenant.

Boston explains that the covenant of grace is intended only for the elect; it is God's response to man's breach of the covenant of works. He uses the terms *covenant of redemption* and *covenant of grace* to name the two sides of the covenant. Boston did not believe the covenant of redemption was separate from the covenant of grace, nor was it "a covenant within the covenant," as some theologians had taught. As with the covenant of works, there are two participants in this covenant: God the Father, representing the offended party, and Christ, the second (or last) Adam, representing the elect.

The covenant of grace was established in eternity in the council of the Trinity, Boston says. The plan and objects of salvation were settled before man was created. The Persons of the Godhead have different roles in the plan of salvation: the Father chooses the objects of salvation, the Son redeems them, and the Spirit sanctifies them, applying redemption.

Christ is the representative head of His seed in the same way that Adam was of his seed, Boston says. The conditions of the covenant between the Father and the Son are the *principal* required in the first covenant—perfect obedience—and the *penalty* of Adam's disobedience to be paid in Christ. The second Adam entered into covenant with God on behalf of His elect; He stood where the first Adam stood but succeeded where the first Adam failed.

In the last section of his treatise on the covenant of grace, Boston explains how sinners become part of that covenant. Most people are strangers to the covenant of grace and have no saving interest in Christ, Boston says, but we may offer the gospel of reconciliation to them. We must, indeed, compel sinners to enter the covenant of grace (Luke 14:23).

Boston taught that saving faith, which is necessary to take hold of Christ, has four components: first, faith in Christ's sufficiency, by which the sinner believes that Christ is fully able to save men from their sins; second, faith in the gospel, by which the sinner believes that Christ is offered to sinners such as he; third, faith in one's right to Christ, whereby one is encouraged to go to Christ; and fourth, faith for salvation, whereby one appropriates Christ as his personal Savior.

David Dickson

(c. 1583-1662)

David Dickson (Dick) was born about 1583 in Glasgow, Scotland. He was the only son of John Dick, or Dickson, a wealthy and godly merchant. He earned a Master of Arts degree from the University of Glasgow, where he studied under Robert Boyd, the great exegete of Trochrig. In 1610, Dickson was appointed professor of philosophy and Greek at the university. He taught for eight years.

In 1617, Dickson married Margaret Roberton, daughter of Archibald Roberton of Stonehall. Together they had three sons. The second son, Alexander, became professor of Hebrew in the University of Edinburgh.

In 1618, Dickson was ordained as minister in Irvine, Ayrshire. His ministry there was extraordinarily fruitful for twenty-three years. His work was interrupted between 1622 and 1623, however, when he was suspended by Archbishop Spottiswood for his strict defense of Presbyterianism. Dickson was banished to Turriff in Aberdeenshire for opposing the Anglican ceremonies imposed by the Articles of Perth. These articles required kneeling rather than sitting at the Lord's Supper, private communion, baptism not withheld longer than one Sabbath and administered privately where necessary, the participation of bishops in confirmation, and the observance of church feast days such as Christmas and Easter.

When Dickson returned from almost a year of exile, a notable revival began. He began preaching on the street on market day, and many people were brought under conviction of sin.

Resistance to the king's efforts to impose a ceremonial worship culminated in the Glasgow Assembly of 1638 and the signing of the National Covenant. Dickson was a prime mover in preparing for the Assembly, drafting a paper insisting that representative ruling elders should be commissioned to the Assembly along with ministers. He became a leader of the Presbyterian movement and was instrumental in upholding Presbyterianism in Scotland. The following year, he became moderator of the General Assembly, when the king made important concessions to the popular uprising.

In 1640, Dickson became professor of divinity at Glasgow University. Ten years later, he accepted a similar position at Edinburgh University and was appointed to the second charge of St. Giles. A large portion of the Church of Scotland's ministers during the time of the Westminster Assembly received their theological training from Dickson.

About the time of his transfer to Edinburgh, Dickson and James Durham produced their famous *Sum of Saving Knowledge* (1650), an important federal presentation of the gospel. The book is still printed in Scottish editions of the Westminster Standards as a model of what to teach and how to evangelize in a manner consistent with the Westminster Standards. *The Sum* would later become instrumental in the conversion of Robert Murray M'Cheyne and scores of others.

After the Restoration, Dickson refused to take the oath of supremacy and was ejected from his university chair in Edinburgh and his ministerial charge in October 1662. These hardships broke his health, yet he believed the gospel's cause was not lost in Scotland. When asked, "What is come of all the blood and prayers of many years, now when all is overturned?" he answered, "There is the Confession of Faith and Catechisms; and these are worth more than all the blood or prayers that have been!"

Dickson died two months after his ejection. On his deathbed, he said: "I have taken all my good deeds, and all my bad, and cast them through each other in a heap before the Lord, and fled from both, and have betaken me to the Lord Jesus Christ, and in Him I have sweet peace" (W.K. Tweedie, ed., *Select Biographies*, 2:12). He was buried on December 31, 1662.

During his years as a professor, Dickson played an essential role in establishing orthodox Christianity throughout Scotland. His writings contributed to that influence, particularly *Therapeutica Sacra*, first published in Latin in 1656, then in English in 1664, and last reprinted in *Select Practical Writings* in the nineteenth century. The English subtitle of that work was *The Method of Healing the Diseases of the Conscience Concerning Regeneration.* Dickson wrote *Praelectiones in Confessionem Fidei* (later published in English as *Truth's Victory Over Error*), the first full commentary on the Westminster Confession of Faith; commentaries on the Psalms, Matthew, Paul's epistles, and Hebrews; and *A Treatise on the Promises.* He also helped Alexander Henderson and David Calderwood write a *Directory for Public Worship* (c. 1643).

Six of Dickson's communion sermons are included in *Select Practical Writings.* In the words of Robert Wodrow, these are "full of solid substantial matter, very scriptural, and in a very familiar style, not low, but extremely strong, plain, and affecting." Dickson was greatly used by God in private as well as public ministry. People greatly valued his spiritual counsel and wisdom. He was gifted in applying godly comfort and encouragement to needy souls.

***

The Epistles of Paul (by James Fergusson) and **Hebrews** (by David Dickson) (BTT; 600 pages; 1978—also published separately, SG; 82 pages; 2005). Dickson's preaching was so popular that his parishioners took thorough notes on his sermons, then circulated them among their friends. Sensing the need for publishing clear and simple expositions of Scripture, Dickson began a project designed "to bring to the common man the ripe fruit of academic work." His first effort on Hebrews (1635) set the pattern for a series of commentaries. His method was to summarize each section of the epistle, then provide a doctrinal exposition, and finally give practical applications. The short volume on Hebrews was printed with the hope that "any success attending this 'piece of hard meat' would encourage others to attempt less difficult Scripture."

James Fergusson (1621-1667), minister at Kilwinning, was first to assist Dickson in this project. Over a period of about ten years, Fergusson produced commentaries on Galatians, Ephesians, Philippians, Colossians, and 1 and 2 Thessalonians. All of those were included with Dickson's work on Hebrews in a volume published in 1850 in Ward's Library of Standard Divinity. This volume is a reprint of that edition.

Spurgeon says of the Fergusson titles, "He who possesses this work is rich. The author handles his matter in the same manner as Hutcheson and Dickson, and he is of their class—a grand, gracious savoury divine." Of the Dickson portion on Hebrews, he writes, "Get it, and you will find abundance of suggestions for profitable trains of thought."

The Gospel of Matthew (BTT; 416 pages; 1981). First published in 1647, this commentary is accurate and compelling. Dickson focuses upon the essential elements of a Scripture passage, explaining the main flow of the text without charting exegetical backwaters. Then he offers an abundance of practical applications. For example, when explaining Matthew 16:25-28, Dickson offers seven succinct reasons why Christians should want to lose their lives for Christ's sake. This work is packed with sound theology, profound love for Christ, and keen pastoral insights. It will edify both the preacher and the ordinary reader.

Spurgeon regarded this commentary as a gem. "The work is, to men of our school, more suggestive of sermons than almost any other we have met with," he says. He later writes, "Dickson is a writer after our own heart. For preachers he is a great ally. There is nothing brilliant or profound; but everything is clear and well arranged, and the unction runs down like the oil from Aaron's head."

The Psalms (BTT; 1,064 pages; 1959). This commentary was written at the height of the controversy between the Resolutioners and Protestors and was first published in three volumes in 1653-54. It has endured throughout the ages as a classic of Scottish exposition. Dickson provides insight into various psalms, though his comments are not as thorough as Henry Ainsworth's *Annotations on the Pentateuch and the Psalms* or Charles Spurgeon's *The Treasury of David*. Dickson's work is written more for the saint than for the scholar. Its concise treatment of the Psalms and simple style is a joy to read.

Spurgeon calls it "a rich volume, dropping fatness. Invaluable to the preacher. Having read and re-read it, we can speak of its holy savour and suggestiveness. We commend it with much fervour."

Truth's Victory over Error (PA; 239 pages; 2002). Dickson has the distinction of writing the first commentary on the Westminster Confession of Faith. He poses the propositions of the Confession as questions, answering them either in the affirmative or in the negative. He then states contrary opinions to the confessional position and refutes them through concise biblical arguments. Dickson's glossary of heresies has been retained and a biography of the author, penned by Robert Wodrow, has also been included.

James Durham

(1622-1658)

J ames Durham, one of Scotland's brightest lights, was born
into a wealthy home. He was the eldest son of Alexander
Durham and Helen Ramsay, daughter of the archdean of
Dunkeld. Durham studied at St. Andrews University but left
without obtaining a degree so he could pursue the life of a
country gentleman.

Durham was converted shortly after he married Anna
Durham of Duntarvie. He came under profound religious conviction while visiting his wife's relatives in Abercorn, near
Edinburgh. His mother-in-law persuaded him to attend
church with her the Saturday prior to the celebration of the
Lord's Supper. Durham went along rather reluctantly, but he
was quite impressed by the service. Upon returning home, he
said to his mother-in-law, "The minister preached very seriously this day. I shall not need to be pressed to go to church
tomorrow." The following morning, Ephraim Melville
preached from 1 Peter 2:7, "Unto you therefore which believe
he is precious." After hearing the fullness and preciousness of
Christ preached, Durham was enabled to "close with Christ"
by faith and to attend the Lord's Table. Durham would later
refer to Melville as "my father."

Durham's experiences on that remarkable Sabbath, combined with his intense study of the Scriptures and his various
experiences as a captain in the Scottish army during the Civil
War of the 1640s, led Durham to assurance of salvation in

Christ. When David Dickson overheard Durham praying with
his soldiers, he was so impressed that he urged Durham to
study for the ministry, saying, "Go home, Sir, for you seem to
be called to another work than this!" (R. Wodrow, *Analecta*,
3:109). Shortly after that, Durham's life was remarkably
spared, first, when his horse was shot and killed from under
him, and second, when an English soldier who was about to
kill Durham saw him dressed in black clothes and, thinking
he was a minister, spared his life.

Durham's growing sense of God's call to the ministry persuaded him to enroll at Glasgow University to study divinity
under Dickson. Neighbors and friends marveled that a man of
his social stature would give up a life of luxury to undertake
theological studies, but Durham was undeterred. By the time
he earned a Master of Arts degree in 1647, he was twenty-five
years of age. That same year, he was ordained as minister to
the south quarter of the Glasgow Blackfriars parish, where he
served faithfully for nearly three years.

In 1650, Durham was appointed Professor of Divinity at
Glasgow University to replace his former teacher, David
Dickson. Before he could take up his duties, the General Assembly appointed him chaplain to the Stuart royal house,
particularly to Charles, son of the king who had been executed the previous year. Meanwhile, trouble was brewing
between England and Scotland. Oliver Cromwell came to
Scotland and defeated the Scots at the Battle of Dunbar. During his stay in Glasgow, Cromwell heard Durham preach and
was greatly impressed. Charles Stuart soon entered England
with a Scottish army, but Cromwell defeated him at the battle of Worcester. Charles escaped to the Continent.

After losing his post as chaplain to the royal house,
Durham inquired about taking up his duties at Glasgow University, but he was denied that opportunity. Instead, in 1651,
he became minister at St. Mungo's, Glasgow, a flock of some

1,500 souls, where he remained for the rest of his life. He soon became known there for his piety, wisdom, and scholarship. He was a powerful preacher and especially gifted in resolving cases of conscience. John Carstairs described him as "a very candid and searching preacher, who [came] into the inmost corners of your bosoms, [albeit] with caution and meekness, without giving any of his hearers the smallest ground to fret and repine at his freedom in dealing with them."

Durham was a humble man. As one story goes, he and Andrew Gray were walking together on a particular Sabbath, each to preach at a different church. Observing that most people were going to the church where Gray was to preach, Durham remarked, "Brother, I perceive you are likely to have a thronged church today."

Gray, who was about age twenty, replied, "Truly, brother, they are fools to leave you and come to me."

Durham replied, "Not so, dear brother, for none can receive such honor and success in his ministry except it be given him from heaven. I rejoice that Christ is preached and that His kingdom and interest is getting [gaining] ground, and that His honor and esteem doth increase though my esteem in people's hearts should decrease; for I am content to be any thing, or nothing, so that Christ may be all in all."

Durham was a very serious man. Some people said he "had the appearance of an old man who seldom smiled." However, one night he was so enjoying the company of William Guthrie at a parishioner's home that he laughed frequently. When Guthrie was asked to pray after dinner and did so with great fervency, Durham said to him, "William, you are a happy man; if I had been so merry as you have been, I could not have been so serious, nor in any frame for prayer for forty-eight hours."

Durham's humility and gravity were especially evident in his preaching and during Communion seasons. Some said that during those times he spoke to them "as a man that had been in heaven, commending Jesus Christ, making a glorious display of the banner of free grace, holding forth the riches of it very clearly and convincingly, and bringing the offers thereof very low." While he was preaching on Matthew 22:4, the "rope or cord of the offer of salvation was let down and hung so low to sinners, that those of the lowest stature amongst them all, might have caught hold of it, who, through grace, had any mind to do so." Indeed, some wondered, when the gospel was so "urgently pressed, on so sweet and easy terms to be embraced," how any could refuse it.

Durham's wife died in 1648. He remarried five years later. His second wife was Margaret Mure, widow of Zachary Boyd, a noted Glasgow minister. They were married only five years before Durham's health broke. For the first half-year of 1658, he was confined to home. During those last months, he finished his massive commentary on Revelation and wrote his classic on scandal as a last effort to bring peace between the Resolutioners and the Protestors in those tumultuous times.

Durham was plagued with doubt on his deathbed. He said to John Carstairs, his brother-in-law and colleague, "Brother, for all that I have preached and written, there is but one scripture I can remember or dare grasp; tell me, if I dare lay the weight of my salvation upon it, *Whosoever cometh to me, I will in no wise cast out.*" In the end, grace triumphed. Just before he died, Durham cried out in holy joy, "Is not the Lord good? Is He not infinitely good? See how He smiles! I do say it, and I do proclaim it" (John Howie, *Lives of Scottish Covenanters*, p. 216).

James Durham died at age thirty-five on June 25, 1658. He was a pastor for only eleven years, but he served well during that time. He studied and worked so hard that some thought it hastened his death. Yet he loved the work. He said that if he could live ten years longer, he would choose to live nine years to study for preaching the tenth year.

Durham was also a prolific writer. Most of his books were published after his death. Some of his unpublished manuscripts are still extant, which supposedly include a number of sermons on the Holy Spirit and fifty-three sermons preached on the fifth chapter of the Song of Solomon. Durham's writings are warmly devotional and experimental and are filled with godly counsel.

———◆◆◆———

The Blessed Death of Those Who Die in the Lord (SDG; 129 pages; 2003). After establishing the certainty of death, this exposition of Revelation 14:13 shows the blessedness of believers who die in Christ and the misery of those who reject Christ. It promotes meditating on death and our preparation for it. Durham provides numerous directions for dying in the Lord and shows what to do when death approaches suddenly. The book concludes with a stirring chapter on "encouragement in death," which shows how each person of the Trinity sanctifies death for the believer.

The Book of Revelation (OP; 1,035 pages; 2000). This massive commentary, originally printed in 1658 and reprinted eight times in the following century, is based on comments on the Scripture reading (called "lecturing") that Durham gave every Sabbath just before the sermon. Robert Baillie, Scottish commissioner to the Westminster Assembly, wrote, "It is not for naught, that the most judicious Calvin and acute Beza, with many other profound divines, would never be moved to attempt any explication of that book [of Revelation], yet I hope I may make bold to affirm, without hazard of any heavy censure, that there is here laid such a bridge over that very deep river, that who ever goeth over it, shall have cause to bless God for the author's labour."

You do not have to agree with all of Durham's interpretations to benefit from reading this work. As Spurgeon said,

"After all that has been written [on Revelation], it would not be easy to find a more sensible and instructive work than this old-fashioned exposition. We cannot accept its interpretations of the mysteries, but the mystery of the gospel fills it with sweet savour."

A bonus in this commentary is Durham's writing on a variety of "Questions and Controversies." For example, his explanation on the call to the ministry (pp. 66-83) is one of the clearest ever written on this often misunderstood subject. These excurses, inserted at Durham's request, comprise nearly one fourth of the commentary.

Christ Crucified: Or the Marrow of the Gospel in 72 Sermons on Isaiah 53 (NP; 704 pages; 2000). First published in 1683, then in 1686, this collection of sermons was reprinted six times in the eighteenth century. The present reprint is carefully and beautifully done; it uses the 1702 edition as the base text but also takes the other editions into account.

This book belongs in the class of Friedrich Krummacher's *The Suffering Savior*. Like Krummacher, Durham was gifted at describing the sufferings of Christ through illustration, though his language is now antiquated. For example, in describing Christ's agony in Gethsemane, he writes, "There was such a striving, wrestling and conflicting, not with man without him, but with inward pressures on his spirit, that he is like one in a barrace, or cock-pit, or engaged in a duel with a mighty combatant, sore put to it, very far beyond aught that we can conceive of, so that he sweat great drops of blood." The sixty-ninth sermon on making use of Christ's intercession is a masterpiece.

This is an excellent book for believers who yearn for a more intimate fellowship with Christ in His sufferings. John Duncan said to a friend who wanted to draw closer to Christ, "Read Durham on the fifty-third of Isaiah at my request. He has much repetition and you may be disgusted with that. But it's repetition of a very fine thing, the eating of Christ's flesh and the drinking of His blood. Well, that's what we must be repeating, in fact, all our life long."

The Marrow of the Gospel is one of the best commentaries ever written on Christ's person and work in redemption. Charles Spurgeon highly recommended this book, saying, "This is marrow indeed. We need say no more: Durham is a prince among spiritual expositors." Others have said this work equals if not excels all of Durham's other publications.

Concerning Scandal (NP; 400 pages; 1990). This work was first published posthumously as *A Dying Man's Testament to the Church of Scotland* (1659). Durham dictated the last part of it from his deathbed. It explains private offenses and scandals, church discipline, the sin of spreading scandalous rumors, and divisions among churches and ways to unite them. Durham also addresses scandalous errors: how they spread, the Lord's purpose with them, Satan's devices in spreading error, and the duties of believers when error prevails. Durham's counsel to ministers on working with the errant is particularly enlightening. He discusses four steps: discovery (or trial), conviction, admonition, and rejection.

Though difficult to read at times, this book is worth careful study. Durham stresses how far each church member and office-bearer should go in serving others to build up the body of Christ. This work was written to help reconcile divided parties (the Resolutioners and the Protestors) within the Church of Scotland, of which Durham was a member. John Macleod said this book "has long been looked upon as the Scottish classic on its topic" (*Scottish Theology*, p. 95).

Lectures on Job (NP; 240 pages; 1995). This work deals with all the chapters of Job and includes practical applications at the end of each chapter. Durham's commentary was last printed in 1759, upon which this edition is based. The various editorial additions by Christopher Coldwell are helpful for the modern reader.

The book is packed with spiritual substance. Durham is not afraid to warn his readers of the wrath to come. Here's one example, taken from Durham's exposition of Job 3: "Observe there's nothing so terrible as the wrath of God, when it looks a soul in the face. This made David roar. And if God is so terrible to his children in the way of trial, how terrible will he be to the wicked when he shall not only hound out one devil, but all the devils in hell, and that without any limitation upon them, and they shall have no peace, nor good conscience as Job had? When the little thing that Job felt is so terrible, what will it be when the wrath of the great and living God, and an unreconciled sinner meet? Fear to meet God [with] the cup of his wrath to drink."

A Practical Exposition of the Ten Commandments (NP; 425 pages; 2002). Durham's writings were popular for nearly two centuries after his death. George Christie said that twenty-six printing presses in eight villages of Scotland, England, and the Netherlands were involved in publishing one or more of Durham's books. "In each decade between his death and the beginning of the nineteenth century, at least one of his books was printed," Christie said ("A Bibliography of James Durham," *Papers of the Edinburgh Bibliographical Society*, 1918, p. 35). Of the seventy printings of Durham's books in those first centuries, his exposition of the Ten Commandments, often published as *The Law Unsealed*, was the most popular title.

Durham's treatment of the moral law is excellent though uneven; eighty-six pages are devoted to the fourth commandment, whereas only eight pages are given to the sixth and the ninth commandments. His sections on family worship (pp. 221-35) and on the change of the seventh day to the first (pp. 249-64) are particularly helpful.

The present edition is the first reprint in two hundred years. The text, based on several earlier printings, is well edited. For the first time this book includes author and Scripture indices. This is a handsome volume, intended for a variety of audiences, and essential for preachers. Few parts of this book sound outdated.

The Song of Solomon (BTT; 460 pages; 1982). First published in 1668, this commentary on the Song of Solomon is thoroughly evangelical, spiritual, and insightful. Durham considered the song in its historical and allegorical sense, giving full weight to the relationship between Christ and His church.

Durham says that four prerequisites enable believers to benefit from the Song of Solomon: knowledge of the whole Scripture, a personal knowledge of the ways of God with men's hearts, a disciplined and tender spirit, and fellowship with Christ in prayer for the illuminating power of the Holy Spirit.

Spurgeon wrote of this book: "Durham is always good, and he is at his best upon the Canticles. He gives the essence of the good matter. For practical use this work is perhaps more valuable than any other key to the Song."

The Unsearchable Riches of Christ (SDG; 375 pages; 2002). Durham originally preached the fourteen sermons in this volume to his congregation in Glasgow as Communion sermons. Each sermon explains the riches of grace found in Christ Jesus. In addition to four sermons on covenanting with God, sermons cover the danger of unworthy communing, the sin of not discerning Christ's body, the strong invitations contained in gospel proclamations, the danger of turning to folly after knowing God's peace, adhering to Christ by faith, remission of sins through Christ's blood, and sweet communion with Christ in heaven.

EBENEZER ERSKINE

RALPH ERSKINE

Ebenezer Erskine (1680-1754) & Ralph Erskine (1685-1752)

D ue to the intertwining of their ministries, the Erskine brothers are considered together. Ebenezer Erskine was born in Dryburgh, Scotland, in 1680. Five years later, his brother, Ralph, was born in Monilaws, near Cornhill, Northumberland, the northernmost county of England. Their father, Henry, was a Puritan minister who had been forced by the Act of Uniformity to vacate his home and pastorate in Cornhill in 1662. Their mother was Margaret Halcro, Henry Erskine's second wife. Both parents were of prestigious background and closely related to Scottish nobility.

The lives of the young boys were disrupted when their father refused to renounce the Solemn League and Covenant. The Scottish Assembly despised the preacher's Puritan principles. When Ebenezer was two years old, his father was arrested and sentenced to imprisonment on the Bass Rock for exercising his ministerial office illegally by "withdrawing from ordinances, keeping conventicles, and being guilty of disorderly baptisms." The Committee of Privy Council questioned Henry Erskine for hours, then finally asked if he would promise not to preach at any more conventicles. Erskine replied, "My lord, I have my commission from Christ, and, though I were within an hour of my death, I durst not lay it down at the feet of any mortal man."

Upon his request, Erskine's sentence to Bass Rock was commuted to exile, due to poor health. He and his family moved to England and settled in Parkridge, near Carlisle. From there they went to Monilaws, where Erskine was arrested again and imprisoned for several months for preaching at conventicles. Erskine then preached in the border parish of Whitsome, where he helped lead Thomas Boston to Christ at age eleven. The king's indulgence of 1687 enabled him to continue his ministry without fear of arrest. In 1690, when Ebenezer was age ten and Ralph, five, their father was admitted to the parish of Chirnside, near Berwick, in southeastern Scotland, where he ministered until his death in 1696 at the age of seventy-two.

Ebenezer Erskine went to Edinburgh University, where he first studied philosophy and the classics, then earned a master's degree in theology in 1697. He served as tutor and chaplain to the God-fearing family of the Earl of Rothes until he was licensed in 1703 by the Presbytery of Kirkcaldy and ordained to Portmoak, near Kinross, where he would minister for the next twenty-eight years. The year he was ordained, he married Alison Turpie, a God-fearing woman who had a profound spiritual influence on him.

Erskine's first years at Portmoak were difficult, mostly due to a spiritual battle that he had with himself after overhearing a conversation on the "deep things of God" between Ralph and his wife. The discussion convinced Ebenezer that he was not yet converted. After a year of spiritual struggle, he finally began to experience what he called "the true grace of God." In the summer of 1708, Erskine wrote in his voluminous diary that he finally "got his head out of Time into Eternity." On August 26, he wrote that God had "brought my heart to give a consent to Him" and that he was now sure that God could never "deny His own covenant" with him. In turn, Erskine made a covenant with God. He wrote:

> Lord, if I have done iniquity, I am resolved through thy grace to do so no more. I flee for shelter to the blood of

Jesus and his everlasting righteousness; for this is pleasing unto thee. I offer myself up, soul and body, unto God the Father, Son, and Holy Ghost. I offer myself unto Christ the Lord, as an object proper for all his offices to be exercised upon. I choose him as my prophet for instruction, illumination, and direction. I embrace him as my great priest, to be washed and justified by his blood and righteousness. I embrace him as my king to reign and rule within me. I take a whole Christ with all his laws, and all his crosses and afflictions. I will live to him; I will die to him; I will quit with all I have in the world for his cause and truth.

From the time of his conversion, Erskine became more diligent than ever in preparing sermons. His delivery also improved; instead of fixing his attention on a stone in the rear wall of the church, he now looked straight into the eyes of his hearers. The results were dramatic. Hundreds of people flocked to hear him, coming from as far as sixty miles, particularly during times of Communion. Scores of people were converted to Christ.

Ebenezer's younger brother, Ralph, was converted at age eleven when his father died. Ralph experienced a profound sense of sin and of deliverance in Christ, as well as remarkable answers to prayer. With this conviction, he made excellent progress at school. He entered Edinburgh University at the age of fifteen to study theology. During his holidays, Ralph stayed with his brother at Portmoak. After earning a master's degree in theology in 1704, Ralph worked for five years as a private chaplain for his relative, Colonel John Erskine.

By 1709, Ralph was old enough to be licensed as a preacher. The Dunfermline Presbytery agreed to allow Ralph Erskine to speak on a trial basis, and after a short time its members became convinced that this young man was sent by God to preach the gospel. Erskine was ordained to the second charge in Dunfermline in 1711 and promoted to the first charge in 1716.

After Erskine was settled in Dunfermline, he was overcome by doubts about his Christian witness and calling. He began scouring the works of godly men to find comfort. Thomas Boston's work on the covenant of grace finally brought him relief. After reading Boston, Erskine was able to plead the promises of God and regain peace of heart.

The assurance gleaned from that experience energized his ministry. So intent was Erskine on studying the Word, praying, and preaching, that he ignored sleep and worked long into the night. He would serve the Dunfermline congregation for more than forty years until his death in 1752. God mightily blessed that work. Within two years of Erskine's ordination, the Spirit was working so powerfully through his preaching that worshipers filled the church and churchyard. A previously dead church came alive. After the evening service, prayer and thanksgiving went on in small groups, sometimes until after midnight. One seeker rose at 2:00 a.m. to pray in secret and found so many people in town on their knees that the countryside hummed like a gigantic hive of bees. Hundreds of penitent sinners were pouring out their hearts to God. The revival proved to be genuine and abiding, though it remained confined mainly to Dunfermline.

Ralph Erskine married Margaret Dewer, a gentleman's daughter, in 1714. Margaret was noted for her kindness. She served at Ralph's side for sixteen years, bearing ten children, five of whom died in infancy. Erskine was shattered by her death at the age of thirty-two. Two years later, he married Margaret Simson of Edinburgh. Three of four sons born to them died in childhood.

While Ralph's ministry was thriving, his brother, Ebenezer, was called to a new charge in Stirling (1731), where he would serve for twenty-two years. Hundreds of people from neighboring parishes joined Erskine's congregation. The Erskines sometimes served more than thirty tables at Communion.

Those whom God greatly blesses He also tries. The troubles for the Erskines would come in three major waves, beginning in the early 1720s and continuing for more than two decades.

The first major trial, which became known as the Marrow Controversy, stirred up the Scottish church from 1717 to 1723. The controversy centered on the Auchterarder Creed. In 1717, William Craig, a divinity student, took issue with the General Assembly about one of the propositions that the Presbytery of Auchterarder required all ordination candidates to sign. The proposition, which was intended as a guard against Arminianism, said: "I believe that it is not sound and orthodox to teach that we must forsake sin in order to our coming to Christ, and instating us in covenant with God." The Assembly sided with Craig, declaring the proposition to be "unsound and most detestable."

In the context of that debate, Thomas Boston told John Drummond of Crieff that he had received aid years ago on the disputed issue from a relatively unknown book titled *The Marrow of Modern Divinity*, written in 1645 by Edward Fisher, a Presbyterian from London. Drummond mentioned the book to James Webster of Edinburgh, who told James Hog of Carnock about it. Hog prefaced a reprinting of the book in 1718.

Fisher's book emphasized an immediate offer of salvation to sinners who looked to Christ in faith. This emphasis was avidly supported by Boston and the Erskines, who were leaders among the church's evangelical minority. Fisher's emphasis, however, raised the opposition of the controlling party of the church, who later became known as the Moderates. The Moderates considered a call to immediate trust in Christ and to full assurance to be dangerously antinomian.

The church's General Assembly condemned *The Marrow of Modern Divinity* in 1720 and required all ministers of the church to warn their people against reading it. The Erskines, Boston, and nine of their colleagues, known as the Marrowmen or Marrow Brethren for their defense of Fisher's book, protested this action, but without avail. They were formally rebuked by the General Assembly in 1722.

The Marrow Controversy quieted down by 1723, but its effects lingered. The Marrow Brethren suffered continuing rejection in the Church of Scotland; nevertheless, they continued to teach and write on the doctrines the Assembly had condemned. Thomas Boston published his copious notes on *The Marrow of Modern Divinity* in the 1726 edition, and Ralph Erskine wrote several tracts defending Marrow theology.

The second major trial that affected the Erskines centered on the issue of patronage. The 1731 Assembly, dealing with an overture "concerning the Method of Planting Vacant Churches," legalized the appointment of ministers by patrons (wealthy landowners) rather than by the vote of church members. Both of the Erskines spoke out against the proposal, arguing strenuously for the right of the people to choose their own ministers. The 1732 Assembly reaffirmed support of patronage, even though the majority of presbyteries that responded had problems with it or firmly opposed it.

Ebenezer Erskine preached against the decision of the 1732 Assembly when he returned to his own congregation in Stirling. In response, the Synod voted to rebuke Erskine. When the 1733 Assembly supported the rebuke of the Synod, Erskine and three of his colleagues lodged a protest. The Assembly responded by insisting that the four repent of the protest. If they refused to do so, a higher censure would be passed against them.

The Assembly later that year carried out that threat by a majority of one. It suspended Erskine and three other ministers from their parishes, declared their churches vacant, and prohibited them from being employed by any church in the Church of Scotland.

The four ministers (Ebenezer Erskine, James Fisher, Alexander Moncrieff, and William Wilson) met at Gairney Bridge, near Kinross, in December of 1733, where they formed the Associate Presbytery, giving birth to the Scottish Secession Church. Ralph Erskine, who was at the Gairney Bridge meeting, continued to fellowship and correspond with the other ministers, though he did not join the Associate Presbytery at that time.

In 1734, the General Assembly softened its stand against the suspended ministers. In 1735, it invited Ebenezer Erskine to serve again as moderator of the Presbytery of Stirling. After lengthy deliberations, Erskine and his three friends declined to return, stating that none of their grievances had been addressed. After much inner conflict, Ralph Erskine formally joined his brother in the Secession in 1737.

On May 12, 1740, both of the Erskines and their colleagues were deposed by the General Assembly. Most of Ralph Erskine's congregation left the established church with him. A new building seating 2,000 was completed in 1741. In 1742, a new minister was ordained in the parish church, all ties were broken, and several hundred people drifted back to the parish church.

Unlike Ralph, Ebenezer Erskine was immediately shut out of his church after he was deposed. Instead of letting his congregation break down the doors, Erskine began preaching outdoors. His congregation grew rapidly in the ensuing months. The Erskines became busier and busier. As they ministered to their own large churches and a variety of other parishes throughout Scotland, the Secession cause grew dramatically, promoting Marrow theology.

The last major trial for the Erskines involved the so-called Burgher conflict. The Burgess Oath of 1744, which endorsed the religion of the realm, was required of all citizens of Edinburgh, Glasgow, and Perth. The oath stated, "Here I protest before God, and your lordships, that I profess, and allow with my heart, the true religion presently professed within this realm, and authorized by the laws thereof: I shall abide thereat, and defend the same to my life's end; renouncing the Roman religion called papistry."

The oath was important because only burgesses were permitted to vote, engage in commerce, or belong to a trade guild. Some members of the Associate Synod (the Seceders) objected to the oath, saying it endorsed practices in the established Church of Scotland that the Seceders had found objectionable. Others, including the Erskine brothers, regarded the oath as an approbation of the Reformed faith, intended only to exclude Roman Catholics from becoming burgesses. The Erskines affirmed the right to take the burgess oath, believing that an anti-burgher position would lead to the abandonment of civic and political duty. Ralph Erskine wrote a greater number of pamphlets than any other member of the Burgher Synod in defense of this position.

After three years of synodical meetings, the issue split the young denomination. Twenty-three church leaders of the Antiburgher party, under the leadership of Adam Gib and Alexander Moncrieff, started a new denomination, commonly known as the Antiburgher Synod, avowing that they were the rightful continuation of the Secession.

What made the split particularly heartbreaking for Ralph Erskine was that his son, John, sided with the Antiburghers and even participated in their Synod's decision to excommunicate the Erskines along with other members of the Burgher Synod. In the years following the controversy, the Burgher Synod redefined its position (in a Revised Testimony), gradually dropped the practice of covenanting, and resumed friendly relations with evangelical ministers in the established church.

Though they were deeply affected by them, controversies were not a priority for the Erskines. Their work was carried on, centered on winning souls, and, for a time, on training young ministers. When Alexander Moncrieff joined the Antiburgher Synod, Ebenezer Erskine was asked to teach divinity for the Associate Synod; he served in that capacity only until 1749, when he resigned for health reasons. Ralph Erskine spent more time training men for the ministry, to the point that in the autumn of 1752, Ralph Erskine's wife begged him to slow down and to spend more time with the family, for he was now sixty-seven years old. He promised to do so, but the following month he became very ill and died. His final words were, "Victory, victory, victory!"

Ebenezer would soon follow, however. After eighteen months of weakness and sickness, he died on June 1, 1754, at the age of seventy-three, after nearly fifty-one faithful years in the ministry.

The Works of Ebenezer Erskine (FPP; 3 vols., 1,500 pages; 2001); *The Works of Ralph Erskine* (FPP; 6 vols., 3,800 pages; 1991). The three volumes of Ebenezer Erskine's sermons (52 sermons) and the six volumes of Ralph Erskine's sermons (168 sermons) profoundly influenced ministers and lay people in the Reformed faith in several countries. They affected tens of thousands of people in Scotland for over a century, and gave direction to the Secession movement, passing on the essence of Marrow theology to subsequent generations. Ebenezer Erskine's *Whole Works*, first printed in Edinburgh in 1761, was reprinted six more times in Scotland. Ralph Erskine's writings, first published in 1764, were reprinted four times in Scotland. John Ker wrote in 1887 that the sermons of the Erskines were scattered throughout Scotland "in almost every farmhouse and cottage where there was an interest in religion."

The Free Church of Scotland, which started in 1843, was also influenced by the Erskines. George Smeaton, an eminent Free Church scholar, warmly introduced a reprinting of *The*

Beauties of Ralph Erskine. Robert Candlish, a leading preacher in the Free Church, recommended reading the Erskines, as did the Free Church minister and theologian Hugh Martin, who wrote in 1875 that the Erskines were still loved by the Scottish people.

In England, men of such stature as George Whitefield, Augustus Toplady, and James Hervey lauded the Erskines for preaching the gospel freely without sacrificing experimental depth. One of Hervey's last tasks was to dictate a preface to a new edition of Ralph Erskine's works, in which he wrote that he had found in his lifetime no human works "more evangelical, more comfortable, or more useful" than those of Ralph Erskine. His sermons were so treasured that, as late as 1879, they were still the best-selling religious books in London.

Many of the sermons of the Erskines, translated into Welsh, helped shape the preaching of two eighteenth-century Welsh preachers, Howell Harris and Daniel Rowland, whose messages were instrumental in the conversion of thousands. The Methodists in Wales "read, borrowed, translated, used and commended the Erskine brothers," wrote Eifion Evans. The Erskines influenced people in Ireland as well, particularly through the ministries of John Erskine, Ralph Erskine's son, and James Fisher, Ebenezer Erskine's son-in-law, who both labored there for some years.

From 1740 on, the writings of the Erskines were translated into Dutch and received a ready reception throughout the Netherlands. On a typical eighteenth-century market day in Rotterdam, farmers inquired at bookstalls for sermons of *Erskeyna.* Alexander Comrie and Theodorus van der Groe were greatly influenced by the Erskines. Van der Groe introduced several translated books of the Erskines, though he had a more restricted view of the promises of God than did the Erskines. By the time of van der Groe's death in 1784, the sermons of the Erskines were outselling those of any English or Scottish divine in the Netherlands.

In the 1830s, Hendrik Scholte, a well-known Secession leader who immigrated to Pella, Iowa, published a number of Ralph Erskine's sermons. In the mid-nineteenth century, volumes of the Erskines' sermons were published three times, finding a ready market among Dutch Reformed Church believers as well as among those who had seceded. Among the Seceders, those who approved of the sermons of the Erskines defended an unconditional, free offer of grace; those who opposed the sermons judged them to be tainted by Arminianism. In 1904, Herman Bavinck, a prominent Dutch theologian and professor at Kampen and the Free University of Amsterdam, wrote a largely commendatory foreword to a compilation of Ebenezer and Ralph Erskine's sermons.

Throughout the twentieth century, the writings of the Erskines have been reprinted frequently in the Netherlands. They continue to prompt discussion in Dutch Reformed circles, particularly in subjects such as how to preach grace to the unsaved and how to teach people about God's promises.

Although the sermons of Ebenezer and Ralph Erskine could have been written by the same hand, the brothers differed a bit, of course. Ebenezer's gifts were not as striking as Ralph's, but Ebenezer had a calm, sure strength that made him a better leader. Ralph was more self-effacing, more devout, and more experimental than his brother, and looked more to the Puritans for guidance. Nevertheless, the substance and spirit of their sermons were so similar—and remained so throughout their careers—that examining them together does no disservice to either.

The Erskines began to publish sermons and other writings in the 1720s to illustrate Reformed doctrines of grace, to explain Marrow theology, and to guard against legalism. Their writings include the Reformation's emphasis on the promises of God, the Puritan emphasis on experimental piety, and the Scottish Second Reformation's emphasis on covenant theology. Their sermons glow with teachings on the love of God and indiscriminate offers of Christ.

The Erskines leaned on the Reformers and Puritans for exegetical help. Luther and Calvin were their favorite commentators among the Reformers and James Durham and Matthew Henry among the Puritans. Some scholars have critiqued the Erskines for focusing more on the doctrines flowing out of a text than on the exegesis of a text, wandering at times beyond the boundaries of the text so that they lost its original intent. More commonly, however, the Erskines showed considerable exegetical skill in their sermons, particularly in expounding texts about salvation in Jesus Christ.

Homiletically, the Erskines followed the Puritan "plain" style of preaching. This style of preaching, according to William Perkins, did three things:

1. It gave the basic meaning of a text of Scripture within its context;
2. It explained points of doctrine gathered from the natural sense of the text;
3. It applied the doctrines "rightly collected to the life and manners of men."

The first part of an Erskine sermon was therefore exegetical, usually providing a short analysis of the text; the second, doctrinal, stating and expounding some doctrine or "observation"; and the third, applicatory. The Erskines usually divided the third part, often referred to as the "uses" of doctrine derived from a text, into sections such as information, trial (self-examination), comfort, exhortation, and advice. For example, in a sermon titled "Present Duty Before Approaching Darkness," based on Jeremiah 13:16 ("Give glory to the Lord your God, before he cause darkness"), Ralph Erskine offered six points of information, two points of self-examination, five points of exhortation, and six points of advice. Because of the nature of the text, no section was offered for comfort.

This homiletical method often led to a lengthy series of sermons on one text. For example, Ralph Erskine delivered fourteen sermons on prayer based on Romans 12:12, thirteen sermons on Christian living based on Colossians 2:6; nine sermons on self-conceit based on Proverbs 30:12, and eight sermons on "The Happy Congregation" based on Genesis 49:10.

The Erskine sermons combined doctrinal and experimental exposition. Doctrinally, they focused on the great, central themes of Christianity: the person and work of Christ, sin and salvation, faith and hope, and God's grace. Experimentally, they dealt with such matters as comfort, assurance, assistance in trials, and the privileges of being a Christian.

The Erskines are best known for sermons that, in keeping with Scottish tradition, focus on the promises of God. The Scots Confession of 1560 spoke of an "assured faith in the promises of God." Writings such as George Hutcheson's *Exposition of the XII Small Prophets*, Andrew Gray's *Great and Precious Promises*, and Thomas Halyburton's *Great Concern of Salvation* made much of God's promises. "God binds Himself to us with His promises," Halyburton had written.

But the Erskines emphasized the promises even more than did those writers. "What is the gospel but a word of promise?" Ebenezer Erskine asked (1:262). "Take away the promise out of the Bible," wrote Ralph Erskine, "and you take away the gospel" (5:118), for "the gospel and the promise is one and the same thing" (5:235).

The Erskines never tired of preaching on the promises of Scripture. Ralph Erskine wrote, "I will look to the promise, and lay stress upon it, and upon a God that promises" (5:236). They found promises everywhere in the Bible, even in texts such as John 17:17, which says, "Sanctify them through thy truth; thy word is truth" (5:103). As Ebenezer Erskine wrote, "All the histories, prophecies and shadows, and types of the

Word—what are they but an opening and an exposition of the promises?" (1:512).

This focus on God's promises impacted the theology of the Erskines in a variety of key doctrines. They viewed God's promises as rooted in eternity past and consequently as being inseparable from each person of the Trinity. The promises are of the very essence of the gospel. There are unconditional promises for every kind of sinner, they taught. They knew how to relate the promises of God to faith, repentance, conviction of sin, the free offer, self-examination, assurance of faith, and sanctification. Read the sermons of the Erskines if you would be comforted with an experiential sense of the value and reality of God's promises.

The Beauties of Ebenezer Erskine, ed. Samuel M'Millan (RHB/CFP; 700 pages; 2001).

When Samuel M'Millan, who ministered in Aberdeen, published *The Beauties of Ralph Erskine* (2 vols.) in 1812, followed by *The Beauties of Ebenezer Erskine* in 1830 (reprinted in 1850), he collected spiritual gems from their Christ-centered sermons. The reprint in 2001 is taken from the 1850 edition; it includes a new fifty-page introduction on the Erskines by Joel R. Beeke.

The Beauties of Ebenezer Erskine offers the best portions of his sermons. The selections focus particularly on different aspects of Christ and His ministry as well as the doctrine and life of faith. The section on assurance of faith is also very helpful. This volume makes for an excellent daily devotional. It is meant to be read slowly; meditate, apply, and practice its weighty and savory truths.

The Assembly's Shorter Catechism Explained by Way of Question and Answer, Ebenezer and Ralph Erskine and James Fisher (Berith; 477 pages; 1998). This excellent work, which consists of thousands of short questions and short answers on the Shorter Catechism, became a classic shortly after its publication. It was originally published in two volumes, the first of which was done primarily by the Erskine brothers (1753), the second, by James Fisher (1765). In this 1998 reprint, both volumes are freshly typeset and conveniently bound in one volume.

The strength of the Erskine-Fisher Catechism is the succinctness of answers given to challenging questions. Here is a typical example taken from the section on assurance under Q. 36 of the Shorter Catechism:

> Q. 8. What is the difference between the assurance of faith, and the assurance of sense?
>
> A. The object of the assurance of faith is "Christ in the promise" (James 2:23), but the object of the assurance of sense is "Christ formed in the soul" (2 Tim. 2:12); or, which is the same thing, the assurance of faith is founded on the infallible word of God, which cannot lie; but the assurance of sense upon the person's present experience of the communications of divine love (p. 195).

The influence of this valuable catechism went far beyond Scotland. It was translated into several languages. In America, converts of the Great Awakening became avid readers of the Erskine-Fisher Catechism. About 30,000 copies designed for children were sold in America by the Presbyterian Board in Philadelphia. John Mason, Scottish preacher in New York and leader in the Associate Reformed Church, which he helped establish, was nourished by this volume, as were scores of other ministers.

Select Sermons of Ralph Erskine (GM; 2 vols., 560 pages; 2000). The twenty-three sermons in these two paperback volumes are some of Ralph Erskine's choicest sermons extracted from his six-volume set of works (see above).

George Gillespie

(1613-1648)

George Gillespie was born on January 21, 1613, at Kirkcaldy, Fife. He was the second son of John Gillespie, "the
thundering preacher" of Kirkcaldy, and Lilias, daughter of
Patrick Simson, minister of Stirling. As a boy, George seemed
to lack the potential to become a pastor, but his father said
upon his deathbed, "George, George, I have gotten many a
brave promise for thee!" Before he died, his father prophesied
that George would become "a great man" in the Church of
Scotland (Wodrow, *Analecta*, 3:110).

Gillespie graduated from the University of St. Andrews at
age sixteen. He was appointed as the Presbytery bursar at the
university from 1629 to 1631. He was unwilling to be ordained
by a bishop, however. Instead, and probably through the influence of Samuel Rutherford, Gillespie obtained work as the
domestic chaplain of John Gordon, the first Viscount Kenmure
(1599-1634). Some years later, Kenmure's wife, Jane Campbell,
would become the recipient of many of Rutherford's renowned
letters. In 1634, Kenmure died, prompting Rutherford to write
The Last and Heavenly Speeches of John Gordon Viscount Kenmure.
Gillespie formed a particularly close friendship with Rutherford. They covenanted to pray regularly for each other and to
write to each other about the life of God in their souls.

In 1634, Gillespie moved to the household of the Presbyterian nobleman, John Kennedy (1595-1668), the sixth earl of Cassilis, to tutor his eldest son, Lord Kennedy. Andrew Bonar described Kennedy as both "a staunch Presbyterian and a staunch covenanter." As a domestic chaplain, Gillespie wrote out his sermons in full, then examined the children and servants of the household each Sabbath evening on his sermons' contents.

While at the Kennedy home, Gillespie published anonymously in the Netherlands his first major work, *Dispute Against the English Popish Ceremonies*, which takes a strong stance against Episcopacy and Anglican ceremonies. The book "appeared in Scotland in the summer of 1637, just as the entire kingdom was in uproar over the introduction of the new Scottish Book of Common Prayer. The *Dispute* created such a sensation that in October of the same year the Scottish privy council ordered all copies of his book to be collected and burnt by the common hangman" (*Oxford DNB*, 22:257). Word was soon out that Gillespie was its author. Even though he disagreed with much of Gillespie's book, Robert Baillie wrote that Presbyterians in Scotland marveled that a young man of twenty-four could write it: "I think he may prove among the best wits of this isle" (*Letters and Journal of Robert Baillie*, 1:90).

In 1638, Gillespie was ordained to the parish of Wemyss in Fifeshire, weeks after the National Covenant had been signed and sworn by thousands in Scotland. In defiance of Episcopacy, Gillespie requested that his ordination take place on the door step of the Episcopal seat of St. Andrews. His was the second non-Episcopal ordination after the signing of the covenant.

In November of 1638, a General Assembly met in Glasgow in what is still regarded as a high watermark in Scottish Presbyterianism. The Assembly included 140 ministers and ninety-eight ruling elders. The Assembly deposed the bishops who had ruled the church, condemned the English ceremonies that

Gillespie had exposed, and restored Presbyterian government. Though Gillespie had been a minister only seven months, he was asked to be one of the preachers at this illustrious meeting.

Shortly after that, Gillespie became a chaplain in the Scottish army. In 1640, he was sent to London as part of a commission to work out a peace accord. In 1642, he was asked to take an important charge at Greyfriars Church in Edinburgh. For the last six years of his life, Gillespie took a leading role in the theological battles of the day. His knowledge of Greek, Hebrew, and other languages of antiquity aided him in this, as did his extraordinary talent for written argument and extemporaneous debate.

Gillespie was one of the four commissioners (along with Robert Baillie, Alexander Henderson, and Samuel Rutherford) sent from the Scottish church to the Westminster Assembly of Divines in 1643. He attended the Assembly for four years, returning to Scotland only once to report to the General Assembly. Despite being the youngest delegate (age thirty), he was a distinguished participant. In *Letters and Journals*, Robert Baillie wrote of Gillespie, "There is no man whose parts [gifts] in public dispute I do so admire. He has studied so accurately all the points ever yet come to our assembly, he has gotten so ready, so assured, so solid a way of public debating, that however there be in the assembly diverse very excellent men, yet, in my poor judgment, there is not one who speaks more rationally and to the point, than that brave youth has done" (2:160).

According to one account, Gillespie was taking part in an intense debate, seemingly speaking from extensive notes. Those sitting next to him could not help but see what he had written, however. The following words were written in Latin: "Lord, send light. Lord, give assistance. Lord, defend Thine own cause."

In 1645, Gillespie and Robert Baillie introduced the Directory of Public Worship to the General Assembly in Edinburgh. Two years later, Gillespie presented the Confession of Faith to the Assembly, which was then formally approved.

In 1647, he returned to Scotland with the reputation of being Scotland's leading theologian. Within a few months, he was chosen to replace the recently deceased Alexander Henderson as minister of the first charge of St. Giles, Edinburgh, one of the most prestigious pulpits of Scotland. The following year he was appointed moderator of the General Assembly. He was also appointed to the commission to promote religious conformity with England. Some months later, however, Gillespie contracted tuberculosis and became so sick it was apparent that he would soon die.

Retiring to Kirkcaldy, Gillespie issued two "dying testimonies" published posthumously by his brother Patrick in 1649, and later collected in his *Works*. K. D. Holfelder summarizes: "In them he warned against confederacies with 'malignants' and urged the kirk to 'purge' itself of all 'enemies to God and his cause.' In the years that followed, these testimonies were to have a profound influence on the course of the covenanting movement, paving the way for the political and military 'excommunication' enjoined by the 1649 Act of Classis and, ultimately the division of the kirk between radicals and moderates during the protester-resolutioner controversy" (*Oxford DNB*, 22:258).

Samuel Rutherford wrote to Gillespie, encouraging him to look only to Jesus. He added, "Christ in and by you hath done more than by twenty, yea, an hundred gray-haired and godly pastors. Believing now is your last (task). Look to that word — Galatians 2:20." On December 21, 1648, at age thirty-five, Gillespie died, full of faith in Jesus Christ and in the strength of His righteousness. He was survived by his wife, Margaret Murray. Twelve years later, the Restoration Parliament took his tombstone and had the public hangman of Kirkcaldy "solemnly break it with a hammer."

————◆◆◆————

The Works of George Gillespie (SWRB; 2 vols., 650 pages; 1991). In addition to the two titles noted above, *Works* includes Gillespie's "A Treatise of Miscellany Questions, Notes of Debates and Proceedings of the Assembly of Divines at Westminster"—a work of historic importance that contains some of Gillespie's best writing; "A Humble Acknowledgment of the Sins of the Ministry of Scotland"; "One Hundred Eleven Propositions Concerning the Ministry and Government of the Church"; and some miscellaneous sermons and polemical pieces. A helpful forty-page memoir of Gillespie written by the Scottish historian William H. Hetherington prefaces the works.

Aaron's Rod Blossoming; Or, The Divine Ordinance of Church Government Vindicated (SPR; 276 pages; 1985). This work, for which Gillespie is best known, was first published in 1646. It addresses the proper nature and relationship of civil and ecclesiastical power. James Walker called it "the *chef d'oeuvre* of Scottish ecclesiastical theology" (*Theology and Theologians of Scotland*, p. 14).

One of the prevailing theological errors of Gillespie's day was Erastianism, which taught that the chief magistrate in a Christian state ought to be the head of the church as well as of the state; consequently, there should be no independent ecclesiastical government or discipline. In response, Gillespie argued the classic Reformed view that, since the state and the church have been instituted by God, it follows that "the supreme end of the magistrate is the glory of God as King of the nations" and that His glory is best served by "a free church in a free state." As the magistrate rules on God's behalf, he must enforce obedience to the moral law to which all men and nations are obliged by virtue of their relationship to God as Creator.

*A *Dispute Against the English Popish Ceremonies* (NP; 575 pages; 1993). This handsome volume was published to coincide with the 350th anniversary of the Westminster Assembly. It is the first of a Naphtali Press series of seventeenth-century Presbyterian reprints of Scottish authors who have contributed significantly to theological literature.

English Popish Ceremonies is divided into four parts, arguing against (1) the necessity, (2) the expediency, (3) the lawfulness, and (4) the indifference of the English-popish ceremonies that Charles I was seeking to impose upon the Scottish church. It is a masterful polemic against human innovation in public worship. The book "fell like a thunderclap, silencing any argument, except that of force, against which the Scots rose up in a defensive war," Roy Middleton writes in a lengthy, helpful introduction. The civil government burned and banned the book but never formally responded to it.

The text of the 1637 first edition has been carefully compared and collated with the 1845 edition. Numerous defects and errors in the earlier editions, particularly in the footnotes, have been corrected. Extensive Latin quotations have been translated, but the Latin is retained in footnotes. Helpful editorial notes and definitions of archaic or Scottish terms are assets to this edition. A glossary of such terms is also provided, as are a complete index of Scripture passages cited, a lengthy subject index, and an extensive bibliography of Gillespie writings and the works he cites.

One problem is that Gillespie covers his ground so well that, at times, he becomes tedious. As John Macleod wrote, "He virtually fought all his battles over again and thrice he slew the slain."

Andrew Gray

(1633-1656)

Andrew Gray was born in Lawnmarket, Edinburgh, to Sir William of Pittendrum, a merchant and staunch royalist, and Egidia Smyth. He was the eleventh child in a family of twenty-one. As a child, he was convicted of the sin of ingratitude by unexpectedly witnessing a beggar pour out his heart to God in a field near Leith. Before long, Gray was brought to rest in the finished work of Christ for his distraught soul.

Gray felt called to the ministry already as a boy. That gave impetus to his studies at Edinburgh and St. Andrews universities. He earned a Master of Arts degree in 1651 and at age nineteen was declared a candidate for the ministry. He was ordained in the Outer High Kirk in Glasgow by the Protestors on November 3, 1653, despite the objections of Robert Baillie and other Resolutioners.

Gray was regarded as a burning light by thousands who heard him preach. William Blaikie, author of *The Preachers of Scotland*, wrote, "His knowledge of Christian experience was wonderfully extensive and minute; he knew well the joys and troubles, the helps and hindrances, the temptations and elusions of the Christian life. He had a remarkable power of probing the conscience; as James Durham remarks, 'he could make men's hair stand on end.'"

Both in preaching and in his personal life, Gray exhibited the need for holiness. He was a genuinely pious man. George Hutcheson spoke of him as "a spark from heaven."

That spark did not stay lit for long. Gray often preached of and longed for heavenly glory. When he was twenty-two, he expressed the desire that he would meet his Master in celestial bliss before his next birthday. Six months later, after a few days of fever, God granted that wish. Gray left behind a God-fearing wife, Rachel Baille (who later married George Hutcheson), and two children, Robert (who would soon die as a child) and Rachel. Gray's body was interred in Glasgow Cathedral.

"We may safely say that never in the history of our country did a man of his years make so deep a mark," said Blaikie. God used Gray mightily in his twenty-seven months of ministry.

The Works of Andrew Gray (SDG; 505 pages; 1992). Most of Gray's sermons were taken down in shorthand. These sermons were first published from a student's notes but contained numerous errors. Later, they were revised from additional sets of notes, including those owned by Gray's wife, and were issued by Robert Traill and John Stirling. Printed as short books (*The Mystery of Faith Opened* [1659]; *Great and Precious Promises* [1669]; *Directions and Instigations to the Duty of Prayer* [1669]; *The Spiritual Warfare* [1671], etc.), Gray's written sermons proved as popular as his preaching, not only in England, Scotland, and North America, but also in the Netherlands. Most of his works were translated into Dutch and are still being reprinted today.

For more than a century, these short books passed through numerous editions until they were collected and printed in 1762 in Glasgow as *The Works of the Reverend and Pious Mr. Andrew Gray*. This work also went through several printings, the most notable being the definitive 1839 edition published by George King in Aberdeen, from which the present reprint is taken.

Since Gray's writings are sermons rather than treatises, they do not offer exhaustive treatments of each subject. They do not offer precise language, either, since Gray did not have the opportunity to edit his own sermons. On the other hand, Gray's sermons were "studied with prayer, preached with power, and backed with success." Moreover, his profound insights, poignant statements, and succinct summaries on various truths are priceless. Gray's gifts are not in propounding new theological insights but in presenting "old truth" in fresh ways.

For example, when explaining assurance of faith, Gray offers the following evidence: (1) the lives of biblical saints that showed assurance; (2) "the great scope of many scriptures, to show how Christians may attain unto assurance"; (3) "commands in Scripture for Christians to be serious in searching after assurance," most notably, 2 Peter 1:10; (4) "the blessed end of God's oath in the everlasting covenant that a Christian might get assurance"; (5) "the ends of the sacraments, that our assurance may be confirmed"; and (6) the very exercises of divine graces that affirm the necessity of assurance. None of these points are new, but no one prior to Gray had compiled such a list.

Gray's writings will warm your soul, convict you of slothfulness, and urge you to godliness. They are full of spirit and life. Unlike many collections of *Works*, Gray is thoroughly readable from the opening series of sermons on the mystery of faith to the closing letter addressed from his deathbed.

*A Door Opening Into Everlasting Life: An Essay Tending to Advance Gospel Holiness, and to Establish the Hearts of True Believers against Their Many Doubts and Fears (NR; 220 pages; 1989). Reprinted for the first time since 1810, this volume is Gray's major work on the doctrine of sanctification. Gray uses a five-pronged approach to spur believers onward in holy living. First, he shows why Christians should pursue sanctified lives. Second, he provides directions for "living holily." Third, he describes marks of grace evidenced in the lives of God's people. Fourth, he answers fears, doubts, and objections raised by those who feel the poverty of their own sanctification. Fifth, he encourages the children of God by showing the privileges and happiness of those who follow after Christ.

Select Sermons (RHB; 625 pages; 2007). These fifty-one sermons, of which only a few are in Gray's *Works*, show why Gray was so popular as a preacher. They make doctrine intelligible and practical. They powerfully speak to the mind and the conscience, comforting the regenerate, arresting the backslider, inviting the unsaved, and unmasking the hypocrite. Above all, they seek to win souls to Christ. As William Tweedie wrote, "Christ was the beginning, the middle, and the end of all his sermons."

Select Sermons was first published in 1765 from handwritten manuscripts obtained by Gray's former wife. A second edition was printed in 1792 by Patrick Mair in Falkirk. The present edition is freshly typeset from the more accurate 1792 edition. (A selection of twelve sermons from this volume was reprinted as *Twelve Select Sermons* by Westminster Standard in Gisborne, New Zealand, in 1961.)

Select Sermons includes the following:

- Five sermons on how to fight spiritual pride
  (2 Cor. 12:7a)
- Four on praying against temptation (2 Cor. 12:8)
- Three on God's way of answering prayer (2 Cor. 12:9)
- Three on precious remedies against Satan's devices
  (2 Cor. 2:11)
- Three on resisting the devil (James 4:7)
- Two on beholding Christ (Isa. 65:1)
- Two on the role of Christian diligence in obtaining
  assurance of faith (2 Pet. 1:10)

- Two on Christ's preciousness to believers (1 Pet. 2:7)
- Several on Communion occasions
- A variety of individual sermons

Some of the more remarkable individual sermons include "The Necessity and Excellency of Delighting in God" (Ps. 37:4), "The Mansions of Glory Prepared for Believers" (John 14:2), "The Christian's Case and Exercise in the Night of Desertion" (Song of Sol. 3:1), "The Intercourses of Divine Love Between Christ and His Church" (Song of Sol. 2:1-2), and "The Necessity and Advantage of Looking Unto Jesus" (Isa. 45:22). The volume concludes with a deathbed letter sent by Gray to Lord Wariston.

We highly recommend this work. This, together with *A Door Opening* and *The Works*, completes the reprinting of Gray's writings, with the exception of a few sermons.

William Guthrie

(1620-1665)

William Guthrie was born in 1620 to James Guthrie, Laird of Pitforthy, Angus. He was the eldest of five sons, three of whom would become ministers of the gospel. He studied under his cousin, James Guthrie, at the University of St. Andrews, graduating with a Master of Arts degree in 1638. He stayed in St. Andrews to study theology under Samuel Rutherford, whom God used to call Guthrie both to salvation and to the ministry. Once called, Guthrie decided to give his family inheritance to a younger brother so that he would be free to minister unencumbered by earthly cares. Meanwhile, he remained close friends with his cousin until James died as a martyr at the gallows, one of the first to be executed in the persecution that followed the restoration of Charles II.

Guthrie was licensed to preach by the presbytery of St. Andrews in 1642. For two years he was tutor to Lord Mauchlin, eldest son of the earl of Loudoun, a leading Covenanter. In 1644, he was ordained as minister in Fenwick, an Ayrshire parish that recently had been established as an offshoot of Kilmarnock. Conditions in the parish were dismal. Ignorance abounded. People did not fear God. Many villagers refused to attend church services and would not take time for catechizing or family worship. Nevertheless, Guthrie served diligently as pastor. He even offered half of a crown to a man who preferred hunting birds on the Sabbath if he promised to attend church. The next Lord's Day, the man came to church. Guthrie promised him the same amount the next week. The man never missed church again. He was converted and later became an elder in the church.

Under Guthrie's twenty-year ministry in Fenwick, the town received a fresh outpouring of the Spirit. The new church was filled. Hundreds of people became regular attenders, were reborn, and grew in the grace and knowledge of Christ Jesus. Matthew Crawford, who was the minister at Eastwood, said that Guthrie "converted and confirmed many thousand souls, and was esteemed the greatest practical preacher in Scotland" (cited by Matthew Vogan, "William Guthrie," *Free Church Witness* [March 2003], p. 4). George Hutcheson, who assisted Guthrie at Communion, said that, if there was a church full of saints on the face of the earth, it was at Fenwick.

Guthrie married Agnes Campbell one year after he settled in Fenwick. Less than a year after he married, he was called to serve as chaplain during the Civil War in the Scottish army. When Guthrie fell seriously ill before his departure, his bride stopped worrying about his safety in the war. She bowed under God's sovereignty, realizing that her husband was in God's hands everywhere. Guthrie was preserved through his time in the army and returned to his parish.

Guthrie suffered numerous physical ailments related to stress. He tried to overcome these, in part, through fishing and bird hunting. Even while hunting, he discussed spiritual truths with fellow sportsmen.

Guthrie's work was marked by zeal and courage. On one occasion, several soldiers who lacked proper credentials approached the Lord's Table. Guthrie talked to them with such loving gravity that they immediately returned to their seats.

In 1647, a treaty was signed between Charles I and some Scottish nobles, binding the king to a limited support of Presbyterianism in exchange for freedom to return to the throne.

Guthrie then joined his cousin James, Samuel Rutherford, and John Livingston, who supported the minority Protestors in opposition to the Resolutioners. In 1654, Guthrie served as moderator of the Protester Synod of Glasgow and Ayr.

Other appointments also came Guthrie's way. In 1649, he was appointed as a commissioner to visit the University of Glasgow. A few years later, he became one of the Triers to approve ministers and lecturers before they assumed their ecclesiastical positions. By that time he had received pastoral calls to several larger parishes, but he declined them all.

In 1657, a collection of Guthrie's unedited notes from his sermons on Isaiah 55 were published without his consent as *A Clear, Attractive, Warning Beam of Light.* In response, Guthrie published those sermons the following year as *The Christian's Great Interest.* John Owen was much impressed with these writings. He said Guthrie's little book contained more divinity than all of his own writings combined. "He is one of the greatest divines that ever wrote," Owen said.

Because of his connection with William Cunningham, earl of Glencairn, Guthrie was allowed to retain his pulpit for several years following the restoration of Charles II. The archbishop of Glasgow, Alexander Burnet, embarrassed by Guthrie's refusal to submit to episcopacy and envious of the crowds that attended Guthrie's services, however, deprived him of his ministry in 1664. On the Wednesday before the Sunday on which the suspension was to take effect, the people of Fenwick observed a day of prayer and fasting. Guthrie preached to them from Hosea 13:9: "O Israel! Thou hast destroyed thyself." The following Sunday he preached his last sermon on the remainder of the text: "but in me is thine help." By the end of the sermon, much of the congregation was in tears.

When twelve soldiers seized Guthrie at noon that Sabbath, he said to one, "The Lord may pardon your countenancing this business." When the soldier responded, "I wish we never do a greater fault," Guthrie replied, "A little sin may damn a man's soul" (John Howie, *Lives of the Scottish Covenanters*, p. 287).

Guthrie lived for about a year in the Fenwick manse. While visiting Pitforthy to settle the family estate due to the death of the brother, he fell very ill and died of kidney disease on October 10, 1665, at age forty-five. He was survived by his wife and two daughters. Four of his children predeceased him.

Most of Guthrie's unpublished writings were seized and destroyed in 1682 by a soldier searching his widow's home. A collection of seventeen of his sermons was printed in 1779, then reprinted in 1880 as *Sermons Delivered in Times of Persecutions in Scotland.*

———⟫◆◆◆⟪———

The Christian's Great Interest (BTT; 207 pages; 1969). This book is a classic on assurance of faith. It has been reprinted more than eighty times and has been translated into several languages, including French, German, Dutch, and Gaelic.

Guthrie's book is divided into two sections. The first part provides numerous biblical tests on how one may know whether or not he is a Christian. Guthrie's use of "Interest" in the title refers to a legal claim in the covenant that Christ makes with believers. He places us in a courtroom setting to be examined by Scripture to determine whether or not we possess saving grace. After proving that believers may be assured of their salvation, Guthrie examines various ways by which sinners are drawn to Christ. He then focuses on saving faith as a most sure evidence of having a saving interest in Christ. He also distinguishes that faith from the faith of hypocrites. He concludes the first part by explaining why some believers doubt their interest in Christ.

The second part deals with how we might attain a saving interest in Christ. In the second chapter, "What it is to Close with God's Gospel Plan of Saving Sinners by Christ Jesus, and the Duty of So Doing," Guthrie reaches the crux of his treatise. This is a helpful chapter for those struggling with the reality of their faith. The next chapter deals with objections one can raise against closing with Christ, such as excessive sinfulness, inability to believe, unfruitfulness, and ignorance. The final chapter describes personal covenanting with God in Christ. The book concludes with a four-page, question-and-answer summary of the work.

Throughout this book, Guthrie distinguishes between the extraordinary and ordinary experiences of the believer. In this he helps sincere believers who have discounted their own salvation because they have been looking for extraordinary experiences upon which to build their salvation rather than relying on a childlike faith that trusts in Christ alone.

This is a wonderful book for people who are searching for spiritual certainty. Thomas Chalmers claimed it was "the best book I ever read." He added, "It has long been the favorite work of our peasantry in Scotland. One admirable property of this work is that, while it guides, it purifies."

Thomas Halyburton

(1674-1712)

Thomas Halyburton was born on December 25, 1674, in Dupplin, Perthshire. He was one of eleven children, all but two of whom died in youth. His father, George Halyburton, was minister of Aberdalgie, Perthshire, until his ejection for keeping conventicles in 1676. He died when Thomas was only seven. Thomas's mother, Margaret, a woman of deep piety, moved the family to Rotterdam in 1685 to escape persecution. There Thomas received a brief classical education at the Erasmus School.

When the penal laws against Protestant dissenters were repealed under the Declaration of Indulgence in 1687, the Halyburtons returned to Scotland. Thomas attended school in Perth for three or four years before going to Gavin Weir's school in Edinburgh. By his mid-teens, he was well-versed in Greek, Latin, and Dutch. He also received thorough religious indoctrination. Halyburton says in his *Memoirs* that he heard three sermons and two lectures on Sundays, additional sermons on Tuesdays and Thursdays, and additional lectures on Mondays and Fridays. Wednesday was prayer meeting and Saturday was catechism. It is little wonder that he grew weary of these daily meetings while he was yet unconverted.

In 1692, Halyburton entered Edinburgh University, where he first began to suffer from a debilitating immobility resulting, most likely, from rheumatoid arthritis. For health reasons, he then transferred to St. Leonard's College, St. Andrews, where he studied under Thomas Taylor and graduated with a Master of Arts degree in 1696. Throughout his university years, he struggled spiritually, especially with religious doubts which he attempted to resolve—in vain—through studying philosophy. Nevertheless, being profoundly influenced by the preaching of Thomas Forrester at St. Andrews and having thought he would follow his father and brother-in-law into the ministry, he began studying for the ministry while serving as family chaplain for Margaret Wemyss, countess of Wemyss. He felt out of his element among the aristocracy, however, and also struggled with how to address several theological issues with which he was confronted—particularly the challenges of deism.

Early in 1698, Halyburton was finally able to embrace the Savior by faith and gained some assurance that he was converted. He then "came to view faith and philosophy as antithetical and to reject any attempt to found the convictions of the heart upon the deliverances of the head as a diabolical temptation" (*Oxford DNB*, 24:732).

The following year, Halyburton was licensed to preach the gospel by the presbytery of Kirkaldy. He was ordained in 1700 as minister of Ceres, Fife, a few miles from St. Andrews. The following year, he married Janet, daughter and heir of David Watson, a St. Andrews heritor. Together they had at least six children, three of whom died in childhood. Halyburton's *Memoirs* show his sanctified struggles during those sad times.

Halyburton's ministry was fruitful, but within a few years his health began to decline. Before the end of the decade, preaching became difficult for him. Out of concern for his health as well as recognition of his abilities, the presbytery installed Halyburton as Professor of Divinity at St. Andrews in 1710. It was too late; Halyburton died at St. Andrews two years later on September 23, 1712, at the age of thirty-seven. Upon his request, he was buried beside Samuel Rutherford.

Their gravestones, only inches apart, can still be seen today in the Old Cathedral's graveyard in St. Andrews.

Although Halyburton was a pastor for only twelve years, he has long been regarded as one of Scotland's most distinguished theologians. John Duncan called him "a minor John Owen." Hugh Martin classified him and William Cunningham as "the two greatest theologians that Scotland has ever produced."

⇒◆◆◆⇐

Halyburton's Works, Volume 1: Faith and Justification (JB; 370 pages; 2000); *Volume 2: Faith and Salvation* (JB; 425 pages; 2002); *Volume 3: Faith and Revelation* (JB; 431 pages; 2003); *Volume 4: Faith and Experience* (JB; 387 pages; 2005).

Volume 1 of this four-volume reprint of Halyburton's writings contains three short treatises related to faith and justification:

1. "An Essay concerning the Nature of Faith; or, The Ground upon which Faith assents to the Scriptures" (pp. 1-74) explains the apostle's determination to preach in such a way "that your faith should not stand in the wisdom of men, but in the power of God" (1 Cor. 2:5). Against the English philosopher John Locke (1632-1704), who taught that reason must be the guide in all things, Halyburton says that true faith rests on God's authority. He writes, "Faith leans only on the testimony of God, approving itself such to the souls of believers by its own glorious power, whereby, without borrowing help from any other signs, it evidences itself to be the Lord's word, with a light so strong as carries the soul into an assent."

2. "A Modest Inquiry whether Regeneration or Justification has the precedency in Order of Nature" (pp. 75-98) shows how the blessings of salvation are connected with the believer's union with Christ provided for in the covenant of grace.

3. "An Inquiry into the Nature of God's Act of Justification" (pp. 99-114) reveals how God makes justification

known to His people, or, in Halyburton's words, "how God gives out sentence in the sinner's favour."

Volume 1 also contains ten sermons (pp. 115-347) showing the biblical moorings and experiential character of Halyburton's theology. The concern of these sermons is to magnify God's grace and to humble sinners before God's mercy seat. Halyburton's Christological focus is particularly evident in his sermons titled "Christ Crucified," "Communion with Christ," and "Christ the Beauty and Safety of Believers."

Volume 2 contains "The Great Concern of Salvation," which details with remarkable clarity how the Holy Spirit works salvation in sinners. The work is divided into three sections that correspond with the Heidelberg Catechism's framework of knowing one's sin and misery, experiencing deliverance in Christ alone, and expressing gratitude to God by a lifestyle of holiness. All of this is preceded by an introductory sermon on Acts 10:29 ("I ask therefore for what intent ye have sent for me?"), considering the designs and motives of a congregation when it calls a minister.

The first part, "A discovery of man's natural state; or, the guilty sinner convicted," based on Romans 3:23, powerfully convicts one of sin and tolerates no excuse for it, showing the graphic results of damnation for the impenitent. The second part, "Man's recovery by faith in Christ; or, the convinced sinner's case and cure," based on Acts 16:29-31, freely offers Christ to sinners and beautifully balances the Spirit's use of law and gospel in salvation. The final part, "The Christian's duty, with respect to both personal and family religion," based on Joshua 24:15, discusses aspects of family life, focusing especially on worship, authority, and baptismal vows. This volume excels in practical, experiential divinity.

Volume 3 contains Halyburton's *magnum opus*, "Natural and Revealed Religion," a major polemic against deism. Its full title is "Natural Religion Insufficient, and Reveal'd

[Religion] Necessary to Man's Happiness in His Present State; or, A Rational Enquiry into the Principles of the modern Deists." First published in 1714 and frequently reprinted, it has become a standard work of apologetics. It clearly affirms the Christian faith, defending it with careful study, sound reasoning, and warmth.

According to Halyburton, deism had its roots in European Roman Catholicism, which soon spread northward into various parts of Protestant Europe. In the seventeenth century, deism was brought to England, where it was embraced by people in the ruling classes, particularly among the Cavaliers, the aristocratic partisans of the Stuart kings, and nominal members of the Church of England. These members of the cultural elite despised the Reformed faith of Puritan England and Presbyterian Scotland and found that new ideas from the Continent were most useful in the fight against Puritanism. Like Arminianism, deism became a stylish alternative to the old-fashioned beliefs and conservative morality of Calvinism.

Deists were a mixed lot, however. Some professed a high regard for the Christian faith, seeking only to purge it of irrational elements. Others were quite willing to use "contempt, buffoonery, banter, and satire" to attack Christianity. Halyburton recognized various types of deists, but in the end concluded that deism was an erroneous, spiritually powerless faith at best, and, at worst, a morally bankrupt libertinism and practical atheism.

Deism became a creed in the hands of the "father of deism," Lord Herbert of Cherbury (1581-1648), who proposed five articles of faith as the universals of natural religion: the belief in a supreme being, the obligation to worship, the obligation of ethical conduct, the need for repentance, and divine rewards and punishments in this life and the next. With Charles Blount (1654-1693), deism became a platform from which to ridicule the teachings of historic Christianity. Others took those ideas forward, vigorously attacking historic Christianity in the name of reason.

Deism flourished for a time, then fell under its own weight, like a diseased and dying tree. It also fell because men like Thomas Halyburton rose to defend Christianity, exposing the errors and emptiness of deism. Today, we see the legacy of deism in the tendency to explain nearly everything in mechanical or naturalistic terms.

John Newton recommended Halyburton's treatise against deism to Thomas Scott, declaring, "I set a high value on this book of Halyburton's, so that, unless I could replace it with another, I know not if I would part with it for its weight in gold" (Burns, "Introductory Essay," *Works*, 1835 edition, p. xxv).

Volume 4 contains Halyburton's memoirs (see below), plus three short pieces not published before in a volume of Halyburton's works: "The Obligation of Oaths to Posterity" and two sermons, as well as "A Short Account of Lady Anne Elcho's Death." The concluding volume also contains subject and Scripture indexes to the entire set.

Memoirs of Thomas Halyburton, edited by Joel R. Beeke (RHB; 344 pages; 1996). Halyburton's *Memoirs*, originally written for himself and his family, were first made public by his wife in 1715, and were frequently reprinted. Most editions after 1718 included a preface by Isaac Watts. John Wesley and George Whitefield added a foreword in an abridged edition in 1739.

Halyburton's *Memoirs* records a remarkable spiritual journey, culminating in one of the remarkable deathbed testimonies ever recorded in church history. On his deathbed, Halyburton wrote, "I bless the Lord that when I stood trembling under the terrors of God's law, He seasonably saved me from despair by some discovery of the blessed way of salvation for self-destroyed sinners through a slain Saviour; even such a discovery as made me resolve to part with all that I might have the field, Christ the treasure hid in it, and pearl of price. There is nothing I dread so much as a mistake in this matter. It is Christ only that will answer me and my case, and without Him I am undone; on Him—the efficacy of His sufferings, the power of His resurrection, and of His whole mediation, as revealed in the Gospel—do I build all my hope."

Nearly seventy pages of these deathbed notes bring the reader near the gates of heaven. Here's one sample: "Come, sweet Lord Jesus, receive this spirit, fluttering within my breast like a bird to be out of a snare. I wait for Thy salvation, as the watchman watcheth for the morning. I am weary with delays. I faint for Thy salvation. Why are His chariot wheels so long a-coming?" (pp. 266-67).

Perhaps the most unique feature of this autobiography is its Word-centeredness. After nearly every recorded experience, Halyburton provides a text that illuminates that particular experience. Often the selection is remarkably well chosen; it helps the reader see the value of examining every experience in light of the Word of God (Isa. 8:20).

This book was widely read in Scotland, England, and America, and is still praised today. John Duncan equated it with Augustine's *Confessions* and Bunyan's *Grace Abounding*. Archibald Alexander wrote, "There is no production of the kind, in which the exercises of the human heart, both before and after regeneration, are so distinctly described." Samuel Miller and Charles Hodge said, "It is worthy of a place in every family."

Samuel
Rutherford
(1600-1661)

Samuel Rutherford was born in 1600 in Nisbet, Rox-burghshire, eldest son of a well-to-do farmer. His parents noted his intellectual gifts and believed that God would call him to the ministry, though they seldom spoke about Christ in an experiential way. Rutherford later wrote that in his birthplace "Christ was scarce named, as touching any reality or power of godliness" (*Letters*, p. 680). Rutherford was educated first at Jedborough, then at the University of Edinburgh, where he excelled in Latin and Greek, and earned a Master of Arts degree in 1621.

In 1623, Rutherford was chosen to serve as Professor of Humanity at Edinburgh, with responsibilities as a Latin tutor. Two years later, he was forced to resign after behaving inappropriately with a young woman named Euphame Hamilton, whom he subsequently married. God apparently used this incident to initiate or further his conversion. In a letter to Robert Stuart (1637), Rutherford wrote, "Ye have gotten a great advantage in the way of heaven, that ye have started to the gate in the morning. Like a fool, as I was, I suffered my sun to be high in the heaven, and near afternoon, before I ever took the gate by the end."

In 1625, Rutherford studied theology at Edinburgh under Andrew Ramsay. Two years later, he was asked to pastor the church in Anwoth by the Solway in Kirkcudbrightshire—the charge with which his name is inseparably bound. John Welsh, the godly son-in-law of John Knox, had ministered at that church from 1595 to 1600. Anwoth was a rural parish; its people were scattered in farms over a hilly district.

Rutherford rose at 3 a.m. each day, devoting many hours to prayer and meditation. He wrote of a favorite place where he often walked to ponder spiritual truths: "There I wrestled with the angel and prevailed. Woods, trees, meadows and hills are my witnesses that I drew on a fair meeting between Christ and Anwoth" (cited in Nigel Clifford, *Christian Preachers*, p. 132).

Rutherford worked effectively and tirelessly for his congregation for nearly a decade. One aged, contemporary pastor wrote, "I have known many great and good ministers in this church, but for such a piece of clay as Mr. Rutherford was, I never knew one in Scotland like him, to whom so many great gifts were given; for he seemed to be altogether taken up with everything good, and excellent, and useful. He seemed to be always praying, always preaching, always visiting the sick, always catechizing, always writing and studying.... Many times I thought he would have flown out of the pulpit when he came to speak of Jesus Christ. He was never in his right element but when he was commending Him. He would have fallen asleep in bed speaking of Christ" (Thomas M'Crie, *The Story of the Scottish Church*, p. 48).

An English merchant put it this way, "I came to Irvine, and heard a well-favored, proper old man [David Dickson] with a long beard, and that man showed me all my heart. Then I went to St. Andrews, where I heard a sweet, majestic-looking man [Robert Blair], and he showed me the majesty of God. After him I heard a little, fair man [Rutherford], and he showed me the loveliness of Christ."

Marcus Loane writes, "Rutherford's ministry while in Anwoth was a noble approach to the splendid ideal of Baxter's

Reformed Pastor or Herbert's *Country Parson*" (*Makers of Puritan History*, p. 70). His years in Anwoth, though, were fraught with affliction. The comfort his ministry and letters brought to thousands was forged in the crucible of personal losses. His wife, Euphame, died in 1630 after suffering intensely for thirteen months. With the exception of one daughter, all the children she and Rutherford had died at an early age. Rutherford himself fell seriously ill with a high fever about this time. Then, in 1635, Rutherford's mother, who had come to live with them, also died.

Rutherford was not always easy to get along with. On the one hand, he was godly and humble. On the other hand, he was a man of strong emotions who occasionally lost his temper and heaped abuse on his opponents. Rutherford himself once told David Dickson, "I am made of extremes." He also frequently suffered from depression. Nevertheless, God used those times to prepare Rutherford to comfort other suffering believers.

Rutherford was politically active during his ministry. Though a minor parish, Anwoth was strategically located. It was home to several influential people, particularly the Gordon family, with whom Rutherford allied himself. Using that connection, Rutherford soon became a strong opponent of Episcopacy. He wrote his own catechism and organized seasons of fasting and prayer in response to the corruption of the church.

In 1630, Rutherford was called to appear before the Court of High Commission in Edinburgh for nonconformity to the Perth Articles. That did not stop him. As John Coffey writes, "He became engrossed in the Arminian controversy, disseminating political information, intervening in burgh elections.... [He] prepared a Latin treatise against the theology of Arminius and the Jesuits, and circulated manuscript treatises he had written to justify the conventicles" (*Politics, Religion, and the British Revolutions: The Mind of Samuel Rutherford*, pp. 41-42).

That put Rutherford in conflict with the church authorities, which were dominated by the English Episcopacy. He was called before the High Court in July 1636. After a three-day trial, he was deprived of his ministerial office, forbidden to preach anywhere in Scotland, and confined to Aberdeen.

Aberdeen was a bastion of Arminianism, was committed to episcopacy, and was strongly opposed to the Reformed Presbyterianism Rutherford held dear. All of that, plus being separated from his congregation, was a sore trial for Rutherford. Sundays were particularly difficult. "The memory of my communion with Christ, in many, many fair days in Anwoth, hath almost broken my faith in two halves," he wrote to the provost of Ayr. During his exile, Rutherford debated Arminianism and ceremonies with Robert Barron, a doctor from Aberdeen, proving himself to be a remarkably effective disputant.

He also wrote many letters to his congregation. We are still blessed today by those letters, particularly by their Christ-centeredness. To the Laird of Cally, he wrote in 1637, "Give Christ your virgin love; you cannot put your love and heart into better hand. Oh! If ye knew Him, and saw His beauty, your love, your liking, your heart, your desires would close with Him and cleave to Him." Rutherford had many sweet times of communion with Christ in Aberdeen. "I never knew, by mine nine years' preaching, so much of Christ's love, as He has taught me in Aberdeen," he wrote to his congregation. "Sweet, sweet have His comforts been to my soul; my pen, tongue, and heart have no words to express the kindness, love and mercy of my Well-beloved to me, in this house of my pilgrimage" (*Letters*, pp. 227, 357).

In 1638, the struggles escalated between England's Parliament and king as well as between Presbyterianism and Episcopacy in Scotland. After the National Covenant was signed, which heralded a new dawn for Christ's cause in Scotland, Rutherford slipped out of Aberdeen and returned to

Anwoth, but not for long. The Church of Scotland General Assembly soon restored Presbyterianism to the land and appointed Rutherford to the strategic position of professor of theology at St. Mary's College, St. Andrews. He accepted the position reluctantly, and only on the condition that he be allowed to preach at least once every Sunday. Leaving Anwoth was difficult for him. "Never did I so much long for death," he wrote. "The Lord help and hold up sad clay." Rutherford shared a pulpit in the university's church with Robert Blair and preached fairly regularly in various pulpits in St. Andrews. His lectures and preaching greatly impacted the theological students. One student spoke for many when he wrote, "God did so singularly second his indefatigable pains, both in teaching and in preaching, that the University forthwith became a Lebanon, out which were taken cedars for building the house of the Lord through the whole land" (cited in Clifford, p. 135).

In 1640, Rutherford married Jean M'Math, described as "a woman of great worth and piety." He had one daughter, Agnes, from his previous marriage, and six more from the second marriage, all of whom died before Rutherford. Two of them died as infants before Rutherford left to attend the Westminster Assembly. Two more died while he and his wife were in London.

When the Westminster Assembly began in 1643, Rutherford was one of six Scottish commissioners invited to attend; he stayed until October 1647, longer than any of the others. Although the Scots chose not to vote, they had a great influence. Rutherford in particular contributed substantially to the theological deliberations and to the Shorter Catechism. He also preached occasionally before the Long Parliament.

During this period, Rutherford wrote at least five books, including *Lex Rex* (1644). This book deals with a magistrate's right to exact obedience from his subjects and a citizen's obligations towards magistrates. It grapples with questions related to natural rights, civil law, Christian obedience, and Christian ethics. Rutherford argues for limitations on the divine right of kings. The crown is bestowed by the voluntary consent of the people; therefore, the people are at liberty to resist a tyrant.

Other books Rutherford wrote during his assembly years include *The Due Right of Presbyteries* (a defense of Presbyterianism against Independency), *The Divine Right of Church Government and Excommunication* (a defense of regulating worship and of permanent obligations of church government by elders and presbyteries), *Survey of the Spiritual Antichrist* (a defense against antinomianism and various sects), and *The Trial and Triumph of Faith* (a book of sermons on Christ's saving work in the Canaanite woman).

Less than two years after he returned to St. Andrews in the fall of 1647, Rutherford was appointed principal of St. Mary's College and, in 1651, rector of the University. He spent the last fourteen years of his life teaching and preaching at St. Andrews. His books brought him fame and invitations in the late 1640s and early 1650s to join prestigious faculties in the Netherlands, including Utrecht, where Voetius was teaching. Rutherford declined every invitation.

Unfortunately, the 1650s were not peaceful; the Church of Scotland was torn by two parties. The Resolutioners supported the Scottish coronation of Charles II and public resolutions brought to the General Assembly of 1651 allowing the supporters of Charles I to return to office. Rutherford and his fellow Protestors opposed those actions. The subsequent strife separated Rutherford from some of his closest friends, including David Dickson and Robert Blair.

When the monarchy was restored in 1660, Rutherford knew persecution awaited him. In 1661, he was charged with treason, deprived of his church, his university chair, and his stipend. *Lex Rex* was ordered to be burned and his presbytery to be overthrown. Rutherford himself was put under house arrest. Ultimately, Parliament, seeking to eliminate all resistance to Charles II, sentenced the most prominent covenantal leaders to hanging. Rutherford anticipated that and considered it a privilege to give his life for his Savior. He was comforted that Lady Kenmure agreed to care for his wife and eleven-year-old daughter, Agnes.

But by the time the summons arrived from the Council in 1661, charging him with treason and demanding his appearance, Rutherford was already on his deathbed. He appealed to a higher tribunal, giving the memorable response: "Tell them I have got a summons already before a superior judge and judicatory, and I behoove to answer my first summons; and ere your day arrive, I will be where few kings and great folks come." When the Council returned and reported to Parliament that Rutherford was dying, Parliament almost unanimously decided that he not be allowed to die in the college. To this, Lord Burleigh responded, "You have voted that honest man out of his college, but you cannot vote him out of heaven" (M'Crie, pp. 51-53).

Rutherford sought to reconcile with those with whom he had quarreled and died peacefully on March 30, 1661, at St. Mary's College, St. Andrews. Some of his last words were, "I shall live and adore Christ; glory to my Redeemer forever. Glory, glory dwelleth in Emmanuel's land." To his fellow ministers he said, "Dear brethren, do all for Christ. Pray for Christ. Preach for Christ. Beware of men-pleasing." With his death, Scotland lost one of its greatest theologians, powerful preachers, devotional writers, and political thinkers.

Rutherford was buried at the Old Cathedral graveyard in St. Andrews. His tombstone, which can still be seen today, bears these memorable words:

What tongue or pen or skill of men
Can Famous Rutherford commend?
His learning justly raised his Fame,
True godliness adorned his name.

    He did converse with Immanuel's love.
    Most orthodox he was and sound
    And many errors did confound.

For Zion's king and Zion's cause
And Scotland's covenantal laws
Most constantly he did contend
Until his time was at an end.

    Then he won to the full fruition
    Of that what he had seen in vision.

Communion Sermons (BB; 362 pages; 1986). Edited by Andrew Bonar in the 1870s, this volume contains fourteen Communion sermons, published from the notes of Rutherford's listeners. Bonar wrote in the preface, "All who relish Rutherford's letters will welcome the reprint of this volume, entitled, when first printed, *Collection of Valuable Sermons Preached on Sacramental Occasions, in the years 1630, 1634, and 1637.*"

Here is an example of that work: "Many have light, as sick men have meat at their bedside, but cannot use it." According to Rutherford, many converts have light in their souls but cannot discern it for their own comfort and consolation. These sermons help believers toward this comfort and consolation. Bonar writes of these sermons, "All breathe the same spirit as the famous 'Letters,' and are full of racy remark and illustration, bearing on scriptural doctrine and Christian experience."

The Covenant of Life Opened (Pur Pub; 518 pages; 2005). With keen insight, Rutherford unfolds the manner in which God covenants with man. He investigates the nature of the covenants of works, grace, and redemption. Along the way, he shows how God's sovereignty, the extent of Christ's work of satisfaction, justification, sanctification, and infant baptism are related to covenant. This edition has been re-typeset from the original 1655 edition, making it much more reader-friendly.

The Letters of Samuel Rutherford (BTT; 768 pages; 1984). A facsimile of the Oliphant edition from the late nineteenth century, this edition contains all of Rutherford's letters. They were originally collected and published by Robert MacWard, a former student, and edited in the nineteenth century by Andrew A. Bonar. In addition to this Banner hardback, an abridged paperback has been printed by the Trust. Its 206 pages contain choice extracts from Rutherford's letters. Other publishers have printed smaller selections of letters under such titles as *Loveliness of Christ* and *Gleanings from the Past.*

Most of Rutherford's letters (220 of 365) were written while he was in exile in Aberdeen. The letters beautifully harmonize Reformed doctrine and the spiritual experiences of the believer. Six topics dominate the letters: (1) Rutherford's love to and desire for Christ ("I would desire no more for my heaven beneath the moon, while I am sighing in this house of clay, but daily renewed feasts of love with Christ," he wrote); (2) his deep sense of the heinousness of sin (he spoke often of his own "abominable vileness": "Only my loathsome wretchedness and my wants have qualified me for Christ!"); (3) his devoted concern for the cause of Christ (to David Dickson he wrote on May 1, 1637, "My sorrow is that I cannot get Christ lifted off the dust in Scotland, and set on high, above all the skies, and heaven of heavens"); (4) his profound sympathy for burdened and troubled souls (to one troubled saint, he wrote, "Our crosses are like puffs of wind to blow our ship home; they convey us to heaven's gate, but they cannot follow it into heaven"); (5) his profound love for his flock (he wrote to Anwoth on July 13, 1632, "My witness is above; your heaven would be two heavens to me, and your salvation two salvations"); and (6) his ardent longings for heaven ("Oh, how long is it to the dawning of the marriage day! O sweet Jesus, take wide steps! O my Lord, come over the mountain at one stride").

During his years in Aberdeen, Rutherford experienced deep communion with God. He wrote of those encounters with astonishing freedom. Here's an example of what he shared with John Nevay in 1637: "I would willingly subscribe an ample resignation to the Christ of the Fourteen Prelacies...to have no other exercise than to lie on a love-bed with Christ, and fill this hungry and famished soul with kissing, embracing, and real enjoying of the Son of God: and I think that then, I might write to my friends that I had found the Golden World" (Letter 272).

Additional letters testify of God's special care, encouraging believers to persevere in faith. The beauty of Rutherford's work is that he saw himself as the chief of sinners and Christ as the only Savior. His favorite theme is the union of Christ and His people as illustrated by courtship and marriage. Richard Baxter, one of Rutherford's most persistent critics, confessed that "such a book of letters the world never saw the like." Robert Murray M'Cheyne used Rutherford's letters as devotional material and saw Christ on every page. Spurgeon considered these letters closer to inspiration than anything else ever written.

Although he did not write these letters for publication, they are Rutherford's most popular work. They have been reprinted more than eighty times in English, fifteen times in Dutch, and several times in German and French and Gaelic.

Lex Rex, or The Law and the Prince (SPR; 307 pages; 1982). This book refutes John Maxwell's *Sacro-Sancta Regnum Majestus*, which supported the divine right of kings. Answering forty-four questions, *Lex Rex* argues for limited government and the restraint of monarchical power. It vindicates the covenant rights of the people against absolute monarchy.

Nearly every member of the Westminster Assembly owned a copy of *Lex Rex*. It remains one of the most comprehensive expressions of Calvinistic political theory. Some scholars say it was a major influence in the formation of modern political theory.

The Power of Faith and Prayer (RP; 88 pages; 1991). This slender paperback, first reprinted since 1713, offers teaching on the miracle of Christ in healing the two blind men (Matt. 9:27-31). Especially instructive are Rutherford's comments in Chapter 5 on the reflex action of the faith of the blind man. This book is written in Rutherford's devotional, Christ-centered, quaint style.

Quaint Sermons of Samuel Rutherford (SDG; 384 pages; 1999). This collection of sermons, published first in 1885, was taken from a volume of manuscripts compiled in shorthand by a listener. Among the eighteen sermons are: "Fear Not," "Weeping Mary at the Sepulcher," "The Forlorn Son," "The Apostle's Choice," and "The Spouse's Longing for Christ." The warmth of Rutherford's preaching is clearly evident in this collection.

Rutherford's Catechism: or, The Sum of Christian Religion (BB; 105 pages; 1998). Like many Scottish divines, Rutherford was a keen catechist. He drafted this catechism for his Anwoth flock. It is a compact primer of Reformed theology.

This edition of Rutherford's catechism is based on Alexander Mitchell's collection, *Catechisms of the Second Reformation* (1886). It is vintage Rutherford; many of the metaphors and quaint words are also found in *Letters*. Noteworthy for its pithiness and numerous scriptural proof texts, this catechism was probably completed at the Westminster Assembly where Rutherford was asked to suggest catechetical materials.

Catechizing was very important to Rutherford. In a letter to his Anwoth flock, he wrote, "If ye fall away and forget [the good doctrine] and that catechism I taught you, the Lord judge between you and me" (Letter 167).

The Trial and Triumph of Faith (BTT; 406 pages; 2001). Originally published in 1645, this book contains twenty-seven sermons on Christ's saving work in the Canaanite woman (Matt. 15 and Mark 7). Rutherford sees the woman as an example of Christ's new creation, "a flower planted and watered by Christ's own hand." He says, "To any seeking Jesus Christ, this text crieth, 'Come and see.'" In nearly every sermon, Rutherford shows the overflowing grace of Christ to Gentiles. He opens up the nature of genuine prayer and addresses practical aspects of the trial of faith. Throughout, he also speaks against antinomianism and other doctrinal errors.

Like *Letters*, these sermons show Rutherford's devotion to Christ as well as the poetic and experiential gifts that made his preaching so moving. Here is one example: "Christ, for this cause especially, left the bosom of God, and was clothed with flesh and our nature, that he might be a mass, a sea, and boundless river of visible, living, and breathing grace, swelling up to the highest banks of not only the habitable world, but the sides also of the heaven of heavens, to over-water men and angels" (p. 11).

Henry Scougal
(1650-1678)

Henry Scougal was born in 1650 at Leuchars, Fife, the second son of Patrick Scougal and Margaret Wemyss. His father, bishop of Aberdeen for more than twenty years after the Restoration, was a close friend of Robert Leighton. He was well known for his purity, humility, and kindness.

From his youth, Scougal valued religious exercises and hard study. He showed remarkable proficiency for Latin, Greek, and Hebrew, and took thorough notes of sermons. He especially enjoyed studying the historical passages of the Old Testament. He would often recite lengthy passages from the Bible. He loved communing with believers and listened attentively to ministers whenever they visited his father's house.

In 1664, Scougal entered King's College, Aberdeen. He became a leader among his peers, who attributed to him "the wisdom of a senator." They frequently asked him to chair their public meetings.

In 1668, Scougal put together a collection of his private reflections. Those were later published in Aberdeen as *Private Reflections and Occasional Meditations* and *Essays, Moral and Divine*. Though Scougal was in his teens when he wrote these reflections, his knowledge of philosophy and love for wisdom is apparent on every page.

After graduating from the college with a Master of Arts degree in 1668, Scougal was asked to be professor of philosophy at age nineteen. He was probably the first professor in

Scotland to teach Baconian philosophy. He openly refuted the erroneous doctrines of the English philosopher Thomas Hobbes (1588-1679). But most of all, he taught a relentless heart-religion. Carefully guarding his students from the subtleties of infidelity, he taught them that philosophy and religion were friends, not enemies.

After teaching for four years, Scougal was ordained in 1673 as minister of the church in Auchterless, Aberdeenshire, a small village twenty miles from Aberdeen. There he revived the practice of lecturing, i.e., commenting on a whole chapter or a large portion of Scripture, believing that to be the most edifying style of preaching. He considered it mandatory that a pastor address his hearers according to their particular dispositions to best impress the truth upon them. In this practice, he proved himself a firm supporter of Puritan casuistry.

One year after accepting the call to Auchterless, Scougal returned to Aberdeen to become professor of divinity at King's College under the sponsorship of Robert Leighton (1611-1684), archbishop of Glasgow. Scougal impressed upon students the holiness of the pastoral office and the vital role of theology. In a sermon preached before the synod of Aberdeen, titled "Of the Importance and Difficulty of the Ministerial Function," Scougal said, "The minister ought to be employed in the exercise of devotion, for the interest of advancing piety, and the honor of our Maker."

Scougal taught for five years until he died of tuberculosis on June 13, 1678. He was buried in the university chapel. He never married. Shortly before his death, he told his friends, "When you have the charity to remember me in your prayers, do not think me a better man than I am; but look on me, as indeed I am, a miserable sinner."

George Gairden preached at Scougal's funeral sermon from Philippians 1:21, "For to me to live is Christ, and to die is gain." Of Scougal's short life, Gairden said, "Length of life is not to be measured by many revolutions of the heavens [viz. many years], but by the progress we have made in the great design for which we are sent into the world. [Scougal] has truly lived much in a few years and died an old man at the age of twenty-eight."

Scougal left his library to the college, revealing the wide range of his interests. He was well-read in philosophy, and admired the church fathers, especially Augustine. He loved Thomas à Kempis's (1379-1471) *The Imitation of Christ*, yet was a careful Calvinist. Though Scougal was an Episcopalian in a Presbyterian land, the Scottish church has claimed him as one of its most radiant lights.

The Works of Henry Scougal (SDG; 378 pages; 2002). The treatises and sermons in this volume illustrate the author's theological depth, experience, and warmth. Scougal's writings have influenced hundreds since their first printing. Various editions of his works appeared in 1765, 1773, 1818, and 1830. Patrick Cockburn, who printed an edition of *The Life of God* in 1726, says that Scougal wrote some tracts in Latin: "A Short System of Ethics," "A Preservative against the Artifices of the Romish Missionaries," and the beginning of a work on pastoral care, but they have since been lost.

The Life of God in the Soul of Man was originally a letter written to a friend explaining the Christian religion and offering spiritual counsel. During the summer of 1667, Scougal met a close friend, Gilbert Burnett, who pressed for its publication. Scougal consented, but only if he could remain anonymous. Burnett sent the first edition to the press, not realizing how influential the work would become.

Several editions of this work have since been printed. Burnett's edition was reprinted no less than seventeen times by 1819, and a plethora of paperback editions have been issued since 1739. John Wesley (1707-1791) said this work

greatly affected his own life. He published an abridged edition of it in 1742, which was reprinted seven times in the next
sixty-six years.

   The Life of God in the Soul of Man has been valued by Christians of all times. George Whitefield said of it, "Though I
fasted, watched, and prayed, and received the sacrament so
long, yet I never knew what true religion was till God sent me
that excellent treatise by the hand of my never-to-be-forgot-
ten friend," Charles Wesley.

   Scougal's classic was translated into French (1722), German (1755), and Welsh (1779). In 1756, Benjamin Franklin
printed another copy of the German translation and distributed it among the German-speaking settlers of Pennsylvania.

   The book is divided into three parts, each of which ends
with a prayer. The first subject Scougal considers is the nature
of true religion. He laments that most people see religion only
as a matter of the mind, formality, or the affections. Instead,
Scougal contends that true religion is a "union of the soul with
God," in which the Christian participates in the divine life.
Thus the life of God in man's soul is permanent and lasting;
those who believe the gospel in their minds but do not practice it from their hearts are deceived. Likewise deluded are
those who are caught up in a rapturous moment and then are
abandoned to their corrupt affections.

   The second subject Scougal deals with is the worth and
profit of religion. Fundamental to religion is its cultivation of
holiness. This holiness is "the right temper, the vigorous and
healthful constitution of the soul." Prior to the soul's union
with God, the soul "wearied itself with endless tossings and
rollings, and was never able to find any rest," but after the
union, "the distemper being removed, it feels itself well." Thus
the renewed man may live a life free from the bondage of sense
and its carnal desires. He can now discern the sense of "invisible things" and properly enjoy them. Paramount to the

excellence of religion is love's object, Scougal says. "Love is that powerful and prevalent passion, by which all the faculties and inclinations of the soul are determined, and on which both its perfections and happiness depend."

The third area that Scougal confronts includes despondency, mortification of sin, watchfulness, self-examination, contemplation, and prayer. Especially noteworthy is his analysis of meditation. To advance the divine life in our souls, Scougal recommends "a deep and serious consideration of the truths of our religion, and that both as to the certainty and importance of them." The believer must work up his mind to a serious belief and full persuasion of divine truth, to the extent that the divine truths make a lasting impression upon his affections.

Nine Discourses on Important Subjects consists of nine sermons preached on various occasions. They are the only sermons of Scougal that have survived. Each sermon begins by stating a problem. After a brief explication of the text, Scougal explores various aspects of the problem. He concludes with an application. His sermons may briefly be summarized as follows:

- "The Superior Excellency of the Religious," on Proverbs 12:16, addresses the rampant contempt of religion in the world.
- "The Indispensable Duty of Loving Our Enemies," on Luke 6:27, discusses the attitude one should take toward enemies.
- "The Necessity and Advantage of Early Afflictions," on Lamentations 3:27–28, explains how to exercise Christ-centered resignation during difficult times.
- "A Small Number Saved," on Luke 13:23, addresses the narrow way of salvation.
- "The Duty and Pleasure of Praise and Thanksgiving," on Psalm 107:15, reveals Scougal's experience in confronting a much-neglected topic.

- "The Nativity of Our Savior," on Psalm 2:11, defends the celebration of Christ's birth, though he cautions that it must be done with sincerity and reverence.

- "The Passion of Our Savior," on Lamentations 1:12, considers the Savior's sufferings and our need to make diligent and saving use of them.

- "A Preparation for the Holy Sacrament," on Joshua 3:5, is incomplete, but what has been preserved is of considerable value for those preparing for the Lord's Supper. For instance, Scougal reminds us that "He who sits with the Father above, is, at the same time, present here below, and gives Himself to all who will receive and embrace Him."

- "The Importance and Difficulty of the Ministerial Function," preached before the Synod of Aberdeen on 2 Corinthians 2:16, is one of Scougal's best sermons. He says that the ministry "is a greater burden lying on our shoulders, than if the greatest affairs of this world were devolved upon us, and we did hold up the pillars of the earth." On the difficulty of ministerial labor, he writes, "The world lies in sin, and it is our work to awaken men out of their deadly sleep—to rescue them out of that dismal condition." The most difficult work of a minister, according to Scougal, is "in applying himself particularly to the several persons under his charge, to acquaint himself with their behavior, and the temper of their souls—to redress what is amiss, and prevent their future miscarriages."

Finally, *Private Reflections and Occasional Meditations* and *Essays, Moral and Divine* consist of personal reflections and essays recorded by Scougal while a student at King's College. The entries bear the stamp of a serious mind that had already arrived at the religious point of view later espoused in *The Life of God in the Soul of Man*.

APPENDIX 3

Dutch Further Reformation Divines

To further their program of active personal, spiritual, ecclesiastical, and social reformation, the writers of the *Nadere Reformatie* [Dutch Further Reformation] produced some of the finest, most profound literature in the Protestant tradition. Furthermore, because the Dutch Reformed piety of the seventeenth century grew out of Reformed orthodoxy and included among its founders and exponents several erudite orthodox theologians—such as Gisbertus Voetius, Petrus van Mastricht, and Johannes Hoornbeek—the works of the *Nadere Reformatie* do not give evidence of the kind of antagonism between theology and piety that belonged to the Pietist phase of German Lutheranism. Rather, the proponents of the *Nadere Reformatie* offered a balance of doctrine and piety as well as theology and life that has seldom been equaled in church history.

—The Dutch Reformed Translation Society

Introduction to the
Dutch Further Reformation

Dutch Calvinism did not flower profusely until it was cultivated by the Synod of Dort (1618-19) and fortified by the *Nadere Reformatie*, a primarily seventeenth- and early eighteenth-century movement paralleling English Puritanism both in time and in substance. The *Nadere Reformatie* dates from Willem Teellinck (1579-1629), often called the father of the movement, to its last brilliant contributors, Alexander Comrie (1706-74) and Theodorus van der Groe (1705-84).

Scholars responsible for the periodical *Documentatieblad Nadere Reformatie* offer the following definition of the *Nadere Reformatie*:

> The *Nadere Reformatie* is that movement within the Nederduits Gereformeerde Kerk (Dutch Reformed Church) during the seventeenth and eighteenth centuries, which, as a reaction to the declension or absence of a living faith, made both the personal experience of faith and godliness matters of central importance. From that perspective the movement formulated substantial and procedural reformation initiatives, submitting them to the proper ecclesiastical, political, and social agencies, and pursued those initiatives through a further reformation of the church, society, and state in both word and deed (*Documentatieblad Nadere Reformatie* 19 [1995]:108).

The term *Nadere Reformatie* is a problem for English writers and readers because it allows for no precise English translation of "nadere." Literally, *Nadere Reformatie* means a nearer, more intimate, or more precise Reformation. Its emphasis is the working out of the Reformation more intensely in people's lives, in the church's worship, and in society.

For many years, we thought that the best translation to use for *Nadere Reformatie* was "Dutch Second Reformation," particularly because it was used by some early Dutch divines of that era and it avoids some of the colored judgments of other choices. Problems with using this terminology are that this translation misses the emphasis on the Reformation as a work in progress, and it can be confusing since "Second Reformation" is often associated with other phenomena that chronologically and historically are distinct from the *Nadere Reformatie.* Examples of the use of "Second Reformation" include, first, the revolution in Scotland in 1638, when Episcopalism was replaced by Presbyterianism upon the instigation of the King and the Covenanters; and secondly, it is sometimes used also for a broad European movement of spiritualists and rationalists who attacked the authority of state churches and the clerical establishment during the seventeenth century. In recent years, Fred van Lieburg, Willem op 't Hof, and other Dutch scholars have gradually persuaded us that "Dutch Further Reformation" is probably a more accurate and fitting translation, providing that we do not understand this as implying that the first Reformation did not go far enough in terms of doctrinal reform. The *Nadere Reformatie* did not intend that. Rather, they sought to *apply* Reformation truths to practical, daily living; hence, they carried the Reformation *further* in terms of heart and life applications. Consequently, in this book we are switching to using the terminology of Dutch Further Reformation.

The Dutch Further Reformation has also been called "Dutch Puritanism." At first glance, that seems helpful, since the *Nadere Reformatie* is the Dutch counterpart to English Puritanism. The link between those movements is strong, historically and theologically. Keith Sprunger has shown that during the seventeenth century tens of thousands of Anglo-Scottish believers of Puritan persuasion lived in the Netherlands. Those believers represented about forty congregations and 350 ministers.

The divines of English Puritanism and the Dutch Further Reformation respected each other. They enriched each other through personal contact and their writings, both their Latin treatises and the many books translated from English into Dutch. Speaking of English Puritan writings translated into Dutch from 1598 to 1622, Willem op't Hof says, "A total of 114 editions were issued of a total of 60 translations. These 60 translations concerned works by...twenty-two English authors.... Two authors are numerically preeminent among them: Cowper (18 editions of 10 translations) and Perkins (71 editions of 29 translations). Indeed, Perkins alone eclipses all the others taken together.... Auction catalogues show that Udemans possessed 20 Puritan books in Latin and 57 in English. Similarly, Voetius possessed 30 Puritan works in Latin and 270 in English.... A rough estimate for the period from 1623-1699 gives 260 new translations, 580 editions and 100 new translators" (*Engelse piëtistische geschriften in het Nederlands,* 636-37, 640, 645). More Reformed theological books were printed in the seventeenth century in the Netherlands than in all other countries combined.

English Puritan and Dutch Further Reformation divines also had similar aims: to foster God-glorifying experiential piety and ethical precision in individuals, churches, and nations. Despite similar outlooks, however, English Puritanism and the *Nadere Reformatie* developed historically and theologically distinct identities. Though English Puritanism was a primary influence on the *Nadere Reformatie*—particularly in its stress on the need for a personal and congregational life of practical godliness—it was not an exclusive influence. Non-

English factors also contributed. In some respects, the Dutch movement was more Puritan than English Puritanism itself. Jonathan Gerstner says, "In England from an orthodox Reformed perspective, for all but a short period under Cromwell, there were always grossly unbiblical things to fight: the presence of bishops, superstitious rites in *The Book of Common Prayer*, vestments, etc. In the Netherlands none of these were present, and the task was all the more subtle. Defenders of the *status quo* were not so clearly unreformed as in England. In this context the true spirit of Puritanism came to the fore."

Divines of the Dutch Further Reformation were less interested in reforming the government and church than were their English brethren, but the essence of the Dutch Further Reformation does match the emphasis of English Puritanism on Reformed spirituality to a remarkable degree. Consequently, we are including the Dutch Further Reformation writers in this volume as an appendix.

Wilhelmus à Brakel
(1635-1711)

Wilhelmus à Brakel was born on January 2, 1635, in Leeuwarden, the only son of Margaretha Homma and Theodorus à Brakel, a Reformed pastor of extraordinary piety who became known for his *De Trappen des Geestelycken Levens* [The Steps of Grace in Spiritual Life]. Wilhelmus and his five sisters were reared in a remarkably God-fearing home.

Wilhelmus was converted as a boy, probably under his father's preaching and his mother's prayers and pleading. He attended the Latin school in Leeuwarden, then entered the academy of Franeker at the age of nineteen in 1654. Upon completion of his studies in 1659, Classis Leeuwarden admitted him into the ministry. Due to a lack of vacancies at the time, à Brakel continued his theological training for a few years in Utrecht under Gisbertus Voetius and Andreas Essenius.

À Brakel served five congregations in the national church of the Netherlands during a ministry of nearly fifty years. His first charge was in Exmorra, Friesland (1662-65), a difficult congregation because of widespread spiritual indifference. During his ministry there, he married Sara Nevius, widow of Henricus Vege, who had pastored at Benthuizen. After the loss of her first husband, Sara lived in Utrecht, where she participated in the Voetian conventicles and became spiritually mature. She was a great boon to à Brakel and his ministry.

À Brakel's second congregation at Stavoren (1665-70) was larger and proved to be a more fruitful pastorate. Next,

WILHELMUS À BRAKEL

à Brakel went to the flourishing port city of Harlingen (1670-73), where his ministry and that of his three colleagues were blessed with numerous conversions.

From 1673 to 1683, à Brakel served the large Reformed congregation at Leeuwarden which met in three different church buildings and had six ministers and thousands of members. Every Sunday three services were conducted in the Grote Kerk (the Great Church), two in the Galileerkerk (the Galilee Church), and two in the Westerkerk (the West Church). Three weekday services were also held each week. The city of his birth and the largest city of Friesland, Leeuwarden boasted a population of nearly 20,000.

In the late 1670s, à Brakel became involved in three controversies. First, as he had done at Stavoren and Harlingen, à Brakel established conventicles in various localities in Leeuwarden. These meetings consisted primarily of God's people sharing their experiences of the inner life of faith and exhorting each other to godliness. À Brakel's consistory, however, feared that these conventicles would promote the idea of churches within the church and ultimately lead to schism; hence, they discouraged the practice, and in 1676, the classis of Leeuwarden admonished à Brakel for continuing to promote them.

Second, à Brakel became involved in the controversy that swirled around Jacobus Koelman, a fiery Further Reformation divine who promoted strong separatistic measures. When Koelman visited Leeuwarden, à Brakel let him preach from his pulpit against the wishes of the consistory, for which he was rebuked by the classis of Leeuwarden in 1677. Eventually, à Brakel came into conflict with the government over Koelman because the government had deposed Koelman from office and à Brakel believed that "no political body had the authority to depose a minister." The government suspended à Brakel from all ministerial duties for four weeks, but à Brakel refused to stop preaching and working. Ultimately, à Brakel signed a statement in which he promised to respect the government and to exhort others to do so as well. The entire conflict became known throughout the Netherlands, and à Brakel's fame spread in the churches for his defense of the rights of the church.

Finally, à Brakel battled David Flud van Giffen, a Cocceian minister who preached from à Brakel's pulpit in 1679 that Psalm 8 was a prophecy of Christ's advent. When the sermon engendered dissatisfaction, à Brakel preached on the same psalm the following Sunday from a more classically Reformed position. He published his sermon under the title, *Davids Hallelujah, ofte lof des Heeren in den achtste Psalm, verklaert* (1680) [David's Hallelujah, or the Praises of the Lord in the Eighth Psalm Expounded]. After van Giffen and à Brakel were reconciled, à Brakel followed up his first publication with an extensive treatment of the covenant of grace in *Hallelujah, ofte Lof des Heeren over het genadeverbond opgesteld* (1681) [Hallelujah, or the Praises of the Lord Relative to the Covenant of Grace].

After twenty-one years of ministering in Friesland, à Brakel accepted a pastoral call in 1683 to Rotterdam, where he remained for the rest of his life. Rotterdam, one of the republic's largest cities with a population of 55,000, provided a major field of labor. Here, too, à Brakel's labors were greatly blessed to the upbuilding of the godly in their faith and the conversion of the unsaved. Those blessings were interrupted in the late 1680s by two major conflicts. The first led to à Brakel's distancing himself from Jean de Labadie and his followers, the Labadists, who were trying to promote an "ideal church" that led them into a variety of excesses, including advising believers not to partake of the Lord's Supper in organized churches which were all deemed to be corrupt. In the second, à Brakel engaged in renewed conflict with the government when he insisted that the church is independent from the government and hence the government has no right to forbid the extension of a pastoral call from a local congregation to a particular minister.

À Brakel devoted his tranquil years in the 1690s to producing his *magnum opus, De Redelijke Godsdienst* (1700; 3 volumes —the third, definitive edition of 1707 was slightly expanded to 2,350 pages), a massive set of books that cover both Reformed systematic theology and Reformed ethics for interested lay people, theological students, and ministers at a level that all can understand. Even though he had difficulty finding a printer for the first edition (finally finding a Roman Catholic publisher!), his work was in demand throughout the Netherlands within a very short time. *Redelijke Godsdienst* became nearly as popular in Dutch circles as Bunyan's *Pilgrim's Progress* became in English circles. For family worship, a typical eighteenth-century Dutch farmer would read a "stukje van Vader Brakel" [a piece or selection from Father Brakel] every night to his family after the reading of Scripture. When he completed the whole, he would return to the beginning, and read it through again. *Redelijke Godsdienst* went through twenty editions in the eighteenth century alone. It has been reprinted several times in Dutch in the nineteenth and twentieth centuries as well. Efforts to translate this large work into English (including a decision to do so by a late eighteenth-century Synod of the Reformed Church of America) never materialized until the late 1980s and were brought to fruition in 1995.

The uniqueness of à Brakel's work lies in the fact that it is more than a systematic theology. À Brakel's intent in writing is inescapable: he intensely wishes that the truth expounded may become an experiential reality in the hearts of those who read. In a masterful way, he establishes the crucial relationship between objective truth and the subjective experience of that truth.

Beside this classic work, à Brakel was best known in his day as a powerful and effective preacher who could hold people spellbound by the thousands with eloquence and intense delivery. His method of preaching was more analytical than synthetic, and was always Christ-centered and experiential. Like the English Puritans, à Brakel applied his sermons to different groups of people, particularly the saved, the unsaved, and the hypocrite. At times, he broke the classification down further. For example, among the unsaved, he distinguished the ignorant, the indifferent, the ungodly, and the seeking sinner. Among the saved, he frequently provided different applications for those who were concerned and possessed "refuge-taking" faith in Christ, and those who were established and possessed full assurance of faith in Christ. He promoted Word- and Christ-centered self-examination, and warned frequently against sins of debauchery and worldliness.

In the summer of 1711, à Brakel became very ill. When asked on his deathbed how his soul fared, he responded, "Very well; I may rest in my Jesus. I am united to Him and I am awaiting His coming for me; meanwhile, I submit myself quietly to Him." He died on October 30, 1711, at the age of seventy-six. Daniël LeRoy and Abraham Hellenbroek preached his funeral sermons.

À Brakel was a popular leading representative of the Puritan-minded Dutch Further Reformation. He was so loved among his people for his fatherly ministry both from the pulpit and in pastoral work that many fondly called him "Father Brakel." That honorary title has stuck until today in the homes of many Dutch people in the Netherlands who still read his classic work and appreciate the Puritan, experiential, and pietistic tradition that he so ably represented.

The Christian's Reasonable Service, ed. Joel R. Beeke, trans. Bartel Elshout (RHB; 4 vols., 2,675 pages; 1992-95). À Brakel derived the title for his classic from Romans 12:1, "I beseech you, therefore, brethren, by the mercies of God, that ye present your bodies a living sacrifice, holy, acceptable unto God, which is your reasonable service." This title expresses his intention to assist believers in serving God in Spirit and in truth—intelligently, experientially, and practically, in subjection to the Scriptures.

The Christian's Reasonable Service is arranged in three parts. The first forms a traditional Reformed systematic theology, dealing mainly with the knowledge of God, the offices and work of Christ, soteriology, the covenants, the church, and eschatology. The strength of this section is threefold: clarity of thought, thoroughness of presentation, and the helpfulness of application. The concluding sections at the end of each chapter that apply the particular doctrines discussed to the lives of believers and unbelievers are highlights. À Brakel's practical casuistry in these applications supersedes any other systematic theologian, both in his day and ever since. Such casuistry represents Reformed, Puritan, experiential theology at its best.

The second part expounds Christian ethics and Christian living. À Brakel writes, "In the first volume we spoke of the purchase of salvation and the application of salvation to the elect. In the second volume we will treat of the life of the true people of the covenant, of its quality and condition." This part includes chapters 42 through 99, covering the concluding section of volume 2, all of volume 3, and most of volume 4 in the English translation. It is the largest and most fascinating section of à Brakel's work, packed with salient applications on a variety of topics pertinent to living as a Christian in this world. In addition to a masterful treatment of the ten commandments (chs. 45-55) and the Lord's Prayer (chs. 68-74), this part addresses topics such as living by faith out of God's promises (ch. 42); how to exercise love toward God and His Son (chs. 56-57); how to fear, obey, and hope in God (chs. 59-61); how to profess Christ and His truth (ch. 63); and how to exercise a host of spiritual graces, such as courage, contentment, self-denial, patience, uprightness, watchfulness, neighbor love, humility, meekness, peaceableness, diligence, compassion, and prudence (chs. 62, 64-67, 76, 82-88). Other topics treated most helpfully include fasting (ch. 75), solitude (ch. 77), spiritual meditation (ch. 78), singing (ch. 79), vows (ch. 80), spiritual experience (ch. 81), spiritual growth (ch. 89), backsliding (ch. 90), spiritual desertion (ch. 91), temptations (chs. 92-95), indwelling corruption (ch. 96), and spiritual darkness and deadness (chs. 97-98).

The third part (vol. 4, pp. 373-538) is devoted to a history of God's redemptive, covenantal work from the beginning to the end of the world. It is reminiscent of Jonathan Edwards's *History of Redemption*, though it is not as detailed as Edwards; à Brakel's work confines itself more to Scripture and has a greater covenantal emphasis. It concludes with a detailed study of the future conversion of the Jews drawn from six passages of Scripture (4:511-38). (In the Dutch volumes, a fourth part, which serves as a kind of 350-page appendix that expounds the book of Revelation, has not been translated into English.)

The Christian's Reasonable Service represents, perhaps more than any other work, the Puritan heartbeat and balance of the Dutch Further Reformation. Here systematic theology and vital, experiential Christianity are scripturally and practically interwoven within a covenantal framework, the whole bearing the mark of a pastor-theologian deeply taught by the Spirit. *The Christian's Reasonable Service* combines the scholarship and preciseness of Gisbertus Voetius, the teaching of Witsius on the doctrines of faith and covenant, and the better insights of biblical theology supplied by Johannes Cocceius. Sweeping in coverage, nearly every subject treasured by Christians is treated in an unusually helpful way, always aiming for the promotion of godliness. If one could only possess one multi-volume set of books, this set would be a wise choice.

Alexander
Comrie
(1706-1774)

Alexander Comrie was born on December 16, 1706, in Perth, the son of Patrick Comrie, an attorney, and Rachell Vause. His parents wanted him to follow his great-grandfather, Andrew Gray, and his mother's stepfather, George Hutcheson, into the Presbyterian ministry. As a youth, Comrie was catechized by Ebenezer and Ralph Erskine, and was greatly influenced by the writings of Thomas Boston.

Comrie postponed his studies at the age of twenty because of financial hardship. He went to the Netherlands, where he worked for a Rotterdam merchant. Three years later, he enrolled at Groningen University, where he studied under Anthonius Driessen and Cornelius van Velsen. In 1733, he transferred to Leiden to study philosophy under W. J. 's-Gravensande. He was awarded a doctorate in philosophy in 1734 after completing a critical study of the thought of Descartes, entitled *De moralitatis fundamento et natura virtutis.*

Comrie was then elected minister of the parish of Woubrugge, where he was pastor for thirty-eight years until 1773, the year before his death, faithfully working among people who deeply appreciated his zeal for the Calvinist faith. He visited each of the 125 families of the church three times per year.

Comrie married three times: first, in 1737, to Johanna de Heyde, who died shortly after giving birth to their only child,

Rachel Cornelia, who died two months before Comrie; second, to Maria van de Pijll (d. 1764) in 1741; and finally, to Catharina de Reus in 1766.

An able, experiential preacher, Comrie often focused on the doctrine of faith and its properties, even as he proclaimed a strong free offer of grace to all gospel hearers. Applications throughout his sermons flow directly from his exposition. His concluding applications are often short and specific, commonly addressing the believer and the unbeliever, though at times he breaks down his applications to the seeker, the unsaved, the strong believer, and the weak believer. The seeker is pointed to Christ, the unsaved are warned, the strong believer is exhorted to godliness, and the weak believer is comforted with gospel promises.

Comrie was more influential as a writer than as a preacher. Like Gisbertus Voetius, he aimed to unite and promote Reformation doctrine, scholastic methodology, and scriptural piety through his writing. He took on four major tasks, the first of which was to help church members progress in Reformed, experiential truth, to which end a collection of his sermons was published in 1749 (*Verzameling van leerredenen*). Secondly, he devoted several treatises to the doctrine of faith and its relationship to justification and assurance. He wrote a book on various biblical terms that describe faith, published as *Het A.B.C. des geloofs* in 1739 (translated as *The ABC of Faith*, 1978, see below); a major work on the scriptural properties of saving faith (*Verhandeling van eenige eigenschappen des zaligmakenden geloofs*, 1744); a commentary on the first seven Lord's Days of the Heidelberg Catechism (*Stellige en praktikale verklaaring van den Heidelbergschen catechismus*, 1753); and an extended tract on justification of sinners by direct imputation (*Brief over de rechtvaardigmakinge des zondaars*, 1761). His distinction between the principle or habit (*habitus*) of faith and the exercise or act (*actus*) of faith served as the foundation of his doctrine of faith.

By emphasizing the principle of faith, he promoted divine grace as the sole cause of faith. He taught that the principle of faith is exercised by knowledge, assent, and trust.

To promote Puritan piety, which was his third objective, Comrie translated several important volumes from English into Dutch. These included Thomas Shepard's *The Ten Virgins*, Walter Marshall's *Gospel Mystery of Sanctification*, Thomas Boston's *The Covenant of Grace*, and George Hutcheson's *Brief Exposition of the Twelve Small Prophets*. Finally, Comrie defended Reformed theology against neonomianism, Arminianism, and rationalism. By focusing on the habit of faith, Comrie aimed to prevent Calvinism from lapsing into neonomianism, which taught that the gospel is a "new law" (*neonomos*) that a sinner must obey by faith, and that this obedience, together with the righteousness of Christ, is the ground of justification. In opposition to Arminianism, Comrie, with Nicolaus Holtius, produced two volumes of dialogues against efforts to reconcile Calvinism with Arminianism by departing from the doctrinal standards of the Dutch Reformed church (*Examen van het ontwerp van tolerantie*, 1753-59). He also wrote against ministers and professors who were advocating rationalism, including Antonius van der Os (*Aanspraak aan Antonius van der Os*, 1752) and Johannes van den Honert (*Banieren vanwegen de waarheid opgeregt tegen den Heer Jan van den Honert*, 1753).

Van der Os, minister of Zwolle, had declared that no church confessions had power to decide in matters of faith, for the Scriptures were the true rule, and each man was at liberty to receive them according to his individual interpretation. He also argued that the Synod of Dort did not mean to set forth truth for all time, but only until further light should be obtained. Van den Honert questioned the fundamental doctrine of justification by faith, which Comrie felt involved the surrender of all that Luther and Calvin had taught on the subject. Despite the strenuous opposition of Comrie and his friends, rationalism advanced steadily among the clergy and professors. But the people of the Netherlands for the most part remained faithful to the gospel that Comrie preached. Today his name is still recognized and his books are still read in the Netherlands by those who advocate Reformed, experimental faith.

Comrie spent the last months of his life as a pastoral assistant in Gouda. He died on December 10, 1774, and was buried, upon his own request, in an unmarked grave at St. Janskerk in Gouda. His funeral sermon was delivered by his successor, Jan Ouboter, from Hebrews 13:7.

━━━━◆◆◆━━━━

The ABC of Faith, trans. J. Marcus Banfield (Zoar; 1978; 200 pages). Comrie's most popular treatise unveils the doctrine and life of faith by devoting a chapter to each biblical description of faith, such as trusting, thirsting, drinking, eating, hearing, choosing, kissing, taking, committing, etc. Repeatedly, the author directs the seeker and the saved to Christ and lifts up the weak in faith.

This treatise is rich doctrinally and experientially. Here is one example: "The grace of faith, as long as it is in any degree in exercise, keeps the soul in a childlike, powerless condition. When pride, haughtiness, a standing upon one's own feet, a following of one's own will can be traced, it is a sign that faith is not in exercise. God indeed permits such to stand upon their own feet and to take a few steps, until they hit their head, and tumble over and hurt themselves to the extent that they must come back with shame; but that little, powerless life is really the life of faith, to be borne as a weak lamb in Christ's arm and bosom (Isa. 40:11)" (p. 88).

Theodorus Jacobus Frelinghuysen

(1691-1747)

Theodorus Jacobus Frelinghuysen's family supported the Reformation from the sixteenth century. Theodorus's great-grandfather pioneered the Lutheran Reformation in the German village of Ergste. His grandfather introduced the family to the Reformed tradition in 1669; they joined a small Reformed church in nearby Schwerte. His father, Johan Henrich, became pastor of a newly established German Reformed church in 1683 at Hagen, Westphalia. Shortly after Johan was ordained, he married Anna Margaretha Bruggemann, daughter of a Reformed pastor. He baptized their fifth child, Theodorus Jacobus, on November 6, 1692.

Frelinghuysen attended the Reformed *gymnasium* at Hamm (influenced by Johannes Cocceius) for two years to study philosophy and theology, then enrolled at the University of Lingen (influenced by Gisbertus Voetius) for theological study. At Lingen, Theodorus became thoroughly committed to Reformed piety and the experimental divinity of the Voetian rather than Cocceian mode.

Frelinghuysen was ordained to the ministry in 1717 at Loegumer Voorwerk in East Friesland, near Emden. Fourteen months later, a flood swept over the area, reducing his parishioners to poverty. After serving for several months as co-regent of the Latin school at Enkhuizen, North Holland, Frelinghuysen accepted the call of Classis Amsterdam of the Reformed Church to four small, Dutch Reformed congregations in New Jersey's Raritan Valley (Raritan, Six Mile Run, Three Mile Run, and North Branch).

Shortly after his arrival in New Brunswick, New Jersey, in 1720, Frelinghuysen married Eva Terhune, the orphan daughter of a well-to-do Long Island farmer. Their union was blessed with five sons and two daughters. All five sons became ministers, and both daughters married ministers.

Frelinghuysen's honeymoon of adjustment in America, however, was short-lived. Many objected from the start to his stress on regeneration, his intense piety, and his probing, experiential style of preaching. He, in turn, objected to some of his members' casual way of living, which included poor church attendance, nominal Christianity, covetousness, and in some cases, gambling and dissipation.

Though Frelinghuysen invited sinners to come to Christ as strongly as he warned them against sin, he taught that only those are truly saved who have *experienced* conversion. The Voetian themes of the narrow gate and the hard way, the life of precision and the scarcity of salvation, and the priority of internal motives which effect external observance appear frequently in Frelinghuysen's sermons as inevitable fruits of the Christian life.

Frelinghuysen viewed the evidences of conversion—repentance, faith, and holiness—as tests for admission to the Lord's Supper. Since, in his judgment, lack of the fruits of godliness revealed that many of his members were unregenerate, he felt obliged to warn them against coming to the communion table. The disciplinary actions of Frelinghuysen and his consistory upset many church members, particularly the wealthy who resented his admonitions against carnal luxury. They complained to influential Reformed ministers in New York, some of whom sided with the complainers—most notably, Gualtherus DuBois (1671-1751) and Henricus Boel (1692-1754). Other colleagues, however—most notably

Guiliam Bartholf (1656-1726), an itinerant, pioneer pastor who was responsible for organizing the four congregations to which Frelinghuysen was called—supported Frelinghuysen, although they cautioned him not to be too harsh in judging the spiritual lives of his people. Matters became extremely tense when Frelinghuysen openly referred to colleagues who opposed him as "unconverted ministers."

In 1723, several disgruntled members of Frelinghuysen's congregation, who became known as the *Klagers* (Complainers or Plaintiffs), charged Frelinghuysen with preaching false doctrines. Frelinghuysen's consistories drew up a summons (*daagbrief*), which they sent to the *Klagers*. In this summons, the *Dagers* (Summoners), as they became known, listed the errors of their opponents and eventually excommunicated four of their ringleaders—an action that sent shock waves throughout the Dutch Reformed community.

In 1725, the *Klagers* finally responded to the summons in a *Klagte* (Complaint)—a document of 146 pages addressed to Classis Amsterdam. The *Klagte* was signed by sixty-four heads of households, representing one quarter of Frelinghuysen's four congregations. The *Klagte* detailed every conceivable criticism of Frelinghuysen that might rouse the disaffection of classis and lead to his dismissal.

The fierce opposition took its toll on Frelinghuysen's health. Especially in the early 1730s, he underwent several debilitating bouts of mental depression, which often left him incapacitated for several months. But Frelinghuysen did not relent. Between breakdowns, he continued to spread his pietistic and controversial teachings by the printed and spoken word.

The controversy between the *Dagers* and the *Klagers* raged intermittently until, through the prodding of Classis Amsterdam, they reached a compromise. On November 18, 1733, the churches served by Frelinghuysen adopted eleven "Peace Articles," which were read from the pulpits on the first three

Sundays of 1734 and then forwarded to Amsterdam for final approval. The articles, to which the *Klagers* subscribed, stated that the consistories should forgive the shortcomings of the *Klagers* and rescind their excommunication, providing the *Klagers* accept Frelinghuysen as an orthodox Reformed minister and return to the church. Though Boel's opposition to Frelinghuysen and the revivals continued, DuBois inaugurated a movement to join the revival party in a petition for independence from Classis Amsterdam. Two parties emerged by mid-century, the *Coetus* and the *Conferentie*. The *Coetus* party was composed mainly of ministers who represented Frelinghuysen's pro-revivalist, progressive piety. The *Conferentie* party represented anti-revivalist, traditional orthodoxy and consisted of those who desired to remain "in conference" with Classis Amsterdam. For decades, the two parties exchanged a series of pamphlets. In the end, the goals of Frelinghuysen and the *Coetus* were reached: preaching in English was sanctioned, ministers were trained and ordained in America, and the American church was granted full autonomy.

While some people were offended by Frelinghuysen's searching preaching, the majority of the people rallied behind him. At least three hundred persons appear to have been converted under his ministry in New Jersey. Several mini-revivals under Frelinghuysen's ministry paved the way for the Great Awakening. His preaching and friendship impacted Gilbert Tennent, a young Presbyterian minister who came to New Brunswick to labor among the English-speaking colonists. The revival begun under Frelinghuysen in the Dutch community spread to the English-speaking settlers under Tennent's ministry, and later blossomed into the Great Awakening. George Whitefield called Frelinghuysen "the beginner of the great work."

In his later years, Frelinghuysen became less judgmental of others; he apologized for calling some of his colleagues unconverted. Reconciliation efforts between Frelinghuysen and DuBois were successful. In the end, Frelinghuysen's indefatigable work, zeal, and piety won the day; even many of his former enemies came to accept him.

⸺⬥⬥⬥⸺

Forerunner of the Great Awakening: Sermons by Theodorus Jacobus Frelinghuysen, ed. Joel R. Beeke. The Historical Series of the Reformed Church in America, No. 36 (Eerdmans; 385 pages; 2000). This book contains a biographical introduction, an updated translation of all twenty-two of Frelinghuysen's extant sermons, and an annotated bibliography of English sources on Frelinghuysen.

Frelinghuysen excelled in distinguishing between true and false religion in his sermons. He developed this skill with the assistance of Dutch Puritan pietistic mentors who divided a congregation into various states and conditions of soul and then made personal applications in preaching to each group. Pioneers of this classification method in Dutch Puritanism were Jean Taffin (1528-1602), Godefridus Udemans (1581-1649), and Willem Teellinck (1579-1629). Frelinghuysen's foremost mentor, Johannes Verschuir (1680-1737), known mainly for his *Waarheit in het Binnenste, of Bevindelyke godtgeleertheit* (Truth in the Inward Parts, or Experimental Divinity), wrote especially for young pastors to help them deal with souls entrusted to their care. Verschuir distinguished between several categories of churchgoers, all of whom need to be addressed by the preacher: (1) the strong Christian (*sterk Christen*) who is converted and has reached a degree of maturity in spiritual life; (2) the concerned Christian (*bekommerde Christen*) who is also converted but struggles with many doubts and lacks assurance of faith; (3) the "letter-learned" (*letterwyse*) who are unconverted but instructed and conversant in truth though not knowing its experience or power; (4) the ignorant (*onkunde*) who are unconverted and unlearned but who may still be persuaded to learn because they have native intelligence. Further distinctions are made among the various types of the wicked.

Frelinghuysen's sermons show that he usually followed Verschuir's method of classification. More preaching is devoted to counselling the concerned Christian than the strong Christian. By the time he spent on encouraging this class of hearers, we may conclude that Frelinghuysen believed that most of the true believers in his congregation were "concerned Christians." Most of his warnings are directed to the "letter-learned." They are viewed as being in great danger because they are "almost Christians," not far from the kingdom of God. They walk with Christians and talk like Christians, but they do not possess the new birth. Despite their outward morality and profession of truth, they will perish if death overtakes them.

Frelinghuysen's conviction that the one thing needful is regeneration constitutes the heart of his theology. In a typical sermon, he exhorts his hearers to examine whether they possess the evidences of the new birth. Closely related to this is the call to *conversion*, by which Frelinghuysen usually does not mean the daily conversion of the believer but the initial conversion of the unsaved. He used conversion in that sense interchangeably with regeneration or the new birth.

Frelinghuysen preached that the new birth must be experimental. That is to say, a convert had to know how he had passed from death to life and was expected to be able to relate what God had done for his soul. These two things—a heavy emphasis on the necessity of the new birth and on classifying churchgoers into various categories—particularly impressed Tennent, Whitefield, and other revival preachers.

All of this is consistent with Frelinghuysen's philosophy of preaching. In the application to a sermon, "Duties of Watchmen on the Walls of Zion," he reflects upon his duty as a preacher:

Though I would prescribe a method of preaching to no one, I am yet of the opinion that the application should be discriminating, adapted to the various states of all hearers (Jude 20, 21; Jeremiah 15). In the church are wicked and unconverted persons, moral persons, Christians in appearance and profession: and these constitute the greater number for many are called but few are chosen. Also are there in the church converted persons: little children and those more advanced. Each one longs and calls, each one must be addressed and dealt with according to his state and frame, according to Jeremiah 15:19. How pernicious general applications are, has been shown by many zealous divines (Ezekiel 13:19-20).

Frelinghuysen's sermons show his strong personality and his conviction to stand for the truth, regardless of the consequences. "I would sooner die a thousand deaths," he declared to his flock, "than not preach the truth." He was an eloquent speaker, a vigorous writer, an able theologian, and a zealous preacher. "By the fervor of his preaching," Leonard Bacon wrote, "he was to win the signal glory of bringing in the Great Awakening." Jonathan Edwards regarded him to be one of the greatest divines of the American church and, under God, attributed the success of the revival in New Jersey to his instrumentality.

ABRAHAM HELLENBROEK

Abraham Hellenbroek

(1658-1731)

Abraham Hellenbroek was born to God-fearing parents on December 3, 1658, in Amsterdam. Both his father, Jan, and his mother, Elizabeth Kluft, came from strong Reformed families. Abraham was the sixth of ten children. His oldest brother was stillborn and his oldest sister died at the age of three. His father wrote at that time, "Those children, dying young, have a blessed destiny, for they are with God all the sooner."

Abraham had extraordinary learning abilities, so his parents sent him to school early. That education was soon interrupted by the plague of 1664 in Amsterdam, which spread for nearly a year and claimed more than 24,000 lives. The Hellenbroek family was graciously spared.

When Abraham was age ten, his parents enrolled him in Amsterdam's best Latin school. Five years later, he passed his entrance examination for the University of Amsterdam. On that occasion, he delivered a speech in Latin on the frailty of human life (*De vitae humanae fragilate*).

Hellenbroek studied Latin, Greek, Hebrew, rhetoric, philosophy, and history under Herman Witsius, as well as several Cocceian professors whose views he would later repudiate. In 1677, he moved to Leiden University, where he studied Cartesian philosophy for some time before turning to theology under the tutelage of Friedrich Spanheim. In the Netherlands, Spanheim became known as one of the most ardent defenders of Calvinian predestination against the views of Amyraldism.

Hellenbroek was declared a candidate for the ministry by the Classis of Leiden on March 17, 1682. Due to a surplus of ministers, he had to wait five months before he received a pastoral call. He was installed in Zwammerdam on February 28, 1683, by Rev. VanKralingen of Rijnsaterswoude and preached his inaugural sermon from Isaiah 40:6. In Zwammerdam, Hellenbroek experienced full assurance of faith and personal reconciliation with a Triune God.

Hellenbroek married Geertruida Van der Hoeven in 1690. Four of their six children died in infancy; the remaining daughters, Elizabeth and Barbara, died at ages nineteen and twenty-five. After the loss of their last daughter in 1725, Hellenbroek said to his friends, "The Lord has determined that we should be left childless; you can call me Mara, for, as Naomi said to the citizens of Bethlehem, 'the Almighty hath dealt very bitterly with me. I went out full, and the Lord hath brought me home again empty.'" Hellenbroek was not bitter, however. Rather, he became known for his meek, Christ-like disposition.

From 1691-1694, Hellenbroek served the Reformed congregation at Zwijndrecht. He was installed by Adrianus Gelosse from Ridderkerk. Those were fruitful years. In March of 1694, he accepted a call to Zaltbommel and was installed there in May by Justus Schalkwijk à Velde. Later that same year, Hellenbroek felt compelled to accept a call to Rotterdam. He had been considered for a call five times there, but had never been chosen; people were suspicious that he was influenced by the philosophy of René Descartes and the theology of Johannes Cocceius, which they knew he had studied. Once the people realized Hellenbroek rejected those teachings, they asked him to be their minister.

Hellenbroek was installed in Rotterdam by Ludolphus de With in January 1695. He served the Rotterdam flock faithfully for thirty-three years until his retirement in 1728. Many young people were converted under his ministry during those years. He reached out into the community as well. For many years, he spoke weekly at an orphanage, held public prayer services monthly, and led gatherings at his home for the godly in his community.

Hellenbroek was best known for his writings, such as his catechism book, *A Specimen of Divine Truths* (*Voorbeeld der Goddelyke Waarheden*, see below), a four-volume work on Isaiah (*De Evangelische Jesaja*, 1702-1710) and a two-volume work on the Song of Solomon (*Verhandeling van het Hooglied van Salomo*, 1718-1720), as well as for his written sermons. Hellenbroek's 279 extant sermons are typical of the Dutch Further Reformation. They are Christ-centered expositions bathed in Reformed, Puritan piety. They focus on the marks of grace and contain extensive applications for God's people and the unconverted. Exegetically, homiletically, and experientially, Hellenbroek's commentaries and sermons show the influence of Gisbertus Voetius, who sought to wed Reformed scholastic theology and heartfelt piety.

Hellenbroek was also known for his leadership. He served as president of the provincial synods of South Holland in 1709 and 1712, and oftentimes as a synodical delegate. The magistrate of Rotterdam appointed him as fellow curator of the local and popular Erasmian schools. He was also offered the position of court preacher at the Hague, but declined the honor.

The last sermon Hellenbroek preached was from Psalm 16:11: "Thou wilt show me the path of life: in thy presence is fulness of joy; at thy right hand there are pleasures for evermore." Upon arriving home, he said, "I have experienced more of that fulness of joy than I have been able to express from the pulpit." His physical condition deteriorated in the ensuing months.

About ten weeks before Hellenbroek died, a friend asked what the preacher was thinking about. Hellenbroek answered, "I am thinking about what it means to be reconciled with a Triune God, and how that the Lord has given me ground to believe that I may share in that great blessing." During his final weeks, Hellenbroek often spoke of his longing to be with Christ. He died on December 14, 1731, highly esteemed by the orthodox Reformed community throughout the Netherlands.

———◆◆◆———

A Specimen of Divine Truths, trans. Joel R. Beeke (RHB; 98 pages; 1998). This classic question book for teenagers and adults has gone through more than fifty editions in Dutch since its first publication in 1706, as well as numerous editions in English. The Classis of New Brunswick (1783) of the Reformed Church in America supervised its first translation into English. That translation was used extensively throughout Reformed denominations for more than a century, and was frequently reprinted until the late twentieth century.

After Hellenbroek died, three items were added to the catechism as appendixes: a chapter on the counsel of peace, an introduction to students on how to profit from catechism class, and a compendium of the principal doctrinal errors of those who do not adhere to Reformed theology. With the appendixes, the enlarged catechism book became known in Dutch as "the big Hellenbroek" (*groot Hellenbroek*). The 1998 translation is based on the 1918 Dutch edition of "the big Hellenbroek."

Hellenbroek organized his catechism according to the six major doctrines of Reformed systematic theology: God, man, Christ, salvation, the church, and the last things. Over the centuries, this structure has proven to be an effective means of teaching young adults the Reformed truths of Scripture.

Johannes Hoornbeek

~~⇒◆◆◆⇐~~

(1617-1666)

Johannes Hoornbeek (or Hoornbeeck) was born at Haarlem in 1617, just prior to the commencement of the renowned Synod of Dort (1618-1619). One of the Dutch Further Reformation's most learned divines, he was a child prodigy who began his study of Latin at the age of six. At sixteen years of age, he studied theology at Leiden University under Antonius Walaeus. Subsequently, he went to study theology at the University of Utrecht under Gisbertus Voetius, by whom he was greatly influenced.

Hoornbeek was ordained into the ministry at Muhlheim-on-the-Rhine in 1639. Shortly after receiving his doctoral degree in theology in 1643, he became professor of Old Testament at Utrecht, and was appointed preacher there as well in 1645.

At Utrecht (and subsequently at Leiden), Hoornbeek proved to be an indefatigable worker and theologian of many interests, famous for his orthodox scholarship, practical theology, and love for missions. Possessing many God-given talents, he mastered thirteen languages and wrote voluminously.

Major works of his Utrecht years, all of which were well-received by the orthodox of his day, include the following: a practical manual of homiletics, *Tractatus de ratione concionandi* (1645); a treatise that opposes the mysticism of Weigel, Schwenkfeld, and others, *De paradoxis et heterodoxies weigelianis commentaries* (1646); a book on how to die well, *Euthanasia ofte*

Welsterven; waar in veel voorbeelden der stervenden en hun laatsten doodtspreuken verhaald worden (1651); an effective three-volume treatise against Socinianism, *Socinianismus confutatus* (1650-64); a concise textbook of Reformed polemics, opposing "unbelievers" (the heathen, Judaists, and Mohammedans), "heretics" (Roman Catholics, Anabaptists, Libertines, Socinians, and the Enthusiasts), and "schismatics" (Remonstrants, Lutherans, Brownists, and Grecians), *Summa controversiarum religionis* (1653); and a compiled volume of theology extracted from other writers who opposed Cocceian theology, *Institutiones theologicae ex optimis auctoribus concinnatae* (1653).

In 1654, Hoornbeek accepted the position of theological professor at Leiden. Here he continued to work avidly, also preaching regularly and undertaking some pastoral work.

Major writings of Hoornbeek's Leiden years include: two volumes that display his love for mission, *De convincendis et convertendis judaeis et gentilibus libri VIII* (1655); *De conversione indorum et gentilium* (1669); three volumes promoting strict Sabbath day observance (in opposition to the abolition of the fourth commandment as advocated by Cocceius), *Heyliginghe van Godts name en dagh* (1655), *De observando a Christianis praecepto Decalogi quarto* (1659), and *Nader bewysinghe van des heeren daghsheyliginghe* (1659); a work against Arminianism and its influence on Socinianism, *Van de oorsprongh der Arminiaensche nieuwigheden* (1662); a two volume work of systematic theology and ethics, *Theologica practica* (1663-66), written along Second Reformation lines that resembles the writings of Voetius and Wittewrongel; and a volume that opposed the canonicity of non-biblical writings, *Miscellanea sacra* (1674).

Hoornbeek wore himself out by 1666, when he died at age forty-eight. His life and work represented well the Voetian school of thought that combined scriptural exegesis, scholastic theology, and godly zeal in promoting Reformed Orthodoxy. An able and well-rounded theologian and richly taught by the Spirit, his influence was understandably great on his students.

In the seminary chair, from the pulpit, and by a godly walk, he modeled Reformed and Puritan doctrine and piety.

———◆◆◆———

Spiritual Desertion, with Gisbertus Voetius, ed. M. Eugene Osterhaven, trans. John Vriend and Harry Boonstra (Baker; 176 pages; 2003). This book was begun by Gisbertus Voetius, who, being in the midst of pressing duties, asked Hoornbeek to complete it. The first edition appeared in 1646, and an improved edition was published in 1659. It was last printed in Dutch in 1898.

Of the present translation supervised by the Dutch Reformed Translation Society, Voetius wrote only twenty-seven pages, focusing on the definition, causes, and kinds of spiritual desertion. He also briefly addressed remedies for spiritual desertion, and questions about such desertion, including why God allows it.

Hoornbeek's contribution of 118 pages focuses in greater depth on three issues: "(1) the abandonment as such; (2) the difficulties that arise from it for the abandoned soul; (3) the conflict that often arises in the soul as a result and continually furnishes work for it so as to spawn continual unrest" (p. 65). Hoornbeek's work is very helpful, reminiscent of the best of Puritan casuistry.

M. Eugene Osterhaven writes in the introduction that *Spiritual Desertion* "was written because of the biblical admonition to rejoice in the Lord and to live victoriously as his children, whereas many fellow Christians manifested a lack of delight in God and were filled with fears and anxieties. The noble intention of Voetius and Hoornbeeck is as relevant today as it was in the seventeenth century. The breakdown of morality, environmental problems, terrorism, and of course, the perpetual problem of indwelling sin, not to mention other concerns, are certain to generate feelings of spiritual abandonment. The message of Voetius and Hoornbeeck is needed today" (p. 23).

Jacobus Koelman

(1631-1695)

Jacobus Koelman was born in 1631 and educated at Utrecht, where he earned his doctorate in philosophy at the age of twenty-four, then studied theology under Gisbertus Voetius, Andreas Essenius, and Johannes Hoornbeek. He left university in 1656 as a confirmed Voetian. That same year, he translated Christian Love's *The Conflict between Flesh and Spirit.*

From 1657 to 1662, Koelman served as chaplain at the Dutch embassies, first at Copenhagen, Denmark, and later in Brussels. From 1662 to 1674, he was minister of the Reformed congregation of Sluis in what is Flemish Zeeland today, but was then one of the areas governed by the States General called the General Territories. In Sluis, he enlarged his vision for the Dutch Further Reformation. He became a staunch advocate of that vision in preaching, writing, and translating Scots and English divines into Dutch.

Koelman opposed governmental interference in church life on several fronts. He rejected the government's right to call ministers and to select elders and deacons. He fought against its low view of Christian living and its lack of maintaining Christian discipline in conjunction with the administration of the sacraments. And he staunchly opposed the observance of church feast days in worship services, as well as irreverent and mechanical form prayers.

Opposition created opponents. From 1673 to 1675, Koelman's opponents worked for his ouster, and finally succeeded. In June of 1675 Koelman lost his pastorate and was banished from Flanders, and in November of the same year, he lost his wife.

For some time, Koelman had no established living. When persecution increased, he eventually settled in Amsterdam under the protection of the mayor, Conrad van Beuningen. He spent his time teaching classes at various churches, leading conventicles at various homes, writing books or translating Puritan works into Dutch, and engaging in preaching itineraries in Groningen and Friesland opened to him by Wilhelmus à Brakel. Eventually, nearly all the provincial synods ruled against his being allowed to preach, teach, or conduct conventicles.

In addition to à Brakel's support, Koelman received encouragement from Jodocus Van Lodenstein. Though Van Lodenstein could not agree with Koelman's fiery opposition against the observance of church feast days, he fully supported his spiritual emphases and his conviction that government ought not interfere in church life.

In 1691, Koelman returned to Utrecht, the city of his birth, where, although still banned from preaching and leading conventicles, he was given permission to preach in homes, conduct Bible expositions ("Bijbellezingen"), and teach catechism. Here, too, he continued to write books and translate. By the time he died in 1695 at the age of sixty-three, he had written forty-four books and translated twenty-three volumes of English and Scots divines (including Christopher Love, Samuel Rutherford, Thomas Hooker, William Guthrie, Hugh Binning, and John Brown). Particularly through his pen, he exercised influence upon his contemporaries, as can be observed by the numerous reprints of his writings and translations.

Koelman's writings and translations reveal a multifaceted individual. He wrote a practical, renowned treatise on parenting (*De pligten der ouders; The Duties of Parents,* see below). He wrote on philosophy, especially against Descartes. He opposed De Labadie. He wrote on faith (*De natuur en gronden des geloofs*) and on the covenant of grace (*Het verbond der genade*). He wrote practical works for office-bearers (*De wekker der leraren; Het ambt en de plicht van ouderlingen en diakenen*) and for teachers (*Schoolmeesters*). He set forth his vision for the Dutch Further Reformation in his *Punten van Nodige Reformatie,* stressing the need for vital godliness in all areas of life. He argued for an orthodox, Puritan, and Voetian understanding of the Sabbath. His Puritan sympathies were particularly strong; hence his translation of so many of them. His translations of two volumes of Francis Rous reveal his mystical tendencies, which, however, were never carried to extreme.

Koelman was buried in the Catherine Church at Utrecht, where Voetius's remains also rest. Koelman was one of the most outspoken and influential of the Dutch Further Reformation divines, as well as one of the most severely opposed.

***

The Duties of Parents, ed. M. Eugene Osterhaven, trans. John Vriend (Baker; 170 pages; 2003). First published in 1679, Koelman's classic on childrearing was often reprinted in Dutch until today and is significant because it was one of the few domestic helps written by Dutch Further Reformation divines. Peter Wittewrongel's *Oeconomia Christiana, or the Christian Household* (1655) is a notable exception. Koelman wrote his work as another major plank in his program to further reform the Dutch Reformed church.

Each chapter is divided into a number of "rules" or sections, numbering 282 in all. Koelman actually intended this book to be read alongside two other books he wrote: first, a catechism for children, and second, twenty stories of godly children who died at a young age. For the most part, however, *Duties of Parents* can stand alone.

Koelman's work ably meets its purpose of impressing upon Christian parents the solemn task of raising their children to embrace a life of godliness. Without denying the necessity of God's accompanying grace, he provides numerous guidelines to help parents labor for the salvation of their children's souls. Though a few of his guidelines now seem harsh, quaint, or even tedious, the vast bulk of them provide sound, challenging advice that is seldom found in contemporary books on childrearing. The chapter on teaching godliness through conversation is particularly good. As the editor notes: "There is much sound advice in this volume, advice good in every age and especially in our time of dysfunctional families, one-parent families, the lack of good discipline, and street children. Koelman speaks to our society today in many of his emphases: the importance of letting children know that parents have their best interests at heart; the need for loving, thoughtful discipline; the need for good schools and good teachers, the latter realizing their great responsibility; and teaching children that their relation to God and their eternal well-being is the purpose of all nurture and admonition" (p. 15). Here is one quote from Koelman's introduction to whet your appetite, if you are a parent:

> Bring your children to God and teach them how they must serve him throughout their whole life. They are the Lord's more than they are yours. The Lord is their Owner as well as their Creator and Sustainer. In baptism you have consecrated them to God. There you have made a solemn promise that you will raise them as his possession, not for the flesh, the world, and the devil, but for him, to serve him and live for him. The covenant whose seal they received demands faith and repentance. Should

you not then nurture them in the knowledge of divine things and for faith and godliness? For you have not wished to lie before the Lord, as I may hope, and you are not sorry that you have dedicated them to God in the sacrament. Then follow your conscience in this matter. Try to save them with all appropriate means prescribed by God; try to turn them away from evil and to spur them on to all good work. From you they have inherited the origin of evil, which is a thousand times worse than leprosy, gall stones, kidney stones, and similar physical ailments they might have inherited from you. It is fair, therefore, for you to do your utmost to seek their healing by trying to surrender them into the hands of the physician of souls, Jesus Christ, by making him known, recommending him, and leading them to him as it were by your hand (pp. 29-30).

It is remarkable that this volume was the first treatise Koelman published to implement his vision and program for further reformation in the Netherlands, since he himself never had children. His marriage to Anna Huss was short-lived, as she died at an early age.

Jean Taffin

(1529-1602)

Jean Taffin, one of the pioneers of the loosely organized Dutch Further Reformation, was born in 1529 into a wealthy Roman Catholic family in Tournai (Doornik, in the Flemish and Dutch languages) in the southern part of the Netherlands (today, the south-central part of Belgium). His father was Denis, a prominent lawyer and a municipal magistrate, and his mother was Catherine Alegambe. He was one of seven children.

After being educated by a highly qualified family tutor, Taffin went to the University of Leuven, where he was exposed to classic and patristic sources and Erasmian Christian humanism. He then moved on to the University of Padua in Italy, and from there, in 1554, to becoming secretary and librarian for Antoine Perrenot, bishop of Atrecht (who later became Cardinal Granvelle). In this position, which he maintained for three years, Taffin was introduced to many prominent people, including members of nobility and political and civic leaders. He was most likely converted to the Reformed faith during these years.

Upon conversion, Taffin resigned his position, provided assistance briefly to a Reformed church in Antwerp (1557), and, having become active in the "churches under the cross,"

was forced to flee persecution in 1558 with other refugees. He
spent some months in Strassburg with Bucer and Capito, and
then went to Geneva to study theology under Calvin and Beza
(1558-59). He pastored churches in Aachen (1560-61) and
Metz (1561-66). While at Metz, he married into the Quintine
family. His only son from this marriage, Samuel, died young.
Meanwhile, the Metz church flourished and Taffin's reputation as a church leader spread, such that he established
friendships with other leading Reformers, including Guido de
Brès (1522-67) and Petrus Dathenus (c. 1532-88). In 1564, he
participated in discussions, initiated by Prince William of
Orange, that sought to merge Lutheran and Calvinistic
thought against a militant Roman Catholicism.

Taffin helped to consolidate reform in Antwerp for most
of 1566 and 1567 while on loan from his Metz congregation.
When civil persecution increased against the Calvinists, he
returned to his family and congregation in Metz (1567-69).
By 1569, the political situation in Metz had degenerated to
the point that Calvinistic worship was forbidden. Taffin settled in Heidelberg (1570-73), where he pastored a small
refugee church.

Taffin was also active in church leadership. He was delegated to several prominent Dutch Synods (e.g., Emden, 1571;
Dort, 1574 and 1578; Middelburg, 1581), where he was often
appointed secretary, but he remained distant from the polemical battles of his day, reflecting his mild, loving character. His
stress was on preparation for eternity and the great resurrection and homecoming of the true Christian in glory, where he
shall finally see God as He is.

Taffin became chaplain to William of Orange in the fall of
1573, a position he held for more than a decade together with
a fellow chaplain, Pierre Loyseleur. The pastors led daily worship services, provided pastoral counsel to the prince's family
and staff, advised and prayed with him on ecclesiastical and

political matters, and carried out assignments as the prince's representatives.

Taffin was instrumental in arranging the marriage of William of Orange to Catherine of Bourbon in 1575. That same year, Taffin's wife died. Two years later he married Nicole Castelin; they had two sons.

Gradually, Taffin became frustrated with the prince's ecclesiastical policy which still left considerable control of the churches to the magistrates. When William decided to downsize his staff and move his court from Antwerp to Delft, Taffin decided to stay on in Antwerp to serve the flourishing Reformed congregation there. When Antwerp fell under Spanish-Catholic control in August 1585, Taffin became a Protestant refugee yet again. As Catholicism continued to make great strides both in property and among the populace, Taffin and his family spent several months in Emden to recover emotionally from these disheartening developments. During this period of respite, he wrote *The Marks of God's Children* in French (see below), which deals extensively with how believers should cope with affliction and persecution.

From 1585 to 1587, Taffin served the Walloon church at Haarlem. Of his ministry there, James DeJong writes, "He often represented the Reformed church at the States General, the parliamentary body that functioned on both provincial and national levels, and on Walloon matters. He was especially grateful for and supportive of the English Duke of Leicester's regime in the Netherlands, for it fostered the adoption of a church order in 1586 more congenial toward Taffin's ecclesiology" (*Marks of God's Children*, p. 17).

In 1587, Taffin accepted a ministerial call to serve the Oudezijdskapel in Amsterdam, a position he maintained until his death fifteen years later. There he interacted with Jacobus Arminius, another Amsterdam pastor, during the early stages of what would become known as the Arminian controversy.

Taffin died suddenly on July 15, 1602. His name became widely known in Reformed and Puritan circles, and his writings were translated into at least four languages. Taffin was more a practical than a systematic theologian. Inwardly experienced piety and sanctification permeated his life and writings. This theme is reflected in his two most prominent works: *Des Marques des enfans de Dieu et des consolations en leurs afflictions* (1586—reprinted seven times in French by 1616; translated as *The Marks of the Children of God, and of Their Comforts in Affliction* [London, 1590; reprinted seven times by 1634, and now freshly translated in 2003 as *The Marks of God's Children*]), and *Traicte de l'amendement de vie* (1594; translated as *The Amendment of Life* [London, 1595], which deals with repentance as a lifestyle). Taffin also wrote a book against the Anabaptists and a booklet on almsgiving.

━━▶◆◀━━

The Marks of God's Children, ed. James A. DeJong, trans. Peter Y. DeJong (Baker; 155 pages; 2003). This book was written to "comfort God's troubled people" after William of Orange's assassination and Spanish-Catholic gains throughout the Netherlands. It was translated from French into Dutch in 1588 as *Van de Merck-teeckenen der kinderen Gods*, and reprinted at least twelve times by 1659.

Taffin describes the felicity of true Christians in three successive stages: first, "peace of conscience and joy in the Holy Ghost" in this life; second, the separated soul with Christ in heaven; third, the ultimate state of bliss when soul and body shall be reunited to serve God eternally. To be prepared for such bliss, a person must have a personal knowledge and experience of the marks of saving grace—external marks, such as church membership conjoined with a willingness to hear the Word purely preached, to receive the sacraments purely administered, and to pray; and inward marks, such as "the testimony of the Holy Ghost in our hearts, the peace and

quietness of our consciences before God, feeling ourselves justified by faith," love to God and our neighbor, a change in
heart, and a steadfast desire to walk in the fear and obedience
of God. In sum, Christians are spiritual pilgrims who strive to
live to God and to die for Him. For Taffin, life and death are inseparable: Christians live to die and die to live.

Such a lifestyle will bring the Christian into spiritual conflict, tempting him to doubt, and will also lead him into
affliction. Taffin discusses six temptations, and then proceeds
to employ more than half of his treatise on the subject of affliction. Here also Taffin strongly emphasizes the need for
heartfelt experience. "Holy affections and desires" are certain
indications that believers have "the Holy Ghost dwelling in us
and consequently that we also have faith." For Taffin, knowledge is important, but love has the last word. It is better to
possess a "learned ignorance" than a "rash knowledge." Finally,
Taffin subjects all knowledge, love, feelings, and experiences to
Scripture as the ultimate guide.

Willem Teellinck
(1579-1629)

Willem Teellinck, often called "the father of the Dutch Further Reformation," was born January 4, 1579, in Zerikzee, the main town on the island of Duiveland, Zeeland, to a godly, prominent family. He was the youngest of eight children. His father, Joost Teellinck, who served as mayor of Zierikzee two years prior to Willem's birth, died when Willem was fifteen years old. His mother, Johanna de Jonge, survived her husband by fifteen years but was often sick when Willem was young. Willem was well-educated in his youth; he studied law at St. Andrews in Scotland (1600) and at the University of Poitiers in France, where he earned a doctorate in 1603.

The following year, Teellinck spent nine months with the Puritan community in England. His lodging with a godly family in Banbury and his exposure to Puritan godliness—lived out through extensive family worship, private prayer, sermon discussions, Sabbath observance, fasting, spiritual fellowship, self-examination, heartfelt piety, and good works—profoundly impressed him and was used for his conversion. An unquenchable zeal for God's truth and Puritan piety was born in his heart. He surrendered his life to the Lord and decided to study theology at Leiden. He trained there for two years under Lucas Trelcatius, Franciscus Gomarus, and Jacobus Arminius.

While in England, Teellinck met Martha Greendon, a young Puritan woman from Derby, who became his wife. She shared Teellinck's life goal of living out the Puritan *praxis pietatis* ("practice of piety") in family life as well as in parish work. Their first son, Johannes, died in infancy. They were then blessed with three sons—Maximiliaan, Theodorus, and Johannes—all of whom became Reformed ministers with emphases similar to their father's. They also had two daughters: Johanna, who married an English minister, and Maria, who married a political official at Middelburg.

Teellinck edified his family by his godly example. He was hospitable and philanthropic, yet he stressed simplicity in furnishings, clothing, and food. He generally steered conversation at mealtimes in a spiritual direction. Family worship was scrupulously practiced the Puritan way. Once or twice a year, the Teellincks observed a family day of prayer and fasting. Teellinck found this practice helpful for moving his family to dedicate themselves entirely to God.

Teellinck was ordained into the pastoral ministry in 1606 and served the Burgh-Haamstede parish on the island of Duiveland for seven fairly fruitful years. There were several conversions, but Teellinck, much like his predecessor, Godfridus Udemans, struggled with village life, which was rough and undisciplined. The classis minutes of that time frequently addressed the problems of alcohol abuse, Sabbath desecration, fighting, carnival attendance, and a general disorderly spirit.

During this pastorate, Teellinck wrote his first books. In his first publication, *Philopatris ofte Christelijke Bericht* (1608; The Love of Fatherland, or A Christian Report), he stressed the Dutch government's need to implement strict laws to combat the sins and faults of the populace. In 1610, Teellinck visited England to renew ties with his Puritan colleagues Thomas

Taylor, Dod, and Hildersham. During that stay, he preached to the Dutch congregation in London. In 1612, he was delegated by Zeeland to go to the Hague to lobby the States General for a national synod dedicated to resolving the growing problems associated with Arminianism.

From 1613 until his death in 1629, Teellinck served as pastor in Middelburg, a flourishing city that had six Reformed churches—four Dutch, one English, and one French. People were drawn to his ministry by his sincere conversation and preaching, faithful visiting and catechizing, godly walk and selfless demeanor, and simple and practical writings. He demonstrated the conviction that a pastor ought to be the godliest person in the congregation—and his godliness involved self-denial. When a pestilence swept through Middelburg in 1624, for example, Teellinck not only called people to public and private repentance but also visited numerous infected homes, even as he urged others not to put themselves at risk by doing so.

Teellinck's hard work in Middelburg bore fruit. Five years after his arrival, he wrote to his congregation in his *Noodwendig Vertoogh* (Urgent Discourse): "We have every reason to thank the Lord. You come to church in large numbers each Sunday; our four church buildings cannot contain all the people. Many of your families may be called 'little churches.' There is good order according to good rules. Many of you use the means of grace diligently and you gladly listen to our admonitions to exercise godliness." Yet Teellinck remained burdened for the indifference in and beyond his flock. The "constant hurt and pain" that he carried in his heart because of the spiritual laxity and carnality that prevailed in church and society moved him to use his prodigious energies and gifts in speaking and writing to bring about a comprehensive reformation in every sphere of life.

In his preaching, Teellinck infiltrated the Dutch scene with English Puritan pathos. His sermons focused on the practice of godliness, and he preached often on the necessity of repentance. He had the gifts to rebuke sin and pronounce God's impending judgments while simultaneously drawing people to the love of God and wooing them to Christ.

Homiletically, Teellinck was influenced by William Perkins, who advocated the Puritan "plain method" of preaching. After exegeting a text, Teellinck drew out various doctrines, explained how these doctrines should benefit the hearer by means of comfort and admonition, and then applied wisdom gleaned from the text to saved and unsaved hearers. Though not an eloquent orator, Teellinck was an effective preacher. After hearing Teellinck preach on a few occasions, Gisbertus Voetius wrote, "Since that time my heart's desire has been that I and all other preachers of this land could duplicate this kind of powerful preaching."

Near the end of his life, Teellinck developed a mystical emphasis that had surfaced only occasionally in his earlier writings. That mysticism became evident in the posthumously published *Soliloquium* (Soliloquy) and *Het Nieuwe Jeruzalem* (The New Jerusalem). The latter book is reminiscent of the writings of Bernard of Clairvaux. Feelings and emotions are accented more than faith; the believing soul becomes one with Christ in tender communion.

Teellinck battled ill health for most of his ministry. He passed away on April 8, 1629, at the age of fifty. He was mourned by thousands and was buried in the churchyard of St. Pieters Church in Middelburg.

The Netherlands was not as ready for Teellinck as England had been for Perkins, however. Teellinck's insistence on connecting the fruits of love with the acts of justifying faith did not appeal to some of his peers. They found his call for renewal in church, school, family, government, and society too intense. So on the one hand, Teellinck's preaching against dead Reformed orthodoxy brought him under suspicion by the orthodox Reformed. On the other hand, Arminians censored him for his devotion to that same Reformed orthodoxy and resented his popularity with laypeople.

Teellinck's goals for the reformation of the church are most evident in his writings. His numerous works sought to build up people in the faith by moving the Reformed Church beyond reformation in doctrine and polity to reformation in life and practice. Even more than Perkins, Teellinck stressed godly living, fruits of love, marks of grace, and primacy of the will.

Teellinck produced 127 manuscripts in all, sixty of which were printed. Those sixty included twenty full-length books. Franciscus Ridderus published a representative anthology of Teellinck's works in 1656 titled *Uyt de Geschriften en Tractaten van Mr. Willem Teellinck* (From the Writings and Tracts of Mr. Willem Teellinck). Three years later Teellinck's sons began printing his works, but they never got beyond three folio volumes titled *Alle de wercken van Mr. Willem Teellinck* (The Works of Mr. Willem Teellinck). Most of Teellinck's writings can be divided into five categories:

• *Exegetical.* Teellinck's exegesis of Romans 7 was published posthumously as *De Worstelinghe eenes Bekeerden Sondaers* (The Wrestling of a Converted Sinner). He published commentaries on Malachi, Judges 13-16, and Isaiah 9:5. His commentary on the Pentateuch, *Verklaeringe Over de Vijf Boecken Moses* (Exposition of the Five Books of Moses), which was ready for print shortly before his death, was lost. All of his exegetical works were written on a popular level. His concern was always for the genuine practice of Christianity.

• *Catechetical.* Teellinck's catechetical writings include his *Huysboeck* (Family Manual), a commentary on the Compendium of the Heidelberg Catechism intended for family devotions, and *Sleutel der Devotie openende de Deure des Hemels voor ons* (The Key of Devotion Opening the Door of Heaven for Us), a two-volume work of dialogues that addresses many questions about spiritual and practical Christian living.

• *Edificatory.* The majority of Teellinck's books were written to edify and instruct believers and usually focused on a single theme. *Een getrouwe Bericht hoe men sich in geval van Sieckte Dragen Moet* (A Faithful Account of How One Should Conduct Oneself in Time of Sickness) provides practical guidance for coping with affliction. *Den Christelijcken Leidsman, Aanwijzend de Practycke der Warer Bekeeringhe* (The Christian Guide, Showing the Practice of True Conversion) was written to challenge Calvinists spiritually and to warn them about Arminian ideas.

• *Admonitory.* In *Wraeck-Sweert* (Sword of Revenge), Teellinck warns of divine judgments that will descend upon the people who fail to repent and turn to God. In *Zions Basuijne* (The Trumpet of Zion), he tells representatives of the provinces that the Netherlands cannot be saved without a spiritual and moral reformation. Teellinck often wrote short books to warn against specific sins. In *Timotheus* (Timothy), he warns about the use of images, and in *Den Spiegel der Zedicheyt* (The Mirror of Morality), he opposes immodesty and extravagance in dress.

• *Polemical.* In *Balaam*, Teellinck warns against Roman Catholicism, and in *Den Volstandigen Christen* (The Mature Christian), against Arminianism. In *Eubulus*, Teellinck opposes Arminians for their man-centered doctrine, though he also points out faults of the Calvinists. Teellinck believed that most Calvinists focused on sound doctrine at the expense of practical godliness. He thought that Calvinists should read practical writers (*praktijk-schrijvers*) such as William Perkins and Jean Taffin. He also stressed that staunch orthodoxy is worthless if confession is not made from the heart. Because of this emphasis, some Reformed leaders charged Teellinck with being too emotionally subjective and put him in league with the Arminians. Teellinck responded to these charges by saying that he emphasized both soundness of doctrine and godliness of life.

Teellinck's writings focused on three major themes: sanctification, the Lord's Supper, and Sabbath-keeping. With regard to sanctification, Teellinck's greatest work is *The True Path of Godliness* (see below). His most extensive work, *Sleutel der Devotie* (The Key of Devotion), offers nearly eight hundred pages on the subject of devotion, which is, for Teellinck, one aspect of sanctification. Teellinck views devotion as commitment to God in Christ, which is man's highest calling.

Teellinck also wrote extensively about the Lord's Supper, particularly in his *Het Geestelijk Sieraad van Christus' Bruiloftskinderen, of de Praktijk van het H. Avondmaal* (The Spiritual Ornament of Christ's Children of the Bridechamber, or The Use of the Holy Supper), which was reprinted eleven times from 1620 to 1665. The book consists of four lengthy sermons, the first of which details a believer's duty toward the Lord's Supper; the second, preparation for the Supper; the third, partaking of the Supper; and the fourth, conduct after the Supper.

Teellinck was offended by how easily the Lord's Day was profaned in the Netherlands. In 1622, he wrote *De Rusttijdt, ofte Tractaet van d'onderhoudinge des Christelijcke Rustdachs, diemen gemeynlijck den Sondach Noemt* (The Time of Rest, or A Tract about Maintaining the Christian Day of Rest, Which Is Generally Called the Sunday). Divided into seven books, *De Rustijdt* urges strict observance of the Sabbath and includes details from Teellinck's own experience on how to prepare for the Sabbath.

Teellinck's major influence was injecting Puritan color into the Dutch Further Reformation. Though he never taught theology at a university, was no scholar at heart, and was not eloquent, his life, sermons, and writings helped shape the piety of the entire movement.

Teellinck was one of the most influential "old writers" (*oude schrijvers*) of the seventeenth century. More than 150 editions of his books were printed in Dutch. Moreover, his practical piety was carried on and reshaped by other major Dutch Further Reformation writers such as Voetius. Several of Teellinck's books were also translated into German. One of Germany's most influential Pietists, Friedrich Adolph Lampe (1683-1729), often used Teellinck to promote the practice of godly living. Thus, Teellinck left his mark on both continental and American pietism.

***

The Path of True Godliness, ed. Joel R. Beeke, trans. Annemie Godbehere. (Baker; 300 pages; 2003). *The Path of True Godliness*, originally titled *Noord-Sterre, aawijzende de juiste richting van de ware godzaligheid* (The North Star, Showing the Right Direction of True Godliness), was printed four times in Dutch: in 1621, at Middelburg by Hans van der Hellen; in 1636, at Groningen by Nathanael Rooman; in 1642, at Groningen by Jan Claesen; and in 1971, at Dordrecht by J. P. van den Tol. This last edition, edited by J. van der Haar (from the 1636 edition), was used as the basis for this translation.

The Path of True Godliness, Teellinck's major work on sanctification, is a Puritan-style manual on how to practice godliness. Teellinck divided this work into nine sections, which he called "books," then subdivided the books into eighty-one "chapters."

Book 1. Since many people boast of their faith but have no saving knowledge of the truth, Teellinck feels a need to address three matters in this book: (1) what true godliness is, (2) how believers should conduct themselves in practicing godliness, and (3) why the exercise of true godliness is of utmost importance.

Book 2. The second book discusses the realm of darkness that opposes the practice of godliness. The three main powers of this realm are our own depraved flesh, the world, and the devil.

Book 3. Teellinck shows how the kingdom of grace, in contrast to the realm of darkness, promotes godliness. The kingdom of grace possesses three powers: the renewed spirit, which wars against the flesh; the church of God, which fights against the world; and the Spirit of God, who opposes the devil. Each of these powers possesses three gifts that oppose and overcome its enemy in the realm of darkness.

Book 4. The fourth book shows us how to respond to these two realms. We must at all times keep life's three major purposes before us: the glory of God, the salvation of our own souls, and the promotion of the salvation of others. Teellinck then explains how the realm of darkness tries to divert people from life's real purposes by influencing them to live without ever knowing those purposes, to pursue wrong purposes, or to pursue the right purposes only halfheartedly.

Book 5. This book describes the means of achieving the true purposes of life: God's holy ordinances, God's works, and God's promises. It also describes people upon whom it is especially incumbent to use those means: civil authorities, church office bearers (especially pastors), and ordinary Christians.

Book 6. This book shows how Christians must attain the right purposes of life through the assistance of the right means described in the last book, all the while living consistently, watching diligently, and struggling against every hindrance.

Book 7. Here Teellinck provides us with a variety of God-centered motivations for practicing godliness. These include the Father's wisdom, omnipotence, and lovingkindness; the Son's incarnation, exemplary life, and kind invitations to come to Him; and the Spirit's promise to give new hearts, to overlook weaknesses, and to graciously reward the practice of godliness.

Book 8. This book contains motivations for practicing godliness and is divided into three major sections: our natural condition, the manifold blessings of God, and the promises we make to God.

Book 9. The last book presents motivations for practicing godliness from the excellence of the godly life, including the glorious God we serve, the glorious work that is accomplished, and the glorious fruits that result; the misery of the godless life, including the awful master that is served, the detestable work that is accomplished, and the shameful fruits that result; and the emptiness of material things with regard to this life, to death, and to life after death.

Throughout this book, Teellinck insists on the need for personal religious experience and the detailed regulation of Christian conduct in life, especially in regard to prayer, fasting, Christian education, and Sabbath observance.

This book should be widely read today. Teellinck's emphasis on promoting biblical, Reformed spirituality serves as a corrective to much false spirituality being marketed today. It also serves as an important corrective to orthodox teaching that presents truth to the mind but does not apply it to the heart and daily life. Teellinck helps us link a clear mind, a warm heart, and helping hands to serve God with the whole person. He fleshes out James's emphasis, saying to us on every page, "Show me your faith by your works" (cf. James 2:18). This is one of the best books available today on how to live a sanctified, Christian life.

Theodorus
van der Groe

(1705-1784)

Theodorus van der Groe is one of the last and most well-known representatives of the Dutch Further Reformation. After attending grade school and a school for Latin in his hometown of Swammerdam, he studied theology at Leiden upon the request of his father who was also a minister. The two professors who influenced him most were Johannes à Marck in church history and Taco Hajo van den Honert in dogmatics.

Van der Groe became a candidate for the ministry in 1729. In 1730, he was installed as a preacher at Rijnsaterwoude, a small village in South Holland. During his first pastorate, he was converted powerfully by God at the age of thirty, which profoundly influenced his preaching. Death in Adam and life in Christ became his primary themes. As one biographer notes, "It rang throughout all his preaching: to count all but loss and dung save the knowledge of Christ. It is no wonder that this manner of preaching met with opposition."

In 1740, van der Groe accepted a pastoral call to Kralingen, where he preached faithfully the whole counsel of God for the remaining forty-four years of his life. He preached an unfettered gospel, but also warned against sin, worldliness, and divine judgment. He was a watchman on Zion's walls, heralding forth law and gospel, breaking down the work of man and building up the work of God, separating saving faith from false forms of faith.

In the eighteenth-century debate on whether assurance of faith is to be regarded as of the essence of faith, van der Groe emphasized the necessity of assurance. He denied that faith was saving if it fell short of assured union with Christ. Van Thuynen and Themmen supported his position. Wilhelmus à Brakel, Driessen, Groenewegen, and Lampe opposed it. Comrie offered a mediating position, agreeing with the former group by maintaining that confidence and assurance certainly belong to the essence of faith, while leaning toward the latter group when he taught that some believers do not obtain full assurance of faith in this life.

Van der Groe was forty-nine years old when he married Johanna Bichon. During their married life, he was often ill, being of a weak constitution. He often wrote instructive letters from his sickbed to dear friends, which contained such experimental outpourings of heart as these: "With Lodenstein, I feel I am merely a dead dog before God. But I lean on Christ and am carried by Him. All my guilt lies reconciled and satisfied through Christ. I cannot bring two words together to form a true prayer, but Christ is my all."

Van der Groe died in 1784 in full assurance of faith, embracing the promises of God in Christ Jesus as his only expectation.

Throughout his writings, van der Groe emphasized the need for experimental application of the three great truths expounded by the Heidelberg Catechism: conviction of sin, deliverance in Christ, and growth in sanctification. His three-volume exposition of the Heidelberg Catechism (*Des Christens eenigen troost in leven en sterven of Verklaring van den Heidelbergsen Catechismus*) and two-volume *Toetsteen der ware en valsche Genade* (Touchstone of True and False Grace) are well-known in Dutch circles, as is his *Beschrijvinge van het oprecht en ziel-zaligend*

Geloove (Description of True, Saving Faith). Sermon volumes include *De genezing van de blinde Bartimeus* (The Healing of Blind Bartimaeus); a two-volume set of forty-eight sermons on the sufferings of Christ (*Acht-en-veertig Predikatien over het lijden van onzen Heere Jezus Christus*); a volume of seventeen sermons on conversion (*De Bekeering*); and two volumes for Prayer Day containing thirty sermons in all (*Verzameling van zestien Biddags-Predikatien; Veertien nagelatene Biddags-Predikatien*). Two volumes of his letters (*Brieven van Theodorus van der Groe*) were first published in 1838 and appeared in one volume in 1984.

Van der Groe showed his support for the translation of English Puritans into Dutch by writing an extensive preface to George Hutcheson's two-volume *Practical Explanation of the Minor Prophets* and his *Explanation of the Book of Job*. He prefaced other works translated from English as well—for example, the works of Ebenezer and Ralph Erskine.

The Prayer of the Publican (Zoar; 48 pages; 1976). This booklet, first published in Dutch as *De gelijkenis van den Tollenaar*, clearly sets forth the stark contrast between the prayer of the publican and that of the Pharisee. The publican's humility is shown through his penitent feet, penitent eyes, and penitent hands, which is then contrasted with the Pharisee's pride shown through his bold feet, bold eyes, and bold hands. The publican is concerned about his relation with God; the Pharisee, his relation with man. The publican pleads upon God's character of mercy; the Pharisee does not really pray at all. The publican goes to his home justified; the Pharisee returns condemned. Here is vintage, experiential Puritan material.

Johannes VanderKemp

(1664–1718)

Johannes VanderKemp is best known as a Dutch "old writer" (*oude schrijver*) for his Heidelberg Catechism sermons, which have been reprinted in Dutch more frequently than any other of the scores of Dutch sermon volumes on the Catechism.

Johannes was born to Cornelis VanderKemp and Trijntje van Andel in March 1664, and was baptized on March 20. Johannes's father died in 1673, and Johannes's mother supported the family as a hatmaker. Because of her industriousness, Johannes was able to study theology.

VanderKemp became a candidate for the ministry in 1691, and passed his classical exam on July 18, 1692. He was ordained that same year as a pastor in the Reformed church of Dirksland, where he remained for all twenty-six years of ministry. On November 17, 1718, he slumped over in the pulpit while preaching from 1 Peter 4:11: "If any man speak, let him speak as the oracles of God; if any man minister, let him do it as of the ability which God giveth: that God in all things may be glorified through Jesus Christ, to whom be praise and dominion for ever and ever. Amen." He died a few hours later, survived by his wife, Alida Rogge.

In addition to his *magnum opus* on the Heidelberg Catechism, VanderKemp wrote *De Verborgentheyd van de Verbonden Gods* (1710; The Mystery of the Covenants of God) and *Schets van 't Gebou der Voorbeelden: In zyne vaste gronden...ter beschouwing v. waerheyt en betrachting v. Godtzaligheidt uit Godts Woordt* (1715; A Sketch of the Building of Types, firmly grounded in God's Word, for the observation of the truth and the practice of godliness). He also published three short, experiential letters (*Drie Ondervindelyke Brieven*), originally written to friends whom he had pastored. Those letters, which deal with justification, were reprinted as recently as 1991 under the editorship of C.R. VandenBerg. Finally, VanderKemp prepared a shorter work on the Heidelberg Catechism using questions and answers, which his grandson Didericus published in 1746 (*De Heidelbergse Catechismus kortelyk geopend en verklaard by wyze van Vragen en Antwoorden*).

Several of Johannes VanderKemp's descendants inherited his love of theology. His son Cornelis (1700-1772) became pastor in Rotterdam, and later became professor at the Latin school there. Cornelis's son Didericus (1731-80) pastored at five Reformed congregations in the Netherlands before he became professor of church history and theology. Didericus's brother Johannes (1747-1811) became a missionary. Didericus's grandson Carel (1799-1862) became a well-known leader among the Reveil men, that is, those associated with the revival inaugurated under the preaching and financial support of Robert Haldane.

⸺◆⸺

The Christian Entirely the Property of Christ, in Life and Death, Exhibited in Fifty-three Sermons on the Heidelberg Catechism, trans. John M. Van Harlingen (RHB; 2 vols., 1,060 pages; 1997). VanderKemp's catechism exposition was first published in 1717, a year before he died. That same year, the theological faculty of Leiden University approved Vander Kemp's work for reading and study. The Leiden committee wrote, "We praise this honorable man's diligence and zeal to edify God's Church by mouth and pen." By 1779, the exposition had been printed nineteen times, and has been reprinted several times since. In 1810, John Van Harlingen, a Dutch Reformed pastor, translated VanderKemp's work into English. The 1997 printing is photolithographed from this edition.

VanderKemp's catechism sermons are remarkably readable even today. In his preface, VanderKemp states that he was already drawn to the Catechism in his youth. He says he was grieved when he heard people degrade the Catechism. In his sermons, VanderKemp emphasizes the biblical, doctrinal, experiential, and practical aspects of the Catechism. He admirably succeeds in writing a balanced work, avoiding the extremes of mysticism, speculation, and academics. Given our distance from VanderKemp's day, however, certain sermons may appear too polemical for our taste.

VanderKemp's sermons excel in heartfelt, pointed, and diverse applications. Preachers can learn much from his ability to bring God's truth to bear upon every sphere of our daily lives. VanderKemp was an educated, godly, and wise divine who still speaks to us today.

GISBERTUS VOETIUS

Gisbertus Voetius
(1589-1676)

Gisbertus Voetius represents the mature fruit of the Dutch Further Reformation and ranks among the most influential Dutch Reformed theologians of all time. He was to the Dutch Further Reformation what John Owen, often called the prince of the Puritans, was to English Puritanism. Though largely unknown and ignored by English-speaking scholarship, Voetius is an in-house name to students of Dutch Post-Reformation orthodoxy. Voetius wedded a Reformed scholastic methodology to heartfelt piety. Standing at the pinnacle of scholasticism immediately prior to its disintegration, Voetius illustrates how orthodox Reformed theologians used scholasticism as a methodology which, contrary to the oft-repeated caricature, promoted neither a departure from Calvin's theology nor a dead orthodoxy. Voetius serves as proof that, historically speaking, the expression "dead orthodoxy" is a misnomer, for such orthodoxy has never been orthodox. Orthodox Reformed scholastics like Voetius have always resonated with a vital warmth and heartfelt piety.

Gisbertus Voetius was born on March 3, 1589, at Heusden, the Netherlands, to a prominent family of Westphalian descent and Reformed persuasion. His grandfather had died in a Spanish prison for the sake of the gospel; his father narrowly escaped a similar fate the month Gisbertus was born, only to be killed eight years later while fighting for Prince Maurice. Not surprisingly, Gisbertus imbibed Reformed doctrine and convictions from early childhood.

Voetius studied theology at the University of Leiden from 1604 to 1611 when it was the focal point of the Arminian crisis. He was particularly influenced by the lectures of Franciscus Gomarus, a staunch Calvinist. He also attended lectures of Jacobus Arminius and other professors whose orthodoxy was called into question. He would later write, "I shall be Gomarus's grateful disciple to the end of my life."

Appointed lecturer in logic while a student at Leiden, Voetius defended orthodox Reformed theology in his teaching. In terms of methodology, he leaned on the humanistic Aristotelianism of Leiden rather than on Ramism, which insisted on the purely instrumental and non-autonomous role of philosophy. Voetius did not accept the conviction of other Calvinists, such as William Ames, who felt that Peter Ramus was a safer guide than Aristotle for methodology in doing theology. He was convinced that the new Aristotelianism had absorbed everything of value in Ramism and consequently regarded the Ramistic controversy as superfluous.

Already in his Leiden years, Voetius showed a keen interest in a more pietistic form of theology. He read Thomas à Kempis's *The Imitation of Christ* with deep appreciation. From that time on, two elements strove for preeminence in his life and work: an intellectual Reformed scholasticism and a piety resembling the *devotio moderna* ("modern devotion") spirit, a form of spiritual life exemplified in à Kempis's classic.

The temporary victory of the Arminians in 1610 had far-reaching consequences for Voetius. His mentor, Gomarus, was forced from the faculty, Arminians were hired, and Voetius's own hopes for an academic career were dashed. For supporting Gomarus and opposing Arminius, he was put out of his dormitory and had to take up lodging with friends. After finishing his studies and returning to Heusden, he attempted in vain to obtain a grant from the magistrates to study in England or other foreign centers of Reformed theology. Instead, he accepted a call from an unorganized group of Reformed-minded folk at Vlijmen, a small town near 's-Hertogenbosch, to whom he was recommended by Gomarus. He was ordained to the ministry on September 25, 1611, at the age of twenty-two. The following year, he organized the Vlijmen flock with the installation of elders and deacons. His first pastorate was not easy, for the village was predominantly Roman Catholic. Though he was instrumental in bringing some Roman Catholics to the Reformed faith, the Vlijmen church remained small during his six years of ministry there.

During these years, Voetius became deeply involved in battling Arminianism. He also continued to apply himself to diligent study, mastering Arabic and reading the works of numerous divines, including a special study of the popular works of William Perkins. In 1612, he married Deliana van Diest, with whom he had sixty-four years of marriage and ten children—two of whom would also become professors of philosophy at Utrecht.

In 1617, Voetius commenced a seventeen-year pastorate in Heusden. His call there was opposed by the senior minister, Johannes Grevius, as well as by Johan van Oldenbarnevelt, a leading statesman, both of whom were partial to the Remonstrants. By 1618, Heusden's internal difficulties were catapulted to national prominence. A failed attempt made by the national government to send Hugo Grotius, a well-known jurist, statesman, and theologian, to Heusden to influence the local magistracy during an election led the consistory of Heusden to take revenge by dismissing Grevius. The government then compelled the reinstatement of Grevius, which led to an open schism that was ended only by the Orangist revolution.

Voetius's hard work in combating the errors of Romanism and Arminianism earned him an appointment to the international Synod of Dort (1618-19) despite his youth. Two items of interest surface in his attendance at Dort: first, his most prominent action was his defense of Johannes Maccovius, whose supralapsarian conception of predestination was of a more logically rigid nature than that of most other delegates. Voetius appealed to the authority of William Ames, who had expressed confidence in Maccovius's intentions, though he regretted some of his terminology. Second, Voetius later wrote appreciatively of close friendships established with a number of English delegates noted for their emphasis on Puritan theology and practice.

Voetius's influence and stature increased after Dort. On several occasions in the 1620s, the Provincial Synod of South Holland appointed him as deputy in matters that related to the Synod of Dort, such as caring for the archives of the Synod; involvement with the final approval of the Church Order of Dort; membership in the commission charged with purging Leiden of Arminian influence; dealing with the holding of conventicles by the Arminian faction in various places; and dealing with Gerhardus Vossius, rector of the Latin school at Dordrecht, whose book on Pelagianism gave the Arminians fodder for their unreformed convictions.

Then, too, Voetius gained renown as a writer during his Heusden years. His pamphlet wars against Roman Catholics and Arminians raised his stature among the Reformed as a first-rate scholastic theologian. His work against the Arminian, Daniel Tilenus, influenced Grotius. Even more importantly, his *Proeve van de Cracht der Godsalichheydt* (1627; Proof of the Power of Godliness) and *Meditatie van de Ware Practijcke der Godsalicheydt of der goede Wercken* (1628; Meditation on the True Practice of Godliness or Good Works) established him as a writer of practical piety who insisted on a converted life as the attestation of an orthodox faith.

One of Voetius's most important accomplishments during his Heusden years was his major role in assisting the reformation of the city of 's-Hertogenbosch. This reform, which he served as an army chaplain, led him into debates and pamphlet wars with Cornelis Jansenis and Samuel Maresius. His debates with Maresius concerning virtually every theological issue of the day were to last four decades until the two theologians united to battle the emergence of Cartesianism in the late 1660s.

While pastoring in Heusden, Voetius revealed his heart for missions. He was influential in persuading various trading companies to send missionaries with the Dutch ships to distant parts of the world. Moreover, as H.A. Van Andel points out, "Voetius attempted not only to sketch the outlines of a solid theology of missions, but he was also the first who attempted seriously to give missiology a legitimate scientific place in the whole of theology" (*De Zendingsleer van Gisbertus Voetius*, p. 19). It is remarkable that the greatest Dutch scholastic of Reformed orthodoxy developed the first comprehensive Protestant theology of missions.

For seventeen years, Voetius kept up a rigorous schedule at Heusden. He preached eight times a week and pastored faithfully and incessantly, especially by giving counsel to weak and disturbed consciences. Meanwhile, he continued to study avidly, keeping up with his Arabic and tutoring students in theology, logic, metaphysics, and oriental languages. After declining calls to other, larger churches, including Rotterdam, Dordrecht, and The Hague, Voetius accepted a professorial post in the new Academy of Utrecht, where he taught for forty-two years until his death in 1676.

In his lectures, Voetius focused particularly on systematic theology, ethics, and church polity. He also taught logic, metaphysics, and the Semitic languages: Hebrew, Arabic, and Syriac. For thirty-six of his forty-two years as professor in Utrecht, Voetius carried a half-time preaching and pastoral schedule. He refused to relinquish visiting the sick and regularly catechized Utrecht's orphan children.

Meanwhile, Voetius' private study and his literary output continued apace. In 1664, he published *Exercitia et Bibliotheca studiosi theologae* (The Exercises and Library of a Studious Theologian), a comprehensive 700-page introduction to theological literature and a four-year program of theological study. Its theme is one with his overall vision: theology must be known and practiced. Voetius's most academic works were published over a twenty-two-year span in his five volumes of selections from his theological debates, *Selectarum disputationum theologicarum* (1648-69). These volumes are the outgrowth of his famous Saturday seminars. These seminars took the following form: Voetius himself composed theses, especially touching on the pressing issues of the day, and appointed debaters who were instructed on how to defend them. Other students sought to challenge the debaters. The five volumes of these debates, similar to medieval debate texts, do not contain verbatim reports, but the final redaction of the whole by Voetius himself. In addition, Voetius published four volumes on church polity, *Politicae Ecclesiasticae* (1663-76), which also grew out of the Saturday debates. He evidenced a working knowledge of all the literature on church government of his day, including polemical works and works dealing with the ancient creeds. More than any other major work, *Politicae Ecclesiasticae* represents the ecclesiastical ideals of the Dutch Further Reformation. Together with these works, Voetius wrote his *Ta Asketika sive Exercitia Pietatis* (1654; "Ascetica" or the Exercises of Godliness), a detailed manual of piety in theory and practice. (Cornelis A. de Niet edited a scholarly edition of *Ta Asketika* in 1996, which includes both the Latin version and a Dutch translation.)

In all these works, Voetius reveals himself as a scholastic, practical theologian who did not fear conflict. While at Utrecht, he unceasingly opposed Johannes Cocceius, the Bremen-born theologian who taught at Franeker and Leiden, and

whose covenant theology, in Voetius's opinion, overempha-
sized the historical and contextual character of specific ages.
He believed that Cocceius's new approach to the Scriptures
would undermine both Reformed dogmatics and practical
Christianity. He battled the philosophy of René Descartes,
which he was convinced placed reason on a par with Scripture at the expense of faith, and therefore was destructive for
the church. He recognized the danger in Cartesianism that ultimately man becomes the measure of all things. He resisted
Jean de Labadie, whose preaching had been the source of spiritual revival in Swiss Reformed churches, for promoting
notions of mystical subjectivism and of separation from the
instituted church. He spoke out against the government when
the rights of the church were at stake, rejecting Erastianism
and demanding that the church be completely independent of
the state and of all patronage.

As a polemical theologian, Voetius's firm position and ve-
hement attacks isolated him. Loneliness assailed him on such
occasions, but he viewed it as part of the price he was called
to pay for taking a stand for biblical, Reformed truth. Over
the decades at Utrecht, however, a group of friends and students, nicknamed the "Utrecht circle," came to appreciate
and support his convictions. By the time of his death on November 1, 1676, dedicated Voetians were to be found in every
university and ecclesiastical province of the Netherlands. He
was mourned by thousands, especially by the Utrecht circle,
and was buried in what is now the Roman Catholic cathedral
of Utrecht.

Cornelis Gentman rightly said of Voetius at his funeral
that he was "a giant among trail blazers." Through his two important offices as professor and preacher, Voetius made
Utrecht a stronghold of orthodoxy. His writings disseminated
his thought throughout and beyond the Netherlands. His

influence was so widespread at the university that it was frequently called the *Academia Voetiana*.

Voetius has been underestimated as a Reformed scholastic and experiential theologian in the Netherlands and throughout Europe, and even more so by British and North American scholarship. Though not a creator of a new theology, he was a competent systematizer who influenced thousands. Moreover, he was instrumental in training hundreds of ministers who, following in his footsteps, strove to maintain a harmonious union between scholasticism and godliness. His teaching also attracted many Presbyterian Scots and nonconformist English students. To many of his students, his theology became a program. His ideals were formulated into what became known (contrary to his wishes) as "the Voetians" or "the Voetian party." With their powerful combination of orthodox doctrine and vital piety, the Voetians were far more successful at reaching the common people than were the Cocceians.

Spiritual Desertion, with Johannes Hoornbeek, ed. M. Eugene Osterhaven, trans. John Vriend and Harry Boonstra (Baker; 176 pages; 2003). See review under Hoornbeek.

Herman Witsius
(1636-1708)

Herman Wits (Latinized as Witsius) was born on February 12, 1636, at Enkhuizen, to God-fearing parents who dedicated their firstborn to the Lord. His father, Nicholas Wits, was a man of some renown, having been an elder for more than twenty years, a member of Enkhuizen's city council, and a writer of devotional poetry. Witsius's mother, Johanna, was a daughter of Herman Gerard, pastor for thirty years of the Reformed church in Enkhuizen. Herman was named after his grandfather with the prayer that he might emulate his godly example.

Witsius began Latin studies at age five. Three years later, his uncle, Peter Gerard, noticing the boy's gifts, began to tutor him. By the time Witsius took up theological studies in Utrecht at age fifteen, he could speak Latin fluently, read Greek and Hebrew, and had memorized numerous Scriptures in their original languages. At Utrecht, he studied Syriac and Arabic under Johannes Leusden and theology under Johannes Hoornbeek, whom he called "my teacher of undying memory." He also studied under Andreas Essenius, whom he honored as "my father in the Lord," and Gisbertus Voetius, whom he called "the great Voetius."

After studying theology and homiletics with Samuel Maresius at Groningen, Witsius returned in 1653 to Utrecht, where he was profoundly influenced by the local pastor, Justus van der Bogaerdt. According to Witsius's later testimony,

HERMAN WITSIUS

van der Bogaerdt's preaching and fellowship brought him experientially to understand the difference between theological knowledge gleaned from study and the heavenly wisdom taught by the Holy Spirit through communion with God, love, prayer, and meditation. Witsius wrote that he was born again in "the bosom of the Utrecht church by the living and eternal Word of God." Through this godly pastor's influence, Witsius said, he was preserved "from the pride of science, taught to receive the kingdom of heaven as a little child, led beyond the outer court in which he had previously been inclined to linger, and conducted to the sacred recesses of vital Christianity."

As a teenager, Witsius had demonstrated his gifts in public debate. In 1655, he defeated some of the leading debaters at the University of Utrecht by showing that the doctrine of the Trinity could be proven from the writings of ancient Jews. The following year, Witsius passed his final examinations and was declared a candidate for the ministry.

In 1657, Witsius was ordained into the ministry at Westwoud. His catechizing of young people there bore special fruit, but he also encountered opposition because of the congregation's ignorance of their Reformed heritage. Medieval customs such as praying for the dead were still evident among the people. These problems convinced Witsius early in his ministry of the need for further Reformation among the people. It also prompted him to publish his first book, 't bedroefde Nederlant (The Sorrowing Netherlands).

In 1660, Witsius married Aletta van Borchorn, daughter of a merchant who was an elder in Witsius's church. They were blessed with twenty-four years of marriage. Aletta said she could not tell what was greater—her love or her respect for her husband. The couple had five children—two sons, who died young, and three daughters: Martina, Johanna, and Petronella.

In 1661, Witsius was installed in the church at Wormer —one of Holland's largest churches—where he succeeded in uniting warring factions and training the people in divine knowledge. He and his colleague, Petrus Goddaeus, took turns teaching a doctrinal class on weekday evenings to "defend the truth of our teachings against false doctrines" and to inculcate "the sanctity of our teachings in terms of God-fearing conduct." The class began in private homes, then outgrew that space and moved to the church. Eventually people had to stand outside the church due to lack of room. These class lectures were eventually published in a book titled *Practycke des Christendoms* (The Practice of Christianity), to which Witsius appended *Geestelycke Printen van een Onwedergeborenen op syn beste en een Wedergeborenen op syn slechste* (A Spiritual Picture of the Unregenerate at His Best and the Regenerate at His Worst).

Practycke des Christendoms explains the primary grounds of godliness, while the appended work applies those grounds by teaching what is laudable in the unregenerate and what is culpable in the regenerate. John Owen said he hoped he could be as consistent as Witsius's unregenerate man at his best and that he would never fall so deeply as Witsius's regenerate man at his worst.

Witsius accepted a call to Goes in 1666, where he labored for two years. In the preface to *Twist des Heeren met syn Wijngaert* (The Lord's Controversy with His Vineyard), published in Leeuwarden in 1669, he said he had labored with much peace in this congregation together with three colleagues, "two of whom were venerated as fathers, and the third was loved as a brother." Of these four ministers working together in one congregation, Witsius noted: "We walked together in fellowship to God's house. We did not only attend each other's services, but also each other's catechism classes and other public services, so that what one servant of God might have taught yesterday, the others confirmed and recommended to the congregation the next day." Under the influence of these four ministers, "all sorts of devotional practices blossomed, piety grew, and the unity of God's people was enhanced," Witsius wrote.

After serving Goes, Witsius went to his fourth pastoral charge, Leeuwarden, where he served for seven years (1668-1675). In 1672, called the "Year of Disaster" (*rampjaar*) because the Dutch Republic was attacked by four enemies who had declared war on the Netherlands (France, England, and the German electorates of Cologne and Munster), Witsius gained renown for faithful ministry in the midst of crisis. Johannes à Marck, a future colleague, said of Witsius that he knew of no other minister whose labors were so owned of God. In 1673, Witsius again teamed up with a renowned colleague— this time, Wilhelmus à Brakel, with whom he served two years. At Leeuwarden, Witsius played a critical role mediating disputes between Voetius and Maresius.

In 1675, Witsius was called to be a professor of theology. He served in this capacity for the rest of his life, first at Franeker (1675-80), then at Utrecht (1680-98), and finally at Leiden (1698-1707). Shortly after his arrival at Franeker, the university there awarded Witsius a doctorate in theology. His inaugural address, *On the Character of a True Theologian* (1675), which was attended by scholars from all over the province, stressed the difference between a theologian who knows his subject only scholastically and a theologian who knows his subject experientially. Under Witsius's leadership the university began to flourish as a place to study theology, especially after the arrival of the twenty-one-year-old professor, Johannes à Marck, in 1678. It soon attracted students from all over Europe.

During his professorship at Franeker, tension between the Voetians and the Cocceians escalated. Witsius's concern about this controversy moved him to publish *De Oeconomia Foederum Dei cum Hominibus* (1677), first printed in English in 1736 as *The Economy of the Covenants between God and Man, comprehending a Complete Body of Divinity*. It was reprinted numerous times, most recently in two volumes by the den Dulk Christian Foundation in 1990 (see below). In governing his systematic theology by the concept of covenant, Witsius uses Cocceian methods while maintaining essentially Voetian theology. In his work on the covenants, Witsius argued against Roman Catholicism, Arminianism, Socinianism, and those Dutch Protestant theologians who, with Hugo Grotius, had exchanged a *sola scriptura* theology for an institutionalized, sacramental view of the church based on traditions that paved the way back to Rome.

Witsius next went to Utrecht, where he labored for eighteen years as professor and pastor. Students from all over the Protestant world attended his lectures; magistrates attended his sermons. On two occasions, his colleagues honored him with the headship of the university (1686, 1697).

In 1685, the States General appointed Witsius as a delegate to represent the Dutch government at the coronation of James II and to serve as chaplain to the Netherlands Embassy in London. While there he met the archbishop of Canterbury as well as several leading theologians. He studied Puritan theology and enhanced his stature in England as a peacemaker. Later, the English church called on him to serve as a mediating figure between antinomians and neonomians—the former accusing the latter of overemphasizing the law, the latter accusing the former of minimizing the law. Out of this came his *Conciliatory Animadversions*, a treatise on the antinomian controversy in England. In this treatise, Witsius argued that God's starting point in His eternal decrees did not demean His activity in time. He also helped facilitate the translation into Dutch of some of the works of Thomas Goodwin, William Cave, and Thomas Gataker and wrote prefaces for them.

Witsius's years at Utrecht were not free from strife. He felt obliged to oppose the theology of Professor Herman A. Roell, who advocated a unique mixture of the biblical

theology of Johannes Cocceius and the rationalistic philosophy of René Descartes. Witsius felt that this combination
threatened the authority of Scripture. Witsius taught the superiority of faith over reason to protect the purity of Scripture.
Reason lost its purity in the fall, he said. Though reason is a
critical faculty, it remains imperfect, even in the regenerate. It
is not an autonomous judge, but a servant of faith. Clearly
Witsius's understanding of who God is affected his understanding of how we know what we know and that Scripture
is the final standard of truth rather than our reason. His
knowledge of God through the Scriptures shaped all his
thinking, as is evident in his defense of the penal substitution
of Christ against the rationalist Socinus.

Subsequently, Witsius opposed rationalism in the teachings of Balthasar Bekker as well as the popular, separatistic
ideas of Jean de Labadie. He admitted that the Reformed
churches were seriously flawed, but he strongly opposed separating from the church.

At Utrecht, Witsius published three volumes of *Exercita-
tiones Sacrae* (Sacred Exercises), two on the Apostles' Creed
(1681) and one on the Lord's Prayer (1689). Second in importance only to his *Economy of the Covenants*, these books stress
the truths of the gospel in a pure, clear manner. The three
works birthed in a seminary setting are known as Witsius's
trilogy (see below).

In the midst of his busy years at Utrecht (1684), Witsius's
wife died. His daughter Petronella, who never married, remained with her father, faithfully caring for him through his
twenty-four years as a widower.

When he was sixty-two years old, Witsius accepted a call
to serve at the university at Leiden as professor. His inaugural
address was on "The Modest Theologian." At Leiden he
trained men from Europe, Great Britain, and America,

including several Native Americans who had been converted through the work of John Eliot.

In 1699, Holland and West Friesland appointed Witsius inspector of the University's theological college. It was a position he held until he retired in 1707 because of ill health. In his last six years he suffered painful bouts of gout, dizziness, and memory lapses. After a serious attack in October of 1708, he told friends that his homecoming was near. Four days later, he died at the age of seventy-two after nearly fifty-two years of ministry. During his last hour, he told his close friend, Johannes à Marck, that he was persevering in the faith that he had long enjoyed in Christ.

Witsius had many gifts. All his life he was a humble biblical and systematic theologian, dependent on the Scriptures. He was also a faithful preacher. For him, Christ—in the university, on the pulpit, and in daily living—took preeminence. As an exegete, he exhibited scriptural simplicity and precision. As a historian, he measured movements against the ideal, apostolic church, bringing history and theology from numerous sources to bear upon his reasoning. As a theologian, he grounded spiritual life in regeneration and covenantally applied the entire order of salvation to practical, experiential living. As an ethicist, he set forth Christ as the perfect example in probing the heart and guiding the believer in his walk of life. As a polemicist, he opposed Cartesianism, Labadism, antinomianism, neonomianism, and the excesses of Cocceianism. As a homiletician, he, like William Perkins, stressed the marks of grace to encourage believers and convict nominal Christians.

Witsius influenced many theologians in his lifetime: Campegius Vitringa and Bernardus Smytegelt in the Netherlands, Friedrich Lampe in Germany, and Thomas Boston and the Erskine brothers (Ralph and Ebenezer) in Scotland. James Hervey commended him as "a most excellent author, all of whose works have such a delicacy of composition, and such a

sweet savour of holiness, [like] the golden pot which had
manna, and was outwardly bright with burnished gold, inwardly rich with heavenly food."

The Apostles' Creed (P&R; 2 vols., 1,170 pages; 1993). More
than a century after Witsius's death, two of his most significant works were translated into English: *Sacred Dissertations on
what is commonly called The Apostles' Creed*, translated by Donald
Fraser, 2 vols. (Glasgow, 1823), and *Sacred Dissertations on the
Lord's Prayer*, translated by Rev. William Pringle (Edinburgh,
1839; see below). Both of these works are judicious, practical,
pointed, and edifying. They are meat for the soul.

Witsius's two-volume work on the Apostles' Creed, originally published in Latin at Franeker in 1681, grew out of
lectures he gave to his students at the University of Franeker.
His exposition of the creed begins with studies that discuss
its title, authorship, and authority; the role of fundamental articles; and the nature of saving faith. The creed's authority is
great but not supreme, Witsius said. It contains fundamental
articles that are limited to those truths "without which neither faith nor repentance can exist" and "to the rejection of
which God has annexed a threatening of destructions." It is
scarcely possible to determine the number of fundamental articles. Some are not contained in the creed but are taken up in
lengthier doctrinal standards.

Witsius again addressed the acts of saving faith, affirming
that the "principal act" of faith is the "receiving of Christ for
justification, sanctification, and complete salvation." He
stressed that faith receives "a whole Christ," and that "he cannot be a Saviour, unless he be also a Lord." He reasserted the
validity of obtaining assurance of faith by syllogistic conclusions and distinguished temporary faith from saving faith.
Because temporary faith can remain until the end of a person's
life, Witsius preferred to call it presumptuous faith. These

kinds of faith differ in their knowledge of the truth, their application of the gospel, their joy, and their fruits (1:56-60).

The remainder of the work follows a phrase-by-phrase 800-page exposition of the creed, accompanied by more than 200 pages of notes added by the translator. Throughout, Witsius excels in exegesis, remains faithful to Reformed dogmatics without becoming overly scholastic, applies every article of the creed to the believer's soul, and, when occasion warrants, exposes various heresies. His closing chapter on life everlasting is perhaps the most sublime. His concluding applications summarize his approach:

- From this sublime doctrine, let us learn the Divine origin of the Gospel
- Let us carefully inquire whether we ourselves have a solid hope of this glorious felicity
- Let us labor diligently, lest we come short of it
- Let us comfort ourselves with the hope of it amidst all our adversities
- Let us walk worthy of it by leading a heavenly life in this world (2:xvi, 470-83).

The Economy of the Covenants Between God and Man (P&R; 2 vols., 960 pages; 1990). Witsius wrote his *magnum opus* on the covenants to promote peace among Dutch theologians who were divided on covenant theology. He sought to be a theologian of synthesis who strove to lessen tension between the Voetians and the Cocceians. He wrote in his introduction that "the enemies of our church...secretly rejoice that there are as many and as warm disputes amongst ourselves, as with them. And this, not very secretly neither: for they do not, nor will ever cease to cast this reproach upon us; which, I grieve to say is not so easily wiped away. O! how much better would it be to use our utmost endeavours, to lessen, make up, and, if it could be, put an end to all controversy!" (1:22-23).

Economy of the Covenants is not a complete systematic theology, though its title claims that it comprehends "a complete body of divinity." Several major doctrines not addressed here, such as Trinity, creation, and providence, were dealt with later in Witsius's exposition of the Apostles' Creed.

For Witsius, the doctrine of the covenants is the best way of reading Scripture. The covenants are for him what J. I. Packer calls "a successful hermeneutic," or a consistent interpretative procedure yielding a proper understanding of Scripture, both law and gospel. Witsius's work is divided into four books:

- Book I: The Covenant of Works (120 pages)
- Book II: The Covenant of Redemption, or The Covenant of Grace from Eternity Between the Father and the Son (118 pages)
- Book III: The Covenant of Grace in Time (295 pages)
- Book IV: Covenant Ordinances Throughout the Scriptures (356 pages).

Throughout his exposition of covenant theology, Witsius corrected inadequacies of the Cocceians and infused Voetian content. He treated each topic analytically, drawing from other Reformed and Puritan systematicians to move the reader to clarity of mind, warmth of heart, and godliness of life.

In Book 1, Witsius discusses divine covenants in general, focusing on etymological and exegetical considerations related to them (*běrîth* and *diathēkē*). He notes promise, oath, pledge, and command as well as a mutual pact that combines promise and law. He concludes that covenant, in its proper sense, "signifies a mutual agreement between parties with respect to something" (Book 1, ch. 1, par. 3-5—hereafter 1.1.3-5). Then he defines covenant as "an agreement between God and man, about the method of obtaining ultimate blessedness, with the addition of a threat of eternal destruction, against anyone contemptuous of this blessedness" (1.1.9). The essence of the covenant, then, is the relationship of love between God and man.

Covenants between God and man are essentially monopleuric (one-sided) covenants in the sense that they can be initiated only by God and are grounded in "the utmost majesty of the most high God." Though initiated by God, these covenants call for human consent to the covenant, to exercise the responsibility of obedience within it and to acquiesce in punishment in case of violation. In the covenant of works, that responsibility is partly gracious and partly meritorious, whereas in the covenant of grace, it is wholly gracious in response to God's election and Christ's fulfillment of all conditions of the covenant (1.1.15).

Nevertheless, all covenants between God and man are dipleuric (two-sided) in administration. Both aspects are important. Without the monopleuric emphasis on God's part, covenant initiation and fulfillment would not be by grace alone; without the dipleuric emphasis of divine initiation and human responsibility, man would be passive in covenant administration. The attempt made by contemporary scholars to force seventeenth-century federal theologians into either a monopleuric or dipleuric concept of the covenant misses the mark, as Richard Muller has shown.

According to Witsius, the covenant of works consists of the contracting parties (God and Adam), the law or condition (perfect obedience), the promises (eternal life in heaven for unqualified veneration to divine law), the penal sanction (death), and the sacraments (Paradise, the tree of life, the tree of knowledge of good and evil, the Sabbath). Throughout, Witsius stressed the relationship of the covenant parties in terms of the Reformed concept of covenant. He claimed that denying the covenant of works causes serious Christological and soteriological errors.

For example, the violation of the covenant of works by Adam and Eve rendered the promises of the covenant inaccessible to their descendants. Those promises were abrogated by God, who cannot lower His standard of law by recasting the covenant of works to account for fallen man's unrighteousness. Divine abrogation, however, does not annul the demand of God for perfect obedience. Rather, because of the stability of God's promise and His law, the covenant of grace is made effective in Christ, the perfect Law-fulfiller. In fulfilling all the conditions of the covenant of grace, Christ fulfilled all the conditions of the covenant of works. Thus "the covenant of grace is not the abolition, but rather the confirmation of the covenant of works, inasmuch as the Mediator has fulfilled all the conditions of that covenant, so that all believers may be justified and saved according to the covenant of works, to which satisfaction was made by the Mediator," Witsius wrote (1.11.23).

Witsius outlines the relationship of the covenant of works to the covenant of grace in his second book. He discusses the covenant of grace from eternity, or, the covenant of redemption as the *pactum salutis* between God the Father and God the Son (2.2-4). In the eternal *pactum*, the Father solicited from the Son acts of obedience for the elect, while pledging ownership of the elect to the Son. This "agreement between God and the Mediator" makes possible the covenant of grace between God and His elect. The covenant of grace "presupposes" the covenant of grace from eternity and "is founded upon it" (2.2.1).

The covenant of redemption established God's remedy for the problem of sin. The covenant of redemption is the answer for the covenant of works abrogated by sin. The Son binds Himself to work out that answer by fulfilling the promises and conditions and bearing the penalties of the covenant on behalf of the elect.

This covenant of grace worked out in time (Book 3) is the core of Witsius's work, and covers the entire field of soteriology. By treating the *ordo salutis* within the framework of the covenant of grace, Witsius asserts that former presentations of covenant doctrine were superior to newer ones. He shows how covenant theology binds theologians together rather than drives them apart.

Though the "internal, mystical, and spiritual communion" of the covenant is established within the elect, there is also an external economy or administration of the covenant. Those who are baptized and raised with the means of grace are in the covenant externally, though many of them "are not in the testament of God" in terms of being saved (3.1.5).

Effectual calling is the first fruit of election, which in turn works regeneration. Regeneration is the infusion of new life in the spiritually dead person. Thus the incorruptible seed of the Word is made fruitful by the Spirit's power. Witsius argued that so-called "preparations" to regeneration, such as breaking of the will, serious consideration of the law and conviction of sin, and fear of hell and despairing of salvation are fruits of regeneration rather than preparations when the Spirit uses them to lead sinners to Christ (3.6.11-15).

The first act of this new life is faith. Faith, in turn, produces various acts: (1) knowing Christ, (2) assenting to the gospel, (3) loving the truth, (4) hungering and thirsting after Christ, (5) receiving Christ for salvation, (6) reclining upon Christ, (7) receiving Christ as Lord, and (8) appropriating the promises of the gospel. The first three acts are called preceding acts; the next three, essential acts; the last two, following acts.

Witsius is solidly Reformed on justification by faith alone. He speaks of the elect being justified not only in Christ's death and resurrection, but already in the giving of the first gospel promise in Genesis 3:15. Applications of justification to the individual believer occur at his regeneration, in the court of his conscience, in daily communion with God, after death, and on the Judgment Day.

Sanctification is the work of God by which the justified sinner is increasingly "transformed from the turpitude of sin, to the purity of the divine image" (3.12.11). Mortification and vivification show the extensiveness of sanctification. Grace, faith, and love are motives for growing in holiness. The goals and means of sanctification are explained in detail. Nevertheless, because believers do not attain perfection in this life, Witsius concludes by examining the doctrine of Perfectionism. God does not grant perfection to us in this life for four reasons: to display the difference between earth and heaven, warfare and triumph, toil and rest; to teach us patience, humility, and sympathy; to teach us that salvation is by grace alone; and to demonstrate the wisdom of God in gradually perfecting us (3.12.121-24).

After explaining the doctrine of perseverance, Witsius ends his third book with a detailed account of glorification. Glorification begins in this life with the firstfruits of grace: holiness, the vision of God apprehended by faith and an experimental sense of God's goodness, the gracious enjoyment of God, full assurance of faith, and joy unspeakable. It is consummated in the life to come.

Book 4 presents covenant theology from the perspective of biblical theology. Witsius offers some aspects of what would later be called progressive revelation, emphasizing the faith of Abraham, the nature of the Mosaic covenant, the role of the law, the sacraments of the Old Testament, and the blessings and defects of the Old Testament. Some of his most fascinating sections deal with the Decalogue as a national covenant with Israel rather than as a formal covenant of works or covenant of grace, his defense of the Old Testament against false charges, and his explanation of the ceremonial law's abrogation and the relationship between the covenant of works and the covenant of grace. He then explains the relationship between the testaments and the sacraments of the New Testament era. He strongly supported the restoration of Israel according to Romans 11:25-27 (4.15.7). He sets Christian liberty in the context of freedom from the tyranny of the devil, the reigning and condemning power of sin, the rigor of the law, the laws of men, things indifferent, and death itself.

In summary, Witsius was one of the first theologians among Dutch Further Reformation divines who drew close ties between the doctrines of election and covenant. He aimed for reconciliation between orthodoxy and federalism, while stressing biblical theology as a proper study in itself.

The Cocceians did not respond kindly to Witsius's efforts to reconcile them and the Voetians. They accused him of extending the covenant of grace back into eternity, thereby helping the Reformed orthodox negate the Cocceian principle of the historical development of redemption.

Witsius's work on covenant theology became a standard work in the Netherlands, Scotland, England, and New England. Throughout this work, he stressed that the motto "the Reformed church needs to be ever reforming" (*ecclesia reformata, semper reformanda*) should be applied to the church's life and not to doctrine, since Reformation doctrine was foundational truth. His emphasis was on experiencing the reality of the covenant with God by faith and the need for godly, precise living.

The Lord's Prayer (P&R; 420 pages; 1994). Like Witsius's work on the Apostles' Creed, *Sacred Dissertations on the Lord's Prayer* was based on lectures delivered to his theological students. As such, it is a bit heavy with Hebrew and Greek words; however, Pringle's translation includes a rendering of most words of the original languages into English.

The Lord's Prayer contains more than its title reveals. In his preface to a 230-page exposition of the Lord's Prayer, Witsius devoted 150 pages to the subject of prayer: "First, to explain what is prayer; next, in what our obligation to it consists; and lastly, in what manner it ought to be performed." Though parts of this introduction seem a bit dated (especially chapter 4), most of it is practical and insightful. For example, Witsius's dissertation "On the Preparation of the Mind for Right Prayer" contains valuable guidance on a subject seldom addressed today.

Throughout this introduction, Witsius established that genuine prayer is the pulse of the renewed soul. The constancy of its beat is the test of spiritual life.

Witsius's exposition of the individual petitions of the Lord's Prayer is a masterpiece. In many instances, the questions receive greater instruction from Witsius's pen than anyone else to date. For example, where else can such insight be found on whether the infant believer and the unregenerate should use the name Father in addressing God (pp. 168-70)?

Witsius stressed that those who would have God hear them when they pray must hear and obey Him when He speaks. Prayer and work must both be engaged in. To pray without working is to mock God; to work without praying is to rob Him of His glory.

On the Character of a True Theologian (RAP; 59 pages; 1994). This 1675 essay was Witsius's renowned inaugural address at Franeker. The Free Church of Scotland valued this address so highly that it distributed nearly one thousand copies to its divinity students free of charge in 1856.

On the Character of a True Theologian is a masterpiece that exemplifies Witsius's own dictum, "He alone is a true theologian who adds the practical to the theoretical part of religion." Like all of Witsius's writings, this address marries profound intellect with spiritual passion. All ministers and theological teachers and students would do well to peruse it prayerfully and repeatedly.

APPENDIX 4

———◈◈◈———

Secondary Sources on the Puritans

"Our books may come to be seen where ourselves shall never be heard. These may preach where the author cannot, and (which is more) when he is not." This prediction by one of the great Puritans has had many fulfilments. An ungodly Welsh clergyman, shopping at a fair in the eighteenth century, bought an article which happened to be wrapped in a page torn from an old Puritan folio. The reading of that one page led to his sound conversion. As Luther said, "Satan hates the use of pens," and never were pens more powerfully wielded in the cause of God than by the Puritan divines of the seventeenth century. Nor have their books outlived their usefulness. Although the original volumes are worn with age, the truths found in them are as fresh as the new formats in which they are now appearing.

—John Brentnall

Secondary Sources on the Puritans

For the sake of space, only a limited number of secondary sources on Puritans and Puritanism printed in the last twenty years are included here, alphabetized by author. For a fuller list of books written on the Puritans, see the bibliography on pages 861-888.

Assurance of Faith: Calvin, English Puritanism and the Dutch Second Reformation, by Joel R. Beeke (PL; 508 pages; 1991); revised and updated as **The Quest for Full Assurance of Faith: The Legacy of Calvin and His Successors** (BTT; 410 pages; 1999). Against the backdrop of the magisterial Reformers, this book examines the theological development of personal assurance of faith from 1600 to 1760 in English Puritanism and its parallel movement in the Netherlands. Studies of William Perkins, William Teellinck, the Westminster Confession, John Owen, Alexander Comrie, and Thomas Goodwin demonstrate that differences between Calvin and English Puritans on assurance rose primarily from a pastoral context rather than from variations in doctrine. A bibliography lists some fifteen hundred titles.

A Short History of the Westminster Assembly, by William Beveridge, edited by J. Ligon Duncan III (RAP; 157 pages; 1993). This brief, popular history of the Westminster Assembly (1643-49) is revised from the original 1904 work. A helpful annotated bibliography is attached.

The Everyday Work of the Westminster Assembly, by Samuel William Carruthers, edited by J. Ligon Duncan III. (RAP; 284 pages; 1994). Despite a busy life as a medical doctor and elder in the Presbyterian Church of England, Carruthers established himself as the leading scholar of the Westminster Assembly. He published the standard edition of the Westminster Confession of Faith in 1937 and followed it up in 1943 with this study, which treats an aspect of the Assembly not adequately dealt with elsewhere. Carruthers says his research aims to tell "in connected fashion the many daily occupations...which filled a large part of the time of the Divines, and which tested and manifested their practical wisdom, as well as their limitations and failings."

John Bunyan on the Order of Salvation, by Pieter DeVries, translated by C. van Haaften (PL; 234 pages; 1994). This is an excellent study of Bunyan's soteriology. It does justice to his experiential emphases.

John Owen on the Christian Life, by Sinclair B. Ferguson (BTT; 300 pages; 1987). This book expounds Owen's teachings on the plan of salvation, sanctification, fellowship with God, assurance of salvation, conflict with sin, the fellowship of the saints, the inspiration and authority of Scripture, the ministry, the sacraments, prayer, apostasy, and perseverance. An opening chapter summarizes Owen's life. This highly readable, revised doctoral dissertation is packed with insights for personal sanctification and for pastoral ministry. It serves as an ideal companion for the reading of Owen's voluminous writings. Ferguson writes, "It is intended in part as something of a 'Reader's Guide to John Owen,' providing a framework to his works and a conducted tour of much of his teaching" (p. xi).

Jonathan Edwards, Evangelist, by John Gerstner (SDG; 192 pages; 1995). This paperback, previously published as *Steps to Salvation: The Evangelistic Message of Jonathan Edwards* (1960), is a thorough study on how the way of salvation was taught in the sermons of Jonathan Edwards. It includes chapters on conviction of sin, seeking salvation, backsliding, regeneration, justification by faith, assurance, and the covenant. Gerstner was an astute authority on Edwards's sermons.

The Puritans in America: A Narrative Anthology, edited by Alan Heimert and Andrew Delbanco (Harvard; 438 pages; 1985). These documents from early American Puritanism cover the changes in Puritan thought in New England. A general introduction describes the Puritan environment, and shorter introductions

preface the six divisions of the collection: Loomings, The Migration, City on a Hill, O New England!, Coming of Age, and The
Dispersion of the New England Way. Thirty-eight writers are fea-
tured, including Cotton, Bradford, Bradstreet, Winthrop, Taylor,
and the Mathers. The testimony of Anne Hutchinson and documents about the witchcraft crisis are also included. These works,
several of which are published here for the first time, have been
updated in spelling and punctuation.

This book shows that Puritanism remains resistant to categories, whether done by Perry Miller, Christopher Hill, or Max
Weber. As an anthology, it skillfully presents the beauty and
power of Puritan literature. Especially noteworthy is John Cotton's *Christ the Fountain of Life* (c. 1628), in which Cotton argues
that as water cools hot tempers, so love softens hard, frozen
hearts (p. 31).

History of the Westminster Assembly of Divines, by William H.
Hetherington (SWRB; 325 pages; 1993). This reprint of the 1843
edition still is the best popular historical account of the Westminster Assembly. In covering the period from 1531 to 1662,
Hetherington masterfully explains what led to the convening of
this body of divines. He details the debates and resolutions that
culminated in the Westminster Confession of Faith, the Shorter
and Larger Catechisms, and other pertinent documents. Also included are a chapter on the theological productions of the
Westminster Assembly and six valuable appendixes.

Who are the Puritans?, by Erroll Hulse (EP; 220 pages; 2000).
The first two parts of this book on the lives of the Puritans are an
excellent introduction to the leading figures and their work. The
third part, titled "Help from the Puritans," will be of interest especially to those who are more advanced in Puritan studies. That
is particularly true of the chapters on spiritual experience and
the warrant and the way of faith.

The Devoted Life: An Invitation to the Puritan Classics, edited
by Kelly M. Kapic and Randall C. Gleason (IVP; 318 pages; 2004).
This collection of essays and excerpts provides a detailed and in-
triguing introduction to some of the greatest classics in Puritan

literature. Following the introduction, which provides a helpful summary of the essence of Puritanism, the book contains eighteen chapters analyzing various Puritan works, and an afterword concerning spiritual renewal. A sampling of the chapters included are "*The Art of Prophesying* by William Perkins" (Paul Schaefer), "*The Marrow of Theology* by William Ames" (Joel R. Beeke & Jan van Vliet), "*Of the Object and Acts of Justifying Faith* by Thomas Goodwin" (Michael S. Horton), "*Pilgrim's Progress* by John Bunyan" (J. I. Packer), "*The Mystery of Providence* by John Flavel" (Sinclair B. Ferguson), and "The Poetry of Ann Bradstreet and Edward Taylor" (Mark Noll).

The Grace of Law: A Study in Puritan Theology, by Ernest E. Kevan (SDG; 294 pages; 1993). Kevan, formerly principal of London Bible College, provides us with a well-documented study on the Puritan theology of law. He also introduces us to many Puritans who are relatively unknown. Notable chapters are "The Law of God for Man," "The Law and Sin," "The Place of Law in the Purpose of God," "The Continuance of Moral Obligation," "The Christian Law-Keeping," and "Christian Freedom." Chapters 3 and 4 are invaluable on the place of law in the purpose of God and on the end of the law in Christ's righteousness. This is an excellent volume to help obtain a clear biblical grasp on the relationship between law and gospel, thereby avoiding both legalism and antinomianism. Kevan successfully argues that God's law and God's grace are not enemies but allies in bringing sinners to faith and repentance at the feet of Christ.

A Spectacle unto God: The Life and Death of Christopher Love, by Don Kistler (SDG; 212 pages; 1994). This is a stimulating, well-illustrated biographical account of the great Puritan and Westminster Assembly divine who was executed by Cromwell's forces for his loyalty to Charles II. It contains numerous letters that Love wrote to his wife and others. It whets our appetite for Love's writings.

The Genius of Puritanism, by Peter Lewis (SDG; 200 pages; 1996). This is an excellent introduction to the Puritans, their writings, and their pastoral work. It examines Puritans as pastors, counselors, and theologians, as well as private people. The section on spiritual depression is detailed and helpful.

The Puritans: Their Origins and Successors, by Martyn Lloyd-Jones (BTT; 436 pages; 1987). This volume brings together addresses given by Lloyd-Jones at the Puritan Studies and Westminster conferences between 1959 and 1978. As J. I. Packer observed, "These studies are of practical value because the Puritans are approached with three important questions in mind: What did they teach and do? Was their teaching biblical? And, what can we learn from them for our life and witness today?"

Minutes of the Sessions of the Westminster Assembly of Divines, by A. E. Mitchell and John Struthers (SWRB; 650 pages; 1991). B. B. Warfield rightly calls this resource "the fundamental authority for the study of the work of the assembly." It includes notes and indexes on the Directory for Church Government, Westminster Confession of Faith, and Shorter and Larger Catechisms, as well as an eighty-six page introduction.

The Puritan Hope, by Iain H. Murray (BTT; 325 pages; 1998). This study in revival and the interpretations of prophecy through Puritan eyes in England and Scotland in the seventeenth and eighteenth centuries argues for the hope of worldwide revival before Christ's second coming. This Puritan hope involves the widespread conversion of the Jews as well as multitudes of Gentiles by the preaching of the gospel and the saving ministry of the Spirit.

The Holy Spirit in Puritan Faith and Experience, by Geoffrey F. Nuttall (UC; 222 pages; 1992). This standard work, first published in 1946, explains the Puritan view of the saving work of the Holy Spirit in the lives of believers. It includes chapters on the Spirit's relationship to the Word and to prayer, the witness and liberty of the Spirit, and the life and fellowship of the Spirit. Nuttall seeks to demonstrate the unity of the Reformation tradition, sometimes even drawing upon the Quaker tradition. Nevertheless, there is much valuable material in this volume not found elsewhere.

John Owen: The Man and His Theology, edited by Robert Oliver (BTT; 190 pages; 2002). This book consists of helpful papers read at the Conference of The John Owen Centre for Theological Study in September, 2000, including Owen's life and times (editor), Owen as theologian (Carl R. Trueman), Owen on the person of Christ and on the Holy Spirit (Sinclair B. Ferguson), Owen and the church (Graham S. Harrison), and Owen facing the challenge of the Quakers (Michael A. G. Haykin).

A Quest for Godliness: The Puritan Vision of the Christian Life, by James I. Packer (Crossway; 366 pages; 1990). In this work, Packer "uncovers the hidden treasures of Puritan life and thought...revealing the depth and breadth of Puritan spiritual life, contrasting it with the superficiality" of our day. Most of the chapters are addresses given at Puritan and Reformed Studies Conferences, Westminster Chapel, London. Several addresses focus on some aspect of John Owen's theology. "The Witness of the Spirit in Puritan Thought" is particularly valuable.

Puritan Papers, edited by James I. Packer (P&R; 5 vols., 250-320 pages each; 2000-2005). These volumes form an attractive reprinting of seventy-six papers read at the annual Puritan and Reformed conferences, Westminster Chapel, London, from 1956-1969, all of which were edited by Packer. They are ideal for those who have recently been introduced to the Puritans, and will whet their appetite to read the Puritans for themselves.

No conference was held in 1970. Reconvened as the Westminster conference in 1971 under the leadership of Dr. Martyn Lloyd-Jones, the papers from 1971 until today have been reprinted in annual paperbacks of about one hundred pages each by Tentmaker Publications. Together they form an invaluable resource.

Worldly Saints: The Puritans as They Really Were, by Leland Ryken (Zondervan; 280 pages; 1986). In this work, Ryken fulfills his threefold purpose: "(1) to correct an almost universal misunderstanding of what the Puritans really stood for, (2) to bring together in a convenient synthesis the best that the Puritans thought and said on selected topics, and (3) to recover the Christian wisdom of the Puritans for today." He not only covers religious topics such as the Puritan view of the Bible, church, preaching, and worship, but also delves into Puritan attitudes towards work, marriage, sex, money, family, education, and social action. Concluding chapters focus on the Puritans' greatest strengths and weaknesses. This is the book to read for an introductory, accurate overview of the Puritans.

The Westminster Assembly and Its Work, by Benjamin B. Warfield (SWRB; 400 pages; 1991). These six articles about the Westminster Assembly were written by a highly esteemed Princeton theologian who stood in the tradition of Archibald Alexander and Charles Hodge. The chapters dealing with the inspiration of Scripture, God's absolutely sovereign decree, and the Holy Spirit are especially relevant for today.

APPENDIX 5

"The Great Tradition": A Final Word on Puritanism and Our Need Today

J. I. Packer provides us with fitting concluding words on Puritanism and our need today, which are reprinted here with permission from the chapter, "The Great Tradition," in his Faithfulness and Holiness *(Wheaton, Ill.: Crossway, 2002), pages 81-82:*

"It is now more than half a century since I began to discern in the developed Puritanism of history a definitive embodiment of New Testament Christianity. By the Puritanism of history I mean the Bible-based, Christ-centered, conversionist, devotional, Church-focused, community-oriented movement that began to take shape with the Elizabethans Greenham and Perkins and Richard Rogers, and that effectively ended with Baxter, Howe, and Henry, who saw the Stuarts out and toleration in, and that produced such as Sibbes, Owen, and Bunyan in old England and Thomas Hooker, Increase and Cotton Mather, and finally Jonathan Edwards in New England. By a definitive embodiment of New Testament Christianity I mean a body of beliefs and a style of life that combined on the grand scale the Trinitarian objectivism of the Fathers, the knowledge of self and sin set forth by Augustine, the knowledge of Christ, of the cross, and of justification by faith that the magisterial Reformers had and shared, and the universal Christian passion for the glory of God in the worshiping life of the Church, with the insight into regeneration, sanctification, and the inner life of the self that was the Puritans' distinctive contribution. I mean a body of beliefs and a style of life that was intensely practical, experiential, conscientious, determined, vigorous, hopeful, hardworking, and visionary in its struggle to achieve and maintain sanctity in all circumstances, walks of life, personal states, relationships, and life activities, and to establish that sanctity everywhere in England and Wales (Scotland and Ireland had their own parallel movements), and beyond Britain too, by every means available. My amazement at the rightness and richness of Puritan Christianity was great from the start, and has only increased as the years have gone by.

"Seeing in this Puritan ideal, and in individual Puritan lives that I have studied, the most complete, profound, and magnificent realization of biblical religion that the world has yet known, and viewing German Lutheran pietism and the English-speaking evangelical movements of the eighteenth and nineteenth centuries as they viewed themselves—namely as partial though incomplete realizations of the Puritan vision of godliness—I have only been able to give two cheers for those many latter-day explorations of the evangelical heritage that treat evangelical religion as beginning in the eighteenth century. The truth is that evangelicalism, so-called, yesterday and today, should be seen as Puritanism continuing, but constantly narrowed—intellectually, culturally, humanistically, aesthetically, relationally—by secularizing pressures and perspectives in the Protestant world, so that increasingly it produces pygmies rather than giants. It is by Puritan standards that our stature should be measured, and our short-comings detected, for those are the standards of the Bible. The pioneers of the Evangelical Revival in Britain and the Great Awakening in New England knew this well, and read, thought, prayed, spoke, and acted accordingly. The fact that today's evangelicals are so largely out of touch with their own history, and so cannot discern how small and dry and lightweight and superficial and childish they are compared with those from whom they take their name, is one of the more glaring of our current shortcomings, all the more so for going constantly unnoticed."

As authors of Meet the Puritans, *our prayer is that the Holy Spirit may bless this book to enable us all to notice the difference between the Puritan age and our own day, as well as to repent and return to the Lord, and be fed and refreshed by the Puritan giants who have gone before us. Soli Deo Gloria!*

Glossary of Terms
and Events in this Guide

Ray B. Lanning

Abbreviations:
  CoE = Church of England; CoS = Church of Scotland;
  q.v. = Latin, quod vide, "which see."

Abjuration Oath: Oath taken by members of Parliament, clergy, and laymen, abjuring or renouncing the claim of the House of Stuart to the British throne.

Act of Toleration: See Toleration, Act of.

Acts of Uniformity: See Uniformity, Acts of.

Amyraldianism: Doctrine of French Reformed theologian Moise Amyraut (1596-1664) of the Academy of Saumur, that Christ's atonement was of infinite value, and therefore "hypothetically universal," but efficacious only for the elect, since only they are given faith to believe and be saved.

Antinomianism: From Greek, *anti* ("against") + *nomos* ("law"), the teaching that rejects the moral law of the Old Testament as a rule of life for believers under the New Testament, in opposition to the view of the law taught in the Westminster Confession of Faith, Ch. XIX, "Of the Law of God."

Archdeacon: (CoE) Church official below a bishop in rank, superintending *deans* (q.v.), in that part of a *diocese* (q.v.) set off as his archdeaconry, with power to impose church censures.

Aristotelianism: Refers to the Christian formulation of knowledge and theology according to the method of the Greek philosopher Aristotle (384-322 B.C.), developed through the Medieval period, and the common intellectual property of Roman Catholics and Protestants at the time of the Reformation.

Arminianism: Doctrine of salvation made popular by Dutch theologian Jacobus Arminius (1560-1609), discarding the Reformed understanding of divine sovereignty, human inability, gracious election, and particular atonement, in order to accommodate the notion of human autonomy or "free will," and to advance the notion of universal atonement while denying universal salvation. Arminius's Dutch followers, who also discarded the Reformed doctrine of the perseverance of the saints, were known as "Remonstrants" because they summed up their views in five points as their "Remonstrance" or protest against the confessional teachings of the national church. The *Synod of Dort* (q.v.) convened in 1618 to address the challenge of the Remonstrants.

Articles of Perth: (CoS) Five articles adopted by the CoS's General Assembly, meeting at Perth in 1618 at the instigation of King James, imposing usages of the CoE ("English popish ceremonies," as George Gillespie termed them) on the Scottish church, such as kneeling at the Lord's Supper, private communion, baptism of infants not later than one Sabbath after birth, episcopal confirmation, and keeping of feast days such as Christmas and Easter. The reforming Glasgow Assembly of 1638 condemned the Assembly of Perth and set aside its five articles.

Assizes: English and Welsh county courts sitting at stated times for the administration of civil and criminal justice.

Auchterarder Creed: (CoS) Doctrinal propositions imposed on candidates for licensure and ordination by the Presbytery of Auchterarder in Perthshire, Scotland. The most important proposition reads: "I believe that it is not sound and orthodox to teach, that we must forsake sin in order to our coming to Christ, and instating us in covenant with God." This article is directed against *preparationism* (q.v.). The act of the General Assembly in 1717, condemning this proposition as "unsound and most detestable," gave rise to the *Marrow Controversy* (q.v.).

Barrowists: Congregationalists holding to the form of *Congregationalism* (q.v.) taught by Henry Barrow (c. 1550-1593), placing the power of church government and the exercise of church discipline in the hands of the officers of the local church; see *Brownists*.

Benefice: (CoE) The living, that is, the property and income, held by a *rector* (q.v.) or *vicar* (q.v.), as the gift of the parish corporation or patron.

Book of Common Prayer: (CoE) Liturgy of the CoE, first issued in 1549, revised in 1552, and reissued in final form in 1662. Use was made compulsory by the *Acts of Uniformity* (q.v.). Intended as a middle way between Rome and the Reformed churches, the Book of Common Prayer occasioned many problems of conscience for the Puritans. The *Westminster Assembly of Divines* (q.v.) proposed that it be laid aside in favor of their *Directory for the Public Worship of God* (1645). Following the *Savoy Conference* (q.v.) in 1661, Richard Baxter produced his own redaction of the BCP, known as "Baxter's Liturgy," reflecting the concerns that Presbyterians had brought to the meeting.

Book of Sports: Declaration of King James I in 1617, intended to resolve disputes over Sabbath day recreations by permitting some of the more innocent amusements of the era while banning others, providing that none of the activities permitted might intrude on hours set aside for public worship, or lead to the neglect of it; for the stricter Puritan view, see Westminster Confession of Faith, Ch. XXI, "Of Religious Worship and the Sabbath Day," and the *Directory for Public Worship*, "Of the Sanctification of the Lord's Day."

Brownists: Congregationalists holding to the form of *Congregationalism* (q.v.) taught by Robert Browne (c. 1550-1633), leaving the power of church government and the exercise of church discipline in the hands of the communicant membership of the local church; see *Barrowists*.

Cambridge Platform: Entitled *A Platform of Church Discipline, Gathered out of the Word of God: and Agreed upon by the Elders: And Messengers of the Churches Assembled in the Synod at Cambridge in New England* in 1648, this church polity document was drafted to protect the New England churches, lest episcopacy be imposed on them for want of any other order. It represents the efforts of *Barrowist* (q.v.) Congregationalists to systematize their practice and overcome some of the disadvantages of Independency; see *Congregationalism.*

Cambridge Platonists: Group of academics at Cambridge University who revived the study and philosophy of Plato in the latter part of the seventeenth century. They shared common quarters with the many Puritans who studied at Emmanuel College, Cambridge, and were themselves of Puritan origin and sympathies, but chose to remain in the established church as a reconciling force, pleading for toleration on all sides. For this they were branded "Latitudinarians."

Casuistry: Theological science of applying the general teaching of Scripture and the requirements of the moral law to specific cases or problems.

Catechist: Minister of the Word or teacher in the local congregation whose specific duty is the instruction of "catechumens," either children who are baptized but not yet admitted to communicant membership, or persons of riper years who desire to be baptized and admitted to communicant membership. Puritan ministers carried the work of catechizing into the home and involved all ages as they visited the families of the congregation or parish under their care.

Cavalier: French, meaning "horseman" or "rider," the term came to denote a gentleman, one of whose accomplishments was good horsemanship. It was applied to the aristocratic English partisans of the House of Stuart. The irreligious, profligate, and highhanded ways of these pro-Stuart Cavaliers made the term a byword for flippant, supercilious, and often godless attitudes and manners.

Chancel: From Latin, *cancelli,* "bounds" or "limits," in church architecture, the portion of the church building where the altar or communion table, pulpit, and lectern are placed, usually raised and railed off and reserved for the clergy and choir.

Chancellor: Academic title for the non-resident head of a university, most of whose duties are performed by a vice-chancellor.

Commissary: (CoE) Ecclesiastical title for someone commissioned to act as the representative of a bishop in part of his see, or in the place of the bishop in his absence.

Commonwealth: Term used for the republican government in England which existed from 1649 to 1660 under Parliament and the Lord Protector, first, Oliver Cromwell, then his son, Richard Cromwell, and therefore called "the Protectorate"; used in the Westminster Confession of Faith for a political entity (Ch. XXIII.II) or "body politic" (XIX.III); see also *Interregnum.*

Confession of Faith: See *Westminster Standards.*

Congregationalism, Congregationalists: Congregationalists hold that each local church is sufficient to itself for all purposes of church government and discipline. Some Congregationalists ("Brownists") left this power in the hands of communicant membership of the church. Others ("Barrowists") placed this power in the hands of ministers and ruling elders, chosen by the communicant membership. In its most basic form, it is called "Independency," and its proponents, "Independents." To overcome the disadvantages of pure Independency, Congregationalists explored various ways for independent churches to work cooperatively, and in time developed a system of associations local, provincial, and national, which closely approximates the courts or assemblies of Presbyterian and Reformed polity, and a loose network of societies or agencies for missions, publishing, Sabbath school work, etc. See also *Cambridge Platform, Savoy Declaration.*

Conventicle, Conventicle Acts: From Latin, *conventiculum,* "a small gathering," "a little meeting place." Term used to characterize secret meetings for worship held by Nonconformists in England and by Covenanters in Scotland. Banned by successive Conventicle Acts after the *Restoration* (q.v.) of Charles II, efforts were taken in hand to suppress such gatherings. Harsh penalties were imposed on those found guilty of holding or participating in them, especially during the period known in Scotland as "the Killing Times" (1660-1688).

Dean: (CoE) Title for the senior clergyman of a cathedral or collegiate church, and for a church official having, as his "deanery," supervision over some portion of the parishes and parochial clergy under the supervision of an *archdeacon* (q.v.).

Decalogue: Literally, "Ten Words," to wit, the Ten Commandments of Exodus 20:1-17; see also Deuteronomy 4:13 and 10:4.

Declarations of Indulgence: See *Indulgence, Declarations of.*

Diocese: (CoE) Territory ruled by a particular bishop, also known as a "see" or "bishopric," as the basic unit of episcopal church government, divided into parishes, which may be grouped into archdeaconries and deaneries as sub-units of the diocese; see *Archdeacon, Dean, Episcopacy* (q.v.).

Dissent, Dissenters: Term used for various groups and individuals who expressed disagreement with, or dissent from, the faith, worship, or polity "as by law established" for the national churches of England and Scotland. Dissenters were also called *Nonconformists* (q.v.).

Divine, Divinity: Here used in the sense of "theologian" and "theology." The Westminster Assembly was a body of theologians, most of them clergyman, though there were some lay theologians among them.

Ejection: See *Great Ejection.*

Episcopacy, Episcopalians: From Greek *episkopos*, meaning "overseer" or "superintendent." Episcopalians place the power of church government and discipline in the hand of bishops, each one sovereign in his own see or diocese, and all united as the church hierarchy or "priestly rulers." All bishops may be called "prelates," but some bishops have more prestige and power, and therefore are called "prelates" because they are preferred above others. Some are "primates" because they rank first above all others. The archbishop of York is "Primate of England," and the archbishop of Canterbury, "Primate of All England." See *Diocese.*

Fellow: In English universities, a graduate of a particular college, elected as an incorporated member of the college, with appropriate rank, privileges, and emoluments; sometimes further distinguished in rank as "major" or "minor." Many fellows had teaching responsibilities.

Five Mile Act: "An Act to restrain Nonconformists from inhabiting Corporations" was passed by the English Parliament in 1665. Nonconformists were forbidden to reside or approach within five miles of a "corporation," i.e., any borough, town, or city represented in Parliament. Nonconformists were also required to take an oath not to take arms against the king, or attempt any "alteration of government" in church or state. Punishments included heavy fines and imprisonment.

Flint Assizes: Sessions of county court in and for the shire of Flint in Wales. See *Assizes.*

Glorious Revolution: Descriptive term for the "revolutionary" decision of the English Parliament, in 1688, to invite William, Count of Nassau, Prince of Orange, and Stadholder of the Netherlands, and his wife, Princess Mary Stuart, to take the throne of the United Kingdom upon the abdication of James II. The commencement of the reign of William and Mary in 1689 as joint sovereigns and committed Protestants meant the end of long years of suffering for Puritans in England and Presbyterians in Scotland.

Great Ejection: On St. Bartholomew's Day, August 24, 1662, in consequence of the Act of Uniformity passed by Parliament in May of the same year, more than 2,000 ministers were "ejected" or expelled from their churches, residences, and incomes because they would not conform to the use of *The Book of Common Prayer* (q.v.) as the uniform order for worship in the Church of England.

Grotianism: Doctrine of Dutch statesman, lawyer, and theologian Hugo Grotius (1583-1645), who espoused the cause of the "Remonstrants" and their *Arminianism* (q.v.). He proposed the "governmental" theory of the atonement in the place of the classic doctrine of penal substitution and satisfaction, holding that Christ's death was intended to be a monumental display of God's detestation of sin, and a terrible example of punishment, to deter men from sin.

Habeas Corpus: Latin phrase, "you must have a body," i.e., evidence that a crime has been committed; formulary in a writ compelling civil authorities to account to a court of law for the arrest or imprisonment of a citizen, as a protection against illegal arrest or imprisonment; one of the rights of British subjects secured by the *Magna Carta* (q.v.).

Hampton Court Conference: Meeting held in January 1604 at Hampton Court Palace, near London, between representative Puritans and members of the church hierarchy, presided over by King James I, to discuss Puritan objections to various usages of the national church. Very little change resulted from the conference, save for the decision of the king to act on Puritan spokesman John Reynolds's proposal that the English translation of the Bible be revised. The "King James Version" of the Holy Bible was completed in 1611.

House of Commons: Lower house of the English Parliament whose members are elected from and represent the common people of the land.

House of Lords: Upper house of the English Parliament, also called the House of Peers, whose members belong to the aristocracy of the nation or the hierarchy of the national church.

Imprimatur: Latin, meaning "let it be printed," used in a formula to certify that the author of a book has been given license or official sanction by authorities of state, church, or other institutions, to publish his work.

Independency, Independent: See *Congregationalism, Congregationalist.*

Indulgence, Declarations of: Proclamations issued occasionally in the years 1669 to 1687, offering indulgence or accommodation to dissenting ministers in the form of amnesty and freedom to preach. The aim was to induce the more amenable sort of ministers back into the national church while further isolating and targeting the more resolute dissenters. In the intervals between such declarations, the government maintained a harsh policy of repression, attempting to enforce conformity to the usages imposed by law on the national church.

Interregnum: Latin, indicating a period between (*inter*) the end of the reign (*regnum*) of one king, and the beginning of another, such as the period of the *Commonwealth* (q.v.).

King Philip's War: "Philip" was the name given by European settlers to Metacomet, son of Massasoit, and chief of the Wampanoag tribe which inhabited today's Rhode Island. In 1675, Metacomet led an uprising against the settlers. The ensuing campaign of raids, killings, and burnings ended with the defeat of the Wampanoag and the death of Metacomet in 1676.

Larger Catechism: See *Westminster Standards.*

Lecturer: The sermons of Puritan ministers who preached under the sponsorship of town corporations, parishes, and individuals, usually on week days and market days, were called "lectures." Those who delivered them on a stated basis were called "lecturers." These lectures were "exposition and direct application of scripture" (R.J. George), that is, discourses on longer passages of Scripture, rather than strictly textual, doctrinal, or topical. *Lectio continua* is the technical term for a series of such lectures on a passage, chapter, or book of the Bible.

License of the Press: See *Imprimatur.*

Living: See *Benefice.*

Long Parliament: Session of the English Parliament so called because it sat, at intervals, from 1640 to 1660; derisively called the Rump Parliament, because only the "rump" remained after "Pride's Purge" drove out Presbyterian members in 1648, leaving it in the hands of Congregationalists more sympathetic to the policies of the Lord Protector; see *Commonwealth.*

Magna Carta: Latin, meaning "Great Charter," constitutional document forced by the English barons upon King John in 1215, formulating and securing their rights and freedoms over against the powers of the monarchy. In time these rights and freedoms were extended to every British subject, and *Magna Carta* became a byword for any landmark document in the history of a nation, institution, or movement.

Marrow Controversy, Marrowmen: (CoS) Refers to the early eighteenth-century debate in Scotland over the free offer of the gospel, faith, justification by faith alone, and assurance, occasioned by republication of a book by English Puritan Edward Fisher, *The Marrow of Modern Divinity,* in response to the 1717 decision of the General Assembly condemning the *Auchterarder Creed* (q.v.). The General Assembly proceeded to condemn the book as well, and the "Marrowmen," led by Thomas Boston (1676-1732), rose in its defense. The conflict was never fully resolved. Defenders of the *Marrow* soon found themselves at a disadvantage when it came to receiving calls to vacant churches where the heritor or patron had power to thwart the congregation's choice if he so desired. Many heritors were "Moderates" who looked on the Marrowmen as errorists and fanatics. The lingering effects of the Marrow controversy led to another controversy over patronage provoked by Marrowman Ebenezer Erskine, which ended in 1733 with his deposition from the ministry and secession from the CoS to form the Associate Presbytery; see *Secession Church.*

Massachusetts Bay Colony: One of two Puritan colonies founded on the shores of Massachusetts Bay in New England, the other being Plymouth Plantation, known as "the Old Colony." The Old Colony was founded by *Separatists* (q.v.), while the fathers of the Bay Colony came from the ranks of *Non-Separating Congregationalism* (q.v.). The two colonies remained distinct in geography, law, administration, customs, and sentiment for a long time.

Monmouth's Rebellion: An uprising of Scottish Covenanters crushed by the forces of the Duke of Monmouth in the battle of Bothwell Bridge, June 22, 1679. Four or five hundred Covenanters were killed, and over 1,200 taken prisoner and held in Greyfriars' Churchyard. Of these, 257 were sentenced to be transported abroad, and most drowned when their ship foundered off the coast of Scotland.

Neonomianism: From Greek, *neo,* "new" + *nomos,* "law," restatement of the gospel as merely a "new law" in the place of the law of the Old Testament, so that faith becomes mere assent to that new law and obedience to it; a view associated with Richard Baxter.

Nonconformist, Nonconformity: Act of refusing to conform to the standard decreed for the national church for faith, worship, or polity; similar in meaning to "dissenting," though dissent has reference to one's views and beliefs, while Non-conformity refers to one's practice. Nonconformists in England often found themselves at odds with people who professed to hold the same articles of faith. Nonconformity later became a collective term for the various "free" churches, Presbyterian, Congregational, Methodist, Baptist, etc., in England and Wales, existing outside the established church. See *Dissent, Dissenter.*

Non-Separating Congregationalism: (CoE) Ministers and other persons belonging to the CoE who adopted Congregationalism as a theory of church polity, but did not feel free in conscience to separate from the national church, lest they be guilty of schism. Many English Presbyterians found themselves in the same predicament.

Parliamentarians: Supporters of the ancient rights and claims of Parliament over against the attempts of the Stuart Kings to absolutize the monarchy, which led to the English Civil War.

Patron, Patronage: Under the system of patronage, the patron held title to the property and tax revenues (tithes) of a parish of the national church in Scotland or England; such titles were held by members of the aristocracy or church hierarchy. Also called the "heritor," since the titles were bequeathed to the patron's heirs from generation to generation. The patron or heritor of the parish could grant the use of the property and its income as a *benefice* (q.v.) to the minister of his choice, whether or not the minister was acceptable to the people of the parish. See *Marrow Controversy.*

Popery, Popish: Refers to the Pope of Rome, the institution of the papacy, and in general, the distinctive teachings, practices, and claims of the papal or Roman Catholic church.

Prebend, Prebendary: (CoE) From Latin, *praebenda,* "pension" or "grant." A prebend is part of the revenue of a cathedral or collegiate church paid as a stipend to one of the clergy attached to said cathedral or church; the recipient of a prebend is therefore a prebendary.

Prelacy: Term of contempt for *Episcopacy* (q.v.).

Preparationism: Tendency in some Puritan divines to propose various things which a sinner must do, various states through which he must pass, or various signs or marks he must look for in himself, prior to saving faith in Christ. In this way the sinner prepares himself for grace, though he may be convinced that he has not yet received grace. Preparationism stresses the common way that God leads sinners to Christ, that is, by means of conviction of sin and a felt sense of the loss of one's own righteousness; it tends to downplay the warrant to believe contained in the gospel promise. See *Marrow Controversy, Marrowmen.*

Presbyterian, Presbyterianism: From Greek, *presbuteros,* "presbyter" or "elder," and *presbuterion,* "presbytery." Presbyterians hold (1) that "bishop" and "presbyter" are used interchangeably in the New Testament to refer to ministers of the Word; (2) that alongside ministers of the Word, there were in the church of both Old and New Testaments other church governors also called elders; (3) that Christ has appointed a government for His church in the hand of these officers; (4) that these officers are to exercise their power jointly through the courts or assemblies of the church; and (5) that just as there are found in Scripture local, metropolitan, provincial, and national churches, so there were local, metropolitan, provincial, and national assemblies to govern them. In practice these came to be designated sessions, presbyteries, particular synods, and general synods or assemblies. These principles are referred to only briefly in the Westminster Confession of Faith (Chs. XXX, XXXI) since they are unfolded more extensively, with Scripture proofs, in the *Form of Presbyterial Church Government* (see *Westminster Standards.*) Strict Presbyterians were called "*jure divino* Presbyterians" because they held this polity as an article of faith, claiming for it a *jus divinum* or "divine authority" from the written Word of God.

Privy Council: From Old French, *prive,* "private," the body of advisors personally chosen by the monarch to serve as his advisors, in distinction from the government, or prime minister and his cabinet.

Probationer: (CoS) From Latin, *probare,* "to prove" or "to demonstrate," referring to candidates for ordination to the ministry who must first sustain trials and be given license to preach in the churches as probationers, giving proof or demonstration of their ability and fitness to be ordained, in the hope of receiving a call.

Proctor: A syncopated form of "procurator"; academic officer at Oxford and Cambridge Universities, charged with the task of enforcing student discipline, acting on behalf of the university authorities.

Prolocutor: (CoE) From Latin, *proloquor*, "to speak for," or "to speak forth"; title of the moderator or presiding officer of an ecclesiastical assembly, so called because he is the spokesman for the house, to whom individual speakers must address themselves, and because he propounds the business to be taken up, and the questions to be decided; title used for the presiding officer of the *Westminster Assembly of Divines* (q.v.).

Protestors: (CoS) Scottish "Remonstrants" (not to be confused with the Arminians of the Netherlands, also called "Remonstrants") who brought a protest or "Remonstrance" to the General Assembly of 1650 against the haste and ease with which King Charles II had been permitted to subscribe the national covenants, without having evidenced any change of principles. They were opposed by the *Resolutioners* (q.v.) who condemned the Remonstrance as an act of high treason. The result was a partial and rancorous schism in the CoS which lasted into the period of the Restoration.

Provost: Derived from Latin, *praepositus*, "one placed at the head"; in English universities, title for the heads of certain colleges; in Scotland, title for the head of a municipal corporation or "burgh."

Ramism, Ramist: System of logic propounded by a French Reformed academic, Petrus Ramus (1515-1572), in opposition to the prevailing Aristotelianism of the western tradition; very influential with certain Puritans, such as William Ames (1576-1633).

Reader: (CoE) Person appointed to read parts of the service from *The Book of Common Prayer* during public worship.

Rector: (CoE) Minister of a parish church which holds title to its property and incomes (tithes); see *Vicar*.

Rector Magnificus: Latin, "Exalted Ruler," academic title for the head of a university on the European continent.

Regius Professor: Latin, "Royal Professor," holder of a chair at a British university endowed or funded by the crown.

Resolutioners: (CoS) Opponents of the *Protestors* (q.v.), so called because they approved of certain notorious "Resolutions" of Parliament. The Resolutioners were stout partisans of King Charles II, believing that his accession to the throne would well serve the cause of Presbyterianism in both Scotland and England. Various undertakings and promises of Charles encouraged them in this belief, but events after the *Restoration* (q.v.) soon showed how mistaken they were.

Restoration: End of the Commonwealth and the Protectorate, with the return or restoration of the monarchy under Charles II in 1660. Many Presbyterians in England and Scotland had looked upon the government of the Cromwells with increasing disapprobation and disaffection, and therefore they welcomed the restoration of the monarchy. Charles quickly set about the task of restoring the old order in church and state, waging war against English Puritans and Scottish Covenanters; see *Protestors* and *Resolutioners*.

Rochet: (CoE) White priestly vestment with long sleeves, resembling a surplice, used chiefly by bishops and abbots, and therefore a fitting symbol for a bishop's office.

Royalists: Partisans of King Charles I in his war against Parliament; supporters of the claims of the monarchy generally.

Rye House Plot: A plot against the lives of King Charles II and his son, James, discovered in 1683; "a scheme to assassinate Charles and James at an isolated house on the high road near Hoddesdon in Hertfordshire as they returned from New Market to London" (P.C. Yorke).

Savoy Conference (1658): Assembly of Congregationalist ministers and laymen at the Savoy Palace in London, which convened on September 29, 1658. The purpose was to formulate their position and systematize their practice, over against *Presbyterianism* (q.v.). The Conference adjourned on October 12, 1658. The result of this meeting was given to the world as the *Savoy Declaration* (q.v.).

Savoy Conference (1661): Meeting at the Savoy Palace, London, from April 15 to July 25, 1661, between equal numbers of Episcopalians and Presbyterians, for the purpose of revising *The Book of Common Prayer* to the satisfaction of both parties. Presbyterian objections to the existing BCP were met with determination on the part of the Episcopalians to defend it down to the least detail. The stalemate dashed all remaining hopes for finding a way for Presbyterians to remain within the pale of the national church, and set the stage for the *Great Ejection* (q.v.).

Savoy Declaration: Approved by the Savoy Conference on October 12, 1658, the document begins with a lengthy preface attributed to John Owen, then presents *A Declaration of the Faith and Order Owned and Practised in the Congregational Churches of England*, a redaction of the Westminster Confession of Faith, with certain chapters omitted, others rewritten, and at least one added. The final section is devoted to an exposition of Congregational church polity in thirty articles under the title *Of the Institution of Churches, and the Order Appointed in Them by Jesus Christ.*

Secession Church: Name for the bodies which resulted from the decision of Ebenezer Erskine (1680-1754) and three colleagues to decline the authority of the General Assembly, and secede from the CoS to constitute the Associate Presbytery in 1733. Hence they and their adherents were called "Seceders." The Secession Church took root and grew vigorously in Scotland and Ireland, and later in North America. Divisions, reunions, and unions resulted in the Associate, General Associate, United Secession, Original Secession, and United Presbyterian Churches of Scotland. In the USA, Seceders organized as the Associate, Associate Reformed, and United Presbyterian Churches.

Separatist: (CoE) Many English Presbyterians and Congregationalists believed it their duty to remain in the national church, but some did not (see *Non-Separating Congregationalism*). Both Presbyterian and Congregationalist churches separate from the national church were formed at an early date. Some believed it a moral duty to separate from the established church, and these are properly called Separatists. Among them were the Pilgrim fathers who went into exile, first in the Netherlands and later as founders of Plymouth Plantation on the shores of Massachusetts Bay.

Sequestered: From Latin, *sequestrare*, "to remove for safekeeping"; the state of one subjected to temporary seizure or confiscation of income, property or goods by the civil authorities.

Shorter Catechism: See *Westminster Standards*.

Sizar: Student at a Cambridge university paying reduced fees in exchange for daily work as a menial servant or "servitor," so called because granted a "size" or ration of food and drink.

Socinianism: Doctrines of Socinus, Italian theologian Faustus Socinus (1539-1604), who, while asserting the authority of Scripture, denied the doctrines of the Trinity and the deity of Christ as contrary to reason. Socinianism and Deism gave rise to Unitarianism among English Baptists and Presbyterians, and among the Congregationalists of New England.

Solemn League and Covenant: A treaty concluded between England and Scotland in 1643, "for Reformation and Defence of Religion, the Honour and Happiness of the King, and the Peace and Safety of the Three Kingdoms of Scotland, England and Ireland." The English sought the Scots' help in defeating the attempt of King Charles I to retake the throne by force. They wished to protect the rights and powers of their Parliament as well. The Scots hoped to see the faith, worship, and order of Presbyterian Scotland maintained and extended into England. They also desired to safeguard the person and claims of King Charles in the hope that he might be brought to submit to the new order of things in Britain. The political and military aspects seemed uppermost to the English, so they called this treaty a "league" or alliance. For the Scots, with a long tradition of covenanting behind them, the religious character and aims of the treaty marked it as a "covenant." In the event the Scots were routed by the king's men, while the English themselves defeated the royalists. The king for safety surrendered himself to the Scots, but they handed him over to the English in exchange for funds with which to pay their soldiers. The English in turn put the king on trial for treason, condemned him, and put him to death. The one lasting fruit of the Solemn League and Covenant was the work of *Westminster Assembly of Divines* (q.v.) in composing the *Westminster Standards* (q.v.), in fulfillment of the expressed desire for a uniformity of faith, worship, and order in the churches of the three kingdoms.

Spectral evidence: Controversial evidence admitted in proceedings against persons accused of witchcraft, e.g., the testimony of persons who claimed to have had supernatural experiences which proved the guilt of the accused. Such "spectral evidence" could be not examined or tested in any way, and had to be taken at face value, if admitted at all.

Synod of Dort: National Synod held at Dordrecht, the Netherlands, 1618-19, to address the growing influence of *Arminianism* (q.v.), and the objections of Arminians to the confessional teachings of the Dutch national church. The result was the doctrinal deliverances known as the Canons of Dort, setting forth the Reformed doctrine of salvation under five headings, in the form of propositions under each head, followed by refutations of error. The Synod also gave final form to the texts of the Belgic Confession of Faith, the Heidelberg Catechism, and the Dutch Reformed liturgy; produced the classic Church Order of Dort, followed as a model by many Reformed bodies since that time; and commissioned a new translation of the Bible with copious notes, glosses, and cross references, known in English as the *Dutch Annotations*.

Teacher: Congregationalism confessed to find two offices in Ephesians 4:11. "The office of pastor and teacher appears to be distinct. The pastor's special work is, to attend to *exhortation*, and therein to administer a word of *wisdom*: the teacher is to attend to *doctrine*, and therein to administer a word of knowledge: and either of them to administer the seals of that covenant, unto the dispensation whereof they are alike called" (*Cambridge Platform*, Ch. VI.5).

Toleration, Act of: Law passed in 1689, early in the reign of William and Mary, granting freedom of worship to dissenting Protestants in Great Britain, marking the end of the long and often brutal campaign to suppress dissent and compel conformity to liturgy and order of the established church. See *Glorious Revolution.*

Uniformity, Acts of: Publication of the successive editions of *The Book of Common Prayer* (1549, 1552, 1662) was accompanied by the passing of an Act of Uniformity, requiring ministers to conform to usages of the BCP or be punished. Most extreme was the Act of 1662, requiring all ministers to give public assent to the use of the BCP, to use it exclusively, and that all ministers must be episcopally ordained. The result was the *Great Ejection* (q.v.).

Vicar: (CoE) Minister serving a parish of which title to the property and income (tithes) is held by a patron or heritor, who may award the use thereof to the candidate of his choice. See *Rector* and *Patron.*

Vice-Chancellor: See *Chancellor.*

Westminster Assembly of Divines: At the call of the English Parliament, the cream of England's theologians or "divines," both clerical and lay, met in the precincts of Westminster Abbey, from July 1, 1643 to February 22, 1649. Most were Presbyterians, but there were also Episcopalians, Independents, and Erastians among them. Also present were a band of commissioners or delegates from the CoS, able men, who, like the Independents, were few in number but highly influential. Initially, the Assembly's task was to revise the Thirty-Nine Articles of Religion, the CoE's confession of faith dating from 1562. Upon the concluding of the *Solemn League and Covenant* (q.v.) between England and Scotland, the Assembly took up the task of drafting new creedal, catechetical, liturgical, and polity documents which would contribute to securing uniformity of faith, worship, and order among the national churches of England, Scotland, and

Ireland. See *Westminster Standards.* The Assembly also adopted a new metrical version of the Psalms which became the principle source for the Scottish Psalter of 1650.

Westminster Standards: Five documents are the lasting fruit of the Westminster Assembly of Divines, adopted as the constitution and subordinate standards of the CoS, and taken from thence to Presbyterian churches around the world. The three major standards are well known: the *Westminster Confession of Faith* (1647); the *Larger Catechism* (1647), "a directory for catechising such as have made some proficiency in the knowledge of the grounds of religion"; and the *Shorter Catechism* (1647), "for catechising such as are of weaker capacity," also known as "the Assembly's Catechism." The Ten Commandments, Lord's Prayer, and Apostles' Creed were appended to the text of the Shorter Catechism. Not so well-known, but well-deserving of notice, are the two minor standards, *The Directory for the Publick* [or, *Publique*] *Worship of God* (1644), intended to replace *The Book of Common Prayer*, and *The Form of Presbyterial Church-Government* (1645). Scottish and American printings of the Westminster Standards long included *The Sum of Saving Knowledge: Or, a Brief Sum of Christian Doctrine, Contained in the Holy Scriptures, and Holden Forth in the Foresaid Confession of Faith and Catechism; Together with the Practical Use Thereof* (c. 1650), a presentation of the Gospel prepared by Scottish divines David Dickson (1583-1663) and James Durham (1622-1658). Never officially sanctioned, *The Sum of Saving Knowledge* filled a place among the Westminster Standards analogous to that of the Canons of Dort among the Three Forms of Unity of the Dutch Reformed Churches.

Yeoman: Legal term for persons who own sufficient free land to qualify for service on juries, vote in elections, etc.; used generally to describe small landowners, farmers, and other persons of the middle class.

Bibliography of Secondary Sources
on the Puritans
<hr/>

In addition to the sources cited in this book, this bibliography contains a selection of secondary source books, including unpublished doctoral dissertations, on the Puritans, as well as a small sampling of the Scottish and Dutch divines of Puritan persuasion. Articles and encyclopedias are not included. Asterisked items (*) are given a brief summary in the section "Secondary Sources on the Puritans" (pages 827-833).

Addison, William. *The Life and Writings of Thomas Boston of Ettrick.* Edinburgh: Oliver and Boyd, 1936.

Affleck, Bert, Jr. "The Theology of Richard Sibbes, 1577-1635." Ph.D. dissertation, Drew University, 1968.

Alblas, Jacques B.H. *Johannes Boekholt (1656-1693): The First Dutch Publisher of John Bunyan and Other English Authors.* Nieuwkoop: De Graaf, 1987.

Alexander, G. M. *Changes for the Better.* 2 vols. Ossett, W. Yorks: Zoar Publications, 1978.

Armstrong, Nancy, and Leonard Tennenhouse. *The Imaginary Puritan: Literature, Intellectual Labor, and the Origins of Personal Life.* Berkeley: University of California Press, 1992.

Barker, William. *Puritan Profiles: 54 Influential Puritans at the Time When the Westminster Confession of Faith was Written.* Fearn, Ross-shire Mentor, 1999.

Bass, William Ward. "Platonic Influences on Seventeenth Century English Puritan Theology as expressed in the thinking of John Owen, Richard Baxter, and John Howe." Ph.D. dissertation, University of Southern California, 1958.

Battis, John Emery. "Troublers in Israel: The Antinomian Controversy in the Massachusetts Bay Colony, 1636-1638." Ph.D. dissertation, Columbia University, 1958.

Beeke, Joel R. *Gisbertus Voetius: Toward a Reformed Marriage of Knowledge and Piety.* Grand Rapids: Reformation Heritage Books, 1999.

_____. *Puritan Evangelism.* Grand Rapids: Reformation Heritage Books, 1999.

*_____. *The Quest for Full Assurance: The Legacy of Calvin and His Successors.* Edinburgh: Banner of Truth Trust, 1999.

Bell, M. Charles. *Calvin and Scottish Theology: The Doctrine of Assurance.* Edinburgh: The Handsel Press, 1985.

Bercovitch, Sacvan. *The American Jeremiad.* Madison: University of Wisconsin Press, 1978.

———. *The Puritan Origins of the American Self.* New Haven: Yale, 1975.

———, comp. *Typology and Early American Literature.* Amherst: University of Massachusetts Press, 1972.

Beveridge, W. *Makers of the Scottish Church.* Edinburgh: T. & T. Clark, 1908.

*———. *A Short History of the Westminster Assembly.* Ed. J. Ligon Duncan III. Greenville, S.C.: Reformed Academic Press, 1993.

Blaikie, William Garden. *The Preachers of Scotland: From the Sixth to the Nineteenth Century.* Edinburgh: T. & T. Clark, 1888; reprint, Edinburgh: Banner of Truth, 2001.

Blench, J. W. *Preaching in England in the Late Fifteenth and Sixteenth Century.* Oxford: Basil Blackwell, 1964.

Boersma, Hans. *A Hot Pepper Corn: Richard Baxter's Doctrine of Justification in its Seventeenth-Century Context of Controversy.* Zoetermeer: Boekencentrum, 1993.

Bogue, Carl W. *Jonathan Edwards and the Covenant of Grace.* Cherry Hill, N.J.: Mack Publishing Co., 1975.

Bouwman, H. *Willem Teellinck en de praktijk der godzaligheid.* Kampen: Kok, 1928.

Bowman, H. O. "William Guthrie, 1620-1665." Ph.D. dissertation, Edinburgh, 1953.

Bozeman, Theodore Dwight. *To Live Ancient Lives: The Primitivist Dimension in Puritanism.* Chapel Hill: University of North Carolina, 1988.

Bradshaw, William. *English Puritanisme and Other Works.* Westmead: Gregg Reprints, 1972.

Brandt, Geeraerdt. *The History of the Reformation and Other Ecclesiastical Transactions in and about the Low-Countries, from the Beginning of the Eighth Century, down to the Famous Synod of Dort.* 4 vols. London: T. Wood, 1720-23.

Bratt, John H., ed. *The Rise and Development of Calvinism.* Grand Rapids: Eerdmans, 1959.

Bremer, Francis, ed. *Puritanism: Transatlantic Perspectives on a Seventeenth-Century Anglo-American Faith.* Boston: Northeastern University Press, 1978.

Breward, Ian. "The Life and Theology of William Perkins." Ph.D. dissertation, University of Manchester, 1963.

Brienen, Teunis. *De prediking van de Nadere Reformatie.* Amsterdam: Ton Bolland, 1974.

_____, et al. *Figuren en thema's van de Nadere Reformatie.* 3 vols. Kampen: De Groot, 1987-93.

_____, et al. *Theologische aspecten van de Nadere Reformatie.* Zoetermeer: Boekencentrum, 1993.

_____, Exalto, K., J. van Genderen, C. Graafland, and W. van't Spijker. *De Nadere Reformatie. Beschrijving van haar voornaamste vertegenwoordigers.* 's-Gravenhage: Boekencentrum, 1986.

Bronkema, Ralph. *The Essence of Puritanism.* Goes, Netherlands: Oosterbaan and LeCointre, 1929.

Brook, Benjamin. *The Lives of the Puritans.* 3 vols. London: J. Black, 1813; reprint, Pittsburgh: Soli Deo Gloria Publications, 1994.

Brown, John. *The English Puritans.* London: Cambridge University Press, 1912.

_____. *Puritan Preaching in England.* New York: Charles Scribner's Sons, 1900.

Brown, Paul Edward. "The Principle of the Covenant in the Theology of Thomas Goodwin." Ph.D. dissertation, Drew University, 1950.

Brown, Robert. *Doctrinal and Experimental Theology.* London: William Wileman, 1899.

Bruggink, Donald J. "The Theology of Thomas Boston, 1676-1732." Ph.D. dissertation, Edinburgh, 1956.

Burrage, Champlin. *The Early English Dissenters in the Light of Recent Research (1550-1641).* 2 vols. New York: Russell & Russell, 1967.

Bush, Sargent. *The Writings of Thomas Hooker: Spiritual Adventure in Two Worlds.* Madison: University of Wisconsin Press, 1980.

Byington, Ezra Hoyt. *The Puritan in England and New England.* Boston: Little, Brown and Co., 1900.

Calderwood, David. *The History of the Kirk of Scotland.* 8 vols. Edinburgh: Wodrow Society, 1842-43.

Caldwell, Patricia. *The Puritan Conversion Narrative.* New York: Cambridge University Press, 1985.

Campbell, Douglas. *The Puritan in Holland, England, and America.* 4th ed. 2 vols. New York: Harper and Brothers, 1892.

Carden, Allen. *Puritan Christianity in America: Religion and Life in Seventeenth-Century Massachusetts.* Grand Rapids: Baker, 1990.

Carroll, Peter N. *Puritanism and the Wilderness: The Intellectual Significance of the New England Frontier, 1629-1700.* New York: Columbia University Press, 1969.

*Carruthers, Samuel William. *The Everyday Work of the Westminster Assembly.* Philadelphia: Presbyterian Historical Society, 1943.

_____, ed. *The Westminster Confession of Faith.* Manchester: R. Aikman & Son, 1937.

Carson, John L. and David W. Hall, ed. *To Glorify and Enjoy God: A Commemoration of the 350th Anniversary of the Westminster Assembly.* Edinburgh: Banner of Truth Trust, 1994.

Carter, Alice. *The English Reformed Church in Amsterdam in the Seventeenth Century.* Amsterdam: Scheltema & Holkema, 1964.

Carter, R. B. "The Presbyterian-Independent Controversy with Special Reference to Dr. Thomas Goodwin and the Years 1640 to 1660." Ph.D. dissertation, Edinburgh, 1961.

Chalker, William H. "Calvin and Some Seventeenth Century English Calvinists." Ph.D. dissertation, Duke University, 1961.

Chan, Simon K.H. "The Puritan Meditative Tradition, 1559-1691: A Study of Ascetical Piety." Ph.D. dissertation, Cambridge University, 1986.

Cherry, Conrad. *The Theology of Jonathan Edwards: A Reappraisal.* Gloucester, Mass.: Peter Smith, 1974.

Citron, Bernhard. *New Birth: A Study of the Evangelical Doctrine of Conversion in the Protestant Fathers.* Edinburgh: University Press, Clarke, Irwin, 1951.

Clifford, K. "The Reconstruction of Puritan Casuistry." Ph.D. dissertation, University of London, 1957.

Clifford, Nigel. *Christian Preachers.* Bridgend: Evangelical Press of Wales, 1994.

Coffey, John. *Politics, Religion and the British Revolutions: The Mind of Samuel Rutherford.* Cambridge: Cambridge University Press, 1997.

Cohen, Charles Lloyd. *God's Caress: the Psychology of Puritan Religious Experience.* New York: Oxford University Press, 1986.

Collinson, Patrick. *The Elizabethan Puritan Movement.* Berkeley: University of California Press, 1967.

_____. *English Puritanism.* London: Historical Association, 1987.

_____. *Godly People: Essays on English Protestantism and Puritanism.* London: Hambledon Press, 1983.

_____. *A Mirror of Elizabethan Puritanism: The Life and Letters of 'Godly Master Dering.'* London: Dr. William's Trust, 1964.

_____. *The Puritan Character: Polemics and Polarities in Early Seventeenth-Century English Culture.* Los Angeles: University of California, 1989.

_____. *The Religion of Protestants: The Church in English Society, 1559-1625.* Oxford: Clarendon Press, 1982.

Come, Donald R. "John Cotton: Guide of the Chosen People." Ph.D. dissertation, University of Illinois, 1956.

Cook, Faith. *Samuel Rutherford and His Friends.* Edinburgh: Banner of Truth Trust, 1992.

_____. *Singing in the Fire: Christians in Adversity.* Edinburgh: Banner of Truth Trust, 1995.

Coolidge, John S. *The Pauline Renaissance in England: Puritanism and the Bible.* Oxford: Clarendon Press, 1970.

Cragg, C. R. *Puritanism in the Period of the Great Persecution, 1660-1688.* London: Cambridge University Press, 1957.

Cramer, J. A. *De Theologische Faculteit te Utrecht ten tijde van Voetius.* Utrecht: Kemink en Zoon, 1932.

Cremeans, Charles D. *The Reception of Calvinistic Thought in England.* Urbana: University of Illinois Press, 1958.

Cressy, David and Lon Anne Ferrell, eds. *Religion and Society in Early Modern England: A Sourcebook.* London: Routledge, 1996.

Crompton, Gordon Douglas. "The Life and Theology of Thomas Goodwin." Th.M. thesis, Greenville Presbyterian Theological Seminary, 1997.

Cross, Wilfred Oakland. "The Role and Status of the Unregenerate in the Massachusetts Bay Colony, 1629-1729." Ph.D. dissertation, Columbia University, 1957.

Curtis, Mark H. *Oxford and Cambridge in Transition 1558-1642.* Oxford: Clarendon Press, 1959.

Daly, Robert. *God's Altar: The World and the Flesh in Puritan Poetry.* Berkeley: University of California Press, 1978.

Damrosch, Leopold. *God's Plot and Man's Stories: Studies in the Fictional Imagination from Milton to Fielding.* Chicago: University of Chicago Press, 1985.

Daniels, Richard W. *The Christology of John Owen.* Grand Rapids: Reformation Heritage Books, 2004.

Dankbaar, W. F. *Hoogtepunten uit het Nederlandsche Calvinisme in de zestiende eeuw.* Haarlem: Tjeenk Willink, 1946.

Davies, Horton. *The Worship of the American Puritans.* Morgan, Penn.: Soli Deo Gloria, 1999.

_____. *The Worship of the English Puritans.* London: Dacre Press, 1948.

_____. *Worship and Theology in England: From Andrewes to Baxter and Fox, 1603-1690*. Princeton: Princeton University Press, 1975.

Davis, J. C. W. "John Owen, D.D.: Puritan Preacher and Ecclesiastical Statesman." M.A. thesis, Liverpool University, 1962.

De Bie, J. P., and J. Loosjes, eds. *Biographisch Woordenboek der Protestantsche Godgeleerden in Nederland*. 5 vols. 's-Gravenhage: Martinus Nijhoff, 1907-43.

De Boer, Johannes. *De Verzegeling met de Heilige Geest volgens de opvatting van de Nadere Reformatie*. Rotterdam: Bronder, 1968.

De Jong, O. J., et al. *Het eigene van de Nederlandse Nadere Reformatie*. Houten: Den Hertog, 1992.

De Jong, Peter Y. *The Covenant Idea in New England Theology, 1620-1847*. Grand Rapids: Eerdmans, 1945.

_____, ed. *Crises in the Reformed Churches: Essays in Commemoration of the Great Synod of Dort, 1618-1619*. Grand Rapids: Reformed Fellowship, 1968.

Delbanco, Andrew. *The Puritan Ordeal*. Cambridge, Mass.: Harvard University Press, 1989.

De Lind van Wijngaarden, J. D. *Antonius Walaeus*. Leiden, 1891.

De Marest, David D. *History and Characteristics of the Reformed Protestant Dutch Church*. 2nd edition. New York: Board of Publication of the Reformed Protestant Dutch Church, 1856.

Demos, John. *A Little Commonwealth; Family Life In Plymouth Colony*. New York, Oxford University Press, 1970.

_____. *Entertaining Satan: Witchcraft and The Culture Of Early New England*. New York: Oxford University Press, 1982.

Den Boer, C. *Om't eeuwig welbehagen (Verhandelingen over de Dordtse Leerregels)*. Utrecht: De Banier, 1983.

Denholm, Andrew T. "Thomas Hooker: Puritan Preacher, 1586-1647." Ph.D. dissertation, Hartford Seminary Foundation, 1961.

Dentz, Fred. Oudschans. *History of the English Church at the Hague, 1586-1929*. Delft: W. D. Meinema, 1929.

Dever, Mark. *Richard Sibbes: Puritanism and Calvinism in Late Elizabethan and Early Stuart England*. Macon: Mercer University Press, 2000.

*DeVries, Pieter. *John Bunyan on the Order of Salvation*. Trans. C. van Haaften. New York: Peter Lang, 1994.

De Vrijer, Marinus Johannes Antonie. *Ds. Bernardus Smytegelt en zijn "gekrookte riet."* Amsterdam: H. J. Spruyt, 1947.

_____. *Schortinghuis en zijn analogieën*. Amsterdam: H. J. Spruyt, 1942.

De War, M. W. "How Far is the Westminster Assembly an Expression of Seventeenth-Century Anglican Theology?" Ph.D. dissertation, Queen's University (Belfast), 1960.

De Witt, John Richard. *Jus Divinum: The Westminster Assembly and the Divine Right of Church Government.* Kampen: Kok, 1969.

Dexter, Henry Martyn. *The Congregationalism of the Last Three Hundred Years as Seen in its Literature.* New York: Harper & Brothers, 1880.

Dexter, Henry Martyn, and Morton Dexter. *The England and Holland of the Pilgrims.* Boston: Houghton, Mifflin and Company, 1905.

Dorioni, Daniel M. "The Godly Household in Puritan Theology, 1560-1640." Ph.D. dissertation, Westminster Theological Seminary, 1986.

Duke, Alastair. *Reformation and Revolt in the Low Countries.* London: Hambledon, 1990.

Duker, Arnoldus Cornelius. *Gisbertus Voetius.* 4 vols. Leiden: E. J. Brill, 1897-1914; reprint, Leiden: J. J. Groen en Zoon, 1989.

Duncan, J. Ligon, III, ed. *The Westminster Confession into the 21st Century: essays in remembrance of the 350th anniversary of the Westminster Assembly.* Volumes 1-2. Fearn: Mentor, 2003-2004.

Earle, Alice Morse. *The Sabbath in Puritan New England.* London: Hodder & Stoughton, 1982.

Ebner, Dean. *Autobiography in Seventeenth-Century England: Theology and the Self.* The Hague: Mouton, 1971.

Eekhof, A. *De Theologische Faculteit te Leiden in de 17de Eeuw.* Utrecht: G. J. A. Ruys, 1921.

Ehalt, David R. "The Development of Early Congregational Theory of the Church with Special Reference to the Five 'Dissenting Brethren' at the Westminster Assembly." Ph.D. dissertation, Claremont, 1969.

Elliott, Emory. *Power and the Pulpit In Puritan New England.* Princeton, N.J.: Princeton University Press, 1975.

Elliott, J. P. "Protestantization in the Northern Netherlands: A Case Study — The Classis of Dordrecht 1572-1640." 2 vols. Ph.D. dissertation, Columbia University, 1990.

Elshout, Bartel. *The Pastoral and Practical Theology of Wilhelmus à Brakel: A Brief Evaluation of The Christian's Reasonable Service.* Grand Rapids: Reformation Heritage Books, 1997.

Emerson, Everett H. *English Puritanism from John Hooper to John Milton.* Durham, N.C.: Duke University Press, 1968.

_____. *Puritanism in America.* Boston: Twayne Publishers, 1977.

_____. "Thomas Hooker and the Reformed Theology: The Relation of Hooker's Conversion Preaching to its Background." Ph.D. dissertation, Louisiana State University, 1955.

Emerson, Everett, ed. *Major Writers of Early American Literature.* Madison: University of Wisconsin Press, 1972.

Engelberts, Willem Jodocus Matthias. *Willem Teellinck.* Amsterdam: Scheffer & Co., 1898.

Everson, Don Marvin. "The Puritan Theology of John Owen." Th.D. dissertation, Southern Baptist Theological Seminary, 1959.

Exalto, K. *Beleefd geloof: Acht schetsen van gereformeerde theologen uit de 17e Eeuw.* Amsterdam: Ton Bolland, 1974.

_____. *De Kracht der Religie: Tien schetsen van Gereformeerde 'Oude Schrijvers' uit de 17e en 18e Eeuw.* Urk: De Vuurtoren, 1976.

_____. *De Zekerheid des Geloofs bij Calvijn.* Apeldoorn: Willem de Zwijger-stichting, 1978.

Fabend, Firth Haring. *Zion on the Hudson: Dutch New York and New Jersey in the Age of Revivals.* New Brunswick: Rutgers University Press, 2000.

Farrell, Frank E. "Richard Sibbes: A Study in Early Seventeenth Century English Puritanism." Ph.D. dissertation, Edinburgh, 1955.

*Ferguson, Sinclair. *John Owen on the Christian Life.* Edinburgh: Banner of Truth Trust, 1987.

Fienberg, Stanley P. "Thomas Goodwin, Puritan Pastor and Independent Divine." Ph.D. dissertation, University of Chicago, 1974.

Fincham, Kenneth, ed. *The Early Stuart Church, 1603-1642.* Hampshire: Macmillan, 1993.

Foster, Stephen. *The Long Argument: English Puritanism and the Shaping of New England Culture, 1570-1700.* Chapel Hill: University of North Carolina Press, 1991.

Fraser, Donald. *Life and Diary of Ebenezer Erskine.* Edinburgh: William Oliphant and Son, 1831.

_____. *Life and Diary of Ralph Erskine.* Edinburgh: William Oliphant and Son, 1834.

Fulcher, John Rodney. "Puritan Piety in Early New England: A Study in Spiritual Regeneration from the Antinomian Controversy to the Cambridge Synod of 1648 in the Massachusetts Bay Colony." Ph.D. dissertation, Princeton University, 1963.

Gardiner, Samuel Rawson. *History of England from the Accession of James I to the Outbreak of the Civil War 1603-1642.* 10 vols. New York: Longmans, Green, and Co., 1896-1901.

Garrett, Christina H. *The Marian Exiles: A Study in the Origins of Elizabethan Puritanism*. Cambridge: Cambridge University Press, 1938.

Geesink, W. *Calvinisten in Holland*. Amsterdam, 1887; reprint, Genevae: Slatkine Reprints, 1970.

George, Charles H. and Katherine George. *The Protestant Mind of the English Reformation, 1570-1640*. Princeton: Princeton University Press, 1961.

George, Timothy. *John Robinson and the English Separatist Tradition*. NABPR Dissertation Series, Number 1, ed. Charles Talbert. Macon: Mercer University Press, 1982.

Gerstner, John H. *The Rational Biblical Theology of Jonathan Edwards*. 3 vols. Powhatan, Va.: Berea Publications, 1991-93.

*_____. *Steps to Salvation: The Evangelistic Message of Jonathan Edwards*. Philadelphia: Westminster Press, 1960; reprint, *Jonathan Edwards, Evangelist*. Morgan, Penn.: Soli Deo Gloria, 1995.

Gerstner, Jonathan N. *The Thousand Generation Covenant: Dutch Reformed Covenant Theology and Group Identity in Colonial South Africa*. Leiden: E. J. Brill, 1991.

Geyl, Pieter. *The Netherlands in the Seventeenth Century*. 2 vols. London: Benn, 1961-64.

Gilmore, Michael T. *Early American Literature: A Collection of Critical Essays*. Englewood Cliffs, N.J.: Prentice-Hall, 1980.

Glasius, B. *Geschiedenis der Nationale Synode in 1618 en 1619 gehouden te Dordrecht*. 2 vols. Leiden: E. J. Brill, 1860-61.

_____, ed. *Godgeleerd Nederland: Biographisch Woordenboek van Nederlandsche Godgeleerden*. 3 vols. 's-Hertogenbosch: Gebr. Muller, 1851-56.

Godfrey, W. Robert. "Tensions within International Calvinism: The Debate on the Atonement at the Synod of Dort, 1618-1619." Ph.D. dissertation, Stanford University, 1974.

Goeters, W. *Die Vorbereitung des Pietismus in der reformierten Kirche der Niederlande*. Leipzig: J. C. Hinrichs'sche Buchhandlung, 1911; reprint, Amsterdam: Ton Bolland, 1974.

Graafland, Cornelis. *Van Calvijn tot Barth: Oorsprong en ontwikkeling van de leer der verkiezing in het Gereformeerd Protestantisme*. 's-Gravenhage: Boekencentrum, 1987.

_____. *De zekerheid van het geloof: Een onderzoek naar de geloof-beschouwing van enige vertegenwoordigers van reformatie en nadere reformatie*. Wageningen: H. Veenman & Zonen, 1961.

Graham, W. Fred, ed. *Later Calvinism: International Perspectives*. Kirksville, Mo.: Sixteenth Century Journal Publishers, 1994.

Gravemeijer, Henricus E. *Leesboek over de Gereformeerde Geloofsleer.*
3 vols. Utrecht: H. Ten Hove, n.d.

Graves, Frank Pierrepont. *Peter Ramus and the Educational Reformation
of the Sixteenth Century.* New York: The MacMillan Company,
1912.

Greaves, Richard. *John Bunyan.* Grand Rapids: Eerdmans, 1969.

Greve, Lionel. "Freedom and Discipline in the Theology of John Calvin,
William Perkins, and John Wesley: An Examination of the
Origin and Nature of Pietism." Ph.D. dissertation, The Hartford
Seminary Foundation, 1976.

Groenendijk, L. F. *De Nadere Reformatie van het Gezin: De visie van Petrus
Wittewrongel op de christelijke huishouding.* Dordrecht: J. P. van den
Tol, 1984.

Gulley, Frank. "The Influence of Heinrich Bullinger and the Tigurine
Tradition upon the English Church in the Sixteenth Century."
Ph.D. dissertation, Vanderbilt, 1961.

Gura, Philip F. *A Glimpse of Sion's Glory: Puritan Radicalism in New
England, 1620-1660.* Middletown, Conn.: Wesleyan University
Press, 1984.

Gustafsson, Berndt. *The Five Dissenting Brethren: A Study of the Dutch Background of Their Independentism.* London: C. W. K. Gloerup, 1955.

Hagans, J. M. "The Marrow of Modern Divinity and the Controversy
concerning it in Scotland." B.D. thesis, Trinity College, Dublin,
1966.

Haley, K. H. P. *The Dutch in the Seventeenth Century.* Norwich, England:
Jarrold and Sons Ltd., 1972.

Hall, David. *The Faithful Shepherd: A History of the New England Ministry
in the Seventeenth Century.* Chapel Hill: University of North Carolina Press, 1972.

———. *Worlds of Wonder, Days of Judgment: Popular Religious Belief in Early
New England.* Cambridge: Harvard University Press, 1989.

———, comp. *The Antinomian Controversy, 1636-1638: A Documentary
History.* Middletown, Conn.: Wesleyan University Press, 1968.

Hall, Edwin. *The Puritans and Their Principles.* New York: Baker and
Scribner, 1847.

Haller, William. *Liberty and Reformation in the Puritan Revolution.* New
York: Columbia University Press, 1955.

———. *The Rise of Puritanism.* New York: Columbia University Press,
1938.

Hambrick-Stowe, Charles E. *The Practice of Piety. Puritan Devotional*

Disciplines in Seventeenth-Century New England. Williamsburg, Va.: University of North Carolina Press, 1982.

Hansen, Maurice G. *The Reformed Church in the Netherlands.* New York: Board of Publication of the Reformed Church in America, 1884.

Hargrave, O. T. "The Doctrine of Predestination in the English Reformation." Ph.D. dissertation, Vanderbilt University, 1966.

Harinck, Cor. *De Schotse Verbondsleer: Van Robert Rollock tot Thomas Boston.* Utrecht: De Banier, 1986.

Harrison, A. W. *The Beginnings of Arminianism to the Synod of Dort.* London: University of London, 1926.

Hart, Darryl G., Sean Michael Lucas, and Stephen J. Nichols, eds. *The Legacy of Jonathan Edwards: American Religion and the Evangelical Tradition.* Grand Rapids: Baker, 2003.

Hasler, R. A. "Thomas Shepard: Pastor-Evangelist (1605-1649): A Study in New England Ministry." Ph.D. dissertation, Hartford Seminary Foundation, 1964.

Hastie, William. *The Theology of the Reformed Church.* Edinburgh: T. & T. Clark, 1904.

Hawkes, Richard Mitchell. "The Logic of Grace in John Owen, D.D.: An Analysis, Exposition, and Defense of John Owen's Puritan Theology of Grace." Ph.D. dissertation, Westminster Theological Seminary, 1987.

Helm, Paul. *Calvin and the Calvinists.* Edinburgh: Banner of Truth Trust, 1982.

Henderson, G. D. *Religious Life in Seventeenth-Century Scotland.* Cambridge: Cambridge University Press, 1937.

Henson, H. Hensley. *Studies in English Religion in the Seventeenth Century.* New York: E. P. Dutton, 1903.

Heppe, Heinrich. *Geschichte des Pietismus und der Mystik in der Reformierten Kirche, namentlich der Niederlande.* Leiden: E. J. Brill, 1879.

*Hetherington, W. M. *History of the Westminster Assembly of Divines.* New York: Robert Carter & Brothers, 1859.

Hicks, John M. "The Theology of Grace in the Thought of Jacobus Arminius and Philip van Limborch: A Study in the Development of Seventeenth-Century Dutch Arminianism." Ph.D. dissertation, Westminster Theological Seminary, 1985.

Hill, Christopher. *Puritanism and Revolution: Studies in Interpretation of the English Revolution of the 17th Century.* New York: Schocken Books, 1964.

_____. *Society and Puritanism in Pre-Revolutionary England.* 2nd ed. New York: Schocken Books, 1967.

A History of the Westminster Assembly of Divines. Embracing an Account of Its Principal Transactions, and Biographical Sketches of Its Most Conspicuous Members. Philadelphia: Presbyterian Board of Publications, 1841.

Hoeksema, Homer. *The Voice of our Fathers: An Exposition of the Canons of Dordrecht.* Grand Rapids: Reformed Free Publishing Association, 1980.

Hofmeyr, Johannes Wynand. *Johannes Hoornbeeck als polemikus.* Kampen: Kok, 1975.

Holifield, E. Brooks. *The Covenant Sealed: The Development of Puritan Sacramental Theology in Old and New England, 1570-1720.* New Haven: Yale University Press, 1974.

Holley, Larry Jackson. "The Divines of the Westminster Assembly: A Study of Puritanism and Parliament." Ph.D. dissertation, Yale University, 1979.

Honders, Huibert Jacob. *Andreas Rivetus als invloedrijk Gereformeerd theoloog in Holland's bloeitijd.* 's-Gravenhage: Martinus Nijhoff, 1930.

Honig, Anthonie Gerrit. *Alexander Comrie.* Utrecht: H. Honig, 1892.

Hopf, Constantin. *Martin Bucer and the English Reformation.* New York: Macmillan, 1947.

Horst, Irvin Buckwaiter. *The Dutch Dissenters: A Critical Companion to their History and Ideas.* Leiden: E. J. Brill, 1986.

Horton, Douglas, trans. and ed. *William Ames by Matthew Nethenus, Hugo Visscher, and Karl Reuter.* Cambridge: Harvard Divinity School Library, 1965.

Howard, Leon, ed. *Essays on Puritans and Puritanism.* Albuquerque: University of New Mexico Press, 1989.

Howie, John. *The Scots Worthies.* Edinburgh: Banner of Truth Trust, 1995.

Huelin, Gordon. "Peter Martyr and the English Reformation." Ph.D. dissertation, University of London, 1955.

Humphrey, Richard Alan. "The Concept of Conversion in the Theology of Thomas Shepard (1605-1649)." Ph.D. dissertation, Drew University, 1967.

*Hulse, Erroll. *Who are the Puritans?* Darlington: Evangelical Press, 2000.

Jacobs, Jaap. *New Netherland: A Dutch Colony in Seventeenth-century America.* Leiden: Brill, 2005.

Janse, L. *Gisbertus Voetius, 1589-1676.* Utrecht: De Banier, 1971.

_____. *Jacobus Koelman, 1632-1695.* Utrecht: De Banier, n.d.

Jenkins, R. B. *Henry Smith: England's Silver-Tongued Preacher.* Macon, Ga.: Mercer University Press, 1983.

Jones, James William. *The Shattered Synthesis; New England Puritanism Before The Great Awakening.* New Haven: Yale University Press, 1973.

Jones, James William, III. "The Beginnings of American Theology: John Cotton, Thomas Hooker, Thomas Shepard and Peter Bulkeley." Ph.D. dissertation, Brown University, 1970.

Kaajan, H. *De Groote Synode van Dordrecht in 1618-1619.* Amsterdam: N. V. de Standaard, 1918.

*Kapic, Kelly M. and Randall C. Gleason, eds. *The Devoted Life: An Invitation to the Puritan Classics.* Downers Grove: InterVarsity Press, 2004.

Karlberg, Mark Walter. "The Mosaic Covenant and the Concept of Works in Reformed Hermeneutics: A Historical-Critical Analysis with Particular Attention to Early Covenant Eschatology." Th.D. dissertation, Westminster Theological Seminary, 1980.

Kaufmann, U. F. *The Pilgrim's Progress and Traditions in Puritan Meditation.* New Haven: Yale University Press, 1966.

Kempff, D. *A Bibliography of Calviniana, 1959-1974.* Potchefstroom: I.A.C., 1975.

Kendall, Robert T. *Calvin and English Calvinism to 1649.* New York: Oxford University Press, 1979.

*Kevan, Ernest F. *The Grace of Law: A Study in Puritan Theology.* London: Carey Kingsgate Press, 1964; reprint, Morgan, Penn.: Soli Deo Gloria, 1993.

Kibbey, Ann. *The Interpretation of Material Shapes in Puritanism: A Study of Rhetoric, Prejudice, and Violence.* New York: Cambridge University Press, 1986.

*Kistler, Don. *A Spectacle unto God: The Life and Death of Christopher Love.* Morgan, Penn.: Soli Deo Gloria, 1994.

Kling, David William and Douglas A. Sweeney, eds. *Jonathan Edwards at Home and Abroad: Historical Memories, Cultural Movements, Global Horizons.* Columbia: University of South Carolina Press, 2003.

Klunder, Jack D. "The Application of Holy Things: A Study of the Covenant Preaching in the Eighteenth Century Dutch Colonial Church." Ph.D. dissertation, Westminster Theological Seminary, 1984.

Knappen, M. M. "Richard Greenham and the Practical Puritans under Elizabeth." Ph.D. dissertation, Cornell University, 1927.

_____. *Tudor Puritanism: A Chapter in the History of Idealism*. Chicago: University of Chicago Press, 1939.

Knight, Janice. *Orthodoxies in Massachusetts: Rereading American Puritanism*. Cambridge: Harvard University Press, 1994.

Knoepp, Walther T. "Jonathan Edwards: The Way of Sanctification." Ph.D. dissertation, Hartford Seminary Foundation, 1937.

Knox, S. J. *Walter Travers: Paragon of Elizabethan Puritanism*. London: Methuen, 1962.

Kromsigt, Johannes Christiaan. *Wilhelmus Schortinghuis. Eene bladzijde uit de geschiedenis van het Piëtisme in de Gereformeerde Kerk van Nederland*. Groningen: J. B. Wolters, 1904.

Kruger, J. C. *Die verhouding van uitverkiesing tot bekering met spesiale verwysing na die Dordtse Leerreels*. Pretoria: Kerkboekhandel, 1974.

Krull, F. A. *Jacobus Koelman: Een kerkhistorische Studie*. Reprint, Amsterdam: Ton Bolland, 1972.

Kuiper, J. *Geschiedenis van het Godsdienstig en Kerkelijk Leven van het Nederlandsche Volk*. Nijkerk: G. F. Callenbach, 1903.

Kuyper, Herman Huber. *De Post-Acts of Nahandelingen van de Nationale Synode van Dordrecht in 1618 en 1619 Gehouden*. Amsterdam: Hoveker & Wormser, [1899].

Lachman, David. *The Marrow Controversy, 1718-1723: An Historical and Theological Analysis*. Rutherford Studies Series One: Historical Theology. Edinburgh: Rutherford House, 1988.

_____. "The Marrow Controversy: An Historical Survey with special reference to the Free Offer of the Gospel, the Extent of the Atonement, and Assurance and Saving Faith." Th.M. thesis, Westminster Theological Seminary, 1973.

Lake, Peter. *Anglicans and Puritans? Presbyterian and English Conformist Thought from Whitgift to Hooker*. London: Unwin Hyman, 1988.

_____. *Moderate Puritans and the Elizabethan Church*. New York: Cambridge University Press, 1982.

Laman, H. W. *Geloofsbezwaren opgelost door Wilhelmus à Brakel*. Kampen: Kok, 1929.

Lang, Amy Schrager. *Prophetic Woman: Anne Hutchinson and The Problem Of Dissent In The Literature Of New England*. Berkeley: University of California Press, 1987.

Lang, August. *Puritanismus und Piëtismus: Studies zu ihrer Entwicklung von M. Butzer bis zum methodismus*. Ansbach: Brugel, 1941.

Laurence, David Ernst. "Religious Experience in the Biblical World of Jonathan Edwards: A Study in Eighteenth Century Supernaturalism." Ph.D. dissertation, Yale University, 1976.

Leith, John H. *Assembly at Westminster: Reformed Theology in the Making.* Richmond: John Knox Press, 1973.

Letham, Robert. "Saving Faith and Assurance in Reformed Theology: Zwingli to the Synod of Dort." 2 vols. Ph.D. dissertation, University of Aberdeen, 1979.

Leverenz, David. *The Language of Puritan Feeling: An Exploration In Literature, Psychology, and Social History.* New Brunswick, N.J.: Rutgers University Press, 1980.

Levy, Babette May. *Preaching in the First Century of New England History.* Hartford, Conn.: American Society of Church History, 1945.

*Lewis, Peter. *The Genius of Puritanism.* Haywards Heath, Sussex: Carey Publications, 1975.

Lindberg, Richard L. "The Westminster and Second London Baptist Confessions of Faith: A Historical-Theological Comparison." Th.M. thesis, Westminster Theological Seminary, 1980.

Lindeboom, Johannes. *Austin Friars: History of the Dutch Reformed Church in London, 1550-1950.* Trans. D. DeIongh. The Hague: Nijhoff, 1950.

*Lloyd-Jones, D. M. *The Puritans: Their Origins and Successors. Addresses delivered at the Puritan and Westminster Conferences 1959-1978.* Edinburgh: The Banner of Truth Trust, 1987.

Loane, Marcus L. *Makers of Puritan History.* Grand Rapids: Baker, 1980. Reprint of edition published in 1961 by Wm. B. Eerdmans, with the title *Makers of Religious Freedom in the Seventeenth Century: Henderson, Rutherford, Bunyan, Baxter.*

Los, Frans Johannes. *Wilhelmus à Brakel.* Leiden: G. Los, 1892.

Lovelace, Richard. *The American Pietism of Cotton Mather.* Grand Rapids: Eerdmans, 1979.

Lowance, Mason I. *The Language of Canaan: Metaphor and Symbol in New England from the Puritans to the Transcendentalists.* Cambridge, Mass.: Harvard University Press, 1980.

Lowrie, Ernest B. *The Shape of the Puritan Mind: The Thought of Samuel Willard.* New Haven: Yale University Press, 1974.

Macauley, George. *Puritan Theology.* 2 vols. London: James Nisbet, 1872.

Martin, John Frederick. *Profits in the Wilderness: Entrepreneurship and the Founding of New England Towns in the Seventeenth Century.* Chapel Hill: University Of North Carolina Press, 1991.

McCahagan, Thomas Arthur. "Cartesianism in the Netherlands, 1639-

1676: The New Science and the Calvinist Counter-Reformation." Ph.D. dissertation, University of Pennsylvania, 1976.

M'Clintock, John, and James Strong. *Cyclopaedia of Biblical, Theological, and Ecclesiastical Literature.* 12 vols. New York: Harper and Brothers, 1894-95.

McCoy, Charles. "The Covenant Theology of Johannes Cocceius." Ph.D. dissertation, Yale University, 1957.

McCoy, Charles S., and J. Wayne Baker. *Fountainhead of Federalism: Heinrich Bullinger and the Covenantal Tradition.* Louisville: Westminster/John Knox, 1992.

M'Crie, *The Story of the Scottish Church from the Reformation to the Disruption.* London: Blackie & Son, 1875.

MacEwen, A. R. *The Erskines.* Edinburgh: Oliphant Anderson & Ferrier, 1900.

McGee, James Sears. *The Godly Man in Stuart England: Anglicans, Puritans, and the Two Tables, 1620-1670.* New Haven: Yale University Press, 1976.

McGowan, Andrew. *The Federal Theology of Thomas Boston (1676-1732).* Edinburgh: Paternoster, 1997.

McKee, William Wakefield. "The Idea of Covenant in Early English Puritanism (1580-1643)." Ph.D. dissertation, Yale University, 1948.

McKerrow, John. *History of the Secession Church.* Edinburgh: A. Fullarton, 1845.

McKim, Donald Keith. *Ramism in William Perkins' Theology.* American University Studies, Series VII, Theology and Religion, no. 15. New York: Peter Lang, 1987.

MacLear, James F. "The Puritan Party, 1603-1643: A Study in a Lost Reformation." Ph.D. dissertation, University of Chicago, 1947.

Macleod, John. *Scottish Theology: In Relation to Church History Since the Reformation.* Reprint, London: Banner of Truth Trust, 1974.

McNally, Alexander. "Some Aspects of Thomas Goodwin's Doctrine of Assurance." Th.M. thesis, Westminster Theological Seminary, 1972.

McNeill, John T. *The History and Character of Calvinism.* New York: Oxford University Press, 1973.

Macphail, Andrew. *Essays in Puritanism.* London: T. Fisher Unwin, 1905.

Malan, C. J. *Die Nadere Reformasie.* Potchefstroom, Republic of South Africa: Potchefstroomse Universiteit vir CHO, 1981.

Maltby, Judith. *Prayer Book and People in Elizabethan and Early Stuart England.* Cambridge: Cambridge University Press, 1998.

Markham, C. C. "William Perkins' Understanding of the Function of Conscience." Ph.D. dissertation, Vanderbilt University, 1967.

Marsden, George M. *Jonathan Edwards: A Life.* New Haven: Yale University Press, 2003.

Marsden, J. P. *The History of the Early Puritans.* 2nd ed. London: Hamilton, Adams, & Co., 1853.

————. *The History of the Later Puritans.* 3rd ed. London: Hamilton, Adams, & Co., 1872.

Martin, Hugh. *Puritanism and Richard Baxter.* London: SCM Press, 1954.

Martin, Ralph P. *A Guide to the Puritans: A Topical and Textual Index to Writings of the Puritans and Some of their Successors Recently in Print.* Edinburgh: Banner of Truth Trust, 1997.

Middlekauff, Robert. *The Mathers: Three Generations of Puritan Intellectuals, 1596-1728.* New York: Oxford University Press, 1971.

Middleton, Erasmus. *Evangelical Biography.* 4 vols. London: Baynes, 1810.

Miller, Glenn. "The Rise of Evangelical Calvinism: A Study in Jonathan Edwards and the Puritan Tradition." Th.D. dissertation, Union Theological Seminary, 1971.

Miller, Perry. *Errand into the Wilderness.* Cambridge: Belknap Press, 1956.

————. *Jonathan Edwards.* New York: William Sloane, 1949; reprint, Westport, Conn.: Greenwood Press, 1973.

————. *The New England Mind: From Colony to Province.* Cambridge: Harvard University Press, 1953; reprint, Boston: Beacon Press, 1961.

————. *The New England Mind: The Seventeenth Century.* Cambridge: Harvard University Press, 1939; reprint, Boston: Beacon Press, 1961.

————. *Orthodoxy in Massachusetts.* Cambridge: Harvard University Press, 1933; reprint, Gloucester, Mass.: Peter Smith, 1965.

Mitchell, Alexander F. *The Westminster Assembly, Its History and Standards.* Philadelphia: Presbyterian Board of Publications, 1884.

Moffatt, Charles L., Jr. "James Hog of Carnock (1658-1734), Leader of the Evangelical Party in Early Eighteenth Century Scotland." Ph.D. dissertation, University of Edinburgh, 1960.

Molhuysen, Philip Christiaan, ed. *Nieuw Nederlandsch Biografisch Woordenboek.* 10 vols. Leiden: A. W. Sijthoff, 1911-37.

Monk, Robert C. *John Wesley: His Puritan Heritage.* Nashville: Abingdon Press, 1966.

Montgomery, Michael S. *American Puritan Studies: An Annotated Bibliography of Dissertations, 1882-1981.* Bibliographies and Indexes in American History, no. 1. Westport, Conn.: Greenwood Press, 1984.

Morgan, Edmund S. *Puritan Political Ideas.* Indianapolis: Bobbs, Merrill, 1965.

_____. *The Puritan Dilemma: The Story of John Winthrop.* Boston: Little, Brown, 1958.

_____. *Visible Saints: The History of a Puritan Idea.* New York: New York University Press, 1963.

Morgan, Irvonwy. *The Godly Preachers of the Elizabethan Church.* London: Epworth Press, 1965.

_____. *Puritan Spirituality: Illustrated from the Life and Times of the Rev. Dr. John Preston.* London: Epworth Press, 1973.

Morris, Edward D. *Theology of the Westminster Symbols.* Columbus, Ohio: Champlin Press, 1900.

Muller, Richard A. *Christ and the Decrees: Christology and Predestination in Reformed Theology from Calvin to Perkins.* Grand Rapids: Baker, 1988.

_____. *Post-Reformation Reformed Dogmatics.* 4 vols. Grand Rapids: Baker, 2003.

Mullinger, James Bass. *The University of Cambridge.* 3 vols. Cambridge: Cambridge University Press, 1873-1911.

Munson, Charles R. "William Perkins, Theologian of Transition." Ph.D. dissertation, Case Western Reserve, 1971.

Murdock, Kenneth B. *Increase Mather: the Foremost American Puritan.* Cambridge: Harvard University Press, 1925.

Murray, Iain H. *Jonathan Edwards: A New Biography.* Edinburgh: Banner of Truth Trust, 1987.

*_____. *The Puritan Hope.* London: Banner of Truth Trust, 1971.

Nauta, D. *Het Calvinisme in Nederland.* Franeker: Wever, 1949.

_____. *De Nederlandsche Gereformeerden en het Independentisme in de zeventiende eeuwe.* Amsterdam: H. J. Paris, 1935.

_____, ed. *Biografisch Lexicon voor de Geschiedenis van het Nederlands Protestantisme.* 4 vols. Kampen: Kok, 1978-88.

New, John F. *Anglican and Puritan: The Basis of Their Opposition, 1558-1640.* Stanford: Stanford University Press, 1964.

Nobbs, Douglas. *Theocracy and Toleration: A Study in the Disputes in Dutch Calvinism from 1600-1650.* Cambridge: University Press, 1938.

Nuttall, Geoffrey F. *The Beginnings of Nonconformity.* London: J. Clarke 1964.

———. *Congregationalists and Creeds.* London: Epworth, 1967.

*———. *The Holy Spirit in Puritan Faith and Experience.* Oxford: Basil Blackwell, 1946; reprint, Chicago: University of Chicago Press, 1992.

———. *The Puritan Sprit: Essays and Addresses.* London: Epworth, 1967.

———. *Richard Baxter.* London: Nelson, 1966.

———. *Studies in English Dissent.* Weston Rhyn: Quinta Press, 2002.

———. *Visible Saints: The Congregational Way, 1640-1660.* Weston Rhyn: Quinta Press, 2001.

Oki, Hideo. "Ethics in Seventeenth Century English Puritanism." Ph.D. dissertation, Union Theological Seminary, 1960.

Oldridge, Darren. *Religion and Society in Early Stuart England.* Aldershot: Ashgate, 1998.

*Oliver, Robert, ed. *John Owen: The Man and His Theology.* Edinburgh: Banner of Truth Trust, 2002.

Ong, Walter J. *Ramus, Method, and the Decay of Dialogue: From the Art of Discourse to the Art of Reason.* Cambridge: Harvard University Press, 1958.

Op't Hof, Willem Jan. *Bibliografische lijst van de geschriften van Willem Teellinck.* Rotterdam: Lindenberg, 1993.

———. *Engelse piëtistische geschriften in het Nederlands, 1598-1622.* Rotterdam: Lindenberg, 1987.

———. *Voorbereiding en bestrijding: De oudste gereformeerde piëtistische voorbereidingspreken tot het Avondmaal en de eerste bestrijding van de Nadere Reformatie in druk.* Kampen: DeGroot, 1987.

Orme, William. *Life of the Rev. John Owen, D.D.* Reprint, Choteau, Mont.: Gospel Mission Press, 1981.

Owen, T. E. *Methodism Unmasked; or, The Progress of Puritanism from the Sixteenth to the Nineteenth Century.* London: Printed for J. Hatchard, 1802.

*Packer, J. I., ed. *Puritan Papers.* 5 vols. Philipsburg, N.J.: Presbyterian and Reformed, 2000-2005.

*———. *A Quest for Godliness: The Puritan Vision of the Christian Life.* Wheaton, Ill.: Crossway Books, 1990.

———. "The Redemption and Restoration of Man in the Thought of Richard Baxter." D.Phil. dissertation, Oxford, 1954.

Parker, Kenneth L. *The English Sabbath: A Study of Doctrine and Discipline from the Reformation to the Civil War.* Cambridge: Cambridge University Press, 1988.

Parrington, Vernon Louis. *Main Currents in American Thought.* 3 vols. New York, Harcourt, Brace and Co., 1927.

Paul, Robert. *The Assembly of the Lord: Politics and Religion in the Westminster Assembly and the Grand Debate.* Edinburgh: T. & T. Clark, 1985.

Pellman, Hubert. "Thomas Hooker: A Study in Puritan Ideals." Ph.D. dissertation, University of Pennsylvania, 1958.

Pettit, Norman. *The Heart Prepared: Grace and Conversion in Puritan Spiritual Life.* New Haven: Yale University Press, 1966.

Phillips, James M. "Between Conscience and the Law: The Ethics of Richard Baxter (1615-1691)." Ph.D. dissertation, Princeton University, 1959.

Pipa, Joseph A., Jr. "William Perkins and the Development of Puritan Preaching." Ph.D. dissertation, Westminster Theological Seminary, 1985.

Platt, John. *Reformed Thought and Scholasticism: The Arguments for the Existence of God in Dutch Theology, 1575-1650.* Studies in the History of Christian Thought, no. 29. Ed. Heiko A. Oberman. Leiden: E. J. Brill, 1982.

Pollard, Alfred William, and Redgrave, G. R., eds. *A Short-Title Catalogue of Books Printed in England, Scotland, and Ireland, 1475-1640.* London: The Biblio-Society, 1946.

Poole, Harry A. "The Unsettled Mr. Cotton." Ph.D. dissertation, University of Illinois, 1956.

Pope, Robert G. *The Half-Way Covenant: Church Membership in Puritan New England.* Princeton, N.J.: Princeton University Press, 1969.

Porter, H. C. *Puritanism in Tudor England.* New York: The MacMillan Co., 1970.

_____. *Reformation and Reaction in Tudor Cambridge.* London: Cambridge University Press, 1958.

Porterfield, Amanda. *Female Piety in Puritan New England: The Emergence of Religious Humanism.* New York: Oxford University Press, 1992.

Prestwich, Menna, ed. *International Calvinism, 1541-1715.* Oxford: Clarendon Press, 1985.

Priebe, Victor L. "The Covenant Theology of William Perkins." Ph.D. dissertation, Drew University, 1967.

Proost, Pieter. *Jodocus van Lodenstein.* Amsterdam: J. Brandt en Zoon, 1880.

Pytches, P. N. L. "A Critical Exposition of the Teaching of John Owen on the work of the Holy Spirit in the Individual." M.Litt. thesis, Bristol, 1967.

Raitt, Jill, ed. *Shapers of Religious Traditions in Germany, Switzerland, and Poland, 1560-1600.* New Haven: Yale University Press, 1981.

Reid, James. *Memoirs of the Lives and Writings of those Eminent Divines who convened in the famous Assembly at Westminster in the Seventeenth Century.* 2 vols. Paisley: Stephen and Andrew Young, 1811; reprint, 2 vols. in 1, Edinburgh: Banner of Truth Trust, 1982.

Reid, W. Stanford, ed. *John Calvin: His Influence in the Western World.* Grand Rapids: Zondervan, 1982.

Rhoades, Donald Hosea. "Jonathan Edwards: Experimental Theologian." Ph.D. dissertation, Yale University, 1945.

Ritschl, Albrecht B. *Geschichte des Pietismus.* 3 vols. Bonn: Marcus, 1880-86.

Rogers, Henry. *The Life and Character of John Howe.* London: Religious Tract Society, 1863.

Rolston, Holmes, III. *John Calvin versus the Westminster Confession.* Richmond: John Knox Press, 1972.

Rooy, Sidney. *The Theology of Missions in the Puritan Tradition.* Grand Rapids: Eerdmans, 1965.

Rutgers, F. L. *Calvijns Invloed op de Reformatie in de Nederland.* Leiden: E. J. Brill, 1899.

Rutman, Darret Bruce. *American Puritanism: Faith and Practice.* Philadelphia: J. P. Lippincott, 1970.

————. *Small Worlds, Large Questions: Explorations in Early American Social History, 1600-1850.* Charlottesville: University Press of Virginia, 1994.

*Ryken, Leland. *Worldly Saints: The Puritans as They Really Were.* Grand Rapids: Zondervan, 1986.

Ryken, Philip Graham. *Thomas Boston as Preacher of the Fourfold State.* Carlisle: Paternoster Press, 1999.

Sceats, David. *The Experience of Grace: Aspects of the Faith and Spirituality of the Puritans.* Cambridge: Grove, 1997.

Schaefer, Paul R. "The Spiritual Brotherhood on the Habits of the Heart: Cambridge Protestants and the Doctrine of Sanctification from William Perkins to Thomas Shepard." D.Phil. dissertation, Oxford University, 1994.

Schmid, Heinrich. *Die Geschichte des Piëtismus.* Nördlingen: C. H. Beck, 1863.

Schneider, Herbert Wallace. *The Puritan Mind*. London: Constable and Co., 1931.

Schoneveld, Cornelis W. *Intertraffic of the Mind: Studies in Seventeenth Century Anglo-Dutch Translation*. Leiden: E. J. Brill, 1983.

Schroeder, Carl J. *In Quest of Pentecost: Jodocus van Lodenstein and the Dutch Second Reformation*. Lanham: University Press of America, 2001.

Schrog, Felix James. *Pietism in Colonial America*. Chicago: The University of Chicago, 1948.

Schuldiner, Michael. *Gifts and Works: The Post-Conversion Paradigm and Spiritual Controversy in Seventeenth-Century Massachusetts*. Macon, Ga.: Mercer University Press, 1991.

Seaver, Paul S. *The Puritan Lectureships: The Politics of Religious Dissent, 1560-1662*. Stanford, Ca.: Stanford University Press, 1970.

_____. *Wallington's World: A Puritan Artisan in Seventeenth-Century London*. Stanford: Stanford University Press, 1985.

Sepp, Christiaan. *Het Godgeleerd Onderwijs in Nederland, gedurende de 16e en 17e eeuw*. 2 vols. Leiden: De Breuk en Smits, 1873-74.

Shaw, Mark. "The Marrow of Practical Divinity: A Study in the Theology of William Perkins." Th.D. dissertation, Westminster Theological Seminary, 1981.

Shea, Daniel. *Spiritual Autobiography in Early America*. Madison: University of Wisconsin Press, 1989.

Shelly, Harold Patton. "Richard Sibbes: Early Stuart Preacher of Piety." Ph.D. dissertation, Temple University, 1972.

Shields, James Leroy. "The Doctrine of Regeneration in English Puritan Theology, 1604-1689." Ph.D. dissertation, Southwestern Baptist Theological Seminary, 1965.

Short, K. R. M. "The Educational Foundations of Elizabethan Puritanism: with Special Reference to Richard Greenham (1535-1594)." Ed.D. dissertation, University of Rochester, 1970.

Shuffleton, Frank. *Thomas Hooker, 1587-1647*. Princeton: Princeton University Press, 1977.

Sinnema, Donald W. "The Issue of Reprobation at the Synod of Dort (1618-19) in Light of the History of this Doctrine." Ph.D. dissertation, University of St. Michael's College, 1985.

Simpson, Alan. *Puritanism in Old and New England*. Chicago: University of Chicago Press, 1955.

Sisson, Rosemary A. "William Perkins." M.Litt. dissertation, Cambridge, 1952.

Smithen, Frederick J. *Continental Protestantism and the English Reformation.* London: J. Clarke & Co., 1927.

Sommerville, C. J. "Conversion, Sacrament and Assurance in the Puritan Covenant of Grace to 1650." M.A. thesis, University of Kansas, 1963.

Solberg, Winton U. *Redeem the Time: The Puritan Sabbath in Early New England.* Cambridge: Harvard University Press, 1977.

Spear, Wayne. "Covenantal Uniformity in Religion: The Influence of the Scottish Commissioners Upon the Ecclesiology of the Westminster Assembly." Ph.D. dissertation, University of Pittsburgh, 1976.

Spronek, H. H. *Wilhelmus Schortinghuis: Eene Bladzijde uit de Geschiedenis van het Piëtisme in de Gereformeerde Kerk van Nederland.* Groningen: Wolters, 1904.

Sprunger, Keith. *Dutch Puritanism. A History of English and Scottish Churches of the Netherlands in the Sixteenth and Seventeenth Centuries.* Studies in the History of Christian Thought, no. 31. Leiden: E. J. Brill, 1982.

_____. *The Learned Doctor William Ames: Dutch Backgrounds of English and American Puritanism.* Chicago: University of Illinois Press, 1972.

_____. *Trumpets from the Tower: English Puritan Printing in the Netherlands 1600-1640.* Leiden: E. J. Brill, 1994.

Stanford, Charles. *Joseph Alleine: His Companions and Times.* London: Jackson, Walford, and Hodder 1861.

Stannard, David E. *The Puritan Way of Death.* New York: Oxford University Press, 1977.

Stam, David Harry. "England's Calvin: A Study of the Publication of John Calvin's Works in Tudor England." Ph.D. dissertation, Northwestern University, 1978.

Stearns, Raymond P. *Congregationalism in the Dutch Netherlands.* Chicago: The American Society of Church History, 1940.

Steenblok, C. *Voetius en de Sabbat.* Gouda: Gereformeerde Pers, 1975.

_____. *Gisbertus Voetius: zijn leven en werken.* 2nd ed. Gouda: Gereformeerde Pers, 1976.

Stephen, Sir Leslie, and Sir Sidney Lee, eds. *The Dictionary of National Biography.* 22 vols. London: Oxford University Press, 1949-50.

Stoeffler, F. Ernest. *German Pietism During the Eighteenth Century.* Studies in the History of Religions, no. 24. Leiden: E. J. Brill, 1973.

_____. *The Rise of Evangelical Pietism.* Studies in the History of Religions, no. 9. Leiden: E. J. Brill, 1971.

Stoever, William K. B. *'A Fair and Easy Way to Heaven': Covenant Theology and Antinomianism in Early Massachusetts.* Middletown: Wesleyan University Press, 1978.

Stout, Harry S. *The New England Soul: Preaching and Religious Culture in Colonial New England.* New York: Oxford, 1986.

Stout, Harry S., Kenneth P. Minkema, and Caleb J. D. Maskell, eds. *Jonathan Edwards at 300: Essays on the Tercentenary of His Birth.* Lanham, Md.: University Press of America, 2005.

Stoute, Douglas Andrew. "The Origins and Early Development of the Reformed Idea of the Covenant." Ph.D. dissertation, Cambridge, 1979.

Stover, Dale Arden. "The Pneumatology of John Owen: A Study of the Role of the Holy Spirit in Relation to the Shape of a Theology." Ph.D. dissertation, McGill University, 1967.

Strehle, Stephen. *Calvinism, Federalism, and Scholasticism: A Study of the Reformed Doctrine of Covenant.* Basler und Berner Studien zur historischen und systematischen Theologie, Band 58. New York: Peter Lang, 1988.

Strickland, D. R. "Union with Christ in the Theology of Samuel Rutherford: an examination of his doctrine of the Holy Spirit." Ph.D. dissertation, Edinburgh, 1972.

Stuart, Robert Orkney. "The Breaking of the Elizabethan Settlement of Religion: Puritan Spiritual Experience and the Theological Division of the English Church." Ph.D. dissertation, Yale University, 1976.

Tanis, James. *Dutch Calvinistic Pietism in the Middle Colonies: A Study in the Life and Theology of Theodorus Jacobus Frelinghuysen.* The Hague: Martinus Nijhoff, 1967.

Ter Haar, Hendrik Willem. *Jacobus Trigland.* 's-Gravenhage: Martinus Nijhoff, 1891.

Tipson, Lynn Baird, Jr. "The Development of a Puritan Understanding of Conversion." Ph.D. dissertation, Yale University, 1972.

Toon, Peter. *The Emergence of Hyper-Calvinism in English Nonconformity, 1689-1765.* London: The Olive Tree, 1967.

_____. *God's Statesman: The Life and Work of John Owen.* Exeter: Paternoster, 1971.

_____. *Puritans and Calvinism.* Swengel, Pa.: Reiner, 1973.

Trimp, J. C. *Jodocus van Lodensteyn, Predikant en dichter.* Kampen: Kok, 1987.

Trinterud, Leonard J., ed. *Elizabethan Puritanism.* New York: Oxford University Press, 1971.

Trueman, Carl R. *The Claims of Truth: John Owen's Trinitarian Theology.* Carlisle: Paternoster, 1998.

Trueman, Carl R. and R. Scott Clark, eds. *Protestant Scholasticism: Essays in Reassessment.* Carlisle: Paternoster, 1999.

Tufft, J. R. "William Perkins, 1558-1602." Ph.D. dissertation, Edinburgh, 1952.

Tyacke, Nicholas. *Anti-Calvinists: The Rise of English Arminianism c. 1589-1640.* Oxford: Clarendon Press, 1987.

_____. *The Fortunes of English Puritanism, 1603-1640.* London: Dr. Williams's Trust, 1990.

Underdown, David. *Fire from Heaven: Life in an English Town in the Seventeenth Century.* London: HarperCollins, 1992.

Van Andel, Huibert Antonie. *De Zendingsleer van Gisbertus Voetius.* Kampen: Kok, 1912.

Van Baarsel, J. J. *William Perkins. Eene bijdrage tot de kennis der religieuse ontwikkeling in Engeland, ten tijde van Koningin Elisabeth.* Amsterdam: Ton Bolland, 1975.

Van der Aa, Abraham Jacob, ed. *Biographisch Woordenboek der Nederlanden.* 21 vols. in 27. Haarlem: J. J. van Brederode, 1852-78.

Van der Haar, J. *From Abbadie to Young. A Bibliography of English, mostly Puritan Works, Translated i/t Dutch Language.* 2 vols. in 1. Veenendaal: Kool, 1980.

_____. *Schatkamer van de Gereformeerde Theologie in Nederland (c. 1600-1800): Bibliografisch Onderzoek.* Veenendaal: Antiquariaat Kool, 1987.

Van der Linde, S. *Jean Taffin. Hofprediker en raadsheer van Willem van Oranje.* Amsterdam: Ton Bolland, 1982.

_____. *Opgang en voortgang der reformatie.* Amsterdam: Ton Bolland, 1976.

_____. *Vromen en Verlichten: Twee eeuwen Protestantse Geloofsbeleving 1650-1850.* Utrecht: Aartbisschoppelijk Museum Utrecht, 1974.

Van der Tuuk Edema, H. *Johannes Bogerman.* Groningen: J. B. Walters, 1868.

Van der Veen, Jerry D. "Adoption of Calvinism in the Reformed Church in the Netherlands." B.S.T. thesis, Biblical Seminary in New York, 1951.

Van der Woude, Cornelius. *Sibrandus Lubbertus, Leven en werken.* Kampen: Kok, 1963.

Van Dorsten, J., ed. *Ten Studies in Anglo-Dutch Relations.* London: University Press for Sir Thomas Brown Institute, 1974.

Van Genderen, J. *Herman Witsius: Bijdrage tot de Kennis der Gereformeer de Theologie*. 's-Gravenhage: Guido de Brès, 1953.

_____. *Het practisch syllogisme: De sluitrede des geloofs*. Alphen a/d Rijn: Buijs, 1954.

Van Gent, W. *Bibliotheek van oude schrijvers*. Rotterdam: Lindenberg, 1979.

Van Gorsel, W. *De IJver voor Zijn Huis: De Nadere Reformatie en haar belangrijkste vertegenwoordigers*. Groede: Pieters, 1981.

Van Itterzon, G. P. *Franciscus Gomarus*. 's-Gravenhage: Martinus Nijhoff, 1930.

_____. *Het Gereformeerd Leerboek der 17de Eeuw: "Synopsis Purioris Theologiae."* 's-Gravenhage: Martinus Nijhoff, 1931.

_____. *Johannes Bogerman*. Amsterdam: Ton Bolland, 1980.

Van Lieburg, Fred. *Confessionalism and Pietism: Religious Reform in Early Modern Europe*. Mainz: Philipp von Zabern, 2005.

_____. *Living for God: Eighteenth-Century Dutch Pietist Autobiography*. Pietist and Wesleyan Series, No. 18. Lanham, Maryland: Scarecrow Press, 2006.

_____. *De Nadere Reformatie in Utrecht ten tijde van Voetius: Sporen in de gereformeerde kerkeraadsacta*. Rotterdam: Lindenberg, 1989.

Van Oort, J., et al. *De onbekende Voetius*. Kampen: Kok, 1989.

Van Schelven, Aart Arnout. *Het Calvinisme gedurende zijn bloeitijd*. 3 vols. Amsterdam: W. Ten Have, 1943-65.

Van't Spijker, W, ed. *De Nadere Reformatie. Beschrijving van haar voornaamste vertegenwoordigers*. 's-Gravenhage: Boekencentrum, 1986.

_____, ed. *De Nadere Reformatie en het Gereformeerd Piëtisme*. 's-Gravenhage: Boekencentrum, 1989.

Van Veen, Sietse Douwes. *Voor tweehonderd jaren. Schetsen van het leven onzer Gereformeerde Vaderen*. 2nd ed. Utrecht: Kemink & Zoon, 1905.

Van Vlastuin, Willem. *De Geest van opwekking: een onderzoek naar de leer van de Heilige Geest in de opwekkingstheologie van Jonathan Edwards (1703-1758)*. Heerenveen: Groen, 2001.

Vaughan, Alden T. and Francis J. Bremer, eds. *Puritan New England: Essays on Religion, Society, and Culture*. New York: St. Martin's Press, 1977.

Vekeman, H. W. J. *Panorama van de Spiritualiteit in en om de Reformatie in de Nederlanden 1530-1800*. Nijmegen, 1982.

Veninga, James Frank. "Covenant Theology and Ethics in the Thought of John Calvin and John Preston." Ph.D. dissertation, Rice University, 1974.

Verboom, J. H. R. *Dr. Alexander Comrie, predikant van Woubrugge.* Utrecht: De Banier, 1964.

Verboom, W. *De Catechese van de Reformatie en de Nadere Reformatie.* Amsterdam: Buijten en Schipperheijn, 1986.

Von Rohr, John. *The Covenant of Grace in Puritan Thought.* Atlanta: Scholars Press, 1986.

Vorster, D. A. *Protestantse Nederlandse Mystiek.* Amsterdam: Meulenhoff, 1948.

Vose, Godfrey Noel. "Profile of a Puritan: John Owen (1616-1683)." Ph.D. dissertation, State University of Iowa, 1963.

Wakefield, Gordon S. *Puritan Devotion: Its Place in the Development of Christian Piety.* London: Epworth Press, 1957.

Walker, James. *Theology and Theologians of Scotland.* Edinburgh: T. & T. Clark, 1888.

Walker, Williston. *The Creeds and Platforms of Congregationalism.* New York: The Pilgrim Press, 1991.

Wallace, Dewey D., Jr. "The Life and Thought of John Owen to 1660: A Study of the Significance of Calvinist Theology in English Puritanism." Ph.D. dissertation, Princeton University, 1965.

_____. *Puritans and Predestination: Grace in English Protestant Theology, 1515-1695.* Chapel Hill: University of North Carolina Press, 1982.

_____, ed. *The Spirituality of the Later English Puritans.* Macon, Ga.: Mercer University Press, 1987.

*Warfield, Benjamin B. *The Westminster Assembly and Its Work.* Cherry Hill: Mack Publishing, 1972.

Watkins, Owen C. *The Puritan Experience.* London: Routledge and Kegan Paul, 1972.

Watts, Michael. *The Dissenters: From the Reformation to the French Revolution.* Oxford: Oxford University Press, 1992.

Weber, Max. *The Protestant Ethic and the Spirit of Capitalism.* Trans. Talcott Parsons. New York: Routledge, 1992.

Weeks, John. "A Comparison of Calvin and Edwards on the Doctrine of Election." Ph.D. dissertation, University of Chicago, 1963.

Weir, D. A. *The Origins of the Federal Theology in Sixteenth-Century Reformation Thought.* Oxford: Clarendon Press, 1990.

Weisiger, Cary Nelson, III. "The Doctrine of the Holy Spirit in the Preaching of Richard Sibbes." Ph.D. dissertation, Fuller Theological Seminary, 1984.

Welles, Judith B. "John Cotton, 1584-1652: Churchman and Theologian." Ph.D. dissertation, Edinburgh University, 1948.

White, B. R. *The English Separatist Tradition: from the Marian Martyrs to the Pilgrim Fathers.* London: Oxford University Press, 1971.

White, Eugene Edmond. *Puritan Rhetoric: The Issue of Emotion in Religion.* Carbondale: Southern Illinois University Press, 1972.

White, Peter. *Predestination, Policy and Polemic: Conflict and Consensus in the English Church from the Reformation to the Civil War.* Cambridge: Cambridge University Press, 1992.

Whyte, Alexander. *The Spiritual Life: The Teaching of Thomas Goodwin.* Edinburgh: Oliphant, Anderson & Ferrier, n.d.

_____. *Thirteen Appreciations.* Edinburgh: Oliphant, Anderson & Ferrier, 1913.

_____. *Thomas Shepard, Pilgrim Father and Founder of Harvard: His Spiritual Experience and Experiential Preaching.* London: Oliphant, Anderson & Ferrier, 1909.

Wilcox, William. "New England Covenant Theology: Its English Precursors and Early American Exponents." Ph.D. dissertation, Duke University, 1959.

Williams, John Bickerton. *Letters on Puritanism and Nonconformity.* 2 vols. London: Jackson and Walford, 1843-46.

_____. *The Lives of Philip and Matthew Henry.* Edinburgh: Banner of Truth Trust, 1974.

Wing, Donald Goddard, ed. *Short-Title Catalog of Books Printed in England, Scotland, Ireland, Wales and British America and of English Books Printed in Other Countries, 1641-1700.* 3 vols. New York: Columbia University Press, 1945-51.

Winslow, Ola. *John Eliot: Apostle to the Indians.* Boston: Houghton Mifflin, 1968.

Wood, Thomas. *English Casuistical Divinity During the Seventeenth Century.* London: Society for the Promotion of Christian Knowledge, 1952.

Woolsey, Andrew. "Unity and Continuity in Covenantal Thought: A Study in Reformed Tradition to the Westminster Assembly." 2 vols. Ph.D. dissertation, University of Glasgow, 1988.

Ziff, Larzer. *The Career of John Cotton, Puritanism and the American Experience.* Princeton: Princeton University Press, 1962.

_____. *Puritanism in America: New Culture in a New World.* New York: Viking, 1973.

Authors and Titles

The index below includes only the authors for whom biographical articles have been written and the titles of their books that have been reprinted since 1956.

DR. JOEL R. BEEKE is President and Professor of Systematic Theology and Homiletics of Puritan Reformed Theological Seminary, pastor of the Heritage Netherlands Reformed Congregation in Grand Rapids, Michigan, editor of *The Banner of Sovereign Grace Truth*, editorial director of Reformation Heritage Books, president of Inheritance Publishers, and vice-president of the Dutch Reformed Translation Society. He has written or edited fifty books and contributed more than 1,500 articles to Reformed books, journals, periodicals, and encyclopedias. His Ph.D. is in Reformation and Post-Reformation theology from Westminster Theological Seminary. He is frequently called upon to lecture at seminaries and to speak at Reformed conferences around the world. He and his wife Mary have been blessed with three children.

———◆◆◆———

RANDALL J. PEDERSON is a member of the Heritage Netherlands Reformed Congregation in Grand Rapids, Michigan. He is currently finishing his Th.M. degree at Calvin Theological Seminary. His thesis, "Francis Rous and the Mystical Current within English Puritanism, 1640-1660," explores a much-neglected theme in Commonwealth Puritan studies. He is the author and co-author of several publications relating to Puritanism, including forewords, articles, introductions, and devotionals. He has worked as a freelance editor for several Christian publishers, including Evangelical Press, Day One Publications, Bryntirion Press, and Crossway Books. He and his wife Sarah have been blessed with a son.

OTHER TITLES AVAILABLE BY THE AUTHORS
FROM REFORMATION HERITAGE BOOKS

Titles available by Dr. Joel Beeke:
An Analysis of Herman Witsius's "Economy of the Covenants"
    (with D. Patrick Ramsey)
Assurance of Faith: Calvin, English Puritanism and the Second Reformation
Bible Doctrine Student Workbook (with James W. Beeke)
Building on the Rock (5 vols., with Diana Kleyn)
The Christian's Reasonable Service (4 volumes; general editor)
Family Guidance:
    Bringing the Gospel to Covenant Children
    A Loving Encouragement to Flee Worldliness
    Family Worship
    The Family at Church: Listening to Sermons and Attending Prayer Meetings
Forerunner of the Great Awakening: Sermons by Theodorus Jacobus
    Frelinghuysen (1691-1747) (editor)
Gisbertus Voetius: Toward a Reformed Marriage of Knowledge and Piety
God's Alphabet for Life: Devotions for Young Children (with Heidi Boorsma)
The Heidelberg Catechism (2 volumes)
Holiness: God's Call to Sanctification
Jehovah Shepherding His Sheep: Sermons on the 23rd Psalm
Knowing and Living the Christian Life (with James D. Greendyk)
Memoirs of Thomas Halyburton (editor)
Overcoming the World: Grace to Win the Daily Battle
The Path of True Godliness (editor)
Portraits of Faith
Puritan Evangelism: A Biblical Approach
Puritan Reformed Spirituality
The Quest for Full Assurance: The Legacy of Calvin and His Successors
A Reader's Guide to Reformed Literature
Reformed Confessions Harmonized (with Sinclair Ferguson)
Striving Against Satan
Teachers' Guide: Bible Doctrine Student Workbook
Teachers' Guide: Truth that Frees
The Three Epistles of John
Truth that Frees: A Workbook on Reformed Doctrine for Young Adults
The Truths of God's Word (with Diana Kleyn)

Titles available by Randall Pederson:
Day by Day with the English Puritans (compiler)
Day by Day with Jonathan Edwards (compiler)